ADMINISTRATIVE
FINANCIAL
MANAGEMENT

ADMINISTRATIVE FINANCIAL MANAGEMENT

JOSEPH F. BRADLEY

Pennsylvania State University

Third Edition

The Dryden Press
901 North Elm Street
Hinsdale, Illinois

*To the Memory
of My Parents*

Preface

The purpose of this book is to present a broader approach to the basic financial management course—to broaden the area of business finance and to integrate it with the overall administration of the firm. This approach alters the traditional approach to finance, which analyzed it solely as a functional area.

The sequence of chapters (except for the first few on background material) places the reader in the position of the financial manager of an enterprise that is already in operation.

The main criterion for inclusion of material is whether it is useful to management in decision making.

This book attempts to give a balanced approach to descriptive and to analytical material. Students in their first course in financial management seem to need a combination of both.

To a certain extent this book is flexible enough to be used in different sequences. Some users might prefer to omit much of the background material; some might prefer to postpone the chapters on working capital until near the end of the course; others might prefer to postpone the chapter on the securities markets until after stocks and bonds have been discussed.

This, the third edition of *Administrative Financial Management*, has a number of features important to both teachers and students.

First: The finance function is discussed within the framework of the administrative processes of planning, managing, evaluating, and taking remedial action.

Second: The text considers several recent developments in the quantitative areas—for example, the use of models and the use of expected value. A separate chapter is given to these subjects, and then the material is further demonstrated in the form of operations research at appropriate places throughout the book. No attempt is made, however, to treat operations research on a sophisticated level.

Third: Capital budgeting is examined early in the text in order to encourage the use of this tool in a variety of decision-making areas, such as management of accounts receivable and management of fixed assets.

Fourth: The sequence of material breaks with tradition, in that short-term credit is considered as part of the area of management of working capital. Management of working capital, also placed relatively early in the text, is treated as one continuous unit.

Fifth: The text presents approximately 200 short problems which are carefully correlated with the material discussed in the respective chapters. In addition, for most of the problems an answer is given, and the student is asked to demonstrate how the solution was arrived at. Working back to the answer in this way, the student is given an immediate feedback on the correctness of his method.

Sixth: The author is convinced that short discussion-type cases provide a useful mechanism for teaching and learning; hence, a limited number of short cases are presented at the end of selected chapters.

The above points sum up the philosophy underlying this book: to provide a clear, comprehensive, and up-to-date survey of the field of financial management.

I wish to acknowledge my appreciation to the following for their assistance in preparing the third edition:

Professor George C. Philippatos, Professor of Finance and Head of the Department of Finance at the Pennsylvania State University, for providing the teaching schedule that made the third edition possible;

Professor Frank Fabozzi of Hofstra University for his many thoughtful comments on organization and content;

Professor James F. Jackson of Oklahoma State University for his suggestions on financial controls and risk;

Professor William Beranek of the University of Pittsburgh for his encouragement in completing the third edition;

Professor Terrence Martell of the University of Alabama for his suggestions on the sections on capital budgeting;

Professor Frank J. Mandell of Point Park College for his helpful suggestions;

Professor Herbert M. Kennedy of Eastern Michigan University for his in-depth analysis and comments;

Professor Larry R. Trussell of Eastern Michigan University for his helpful suggestions;

Professor Robert D. Hummer and Professor Thomas Duda of the Pennsylvania State University for their helpful comments;

Professor Santo J. Pullara of the Lowell Technological Institute for his helpful comments;

Professor Albert A. Zanzuccki of St. Francis College for suggestions on this and previous editions;

Professor Albert L. Sheaffer of Greenfield Community College for valuable suggestions for improving the coverage of the manuscript;

Professors Robert M. Fryer, Joseph W. Mirabile, and William Bryce, all of the Pennsylvania State University for valuable suggestions on coverage and presentation;

Professor Joseph P. Giusti of the Pennsylvania State University for his comments on this and previous editions;

Professor Lucille Mayne for suggestions on the second edition that were carried over to the third edition;

Gary D'Amico for suggestions on the presentation of break-even analysis;

Jo-Anne Naples for making especially helpful editorial suggestions on improving the entire manuscript;

Miss Rosalind Sackoff, Development Editor of Holt, Rinehart and Winston, for her help with the third edition.

Jere Calmes, Associate Publisher of Dryden Press, for doing a fine job in expediting this the third edition.

I am also indebted to my wife, Ethel, for her valuable assistance in the preparation of the text.

Contents

DISCUSSION CASES

ADMINISTRATIVE FINANCIAL MANAGEMENT

BACKGROUND MATERIAL

The Scope of Administrative Financial Management

The purpose of this book is to present accurately and interestingly the essentials of financial management. The aim is to present principles of finance of lasting value to students of all phases of business administration. This book, therefore, is not a treatise on the techniques of business finance. It is better to obtain these techniques in advanced courses aimed at training specialists or through practical experience. Not only persons who actually conduct business operations but others, including investors, labor leaders, consumers, and the general public, should have a grasp of the basic principles of the financial operations of the profit-seeking firm.

The following will be discussed in this chapter:

1. The nature of financial management
2. Risk versus return
3. The goals of the firm
   a. Increasing the financial welfare of the owners
   b. Assuming social responsibility

THE NATURE OF FINANCIAL MANAGEMENT

The *administrative process* is a systematic method of thinking that enables an executive to guide the firm toward its goals. This logical mode of thought consists of four steps: planning, managing, evaluating, and taking remedial action. *Planning* means establishing goals or targets as well as establishing proposed actions to reach the objectives; *managing* means taking the required actions to make the plans come true; *evaluating* means testing the results against the plans and against other relevant standards; *taking remedial action* means either making adjustments in the firm's activities so that future operations will come closer to matching the planned results or modifying the plans. The administrative approach to financial management gives this functional area a forward look, and it stresses the changes that are constantly occurring in business. This approach also has the advantage of focusing the discussion on top-management problems. For these reasons, the administrative process will be used as a framework for discussing the various subdivisions of financial management (see Figure 1-1).

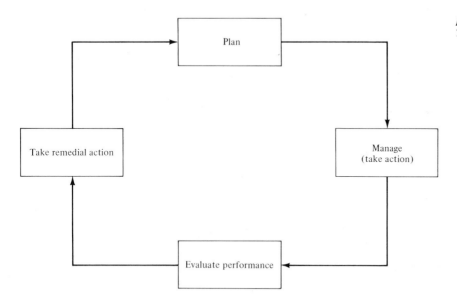

FIGURE 1-1
The Administrative Process

Financial management is the area of business administration devoted to enabling the spending unit to achieve its goals. It is applicable to such spending units as governments, universities, churches, labor unions, and business firms, although in this book we will be limited to the financial management of profit-seeking firms.

The activities of financial management focus on two areas. First is the area of managing assets for growth and survival. Included in this domain is the determination of:

the optimum size of the firm

the composition of the assets, that is, the best places for the firm to allocate its scarce resources

the line of business in which the firm will engage

the most efficient use of current and fixed assets, after they are acquired

whether to purchase asset A or B

criteria for measuring management's success in handling the company's affairs

Second is the area of selecting the sources of funds to finance assets, both those on hand and new ones to be acquired. Included in this domain is the determination of:

whether to issue common stock, preferred stock, or bonds

the amount to be paid in dividends

whether to lease or buy assets

the optimum amount of trade credit and bank loans

how to deal with banks

how much control to give outsiders

the best terms to offer in a merger

From the above, it can be seen that the role of financial management is a vital one in the modern firm.

RISK VERSUS RETURN

In managing assets and obtaining funds, the financial manager must take into consideration the interrelationship between risk and return. The interrelationship is this: *As the rate of return sought on assets increases, the risk increases.* Following are some examples of what is meant by risk. On the one extreme is the conservative businessman who deploys all the firm's funds in a portfolio of U.S. government bonds and safe common stocks. He predicts a modest rate of return of 7 percent, but he is wise enough to know that the realized rate of return might be as low as 5 percent and as high as 9 percent. At the other end of the spectrum is the highly venturesome businessman who deploys the company's money into the stocks of uranium mining companies. He predicts a rate of return of 25 percent, but he is experienced enough to know that the realized rate of return might be as low as 0 percent and as high as 65 percent. This latter use of the company's cash (in uranium mining shares) is said to be risky because the *realized rate* of return in the future might vary widely from the *predicted rate*. The former use of the firm's cash (in government securities and safe common stock) is said to contain little risk because the *realized rate* of return in the future is not likely to be far from the *predicted return*. In summary, risk is a set of beliefs about the future. The two beliefs are: (1) as the expected rate of return on assets increases, the risk increases; (2) risk is the possibility that the realized rate of return on assets might be much higher or lower than the predicted rate.

THE GOALS OF THE FIRM

The *goals* of the business firm may be summarized in the following formula:

Primary Goals

$$\text{Goals of firm} = \frac{\text{Increasing financial}}{\text{welfare of owners}} + \frac{\text{Assuming}}{\text{social}} \\ \text{responsibility}$$

A firm increases the financial welfare of its owners when it distributes or has good prospects of distributing either cash or other items of value as profits to the owners. If the firm performs well, by delivering or having good prospects of delivering profits, the positive differential between the market value of the owner's commitment and what he paid for it will tend to increase. Thus, if a stockholder paid $1,000 for shares of stock in Lukens Steel Company, his financial welfare is increased if the market value of this investment increases to, say, $2,000. This example sets one of the main themes of this book—that a central aim of business decision making is to generate for the residual owners a net gain in value, that is, to increase the market value of an equity commitment over what was paid for it.

The modern firm has another goal—to assume social responsibility by becoming a good citizen. Basically, this means that the firm is expected to donate some of its funds to worthy causes and to use its funds to otherwise advance the public welfare. An annual report of Lukens Steel Company has this to say about the company's goals:

> First ... to promote reasonable and improving corporate earnings through productive effort applied primarily but not limited to the manufacture of steel plate, steel plate specialties, fabricated parts, and partially or fully assembled units.
> Second ... to conduct the business in a manner that earns recognition as a constructive and honorable corporate citizen in its relations, designed to be mutually profitable with stockholders, employees, customers, suppliers, community, and government.

In recent years more and more attention has been given to the role of the firm as a constructive citizen.

In addition to advancing the financial welfare of the owners and to assuming social responsibility, management may have other nonfinancial motives such as obtaining prestige for themselves, appointing their successors, and outwitting their business rivals. These motives are difficult to pinpoint, although their presence is generally conceded. In this book we will not give any further attention to this phase of the goals of the firm; instead, we will focus our attention on the duty of the business to increase the financial welfare of the owners and to assume social responsibility.

Contributory Goals

In an effort to reach the primary goals spelled out in the previous section, management must plan the use of capital. Two convenient guideposts are: (1) planning for profits and (2) planning for solvency. These two guideposts will be called *contributory* goals because they are not an end in themselves but instead contribute to the primary goals. These contributory goals are necessary stepping-stones to the primary goals. In fact, a firm must reach the contributory goals before the primary goals can be attained.

Profits are of such tremendous importance that management must focus its attention on creating them. There is a direct connection between profits and the primary goals of the firm, since profits are a basic source of returns for owners and since profits are usually necessary for a firm to fulfill its obligations as a responsible citizen.

Maintaining solvency is the second of the contributory goals. Solvency also contributes to the primary goals, for a firm must have sufficient cash to be able to distribute returns to owners, as well as for operating purposes. In business finance there is considerable emphasis on one form of capital—cash. But to understand the nature of cash flows, one must be able to see the broad picture of business operations. The study of cash flows, therefore, is not a narrow technical problem of business operations. Instead, it focuses on the entire business process.

The concept of increasing the financial welfare of the owners is generally broad enough to encompass the contributory goals. The advantage of focusing attention on primary goals is to give a beacon light toward which all the activities of the firm may be directed (within the framework of assuming social responsibility).

INCREASING THE FINANCIAL WELFARE OF OWNERS

The *primary* goals of the business firm are to:

1. Increase the financial welfare of the owners
   a. Distribute profits
   b. Distribute higher salary and fringe benefits than the owner could obtain working for another employer
   c. Increase the market value of the owner's investment in the firm
2. Assume social responsibility

Owners of the firm have an intriguing problem in determining what combination of the three forms of return is best for them. Although an individual owner welcomes any of the three kinds, he often has a preference for one of them. His preference depends on a number of factors such as his tax status, his income from other sources, and his family needs. Thus, some owners prefer high current income in the form of profit distribution. Others prefer that the bulk of the profits remain in the business, the owners in this case expecting to remove the profits later or to sell their equity at a profit. Or a single proprietor, partner, or stockholder (in a family corporation) may have contrived a scheme for the firm to pay generous fringe benefits.

The owner's criterion for choosing the best combination of these returns is the maximization of the *net present value of the expected flow of future benefits to himself*. In order to illustrate the concept of net present value, assume that a person paid $10,000 for an equity in a firm and that the present value of the flow of payments (a, b, and c above) to this investor is assumed to be $20,000. The formula for computing net present value is:

$$\text{Net present value} = \frac{\substack{\text{Present value} \\ \text{of expected flow} \\ \text{of Financial Returns} \\ (a + b + c, \text{above})}}{} - \text{Price paid for investment}$$

$$= \$20,000 - \$10,000$$
$$= \$10,000$$

One of the methods by which a firm increases the financial welfare of its owners is to distribute profits to them. A single proprietorship, for example, might distribute $10,000 a year in the form of profits.

The stockholders, owners of a corporation, may receive distributions of profits called dividends. Thus, an investor in American Telephone and Telegraph Company may receive $3.60 annually in dividends for each share of stock owned in this company. In a like manner, the holders of common stock of Greyhound Bus Corporation may receive annual dividends of $1 on every share held. Indeed, one reason for purchasing common stock is the expectation of receiving distributions of profits; the other two reasons are to gain control of a firm so that one may obtain a high salary and generous fringe benefits and to sell the stock at a higher price than its cost. One criterion used to evaluate the effectiveness of decision making is the actual profit distributions made by the firm.

A second method by which a firm can increase the financial welfare of its owners is to pay generous salaries and high fringe benefits to these owners. If the salary and other forms of compensation are higher than the owner could obtain by working as an employee for someone else, the excess is a special kind of return that accrues because the recipient is an owner. If, for example, the owner of a business can pay himself a salary of $15,000, and if he could earn only $10,000 as an employee for another firm, the $5,000 difference is a benefit that accrues to him because of his position as an owner. Or, to take another example, if an owner is able to have an expense account of $2,000 a year and if he would be able to obtain only $1,000 in such an account by working as an employee for someone else, the $1,000 difference is a benefit that arises because of his status as an owner. *These excesses could also be viewed as profit distributions, but since businessmen place such separate emphasis on high salaries and fringe benefits, we will consider them to be separate forms of return.* The paying of high salaries and generous fringe benefits to owners is an alternative available mainly to family-controlled firms.

A third method of increasing the financial welfare of the owner is for the firm to promote policies that will increase the market value of his equity. A single proprietor or partner, for example, might find that after several years he can sell his investment in a business for $100,000, even though he paid a total of

$60,000 for it. An owner of a share of stock may have the same expectations, namely, that the company will follow policies that increase the positive differential between the current market value of the stock and the cost of the stock to him. Since the management of a corporation has no control over what a stockholder pays for his shares, it must concentrate on policies that maximize the market value of each share, assuming a given number of shares of stock outstanding. The stock of American Telephone and Telegraph Company (AT&T) may also be used to illustrate this type of return to the owner. At one point in time this stock could be bought for $75 a share. Several years later the issue had a market value of $110 a share. The increase of $35 represented a differential that could have been converted into a cash gain if the owner so wished. Despite the rise in the market price of AT&T common stock, this firm is known best for the annual profit distributions it makes to its owners. On the other hand, many single proprietorships, partnerships, and corporations have a policy of stressing the third form of financial return, namely, maximizing the market value of the owner's investment in the business. International Business Machines Corporation (IBM), for example, has a policy of attempting to increase the market value of the owner's commitment, and it distributes only a moderate amount of its profits to the owners. A large percentage of the profits is retained in this firm, with the expectation of creating expanded earnings which in turn will cause the price of the stock to rise sharply. Many owners prefer to receive their financial gain through sale of the investment at a profit rather than through direct distribution of profits. (See Table 1-1.)

TABLE 1-1
Importance of
Capital Gains

		Percent of Annual Income
WHERE	Capital gains	60.1%
MILLIONAIRES	Dividends	29.1%
GET THEIR	Salaries, wages	3.9%
MONEY	Interest	2.6%
	Other sources	4.3%

		Percent of Total Assets
. . . AND WHERE	Stock in corporations	59.1%
THEY INVEST	Real estate	8.6%
THEIR	Tax-exempt bonds	6.1%
ASSETS	Savings and checking accounts, and cash	5.1%
	U.S. Treasury bonds	3.6%
	Mortgages, notes	1.7%
	Insurance	1.4%
	Corporate and other bonds	0.5%
	Other assets	13.9%

Source:
Courtesy of U.S. News
and World Report.

Many newspapers give the market value of the stocks of large corporations. Although the ways of presenting these values vary slightly, all stock quotations give substantially the same information. Table 1-2 lists several stocks and their market values. It should be noted that a point in the stock market is $1 and that an eighth of a point is 12½ cents. The market values of the securities of different corporations vary widely, ranging in price from one cent up to several hundred dollars per share. Since different firms appear to have different profit prospects and different numbers of shares outstanding, we would expect the prices of their shares to vary accordingly. It is buyers' and sellers' expectations as to the future that leads them to buy or sell shares at a given price. Because numerous factors affect expectations, the market prices of shares of stock are unstable. In inspecting Table 1-2, the reader should understand that newspapers can give only limited information about the price performance of a share of stock; for long-term price movements it is necessary to go to other sources.

Some stock quotations are presented in terms of bid and asked prices. A bid price refers to the amount that a buyer is willing to pay for a share, while the asked price refers to the amount a seller seeks to obtain for his shares. Recently Ozark Air Lines common stock had a bid price of $9.62½ and an asked price of $9.87½. In order to complete the deal, a buyer may pay a little more than his bid price and the seller may take a little less than his asked price. Bid and asked quotations do not represent transactions; they are intended as a guide to the approximate range within which the securities could have been bought or sold at the time of compilation.

TABLE 1-2
Typical Stock Market
Quotations

High	Low	Stocks	Div.	P-E Ratio[1]	Sales in 100s	High	Low	Close	
84⅝	63¾	GnMot	4.55	7	1533	64½	63	64½	+⅝
78½	72	GnMot 5pf	5		6	74¼	72¾	73⅞	+⅛
22¼	19⅝	GPubUt	1.60	8	257	19¾	19⅝	19¾	...
7⅞	5	Gen Refract		9	7	5⅛	5	5⅛	...
57¼	38½	GnSignal	.65	18	34	42⅞	41¼	41¼	−1

There is a tax advantage in receiving a financial gain through the sale of one's investment instead of through distribution of profits. If an owner receives cash which represents a distribution of profits, he must include these profits (except for the dividend exclusion) in his taxable income. If Robert Smith, a stockholder who has investments in many companies, receives $550 in dividends and is in the 70 percent federal tax bracket, he must pay a tax of over $300 on this increment of income. But the tax on profit from the sale of securities, called a long-term *capital gain* if the securities are held for six months or more, is much lower. On these capital gains, Smith may avail himself of either of the following alternatives:

Increasing the Market Value of the Owner's Equity (II)

1. P-E ratio is the current market price per share divided by what the firm is earning per share.

1. He may report as taxable income only half the gain, add this gain to all his other taxable income, and then have the total taxed at rates that apply to him. Assume that Smith purchased stock several years ago for $500 and sold it this year for $1,000. Also assume that Smith is in the 70 percent federal income tax bracket. If he reports half his profit as income, his tax will be $175 (70 percent of $250).

2. He may pay a flat tax of 25 percent on the entire profit instead of reporting the gain in his taxable income. If Smith takes this course of action, his tax will be $125 (25 percent of $500).[2]

Of course, he will elect the lower of the two alternatives and pay a tax of $125 on the transaction. (If he holds the securities for less than the required holding period, there is no favorable tax concession and the entire gain is taxed at regular rates, the same as wages.) The important point is that the tax on $500 of dividends is considerably higher than the tax on $500 of profit from the sale of securities. *In summary, the tax laws result in a situation in which many owners prefer to obtain their financial profits through capital gains.*

Summarizing the Goals via an Anticipated Composite Rate of Return

We stated that one of the primary goals of the firm is to increase the financial welfare of the owners and that the financial welfare of the members of this group is increased when they receive a distribution of profits, when they sell their investment at a profit, and when they receive larger than normal salaries and fringe benefits. We can summarize these three objectives of the business firm by stating that one mission of the firm is to provide the owners with an adequate composite rate of return on the price they paid for their investment. Although owners have varying preferences as to the form in which they prefer their return, all owners seek to obtain an adequate composite rate of return on the amount they have paid for their ownership interest. Thus, an investor who places $100 in a share of stock might estimate that he will receive a composite rate of return of 10 percent; a single proprietor or a partner might invest $10,000 in a grocery store on the expectation that he will receive a composite return of 20 percent. But how does one determine how to combine the three forms of return into the common denominator, which we will call the anticipated composite rate of return?

The anticipated composite rate of return is that rate which shows the relation between (1) the sum of the three types of financial benefits expected to be received and (2) the amount spent for a full ownership or a fractional ownership in the business. Assume, for example, that a person purchased one share of Greyhound Bus Corporation. At one time a share of this company could be purchased for $38. A person who made such a purchase would become a part owner of the firm. Under our business system, what is the goal of this firm as seen through the eyes of the part owner? Since this buyer would not receive a

---

2. Under this option, rates higher than 25 percent may apply on very large long-term capital gains.

salary or fringe benefits as a direct result of his ownership, we may limit the obligation of Greyhound Bus Corporation to paying dividends and engaging in policies that will help the price of the stock to rise.

A person who bought this stock would have received a cash dividend of $1.30 at the end of the first year, a current yield of only 3.42 percent. Obviously, this rate of return could not explain the motive for making the purchase, because the investor could have obtained almost 6 percent on government bonds, which are a perfectly safe investment. Our stockholder, then, must have other expectations than $1.30 in cash dividends. Let us assume that he looks ahead for five years and that he expects his annual cash intake from dividends to be these amounts: $1.30, $1.40, $1.40, $1.90, and $2.10. The average of these is $1.62 a year. Also assume that he expects to be able to sell his stock for $78 at the end of the five years, thus making a capital gain profit of $40. This is an average gain of $8 a year. If these are his expectations as to future capital gains, what is his antici-pated composite rate of return? The formula for obtaining the answer to this question is:

$$
\begin{array}{l}
\text{Anticipated} \\
\text{composite} \\
\text{rate of} \\
\text{return}
\end{array}
=
\frac{
\begin{array}{c}
\text{Anticipated} \\
\text{average} \\
\text{annual} \\
\text{receipt of} \\
\text{distribution} \\
\text{of profits}
\end{array}
+
\begin{array}{c}
\text{Anticipated} \\
\text{average} \\
\text{annual gain} \\
\text{in market} \\
\text{value of} \\
\text{owner's equity}
\end{array}
+
\begin{array}{c}
\text{Anticipated} \\
\text{average fringe} \\
\text{benefits and} \\
\text{salaries that} \\
\text{are larger than} \\
\text{normal}
\end{array}
}{\text{Amount of outlay for ownership equity}}
$$

$$
= \frac{\$1.62 + \$8 + \$0}{\$38}
$$

$$
= 25 \text{ percent}
$$

Our investor, then, is expecting a composite rate of return of 25 percent. Some investors may place their expectations so high that the management cannot possibly reach them. Also, some owners pay such a high price for their owner-ship equity that the management cannot possibly perform in a manner that would make the realized composite rate of return even approximate the antici-pated one. Another point worth mentioning is that the expectations given above apply only to one stockholder; other stockholders may use an entirely different set of predictions. Despite all these difficulties, we may say that one goal of the firm is to enable the owners to obtain a satisfactory composite rate of return.

The main advantage of the anticipated composite rate of return is its sim-plicity; its main disadvantage (as presented above) is that it does not give any emphasis to the time value of money—that is, the capital gain is not discounted back to its present value.

One side benefit of using the anticipated composite rate of return is that it points out the incompleteness of data that stress only dividends and yield on stock.

Businessmen are being asked to broaden their concept of social responsibility. Although there is no exact definition of this expanded term, it is possible to give examples that are being widely discussed in business circles. *Social responsibility* means using the firm's resources (both money and talent) for these typical purposes: aiding local hospitals, eliminating poverty, improving slum areas, hiring minority groups, helping solve urban problems, producing products that are really good for the consumer, and enhancing the quality of life in general. The argument is that the business firm should develop a social conscience. It goes on to state that while the profit motive is still valid, it is not enough for a firm to make a good product, deliver it at a good price, and earn a good profit. As the *Wall Street Journal* has stated, corporations increasingly are being held to account not just for their profitability but also for what they do about an endless series of social problems.

Numerous citizen groups and consumer groups are demanding that business firms broaden the traditional concept of social responsibility. One example of such a demand is that business firms cease using their assets in a manner that pollutes the air and poisons the drinking water. Such citizen and consumer groups argue that the firm can earn a reasonable return for owners and still meet this type of challenge.

The following examples illustrate how several companies are coping with social responsibility issues. Xerox Corporation has begun a "social service leave program" that will grant employees up to a year's leave at full pay to pursue a self-selected volunteer project. The president of the company said that the program is a logical extension of the company's involvement in the problems of society and that in an effort to put something back into society, his firm is giving the most important asset it has—the time of its people. To give another example of social concern, an annual report of Pfizer Incorporated stated that the firm exceeded its year-end goal of 14 percent minority group employees. Finally, in another example, Smith, Kline and French in Philadelphia has rehabilitated the slum area in the immediate vicinity of its headquarters: 70 abandoned houses were converted into 200 livable apartments at low rents. In addition to the above examples, numerous companies point to their contributions in solving problems of pollution, poverty, and the like.

The introduction of expanded concepts of social responsibility has several potential implications for financial management. First is the impact on financial theory. Current theory is based on the assumption that a firm's primary responsibility is to maximize the market price of the shares by using its assets to increase the net present value of the firm. Although those interested in financial theory have always been aware of the multiple-purpose nature of the firm, social responsibility, in the context described above, has previously been given a minor role in explaining how the firm should behave. If the current trend continues, financial theory will have to be drastically restructured to allow for social responsibility in model building.

Second, all capital budgeting models will have to be drastically revised, for it will be necessary to incorporate qualitative considerations into the models which rank proposed expenditures. Otherwise, the models will be meaningless exercises in mathematics.

Third, the criteria for evaluating managerial performance will have to be changed. As presently constructed, the balance sheet and the profit and loss statement will be incomplete reports on what the company is supposed to have done in the previous period. An officer of the Bank of America has stated that within a few years, corporations will be reporting the company's social outlays as a separate item; he also foresees complete social audits of firms by outside consultants, just as outside accountants conduct financial audits today. Furthermore, the *Wall Street Journal* has reported that a number of businessmen believe that eventually ratings of a company's social performance will be as readily available as ratings of its credit worthiness.

Professor Phillip Blumberg has called attention to the emergence of a "socially oriented power base." He points out that this situation has been fueled by the large accumulation of stock ownership by nonprofit institutions—churches, foundations, and universities—which tend to be especially sensitive to social issues and noneconomic values. Professor Blumberg also contends, as reported in the *Wall Street Journal*, that small shareholders typically have such a minor economic stake in the individual companies whose shares they hold that they, too, may be responsive to social responsibility issues. Socially concerned individual holders, when combined with nonprofit institutional investors, make up a "formidable base of potential support for social reform."

Virtually all businessmen who argue for social responsibility, in its expanded connotation, believe that this activity can be conducted within the profit-making system.

The main issues of social responsibility have been presented here because they are widely discussed by top executives, who must temper social responsibility concepts with the decisions suggested by capital budgeting procedures.

In summary, social responsibility issues affect the goals of the firm, which are a pillar on which financial management is built.

Administrative financial management stresses the financial process from the viewpoint of top management, which represents the owners of the firm. The intellectual tools of planning, managing, evaluating, and taking remedial action provide guidance in using assets and in obtaining assets on advantageous terms. All business decisions should be made with the intent of advancing the goals of the firm.

An important point is that owners look to the future and expect a satisfactory composite rate of return.

The goals of the firm are to increase the wealth of the owners by increasing the market value of their equity (shares), to assume social responsibility, and to engage in nonfinancial activities. Although the suggestion is often made that the goals of the firm can be stated solely in terms of increasing the owners' wealth, this approach does not adequately allow for the role of the behavioral sciences in

HIGHLIGHTS OF THIS CHAPTER

explaining the destiny of the individual firm. Nonetheless, the goal of increasing the market value of the owner's equity does provide an insight into the normative decision-making process.

REVIEW QUESTIONS 1-1. An investor purchased 28 shares of Ford Motor Company common stock. The firm pays out approximately 50 percent of its profits as dividends. The stockholder sold his shares in two years. He claimed that he was mistreated because future stockholders will benefit from the 50 percent of the profits retained during his holding period. Is his complaint justified? Explain.

1-2. Recently the common stock of National Cash Register Company was selling at $40 a share; at the same time the common stock of IBM was selling at $300 a share. Suggest several reasons for the wide difference in the price of these shares.

1-3. Company X pays virtually no dividends; its competitor pays 60 percent of its profits in dividends. Can an investor generalize that the competitor firm is more profitable than Company X?

1-4. A college student purchased 10 shares of Greyhound Bus Company common stock at $20 a share. What is the current market price of these shares? (Look this up in a newspaper.)

1-5. What specific contribution, mentioned in this chapter, is Xerox Corporation making to the solution of the poverty problem?

1-6. Is the concept of social responsibility inconsistent with the capitalistic system?

REVIEW PROBLEMS[3] The answers to the problems appear at the end of this section. *For each problem, show how you obtained the answer.*

1-1. John Thomas is operating a successful bookstore in which he invested $100,000, and which he purchased five years ago. His profits have averaged $15,000 annually, and he has withdrawn an average of $10,000 in profits each year. He estimates that he could now sell the business for $150,000. Thomas also believes that he has been able to obtain $1,000 a year in fringe benefits that he could not have obtained as an employee working for another firm (such as entertaining for business purposes). Determine his composite rate of return, ignoring federal income taxes and the capital gains tax.

1-2. William Finley buys a share of stock in the First National Bank of his

---

3. In problems 1-3 and 1-4, assume that one of the options is to elect to have the long-term capital gain taxed at a flat 25 percent.

hometown for $50. He expects the stock to rise to $75 in five years, and he believes that the average dividends for the next five years will be $3 a share. If these are his expectations, what anticipated composite rate of return does he expect?

1-3. Chester Jones bought $500 worth of stock five years ago. He sells this stock today for $1,000. If he is in the 60 percent tax bracket, how much in taxes will he pay on this transaction, assuming that he will minimize his taxes?

1-4. Tom Smith purchased $1,000 of stock three years ago, He sells this stock today for $2,000. If he is in the 30 percent tax bracket, how much in taxes will he have to pay on this transaction, assuming that he will minimize his taxes?

Answers: 1-1, 21 percent; 1-2, 16 percent; 1-3, $125; 1-4, $150.

2 Promotion and the Forms of Organization

The decision to start a business merits careful consideration and a great deal of preliminary planning. It should be based on a thorough analysis of the known economic forces that will affect the success of the venture. However, there will always be many unknown economic forces that will influence the profitability of the proposed project.

The promoter takes the responsibility of nursing the money-making idea into a full-fledged business enterprise, although he may invite others to assist him. For his efforts in creating the new business, the promoter expects to receive economic rewards. The expected rewards may take a number of forms. He may expect to get on the payroll as an officer; he may expect to receive stock if a corporation is being formed; and he may expect to receive royalties if the firm is going to sell or manufacture a product patented by him.

In this chapter, the following will be discussed:

1. Promoting a new business
2. Selecting the organization for the new business

DISCOVERY OF THE IDEA
An example of a typical promotion is the Trad Cabinet Corporation. This company was organized to manufacture cabinets for television sets. It planned to make about 400 cabinets per week and to hire 35 to 40 workers. Some promotions are highly speculative, such as the Utah Uranium Corporation. This company was organized to develop uranium mining properties. It should be observed that many of our accepted industries are based on what were at one time considered impractical ideas, examples being the automotive industry, the television industry, and the chemical industry. Most new promotions do not attempt to develop a completely new idea. The vast majority of them consist of the establishment of new selling outlets for established products or the formation of new companies to manufacture an established product.

After conceiving the idea that a particular project can be developed into a business, the next step is to study carefully the economic factors that will have a bearing on the success of the company. The only practical way to study these economic forces is to translate them into costs and revenues. When a small business is being formed, the owner makes the study himself; when a large business is being started, independent experts participate in the investigation.

In calculating future net profits, the long-range aspects must be considered. It is well known that few firms are able to make any profit during the first years of their existence; many firms incur losses while building customer lists, earning a reputation, and improving production methods. Later, if the company entrenches itself in the field, profits begin to be earned.

The matter of timing should be considered carefully by the promoters. At certain periods business conditions are excellent and consumers have plenty of money to spend. But at other times business is slack and consumers have considerably less to spend. During periods of slack economic activity many firms find it difficult to reach the break-even point. Hence these businesses yield an inadequate return for their owners or may actually fail. The best time to start a business is when the economy is very active and consumers have large paychecks. At this period of the business cycle it is not so difficult to reach the break-even point, even if there are cost problems to be solved.

Should the promoter go ahead with the new venture? The answer depends mainly on the outcome of a comparison between the income he could expect to receive as an employee with what he could expect to receive as an independent businessman. Expected profits (including salaries) should be compared with the total return that could be expected if the promoter assumed the status of an employee and invested his money elsewhere at 6 percent. Assume that Paul Hogan can earn a salary of $10,000 and that he and his wife have combined savings of $15,000. If these savings were invested at 6 percent, the family would have an annual income of $10,900. If the profit prospects of the new venture do not exceed this amount, Hogan is not improving his financial position. Unless nonfinancial considerations enter the picture—such as the fact that Hogan might want to be his own boss—he should not go ahead with a venture that does not promise to increase his total income.

One of the most important phases of promotion is planning to raise cash for the new business. First, there must be an estimate of the amount of cash needed; second, the sources of cash must be planned. The following discussion indicates the main factors that will be taken into consideration when determining the amount of funds needed to start a new business in the retail field.

It may be necessary for the organizer to spend cash for such purposes as travel expenses to and from proposed locations, entertainment expenses, lawyers' fees, and market surveys. In many cases none of these organization expenses would be incurred. In other promotions, a great many similar expenses would also be encountered.

Cash Outlays for Assets

Because of the possibility of renting space, the cash outlay needed to acquire the use of fixed capital varies greatly. Furthermore, assuming that much of the furniture and fixtures is purchased, there is the further factor that some of the equipment may be acquired on the installment plan, thus lessening the cash outlay needed in the early life of the business. Cash will be needed to acquire inventory, to provide a checking account, and to carry customers who will not pay for their purchases immediately. The size of the inventory and the amount of credit to be granted are the two main determinants of the amount of cash needed to finance the acquisition of circulating assets. Since some of the inventory may be acquired on account, the entire inventory requirements need not be financed through immediate cash outlays.

Sources of Cash

A conventional classification distinguishes funds advanced by owners from funds supplied by creditors. The promoter himself may advance a considerable amount of cash to the business. If the amount needed is large, the promoter may form a partnership, thereby inviting others to become co-owners of the business. Or if a larger sum is needed, a corporation may be formed, thereby appealing to perhaps thousands of investors to become part owners of the company. Creditors, the second group, lend their money to the business under a number of conditions. Some of the sources of loans are commercial banks, private lenders, the U.S. Small Business Administration, and a number of specialized institutions, such as commercial credit companies. Several promotions and their sources of funds appear in Table 2-1.

TABLE 2-1
Promotions and Their Sources of Funds

Type of Business	Source of Funds
Small grocery store	Owner used small inheritance to go in business for himself.
Small clothing store	Two men pooled their savings and started a partnership.
Automotive service station	Owner used savings and obtained a small bank loan. In addition, a local businessman lent money with the agreement that he would have a share in the profits.
Television sales and repair shop	The 3 promoters sold shares of stock to about 35 local residents.

SURVEYING THE ORGANIZATIONAL NEEDS

Businessmen have a number of kinds of organization from which to select when a venture is established; the three main ones are the single proprietorship, the partnership, and the corporation. Before businessmen can select the best form of organization, they must study their specific needs and then attempt to find the one structure that comes closest to filling their requirements.

Of the three forms of organization, the corporation is the most complex; it is an association which is organized under special provisions of the law for the purpose of achieving specified objectives. Thus General Motors Corporation is an association of stockholders organized under the Delaware law for the purpose of conducting a business in the automotive and related fields. Those who are owners of the business are known as stockholders; the stockholders elect directors who determine the policies of the business; the directors in turn select operating officials (such as the president) who supervise actual operations.

In recent years there has been interest in the question of the merits of "inside" versus "outside" directors. An *inside director* is one who is also an officer in the corporation, while an *outside director* is one who is not an officer of the corporation. The main alleged advantage of having inside directors is their technical knowledge of the business. The main alleged advantage of having outside directors is the probably broader viewpoint of those who are not officers. American Tobacco Company is an example of a large corporation with all inside directors. On the other hand, General Foods Corporation has both inside and outside members on the board of directors. Since boards have traditionally consisted of inside directors, the current discussion over the composition of the board centers around the number of outside members that should be allowed on the board.

Although directors are given sweeping powers in managing the corporation, stockholders do reserve for themselves the right to make a few basic decisions, such as whether to liquidate the corporation, whether to amend the charter, and whether to sell all the assets. State law, judicial decisions, and the charter determine the boundaries of authority of directors and stockholders.

The following will be discussed briefly in the remainder of this chapter:

1. Forms of organization and how they meet the needs of businessmen
   a. Meeting the need for limited liability
   b. Meeting the need for transferability
   c. Meeting the need for funds
   d. Meeting the need for minimum taxes
2. The charter
3. Rights of common stockholders
4. The resuscitation of the business trust

An important feature of the *single proprietorship* is the liability of the owner for unpaid business debts. Assume that business debts exceed the amount of cash obtainable from the business. If the owner has a home and a savings account, might he have to give up these assets to satisfy the debt? The answer is yes. This feature of the single proprietorship is known as *unlimited* liability; that is, the owner's possible loss is not limited to the amount he invests in the business. Instead, unpaid business creditors can reach beyond the assets used in the business and seize any available property and investments the owner might hold, except certain essentials (such as a carpenter's tools) which are protected by state laws from seizure by creditors. Unlimited liability is generally considered to be a disadvantage of the single proprietorship, despite the fact that this very feature may give creditors more confidence in the debt-paying ability of the proprietorship.

A general rule is that when a partnership does not have sufficient cash to meet its debts, any or all of the partners may be called on to dip into their

*MEETING
THE NEED FOR
LIMITED LIABILITY*

*The Single Proprietorship
and the
General Partnership*

personal assets to pay the creditors of the partnership. In this respect, a *general partnership* resembles a single proprietorship. Assume that John Anderson and Harry Bell are members of a partnership. If business debts exceed business assets, might either of the partners have to sell his home or give up his investments to pay creditors of the partnership? The answer is yes. If Helen Jones falls on the ice in front of the business and a court awards her damages, and if the business does not have sufficient resources to pay the claim, then she can look beyond the business assets and seize the home and savings account of either Anderson or Bell. Thus the partners are said to have unlimited liability. As in the case of the single proprietorship, the owners' losses are not limited to the amount invested in the business; instead, creditors may reach beyond the business and seize available personal assets if this course of action is necessary. Unlimited liability is a serious disadvantage of the partnership form of organization.

The unlimited liability feature of the single proprietorship and the general partnership arises from the fact that at law these two forms of organization are not regarded as legal entities—the owner and the business are not regarded as separate. In the single proprietorship it is the owner—not the business—that borrows money, makes contracts, and decides on policies. Since it is the owner who does all these things, the courts hold the owner liable for the results of his actions. Likewise, the courts, for most purposes, do not regard the partnership as being something different and separate from the partners. When this view is adopted, it follows that the partners—not the partnership—are liable for unpaid business debts. The partners—not the partnership—borrow money, make contracts, and engage in other actions. The lack of legal entity status for most purposes is an important feature of the partnership.

The Limited Partnership

A special form of partnership known as the *limited partnership* provides limited liability for one or more members of the firm. Thus, if Jerry Altman is a limited partner who has $3,000 invested in the business, he cannot lose more than $3,000 in the venture. In other words, if the partnership fails, Altman will not have to fear that any of his personal assets will be attached. Partnership creditors cannot reach beyond the business assets and seize the personal assets of a limited partner.

Some additional features of the limited partnership are (1) there must be at least one partner with unlimited liability, (2) limited partnerships are formed in accordance with state law, and it is customary to require the filing of the partnership agreement in the county courthouse in the area in which the firm is to do business, (3) limited partners cannot participate in the management of the firm if they are to maintain their status as limited partners, and (4) the partnership is not necessarily dissolved when a limited partner sells his interest or dies.

The Corporation

From the investor's viewpoint, a most important feature of corporations is that they confer only limited liability on the shareholders. This means that creditors of the corporation can look only to the corporation for payment of their claims; creditors cannot seize (except in a few special situations) the owners' (stockholders') personal assets to pay for business debts. Assume that Robert Jones purchased stock of the Adams Corporation at $5 a share and that Jones had a home and a savings account. When the Adams Corporation failed, creditors of the corporation could not seize Jones's home and savings account to satisfy their unpaid claims. If the creditors' claims are not paid in full when a corporation fails, the creditors must bear the loss. Jones lost all the money he invested in the stock of the Adams Corporation. This was bad enough, but the debacle would have been even worse if he had had to use part of his personal assets to pay business creditors. Limited liability is said to exist in the corporation because the individual shareholder's possible loss is—with two minor exceptions—limited to the cost of the securities purchased. The limited liability feature of corporations gives this form of organization an advantage over the single proprietorship and the general partnership.

The two minor situations in which stockholders do not have limited liability are: (1) the stockholders may be liable when they purchase unissued stock from a corporation at a figure that is below the par or stated value of the security, the amount of the liability being equal to the difference between the par or stated value of the shares and the amount paid for them; and (2) in some states stockholders may be assessed for unpaid wages of labor earned within a period of several months prior to bankruptcy.

The limited liability feature of the corporation stems from the fact that the latter is considered to be a *legal entity*. This means that the corporation is regarded as something separate and apart from the owners. Assets used in the business are owned by the corporation—not by the stockholders. The stockholders own the corporation but not the assets of the corporation. Also, debts are contracted by the corporation—not by the stockholders. Likewise, policies are made by the corporation—not by the stockholders. Because it is the corporation that owns assets, goes into debt, and makes policies, the stockholders, as a general rule, are not liable for any unpaid debts of the corporation.

The corporation has many of the rights and privileges of a human being. It can make contracts, sue, be sued, own real estate, and do many other things that an individual might do. For these reasons, the corporation is often referred to as an artificial person.

An owner of a single proprietorship can sell his business, but the transfer may be a slow process. Some aspects of the negotiation may take time. A buyer must be sought, an agreement must be reached on the price, and debts of the business must be paid. Compared to the speed with which the shares of stock of a large corporation may be sold, selling a single proprietorship takes considerable time.

As a general rule, the disposition of an interest in a partnership is a slow process because of the difficult problems of valuation. A further obstacle is that each partner has the right to approve of persons who are about to become his partners. This right to select one's partners is known as *delectus personae*. Assume that a partnership consisting of four members is considering John Edge for admittance to the partnership. Each of the four members of the firm must approve of the admittance of Edge. If any member is opposed to him, he cannot become a partner. The right to choose one's partners is one of the most valuable rights of a partner, because it enables each person to choose those whom he wants as colleagues.

MEETING THE NEED FOR TRANSFERABILITY

The Single Proprietorship and the Partnership

The Corporation   A person may transfer his ownership interest in a corporation without the approval of the corporation or other stockholders. *Delectus personae*, which exists in general partnerships, does not apply to corporations. From the selling stockholder's viewpoint, it is easier to find buyers for the shares of some companies than others. If, for example, a person owns shares of stock in General Motors Corporation, he can sell these shares within a few minutes by notifying a stockbroker of the intent to sell. On the other hand, a stockholder may have difficulty in finding a buyer for shares in a not too well-known company. However, the relative ease with which an owner (stockholder) may sell his interest in a corporation encourages people to invest in these organizations. (See Figure 2-1.)

MEETING THE NEED FOR FUNDS   The size of the single proprietorship is limited to the amount of funds that can be raised from the owner's personal resources plus the amount that can be borrowed from creditors. The owner might, for example, contribute some of his own funds, borrow from a bank, borrow from friends, and borrow from local businessmen; but there is usually a limit to the amount that he can borrow. A disadvantage of the single proprietorship may be the difficulty in raising enough cash to permit the most efficient level of operations.

The Single Proprietorship and the Partnership

FIGURE 2-1
Face of
Stock Certificate

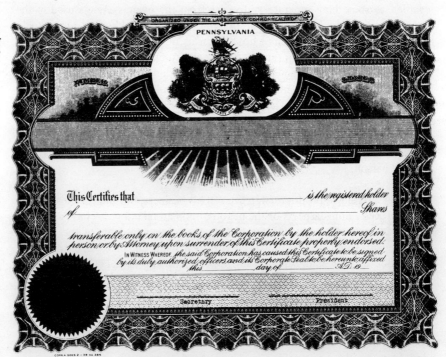

The partnership has an advantage over the single proprietorship in that two or more partners are often able to muster more cash than any one individual can raise. The combined resources of the partners may enable the firm to operate at a more efficient size than could be achieved under a single proprietorship. But, as in the case of the single proprietorship, there is a limit to the amount of funds that can be raised. The upper limit consists of the amount that can be marshaled by the partners plus whatever can be borrowed. Business ventures that require large aggregates of capital, such as automobile manufacturing, could not operate as partnerships, because this form of organization would not supply the mechanism whereby funds could be raised to acquire the assets.

If the corporation appears to be in a position to make profits, the public is quite willing to buy shares of stock in the company with the expectation of sharing in these profits. Whenever a business is going to need large sums of cash to commence operations, it is customary to form a corporation. The corporation, because it can appeal to many investors, is in a much better position to raise funds than the single proprietorship and the partnership. *There are three main reasons why corporations can raise funds so readily: the stockholders have limited liability; the stockholders can transfer their equity with relative ease; and the corporation, being a permanent form of organization, engenders investor confidence.* The ability to raise large sums of cash is one of the outstanding advantages of the corporate form of organization.

The Corporation

A businessman seeks to minimize, over a period of time, the sum of (1) his personal federal income taxes, and (2) the federal taxes paid by the corporation on his share of the profits.

MEETING THE NEED FOR MINIMUM FEDERAL TAXES

The single proprietorship itself does not pay federal income taxes; instead, the businessman reports on his personal federal income tax return the profits earned by his single proprietorship. Even if the owner does not remove the net income from the business, he must pay a tax on the total earnings. For example, if a single proprietorship has profits of $20,000, and if the owner withdraws only $10,000, he must still pay taxes on the total net profits of $20,000.

The Single Proprietorship and the Partnership

The taxation of profits earned by a partnership is basically the same as that of a single proprietorship. The partnership pays no federal income tax; the partners include on their personal income tax return their share of the profits (or losses).

The lowest tax rate on a personal income tax return is 14 percent, while the highest rate is 70 percent. The tax rate on marginal increments of taxable income gradually increases from 14 to 70 percent as the taxpayer's taxable income gradually increases. However, if the income from a business is from personal services, the maximum tax rate is 50 percent. Thus the services performed by a partnership of doctors would result in income from personal services, and it would be taxed at a rate not higher than 50 percent; but the income from a partnership that manufactured pots and pans would not be income from personal services, and such income could be taxed at a marginal rate as high as 70 percent.

The Corporation   Legally speaking, corporations are subject to a normal tax of 22 percent on all taxable income, plus an additional surtax of 26 percent on all taxable income over $25,000. For computational purposes and for decision-making purposes, the tax rate is 22 percent on the first $25,000, plus 48 percent on all taxable income over $25,000. Thus a firm with $60,000 of taxable income would pay a tax of $22,300:

$$22\% \times \$25,000 = \$\ 5,500$$
$$48\% \times\ \ \ 35,000 = \underline{\ 16,800}$$
$$\$22,300$$

The corporate tax rate structure is relatively simple, for there are only the two rates. This is in contrast with the individual personal income tax table, which has numerous rates depending on the size of the taxable income.

Ordinarily the net profits of a corporation are subject to double taxation— once when the corporation earns them and again when the stockholder receives them as dividends. The fact that the investor can exclude the first $100 of dividends ($200 if a joint return is filed) from taxable income is only slight relief from the double taxation.

At the lower and moderate taxable income levels, the personal income tax rates are lower than the corporate tax rates; but at very high levels of taxable income, the maximum rate of 48 percent on corporate taxable income is lower than the maximum rate of 70 percent (or 50 percent) on the personal income tax return.

Attempts to Neutralize Income Tax Considerations   The U.S. government is seeking to neutralize (for small businesses) the federal income tax factor when the taxpayer is determining the best form of organization. In congressional hearings it was stated that small businesses should be able to select the most advantageous form of organization "without the necessity of taking into account major differences in tax consequences." A provision in the tax law, widely known as Subchapter S, permits small corporations to be taxed as a partnership or as a single proprietorship. Basically, this means that the corporation is excused from paying taxes, provided the stockholders include in their personal income tax returns their proportionate share of the corporation's gains or losses. If one person owns the corporation, a similar concept applies if he agrees to report in his personal tax return the profits or losses incurred by the corporation. Subchapter S is a significant feature of the tax laws because it states that under certain conditions a corporation may elect to be taxed as an unincorporated business. This tax development may accelerate the trend toward incorporation to gain the advantage of limited liability, without incurring the possible disadvantage of being subject to the corporate tax rates.

Congressional intent is that the provisions of Subchapter S will apply to "small business corporations." But small business is not defined in terms of level of economic activity, such as volume of sales or total assets; instead, it is defined as a corporation that does not violate certain conditions, three of which are:

1. There must not be more than ten stockholders
2. There must be only one class of stock (no preferred)
3. The income must come from certain sources

The major advantages of a small business corporation electing to be taxed as a partnership are twofold: first, the profits may be taxed at a lower rate, since the tax rate on personal income may be lower than the tax rate on corporate income; and second, the net profits of the corporation are taxed only once, for when these corporate profits are eventually distributed as dividends, they are not subject to a second tax (double taxation is eliminated).

Over 300,000 small corporations are now electing to be taxed as partnerships.

In conclusion, Subchapter S has reduced substantially the federal income tax factor as an element in decision making on the best form of organization to select.

THE CHARTER

The *charter* is a basic contractual document in that it defines the rights, duties, and limitations of the corporation. The corporate charter must be in agreement with the federal Constitution and the laws of the state from which the charter was obtained.

The incorporators must select the name under which they intend to do business. The name should not be exactly the same as that used by some other corporation, and it should be carefully selected because it may influence the purchasers of the commodities sold or services rendered by the corporation. In many states the term "corporation" or "incorporated" must accompany the name selected. In most charters the naming of the corporation is taken care of in a single sentence. After a name has been chosen, it may be changed only by amending the charter.

The second feature of a charter is a brief statement of the "principal office" of the corporation. This office is not always the place where most of the business is conducted; instead, it is a mailing address to which the state and other parties can send legal notices.

All corporate charters contain statements as to the purpose or purposes for which the corporation is being formed. The powers granted to the corporation may be broad or narrow, depending on the intent of the incorporators. Article 3 of the certificate of incorporation of General Motors Corporation contains nine paragraphs on the nature of the business that may be conducted by the company. In addition to the specified powers permitted by the charter, a corporation is presumed to have implied powers. For example, the right to borrow money is an implied power and need not be stated in the charter. There is a tendency to grant broad powers to corporations and to give directors a maximum amount of freedom in managing the corporation's affairs.

A company must state in its charter the maximum amount and kind of stock that it will issue. It is not necessary that all the stock be issued at the time the business commences operations. The charter places an upper limit on the amount of stock that may be issued as long as the terms of the charter are in effect. If a company finds that it needs to issue more than the authorized shares, the charter can be amended.

Charters usually require a statement of the names and addresses of the original incorporators and of the original subscribers to the stock.

Most states grant perpetual charters; that is, the life of the corporation is not limited to a certain number of years. However, the term *perpetual* must be used with care, as a number of events, such as bankruptcy, may lead to the termination of the legal existence of the corporation.

Those who are active in the formation of the corporation and who sign the application to become a corporation are known as the incorporators. In most states, before a corporation can be formed there must be at least three incorporators. After the application for incorporation is signed by the incorporators, it is sent to the secretary of state or some comparable state official, who, after approving the formation of the corporation, returns a copy of the application to the incorporators. This application, which now has been approved by the state, becomes the corporation charter. Upon receipt of the charter, the corporation is permitted to begin its business transactions.

RIGHTS OF COMMON STOCKHOLDERS

Common stockholders come into possession of a variety of rights and privileges when they become stockholders in a corporation. The exact nature of these rights and privileges is determined mainly by provisions in the federal Constitution, state law, the corporate charter, and the bylaws of the corporation.

Right to Share in Profits When Distributed as Dividends

The right to share in corporate profits paid as dividends is one of the most important rights of common stockholders. If the corporation is successful and makes large profits, the stockholders expect to benefit through dividends and an increase in the market value of their shares. Even though the corporation is earning large profits, the stockholders may not be receiving dividends because the directors of the corporation sometimes decide to retain all the profits in the business. It is a well-established principle of law that directors have the right to declare or not to declare dividends and that only in very rare cases will the courts force the directors to declare a dividend. Courts take the view that directors are presumed to be acting in the best interests of the corporation when profits are withheld from stockholders.

Voting Rights

Stockholders vote on such matters as selecting the directors, amending the charter, and approving bonus plans for officers. The corporate charter and state law determine the matters on which stockholders have the right to vote.

Preemptive Right

The *preemptive right* gives the stockholders of a corporation the first chance to purchase newly issued common stock and newly issued securities convertible into common stock. The amount of newly issued securities that can be purchased by a stockholder is determined by the number of shares already owned in relation to the total shares outstanding. For example, if Corporation X has 1,000 shares of common stock outstanding, and if Gerald Ashforth already owns 100 of these shares, Ashforth would be entitled to purchase one-tenth of all new shares of common stock and one-tenth of all securities convertible into common stock. He would not have to purchase these securities; he could purchase them if he cared to do so, assuming that he had the preemptive right.

As with many stockholders' rights, it is possible for stockholders to waive the preemptive right at the time the common stock is bought. If the charter denies the preemptive right (as does the charter of General Motors Corporation), the stockholders automatically waive this right at the time the stock is purchased. The exact status of the preemptive right varies somewhat from one state to another. Delaware promoters may deny the preemptive right through a provision in the charter to this effect; in Indiana, the stockholders are assumed not to have the preemptive right unless it is specifically granted in the charter or granted by resolution of the board of directors. There is a growing tendency for charters to deny the preemptive right in states that permit its waiver. Even when stockholders have the preemptive right, at times they waive it, as, for example, when the company desires to sell stock to employees under an employee stock-ownership plan.

Management usually prefers not to have to abide by the preemptive right when selling securities. When this right is absent, management has more flexibility in selling the securities to the buyer who makes the best and quickest offer. The absence of the preemptive right also eliminates the possible problem of allocating new securities when there are several classes of shares already outstanding.

Common stockholders have the right to inspect the books of the corporation of which they are part owners, although the exact amount of information obtainable is determined by state laws and court interpretations of these laws.

Right to Inspect the Corporation's Books

Stockholders are usually granted the right to look over the part of the corporation records that contains a list of names and addresses of stockholders. When a stockholder seeks to inspect detailed records pertaining to costs and sales, the corporation's officers might object on the grounds that this information is confidential and would injure the company if publicized. Most large corporations make regular and reasonably detailed reports to stockholders, so that only on rare occasions does the stockholder seek personal inspection of the corporate records.

A stockholder can stop his corporation from engaging in acts *ultra vires*, that is, acts beyond the powers of the corporation as stated or implied in the charter. A stockholder might, for example, invest in a corporation because he believes the corporation is going to engage in money-making activities, as stated in the charter. But if the corporation engages in some activity beyond its power in the charter, an investor might decide that the corporation has broken its contract

Right to Prevent Acts Ultra Vires

with the stockholder to engage in only specified activities. If the corporation has already engaged in the act *ultra vires*, the stockholder can take legal action against the directors who willingly permitted the corporation to commit an act beyond its powers. The chance of a corporation's engaging in an act *ultra vires* is considerably decreased in modern times because of the ease with which a charter can be amended and because of the wide powers now granted in corporate charters.

Right to Transfer Certificates

The right to transfer shares is one of the most important rights of stockholders. The corporation does not make any promise to return the common stockholders' money at a specified time, the funds being committed to the company permanently. Hence, if a stockholder wants to sell his shares, he must seek out some other purchaser. The right to transfer one's stock without permission from the corporation facilitates the shifting of shares to others when one desires to convert his securities into cash.

In special instances the stockholders may waive the right to transfer their stock to the general public. For example, a stockholder might agree to offer to sell his shares first to other stockholders in the corporation before selling them to nonstockholders. This situation is most likely to exist in a close corporation. Thus the three main stockholders of the Dodgers baseball club had an agreement whereby if any of them decided to sell, they would give the other two stockholders the first chance to purchase the stock. When Branch Rickey parted company with the Dodgers, his 25 percent of the stock was purchased by the two other parties to the agreement. Arrangements of this sort are advantageous when there are only a few stockholders and they do not wish outsiders to have even a minority interest in the corporation.

THE RESUSCITATION OF THE BUSINESS TRUST

Closely resembling the corporation is the *business trust*, also known as a *Massachusetts trust* or a *voluntary association*. The business trust is formed by drafting a trust agreement which is signed by the creators of the trust. The trust agreement serves the same purpose as the charter serves in the corporation. The business trust issues both stocks and bonds, although the shares are often called *certificates of beneficial interest*. The shares of a business trust are as readily transferable as the shares of a corporation. The holders of shares in a business trust have the same limited liability as the stockholders in a corporation.

One of the outstanding features of the business trust is that shareholders are not permitted to vote for the board of trustees who manage the business. If the shareholders vote for the trustees or otherwise participate in the management, they no longer have limited liability, the courts holding the organization to be a partnership. The inability of shareholders to elect trustees is one of the main differences between the business trust and the corporation. The trustees in a business trust are self-perpetuating; that is, when a vacancy occurs, the remaining trustees fill the position by selecting an additional trustee.

Unlike the corporation, the business trust has a limited life. An example is the

Northwestern Leather Company, which will terminate 21 years after the death of the last survivor of the original seven trustees. At the end of that time, the agreement may be renewed by the current trustees if they so desire.

Business trusts are now widely used in financing real estate transactions in the United States. Congress has encouraged the development of business trusts (engaged in real estate transactions) by giving *eligible* ones a tax-free status, provided they distribute at least 90 percent of their profits to holders of the certificates of beneficial interest.

When the business trust engages in real estate transactions, it is commonly referred to as a *real estate investment trust (REIT)*. This special organization is quite similar to an investment company in that both seek diversification for investors; the difference is that the REIT seeks diversification by participating in a number of real estate transactions, whereas the *investment company* seeks this objective by purchasing the stocks and bonds of a large number of corporations.

The single proprietorship and the general partnership enjoy several advantages. They are relatively easy to start; no federal income tax is necessarily levied on them; both are relatively free from government regulation; and both are relatively easy to dissolve. The two main disadvantages are the unlimited liability feature and the difficulty of raising large sums of money.

The main advantages of the corporate form of organization are that stockholders have limited liability; the corporation is better able to raise large sums of cash than the single proprietorship or the partnership; the corporation is a relatively permanent form of organization; the shares of many corporations are readily transferable; and, in certain cases, the corporation has a tax advantage over the partnership and the single proprietorship. On the other hand, certain disadvantages are attached to this form of organization. The corporation is subject to heavy taxes; it is unable to do business in other states without first qualifying as a foreign corporation (the partnership and the single proprietorship, however, do not need to qualify in states in which they do business); and the corporation is not as flexible as the single proprietorship and the partnership, for corporations can engage only in acts allowed by the charter. Despite several disadvantages, the corporate form of organization continues to grow in importance.

HIGHLIGHTS OF THIS CHAPTER

2-1. Explain the meaning of these terms:

REVIEW QUESTIONS

limited liability
delectus personae
act *ultra vires*
outside director
certificate of beneficial interest
legal entity
preemptive right

2-2. Why is General Motors Corporation operated as a corporation, rather than as a general partnership?

2-3. Answer these questions on organization: (a) Can one person own a corporation? (b) Can the president fire the board of directors? (c) Can the number of directors exceed the number of employees?

2-4. Stephen Clark and Louis Webster, two engineers, decided to start a business that would manufacture expensive thermometers and other equipment of high quality. The two men estimated that they would need about $40,000 to begin operations on an economical scale. Each had his home paid for and each had about $10,000 in the bank and approximately $60,000 in other assets. The two men believed that their venture would be a success, but they were not sure enough to risk all their personal fortune. If they could find backers for their project, each would be willing to place a temporary annual limit of $20,000 on his salary. Which of the following forms of organization seems best suited to their needs: the corporation, the single proprietorship, or the general partnership?

2-5. Five college students have decided to establish a corporation to operate a bookstore on their campus. They will need, according to informed estimates, $128,500 in assets to commence operations at an efficient level. Most of the assets will be supplied by trade creditors, commercial banks, stockholders, and others. But the students will need $15,000 in cash to launch this enterprise. Answer these questions. (a) What are the advantages of operating the bookstore as a corporation instead of a general partnership? (b) What would be some advantages of including a local banker, a local lawyer, and a local accountant on the board of directors? (c) Where will the students obtain the $15,000?

REVIEW PROBLEMS   The answers to the problems appear at the end of this section. *For each problem show how you obtained the answer.*

2-1. George Vickers has committed $10,000 of his savings to a new small business that he has established. Last year, his taxable income from the business was $15,000. He could have earned 6 percent if he had placed his $10,000 in a commercial bank; he could have earned a salary of $10,000 working for a large firm. What are his "true profits," before taxes?

2-2. Company R, a corporation, had taxable income of $100,000, subject to these tax rates: 22 percent on the first $25,000 and 48 percent on all income over $25,000. How much in income taxes did this firm pay?

Answers: 2-1, $4,400; 2-2, $41,500.

John Crosley and Frederick Wicksell formed a partnership for the purpose of producing and selling detergents and allied products to drugstores, restaurants, hotels, and similar establishments. The business grew steadily, and after some months, at the suggestion of a customer, they added paper toweling, paper cups, paper tissues, and other janitorial supplies to their list of products. Crosley did the production work, kept the books, tended the storeroom, and did the shipping. Wicksell was the salesman, and he did an excellent job. The partners had agreed orally to contribute equal capital and to share equally any profits or losses. They had also agreed that each would take the same compensation.

Wicksell suddenly announced to Crosley that he intended to form a corporation with 3,000 shares of stock to be issued, of which he would take 1,500 shares, his wife would be allotted 30 shares, and Crosley would be given 1,470 shares. He informed Crosley, in addition, that he intended to control the corporation with the 51 percent of the stock and to be a director and also president. He announced that Crosley could work for the corporation but could not be a director. Finally, Wicksell informed Crosley that if he, Crosley, would not go along with this proposition, he would dissolve the partnership and liquidate the assets, which would probably net about $15,000. Crosley reluctantly signed, as one of the three incorporators, the articles of incorporation. The assets of the partnership were to be transferred to the corporation as consideration for the stock.

Required: (a) Discuss the principal issues involved; (b) How might this situation have been avoided?

Need a contract that will indicate what procedure will occur in case of Breakup.

Alfred Johnson, married and 53 years old, is reviewing his business activities with the purpose of deciding whether to change the form of organization of some or all of his ventures. Johnson has in mind not only his own financial future but also that of his family, which consists of his wife, Mary, age 52; a daughter, Sue, age 30; and a son, Harold, age 23. Johnson had been thinking of making this evaluation for some time, but he procrastinated until the death of one of his partners brought the problem into focus.

Thirty years ago Johnson began his business career as a salesman in a firm which at that time was known as the Clark Company. This business has continued to the present day its specialized operations of exterminating bugs, rats, mice, and other pests. The Clark Company carries on a profitable activity by servicing hotels, restaurants, public buildings, and, to some extent, homes. The company has yearly contracts with most of its customers and makes monthly service visits to them. The firm has no competitors, and by using low-cost labor it is able to prosper. At the end of his third year with the Clark Company, Johnson was earning $4,800 a year, a sum which he thought was too low. After careful consideration, he decided to resign and to start a competing service. He gave his employer one month's notice and in the meantime began to make arrangements to start his own business. When Clark heard of these actions, he became alarmed and offered to take Johnson in as an equal partner. Johnson accepted this offer, and the firm was renamed Clark and Johnson Company. Actually both men were pleased with the new general partnership because each had a secret fear that the other might obtain the bulk of the business. Over the years the business has grown and prospered, mainly because of the lucrative contracts with a number of large hotels in the area. Presently, each partner is receiving an annual income of $18,000 as his share of the profits, and each has invested $20,000 in the firm. An outsider recently offered to buy the business for $120,000. The prospects for the continued success of the business look bright. Tragedy occurred when Clark died a month ago from a heart attack. This was the event that led to Johnson's decision to review the form of organization of all of his activities.

Early in his marriage Johnson inherited $16,000, a sum which was invested in a $40,000 apartment house. The couple used $5,000 of their savings, and they obtained a $19,000 mortgage to finance the purchase. The rents received gradually liquidated the mortgage, and the building is now debt free. The estimated current market value of the structure is $55,000. The apartment business is conducted technically as a single proprietorship.

Ten years ago the owner of one of the local drugstores died. Johnson was anxious to acquire this business because of its excellent location and profit possibilities. Johnson and a young registered pharmacist from another drugstore in town decided to form a general partnership and to buy the business from the wife of the deceased owner. The two were able to acquire the drugstore for $30,500 (each partner supplied half this amount). A few years later, the young pharmacist married Johnson's daughter Sue. Johnson is attached to his son-in-law, but he does not consider him to have much business sense, although the druggist is an excellent technician. The drugstore has been expanded over the years and is now quite profitable; each partner's share of the net income is $12,000. Both men estimate the business could now be sold for $100,000. The town in which this drugstore is located is growing; hence the outlook is bright for this enterprise.

Johnson also has a successful real estate operation. Five years ago he bought a large tract of land for $35,000. This land is being subdivided and sold as lots for residential purposes. Johnson estimates that within the next few years he will be able to sell all the original land for a total of $225,000. There is, however, still a $12,000 mortgage on the property, as Johnson financed this deal mainly through his local bank. Johnson's son Harold (unmarried) has been devoting all his time to selling these lots. Harold is a college graduate, and he has had two years' experience with a public accounting firm. These real estate operations are conducted as a single proprietorship.

Although Johnson has some personal assets, most of his wealth is in his business ventures. His personal balance sheet appears in Table 2-2.

Required: What program of action do you recommend for Johnson? (Remember that he must find a way to settle Clark's widow's claim of $60,000.)

TABLE 2-2
Alfred Johnson's
Personal Balance Sheet

Assets (at Market Value)

Cash in bank	$ 4,000
United States government bonds	9,000
Residence	25,000
Stocks of corporations	15,000
Cash surrender value of life insurance	18,000
Equity in Clark and Johnson Company	60,000
Apartment house	55,000
Equity in drugstore	50,000
Real estate project	225,000
Other assets	15,000
Total	$476,000

Liabilities

Mortgage on land	$ 12,000
Personal loan at bank	25,000
Total	$ 37,000

Net Worth

Estimated equity	$439,000

Principles of Valuation

Many business transactions require that a value be placed on income-producing property. This valuation process is called capitalizing income. In the discussion to follow, the term *income-producing property* will include such items as business firms, real estate, bonds, common stock, and preferred stock. A value can be assigned to these items based on the net income that they are expected to produce in the future and on the *rate* of return that a given investor expects to earn on them. This value is called the capitalized value. The capitalization of income may be classified into two situations: (1) when the income produced by the property is expected to continue without a time limit, as when a business firm is expected to earn an average of $40,000 a year indefinitely; and (2) when the return from income-producing property is expected to continue for a limited period of time, as when a bond contract promises to pay its holder $40 a year for 20 years, plus $1,000 at maturity. Capitalization of income is a valuable planning tool in the area of quantitative decision making.

The capitalization of income can be applied only to property that has prospects of producing a net income in the future. Whether or not the capitalization process can be used depends on the use to which the property is put rather than its nature. Thus a wedding ring is income-producing property to a jewelry store but not to a wife who wears it. The process of capitalizing income can be used by the jeweler in placing a value on the ring, but it cannot be used to indicate the wife's sentimental valuation of the item. In this chapter we will be concerned with the problem of placing a value on property used for business purposes. The following phases of capitalizing income will be discussed:

1. Capitalizing a stream of returns that is expected to continue indefinitely
    a. Formula for capitalizing income
    b. Estimating the stream of net returns
    c. Determining the capitalization rate

2. Capitalizing a stream of returns that is expected to continue for a limited period of time
    a. Factors affecting the capitalization rate
    b. The compound amount of $1
    c. The present value of $1
    d. The present value of an annuity of $1
3. Forces that cause changes in capitalized values
4. Some applications of capitalizing income

CAPITALIZING A STREAM OF RETURNS THAT IS EXPECTED TO CONTINUE INDEFINITELY

Formula for Capitalizing Income

Capitalizing income is the process of placing a value, called the capitalized value, on income-producing property by estimating the future net income that will be produced by this property and then dividing this estimate by the rate of return that a given person expects to earn on his investment. An income-producing property is expected to have a stream of net income, a certain amount being earned each year. The prospective income has value to those who are entitled to share in it. This anticipated flow of returns is the source from which the value of an income-producing unit arises. The *capitalization rate* is the rate of return that a given person expects to receive on his money, assuming an investment with a given degree of risk. For example, assume that a person believes that an income-producing property will yield an average annual profit of $10,000 for an indefinite number of years and that he expects a 10 percent return on his money. What is the capitalized value of this property?

$$\text{Capitalized value} = \frac{\text{Expected average annual net income}}{\text{rate of return expected on investment (capitalization rate)}}$$
$$= \frac{\$10,000}{.10}$$
$$= \$100,000$$

The capitalized value of the property is $100,000. The process of capitalizing income requires two sets of data: (1) the estimated future annual net return and (2) the capitalization rate. The formula for capitalizing income is useful because it summarizes into two classes the thousands of forces that affect the capitalized value of an income-producing property.

Capitalized value is different from market value; only by coincidence will the two be the same. This is because capitalized value is a rational process of determining the worth of an income-producing property, whereas market value is determined by a mixture of rational and irrational processes. Capitalized value might be described as a reasonable value rather than a necessarily actual value.

Estimating the Stream of Annual Net Returns

In capitalizing income only *future* annual net returns should be used. The task of estimating future returns is a difficult one. The starting point in making such a prediction is the past, as past earnings are useful partial evidence of what future returns will be. Thus in some transactions the net operating earnings of the previous five years are averaged and used as a starting point in predicting the future performance of the company. But in compiling these historic figures, care is taken to remove nonrecurring gains, such as a gain realized on the sale of a building. Usually, only earnings attributable to operations of the firm are included in the figure that is to be capitalized. Also, federal income taxes are deducted from the earnings figure before the capitalization rate is applied. The net income figure is further adjusted for any other factors that would make the adjusted amount more representative of the expected future earnings. The long-run prospects of the company must be taken into consideration. If the firm's profits have an upward trend, recent earnings are given more weight; and a historical period, such as five years, need not be used. In the same way, if the trend of earnings is downward, the earnings of the last year or two are often more indicative of the firm's future than a five-year average or longer. These comments may be illustrated by referring to Table 3-1. Company A has shown little growth over the five-year period. Hence, the average of the five-year span might be taken as typical of what the future will be like, unless the investor has some information to the contrary. Company B has been on the decline, and a five-year average would not be a suitable figure to capitalize. Probably the earnings of the last two years should be averaged to obtain an amount that could be capitalized. Even this amount would be too high if the decline were expected to continue at the present rate. Company C, in contrast, has been improving the trend of its earnings. The average of the last five years would not be a suitable amount to capitalize because it probably understates the future annual income to the firm. In this case the average for the past two years could be used as a starting point, and adjustments could be made for whatever amount the investor believes will be added to this amount in future years. Past earnings, then, are useful only as a starting point in predicting future earnings. The investor must use his judgment in bridging the gap between the past and the future. Although the capitalization process looks to the past for guidance, only anticipated future earnings are of any use in the capitalization process.

TABLE 3-1
Earnings Trend of
Three Companies

	Company A	Company B	Company C
One year ago	$6,500	$ 7,000	$11,000
Two years ago	6,400	8,000	10,500
Three years ago	6,400	10,000	10,000
Four years ago	6,500	10,500	8,000
Five years ago	6,400	11,000	7,000

Determining the
Capitalization Rate

Capitalization rates are found by studying the return earned by companies in a similar line of activity. Such a study involves an analysis of the return being earned on stocks, bonds, small businesses, and other forms of income-producing property. In general, capitalization rates range from approximately 4 to 25 percent.

4 to 5%

If a value is to be placed on an income stream that is expected to continue forever, the valuation process consists of dividing the expected future average annual cash flow by the capitalization rate. However, since most business transactions are expected to give annual cash flows for a *limited* number of years, this procedure must be modified. The modification consists of using compound interest tables for finding the capitalized (discounted) value of this kind of investment (that is, one that is expected to emit a cash flow for a relatively limited period of years).

CAPITALIZING A STREAM OF RETURNS THAT IS EXPECTED TO CONTINUE FOR A LIMITED PERIOD OF TIME

Limited # of yrs.

The actual capitalization rate used in a specific transaction depends on a number of factors, the most important of which are: (1) the risk involved in the commitment and (2) the supply and demand of funds in the money market.

Factors Affecting the Capitalization Rate

An investor uses an increasingly larger capitalization rate as the risk of the transaction increases. The risk increases as the uncertainty of actually receiving the estimated future income increases and as the variability of the flow of estimated future income increases. Thus an investor might be satisfied with a 5 percent return on United States government securities because he is virtually certain of receiving the same dollar income each year. On the other hand, an investor might expect a 7 percent return over a period of time on the common stock of Greyhound Bus Corporation because the return is more uncertain on this security. Or an investor might expect a 20 percent return on an investment in a small grocery store because the high competitive risks in this situation make the possibility of receiving any profits very uncertain.

Risk

An important factor that affects risk is the time element, that is, the time at which the investor expects to receive the returns. Generally speaking, the distant future has more risk than the near future. Therefore, a promise to an investor to pay him $100 twenty years from now has less certainty of completion than a promise to pay him $100 two years from now. Investors, therefore, capitalize at a higher rate income that is expected to be received in, say, twenty years than income expected to be received in, say, two years. An investor might capitalize at 6 percent income that he expects to receive twenty years from now, whereas he might capitalize at 5 percent income that he expects to receive two years from now, assuming all factors are the same except the maturity date. An example of these comments can be seen in Table 3-2, in which yields (capitalization rates) increase as the time span increases.

Another factor that influences capitalization rates is the supply and demand of funds in the economy. If those who have funds have a surplus of them, they

Supply and Demand of Funds

Year Due	Amount Due	Yield (Capitalization Rate in Percentages)
1983	$1,000,000	4.5
1984	1,000,000	4.6
1985	1,000,000	4.7
1986	1,000,000	4.8
1987	1,000,000	4.9

may, in their eagerness to keep their money invested, lower the rate of return that they will accept on their investment. Contrarily, if those who have funds to invest find that the demand for funds is great, they may charge a higher rate and still be able to invest their money. Supply and demand explains why the capitalization rate used on long-term United States government bonds varies between 5 and 8 percent.

Using the Table That Shows the Compound Amount of $1 (Table 3-3)

Table 3-3 answers the question: If a person or business firm invests a fixed sum in the present, how much will it amount to at a certain date in the future, assuming interest is earned at a fixed rate and is compounded yearly (n being the number of years the money is invested)? The table is used as follows.

TABLE 3-3
Compound Amount of $1
(with Interest
Compounded Yearly)

3%	3½%	4%	5%	6%	n
1.0300	1.0350	1.0400	1.0500	1.0600	1
1.0609	1.0712	1.0816	1.1025	1.1236	2
1.0927	1.1087	1.1249	1.1576	1.1910	3
1.1255	1.1475	1.1699	1.2155	1.2625	4
1.1593	1.1877	1.2167	1.2763	1.3382	5
1.1941	1.2293	1.2653	1.3401	1.4185	6
1.2299	1.2723	1.3159	1.4071	1.5036	7
1.2668	1.3168	1.3686	1.4775	1.5938	8
1.3048	1.3629	1.4233	1.5513	1.6895	9
1.3439	1.4106	1.4802	1.6289	1.7908	10

Step 1. Find the rate of interest to be earned and the number of years the money is to be invested. Then look under the corresponding dollar column. The dollar column will give the accumulated amount if $1 is invested at compound interest for the number of years at the stated rate.

Step 2. Multiply original amount invested by the accumulated amount of $1, which has already been found in step 1.

Illustration If Robert Adams invests $1,500 at 4 percent compound interest, how much will his fund amount to at the end of six years?

Step 1. If Adams had invested $1, his original investment would have grown to $1.2653.

Step 2. Since Adams is investing $1,500, his total investment will be 1,500 multiplied by $1.2653, or $1,897.95.

Answer: Adams will have $1,897.95.

Richard Evans purchased a nondividend-paying stock five years ago for $10; today the stock is worth $13.382 per share. At what annual rate is this stock growing in value?

Problem

The answer is 6 percent, determined as follows. Divide $13.382 by the original price of $10. The quotient is 1.3382. Begin on the left-hand side of the five-year line and move to the right until the number closest to the quotient appears. Then look to the percentage figure at the top of the column containing the factor. In this example, the factor in the table happens to be the same as the quotient; the interest rate at the top of this column is 6 percent.

Solution

Table 3-4 answers the question: How much will have to be set aside in the present to have a certain sum available at a fixed date in the future, assuming that the investment earns interest compounded yearly (n being the number of years the money is invested)? The table is used as follows.

Using the Table That Shows the Present Value of $1 (Table 3-4)

TABLE 3-4 Present Value of $1 (with Interest Compounded Yearly)

3%	3½%	4%	5%	6%	n
.97087	.96618	.96154	.95238	.94340	1
.94260	.93351	.92456	.90703	.89000	2
.91514	.90194	.88900	.86384	.83962	3
.88849	.87144	.85480	.82270	.79209	4
.86261	.84197	.82193	.78353	.74726	5
.83748	.81350	.79031	.74622	.70496	6
.81309	.78599	.75992	.71068	.66506	7
.78941	.75941	.73069	.67684	.62741	8
.76642	.73373	.70259	.64461	.59190	9
.74409	.70892	.67556	.61391	.55839	10

Step 1. Find the rate of interest to be earned and the number of years the money is to be invested. Then look under the corresponding dollar column. The dollar column will give the amount that would have to be set aside in the present in order to accumulate $1 at a future time.

Step 2. Multiply the sum desired at the future date by the present value of $1, which has already been obtained in step 1.

Illustration James Johnson wishes to have a fund of $5,000 five years from now. How much will he have to set aside now in order to have the $5,000, assuming the sum set aside in the present earns 3 percent compound interest during the five-year period?

Step 1. If Johnson wanted to have $1 available, he would have had to set aside $0.86261.

Step 2. Since Johnson wants to have available $5,000, he will have to set aside 5,000 multiplied by $0.86261, or $4,313.05.

Answer: Johnson will have to set aside $4,313.05.

The present value of a single cash receipt to be received in the future is the amount of cash that must be set aside today in order to have this specified amount at the future date. Another way to say this is that present value gives the worth today of a promise to receive a certain sum in the future. In the above example, $4,313.05 is the present value of $5,000. The amount set aside today is always less than the amount of cash to be received at the future date because interest is earned on the initial cash deposit. The term *discount* also arises in connection with present value; to discount means to go through the process of computing present value. In theory, *discount* means the thought process of obtaining present value; in practice, it means using interest tables (or formulas) to obtain the present value. In other words, to discount means to subtract something from an item. In the above example, $5,000 is discounted to its present value of $4,313.05. In practice, the terms *discounted value* and *present value* are frequently used as synonyms: $4,313.05 is the present value of $5,000; $4,313.05 is also the discounted value of $5,000.

Using the Table That Shows the Present Value of an Annuity of $1 (Table 3-5)

Table 3-5 answers the question: In order to receive specified payments for a certain period of years, how much will have to be invested, assuming that interest is being earned on the diminishing balance and payments will begin one year after the date of depositing the money?

TABLE 3-5
Present Value of an Annuity of $1 (with Interest Computed Yearly)

3%	3¼%	4%	5%	6%	n
0.9709	0.9662	0.9615	0.9524	0.9434	1
1.9135	1.8997	1.8861	1.8594	1.8334	2
2.8286	2.8016	2.7751	2.7232	2.6730	3
3.7171	3.6731	3.6299	3.5460	3.4651	4
4.5797	4.5151	4.4518	4.3295	4.2124	5
5.4172	5.3286	5.2421	5.0757	4.9173	6
6.2303	6.1145	6.0021	5.7864	5.5824	7
7.0197	6.8740	6.7327	6.4632	6.2098	8
7.7861	7.6077	7.4353	7.1078	6.8017	9
8.5302	8.3166	8.1109	7.7217	7.3601	10
12.5611	12.0941	11.6523	10.8378	10.1059	16
13.1661	12.6513	12.1657	11.2741	10.4773	17
13.7535	13.1897	12.6593	11.6896	10.8276	18
14.3238	13.7098	13.1339	12.0853	11.1581	19
14.8775	14.2124	13.5903	12.4622	11.4699	20

Illustration   Jack Edwards has a son who wants to study for eight years to be a medical doctor. The father desires to provide his son with an annual income of $2,000 for the period. Assuming that the son is to enter college one year from now and that the father wants him to have $2,000 at the beginning of each year, how much of a lump sum will the father have to set aside immediately, if 5 percent is earned on the money?

Step 1. Find the rate of interest and the number of years for which the payments will continue. Then find the corresponding "present value of an annuity of 1," which is $6.4632 in this problem.

Step 2. The figure of $6.4632 is the amount that would have to be set aside in the present to obtain $1 of income for a period of eight years. Since Edwards wants an income of $2,000 for his son, he would multiply 2,000 by $6.4632. The product of this multiplication is $12,926.40.

Answer: Edwards will have to set aside a sum of $12,926.40.

The present value of an annuity is the amount of cash that one must set aside today in a lump sum in order to get back a series of equal cash receipts over a period of years. The known variable is the size of the annual receipts that will be coming in each year; the unknown variable is the lump sum that must be placed aside currently to attain this objective. In the above example, the present value of the annuity of $2,000 a year is $12,926.40. The term *discount* also applies here; the series of equal payments of $2,000 each is said to be discounted to their present value of $12,926.40.

An increase in the capitalization rate or the discount rate will lower the capitalized value of an income-producing property. (In the remainder of this section we will refer to both of these rates as capitalization rates.) Assume that a property is expected to emit a flow of payments of $15,000 a year and that the capitalization rate is 10 percent; the capitalized value is therefore $150,000. But if the capitalization rate increases to 15 percent, the capitalized value will fall to $100,000 ($15,000 ÷ .15). On the other hand, a decrease in the capitalization rate will raise the capitalized value of an income-producing property. A decrease in the capitalization rate from 10 percent to 5 percent will cause the capitalized value to increase to $300,000 ($15,000 ÷ .05). An axiom of finance is that low capitalization rates generally lead to high values and high capitalization rates generally lead to low values.

This phenomenon explains why the price of United States government bonds, the safest investment in the world, fluctuates rather widely. A long-term marketable bond issued by the federal government at $1,000 is likely to fluctuate between $940 and $1,080 over a span of several years. An investor who bought one of these might be irked if he had to sell at a loss a security that is perfectly safe. The reason for this type of fluctuation is that the supply and demand for funds in the economy changes capitalization rates. If an investor has to sell his securities at a time when interest rates (capitalization rates) are high, he will find

FORCES THAT CAUSE CHANGES IN CAPITALIZED VALUES

that the market value of his investment has declined, because rising capitalization rates lower the value. In reverse, he might be fortunate to have to sell his bond at a time when interest rates (capitalization rates) are low, resulting in a high value on his investments. An important point to observe is that this investor encounters price fluctuations only if he sells his bond before maturity. If he holds the bond until maturity, he will not be concerned with the day-to-day fluctuations in the bond market.

An increase in expected average future annual earnings will raise the capitalized value. Assume, to begin, that a firm is expected to have future earnings of $15,000 a year and that these are capitalized at 10 percent. Such a capitalization results in value of $150,000. If future annual net returns are estimated to be $20,000 instead of $15,000, the capitalized value will rise to $200,000. Conversely, a decrease in anticipated future average annual profits will lower the capitalized value. If future profits are estimated to be $10,000 instead of $15,000, the capitalized value of this firm will fall to $100,000. Another axiom of finance is that high prospective future earnings generally result in high capitalized values and low prospective future annual earnings generally result in low capitalized values.

SOME APPLICATIONS OF CAPITALIZING INCOME

Valuation for Purposes of Buying a Business

Fred Underwood, who expects to earn 10 percent on his money, is considering buying a retail store and is estimating the most he will pay for the firm. He believes that under his management future average annual net earnings will be $10,000, the profits to continue indefinitely. He believes that after he acquires the business he can sell idle assets for $1,000. But he also expects to invest an additional $3,000 in new counters and other improvements. Underwood must look on the purchase of the business as a package; that is, he must consider the transaction as extending through a period of time long enough to include the sale of the excess assets and long enough to include his additional investment for improvements. What is the most he should pay for this firm? First, he must capitalize the income as follows:

$$\text{Preliminary capitalized value} = \frac{\text{Expected average annual net profits}}{\text{Rate of return desired on investment}}$$
$$= \frac{\$10,000}{.10}$$
$$= \$100,000$$

Next, he must make adjustments for the cash he will receive from selling the idle assets and for the cash he will have to invest in the firm. These adjustments are made as follows:

Preliminary capitalized value	$100,000
Add cash value of idle assets	1,000
Total	$101,000
Less additional funds to be invested	3,000
Maximum value to Underwood	$98,000

The most Underwood should pay for the business is $98,000. If he pays more, his return will be less than 10 percent, assuming the firm actually has net profits of $10,000 in the future. He should be willing to pay less than $98,000 for the firm because he will earn a return of more than 10 percent, still assuming that future annual profits will be $10,000. The capitalization of income procedure is a widely used tool in valuing firms for purchase or sale.

Assume that George Aiken, a person with money to invest, is studying whether or not he should buy common stock of IBM. This stock was selling at approximately $300 at the time of this writing. If Aiken's opinion is that this stock is really worth more than $300, he will buy it, because he believes this issue is underpriced. The amount that he thinks the stock is really worth is the present value of the benefits he anticipates he will receive in the future as a result of owning this stock. If, for example, he thinks the present value of one share of IBM stock is $470.30 (how he arrived at this estimate is explained below), he will buy the stock because he will have a *net present value* of $170.30; if he thinks the present value of the stock is less than $300, he will not buy it; if he thinks the present value is just $300, there is no incentive for him to buy it. Assume the following information:

Evaluating a Share of Stock

Current price of IBM common stock	$300
Rate of return expected by Aiken	6 percent
Expected future average annual dividends per share	$10
Expected price of IBM stock four years from now	$550

Aiken believes that the future dividends on IBM stock will average $10 a year. He also believes that the price of this stock will rise to $550 by the end of the fourth year. Since IBM has the current policy of reinvesting a considerable part of its net profits, Aiken reasons that his expectations should move in the direction of seeking a capital gain rather than large annual cash dividends.

If this is so, Aiken's opinion on the present value of IBM stock is determined as follows:

Discounted value of dividends (3.4651 × $10)	$34.65
Discounted value of selling price (0.79209 × $550)	435.65
Present value of one share of IBM stock	$470.30
Less cost of one share	300.00
Net present value	$170.30

Aiken's opinion is that the present value of the stock is greater than its cost. Observe in the preceding example that:

Net present value = Present value − Cost (current market price)
  = $470.30 − $300.00
  = $170.30

If there is a net present value, the stock is underpriced and should be purchased. The greater the net present value, the greater the bargain. Aiken will compare other stocks with IBM and attempt to find ones that might have a greater net present value, assuming the same degree of risk.

The above illustration is only one of many approaches to estimating the intrinsic worth of a share of stock.

HIGHLIGHTS OF THIS CHAPTER

Much of business planning is concerned with the receipt of cash in future time periods. Compound interest tables place on a common denominator basis these probable future cash intakes. In order to be effective, financial planning must take into consideration the time value of money.

An income-producing property may be valued on the basis of the net profit that it is expected to earn in the future.

Four important rules in finance are: (1) a low capitalization rate tends to give a high valuation; (2) a high capitalization rate tends to give a low valuation; (3) a low estimate of future net income tends to give a low valuation; and (4) a high estimate of future net income tends to give a high valuation.

The market price of an income-producing property changes because of changes in the capitalization rate and/or changes in expected future annual profits.

The heart of financial management is that of valuation, that is making decisions that will (1) increase the net present value of a share of stock, or (2) increase the net present value of an equity in a partnership or a single proprietorship.

REVIEW QUESTIONS

3-1. Mr. X is about to buy a business. Will he hope to have the purchase price based on a high or a low capitalization rate?

3-2. A few years ago a businessman bought an income-producing property for $100,000. He now estimates its capitalized value to be $200,000 and its market value to be $180,000. When it comes time to pay his local taxes he argues that the property is worth only $100,000; when he attempts to borrow from a bank and use the property as collateral, he argues that the property is worth $180,000. Is this businessman honest?

3-3. A saver wants to know how much he will have in the bank five years from now, assuming that he invests $10,000 today. Which of the following interest tables would he use to obtain the answer? (a) present value of $1; (b) compound amount of $1; (c) present value of an annuity of $1.

3-4. Two interest tables are the present value of $1 and the present value of an annuity of $1. (a) Under what conditions is each used? (b) Give a hypothetical example demonstrating the use of each.

3-5. Obtain a circular on U.S. government series E and series H bonds from a post office (or some other source). Answer these questions: (a) What is the annual rate of interest on each? (b) What are some differences between these two kinds of bonds? (c) How is the interest taxed on each? (d) Who should be notified in the event that the bonds are lost or stolen? (e) Are these bonds transferable to another investor?

The answers to the problems appear at the end of this section. *For each problem, show how you obtained the answer.*

3-1. Robert Bowers has an investment for which he paid $20,000. If the profits of $2,000 a year from the investment are expected to continue forever, what rate of return is he earning on his investment?

3-2. Richard Fox purchased a nondividend-paying stock 10 years ago for $100 a share; today a share is worth $162.89. At what annual rate is this stock growing in value?

3-3. Paul Kelly places $10,000 in a savings account today, which he plans to keep in the bank for seven years. At the end of this period, how much will be in his account if the bank pays 4 percent interest, compounded annually?

3-4. Tom Aldrich wishes to have $5,000 at the end of six years. How much must he place in a savings account today to have this sum on the desired date, assuming that the financial institution will pay him 3 percent, compounded annually?

3-5. Henry Davis wishes an income of $2,000 a year for 10 years. How much must he set aside today in a lump sum to receive this income, assuming the financial institution in which he places it pays 3 percent interest, compounded annually?

3-6. Discounting income may be used in estimating the amount of damages that should be awarded to an aggrieved party who has just won a damage suit in court. Thus, if Rod Beaver is struck and permanently disabled by an automobile driven by a negligent driver, the court may award him damages. The damages might be based on the fact that had it not been for the accident, he could have earned a salary of $20,000 a year for the remaining years of his estimated working life (assumed to be 20 years). If these expected salary figures are discounted at 5 percent interest, how much in lump-sum damages would the court award him?

3-7. Seth Adams is using the present-value process to determine the amount of life insurance he should carry. He assumes that his beneficiaries need an annual income of $10,000 for the next 20 years. If the life insurance company pays 4 percent interest, how much insurance should he carry?

Principles of Valuation   45

3-8. A pizza business is for sale. Two juniors in the college of business administration are considering taking over the business and managing it during their senior year. If they did, each would receive a salary of $7,200. A local businessman would provide the financing; he is willing to grant the juniors an option to buy the firm when they graduate. The option price has not yet been determined. A study indicates that 50,000 pizzas could be sold each year, at $1 apiece. Business firms in this endeavor normally earn a 25 percent profit on sales (before taxes). The businessman expects a 20 percent return (before taxes) on his investment. What is the *most* he would be willing to pay the previous owner for this business? (Of course, he will bargain and seek to obtain the business for less.)

3-9. AT&T stock, now selling at $50 a share, has passed a preliminary screening test by the trust department of a large bank. AT&T is in a growth industry, and the management is excellent. But the trust officer is worried about the issue being overpriced, for it is possible to pay too much for even a high quality issue. Upon the advice of a college student who is familiar with modern decision-making tools, the issue will be considered overpriced if the cost per share exceeds the present value of the share; if this happens, the issue will not be purchased. On the other hand, the issue will be an advantageous purchase if the cost per share is less than the present value of the share; if this happens, the issue will be purchased. AT&T is expected to pay dividends of $3 a year for the next eight years and to be selling at $60 a share at the end of the eighth year. The banker uses a discount rate of 6 percent. The student recommends that the common stock of AT&T be purchased because the present value (discounted value) of the shares is greater than the cost per share by $6.27. Show how this figure was obtained.

3-10. George Ritter, a wealthy local businessman, is considering purchasing a greeting card business near a military camp that is expected to close down five years from now. The venture is expected to produce $10,000 a year in cash flow for each of the five years. The business has $1,000 in idle assets which will be immediately sold for cash; furthermore, Ritter will have to spend $3,000 for new counters. Ritter expects that on the closing of the military camp, the greeting card business will become worthless, except that the assets will be liquidated for $1,000 in cash (ignore taxes on the liquidation value). Assume that the would-be purchaser uses a 6 percent rate for decision-making purposes and that he can purchase the business for $30,000. Ritter should buy the business because the discounted value of it exceeds the cost by $10,871.26. Show how this figure was obtained.

Answers: 3-1, 10 percent; 3-2, 5 percent; 3-3, $13,159; 3-4, $4,187.40; 3-5, $17,060.40; 3-6, $249,244; 3-7, $135,903; 3-8, $62,500.

CASE ON DETERMINING HOW MUCH TO PAY FOR A SMALL BUSINESS

John Harvey is planning to acquire a retail candy store. He knows of a business that is already in operation and that has an established clientele. The owner of this business died recently, and the widow has taken over the operation of the store on a temporary basis. She is anxious to sell it, for she does not want to assume this responsibility permanently. Harvey's main problem is to estimate the maximum amount he should pay for the enterprise.

Harvey decides to take a salary of $10,000, since he could earn this much as an employee in another business. In addition, he expects to earn at least 20 percent on any funds he invests in the business. This rate, in effect, means that he believes the candy store to be worth no more than five times its profits. The widow, of course, does not know of Harvey's expectations.

The store under consideration has the following assets:

Cash	$ 5,000
Accounts receivable	4,000
Inventory	25,000
Fixtures	8,000
Other assets	4,000
Total	$46,000

There are only a nominal amount of accounts payable ($1,000), and the widow has agreed to pay these bills before the firm is transferred. In return, she also expects to take all the company cash. (This is a typical transaction, for when an unincorporated business sells its assets, cash is seldom sold along with other assets.) The widow expects to obtain the selling price plus $5,000. Other than accounts payable, the firm has no business debts. Since the widow will not sell the cash, Harvey will have to pump $5,000 into the business immediately upon its acquisition.

After inspecting the books, Harvey believes that he can earn a salary of $10,000 and that, in addition, he can earn profits of $12,000 per year.

The widow, being a shrewd bargainer, will set the proposed selling price higher than she really expects to receive. Harvey is well aware of this bargaining process; therefore, he will make a preliminary offer that is really lower than he expects to pay.

Required: (a) What price would you recommend that the widow establish to begin the negotiations? (b) What is the maximum price Harvey should be willing to pay? (c) What price would you recommend that he offer to begin the negotiations? (d) Suggest a compromise that might be agreeable to both the widow and Harvey.

A Refresher on Financial Ratios

This chapter is devoted to refresher material on selected financial ratios. In order to give a clear picture of the trends in business performance, financial ratios should cover a span of approximately five years; however, to shorten the discussion, the material in this chapter will be based mainly on a two-year comparison. The following ratios are reviewed:

1. Tests to measure profitability
   a. Total net profits after taxes
   b. Earnings per share on common stock
   c. The price-earnings ratio
   d. Rate of return earned on assets (earning power)
   e. Rate of return earned on common stockholders' equity
   f. Dividends per share on common stock
   g. The payout ratio
   h. Yield on stock
2. Tests to measure solvency
   a. Cash on hand
   b. Cash flow
   c. The current ratio
   d. The acid test ratio
   e. Net working capital
   f. Times interest earned
3. Additional terminology

Considerable variation exists in the details of methods used to compute relations designed to indicate a firm's capacity to earn profits and to meet its commitments to pay cash. A person who can read meaning into financial statements should be able to alter, if the individual circumstances warrant, the tests to be discussed. The explanation of ratios in this chapter is based largely on Table 4-1.

Total net profits of Company A (see Table 4-1) decreased in the more recent year, despite an increase in sales. The profits for the two years were $33 million and $40 million, respectively. When total net profits decrease, stockholders expect an explanation in the annual report. Company A explained that there were higher than usual sales promotion expenses and high preoperating expenses relating to new and expanded factories.

Total profit figures may be misleading unless accompanied by other data, such as earnings per share. Aggregate profit data may be misleading because they do not take into consideration the possibility that owners may have injected more funds into the firm. If this happened, total profits could be increasing while earnings per share would be decreasing. Nevertheless, a simple comparison of net profits over two previous fiscal years is still one of the most frequently used measures of the officers' ability to manage the firm.

TESTS TO MEASURE PROFITABILITY

Total Net Profits after Taxes

	December 31		*TABLE 4-1 Summary Data on Company A* (Millions of Dollars)*
	One Year Ago	Two Years Ago	
Current Assets			
Cash	$ 25	$ 25	
U.S. government securities	42	63	
Accounts receivable–net	51	45	
Stocks listed on exchanges	22	21	
Inventories	81	71	
Prepaid expenses	3	2	
Total current assets	224	227	
Current Liabilities			
Accounts payable	$ 23	$ 25	
Long-term debt due within a year	1	1	
Salaries and wages payable	13	12	
Accrued federal taxes	14	26	
Other	5	5	
Total current liabilities	56	69	
Other Data			
Average annual interest on long-term debt	$ 4	$ 4	
Average annual preferred stock dividends	3	3	
Average number of shares of common outstanding (million)	7	7	
Total dividends on common ($2.50 a share)	17.5	17.5	
Total assets	492	492	
Common stockholders' equity	242	228	

Profit and Loss Data

Sales and other income	568	552
Less:		
Depreciation	19	18
All other deductions, except interest	484	450
Interest	4	4
Total deductions for tax purposes	507	472
Taxable income	61	80
Less income tax	28	40
Net profits after taxes	33	40
Less dividends on preferred stock	3	3
Earnings available for common stock	30	37

*Market value of common stock at time of this study was $100.

Take a Number . . .

Table 4-2 illustrates an actual case—modified to mask company identity—of how different bookkeeping methods can greatly change the bottom line of the income statement. Same company, same sales volume, same operating policies, but very different net earnings.

Earnings per Share on Common Stock

Earnings per share on common stock is one of the most significant measures of the success of officers in managing the firm. The formula for computing this ratio is:

$$\text{Earnings per share on common stock} = \frac{\text{Net profit after taxes} - \text{Preferred stock dividend requirements (if any)}}{\text{Appropriate number of shares of common}}$$

$$= \frac{\$33 - \$3}{7}$$

$$= \$4.29$$

Earnings per share of common stock were $4.29 for the most recent year and $5.29 two years ago. Hence, Company A was not as successful in earning profits in the more recent year. The ease with which stockholders can grasp the meaning of earnings per share explains, in part, the popularity of this test. In interpreting earnings per share figures, one must be on guard to detect the impact of changes in inventory valuation methods, in methods of computing depreciation, in methods of handling nonrecurring gains and losses, and in the number of shares outstanding. (See Table 4-2.) *The earnings-per-share test is one of the most important tools in all of finance.* Both present and past figures are often studied carefully so that estimates can be made of future earnings per share, a factor that has a direct bearing on the market price of the common stock.

TABLE 4-2
Golden Fleece
Manufacturing Company

	Method A (Conservative)	Method B (Liberal)
Net sales	$240,809,200	$243,924,600
Cost of goods sold	201,287,300	199,248,200
Gross profit	39,521,900	44,676,400
Other operating income		1,191,000
Total	39,521,900	45,867,400
Selling, general and administrative expenses	24,210,700	26,468,300
Total	15,311,200	19,399,100
Other income (expenses):		
Interest expense	(1,810,900)	(1,873,400)
Net income–subsidiaries	538,900	
Amortization of goodwill	(170,000)	
Miscellaneous	(269,000)	(229,200)
Total	(1,711,900)	(2,102,600)
Net income before taxes	13,599,300	17,296,500
State income taxes	638,000	812,900
Federal income taxes–deferred		348,900
Federal income taxes–current	5,238,000	6,440,000
Charges equivalent to tax reductions from:		
Investment tax credits	775,000	
Tax loss carryovers	990,000	297,000
Total	7,641,000	7,898,800
Net income	$ 5,958,300	$ 9,397,700
Earnings per share	$1.99	$3.14

Source:
Courtesy of Practicing
Law Institute,
New York, N.Y.

The "appropriate" number of shares in the denominator depends on whether the firm has warrants or convertibles outstanding. If the firm has neither, the weighted average of the number of shares is used, as was done in the above example. But if either or both of these instruments are outstanding, the number of shares in the denominator may be increased, and two earnings-per-share figures may be reported—*primary* and *fully diluted*. These two show the impact of varying degrees of dilution that will take place in the future, if investors use their option to exercise their warrants or to convert their securities. In summary, the investor is being alerted to the possibility that future earnings per share may drop sharply if the firm has *common stock equivalents* (that is, warrants, certain convertible preferreds, or certain convertible bonds).

The price-earnings ratio relates the market price of the stock to the earnings per share of common stock. Again assume that the market price of Company A stock is $100. The formula for determining this ratio is:

The Price-Earnings Ratio

$$\text{Price-earnings ratio} = \frac{\text{Market price of a share of common stock}}{\text{Earnings per share of common stock}}$$

$$= \frac{\$100}{\$4.29}$$

$$= 23$$

The price-earnings ratio of Company A stock is therefore 23. (See Table 4-3 for several additional price-earnings ratios.) A high price-earnings ratio indicates that investors are convinced that future earnings per share will increase. Conversely, a low price-earnings ratio indicates that investors are pessimistic about the possibility of earnings per share increasing. The price-earnings ratio, in addition to varying from company to company, also varies with the business cycle and with secular (indefinite long-term) changes.

TABLE 4-3
Price-Earnings Ratios

	Latest Price	Earnings per Share	Price-Earnings Ratio
American Airlines	23¾ ÷	$ .67 =	35
IBM	401½ ÷	$10.31 =	38
Occidental Petroleum	13¾ ÷	Loss =	0
Polaroid	113¾ ÷	$1.53 =	74
Superior Oil	326 ÷	$1.35 =	241
United Aircraft	42¼ ÷	Loss =	0

Source:
New York Times and New York Stock Exchange.

In everyday analysis considerable emphasis is placed on the price-earnings ratio, particularly from the investors' viewpoint. A high ratio is a sign that stock prices are relatively high in relation to recent earnings per share; a low ratio is a sign that stock prices are relatively low in relation to recent earnings per share. Many newspapers imply that stockholders are foolish to purchase shares when the price-earnings ratio is very high, such as 40. IBM common stock, for example, often sells at a ratio of 40. The purchase of stock with a high price-earnings ratio does not always imply that investors are engaging in thoughtless speculation. Such investors may be acting quite logically, because the ultimate performance of a share of stock depends on future earnings per share and not on recent historical earnings per share. A logical investor may be relating current market price to future earnings per share. If these future earnings per share do increase, the ratio may not be excessively high. The central problem, then, is to predict the rate of growth in earnings per share, a necessary, but admittedly difficult, task.

Rate of Return
Earned on Assets
(Earning Power)

Another significant ratio is rate of return earned on assets (earning power), the formula for which is:

$$\text{Rate of return earned on assets} = \frac{\text{Total net profit}}{\text{Total assets}}$$

$$= \frac{\$33}{492}$$

$$= 6.71 \text{ percent}$$

In the more recent year Company A earned 6.71 percent on its total assets; the corresponding figure for two years ago was 8.13 percent. The rate of return earned on assets is a clue to the efficiency of the firm in managing its affairs. It is a useful test when comparing the efficiency of operations over a number of years and when comparing the efficiency of the firm with others in the same industry.

An alternate but more meaningful method of computing the rate of return earned on assets is:

$$\text{Rate of return earned on assets} = \text{Turnover of assets} \times \frac{\text{Net profits per dollar of sales}}{}$$

$$= \frac{\text{Total sales}}{\text{Assets}} \times \frac{\text{Total net profits}}{\text{Total sales}}$$

$$= \frac{568}{492} \times \frac{33}{568}$$

$$= 1.154 \times .058$$

$$= 6.71 \text{ percent (amount rounded)}$$

This method of computing rate of return earned on assets gives the same answer as the first formula. But the second formula is more meaningful because it includes the components that eventually result in a certain rate of return. That is, it groups the many individual items that enter into rate of return on assets into two main classes: 1) turnover of assets and 2) net profits per dollar of sales. *Turnover of assets* is found by dividing total net sales by total assets. *Net profit per dollar of sales* is found by dividing total net profits by total net sales. (Net profit per dollar of sales is also known as margin.) Some industries, like the retail jewelry trade, tend to have a low turnover of assets but a high profit per dollar of sales. Other industries, like the food supermarkets, tend to have a high turnover of assets but a low net profit per dollar of sales. A firm seeks to increase the rate of return earned on its assets by finding the best combination of turnover of assets and net profits per dollar of sales.

Some companies, such as E. I. du Pont de Nemours and Company, apply the rate of return on assets to each of their divisions, each division being treated as though it were a separate company. This type of analysis enables top management to compare the relative profitability of the component parts of the enterprise. Only the larger companies, however, tend to use the rate of return earned on assets in this manner.

Although the earning-power test is useful, it has a major limitation as an indicator of overall profitability—it does not take into account the size of the corporate profits. Thus a firm with assets of $1,000 and net profits after taxes of $200 might erroneously appear to be better off than a firm with $100 million in assets and with net profits after taxes of $15 million. This is because the former firm would have an earning power of 20 percent while the latter would have an earning power of 15 percent.

As is generally true, before one can reach a conclusion about the profitability of a firm, it is necessary to consider numerous ratios; the user of financial information is never safe in focusing attention on one or two ratios to the exclusion of others.

Rate of Return Earned on Common Stockholders' Equity

The formula for determining this ratio is:

$$\text{Rate of return earned on common stockholders' equity} = \frac{\text{Net profits available for common stockholders}}{\text{Common stockholders' equity}^1}$$

$$= \frac{\$30}{242}$$

$$= 12.40 \text{ percent}$$

Company A earned 12.40 percent on the equity of the common stockholders during the latest year; the corresponding figure for two years ago was 16.23 percent. The rate of return earned on common stockholders' equity is often higher than rate of return earned on assets. This occurs when a firm borrows money at one rate and earns on it a higher rate than is paid for its use. Thus Company A earned 6.70 percent on its assets in the more recent fiscal period, but the firm paid bondholders who supplied a considerable part of the assets only 4 percent. The difference between the two rates accrued to the benefit of the common stockholders. Of course, if the firm is earning less on its assets than it is paying in interest, the rate earned on common stockholders' equity falls sharply and may even wipe out entirely the dollar profits earned on investment. One conclusion, developed more thoroughly in later chapters, is that a certain amount of debt is desirable because of the possibility that the rate on the residual owners' investment will be increased. Our brief comments here are intended to indicate that the rate of return on residual owners' equity is sometimes higher than the rate of return earned on assets.

Dividends per Share of Common Stock

Dividends per share on the common stock of Company A were $2.50 during both fiscal periods. Many large corporations (such as Company A) which have profits available for distribution pay dividends quarterly. Stockholders receive checks, usually four times a year, from these companies, the amount of the check depending on the number of shares owned multiplied by the dividends per share.

When the data cover a short period of time, dividends per share on the common stock are a poor measure of the officers' ability to manage the capital. This

1. Equal to the sum of common stock, surplus, and net worth reserves.

is because dividends per share do not take into consideration the fact that corporations may follow a policy of reinvesting a large percentage of the profits. Furthermore, it is possible for a firm to pay dividends even though there have been no earnings for the last several years. Consequently, short-run dividends in themselves do not indicate the officers' ability to direct the capital of a firm toward its goals. More meaning can be read into dividends per share when supplementary information is given, such as earnings per share.

The Payout Ratio

The payout ratio indicates the percentage of profits available for common stock-holders that is paid as cash dividends to this group of security holders. The formula for determining this ratio is:

$$\text{Payout ratio} = \frac{\text{Dividends per share of common stock}}{\text{Earnings per share}}$$
$$= \frac{\$2.50}{\$4.29}$$
$$= 58 \text{ percent}$$

Company A paid out as cash dividends 58 percent and 47 percent of its available profits in the two respective years. An alternate method of determining this ratio is to divide total cash dividends paid to common stockholders by total earnings applicable to common stock. The payout ratio is an important concept because it describes the cash dividend policy and because it sheds light on the amount of funds being reinvested in the business—a factor that influences the future market price of the stock.

Yield on Stock

Yield on stock measures the rate of return on an investment in stock. To compute yield, one must know the cost of the stock and the sum received per share during a one-year period. Assume that in this year Henry Smith purchased one share of stock of Company A at $100 and that the annual dividends on these shares for this year were $2.50. What is his yield for this year? The formula for measuring yield is:

$$\text{Yield on a share of stock} = \frac{\text{Amount of dividends received annually per share}}{\text{Cost per share}}$$
$$= \frac{\$2.50}{\$100}$$
$$= 2.50 \text{ percent}$$

Smith's yield for this year is 2.50 percent, a rather moderate yield because he could earn a higher return on United States government bonds. Smith, however, is looking to the future, and his expectations are that annual dividends paid by this firm will increase substantially. If his expectations materialize, his yield over a period of future years will be much larger than 2.50 percent. An investor always focuses his attention on the future rather than on the present or the past.

Two additional features of yield should be noted. The yield on the stock can vary from person to person, depending on how much was paid for the shares; and the yield can vary from year to year, depending on how much is received in dividends each fiscal period.

Thus if Stuart Jones bought stock in Company A during this year for $95 a share, and if dividends were $2.50, the yield to Jones would be 2.63 percent. The reason for the difference is that Smith and Jones bought their shares at different times and paid different prices for them.

Assume that this same stock will pay an annual total of $5 in dividends next year. If this is the case, the yield for next year would be 5 percent to Smith and 5.26 percent to Jones. Again the difference in yield is due to the difference in the cost of the stock.

TESTS TO MEASURE SOLVENCY

Cash on Hand

The simplest test of solvency is to observe the amount of cash on hand. Company A had a cash balance of $25 million at the end of the two respective years. This is a substantial amount in relation to total current liabilities of $56 million and $69 million, respectively. Although there is no general rule as to the amount of cash a firm should have, a conservative practice would be to have sufficient cash on hand to pay all bills maturing within the next 60 days.

Cash Flow

In recent years, more attention has been paid to the cash flow of the firm. The formula for determining this is:

$$\text{Total cash flow} = \text{Net profits after taxes} + \text{Depreciation}$$
$$= \$33 + \$19$$
$$= \$52$$

The total cash flow for Company A for the two fiscal periods was $52 million and $58 million, respectively. Cash flow gives an overall picture of the amount of cash available for such purposes as dividend payments and expansion. Observe that the cash flow test applies to a period of time, such as a one-year period. This is in contrast with several other tests of solvency which stress liquidity as of the point of time the balance sheet was prepared. A firm with a large cash flow is in a very flexible position on paying dividends, acquiring new subsidiaries, adding new product lines, engaging in costly research, and moving plants to new locations. Many corporate annual reports also give cash flow *per share* of common stock. The formula for obtaining this information is:

$$\text{Cash flow per share} = \frac{\text{Total cash flow}}{\text{Average number of shares of common stock outstanding}}$$
$$= \frac{\$52}{7}$$
$$= \$7.43$$

Cash flow per share for Company A for the two fiscal periods was $7.43 and $8.29, respectively.

The Sheraton Corporation of America is an example of a firm that places considerable emphasis on cash flow per share. In an interview with a newspaper reporter, the president of this company said: "We try to hold our reported earnings down, you know. Actually we only attempt to cover our 60-cent dividend to satisfy our stockholders. . . . By limiting our reported earnings, we actually fatten our asset value and strengthen our entire financial structure." In the Sheraton Corporation of America we have a case of profits decreasing slightly and dividends remaining almost stable, but the market value of the stock increasing.

In order to illustrate further how depreciation (or depletion) is a source of funds, assume the following facts about a company's cash flow:

Cash sales		$100
Less expenses:		
Cash expenses	$70	
Depreciation	20	90
Income before taxes		$ 10
Income taxes		5
Net profit		$ 5

This firm will have $25 in cash to spend—$5 from profits and $20 from depreciation. Financial usage over many years is the reason for stating that depreciation is a "source of funds" to the extent of $20. A more accurate way of expressing this phenomenon might be to state that cash from sales to customers is the true source of funds in the above illustration and that any cash not spent for expenses is available for expansion of assets, repayment of debts, or some other purpose.

The Current Ratio

Current assets consist of cash; assets that will be converted into cash within a year and in the normal course of business operations; and prepaid expenses, such as prepaid insurance. While prepaid expenses will not be converted into cash, these items lessen the drain on cash in the future.

Current liabilities, like current assets, are given a prominent position in most balance sheets. *Current liabilities* are debts that must be paid within a year from the date of the balance sheet. Examples of current liabilities are bank loans, accounts payable, taxes payable, and dividends payable.

The current ratio shows the relation between total current assets and total current liabilities. The formula for computing it is:

$$\text{Current ratio} = \frac{\text{Total current assets}}{\text{Total current liabilities}}$$
$$= \frac{\$224}{\$56}$$
$$= 4$$

The current ratio for Company A for the two year-ends was 4.00 and 3.29, respectively. For many lines of business, a current ratio of at least two to one is considered desirable. Hence, the above ratios are satisfactory. A high current ratio is a clue that the company will be able to pay its debts that mature within a year. On the other hand, a low current ratio points to the possibility that a firm may not be able to pay its short-term debts.

An excess of current assets over current liabilities does not necessarily mean that debts can be paid promptly. If current assets contain a high proportion of uncollectible accounts receivable or unsalable inventories, there will be a slow-down in the intake of cash. Therefore, it is necessary to inspect the composition of the current assets and evaluate the probability of their being converted into cash in the near future.

The Acid Test Ratio

An informative test that is often used to supplement the current ratio is the acid test ratio. The formula for determining it is:

$$\text{Acid test ratio} = \frac{\text{Cash} + \frac{\text{Marketable}}{\text{securities}} + \frac{\text{Accounts and}}{\text{notes receivable}}}{\text{Current liabilities}}$$

$$= \frac{\$25 + 42 + 22 + 51}{\$56}$$

$$= \frac{\$140}{\$56}$$

$$= 2.50$$

The acid test ratio for Company A was 2.50 and 2.23 at the end of the two respective years. Observe that the acid test ratio *excludes* inventories and prepaid expenses. This exclusion makes it possible to relate items that are highly liquid to current liabilities. For many firms, an acid test ratio of one or more is considered desirable. Hence, the ratios for Company A are satisfactory. The acid test ratio, like the current ratio, is an evaluation of the firm's ability to pay debts that mature within a year. The acid test ratio is also known as the *quick ratio*. The items of cash, marketable securities, and accounts receivable are sometimes called *quick assets*, the term *quick* emphasizing immediate or nearly immediate liquidity.

Net Working Capital

The formula for computing net working capital is:

Net working capital = Total current assets − Total current liabilities
= $224 − $56
=$168

Net working capital for Company A was $168 million and $158 million at the end of the two respective yearly periods. Net working capital is often called *net current assets* or *working capital*. Although accountants generally prefer the term *working capital* financial manuals and reports of the Securities and Exchange Commission are favoring the term *net working capital*. In many lines of business we would expect the total current assets to exceed the total current liabilities by a substantial amount. *The net working capital is the amount by which the current assets could decrease and still leave an amount equal to the current liabilities.*

The amount of net working capital needed by a particular firm depends on a variety of circumstances, the main one being the regularity of the flow of current assets into cash. If a business has a steady conversion of current assets into cash, it is possible to get along with less net working capital than might otherwise be the case. When there is a steady exchange of current assets into cash, there is less need for a large margin of safety. Assume that a water company and a department store have the same amount of total assets. The water company could get along with less net working capital than the department store because of the steady flow of cash it receives. On the other hand, the department store would need a larger margin of net working capital because of the possible danger of being unable to sell its inventory at a profit. When a firm can synchronize its cash intake with its cash payments, it is possible to get along with a minimum of net working capital (net current assets or working capital).

Since interest is a fixed cash outlay, a firm must meet this payment or face legal action. Over a period of time interest payments are made out of funds generated by operations. Analysts often assume that net profit is, or was at one time during the fiscal period, equivalent to cash. Hence, an important clue to a firm's ability to make this payment is the relation between net income available for bondholders and the cash outflow needed to pay the interest. This relationship is commonly called the *number of times interest is earned*. One formula for measuring it is:

Number of Times Interest is Earned

$$\text{Number of times interest earned} = \frac{\text{Net income after taxes} + \text{Interest}}{\text{Interest}}$$

$$= \frac{\$33 + \$4}{\$4}$$

$$= \frac{\$37}{\$4}$$

$$= 9.25$$

Company A has earned its interest 9.25 times during the latest year and 11 times during the fiscal period of two years ago. The small decline in the ratio was caused by the decrease in net income during the more recent period. The higher the ratio, the greater the probability that a firm will be able to continue to pay its interest. Many analysts expect an industrial firm to earn its interest at least four times, a railroad at least three times, and a public utility at least twice. Investors have subjective standards as to their expectations on the number of times interest should be earned.

The times-interest-earned test may be computed on a *before*-tax basis or an *after*-tax basis. If one uses the pretax figures for comparison, the ratio will be larger than if after-tax figures are used. Either method is correct. Financial services such as Moody's give the results of both kinds of computations. The justification for using pretax figures is that interest is deducted on the profit and loss statement before federal income taxes are computed. However, the case for using after-tax amounts is also a good one. Even though it is true that bond interest precedes taxes on the income statement, this does not mean that the bondholders are paid their interest before the government is paid the taxes due it. Actually a going concern that remits its taxes on a pay-as-you-go basis may have a quarterly cash outflow as a payment for taxes before bond interest is paid, especially if it pays bond interest semiannually or annually. We will use net earnings after taxes for most of our computations. This method is more conservative than the pretax method, and it presents a picture that is closer to reality, assuming that we are interested primarily in obtaining clues to the solvency of the firm.

In the above formula, interest was added to net income after taxes because the sum of these two items is the amount of adjusted net income available for bond interest.

INDUSTRY AVERAGES

Another useful tool is industry averages. This type of statistical material shows operating data for a sample of firms in the same line of economic endeavor. Averages are available for businesses such as restaurants, motels, bookstores, and jewelry stores. The averages show a variety of financial data, including amount of sales, amount and kinds of expenses, and amount and rate of net profit earned. Table 4-4 shows selected average ratios. Industry averages are one kind of quantitative device that have been used more and more in recent years to improve decision making.

TABLE 4-4
Selected Financial Ratios

Line of Business (Number of Concerns in Parentheses)	Interquartile Range	Current Assets to Current Debt (Times)	Net Profits on Net Sales (Percent)	Net Profits on Tangible Net Worth (Percent)	Net Profits on Net Working Capital (Percent)
Clothing, men's and boys' (162)	Upper quartile	5.10	4.69	10.15	15.17
	Median	*2.88*	*2.07*	*3.78*	*4.92*
	Lower quartile	2.00	0.21	0.51	0.56

Source: Reprinted by permission of Dun & Bradstreet, Inc.

There are many sources from which one can obtain industry averages, several of which are:

1. Dun & Bradstreet, Inc., publishes annually a series of ratios for 72 lines of

business in manufacturing, wholesaling, and retail fields. In addition, this firm prepares 28 special retail surveys from time to time. Dun & Bradstreet studies cover ratios for such lines of activities as bakeries, gasoline service stations, meat markets, and so on. Usually single copies of these studies are available free upon request.

2. The U.S. Small Business Administration also has assembled data on comparative business ratios. A few examples of the industries about which a person can obtain information are hotels, laundries, department stores, and automobile dealers.

3. Long noted among the banking fraternity for extensive work in the field of ratio compilation and analysis is Robert Morris Associates, the national association of bank loan officers and credit men. Robert Morris Associates has developed ratio studies for some 173 lines of business, a few of which are meat-packing, lumberyard operations, petroleum refining, and soap and detergent manufacturing.

4. Trade associations are also an important source of information on financial ratios. Over 200 trade associations assemble information on industry averages. A few such groups are the Laundry and Cleaners Allied Trades Association, the National Association of Food Chains, and the National Association of Tobacco Distributors.

Many other sources of information are available. In fact, there are so many sources of information that the U.S. Small Business Administration has published a 55-page booklet devoted mainly to listing other booklets that contain industry averages (*Ratio Analysis for Small Businesses*, U.S. Small Business Administration, Washington, D.C.).

After-tax cost is a phrase that means the true cost of an item is reduced if the firm obtains an income tax deduction for it. Let us illustrate with an example (see Table 4-5).

ADDITIONAL TERMINOLOGY

After-Tax Cost

TABLE 4-5
After-Tax Cost
of Advertising

	Tax without Additional Expense (Advertising)	Tax If Additional (Advertising) Expense Is Incurred
Sales	$100	$100
Less all expenses, except advertising	30	30
Advertising	0	10
Total expenses	$ 30	$ 40
Taxable income	$ 70	$ 60
Tax (30 percent)	$ 21	$ 18
Net after taxes	$ 49	$ 42

In this table, the question is: What is the after-tax cost of the advertising? If this expense is incurred, the firm pays out $10 for it, but this results in lowering taxes from $21 to $18, a tax savings of $3. The outlay of $10 for the expense is matched against the saving in taxes of $3; hence, it may be said that the net after-tax cost of the advertising is $7.

Assume that a firm is planning to incur an interest expense of $4,000 and that this firm is in the 40 percent tax bracket. What is the after-tax cost of the transaction? In order to determine the after-tax cost of an expense without constructing a pro forma income statement (which will be discussed in Chapter 5) the following formula may be used:

$$
\begin{aligned}
\text{After-tax cost} &= (\text{Amount of annual expense}) \times (1 - \text{Tax rate}) \\
&= \$4,000 \times (1.00 - .40) \\
&= \$2,400
\end{aligned}
$$

The after-tax cost is $2,400. After-tax cost is widely used in the decision-making process.

Net Worth	The total of stock, surplus, and other ownership accounts is called *net worth* or *stockholders' equity*. This section of the balance sheet indicates the amount of the owners' contribution toward the assets. Outstanding bonds are never part of net worth.
Par-Value Stock and No-Par-Value Stock	*Par value* means the nominal value of a share of stock as stated in the charter and on the face of the stock certificate. The par of a stock may be for any amount, depending on the plans of the organizers and on state law. Par value may range all the way from one cent up to several hundred dollars. Once par-value stock is issued by the corporation, the market value will probably be different from the par value. This happens because the market value of a security is based on expected future happenings, whereas par value is based on past events. The market value of a security may be above, equal to, or below the par value, depending on stockholders' appraisal of the corporation's profit prospects. No-par-value stock comprises shares that lack any nominal value on the certificates or in the charter. An issuer can sell no-par-value stock at any amount per share. This is in contrast with par-value stock which, according to many state laws, must be sold at or above this value. The use of no-par-value stock gives management more flexibility in establishing the unit price of future issues.
Book Value	The *book value* per share is the value of a share as per the accounting records of the firm. The formula for determining book value is:

$$\text{Book value of a share of stock} = \frac{\text{Assets available for that class of stock}}{\text{Number of shares outstanding}}$$

Book value per share is likely to be different from par value and from market value per share.

Treasury stock consists of shares that were once issued and fully paid for and that have been reacquired by the issuing company, through purchase or gift (usually the former). For example, assume that a company is authorized to issue 1,000 shares of stock, that 800 shares have been issued, and that 100 shares have been reacquired by the corporation. The 100 shares reacquired are called treasury stock. In this example, the issued stock is 800 shares because treasury stock is considered to have been issued even though it is back in the hands of the corporation. However, the outstanding stock is only 700 shares. In Table 4-6, which shows the net worth section of the Borden Company, we can see that this firm has 439,687 shares of treasury stock. There is usually an upper limit on the amount of treasury stock that a corporation can purchase, the general rule being that a corporation can purchase treasury stock in an amount not greater than the earned surplus. A corporation does not pay itself dividends on treasury stock, nor does it vote shares held in its treasury.

Capital stock–par value $7.50 per share, 16 million shares authorized:		
Issued	10,347,187	
Less treasury stock	439,687	
Outstanding	9,907,500	$ 74,306,250
Capital surplus		40,677,020
Earned surplus		145,642,326
Total net worth		$260,625,596

*TABLE 4-6
Net Worth of
Borden Company*

It is common practice to compare one year's profits with another year's. Thus, this year's profits of Company A may be $100,000 and last year's may have been $90,000. Although this is one of the easiest concepts for stockholders to understand, it has a serious drawback. It does not take into consideration additional capital injected into the business. If stockholders had $1 million invested in Company A last year and $2 million invested this year, the earning power of the firm has actually declined, because last year 9 percent was earned on the investment, whereas this year only 5 percent was earned. In a case like this, earnings and dividends per share could be falling while total profits are actually increasing. When earnings of one year are compared with those of another, supplementary data on total stockholder investment should be given. Nevertheless, a simple comparison of profits over two recent successive years is still one of the most widely used measures of the officers' ability to manage the assets astutely.

Earnings per share is one of the most important measures of the success of officers in managing the assets. This test automatically reflects new capital injected into the business, and it reflects most other changes in the net worth accounts.

The current ratio shows the relationship between total current assets and total current liabilities. If current assets are $100,000 and current liabilities are $50,000, the current ratio is two to one; that is, current assets are twice current liabilities. Another way of stating this relationship is to say that current assets are 200 percent of current liabilities. Still another way of expressing this relationship is to say that current liabilities are 50 percent of current assets. For many lines of business, a current ratio of at least two to one is considered desirable.

REVIEW QUESTIONS

4-1. The Parison Corporation, started by two college of business administration students, planned to operate a wholesale greeting card business; the firm would buy from manufacturers and sell to retail drugstores. The students hoped to raise $14,000; they offered $0.20 par-value shares at $3.50 each. (a) Suggest a reason for establishing such a low par value. (b) Suggest a reason why the students selected a $3.50 offering price, rather than $24.50.

4-2. Answer these questions: (a) Can total retained profits exceed total cash on hand? (b) Can dividends per share for a given year exceed earnings per share for that year? (c) Can dividends per share for a given year exceed par value per share? (d) Does a firm pay itself dividends on treasury stock?

4-3. Answer these questions: (a) Can cash flow per share exceed earnings per share? (b) Are bonds payable ever part of net worth? (c) What is the advantage of the acid test ratio over the current ratio? (d) Are bonds payable ever a current liability? (e) What is meant by the pay-out ratio?

4-4. The *Wall Street Journal* and the *New York Times* give the price-earnings ratio for selected large companies. Obtain one of these newspapers and answer these questions: (a) What are the price-earnings ratios for any three companies? (b) Suggest several reasons why the price-earnings ratios differ from company to company.

REVIEW PROBLEMS

The answers to the problems appear at the end of this section. *For each problem, show how you obtained the answer.*

4-1. Stephen Lewis buys a share of common stock for $100; it has earnings per share of $10 and pays $5 a share annually in dividends. What is the yield on this stock?

4-2. Company K pays $1 per share in dividends quarterly. If the stock is selling at $20 a share, what is the yield?

4-3. The following data apply to Company P: sales are $100,000; net profits after taxes are 10 percent of sales; and turnover of assets is 2. What is the earning power (that is, the percentage of net profits to total assets)?

4-4. The following data apply to Company G:

Cash	$ 20,000	Bank loans	$ 20,000
Accounts receivable	20,000	Accounts payable	20,000
Inventories	20,000	Bonds	20,000
Fixed assets	40,000	Retained profits	20,000
		Common stock	20,000
Total	$100,000	Total	$100,000

(a) Current assets are $60,000; (b) current liabilities are $40,000; (c) the current ratio is 1.5 to 1; (d) the acid test ratio is 1 to 1; (e) current assets are 60 percent of total assets; (f) stockholders' equity is $40,000; and (g) debt is 60 percent of total assets. Show how these answers were obtained.

4-5. Mr. P, a restaurant owner, is considering opening a small restaurant that will sell hoagies. His experience leads him to believe that the annual cash sales will be $50,000; his son informs him that Dun & Bradstreet ratios indicate that similar firms earn on sales a 30 percent pretax profit (after the owner's salary but before income taxes). If Mr. P expects to earn 25 percent on his investment, what is the most he should be willing to pay for the business?

4-6. Mr. X has studied some statistics released by a trade association; the data indicate that the average annual profits earned by manufacturers of plastic spoons is $10,000 (after the owner's salary but before federal income taxes). In this kind of business, the average annual profits (after the owner's salary but before taxes) are 25 percent of sales. The trade association statistics indicate that for such a business, the asset turnover is 4. (a) How much in assets are needed to start this business? (b) If Mr. X can borrow one-eighth of his needs from a bank and obtain one-eighth from trade creditors, how much of his savings will he have to use?

4-7. The King Company has just floated a bond issue on which the annual interest charges are $60,000. If this firm is in the 42 percent federal income tax bracket, what is the after-tax cost of the loan?

4-8. Company V's common stock has a market price of $30 a share; the price-earnings ratio is 10; earnings per share are growing at the annual rate of 6 percent. If the price-earnings ratio continues at the same level, what will be the market price of the common stock in five years?

4-9. The following data apply to Company R: sales are $100,000; total assets are $50,000; net profits after taxes are $20,000. (a) What is the margin, in percentage? (b) What is the asset turnover? (c) What is the return on total assets (also known as rate of return on investment [ROI]?

4-10. Given the financial data below, determine (a) the number of shares of common stock outstanding; (b) earnings per share on the common stock; (c) the rate of return earned on common stockholders' equity; (d) the pay-out ratio; (e) the yield on the common stock; (f) the price-earnings ratio on the common stock; (g) the cash flow per share; (h) the current ratio; (i) the acid test ratio; (j) net working capital; (k) times interest earned on bonds; (l) the ratio of debt to net worth; (m) the earning power by two different methods, assuming that net profit per dollar of sales is found by dividing total net profits by total sales and that turnover of assets is found by dividing total net sales by total assets.

Financial data are as follows:

Cash	$ 20,000	Accounts payable	$ 10,000
Accounts receivable	40,000	Notes payable	5,000
Marketable securities	10,000	Accruals	10,000
Inventories	50,000	Federal taxes due	10,000
Plant and equipment	235,000	5% first mortgage bonds	100,000
		5% preferred stock	20,000
		Common stock,	
		$10 par value	100,000
		Retained profits	100,000
Total	$355,000	Total	$355,000

Sales	$400,000
Less: Operating expenses, except depreciation	290,000
Depreciation	10,000
Operating income	$100,000
Less interest	5,000
Taxable income	$ 95,000
Federal income tax	44,000
Net after taxes	$ 51,000

Market price per share of common	$50
Quarterly dividends on common	1

Answers: 4-1, 5 percent; 4-2, 20 percent; 4-3, 20 percent; 4-5, $60,000; 4-6a, $10,000; 4-6b, $7,500; 4-7, $34,800; 4-8, $40.15; 4-9a, 20 percent; 4-9b, 2; 4-9c, 40 percent; 4-10a, 10,000; 4-10b, $5; 4-10c, 25 percent; 4-10d, 80 percent; 4-10e, 8 percent; 4-10f, 10; 4-10g, $6.10; 4-10h, 3.43; 4-10i, 2.00; 4-10j, $85,000; 4-10k, 11.20; 4-10l, 61 percent; 4-10m, 14.4 percent; (other reasonable answers are also acceptable).

THE ROLE OF PLANNING

2

5 Planning the Level of Operations (I)

Planning is the mental process of visualizing a set of events that one is determined to make happen in the future. This process requires that the officers prepare carefully conceived quantitative projections of the goals of the firm for a selected number of years and that they plan the activities of the firm so the personnel will have a map to guide them in directing the firm toward its goals. By emphasizing primary goals, management gives a sense of purpose to the operations of the firm. All decisions on the use of assets and the raising of funds on advantageous terms can then be made with the intent of advancing the primary goals of the enterprise. Subsidiary decisions take on more meaning if the officers, the partners, or the proprietor understand the primary mission of the firm. Planning is, therefore, more than idly speculating on what will happen in the future; instead, it is a combination of determining what desirable events should happen and then setting in motion a program of action to make these expected events a reality.

Planning is being given more and more attention in the world in which we live. In order to give this field more recognition, a number of firms have incorporated planning as a separate area in their organizational structure. Thus a common practice for large firms is to have a vice president in charge of planning.

Our discussion of planning statements will be concentrated on how management uses these tools rather than on the mechanics of their construction. Since profits and solvency are so closely related, they will be discussed concurrently.

The following will be discussed in this chapter:

1. Company historical data as a planning tool
2. Planning the level of aspirations (goals)
3. Planning statements used by executives
   a. The cash budget
   b. Pro forma statements

The starting point in planning the use of a going concern's affairs is a careful study of its own past. Each business has an aggregate of assets, a team of workers, and a line of products or services, all of which will influence the firm's pattern of action in the near future. While the past never exactly repeats itself, future events will be affected to a considerable extent by the recent past. Hence, to predict the future one may study the past for a special reason—to improve on past performance. The past, then, is studied not as an end in itself but as a means to attain aspirations in the future.

The historical data come from such statements as balance sheets, profit and loss statements, and cash receipts and disbursements statements. In analyzing data from these statements, the information of recent years should be given the most weight, as the recent past has more relevance than the distant past. Also, any trend in the data should be carefully noted. There is no scientific formula for determining how far back in the past the officers should go in obtaining historical information. But data older than 10 years seldom are very relevant in a dynamic world.

In searching for wisdom through an analysis of the past, one useful tool in analyzing records is to study the sales history of the firm. *Sales are a matrix point in planning for the goals of the firm.* Out of the sales dollars must come sufficient profits and cash to enable the firm to reach its primary goals. A historical analysis of sales is the starting point of predicting sales for the following year or two. In essence, this means that business planners begin with past sales and that expected future changes are applied to the old data in order to estimate future sales. Special attention should be given to the trend in dollar volume of sales. If the trend is upward, this is partial evidence that the firm will be successful in the future. If the trend is downward, the firm will be less successful and might even fail.

Recent historical *percentage* relationships between sales and other financial data are also of help in planning for the future. Let us illustrate this point with several examples. First, assume that a firm's sales averaged $200,000 in the last three years and that its net profits after taxes ranged between $10,000 and $16,000 (that is, between 5 and 8 percent of sales). Now, if the management of the business estimates that next year's sales will be $220,000, a reasonable prediction is that next year's profits after taxes will have a good statistical chance of falling between $11,000 and $17,600. In order to further illustrate this type of percentage analysis, let us look at a second example. Assume that in 1976 a chemical manufacturing company had sales of $1 million, total fixed assets of $500,000, net profits of 10 percent (after taxes) on sales, and 100,000 shares of common stock outstanding. During 1976, the price-earnings ratio reached a high of 10 and a low of 8. That is, the market price ranged between 10 and 8 times higher than earnings per share. Hence, in 1976 the earnings per share were $1 and the price of the stock ranged between $10 and $8. This firm is planning to increase its fixed assets by $500,000 by 1979. The management believes that the firm will have the same number of shares of common stock outstanding for the next several years and that all ratios will continue to be about the same for several years. On the basis of these data, how could the management predict the probable price of the stock as of 1979?

If $1 of assets continues to create $2 in sales, the sales will rise to $2 million by 1979. Actually, the decision to expand the assets and the projected sales data are highly interrelated. In the case under consideration, the management projected the sales and then estimated the amount of assets needed to support this volume of activity. Since the total sales are expected to be $2 million, total profits after taxes are expected to rise to $200,000—assuming that the 10 percent relationship still holds. With 100,000 shares of common stock outstanding in 1979, earnings per share should be about $2. On the basis of the historical price-earnings ratios of 10 and 8, respectively, the high and the low price of the common stock for 1979 is expected to be between $20 and $16. Predictions based on constant-percentage analysis are approximations, especially if such predictions are made for more than a year in advance. The reason for this word of caution is that percentage relationships do not necessarily remain constant. Good judgment, therefore, must be used to provide insight and guidance when using percentage relationships. But percentage analysis, despite its pitfalls, does offer quantitative clues as to what to expect in the years ahead. A wise use of historical data provides a valuable tool for planning the future. But one should not become a slave to the past. In fact, one of the best uses of the past is to use it to create a set of aspirations that will surpass past performance.

Problem Complete the following balance sheet, assuming that only the common stock and retained profit figures are given.

Cash	———	Accounts payable	———
Accounts receivable	———	Common stock	$300,000
Inventories	———	Retained profits	300,000
Fixed assets	———	Total liabilities and	
Total assets	———	net worth	———

Additional information: Total debt is two-thirds of net worth; turnover of total assets is 1.8; 30 days' sales are on the books in the form of accounts receivable; turnover of inventory[1] is 5; cost of goods sold per year is $900,000; and the acid test ratio is 1 to 1.

Solution

Cash	$ 250,000 (6)	Accounts payable	$ 400,000 (1)
Accounts receivable	150,000 (5)	Common stock	300,000
Inventories	180,000 (4)	Retained profits	300,000
Fixed assets	420,000 (7)		
Total	$1,000,000 (3)	Total	$1,000,000 (2)

1. Inventory turnover is found by dividing annual cost of goods sold by the average inventory.

1. If total net worth is $600,000, then total debt is $400,000 ($600,000 × ⅔). Hence, accounts payable, the only form of debt, is $400,000.

2. Total liabilities and net worth amount to $1 million.

3. Because total liabilities and net worth are $1 million, total assets must be the same amount.

4. If cost of goods sold is $900,000 and if inventory turnover is 5, then average inventory is $180,000 ($900,000 ÷ 5).

5. Total sales are $1,800,000 (asset turnover of 1.8 × total assets of $1 million). If total sales are $1,800,000, then average daily sales are $5,000 ($1,800,000 ÷ 360). The amount of accounts receivable on the books is $150,000 (30 days × average daily sales of $5,000).

6. If the acid test ratio is 1 to 1, the sum of the cash and accounts receivable is $400,000. The cash on hand must be $250,000 ($400,000 − $150,000).

7. The cash receivables and inventory amount to $580,000. Hence, fixed assets, the only remaining item on the balance sheet, must be $420,000 ($1 million − $580,000).

PLANNING THE LEVEL OF ASPIRATIONS (GOALS)

Many factors enter into the level of aspirations established by a firm for itself. Such factors as health and educational level of the management, existing size of the firm, and competition all influence the level of the primary goals. Of particular importance is the role of competition. In planning its level of aspirations, a firm must consider the role of competition and potential competition. While a firm may hope to increase its share of the market, a realistic factor is that a reasonable period of time may be required to reach this goal. Thus when Ford plans a production schedule, it considers the well-entrenched position of General Motors and Chrysler. Also, a hotel that is thinking of expanding must take into account the share of the market now held by a competing hotel. Even when a firm creates a new product, competition soon arises, for business rivals soon find methods and products that will be effective competitive products. Also, when a firm plans to change its prices, the reaction of competitors must be considered. Thus Ford could not capture the entire automobile market by substantially lowering the price of its automobiles, because competing firms would soon follow suit, and the effect of this course of action would be nullified. In summary, the planning process requires a tentative statement of plans of action, a visualization of the impact of these proposed actions on competitors, a modification of the original plans, and then a restatement of the plans in terms of what a firm can be reasonably expected to achieve.

THE CASH BUDGET

A cash budget is a written prediction of a firm's expected sources of cash intake, the expected purposes for which the cash is to be spent, and the expected cash balance at various dates. This device has a forward look; it attempts to predict an important aspect of business operations—the flow of cash. A cash budget is different from a predicted profit and loss statement. The former shows only the movement of cash; the latter shows how revenue and expenses are matched and how much profit, if any, is expected to be earned in a future period. The cash budget contains some items that are not in the anticipated profit and loss statement, and the anticipated profit and loss statement contains some items that are not in the cash budget. Such items as receipts from the sale of stocks and bonds and receipts from the sale of fixed assets appear only in the cash budget. On the other hand, items like depreciation and amortization of patents appear only in the anticipated profit and loss statement. Both statements are useful managerial devices, but they predict different phases of a company's future operations.

While there is no rigid rule as to the span of time that a cash budget should encompass, many firms commonly budget for a one-year period. Cash budgets may also be prepared for spans of time longer than 12 months. A company, for example, committed to begin construction of a large building 18 months from now would probably want to prepare a budget that covers a span of at least three years. After determining the total *span of time* to be covered, the next step is to formulate the *unit of time* into which the total span is to be divided. Monthly periods constitute a convenient unit because they synchronize with the conventional accounting period of a month and because they are short enough to include periods when there is a seasonal expansion in inventory. Periods of seasonal expansion in inventory are apt to be ones in which there will be a need for additional financing because money committed to inventory will not be recovered until sales are made and funds collected. Some firms budget their cash in terms of units of one day. A firm that plans ahead on the basis of daily time periods tends to limit these projections to one month and to use monthly intervals for the remainder of the budget period. Then, as the second month approaches, a cash budget based on daily time periods is prepared for this month. This process is repeated for each succeeding month. In summary, the total span of time covered by the budget and the units of time into which it is divided should enable management to take positive action well in advance of the need for additional financing, as well as predict periods when the firm will have more cash than its minimum needs.

Preparation of the Cash Budget

The preparation of a cash budget, based on monthly intervals of time, involves these main steps:

1. Estimating monthly receipts, assuming no additional financing
2. Estimating monthly expenditures
3. Comparing monthly receipts with monthly expenditures, assuming no additional financing
4. Estimating end-of-month cash balances, assuming no additional financing
5. Forecasting the amount of financing needed to maintain the minimum balance and determining the months in which the firm will have excess cash

A cash budget is organized to indicate broad classes of data rather than the thousands of transactions that constitute the business process.

Table 5-1 shows a cash budget for a six-month period for the Woodward Company, a partnership in the retail field.

	Jan.	Feb.	Mar.	Apr.	May	June	TABLE 5-1 *A Cash Budget (Thousands of Dollars)*
Data for receipts:							
Cash sales	10,800	18,000	21,600	25,200	32,400	18,000	
Collections, receivables	13,000	17,000	28,000	35,000	41,000	52,000	
Miscellaneous	5,000	10,000					
Total receipts	28,800	45,000	49,600	60,200	73,400	70,000	
Data for disbursements:							
Payment on purchases	21,600	36,000	43,200	50,400	64,800	36,000	
Other outlays	7,270	9,760	8,390	11,810	11,660	8,010	
Total outlays	28,870	45,760	51,590	62,210	76,460	44,010	
Surplus or deficit	−70	−760	−1,990	−2,010	−3,060	+25,990	
Opening balance	4,000	3,930	3,170	3,000	3,000	3,000	
Surplus or deficit for month	−70	−760	−1,990	−2,010	−3,060	25,990	
Balance before financing	3,930	3,170	1,180	990	−60	28,990	
Bank loan (L) or repayment (R)			1,820L	2,010L	3,060L	6,890R	
Closing balance	3,930	3,170	3,000	3,000	3,000	22,100	

An interesting feature of business finance is that a firm which is having rapidly increasing sales often has a temporary problem of maintaining an adequate cash balance. In a manufacturing concern money must be spent for labor, material, and overhead to create the inventory that will be sold later. Merchandising concerns have a similar problem. Even though the cash to pay the corresponding accounts payable need not be expended for, say, a month after the date of purchase, many of the expenses will have to be paid for before most of the money from the sales comes into the firm. It is this lag in receipts that often requires the injection of new funds into the business—usually on a temporary basis.

There are a number of significant reasons for planning for cash. The first one is to determine in advance the months, if any, in which the bank balance will fall below the minimum established by management. For example, a firm that has a seasonal bulge in sales will have to finance the additional inventory from internal sources or external sources. Since cash planning indicates whether or not additional funds will have to be obtained, management can plan to raise the funds or change its plans. National Dairy Corporation, for example, plans annually to finance its summer expansion in inventory through bank loans. On the other hand, in a small restaurant in an eastern city, the owner postponed acquiring another outlet because his plans for renovating his present restaurant called for large cash outlays in the next few months. This proprietor believed that his enterprise should expand mainly from internal rather than from outside sources.

The Cash Budget as a Planning Tool

A second reason for planning the flow of cash is to indicate, if necessary, whether the need for funds is permanent or temporary and the most likely source from which the funds can be obtained. A firm that has only a temporary need for funds will use a source different than would be the case if the need were permanent. Temporary needs for funds are often met through bank loans, while permanent needs are often met by selling stocks and bonds. In addition to indicating the amount and type of financing, planning for cash may engender the confidence of suppliers of cash and credit to such an extent that they are more likely to extend the funds. Bankers in particular are likely to consider cash planning as a sign of competence on the part of the management of the prospective borrower.

A third reason for planning the flow of funds is to determine the months, if any, in which there will be a surplus of cash. Although a reasonable amount of cash adds to a firm's debt-paying power, excess cash for any length of time is largely a wasted resource because it is not earning a return. A wise move is to remove this idle cash and invest it in United States government bonds or some other asset that adds to the company's profits.

A fourth reason for planning for cash is that the cash budget used to make the prediction can also be used to act as a control device. As time proceeds, management can compare actual levels of cash with anticipated levels. Differences between the two are studied to determine the reasons for the variation, if any. The many worthwhile reasons for planning the flow of cash more than compensate for the time and accompanying costs in preparing the plans.

PRO FORMA STATEMENTS AS PLANNING TOOLS

Meaning of Pro Forma Statements

In addition to the cash budget, the planning process requires that two additional statements be prepared: (1) the pro forma profit and loss statement and (2) the pro forma balance sheet. Since the term pro forma means projected or anticipated, these two statements reflect what management expects to happen in the future. As usual, our approach will be to stress the use of these tools rather than their construction. If this approach is taken, administrative financial management is seen in its broadest and clearest setting.

Executives obtain relevant data from division heads and then coordinate the departmental plans into pro forma statements for the firm as a whole. Very commonly such statements are prepared for a span of a year, with the data classified into monthly time periods. The preparation of pro forma statements requires the cooperation of production officers, marketing officers, and finance officers. Each division must make known its plans to the person or team of persons in charge of preparing the planning statements. Top management must in turn unveil its plans for major changes in policies. Preparing a set of written plans is a task that requires a spirit of cooperation and patience on the part of all the participants.

Tables 5-2 and 5-3 show the pro forma profit and loss statement and the pro forma balance sheet for the Woodward Company, for whom a cash budget was shown in Table 5-1. Observe that the cash outlays for this company do not necessarily coincide with the expenses for the items. The reader will recall that an expense and a cash outlay are different concepts, even though the amounts may happen to be the same.

Sales (gross of $350,000–sales discounts of $14,000)		$336,000
Less cost of goods sold:		
Opening inventory	$ 24,000	
Add purchases	$288,000	
Less purchase discounts	28,000	260,000
Total available	$284,000	
Less closing inventory	32,000	
Cost of goods sold		252,000
Gross profit		$ 84,000
Less other expenses:		
Salaries and wages	$ 39,100	
Advertising	3,050	
Rent	3,000	
Heat	920	
Insurance	500	
Light and power	850	
Telephone	240	
Taxes (estimated)	1,000	
Repairs	2,300	
Depreciation on equipment	4,000	
Other expenses	1,200	
Total expenses		56,160
Net profit		$ 27,840

TABLE 5-2
Woodward Company **Pro Forma** *Profit and Loss Statement January 1 to June 30, 1977*

Assets

Cash	$ 22,100
Accounts receivable	39,000
Inventories	32,000
Fixed assets	40,000
Total assets	$133,100

Liabilities and Net Worth

Accounts payable	$ 32,000
Other current debts	8,000
Partners' equity	93,100
Total liabilities and net worth	$133,100

TABLE 5-3
Woodward Company **Pro Forma** *Balance Sheet June 30, 1977*

The pro forma profit and loss statement indicates the aspirations of management as to sales, expenses, and net profits. It is concerned only with the generation of profits in future periods of time; past profits are important only if they aid in predicting the future.

The Pro Forma Profit and Loss Statement

The pro forma profit and loss statement shown in Table 5-2 indicates that management has set these goals for itself: gross sales of $350,000; gross profits of $84,000; expenses of not more than $56,160; and net profits of $27,840. Actually, management will attempt to surpass these goals. Six months from now the officers will compare the performance of the firm with these planned goals and with other relevant standards, especially industry averages.

The Pro Forma Balance Sheet   The pro forma balance sheet indicates management's aspirations as to the total amount of assets needed, the composition of the assets, and the sources of assets. The typical balance sheet does not show leased property and other similar items to which title is not held. The pro forma balance sheet is used for expressing a number of goals, although in this chapter we are limiting ourselves to the use of assets in the quest for profits and solvency. At this point, we are concerned only with the ability of the pro forma balance sheet to predict the amount of assets expected to be in use and the expected sources of funds. The pro forma balance sheet is said to be the capstone of the planning statements.

HIGHLIGHTS OF THIS CHAPTER   *The basic reason for planning the use of assets is to increase the probability of the firm reaching its primary goals. Since pro forma statements place these plans in writing, these pro forma reports make a contribution toward the firm reaching its objectives. There are several reasons for believing that there is a connection between planning for the use of assets and reaching the primary goals. First, there is the psychological factor. If plans are prepared properly and are made known to a large segment of the key personnel, there is a tendency for the officers to be stimulated to do their best to reach the goals. Without a set of objectives, expressed in pro forma statements, there is some risk that the officers may not be doing their utmost to increase profits. Planning enables personnel to determine quickly which activities are of an inconsequential nature and which seem to aid the firm in reaching its goals. Second, planning forces officers to anticipate future problems with costs, revenues, and cash flows. By planning ahead management becomes conscious of problems caused by shifts in population, possible new competition, and obsolete equipment. If future problems can be foreseen, advance action might be taken to avert a crisis. Third, planning may be a valuable educational device for a number of persons in the firm, thereby providing a pool of people that can be drawn on to provide management succession. Planning requires the cooperation and interchange of ideas of persons from a number of departments. Each participant learns the impact of the activities of his division on other divisions and on the entire firm. Fourth, planning for profits and for solvency provides a set of objective standards which are useful as controls in evaluating the performance of the firm. As time passes, it is necessary to pass judgment on how successful the officers are in directing the affairs of the business. If the budget calls for expected sales of $50,000 next June, this same figure can be used later to determine the efficiency of the officers. Hence, plans provide a set of standards against which performance can be matched. Planning,* of course, is not *a sure* method of solving all the firm's problems. But a firm that plans is more likely to be a financial success than one that drifts along without specific goals.

In summary, plans must be placed in writing if they are to serve any useful purpose. The preparation of written plans results in more careful forecasting and in supplying officers with a set of targets to which reference can be made as needed and against which performance can be compared as the fiscal period progresses.

5-1. What does the term *pro forma* mean? *REVIEW QUESTIONS*

5-2. Should students and faculty be permitted to participate in preparing cash budgets for universities and thereby influence the relative amounts spent on research and on teaching?

5-3. When a firm's seasonal sales are rising, does this result in a seasonal shortage or surplus of cash?

5-4. Name two items which appear on the cash budget that do not appear on the pro forma profit and loss statement.

5-5. *Fortune* contains write-ups on successful business firms. Read about one such company and answer these questions: (a) Does it have long-range plans? (b) Does it have a strong research and development program? (c) Are its activities well diversified? (d) Is the management aggressive? (e) Why does this firm appear to be successful?

5-6. *Forbes* contains write-ups on successful businessmen and how they handle the affairs of the firm. Read about one such person and answer these questions: (a) Is he a long-run planner? (b) What experience has he had with other firms? (c) What plans does he have for expanding the firm?

Answers to some of the problems appear at the end of this section. *For each problem, show how you obtained the answer.* *REVIEW PROBLEMS*

5-1. In the month in which Company Z sells goods, it receives 90 percent of the proceeds; it collects the remaining 10 percent the following month. Below is a balance sheet at the end of April:

Cash	$ 100,000	Current liabilities	$ 300,000
Accounts receivable	200,000	Owner's equity	700,000
Inventories	300,000		
Fixed assets	400,000		
Total	$1,000,000	Total	$1,000,000

If sales in May were $1,500,000: (a) How much cash will be taken in during the month of May? (b) How much were the sales for April?

5-2. Company B is planning a seasonal increase in sales of $1 million. Naturally, the firm's assets will expand and the firm will also have to make provision for financing the expansion in the assets. The following relationships are expected to apply to the incremental sales (not the previous sales). Additional cash needed will be 10 percent of additional sales; additional accounts receivable will be 20 percent of additional sales; additional inventories needed will be 20 percent of additional sales; fixed assets will remain the same; and additional accounts payable will be 10 percent of additional sales. When all of these changes are incorporated in a pro forma balance sheet, the firm will have to borrow. Assume that all borrowing is from the local bank. How much in additional bank loans will the firm need to obtain? Below is the firm's balance sheet before the seasonal expansion:

Cash	$100,000	Accounts payable	$100,000
Accounts receivable	200,000	Bank loans	200,000
Inventories	200,000	Common stock	200,000
Fixed assets	100,000	Retained profits	100,000
Total	$600,000	Total	$600,000

5-3. Complete the following balance sheet. Only the common stock and retained profit figures are given:

Cash	(6)	Accounts payable	—— (1)
Accounts receivable	(5)	Common stock	$600,000
Inventories	(4)	Retained profits	600,000
Fixed assets	(7)	Total liabilities	
Total assets	(3)	and net worth	—— (2)

Additional information: Total debt is two-thirds of net worth; turnover of total assets is 1.8; 30 days' sales are on the books in the form of accounts receivable; turnover of inventory is 5; cost of goods sold per year is $900,000; and the acid test ratio is 1 to 1. *Suggestion*: Proceed in the sequence of numbers to the right of the accounts in the above balance sheet.

5-4. In the past three years, Company F's sales have averaged $300,000 annually, and its profits after taxes have fluctuated between $15,000 and $20,000 a year. The management predicts that next year's sales will be $330,000. What minimum and maximum profit might the management predict for next year?

5-5. The following information applies to Company Z: unit variable costs are $2; total fixed costs are $100; unit selling price is $12; maximum demand for the product is 700 units; production capacity is 450 units; cash on hand is $600; all expenses must be paid in the current production period; the cash from all sales is collected in the following period. For Company Z the optimum level of production, after considering all the constraints, is how many units?

Answers: 5-1a, $1,550,000; 5-1b, $2,000,000; 5-2, $400,000; 5-4, between $16,500 and $22,011; 5-5, 250 units.

Oscar Harvey, an employee in the laundry of a large hospital, is planning to leave his job and establish a self-service laundry. Harvey is 23, and he has $8,000 in the bank. His two basic problems are to determine the amount of cash needed to establish the laundry and to estimate the profit that he will receive from it.

Harvey also plans to establish an additional self-service laundry with the *available profits* (defined later) from the first one.

Since he expects to rent most of his equipment, as well as the storeroom, his outlays for fixed assets will be nominal.

Below are data for estimating the amount of cash that will be needed to form the business:

CASE ON PLANNING THE LEVEL OF OPERATIONS FOR A NEW SMALL BUSINESS

Equipment financed by a 25 percent down payment on these items:	
8-pound-capacity machines	$5,000
Automatic dryers	1,000
Water extractors	1,000
Water heating system	1,000
Equipment for which cash is needed:	
Scale	$ 200
Plumbing and heating	1,600
Electrical work	800
Carpentry, painting, signs	1,200
Other equipment	1,000
Safety margin in cash for three months' expenses	$2,800
Estimated net profits for a single laundry:	
Annual gross from all services	$36,000
Expenses	16,000

A further factor is that Harvey is committed to paying the balance of his equipment obligations by making a payment of $3,000 at the end of the first year and a similar payment at the end of the second year.

Harvey will not take a salary but will withdraw profits to meet his annual living expenses, which he believes will be $10,000 (over and above personal taxes).

Out of each year's profits, Harvey must pay federal income taxes. He estimates that his personal allowable deductions will amount to $2,000 a year, consisting of contributions, medical deductions, and so on; in addition he will be allowed a $750 exemption for himself. The partial tax table below applies to Harvey:

Over	But Not Over		of Excess Over
$10,000	$12,000....	$2,090 plus 27%	$10,000
$12,000	$14,000....	$2,630 plus 29%	$12,000
$14,000	$16,000....	$3,210 plus 31%	$14,000
$16,000	$18,000....	$3,830 plus 34%	$16,000
$18,000	$20,000....	$4,510 plus 36%	$18,000
$20,000	$22,000....	$5,230 plus 38%	$20,000

At the end of each year, he will place *available profits* in a savings and loan association until the fund is large enough to start the second laundry. Available profits are measured in this manner:

Annual profits		———
Less:		
Income taxes	———	
Personal living expenses	$10,000	
Installment paying on equipment	———	
Total	———	———
Available profits (amount placed in		
savings and loan association)		———

These data are relevant because they affect the funds that will be available for financing the second laundry.

Required: (a) Estimate the amount of cash needed to establish the first laundry. Where should the funds be obtained, assuming that Harvey does not use more than $6,000 of his $8,000 savings? (b) How much in federal income taxes will Harvey pay at the end of the first year? (c) At the end of the first year, how much will Harvey place in the savings and loan account? (d) In how many years will Harvey be able to establish the second laundry? (Assume he finances the second one entirely from the *available profits* of the first one.)

Planning the Level of Operations (II)

Leverage means that a percentage change in one amount causes a relatively larger percentage change in other amounts. One example of leverage is the situation in a restaurant where the owner might find that a 10 percent increase in sales will lead to a 20 percent increase in pretax profits. This phenomenon is a result of certain expenses being fixed. Thus rent usually remains the same regardless of a sales increase or decrease. The essence of leverage is that under certain conditions costs do not rise as fast as an increase in sales or fall as fast as a decline in sales. *It is important to observe that a fundamental condition must be met before leverage is operative; namely, the cost structure must not change significantly as a result of the change in sales.* Because of leverage, business profits tend to be magnified in a period of rising sales and losses tend to be magnified in a period of sharply declining sales.

Leverage is one of the tools that can be used to plan, since the concept means that a change in the independent variable leads to a predictable change in the dependent variable. Businessmen are constantly asking the question: If there is a change in one amount, what change will there be in another amount? Leverage provides a reasonably accurate answer to this kind of question.

Closely related to the concept of leverage is that of *break-even analysis*. This latter planning tool shows relationships among volume, costs, and profits. The connection between break-even analysis and leverage is that both concepts are a result of the role of fixed costs in planning.

The following will be discussed in this chapter:

1. The use of leverage
    a. Composite leverage
    b. Operating leverage
    c. Financial leverage
2. Break-even analysis

a. Interpretation

b. The break-even chart as a planning tool

While financial managers are familiar with the concept of leverage, it is useful to carry this thought a step further and attempt to quantify the relationship between changes in one amount and changes in another. This relationship, when quantified, is known as the *degree of leverage*. The degree of leverage may be used as a predictive device. It is possible to predict the future by studying relationships that hold constant over reasonable levels of sales.

As the basis for an example showing how the degree of leverage is determined, let us examine Table 6-1. This table shows expenses classified into the useful grouping of (1) operating expenses and (2) financial expenses. Observe that interest is treated as a financial expense rather than an operating outlay. Also notice that variable costs are subtracted from sales to obtain a *remainder*. Then, fixed operating costs are substracted from the remainder to obtain operating income. The reader will recall that a synonym for "operating income" is "earnings before interest and taxes" (EBIT). Interest is subtracted from EBIT to obtain taxable income, which is then subjected to the income tax so that the profit available for owners may be obtained.

Composite leverage shows the relationship between a change in sales and the corresponding change in taxable income. The president of a company might be interested in knowing the relationship between a certain percentage change in sales and the resulting percentage change in taxable income. From what has already been said, he would expect that a given percentage change in sales would lead to a greater percentage change in taxable income. The formula for establishing this quantitative relationship is:

$$\begin{array}{l} \text{Percent increase in} \\ \text{taxable income} \end{array} = \begin{array}{l} \text{Percent increase} \\ \text{in sales} \end{array} \times \begin{array}{l} \text{Degree of} \\ \text{composite leverage} \end{array} \qquad (1)$$

In order to complete the above formula, it is necessary to determine the degree of composite leverage, found by the following formula:

$$\begin{array}{l} \text{Degree of composite} \\ \text{leverage at} \\ \text{starting point} \end{array} = \frac{\text{Remainder}}{\text{Taxable income}}$$
$$= \frac{\$440,000}{10,000}$$
$$= 44 \qquad (2)$$

The degree of composite leverage of 44 is then substituted in formula (1). If sales increase by 2 percent, then taxable income will increase by 88 percent. Formula (1) then reads:

$$\text{Percent increase in taxable income} = 2 \times 44$$
$$= 88 \text{ percent}$$

This answer may be checked in Table 6-1. Sales increase from $1,100,000 to $1,122,000 (an increase of 2 percent); taxable income increases from $10,000 to $18,800 (an increase of 88 percent). In a similar manner, if sales had increased by 3 percent, taxable income would have increased by 132 percent, assuming a degree of composite leverage of 44. Leverage is always measured from a specific starting point; hence, it is necessary to state the degree of leverage at a certain level, such as at the $1,100,000 level of sales. When different starting points are used, different degrees of composite leverage are obtained. In general, as the volume of sales increases, the degree of composite leverage decreases, assuming that fixed costs stay the same. This is true because leverage is caused by the presence of fixed charges; as the relative importance of these fixed charges to sales decreases, the magnitude of leverage decreases.

If two firms have the same amount of sales, the one with the larger proportion of fixed expenses will have the higher degree of composite leverage.

Since the president of a firm may be more interested in the dollar figure of taxable income than in the percentage change in taxable income, he is interested in the fact that a 2 percent increase in sales will result in his taxable income rising from $10,000 to $18,800, which, of course, is an 88 percent increase. Composite leverage, then, may be used to predict the new level of taxable income as a result of a given percentage increase in sales. Of course, only insiders have enough information to use this tool; the public at large does not have the

TABLE 6-1
Financial Data for Company X

	Starting Point	2 Percent Increase over Starting Point
Sales at $20 a unit	$1,100,000	$1,122,000
Less variable costs (60% of sales)	660,000	673,200
Remainder	$ 440,000	$ 448,800
Less fixed operating costs	400,000	400,000
Operating income (EBIT)	$ 40,000	$ 48,800
Less interest	30,000	30,000
Taxable income	$ 10,000	$ 18,800
Less tax (30% rate)	3,000	5,640
Net after taxes	$ 7,000	$ 13,160
Shares of common stock outstanding	5,000	5,000
Earnings per share on common (EPS)	1.40	2.63
Capitalization rate on EPS (in %)	9.50	9.50
Market price of common	$ 14.74	$ 27.68

necessary breakdown of costs into fixed and variable to compute the degree of composite leverage.

The reason for the dramatic results of composite leverage in this example is that fixed costs were intentionally made high so as to dramatize the principle. In a more normal situation, fixed costs might not be so large and the results would not be so dramatic.

Operating leverage shows the relationship between changes in sales and changes in operating income. Another way to state this is that operating leverage takes into account the impact of only fixed operating expenses; interest costs are not considered.

The formula for determining the consequences of operating leverage is:

$$\text{Percent increase in operating income} = \text{Percent increase in sales} \times \text{Degree of operating leverage} \tag{3}$$

$$
\begin{aligned}
\text{Operating leverage at \$1,100,000 level of sales} &= \frac{\text{Remainder}}{\text{Operating income}} \\
&= \frac{\$440,000}{40,000} \\
&= 11
\end{aligned} \tag{4}
$$

The degree of operating leverage at a particular level of sales is then used in formula (3) to answer the question of what the percentage change in operating income is if there is a given percentage change in sales. Thus, if sales increase by 2 percent, operating income will increase by 22 percent (11 × 2). A 2 percent increase in sales and its impact on operating income can be checked in Table 6-1. If sales increase from $1,100,000 to $1,122,000 (a 2 percent increase), operating income increases from $40,000 to $48,000 (a 22 percent increase). In a similar manner, if sales increase 4 percent from the starting point, operating income will increase by 44 percent.

The reader is again reminded that the tool of degree of operating leverage will hold true only as long as the cost relationships do not change with varying levels of production or sales. Although this situation seldom occurs in real life, the answers obtained by making the assumption are very close to reality. The margin of error is small in making the unrealistic assumptions of an unchanging cost structure. The small errors in the answers do not void the usefulness of operating leverage as a planning tool.

Financial leverage shows the changes that take place in taxable income as a result of changes in operating income. More specifically, the degree of financial leverage is the percentage change that takes place in taxable income as a result of a given percentage change in operating income. Financial leverage takes into account only one fixed charge—interest. The formula for determining financial leverage is:

$$\begin{array}{l}\text{Percent increase in} \\ \text{taxable income}\end{array} = \begin{array}{l}\text{Percent increase in} \\ \text{operating income}\end{array} \times \begin{array}{l}\text{Degree} \\ \text{financial} \\ \text{leverage}\end{array} \qquad (5)$$

The formula for determining degree of financial leverage is:

$$\begin{array}{l}\text{Degree of financial} \\ \text{leverage at the} \\ \text{\$1,100,000 level} \\ \text{of sales}\end{array} = \frac{\text{Operating income}}{\text{Taxable income}}$$

$$= \frac{\$40,000}{\$10,000} \qquad (6)$$

$$= 4$$

The degree of financial leverage of 4 is then substituted in formula (5). If operating income increases by 22 percent, then taxable income increases by 88 percent. Formula (5) then reads:

$$\begin{array}{l}\text{Percent increase} \\ \text{in taxable income}\end{array} \begin{array}{l}= 22 \times 4 \\ = 88 \text{ percent}\end{array}$$

In a similar manner, a 1 percent increase in operating income will result in a 4 percent increase in taxable income.

The reader will recognize the different kinds of leverage as an application of the rules of proportion found in elementary algebra. Because of this, numerous other interrelationships may be discovered, such as the relationship between a change in sales and a change in net after taxes, between a change in sales and a change in earnings per share, and between a change in sales and the market price of the common stock (provided the change in sales is not very large).

The following data apply to Company Z (assume that variable expenses are one-third of sales): *Problem*

Sales	$1,200,000
Less variable expenses	400,000
Remainder	$ 800,000
Less fixed costs, except interest	400,000
Earnings before interest and taxes	$ 400,000
Less interest	200,000
Taxable income	$ 200,000

Required: (a) Using the concept of composite leverage, by what percentage will taxable income increase if sales increase by 3 percent? (b) Using the concept of operating leverage, by what percentage will EBIT (operating income) increase if there is a 3 percent increase in sales? (c) Using the concept of financial leverage, by what percentage will taxable income increase if EBIT increase by 6 percent?

Solution   (a) Composite leverage is 4 (remainder of $800,000 ÷ taxable income of $200,000). If sales increase by 3 percent, taxable income will increase by 12 percent (composite leverage of 4 × percentage increase in sales). (b) Operating leverage is 2 (remainder of $800,000 ÷ EBIT of $400,000). If sales increase by 3 percent, EBIT will increase by 6 percent (operating leverage of 2 × percentage increase in sales). (c) Financial leverage is 2 (EBIT of $400,000 ÷ taxable income of $200,000). If EBIT increase by 6 percent, taxable income will increase by 12 percent (financial leverage of 2 × percentage increase in EBIT).

BREAK-EVEN
ANALYSIS

Interpretation

A *break-even chart* is a pictorial presentation of the amount of profits or losses that a firm can reasonably expect at varying levels of output. The device obtains its name from one point on the chart that is of special significance—the level of output at which a firm's total sales are exactly equal to its total costs. At this point the firm makes neither a profit nor a loss. The chart contains summary material on total sales, total fixed costs, total variable costs, and total output. Like other visual aid material, the chart aids thinking by concentrating attention on a limited number of business forces. The break-even chart gives a composite view of a firm's operations by focusing attention on a few, but vital, classes of data. The grouping of income and expense data into a few classes has the advantage of eliminating thousands of details. Management is thus able to gain perspective on the broad economic characteristics of a particular firm.

Table 6-2 gives new data for a firm that will be used as an example for the discussion of break-even analysis. As can be seen in the table, this company has prepared an anticipated profit and loss statement. The company expects to sell 60,000 units at $20 a unit, resulting in anticipated total sales of $1,200,000. At

TABLE 6-2
The Small-Business
Specialties Company
Condensed Income
Statement for
Year Ending
December 31, 19——

Net sales (60,000 units @ $20 per unit)			$1,200,000
Less costs and expenses:	*Variable*	*Fixed*	
Direct material	$195,000		
Direct labor	215,000		
Manufacturing expenses	100,000	$200,000	
Selling expenses	50,000	150,000	
General and administrative expenses	160,000	50,000	
Total	$720,000	$400,000	1,120,000
Net profit before federal income taxes			$ 80,000

Source:
Courtesy of U.S. Small
Business Administration,
Washington, D.C.

this level of activity total expenses are predicted to be $1,120,000, consisting of $720,000 in variable and $400,000 in fixed expenses. Net profits are expected to be $80,000 under these conditions. The unit selling price will be $20 at all levels of sales, the unit variable costs will be $12 at all levels of sales, and the unit fixed costs will depend on the volume of sales. In this firm, variable costs are 60 percent of selling price at all levels of sales. The company under consideration makes only one type of product, and all goods produced are assumed to be sold. Actually, nearly all businesses sell a number of different kinds of products. In these situations, the sales as well as the costs and expenses for each product are consolidated, and the totals for the firm are used in financial planning. Also, in break-even analysis, all goods produced are assumed to be sold. In the following discussion, the terms *produced* and *sold* will be used synonymously; the terms *income* and *sales* will also have identical meanings. The data given in Table 6-2 are plotted on the break-even chart shown in Figure 6-1. In addition to the predicted net profits of $80,000, the management of the company wants reasonably correct answers to these questions about future operations: (a) At what level of sales will the firm just cover all costs and expenses, that is, break even? (b) If selling price is changed or if costs and expenses are changed, what will be the effect on profits? (c) In order to earn a certain dollar profit, how much will sales have to be?

Break-even charts supply answers to these questions. The first step in preparing data for a break-even chart is to separate costs and expenses into fixed and variable. Fixed items are those that are relatively stable regardless of output. For example, officers' salaries, property taxes, and fire insurance premiums are likely to continue at the same amount for a one-year period regardless of the quantity of goods produced or sold. Table 6-2 indicates the composition of the $400,000 in fixed costs and expenses for this particular firm. Management considers certain costs as inflexible over a one-year period, even though they might be changed in part if the officers were willing to undergo the inconvenience and unpleasantness of change. The assumption that certain costs are rigid is reasonably realistic and it facilitates short-run planning. Variable costs and expenses, the second classification, are items that change with the level of output. Direct materials and direct labor are variable in the sense that they increase or decrease as production rises or falls. The separation of all items into either fixed or variable costs and expenses is not an easy assignment.

The sales data and operating expense data are based on recent experience, but after adjustments are made in the data for expected changes in the future. Only the revised data are plotted on the break-even chart. Since business conditions are changing constantly, management must revise the break-even chart at reasonable intervals if the predictive data shown by it are to serve effectively their function as a planning tool. Our brief comments on the construction of the break-even chart have been for the purpose of providing insight into the *interpretation* of this instrument rather than to give a detailed explanation of the mechanics of its construction.

Although the break-even chart shown in Figure 6-1 gives the appearance of being an exact tool, actually it gives only approximate results. This is true for a number of reasons. The chart assumes unit selling price is the same at all levels of sales; it does not apply to a rapidly growing concern whose cost structure changes rapidly; it assumes that the future will be very similar to the past; and it

FIGURE 6-1
Break-even Chart

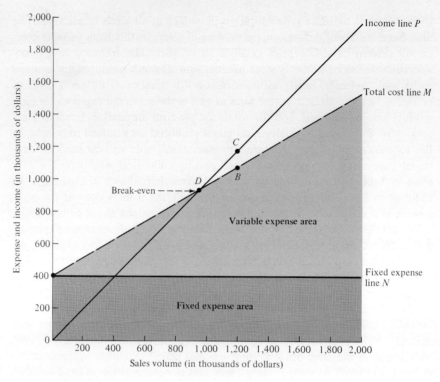

assumes that total fixed costs and unit variable costs stay the same at all levels of output. A sound approach is to view the break-even chart as giving fairly reliable but not precise results. Within these limitations, the chart is a useful visual planning tool in anticipating the future.

The Break-even Chart as a Planning Tool

A first use of the break-even chart is to derive from it the estimated level of sales at which the firm will break even. An inspection of Figure 6-1 shows that this firm has neither a profit nor a loss at point D, where the total cost line is crossed by the total income line. To determine the total income from sales at which this firm breaks even, a perpendicular line is dropped from point D to the base line. Accordingly, when income from sales is $1 million, the break-even point is reached, for at this point total costs and expenses are also $1 million, as can be determined by again beginning with point D but moving to the left axis. As income from sales surpasses $1 million, net profits increase; as income from sales falls below $1 million, net losses occur. The break-even point in terms of total income from sales can also be determined by the following formula (the left side of the equation is total income from sales and the right side is total costs and expenses):

$$S = F + V$$

where S equals sales at the break-even point, F equals total fixed costs and fixed expenses, and V equals total variable costs and variable expenses, as a percentage of sales. Substituting, we have:

$$S = \$\ \ 400{,}000 + 0.60S$$
$$10S = \$4{,}000{,}000 + 6S$$
$$4S = \$4{,}000{,}000$$
$$S = \$1{,}000{,}000$$

Therefore, the break-even point in terms of net income from sales is $1 million. This checks out because the $1 million in sales is exactly offset by total costs and expenses of $1 million ($400,000 fixed and $600,000 variable).

A second use of the break-even chart is to obtain a quick visual picture of the impact of changes in sales, fixed costs, and variable costs on profits. These changes in profits can be illustrated by adding revised data to the chart or constructing a new one. The president of this company, for example, can determine the impact of a 16²/₃ percent increase in sales on net profits. If sales increase from $1,200,000 to $1,400,000, what is the impact of this change on profits? An inspection of the chart shows that at a sales volume of $1,200,000, profits are $80,000 and at a sales volume of $1,400,000, profits rise to $160,000. A 16²/₃ percent increase in sales results in a 100 percent increase in profits. What causes this favorable situation? The answer is that part of the costs are fixed and do not increase with rising sales. Look at the matter this way. Unit selling price is $20 and unit variable costs are $12 per unit, both at all levels of output. But unit fixed costs fall as sales increase, since the total of $400,000 is constant at all levels of sales. The amount by which the unit fixed costs decrease becomes profits. A firm that has a relatively large amount of fixed costs is said to have high *operating leverage*. A company with high operating leverage will find that after the break-even point is passed, a certain percentage increase in sales will result in a larger percentage increase in net profits. The railroad industry is an example of an industry with high operating leverage.

Another important point about firms with high operating leverage is that a small percentage decrease in sales will result in a larger percentage decrease in profits. A company that has a relatively large proportion of its costs as variable will find that changes in sales will result in changes in net profits, but the percentage changes in profits will not be as great as would have been the case if there had been high operating leverage. Generally speaking, management prefers a low break-even point, assuming that the firm's operations are being conducted as efficiently as possible. One would not need a break-even chart to demonstrate how fixed costs affect profits. But this chart does dramatize vividly this facet of the economics of the firm. In addition to indicating how changes in income from sales will change profits, the break-even chart is a useful tool for showing how changes in fixed and variable costs affect profits.

A third use of the break-even chart is to show visually the amount of sales needed to attain a certain level of profits. Assume that a firm wants to know the amount of sales needed to earn a profit of $160,000. Using a ruler, one calculates from either the vertical or the horizontal line the linear distance equivalent to $160,000. One then moves the ruler to the profit area and finds the place where the distance between the total income line and the total cost and expense line is equivalent to $160,000. Next, from this observation point, an imaginary line is dropped perpendicular to the base. The scale of operations needed to reach this profit goal is $1,400,000 and can be read from the chart. Break-even charts are growing in use, in keeping with the increasing use of symbols by businessmen to guide them in their thinking.

HIGHLIGHTS OF THIS CHAPTER

Leverage means that a percentage change in one amount leads to a greater percentage change in another amount. Thus a 5 percent increase in sales might lead to a 10 percent change in taxable income. Leverage is caused by the presence of fixed charges. The impact of leverage is especially great around the break-even point. As sales volume increases substantially past the break-even point, leverage becomes less potent because fixed charges become a smaller percentage of sales and therefore less significant in the overall picture.

The break-even point is useful in determining the level of sales necessary for a firm to break even. While no firm considers this level of volume an achievement, nonetheless, management may wish to know how far sales can fall before the firm begins to suffer losses. Break-even analysis, broader than merely the determination of the break-even point, is useful in predicting the impact of changes in sales on operating profits, of changing unit variable costs on profits, of changes in unit selling prices on profits, and so on.

Both leverage analysis and break-even analysis should be used with care because both rely on the assumption that cost-price relations are not changing. Since this assumption may be unreal, both leverage and break-even analysis should be regarded as approximations only.

REVIEW QUESTIONS

6-1. Company P has operating leverage of 3. How can this figure be used for forecasting purposes?

6-2. On what basic assumption does the concept of leverage rest?

6-3. As a firm produces beyond its break-even point, does operating leverage increase or decrease? Why?

6-4. Suggest *several* uses of break-even analysis by a small restaurant in the area in which you live.

6-5. The U.S. Small Business Administration in Washington, D.C., has compiled the break-even point for many types of small businesses such as laundries, clothing stores, and motels. Write to this agency and obtain information on the kind of firm that interests you. Answer these questions: (a) What is the break-even

point in dollars for the firm you selected? (b) Is a high break-even point a good
or a bad situation? (c) Is it more important to consider a break-even point based
on past data or on future data?

Answers to some of the problems appear at the end of this section. For each **REVIEW PROBLEMS**
problem, show how you obtained the answer.

6-1. Company R has sales of $1 million, variable costs of $500,000, fixed operating costs of $200,000, and interest expenses of $200,000. The firm assumes that its variable costs will remain at 50 percent of sales. Determine (a) the composite leverage; (b) the operating leverage; (c) the financial leverage.

6-2. The following data apply to Company P at the 10,000 level of output: total sales $100,000; total variable expenses $60,000; fixed operating costs $30,000; total interest $5,000; variable costs 60 percent of sales. If sales increase by 10 percent: (a) By what percentage will EBIT increase? (b) By what percentage will taxable income increase? Find the answer by using leverage.

6-3. Company Z has a unit selling price of $6, total fixed costs of $4,000, and unit variable costs of $2. What is the break-even point in units?

6-4. Company M breaks even at a $120,000 volume; it has fixed operating costs of $40,000 and a unit sales price of $3. How much are the unit variable costs?

6-5. Determine the break-even point of Company X, given the following facts: total fixed costs $60,000; variable unit costs 40 cents; selling price per unit 60 cents; opening inventory 10,000 units; closing inventory 5,000 units; fixed assets $80,000; and net worth $25,000.

6-6. Determine the unit variable costs of Company K, given the following information: break-even point 10,000 units; unit selling price $10; and total fixed costs $60,000.

6-7. The following data apply to Company S:

Sales	$600,000
Less variable expenses	200,000
Remainder	$400,000
Less fixed costs, except interest	100,000
Earnings before interest and taxes	$300,000
Less interest	100,000
Taxable income	$200,000

Assume that variable expenses are one-third of sales. (a) Using the concept of composite leverage, by what percentage will taxable income increase if sales increase by 6 percent? (b) Using the concept of operating leverage, by what percentage will EBIT (operating income) increase if there is a 6 percent increase in sales? (c) Using the concept of financial leverage, by what percentage will taxable income increase if EBIT increases by 8 percent?

6-8. The following data apply to Company T:

Sales	$1,000
Less variable expenses	400
Remainder	$ 600
Less fixed operating expenses	200
Operating income (EBIT)	$ 400
Less interest expense	100
Taxable income	$ 300

(a) Prepare a new income statement showing how a 20 percent increase in sales will affect the operations of the firm. (Assume variable expenses are 40 percent of sales.) (b) At the $1,000 level of sales, determine the composite leverage, the operating leverage, and the financial leverage. What do these leverage figures mean? (c) Without preparing an income statement, determine (1) the percentage increase in operating income caused by a 20 percent increase in sales and (2) the percentage increase in taxable income caused by a 20 percent increase in sales. (d) Do your answers check with the information shown in the income statement you prepared in part (a) of this problem?

6-9. Determine the break-even point in both units and dollars for Company H, given the following information: total fixed costs $3,000; unit selling price $5; and unit variable costs $2.

6-10. A businessman, Mr. X, needs an automobile for business purposes. He is interested in the comparative cost of leasing versus owning the vehicle. He reads an advertisement in the *Wall Street Journal* which shows Cadillacs renting for $162 per month, with the user buying his own gasoline and oil (which would amount to $0.02 per mile). If Mr. X purchases a Cadillac, his fixed annual costs will be $1,000, plus variable costs of $0.12 per mile. What is the least number of miles per year he would have to drive in order to make renting cheaper than owning? (Note that he needs to drive the car one mile more than the break-even point.)

6-11. Company A is producing 10,000 units and selling them at $25 each; unit variable costs are $10; total fixed costs are $100,000; aggregate profits are $50,000. The firm has just concluded a labor union agreement which will increase variable costs by $5 a unit and total fixed expenses by $10,000. Company A plans to increase the selling price to offset the additional labor costs;

furthermore, the management plans to add a little extra to the price increase so as to raise profits to $60,000. The management expects to sell the same number of units (10,000). To accomplish these goals, at what level should the management set the new selling price?

6-12. An alternate formula for determining the break-even point in units is:

$$Q = \frac{F}{S - V}$$

where Q is the break-even point in units, F is total fixed costs, S is the unit selling price, and V is variable unit cost. Using the above formula, determine the break-even point in units for Firm B, given the following: total fixed costs $10,000; unit selling price $4; and unit variable cost $2.

Answers: 6-1a, 5; 6-1b, 5/3 ; 6-1c, 3; 6-2a, 40 percent; 6-2b, 80 percent; 6-3, 1,000 units; 6-4, $2; 6-5, 300,000 units; 6-6, $4; 6-10, 9,441 miles; 6-11, $32; 6-12, 5,000 units.

Fred Alton, a salesman for a food wholesaler, and Charles Peters, a salesman for a manufacturer, are former college classmates. Each has been moderately successful in his job. Alton earns an annual salary of $8,600 and Peters an annual salary of $8,400. Both men believe that they will have to change employment if they are to advance financially. After studying a number of projects, the two decide to start a restaurant. They believe that their background will contribute to their success.

CASE ON BREAK-EVEN ANALYSIS FOR A NEW RESTAURANT

The two young businessmen know of a fully-equipped restaurant available for rent. The owner of the building in which the restaurant and its contents are located is anxious to rent the restaurant space and its equipment, for he does not wish to operate this kind of venture. Alton and Peters decide to rent the restaurant, since this course of action will lead to a minimum initial cash outlay on their part.

Alton has $8,000 from an inheritance available for investment in the business. Peters also has $8,000 available for investment in the new firm. This money really belongs to his wife, but she is permitting him to use it.

Alton will buy the food and plan the menus. Peters will keep the books and hire the help. The two partners also agree to divide other managerial and employee chores between themselves.

The two men make a careful study of available data on volume and costs of successful restaurants. They study trade association figures, obtain an opinion on sales-cost relationships from a local certified public accountant, and receive data from Alton's uncle, who operates a successful restaurant in a distant city. Their main problem is to estimate the break-even point.

The restaurant is in a section of the city where many businessmen eat breakfast and lunch and might be expected to drop in for a 15-cent cup of coffee.

Under their management, the restaurant also will be active in serving $4-per-person banquets to bowling leagues, college honor societies, and numerous other groups. The restaurant will be open 9 hours a day, 360 days a year. After taking the above information into consideration, Alton and Peters believe that the average amount spent by each customer will be approximately $1.25.

Next, the two young businessmen estimate their fixed charges. Three full-time cooks will be hired at an annual wage of $7,000 each. In addition three cooks' helpers will be hired at an annual wage of $5,000 each. The cooks' helpers will also wash dishes and perform other general duties. Three full-time waitresses will be hired at an annual rate of $5,000 each. Part-time waitresses will also be hired, but their wages will be treated under variable expenses.

Each partner will take a salary of $9,500, which will also be a fixed expense. They are willing to take a moderate salary in the first year or so, hoping later to earn as much as $20,000 each.

The two promoters are investing a total of $16,000 in the business—$6,000 in current assets and $10,000 in fixed assets. Total annual depreciation is $1,000.

The landlord is charging an annual rental of $5,000; he has insisted on the partners signing a five-year lease, which will give them the use of the restaurant space and all the restaurant equipment.

All other fixed expenses will amount to $2,000 a year.

After studying the fixed expenses mentioned in the preceding paragraphs, the two young businessmen have concluded that the total annual fixed expenses will be $78,000.

Next, they estimate their variable expenses. These include food, part-time waitresses, and other items. Their best estimate is that variable expenses will be 45 percent of sales.

Required:
1. Determine the following for the first year of operation:
   a. The annual dollar volume of sales necessary to break even and the average number of meals per day that will have to be served to break even
   b. The level of sales necessary to earn a profit of $10,000 (after subtracting all expenses, including the salaries of the two owners)
   c. The profit that would be earned if the firm were fortunate enough to have sales of $200,000
   d. The break-even point in dollars if total fixed costs could be reduced by 10 percent
   e. The break-even point (in number of meals) if the average sale could be increased to $1.40, but the other original data stayed the same

2. Determine the impact, if any, of the establishment of a new restaurant on these groups: creditors of competitors of the firm, competitors of the restaurant, the community at large, labor unions, and the economic system as a whole.

Modern Tools for Planning

One trend in finance is the use of quantitative tools to solve managerial problems. This chapter is devoted to a brief discussion of selected mathematical tools that are becoming increasingly important in business finance. These tools, when combined with sound judgment, are valuable aids in enabling a firm to reach its goals. The approach will be to acquaint the reader with the use of selected concepts and to enable him to recognize some of the new terminology used in scholarly and business journals and in conversations with business executives. No attempt will be made to teach the mechanics of the many interesting new quantitative devices.

The following will be discussed in this chapter:

1. The use of models
2. Decision making
   a. Models under certainty
   b. Models under risk
   c. Models under uncertainty

A model is a representation of reality. Examples of models are formulas representing economic forces that determine profits, road maps representing highways, and miniature ships representing battleships. Models may be classified according to their degree of abstractness. The mathematical model is quite abstract. An example is the following formula:

$$P = 2X + 4Y$$

where P equals total profit, \$2 is the net profit on each item of X sold, and \$4 is the net profit on each item of Y sold. Less abstract than the mathematical model

USE OF MODELS

is the analog model, a simplified visual presentation of reality. An example is a U.S. map with different colors representing the states and the regions of the country to which the states belong. Unlike mathematical models, analog models cannot be manipulated to solve problems. The least abstract model is the physical model, such as the miniature ship representing a particular battleship. These models are especially useful in the physical sciences and in the technological fields. Certain experiments can be conducted that could not be performed on the actual object, such as determining the amount of water a ship will hold before it sinks. Models are a compromise between an excessive amount of detail and an oversimplification. If they contain too much detail, they are difficult to comprehend; if they are an oversimplification of reality, they lose their precision. But by their very nature, most of them contain relatively few variables and hence to some extent are an oversimplification of reality. This does not detract from their usefulness, however, because models clarify issues and focus attention on key variables.

Of special interest in business are the mathematical models, which may be divided into two kinds: the *definitional model* and the *decision-making model*. The definitional model is one with which the reader is already familiar; the famous equation of assets equals liabilities plus net worth is such a model; it is always true by definition. Considerable interest now centers around the decision-making model. This tool attempts to determine and simplify interrelations and place them in formula form. Then, by manipulating the formula, one can ascertain an optimum procedure; that is, the formula proposes an alternative which will result in the lowest costs or highest sales. Mathematical models are helpful guides in determining the best way to allocate scarce resources.

Preparing a mathematical model involves several steps. First, it is necessary to define the problem to be solved. Thus a firm might be interested in developing a model that will give guidance on the best quantity of inventory to order at a time so as to minimize combined inventory-carrying costs plus procurement costs. That is, should the firm place many orders for small amounts or should it place few orders for large amounts? Each alternative has its advantages. Second, the variables that affect the problem should be isolated and quantified, if possible. In an inventory model, there are three major considerations: storing costs, procuring costs, and the sum of these two items. A firm that purchases inventory in large quantities knows that it will have larger average inventories on hand and that carrying costs such as insurance and taxes will increase. This is a force that tends to discourage the carrying of large inventories and to discourage relatively few but large purchase orders. On the other hand, the purchasing department that prepares the procurement orders to buy the inventories finds that its costs are lower if relatively few but large orders are submitted. Obviously, it requires less paper work to prepare 5 orders than to prepare 50. This is a force tending to encourage the submission of relatively few but large purchase orders. The problem is to minimize the *sum* of these costs by obtaining a balance between the two opposing cost forces, that is, storing costs and procuring costs. In order to construct a model, the firm must have the internal cost figures on the above variables. (Nevertheless, there may be circumstances where the variables are intangible and hence cannot be incorporated in the model.) The third step in model building is to study the interrelations and then construct a formula. After the model has been constructed, it must be studied carefully to make certain that it is realistic and that it will give correct answers. Models are virtually always subject to improvement by adding additional variables and by changing the structure of the formula.

As an example of a model, let us construct an inventory model, that is, a formula that will give guidance on the optimum amount of inventory to purchase with each order. The first step is to define the problem. In this case we have already stated that the problem is to determine the optimum number of goods to purchase with each purchase order. The second step is to identify the relevant variables, which are represented by letters to facilitate the computations. The formula for determining the optimum quantity to order is:

$$Q = \sqrt{\frac{2UP}{H}}$$

where U equals total units sold each year; P equals Cost in dollars of preparing a purchase order; H equals Cost in dollars of storing a unit of inventory; and Q equals Number of units that should be purchased with each order so that costs will be minimized.

The above formula is a model. By substituting money values for the letters, the formula suggests the most economical quantity to order. In the remainder of this book, the student will not have to derive models, although he should understand their use.

Let us illustrate with a more specific example. If 40,000 units of inventory are needed in one year, if the cost of placing an order is $100, and if the carrying cost of one unit for one year is $2, find the number of orders and the quantity with each order so that the sum of the acquisition costs and the holding (storing) costs will be at a minimum.

$$Q = \sqrt{\frac{2 \times 40,000 \times 100}{2.00}}$$
$$= 2,000$$

The optimum quantity to order is 2,000; the optimum number of orders per year is 20 (40,000 ÷ 2,000).

In conclusion, it should be remembered that models give guidance on the best course of action to take. When used along with sound judgment, models assist a firm in reaching its goals of optimizing the market value of the owner's equity.

As the businessman looks ahead and predicts the future, he is not always assured that things will work out as he hopes. He may or may not feel certain that a particular situation will prevail in the future. Generally, this "situation" refers to a future transaction or set of transactions. For certain purposes it is useful to

DECISION MAKING UNDER CERTAINTY, RISK, AND UNCERTAINTY

classify the businessman's degree of assuredness into three categories: certainty, risk, and uncertainty.

The first condition is that of *certainty*. This means that the businessman can predict with almost 100 percent reliability that a future transaction will occur. An example of this situation is that of a payment of $908 on a bank loan that is coming due at the end of the year. Or a businessman might buy a government bond that pays $50 twice a year. The payment of the $908 on the bank loan and the receipt of $50 in interest are transactions that are almost 100 percent certain to take place. Under certainty, there is often a legally binding contract whose terms must be met. There are not many transactions that fall under the classification of certainty.

The second condition under which decision making is made today is that of *risk*, which means that the businessman is aware of several possible transactions that might take place in the future and that he can assign probabilities to the likelihood of these different events occurring. For example, assume that an enterprising young man decides to sell Christmas trees during the holiday season. He is not exactly sure of how many he can sell, but his best estimate is that there is a 30 percent probability that he will sell 4,000, a 60 percent probability that he will sell 5,000, and a 10 percent probability that he will sell 6,000. The probabilities may be obtained from previous experience or from his best estimate; he will use the method in which he has the greater confidence. When sufficient information is given on selling prices, costs, and probabilities, all the variables are merged into a working tool called *expected value*, a concept discussed in the risk section of this chapter.

Uncertainty, the third of the trio, is the situation that exists when the businessman is unable to assign probabilities to the likelihood of a future event. An example of uncertainty might be the situation of management trying to guess whether there will be a strike six months from now. Most decisions must be made under conditions on the borderline between risk and uncertainty. Uncertainty is a major problem confronting businessmen, and research workers are putting considerable effort into finding arrangements that will transfer decision making from the uncertainty to the risk classification and if possible to the certainty classification.

Models under Certainty

The reader may be surprised to learn that he is already familiar with the model under certainty, often called a definitional model. The outcome has a probability of 1; that is, given the input data, the answer may be obtained by substituting the information in a formula and then completing the solution.

Problem

Assume that the following information is given about a firm's financial activities:

S = Total sales by company = $100,000
E = Total expenses = $50,000
T = Taxes paid = $15,000
U = Shares of common stock outstanding = 10,000
X = Earnings per share

Required: (a) Using the letters *S, E, T, U,* and *X,* prepare a model for determining earnings per share. (b) Compute the actual earnings per share.

(a) $X = \dfrac{S - (E + T)}{U}$

(b) $X = \dfrac{\$100,000 - (\$50,000 + \$15,000)}{10,000}$

$= \dfrac{\$35,000}{10,000}$

$= \$3.50$

Models under risk incorporate probabilities into the solutions. To stress the idea of the use of probabilities, our problems will be presented in tabular form rather than in the form of equations. The tables are quantitative models, however.

    A businessman takes a course of action today with the hope that something favorable will happen in the future as a result of his decision. Before he makes a decision, he usually considers a number of alternatives. Through a process of placing *expected values* on the alternatives, he may be able to obtain guidance on the best alternative to select.

Models under Risk

A wealthy investor is considering whether to place his money in the stock of Company M, a munitions manufacturer, or in the stock of Company H, a manufacturer of hair tonic. If there is a war, the former stock will perform better; if there is peace, the latter will perform better. Our investor believes that there is a 60 percent chance of war and a 40 percent chance of peace. His estimates of his gains and losses are summarized in Table 7-1.

Problem

	Probability of War or Peace	Gains and Losses	
		Investment in Munitions Firm	Investment in Hair Tonic Firm
War	.60	$100	−$50
No war	.40	−40	90

TABLE 7-1 Summary of Investment Information

The information in Table 7-1 states that if he invests in the stock of the munitions firm, he will make $100 if there is a war, but he will lose $40 if there is no war. Similarly, if he invests in the hair tonic firm, he will lose $50 if there is a war, but he will make $90 if there is no war. The dollar figures in the table may be called conditional values. Where should the investor place his money if he uses expected value as his criterion for decision making?

The investor should find the expected value that would result if he invested in the munitions stock; then he should find the expected value if he invested in the hair tonic firm. The expected value of the investment in the munitions firm is

Solution

found by multiplying the **probability** of the events (war versus peace) by the corresponding conditional values and then totaling these products, as shown in Table 7-2. The expected value of the investment in the hair tonic firm is computed similarly, as is also shown in Table 7-2. Column 2 of the table should be completed and then column 3.

TABLE 7-2 *Computation of* *Expected Value*	*(1)* *Probability* *of War* *Peace*	*(2)* *Expected* *Value of* *Investment in* *Munitions Firm*	*(3)* *Expected* *Value of* *Investment* *in Hair Tonic* *Firm*
War	.60	.60 × $100 $ 60	.60 × −$50 −$30
No war	.40	.40 × −40 −16	.40 × 90 36
Expected value		$ 44	$ 6

The expected value of the investment in the munitions firm is $44; the expected value of the investment in the hair tonic firm is $6. Therefore, he should invest in the munitions company because it has the higher expected value.

Notice again that if the investor did not use expected value as his criterion, he might make a different decision.

If the investor was unable to assign subjective probabilities to the likelihood of war or peace, expected value could not be computed; he would then be operating under the condition of uncertainty. If this were the case, there would be no way of making an appraisal of expected values.

In problems that involve selecting from alternatives that will give the lowest cost, the alternative that gives the lowest expected value might be the one selected.

The concept of expected value, then, incorporates probability analysis into the decision-making process. Since most business decisions are made within the framework of risk and uncertainty, this type of analysis has been increasing in importance. It is being used as one tool in determining the best level of inventory to stock, the optimum line of credit to obtain at a bank, whether to carry additional insurance, and other decisions. Yet one should not believe that expected value will replace judgment in decision making; sound judgment considers many aspects of a problem, while expected value considers only one or two.

Expected value is a useful tool to incorporate in the decision-making process. Nonetheless, it has one major disadvantage—it does not always take into account the businessman's attitude toward making or losing money. To solve this problem, it may be necessary to substitute the concept of *expected utility* for that of expected value, as is done in the appendix of the next chapter.

Models under
Uncertainty

Under uncertainty conditions the businessman does not know the probabilities; therefore, he cannot use them. Nonetheless, certain criteria may be used to make a decision. Two of these are the criterion of pessimism (maximin principle) and the criterion of optimism (maximax principle). Numerous other criteria may be used, although they will not be discussed here; the reader is referred to advanced work in decision theory for an elaboration of decision making under uncertainty.

Pessimistic Criterion (Maximin Principle) This criterion is followed by those who wish to be guaranteed of some minimum result; they are willing to sacrifice major potential gains that might not materialize for some minimum return that is almost certain to occur. Assume that a person intends to invest in the common stock of one of the following types of companies: a company that makes dynamite, a company that makes candy, or a company that makes oatmeal. The success of each investment depends on whether there will be war with prosperity, peace with prosperity, or peace with a depression. Table 7-3 shows expected returns under various combinations of events. The table states that if the person invests in the dynamite stock, he will make $18 if there is war with prosperity, he will gain $4 if there is peace with prosperity, and he will lose $2 if there is peace with depression. If he invests in the candy stock, he will make $5 if there is war with prosperity, he will gain $9 if there is peace with prosperity, and he will have a zero gain if there is peace with depression. If he invests in the oatmeal stock, he will have a gain of $3 regardless of the economic and political climate.

	Dynamite Stock	Candy Stock	Oatmeal Stock
War with prosperity	$ 18	$5	$3
Peace with prosperity	4	9	3
Peace with depression	−2	0	3

TABLE 7-3
Consequences of Investing in Three Companies

Since the investor has no really good idea concerning the probabilities of such complicated events as war, peace, and economic conditions, he is unable and unwilling to assign probabilities to what the environment will be like in the future.

The first step in the maximin principle is to determine the worst that could happen with each of the respective investments. This information is given in Table 7-4. The table states that if the investor chooses the dynamite stock, the worst that can happen is a loss of $2; if he invests in the candy stock, the worst that can happen is no gain; and if he invests in the oatmeal stock, the worst that can happen is a $3 gain.

	Worst Possible Outcome
Dynamite stock	$−2
Candy stock	0
Oatmeal stock	3

TABLE 7-4
Worst Possible Outcome of Investments

In appraising the results in Table 7-4, the investor might reason that he will select the alternative that is the most desirable of the group of undesirables. If he buys the oatmeal stock, he will always make $3. This is better than losing $2 or gaining nothing. He is said to be maximizing the minimum, or using the maximin principle.

Optimistic Criterion (Maximax Principle) Instead of being a pessimist, a person might be at the other extreme and be a complete optimist. This means that he would analyze the information in Table 7-3 and seek the investment that *might* give him the highest return. It can be seen that the highest possible return is $18 and that this could be sought by purchasing the dynamite stock. Hence, he would be using the so-called optimist's approach.

There is no one "best" criterion to use under uncertainty; the best one depends on the philosophy, experience, and judgment of the businessman.

HIGHLIGHTS OF THIS CHAPTER	*A model is a representation of reality. Its purpose is to classify the significant variables in a problem; detail is not considered. Because models do not include all the information in a problem, the user of such mathematical devices must be careful to state the assumptions underlying his model. Actually, the inclusion of models in operations research is one of the main differences between current problem-solving and problem-solving in the past.*

Decisions may be made under certainty, risk, or uncertainty. Under certainty, the outcome can be predicted with 100 percent accuracy; under risk, the outcome may take on a number of values and at the same time the businessman is able to assign probabilities to these outcomes; under uncertainty, the businessman is unable or unwilling to assign probabilities to outcomes. Considerable research is currently being conducted to improve decision making under risk and under uncertainty.

REVIEW QUESTIONS

7-1. Distinguish between certainty, risk, and uncertainty.

7-2. What is the difference between the maximax and the maximin criterion?

7-3. Explain how expected value is computed.

7-4. The inventory model seeks to minimize the sum of what two major costs?

REVIEW PROBLEMS

The answers appear at the end of this section. *For each problem show how you obtained the answer.*

7-1. Using the data given below, determine the optimum amount of inventory Company X should order at one time.

Number of units used per year	10
Cost of preparing one purchase order	$5
Storing (holding) cost of one unit	$4

7-2. James Bloom is considering investing in either offensive or defensive securities. If there is inflation, the offensive securities will perform extremely well, but the defensive ones will have only an average performance. Conversely, if there is a stable price level, the defensive securities will perform extremely well; but the offensive securities will have only an average performance. Assume that Bloom will earn $1,000 if there is inflation but only $600 if there is a stable price level. Likewise, if he invests in the defensive securities, he will earn $500 if there is inflation but $900 if there is a stable price level. Bloom believes that there is a 60 percent chance of inflation and a 40 percent chance of a stable price level. What is the expected value of investing in (a) offensive securities? (b) defensive securities? (c) Which should he invest in?

7-3. Philip Adams is considering investing in the stock market. He does not know the probabilities of the outcomes, but he is still considering investing in one of the three kinds of firms listed below. He believes that the outcome of his investment will depend on whether there is war with prosperity, peace with prosperity, or peace with depression.

TABLE 7-5
Consequences of
Investing in
Three Companies

	Explosives	Typewriters	Suspenders
War with prosperity	$ 19	$ 6	$4
Peace with prosperity	5	10	4
Peace with depression	−2	0	3

The factors relevant to his decision appear in Table 7-5. The table states that if there is war with prosperity, he will make $19 if he invests in the company that makes explosives; $6 if he invests in the company that makes typewriters; and $4 if he invests in the firm that makes suspenders. The data are interpreted similarly if there is peace with prosperity or peace with depression. Which investment should Adams select if he uses (a) the maximin principle? (b) the maximax principle?

7-4. Company R, a large corporation, is considering producing a product developed by its research and development department. It is necessary for the management to look to the future and estimate selling price, unit variable cost, and total fixed costs. The officers are willing to assign probabilities to these events. Given the information in Table 7-6, what is the expected value of the break-even point?

7-5. Mr. X is vice president of a bank; he has an expense account for taking businessmen to dinner, with the hope that these businessmen will become de-

TABLE 7-6
Company R's
Price and Cost
Estimates

Selling Price		Unit Variable Costs		Total Fixed Costs	
Probability	Amount	Probability	Amount	Probability	Amount
.10	$40.00	.15	$10	.05	$10,000
.20	60.00	.20	15	.20	12,000
.50	72.00	.40	20	.40	16,000
.20	82.50	.25	24	.35	20,000

positors in the bank. The bank is in the 50 percent tax bracket, and it earns an annual profit (after taxes) of 1 percent on all new checking accounts. However, to make the model more useful for incremental analysis, the 1 percent does not include the entertainment expenses of the vice president. The banker's experience leads him to believe that the information in Table 7-7 will apply.

TABLE 7-7
Probability of
Acquiring
New Depositors

Probability That Businessman Will Deposit Amount Shown in Next Column	Amount of Deposit
.10	$ 0
.15	1,000
.50	10,000
.25	15,000

Assuming that only the first year is taken into consideration, what is the most the banker can afford to pay (including the tip) for the combined cost of his own dinner and that of his guest?

Answers: 7-1, 5; 7-2a, $840; 7-2b, $660; 7-3a, suspenders; 7-3b, explosives; 7-4, 326 units; 7-5, $178.

7-5

$.10 (0) = 0$

$.15 (1,000) = 150$

$.50 (10,000) = 5000$

$.25 (15,000) = 3750$

$EV(Depist) = \$18,900$

$EV(Profit) = .01 \left[EV (Deposit) \right]$

$= .01 (18,900) = \$189$

$EX_{INITIAL} (1-\tau) = EX_{POSTTAX}$

$\dfrac{(189.50)}{.50} = \$89$

$\dfrac{}{178}$

Capital Budgeting as a Planning Tool (I)

Mgt.
Fin.
Mkt
Bus. 100

A significant area of decision making is to determine whether or not a firm should expand. In some situations, the goals of the firm will be advanced by increasing the firm's total assets; in other situations, goals are better served by rejecting the expansion. A firm should expand if marginal revenue from the expansion exceeds marginal cost of the expansion. The company should reject expansion proposals when the anticipated marginal cost exceeds anticipated marginal revenue from them. Assuming that the projects are economically sound, the firm should accept those that have the greatest excess of marginal revenue over marginal cost. By following these principles, management is advancing the goals of the firm, one of which is to increase the earnings and dividends per share of common stock. The problem, however, is for management to find some way of estimating when marginal revenue will exceed marginal cost and some way of determining which projects will yield the greatest net marginal revenue. Department heads, for example, may be submitting capital expenditure proposals for the consideration of top management. These projects usually have different costs, different economic lives, and other differences. Such projects must be ranked in order of their relative desirability, and some effort must be made to determine the amount by which total assets should be expanded. Business firms have been using a technique called capital budgeting to obtain solutions to these problems.

The following will be discussed in this chapter:

1. A preview of capital budgeting
2. The role of interest tables in capital budgeting
3. A problem in capital budgeting
4. Analytical tools for ranking major cash outlays according to their relative desirability
   a. Anticipated net present value (anticipated index of profitability)

b. Anticipated yield (internal rate of return)

c. Anticipated pay-back period

5. Expected utility

The main part of this chapter will be concerned with analyzing criteria for ranking proposed expenditures of large sums of money. A firm may (and frequently does) use adaptations of the tests mentioned in Number 4 above, use them in combination, or use entirely different ones.

A PREVIEW OF CAPITAL BUDGETING

Capital budgeting is an intellectual process that contains a set of criteria to aid management in (1) ranking capital expenditures in order of their relative desirability and (2) determining how much total assets should expand.

For the first point, assume that management wishes to compare the relative desirability of the following proposed capital expenditures: a new lathe, 50 electric calculators, a fleet of new automobiles, and a cement walk in front of the building. The expected benefits yielded by such projects can often be expressed quantitatively. The projects are ranked from high to low, according to their relative desirability. A careful analysis of the four projects just mentioned might indicate the following:

Project	Expected Rate of Return (Percent)
Lathe	28
Calculators	20
Automobiles	4
Sidewalk	Not applicable

A considerable part of this chapter will be devoted to explaining how such rates of return and *other* quantitative criteria for ranking proposed capital expenditures are estimated. Observe that not all the proposed capital expenditures can be converted into a rate of return—the sidewalks, for example. In a situation like this, management must substitute its experience and judgment for quantitative criteria. Of course, in the final analysis all managerial decisions are to some extent a matter of judgment. But more and more decisions are supported by quantitative evidence. Capital budgeting, then, has the advantage of placing on a systematic basis the comparison of various proposed capital expenditures.

For the second point, capital budgeting provides quantitative evidence as to how much a firm should expand its total assets. Assume for the sake of argument that the *cost of capital* for a particular firm is 6 percent (the procedure for estimating the cost of capital is discussed in the next chapter). If this is the case, all projects that yield a higher rate of return than 6 percent might be accepted. In the above situation, total assets should be expanded to include the acquisition of the lathe, the calculators, and possibly the sidewalks, although the last of the three is a decision based on subjective evidence. Clearly, the new automobiles should not be acquired because the marginal revenue generated by their acquisition (4 percent) is less than the marginal cost of acquiring them (6 percent). The percentage return assigned to the projects is only one method of ranking; other methods will also be analyzed.

Business firms often have transactions in which the interest rate is the unknown variable and the datum to be found. Assume that a firm has an opportunity to receive a single lump sum of $3,000 at the end of two years from now and that this return requires an immediate cash outlay of $2,308. If the firm accepts this proposition, what rate of return is being earned on this investment? That is, what rate of interest will result in $2,308 being the present value of $3,000? Stated still differently, what rate of interest equates the $3,000 to the $2,308? An answer to this question will inform the businessman what rate of return he will earn on his investment.

One must begin to seek an answer by a trial and error procedure, that is, by guessing at succeeding interest rates until the rate is found that equates or comes closest to equating the two cash flows involved. Thus one might guess that 13 percent is the rate that will discount (equate) $3,000 back to $2,308. An inspection of Table 8-1 indicates that a 13 percent rate gives a value of $2,349 ($3,000 X .78315), an amount that is too high. Next, the businessman might estimate that 15 percent is the rate that will equate the cash outflow with the cash inflow. A 15 percent rate gives a present value of $2,268 ($3,000 X .75614); a

THE ROLE OF INTEREST TABLES IN CAPITAL BUDGETING

The Present Value of $1 Due at the End of N Years

TABLE 8-1
Present Value of $1 Due at the End of N Years

	N	4%	5%	6%	7%	8%	9%	10%	11%	12%	13%
Years	01	0.96154	0.95238	0.94340	0.93458	0.92593	0.91743	0.90909	0.90090	0.89286	0.88496
of	02	0.92456	0.90703	0.89000	0.87344	0.85734	0.84168	0.82645	0.81162	0.79719	0.78315
Life	03	0.88900	0.86384	0.83962	0.81630	0.79383	0.77218	0.75131	0.73119	0.71178	0.69305
of	04	0.85480	0.82270	0.79209	0.76290	0.73503	0.70843	0.68301	0.65873	0.63552	0.61332
Project	05	0.82193	0.78353	0.74726	0.71299	0.68058	0.64993	0.62092	0.59345	0.56743	0.54276
	06	0.79031	0.74622	0.70496	0.66634	0.63017	0.59627	0.56447	0.53464	0.50663	0.48032
	07	0.75992	0.71068	0.66506	0.62275	0.58349	0.54703	0.51316	0.48166	0.45235	0.42506
	08	0.73069	0.67684	0.62741	0.58201	0.54027	0.50187	0.46651	0.43393	0.40388	0.37616
	09	0.70259	0.64461	0.59190	0.54393	0.50025	0.46043	0.42410	0.39092	0.36061	0.33288
	10	0.67556	0.61391	0.55839	0.50835	0.46319	0.42241	0.38554	0.35218	0.32197	0.29459

	N	14%	15%	16%	17%	18%	19%	20%	21%	22%	23%
Years	01	0.87719	0.86957	0.86207	0.85470	0.84746	0.84034	0.83333	0.82645	0.81967	0.81301
of	02	0.76947	0.75614	0.74316	0.73051	0.71818	0.70616	0.69444	0.68301	0.67186	0.66098
Life	03	0.67497	0.65752	0.64066	0.62437	0.60863	0.59342	0.57870	0.56447	0.55071	0.53738
of	04	0.59208	0.57175	0.55229	0.53365	0.51579	0.49867	0.48225	0.46651	0.45140	0.43690
Project	05	0.51937	0.49718	0.47611	0.45611	0.43711	0.41905	0.40188	0.38544	0.37000	0.35520
	06	0.45559	0.43233	0.41044	0.38984	0.37043	0.35214	0.33490	0.31863	0.30328	0.28878
	07	0.39964	0.37594	0.35383	0.33320	0.31392	0.29592	0.27908	0.26333	0.24859	0.23478
	08	0.35056	0.32690	0.30503	0.28478	0.26604	0.24867	0.23257	0.21763	0.20376	0.19088
	09	0.30751	0.28426	0.26295	0.24340	0.22546	0.20897	0.19381	0.17986	0.16702	0.15519
	10	0.26974	0.24718	0.22668	0.20804	0.19106	0.17560	0.16151	0.14864	0.13690	0.12617

figure that is too low. Next, a person might try 14 percent, a rate that happens to give a present value of $2,308 ($3,000 X .76947). This is the rate of interest for which the businessman has been searching; it will equate the $3,000 to the investment outlay of $2,308. The businessman will earn a rate of 14 percent if he invests $2,308 today and receives $3,000 at the end of two years.

In the quest for the rate of return in Table 8-1, two rules are of assistance in the elimination process.

1. A lower interest rate gives a higher present value.
2. A higher interest rate gives a lower present value.

The reader can test these assertions by inspecting the values on the two-year line of Table 8-1. As one moves to the right and so toward higher rates of interest, the amounts (present values) decrease. Conversely, as one moves to the left on this line and so toward lower rates of interest, the amounts increase. By keeping in mind the inverse relationship between rate of interest (capitalization rate) and value, a businessman speeds up the elimination process by not having to experiment with all the rates in the table.

Very seldom will one be fortunate enough to find in the table the exact rate of interest discounting a future sum to a present value that is equal to the sum invested in the project. Therefore, in a number of situations, one must either interpolate (we will not use the process in this chapter) or accept the rate that is closest to the true rate. As an example of the latter, assume that a firm invests $620 today and is promised $1,000 at the end of five years from now. What is the rate of return being earned on the investment of $620? A 10 percent rate applied to $1,000 results in a present value of $621, an amount that is close enough (to $620) to warrant accepting 10 percent as the rate.

Following is another type of common business transaction. Assume that a firm buys an asset today for $6,340 and that the project will yield an annual net cash return of $2,000 each year for a four-year period. After the fourth year, the businessman will receive nothing. What rate of interest is being earned on this commitment? That is, what rate of interest will result in $6,340 being the present value of a stream of four annual payments of $2,000 each? An answer to this question will indicate to the businessman the rate of return that he will earn on this project. He also can obtain this rate from Table 8-1. One can begin the solution to this problem by guessing a certain rate and then trying other rates until the correct one is found. Our businessman might begin with 9 percent. The present value generated by 9 percent is found by this procedure:

$2,000 X .91743 = $1,835
 2,000 X .84168 = 1,683
 2,000 X .77218 = 1,544
 2,000 X .70843 = 1,417
                 _____
                 $6,479

Since the present value we are seeking is $6,340 (the amount invested in the project), the present value of $6,479 generated by 9 percent is too high. Next, the businessman might try the 11 percent rate. The present value generated by this rate is determined as follows:

$2,000 × .90090 = $1,802
 2,000 × .81162 = 1,623
 2,000 × .73119 = 1,462
 2,000 × .65873 = 1,318
              $6,205

The present value of $6,205 is too low. Hence the 11 percent rate is still not the correct one. But evidently the rate he is seeking is between 9 and 11 percent. Finally, he might try 10 percent as the rate that will discount the flow of $2,000 back to $6,340. The present value emanating from a 10 percent return is determined as follows:

$2,000 × .90909 = $1,818
 2,000 × .82645 = 1,653
 2,000 × .75131 = 1,503
 2,000 × .68301 = 1,366
              $6,340

The present value generated by 10 percent gives the answer he is seeking—the rate that gives a present value equal to the cash invested in the project. Hence, the rate of return earned by this firm is 10 percent if it buys an asset for $6,340 and receives net annual cash flows of $2,000 a year for a four-year period.

The Present Value of $1 Received Annually for N Years (Present Value of an Annuity)

Table 8-2 can also be used to determine the expected rate of return on a proposed capital expenditure, particularly as a shortcut when a firm is to receive *equal* annual net cash receipts from a project. Assume again that a firm has the opportunity to invest $6,340 in an asset and that this asset will return a net annual cash flow of $2,000 a year for a four-year period. Although the answer to this question has been found from Table 8-1, we will indicate how the answer can also be obtained from the use of Table 8-2. The businessman might begin by guessing that 9 percent is the desired rate. According to Table 8-2, a 9 percent rate gives a present value of $6,479 ($2,000 × 3.2397), an amount that is too high. Next, the businessman might estimate that 11 percent is the rate of return that he will earn on his project. This rate gives a value of $6,205 ($2,000 × 3.1024), a discounted value that is too low (in relation to $6,340, the amount that he is seeking). Next, he might try 10 percent, a rate that gives a discounted value of $6,340 ($2,000 × 3.1699), an amount that is the desired value. This firm will earn 10 percent if today it buys an asset for $6,340 that returns a net cash inflow of $2,000 a year for four years. In other words, 10 percent is the rate that equates the flow of annual $2,000 receipts to the initial outlay of $6,340.

If the annual cash receipts from a proposed project are equal, a short-cut method may be used in place of the trial and error method just described. It consists of these steps:

1. Divide the cost of the asset by the annual cash inflow and obtain a quotient.	$\dfrac{\$6,340}{\$2,000} = 3.17$
2. Go to the interest table and find the correct row, which will be to the right of the number of years that the project will last.	Go to the row of numbers which is to the right of 4 years.
3. Proceed to the right along the correct row until the number is reached that is closest to the quotient.	Proceed to the right until the number 3.1699 is reached; this is the closest number to the quotient of 3.17. For lack of a better name, let us refer to the 3.1699 as the factor.
4. After completing step 3, proceed to the top of the table and find the interest rate that heads the column in which the factor is located.	The interest rate at the head of the column that contains the factor is 10 percent, the rate of return for this particular firm.

The businessman may not be able to find in Table 8-2 the exact rate of return needed. In such a situation, as in the use of other interest tables, he must either interpolate or accept the rate that gives the closest answer. As an example of the latter, assume that a firm invests $18,000 in a project and that this capital expenditure will return to the company a net cash flow of $5,000 annually for a five-year period. What rate of return is being earned on this investment? A 12

TABLE 8-2
Present Value of $1 Received Annually for N Years

Year	4%	5%	6%	7%	8%	9%	10%	11%	12%	13%
1	0.9615	0.9524	0.9434	0.9346	0.9259	0.9174	0.9091	0.9009	0.8929	0.8850
2	1.8861	1.8594	1.8334	1.8080	1.7833	1.7591	1.7355	1.7125	1.6901	1.6681
3	2.7751	2.7232	2.6730	2.6243	2.5771	2.5313	2.4868	2.4437	2.4018	2.3612
4	3.6299	3.5459	3.4651	3.3872	3.3121	3.2397	3.1699	3.1024	3.0373	2.9745
5	4.4518	4.3295	4.2123	4.1002	3.9927	3.8896	3.7908	3.6959	3.6048	3.5172
6	5.2421	5.0757	4.9173	4.7665	4.6229	4.4859	4.3553	4.2305	4.1114	3.9976
7	6.0020	5.7863	5.5824	5.3893	5.2064	50.0329	4.8684	4.7122	4.5638	4.4226
8	6.7327	6.4632	6.2098	5.9713	5.7466	5.5348	5.3349	5.1461	4.9676	4.7988
9	7.4353	7.1078	6.8017	6.5152	6.2469	5.9852	5.7590	5.5370	5.3282	5.1317
10	8.1109	7.7217	7.3601	7.0236	6.7101	6.4176	6.1446	5.8892	5.6502	5.4262

Year	14%	15%	16%	17%	18%	19%	20%	21%	22%	23%
1	0.8772	0.8696	0.8621	0.8547	0.8475	0.8403	0.8333	0.8264	0.8197	0.8130
2	1.6467	1.6257	1.6052	1.5852	1.5656	1.5465	1.5278	1.5095	1.4915	1.4740
3	2.3216	2.2832	2.2459	2.2096	2.1743	2.1399	2.1065	2.0739	2.0422	2.0114
4	2.9137	2.8550	2.7982	2.7432	2.6901	2.6386	2.5887	2.5404	2.4936	2.4483
5	3.4331	3.3522	3.2743	3.1993	3.1272	3.0576	2.9906	2.9260	2.8636	2.8035
6	3.8887	3.7845	3.6847	3.5892	3.4976	3.4098	3.3255	3.2446	3.1669	3.0923
7	4.2883	4.1604	4.0386	3.9224	3.8115	3.7057	3.6046	3.5079	3.4155	3.3270
8	4.6389	4.4873	4.3436	4.2072	4.0776	3.9544	3.8372	3.7256	3.6193	3.5179
9	4.9464	4.7716	4.6065	4.4506	4.3030	4.1633	4.0310	3.9054	3.7863	3.6731
10	5.2161	5.0188	4.8332	4.6586	4.4941	4.3389	4.1925	4.0541	3.9232	3.7993

percent rate gives a discounted value of $18,024 ($5,000 × 3.6048), a value that is very close to the desired amount of $18,000. Hence, the project would be said to be earning approximately 12 percent. Even when more refined interest tables are used, a businessman may have to use the rate that gives him the closest answer.

Table 8-3 shows two alternatives under consideration—the acquisition of electric typewriters for use in the offices of the firm and the acquisition of a machine to manufacture dolls. Which should be given priority?

A PROBLEM IN CAPITAL BUDGETING

TABLE 8-3 Data on Two Proposed Capital Expenditures

	Electric Typewriters	Machine for Making Dolls
Cash Outlay for Projects		
Cost of electric typewriters (scrap value $1,000)	$10,000	
Cost of machine to make toy dolls (no scrap value)		$15,000
Freight in		500
Installation costs		500
Additional current assets		4,000
Estimated Cash Inflow from Projects		
Cash gain before depreciation and before federal income taxes:		
Electric typewriters, annually for three years	5,000	
Machine for making dolls, annually for four years		10,000
Depreciation:		
Typewriters, three-year life	3,000	
Doll-making machine, four-year life		4,000
Taxable income	2,000	6,000
Federal taxes, 50 percent	1,000	3,000
Income from project after taxes	1,000	3,000
Net cash inflow from project (net income plus depreciation)	4,000	7,000

Table 8-4 also summarizes data helpful for the solution of the problem. The firm will have to expend $10,000 in cash to acquire the electric typewriters. Management also estimates that the new typewriters will result in a cash saving in labor costs equal to $5,000 a year (before depreciation and before federal income taxes).

TABLE 8-4 Cash Flow Data for Capital Budgeting*

Project	Initial Cash Outlay	Amount of Net Cash Proceeds by Year			
		1st	2nd	3rd	4th
Electric typewriters	$10,000	$4,000	$4,000	$4,000 1,000	None
Machine for making dolls	$20,000	$7,000	$7,000	$7,000	$7,000 4,000

*Data derived from Table 8-3.

The savings will come about from the dismissal of one part-time clerk. Such factors as social security taxes and related items are included in this amount. Because of the rapid rate of obsolescence in electric typewriters for this firm, management believes that it can count on only three years of economic service from them. Furthermore, indications are that the typewriters will have a cash junk value of $1,000 at the end of the third year. Observe in Table 8-3 these additional expectations about the typewriters: annual taxable income from the project will be $2,000; annual federal income taxes will be $1,000; annual net income after taxes will be $1,000; and net annual cash flow (net income after taxes plus depreciation) resulting from the project will be $4,000.

The firm will have to expend $16,000 for the machine to manufacture dolls, a sum that includes freight and installation costs. A project of this kind, however, requires additional current assets of $4,000 for such items as inventories and accounts receivable. The additional current assets raise the outlay for the project to $20,000. Observe that the $4,000 in additional current assets is *not* depreciable, as this amount will be recovered at the end of the life of the project (we will ignore minor leakages). Management estimates that the new machine will result in an annual gain of $10,000 in cash (before depreciation and before federal income taxes) and that by the end of the fourth year the machine will be obsolete and the economic usefulness of the project will be ended. Therefore, the prediction is that the project will yield an annual stream of $10,000 for a four-year period only. A further assumption is that the doll-making machine will have no junk value at the end of its life. Also notice from Table 8-3 these anticipations of annual performance of the project: taxable income of $6,000; federal income taxes of $3,000; net income after taxes of $3,000; and net annual cash flow (net income after taxes plus depreciation) generated from the project of $7,000.

THE NET-PRESENT-
VALUE TEST:
THE INDEX OF
PROFITABILITY

General Nature

One method of ranking proposed capital expenditures is to give the highest priority to those that offer the highest positive net present value. In computing the net present value of a specific proposed capital expenditure, two kinds of information must be assembled: (1) the discounted values of the expected stream of net cash inflows and (2) the discounted value of the cash cost of the asset. (In this example, we are assuming that the entire cash cost is paid out immediately—not over a period of several years.) An important point to keep in mind is that the key variables are *present and future cash flows* associated with the project under consideration. Thus, to repeat, the cash inflow for the electric typewriters, as determined in Table 8-3, consists of adding to the net profit after taxes the amount of depreciation on this equipment. (The terms *discounted value* and *present value* may be used interchangeably.) Net present value is determined as follows:

Discounted value of expected future cash inflows	$XX
Less discounted value of cash cost of asset	XX
Remainder (net present value of project)	$XX

If the project has a positive net present value, it should be accepted, because it will add value to the firm; furthermore priority should be given to the proposed capital expenditures having the greatest net present value.

Net present value for the electric typewriters is found by this formula:

$$\text{Net present value} = \frac{\text{Discounted value}}{\text{of net cash inflows}} - \begin{array}{l}\text{Cost of asset (if asset is} \\ \text{paid for in full at beginning} \\ \text{of period)}\end{array}$$

$$= \$11,532 - \$10,000$$
$$= \$\ 1,532$$

The data for the net-present-value formulas for both projects are obtained from Table 8-5. In this table are shown the calculations for converting the net cash inflows into a present value. Observe that the net cash inflows for the typewriters consist of $4,000 a year from operations plus $1,000 at the end of the third year (from the scrap value). These net cash inflows are converted into present values by applying an assumed discount rate of 6 percent. Then the individual present values are combined to obtain a total present value of $11,532. Since the typewriters cost $10,000, this sum is subtracted from the present value of $11,532 to obtain the net present value of $1,532. In our example, we assumed that the entire $10,000 was expended immediately to pay for the project. If the payments were spread out over a period of several years, then we would have to obtain the discounted value of these payments and use this revised cost figure in the formula.

TABLE 8-5
Net Present Value of Two Alternatives

	Electric Typewriters (Cost $10,000)				Machine for Making Toy Dolls (Cost $20,000)		
Year	Amount	Discount Factor*	Present Value	Year	Amount	Discount Factor*	Present Value
1	$4,000	0.94340	$ 3,774	1	$7,000	0.94340	$ 6,604
2	4,000	0.89000	3,560	2	7,000	0.89000	6,230
3	4,000	0.83962	3,358	3	7,000	0.83962	5,877
3	1,000	0.83962	840	4	7,000	0.79209	5,545
				4	4,000	0.79209	3,168
	Total		$11,532		Total		$27,424

Net present value of electric typewriters is $1,532 ($11,532 − $10,000).
Net present value of machine for making dolls is $7,424 ($27,424 − $20,000).

*From Table 8-1.

In a like manner, the net present value of the doll-making machine is determined by the following formula:

$$\text{Net present value} = \frac{\text{Discounted value}}{\text{of net cash inflows}} - \begin{array}{l}\text{Cost of asset (if asset is}\\ \text{paid for in full at beginning}\\ \text{of period)}\end{array}$$

$$= \$27,424 - \$20,000$$
$$= \$\ 7,424$$

Since this project is expected to have a net annual cash inflow of $7,000 from operations and $4,000 from return of working capital at the end of the fourth year, these receipts are the items to be converted into present values at the assumed discount rate of 6 percent. The sum of the individual present values is $27,424, from which is subtracted $20,000, the cost of the project, leaving a net present value of $7,424. Again we have assumed that the entire $20,000 for the cost of the project was spent immediately. If, instead, the project were paid for over a period of several years, the payments would have to be discounted to their present value and then combined to obtain a revised cost figure, which would be used in the above formula.

The net present value of the electric typewriters is $1,532; the net present value of the doll-making machine is $7,424. Hence, on the basis of this test, the latter alternative is the more desirable of the two. Since the doll-making machine has the greater net present value, it will add more value to the firm than will the electric typewriters.

The main advantage of the net-present-value method of ranking projects is that it focuses attention on one of the goals of the firm, that is, increasing the market price of the shares of common stock. The main disadvantage of this procedure is that it requires an estimate of the company's percentage cost of capital in order to discount the flow of cash intake.

A variation of the net-present-value test is to find an index of profitability by using this formula:

$$\begin{array}{l}\text{Index of profitability}\\ \text{of typewriters}\end{array} = \frac{\text{Present value of flow of net cash receipts}}{\text{Present value of cost of project}}$$

$$= \frac{\$11,532}{\$10,000}$$
$$= 1.15$$

$$\begin{array}{l}\text{Index of profitability}\\ \text{of machine for}\\ \text{making toy dolls}\end{array} = \frac{\$27,424}{\$20,000}$$
$$= 1.37$$

An index of profitability of less than 1 means that the project should be rejected. *An index of profitability of more than 1 means that the project probably should be accepted.* Furthermore, the projects with a scale of higher than 1 can be ranked from highest value to lowest value. In the examples just given, the machine for making toy dolls has the higher index of profitability.

The yield method is another way of ranking proposed projects according to their relative desirability. An attempt is made to determine the percentage that each project will earn, such as 20 percent or 10 percent. A high rate of return is a favorable indicator. Also, those proposed projects with higher percentage returns are given a higher ranking than those with a lower return. *If a project earns more than the cost of capital to the firm, acceptance of the project will advance the goals of the firm.* The reader is reminded again that the cost of capital to the firm is assumed to be 6 percent throughout this chapter.

The cash flow approach for computing the anticipated rate of return on the project consists of the following:

1. Predict the firm's cash outlay to acquire the project. Only actual cash outlay is considered. Such factors as losses on the sale of machines are not directly relevant to the particular problem at hand.

2. Predict the firm's annual net cash inflow from the project and predict the number of years the annual net cash inflow is expected to continue. Again only actual cash transactions are considered. Such items as allocation of overhead are not directly relevant.

3. Find from interest tables the rate of return earned on the project. *That is, seek the rate of interest that comes closest to discounting the flow of annual net cash receipts to the amount invested in the project.*

The cash outlay to acquire the projects is $10,000 in the case of the typewriters and $20,000 in the case of the machine for making dolls. These outlays can be determined to a relatively high degree of accuracy in most cases. There are some situations, however, in which the cash outlay may have to be estimated. This would be true of a very complicated project that might take several years to complete, such as a large office building in New York City. In a case such as this it is also probable that the cash outlay will be spread out over a period of several years rather than paid in a lump sum. In our illustration, we will assume that the entire outlays for the two proposed projects will be made in a lump sum and in the current year.

Predicting the annual net cash inflow resulting from each project is a more involved assignment. In our example, we will take estimates of management as being reliable. Management's prediction is that the electric typewriters will result in a net cash inflow of $4,000 a year for a three-year period. Notice again that the typewriters have a junk value that will result in a $1,000 cash intake at the end of the third year. Also, management's prediction is that the machine to make dolls will result in a net cash inflow of $7,000 a year for a four-year period and that there will be an additional cash inflow of $4,000 at the end of the fourth year as a result of the recovery of working capital. The two streams of cash intake are summarized in Table 8-4.

Interest tables are then used to determine the rate of return earned on the project. Experiments are made with different interest rates (on a trial and error basis) until one is found that comes closest to equating (discounting) the stream of net annual cash inflows to a present value that is equal or approximately equal to the cash invested in the project. As can be seen in Table 8-6, the return earned on the typewriters is 14 percent and that earned on the machine to make dolls is 20 percent.

Actually, both projects might be accepted by management. But if one had to choose between the two, the machine to make dolls would be the better alternative.

TABLE 8-6
Computing Rate
of Return
(Time Adjusted)
on Two Projects

New Electric Typewriters	Machine for Making Dolls
FIRST GUESS, 15 PERCENT	**FIRST GUESS, 21 PERCENT**
$4,000 × .86957 = $ 3,478	$7,000 × .82645 = $ 5,785
4,000 × .75614 = 3,025	7,000 × .68301 = 4,781
4,000 × .65752 = 2,630	7,000 × .56447 = 3,951
1,000 × .65752 = 658	7,000 × .46651 = 3,266
	4,000 × .46651 = 1,866
Total $ 9,791	Total $19,649
SECOND GUESS, 13 PERCENT	**SECOND GUESS, 19 PERCENT**
$4,000 × .88496 = $ 3,540	$7,000 × .84034 = $ 5,882
4,000 × .78315 = 3,133	7,000 × .70616 = 4,943
4,000 × .69305 = 2,772	7,000 × .59342 = 4,154
1,000 × .69305 = 693	7,000 × .49867 = 3,491
	4,000 × .49867 = 1,995
Total $10,138	Total $20,465
THIRD GUESS, 14 PERCENT	**THIRD GUESS, 20 PERCENT**
$4,000 × .87719 = $ 3,509	$7,000 × .83333 = $ 5,833
4,000 × .76947 = 3,078	7,000 × .69444 = 4,861
4,000 × .67497 = 2,700	7,000 × .57870 = 4,051
1,000 × .67497 = 675	7,000 × .48225 = 3,376
	4,000 × .48225 = 1,929
Total $9,962	Total $20,050

Evaluation   The main advantage of the yield method is its relative simplicity; that is, management finds it convenient to have one proposed project assigned a yield of 14 percent, another assigned a yield of 20 percent, and so on. This arrangement facilitates ranking projects from high to low, and the process gives guidance on which projects should be given priority. The yields so obtained are ranked from high to low and then compared with the firm's cost of capital. *All projects yielding a return higher than the cost of capital are acceptable, but projects with the highest yields are the most acceptable.*

The yield method has some limitations, however. First is the implicit assumption that the firm can reinvest the annual net cash inflows at a rate equal to the yield. In the case of the electric typewriters, which have a yield of approximately 14 percent, the interest tables assume that the firm is able to earn this rate on the annual cash inflows of $4,000 and $1,000; similarly, in the case of the doll-making machine, the interest tables assume that the firm is able to earn an annual return of 20 percent on the respective cash inflows for this proposed capital expenditure. If a firm is unable to earn a return equal to the yield (on the net cash inflows), the yield method may give distorted answers. Second, the yield method does not give sufficient consideration to the size of the investment. If taken too literally, a firm might be tempted to prefer an investment of $400 that gives a return of 20 percent over an investment of $50,000 that offers a return of 18 percent. A third pitfall in using the yield method is that under conditions of irregular net cash inflows, this method may give two or more answers. The point is not proved here, but the reader may be able to visualize a condition under which the solution to the yield model becomes involved in quadratic equations that may give more than one answer (or none that is a real number). This peculiar situation did not occur in our examples because we assumed that the net cash inflows were positive for all periods. Despite its pitfalls, the yield method is applicable in most cases.

Observe that the test just discussed is based on annual *cash flows* and not on annual *net income* generated by the project.

A widely used criterion for ranking capital expenditures in order of their relative desirability is the pay-back period—*a financial test that estimates the period of time in which a project will generate cash equal to its cost*. In other words, the pay-back period is a prediction as to how long a company will have to wait in order to recover sufficient cash from the project to equal the cash invested in it. Thus one project may be expected to have a pay-back period of two years while another may be expected to have a pay-back of four years. A short pay-back period is generally a favorable sign, for the following reasons: It is indirect evidence that the proposed expenditure will be profitable; the risk to the firm is less because the company will recover its capital in a shorter period; and the cash flow generated by the project will alleviate the stringent solvency position of a firm that tends to be short of cash. Because of the relative simplicity of the concept of the pay-back period, it is used widely.

THE PAY-BACK TEST

Meaning and Computation

If the annual cash inflow generated by the asset is not in equal amounts, then one compiles cumulative cash gains resulting from the project until the year in which the running total is equal to the amount of the expenditure. If the annual cash inflow from the project is in equal annual amounts, as in Table 8-4, the following formula may be used to determine the pay-back period:[1]

1. Many adaptations of the pay-back period test are in use, such as the inclusion of current assets in the numerator. The reason for not including current assets in the numerator in this example is the assumption that in an emergency the current assets may be immediately liquidated for cash.

Capital Budgeting as a Planning Tool (I)   119

$$\text{Pay-back period (for electric typewriters)} = \frac{\text{Cost of project}}{\text{Net income after taxes} + \text{depreciation}}$$

$$= \frac{\$10,000}{\$\ 4,000}$$

$$= 2.50 \text{ years}$$

The pay-back period for the machine to produce dolls is determined as follows:

$$\text{Pay-back period (for doll-making machine}} = \frac{\text{Cash outlay for project}}{\text{Net income after taxes} + \text{depreciation}}$$

$$= \frac{\$16,000}{\$\ 7,000}$$

$$= 2.29 \text{ years}$$

The pay-back period is 2.50 years for the electric typewriters and 2.29 years for the machine to produce dolls. On the basis of this information, the outlay for the machine to produce dolls will be recovered before the outlay for the electric typewriters. Hence, the doll-making machine would be given priority over the electric typewriters. The pay-back period is useful because it places a number of alternatives on a common denominator basis by assigning a single quantitative test that may be used to compare projects that have different dollar costs and different dollar cash inflows.

Firms that use the pay-back period test may have a policy of rejecting all proposals that do not pay for themselves within a certain period of time, such as three years. The pay-back period at which proposals are rejected is known as a cutoff point. Of course, exceptions are always allowed, such as for buildings, which normally have a very long pay-back period. Each firm must establish a series of cutoff points to allow for projects that have different expected lives and substantially different degrees of risk.

Evaluation   The main advantage of the pay-back period test is that it may help keep the firm solvent. The test, however, has two serious disadvantages. First, it considers the present value of cash inflows of different years to be of equivalent value. Thus $1 cash income received three years from now is considered to be the same as $1 received today. Second, the test fails to consider the net cash inflow that may arise after the pay-back period. The disadvantages of the pay-back period may be demonstrated by referring to Table 8-7, in which three proposed projects—X, Y, and Z—are compared. Each proposed project has the same pay-back period of

TABLE 8-7
Hypothetical Projects

Project	Dollar Outlay for Acquisition	Yearly Cash Inflow 1	2	3	Pay-back Period in Years	Relative Rank of Project
X	$8,000	$6,000	$2,000		2	1
Y	8,000	2,000	6,000		2	1
Z	8,000	6,000	2,000	$2,000	2	1

two years; therefore, all are tied for first place in a ranking based on the pay-back criterion. But the three alternatives are not equally desirable. If one takes into consideration the time value of money, projects X and Z are superior to project Y because most of the funds are recovered in the first year. As between the two more desirable projects, Z is superior to X because the former has an additional cash flow beyond the pay-back period. Hence, while the pay-back period test serves a useful purpose, it may not lead to the best decision in capital budgeting. The test overemphasizes solvency and underemphasizes profitability.

Problem

Company Q is considering buying either machine A or machine B. Since they are mutually exclusive, only one will be acquired. The data appear in Table 8-8.

TABLE 8-8 Machine A or Machine B?

	Machine A	Machine B
Cash cost	$24,483.38	$25,115.20
Net cash benefits per year		
1	$10,000.00	$11,000.00
2	$11,000.00	$11,000.00
3	$12,000.00	$11,000.00
Cost of capital (percent)	10.00	10.00
Life of asset (years)	3.00	3.00

Determine for each: (a) the net present value, (b) the index of profitability, (c) the internal rate of return.

Solution

See Table 8-9. (a) $2,714.19 and $2,239.60 respectively, (b) 1.11 and 1.09 respectively, (c) 16 and 15 percent, respectively. *Required:* Show how these answers were obtained.

TABLE 8-9 Solution to Company Q's Problem

Machine A		Machine B	
Net Present Value		**Net Present Value**	
0.90909 × $10,000 =	$ 9,090.90	2.4868 × $11,000 =	$27,354.80
0.82645 × 11,000 =	9,090.95		
0.75131 × 12,000 =	9,015.72		
Present value	$27,197.57	Present value	$27,354.80
Less cost	24,483.38	Less cost	25,115.20
Net present value	$ 2,714.19	Net present value	$ 2,239.60
Index of Profitability		**Index of Profitability**	
$I = \dfrac{27,197.57}{24,483.38}$		$I = \dfrac{27,354.80}{25,115.20}$	
1.11		1.09	
Internal Rate of Return (16%)		**Internal Rate of Return (15%)**	
0.86207 × $10,000 =	$ 8,620.70	2.2832 × $11,000 =	$25,115.20
0.74316 × 11,000 =	8,174.76		
0.64066 × 12,000 =	7,687.92		
Cost	$24,483.38	Cost	$25,115.20

Capital budgeting is the process of ranking proposed projects in order of their relative desirability to the firm. Several ranking techniques are the net-present-value test, the index of profitability, the yield test, and the pay-back test.

Each of the above tests has a place in advancing the goals of the firm, which are assumed to be mainly increasing the market value of the enterprise. Because these techniques quantify data, management may be able to make better decisions.

Although the examples used in this chapter relate to fixed assets, capital budgeting is not limited to this area. Capital budgeting may give guidance on such matters as the optimum amount of accounts receivable to have, whether to refund a bond issue, and the profitability of a merger.

The first step in capital budgeting is to use the pay-back test as a first screening device. If the pay-back period is greater than the economic life of the project, the project should be immediately rejected, because the firm will decrease its profitability if it acquires an asset that never pays for itself. Furthermore, if this is the case, the project will fail all the other tests (net-present-value, index of profitability, and internal rate of return). But if the pay-back period is less than the economic life of the project, the proposal should be kept in the running for further consideration and should be subjected to a second screening provided by the other tests just mentioned. It is possible that some of the proposals that survived the first screening might not survive the second screening. The projects that do survive the second screening may then be ranked.

A theoretically sound method is the net-present-value test and its extension, the index of profitability. If the project offers a positive net present value, its acceptance will increase the market value of the firm.

Generally, a firm should give the highest priority to projects with the highest index of profitability–provided it is above 1.

If the internal rate of return is used, projects should be accepted when this rate is above the firm's cost of capital; also, projects with the highest internal rates of return should be given priority over projects with lower rates.

In summary, capital budgeting offers additional tools to individual businessmen to increase profits and solvency (and market value of the common stock) for a particular firm at a particular time and in a particular place.

8-1. Suggest several criteria for ranking major cash outlays in order of their relative desirability.

8-2. What is the difference between "the present value of $1 due at the end of N years" and "the present value of $1 received annually for N years"? (See Tables 8-1 and 8-2.)

8-3. Which of the following does not require discounting cash flows? (a) Net present value, (b) index of profitability, (c) internal rate of return (yield), (d) pay-back?

8-4. Other factors being the same, is a high pay-back period better than a low pay-back period?

8-5. Arrange an interview with a vice president in charge of finance (or a similar high-ranking officer) and seek answers to these questions: (a) Does his firm use any of these analytical tools—net present value, index of profitability, internal rate of return, pay back? (b) If his firm uses any of these four tools, how are they modified to meet the needs of his company? (c) What criteria does his firm actually use in ranking proposed large expenditures in order of their relative desirability? (d) Who in the company makes the decision on authorizing large expenditures of cash for projects to be undertaken during the forthcoming year?

Answers to some of the problems appear at the end of this section. *For each problem, show how you obtained the answer.* **REVIEW PROBLEMS**

8-1. A firm in the 50 percent tax bracket is considering buying an asset with a factory price of $10,000; in addition, the purchaser must pay freight of $1,000 and installation costs of $1,000. The asset will result in annual cash savings of $6,000 (before depreciation and taxes) for a period of six years. The firm's cost of capital is 10 percent. Using the following format to obtain some of the information, determine the net present value of the project.

1. Annual savings before depreciation and taxes	————
2. Depreciation	$ 2,000
3. Taxable income	————
4. Income Tax	————
5. Net profits after taxes	————
6. Plus depreciation	————
7. Annual cash inflow (annual cash benefits)	————
8. Present value of amount on line 7	————
9. Present value of cash cost of asset	$12,000
10. Net present value	————

8-2. Company Z may purchase an asset for $15,163, which will result in annual cash benefits of $4,000 for a five-year period. The yield on this asset is approximately 10 percent. Demonstrate a short-cut method of obtaining this answer, that is, without using numerous trial and error steps.

8-3. Company M is considering purchasing an asset for $15,186.50, which will result in annual cash benefits (annual cash inflows) of $5,000 a year for a four-year period. Using a short-cut method, determine the yield on the project. (Observe that the short-cut method gives accurate results only when the annual cash benefits are equal; nevertheless, the method may be used as a starting point even when the annual cash benefits are not equal.)

8-4. Company P is planning to buy an asset that will have a cash cost of $1,000. The asset will last for three years and will result in net cash inflows (cash benefits) of $400 a year. If the firm has a cost of capital of 10 percent, should the project be accepted, assuming that the firm is using only the net-present-value test?

8-5. Company R is considering buying an asset that has a cash cost of $2,000 and a life of five years. The net difference in cash inflow (savings) before depreciation and before taxes is $800; the corporation is subject to a 50 percent tax rate; the firm's cost of capital is 10 percent. The annual cash flow (annual cash benefits) amounts to $600. Show how the $600 figure was obtained.

8-6. Company Q is considering purchasing an asset for $3,169.90. The asset will last four years and has expected annual cash benefits of $1,000. The yield (internal rate of return) on this proposal is 10 percent. Show how the 10 percent figure was obtained.

8-7. Company A is considering buying an asset that has a cash cost of $1,200 and that will result in annual cash benefits of $400. The proposed project will have a life of six years. What is the pay-back period?

8-8. Company B is purchasing an asset that will result in annual cash benefits of $1,000, and will last four years. The firm's cost of capital is 12 percent. So that the firm will not lose money (under the net present value rule), what is the maximum the business should pay for the asset?

8-9. The following data apply to project K: index of profitability 2; present value of annual cash benefits $4,000; pay-back period two years. What is the dollar amount of the annual cash benefits?

8-10. The following data apply to project X: net present value $4,000; present value of annual cash benefits $14,000; firm's cost of capital 12 percent. What is the cost of the asset?

8-11. The net present value of a project is $5,000; the cost of the project is $10,000. If the firm's cost of capital is 12 percent, what is the index of profitability?

8-12. Company G is planning to purchase an asset that has a cash cost of $3,206.40. The asset will have a life of seven years and will result in annual cash benefits of $1,000. The firm's cost of capital is 8 percent. What is the net present value of the project?

8-13. Company C has a cost of capital of 10 percent. The firm is considering purchasing an asset for $10,000 cash. This asset will result in cash savings of $3,000 a year for a period of three years; there is no scrap value. Based on the yield method: (a) Should the company purchase the asset? (b) Is it necessary to use interest tables to answer this problem?

8-14. Company D, in the 50 percent tax bracket, is considering purchasing an asset that will have a cash cost of $4,000 and a life of four years. The asset will result in annual cash savings of $2,000 (before depreciation and taxes). What is the pay-back period of this asset?

8-15. Company F is comparing projects X and R. Data on each are given in Table 8-10.

Project	Outlay	Net Cash Benefits	
		1st Year	2nd Year
X	$5,000	$6,000	$4,000
R	5,000	4,000	6,000

TABLE 8-10
Comparison of
Projects X
and R

Which project should be given priority, assuming both carry the same degree of risk?

8-16. Company L has the possibility of buying an asset for a cash outlay of $4,000. The life of the asset is three years. Net cash benefits are $1,000 per year. Should the firm buy this asset? (Assume no scrap value.)

8-17. Project A, which costs $1,000 in cash, has an anticipated life of 10 years and is expected to result in a yearly net cash benefit of $200 per year. If the firm has a policy of accepting projects with a pay-back period of not more than six years, should the project be accepted?

8-18. Project D, which costs $2,000 in cash, has an anticipated life of eight years. It is expected to result in net cash benefits as follows: first year $200; second year $400; third year $600; fourth year $1,200; remaining years $400 annually. If the company has a policy of accepting projects that have a pay-back period of not more than six years, should this project be accepted?

8-19. Using the pay-back test, rank the four projects in Table 8-11 in order of their relative desirability, assuming all carry the same degree of risk.

Project	Cash Outlay	Annual Net Cash Benefits			
		1st Year	2nd Year	3rd Year	4th Year
A	$10,000	$ 2,500	$ 2,500	$ 2,500	$2,500
B	20,000	6,000	4,000	10,000	8,000
C	30,000	10,000	15,000	5,000	5,000
D	10,000	2,000	8,000	4,000	1,000

TABLE 8-11
Cash Outlay
and Benefits
of Four Projects

Answers: 8-1, $5,421.20; 8-3, 12 percent; 8-4, rejected, because net present value is $-$ $5.28; 8-7, 3 years; 8-8, $3,037.30; 8-9, $1,000; 8-10, $10,000; 8-11, 1.5; 8-12, $2,000; 8-14, 2.67 years.

CASE ON RANKING
PROJECTS IN ORDER
OF THEIR RELATIVE
DESIRABILITY
(CAPITAL BUDGETING)

Joseph Clark, president of the Zenith Company, is deciding which of these two proposed capital expenditures he should give priority to: installation of a set of bookkeeping machines or installation of a set of machines that will add a new product, a special kind of gold-plated mechanical lead pencil. The Zenith Company is a moderate-sized manufacturer of stationery. Clark is interested in diversifying his firm's output and hence is willing to consider the machines for manufacturing pencils.

The cost of the bookkeeping machines is $20,000. There is no freight to be paid by the Zenith Company, nor will the purchaser have to pay any installation costs.

The office manager of Zenith has made a careful study of the possible savings from the use of the bookkeeping machines. These machines will enable the user to maintain continuous balances of accounts receivable, as well as provide other labor-saving services. The office manager estimates that the acquisition of the machines will enable his firm to dismiss one bookkeeper. He estimates that this action will result in annual savings of $10,000 (before depreciation on the new bookkeeping machines and before federal income taxes on these savings). He has checked his data very carefully and is satisfied with their accuracy.

The Zenith Company is growing rapidly, and the officers were considering the possibility of installing elaborate electronic data processing machines. But the management decided that Zenith Company would wait three years to shift to this more expensive kind of equipment. The best estimate of the useful economic life of the bookkeeping machines is three years. Furthermore, because of the uncertainty of the economic usefulness of the bookkeeping machines at the end of three years, the best estimate of their cash value at the end of this period is $2,000. Annual depreciation must be known in order to compute federal income taxes, which in turn affect cash flow. The Zenith Company is in the 50 percent federal income tax bracket.

The machines for manufacturing special pencils constitute the other alternative. The pencils are patented by another firm, which would give the Zenith Company permission to produce the items for a royalty of 50 cents on each one manufactured. Zenith, in turn, would expect to sell these gold-plated pencils at $5 to wholesalers. The agreement with the owner of the patent would be for four years only. In all of its planning the Zenith Company has to assume that the agreement might not be renewed at the end of the period and that the pencil-making machines, with their specialized use, would for all practical purposes have no scrap value.

The factory price of the machines for manufacturing pencils is $27,000. Zenith would have to pay $200 for freight and $800 for installation costs. The president estimates that an additional $6,000 in circulating assets would be required if the machine were acquired. This amount would, however, be recovered in full by Zenith at the end of four years.

The president also estimates that if the machines for producing pencils were acquired, the annual profits from this project (before depreciation on these specific machines and before federal income taxes on the profits produced by them) would be $17,000. This estimate came from discussions with a marketing research agency and from the company's internal records. But net cash flow would be less than $17,000 because taxes have not yet been subtracted.

The Zenith Company would have to obtain a 6 percent bank loan to finance the acquisition of either kind of machine.

The company has 260 employees, 15 of whom are in the accounting department. All employees who are not executives are members of a labor union. In general, Zenith has had good relations with the union, although union officials have been watching carefully both possible alternatives.

Required: Which set of machines should be given priority? Give quantitative evidence to support your decision.

APPENDIX TO CHAPTER 8: EXPECTED UTILITY

In order to improve on a weakness of expected value, another new managerial tool has come into prominence—expected utility. The concept of expected utility improves on expected value by taking into consideration management's attitude toward such outcomes as the possibility of losing a large sum of money. In order to give practice in developing the information for expected value and expected utility, still another example will be used. Table 8-12 shows a comparison of projects Y and Z. If expected value were used as the selection criterion, project Y would be given preference, because it has an expected value of $3,000 while project Z has an expected value of $2,400. Since both give positive results, the acceptance of either would benefit the firm; however, the acceptance of Y

*TABLE 8-12
Expected Value,
Projects Y and Z*

Project Y			Project Z		
(1)	(2)	(3)	(4)	(5)	(6)
Net Present Value of Possible Outcome	Subjective Probability of Outcome in (1) Occurring	Expected Value (1 × 2)	Net Present Value of Possible Outcome	Subjective Probability of Outcome in (4) Occurring	Expected Value (4 × 5)
$-8,000	.10	$-800	$-1,000	.10	$-100
0	.10	0	0	.10	0
4,000	.50	2,000	3,000	.70	2,100
6,000	.30	1,800	4,000	.10	400
	1.00	$ 3,000		1.00	$ 2,400

would be more beneficial than Z. The weakness of expected value is that a particular manager might so dread the loss of $8,000 that he would give this factor overwhelming consideration regardless of what expected value figures show. He might incorporate this dread into a systematic analysis. Let it be assumed that the businessman is considering projects Y and Z and that he has a certain attitude toward the outcomes in columns 1 and 4 of Table 8-12. A scale may be designed to represent his attitude toward each of these outcomes. His attitude, measured in points, is shown in columns 3 and 7 of Table 8-13. Column 3 of Table 8-13 indicates that the businessman has such a dread of losing $8,000 that he assigns -100 points to his satisfaction of having this happen; he assigns no points to the desirability of just breaking even; he assigns 10 points to the desirability of earning $4,000; and he assigns 16 points to the satisfaction he would obtain from earning a profit of $6,000. In a similar manner, this same businessman might let the points in column 7 of Table 8-13 reflect his attitude toward the events in column 5 happening if project Z is accepted. His attitude toward the satisfaction of a loss of $1,000 is reflected in his allowing -5 points for this undesirable event. Similarly, in Table 8-13, his attitude toward the other events in column 5 is reflected by the scale in column 7. The scales shown in columns 3 and 7 of Table 8-13 vary from one businessman to another; they also differ within the same person at different times and under different circumstances. The important matter is that the attitude of management toward risk is incorporated into the process. The exact numbers used are not important as long as they are internally consistent along a relative scale.

The next step in Table 8-13 is to determine the expected utility for project Y; this is done by multiplying column 3 by column 2 and then adding together these products. The expected utility of project Y is -0.2. The expected utility for project Z is determined by multiplying column 6 by column 7 and then adding together the products; the expected utility is 6.10. Project Y is superior under the expected value test; but under the expected utility test, project Z is

TABLE 8-13
Expected Utility

Project Y				Project Z			
(1)	(2)	(3)	(4)	(5)	(6)	(7)	(8)
Net Present Value of Outcome	Subjective Probability of Outcome in (1) Occurring	Attitude of Management toward Outcome in (1) Occurring	Expected Utility (2 × 3)	Net Present Value of Outcome	Subjective Probability of Outcome in (5) Occurring	Attitude of Management toward Outcome in (5) Occurring	Expected Utility (6 × 7)
$-8,000	.10	-100	-10.0	$-1,000	.10	-5	-0.50
0	.10	0	0.0	0	.10	0	0.00
4,000	.50	10	5.0	3,000	.70	8	5.60
6,000	.30	16	4.8	4,000	.10	10	1.00
	1.00		-0.2		1.00		6.10

superior. If expected utility is the criterion, then project Z would be accepted and project Y ruled out because it is lower in rank than Z; even worse, Y has a negative expected utility.

Expected utility has the advantage of incorporating the businessman's attitude toward losses and gains; expected value does this only partially, if at all.

Both expected value and expected utility are valid tools, and the businessman is justified in using either of them. But he is also justified in rejecting both of them as decision tools. He may use some other criterion in making his decision, such as the maximin principle discussed in Chapter 7.

Capital
Budgeting as a
Planning Tool (II)

In the previous chapter we assumed that the percentage cost of capital was given; in this chapter we will give a procedure for estimating this rate of sacrifice. The percentage cost of capital is an important variable in the planning process, as one must have some measure of this cost before an intelligent decision can be made on whether or not to expand. Management must be able to estimate whether its cost of capital is 6, 10, 12, or some other percent. If management accepts projects that add net present value to the firm, a percentage cost of capital must be used in discounting the net cash flows back to their present value. If management accepts projects whose yield exceeds the cost of capital, the percentage cost of capital must be estimated before the worthwhileness of the project can be determined. Only under the pay-back criterion is it unnecessary to have this percentage cost. The cost of capital, then, is an important element in the decision-making process.

The following will be discussed in this chapter:

1. A preliminary example of the use of the percentage cost of capital concept
2. Estimating the weighted average cost of capital for the firm
   a. Determining the component costs of common stock and retained earnings, preferred stock, bonds, and short-term debt
   b. Combining the component costs into an average for the firm
3. Optimum capital structure and the weighted average cost of capital
4. Other cost of capital rates
5. Incorporating common sense in the capital budgeting process
6. Limitations of capital budgeting

The methods of determining the cost of capital explained in this chapter are not the only ones in use. Furthermore, estimating the cost of capital for an individual firm is never a precise procedure, since the estimates are based on predictions of a firm's future. Finally, our analysis will be concerned with the cost of *additional capital* for the firm, rather than with its historical costs.[1]

A PRELIMINARY USE OF THE PERCENTAGE COST OF CAPITAL CONCEPT

If a firm has already ranked a number of projects according to their prospective yield, the cost of capital may be used to determine the cutoff point, that is, how far down the list of proposed capital expenditures management should go in making a selection. Suppose that a firm has a weighted cost of capital of 12 percent and that it has the following projects under consideration:

Project	Anticipated Percentage Rate to Be Earned on Project
A	22
B	20
C	18
D	10
E	2

If the weighted cost of capital tool were injected into the analysis, management would accept projects A, B, and C and would reject projects D and E. If the market price of the common stock is not to decrease, the least a capital expenditure can earn is the firm's cost of capital. *Another way to state this is that the cost of capital provides information on the rock-bottom rate of return that a project should earn in order to prevent a decline in the price of a share of common stock.*

ASSIGNING WEIGHTS TO EACH SOURCE

The first step is to determine the weight (importance) to assign to each source of funds. The various sources that have a cost of some sort are listed, as in Table

TABLE 9-1 Estimating the Weighted Average Percentage Cost of Capital

Source	(1) Market Value of Source	(2) Percent of Each Source to the Total Sources	(3) Percentage Cost of Capital	(4) Weighted Cost (Percent) (2 × 3)
Common stock	$ 60,000	60	20	12.00
Preferred stock	10,000	10	7	.70
Long-term debt	20,000	20	3	.60
Short-term debt	10,000	10	2½	.25
	$100,000	100		13.55

1. Chapter 22 contains a further discussion on interrelationships between the various forms of financing.

9-1, at market value. The individual amounts are obtained and totaled, and then the percentage of each component to the total is obtained. Thus in Table 9-1 the market value of the common stock is $60,000, a sum that represents 60 percent of the market value of all the sources ($100,000).

ESTIMATING THE COST OF EACH SOURCE

Depending on the form of organization, the main components entering into cost of capital computations are common stock and retained earnings (taken as a package), preferred stock, bonds, short-term credit on which there is an interest charge, market value of the single proprietorship, and market value of the partnership.

COMMON STOCK AND RETAINED EARNINGS

The cost of common stock is found by dividing anticipated future earnings per share by the proceeds that would be received if additional shares were sold:

The Formula

$$\text{Cost of common} = \frac{\text{Anticipated future earnings per share}}{\text{Proceeds per share}}$$

In this example, we will assume that expected future earnings per share will be $4 and that the proceeds per share from a new issue will be $20. Hence the cost of capital is:

$$\text{Cost of common} = \frac{\$\ 4}{\$20}$$
$$= 20 \text{ percent}$$

The expected future earnings per share represents management's best estimate of what future earnings per share will be without the additional financing. We will assume that the $4 represents such an average.

There is considerable discussion concerning whether to use future earnings per share or future dividends per share. We will use the former on grounds of expediency. Nonetheless, from a theoretical viewpoint there is a good case for using future dividends per share, because this is a form of cash flow; and to be consistent in capital budgeting all data should be translated into cash flows. *Because it is easier to predict earnings per share, however, it is often used as a substitute for the more correct concept of future dividends per share.* Either concept can be defended; both are correct.

Observe that the proceeds to the company per share is different from the market price per share. The proceeds per share is usually lower than the market price because the company must pay investment banking fees to have the shares sold and the company may have to sell the shares at bargain prices to stimulate interest in the issue.

A most difficult task in measuring the weighted average cost of capital is estimating the cost of capital of the common stock component. Here the businessman must use good judgment, for in some cases the cost of the common will turn out to be an absurd figure, such as 62 percent or 1 percent. The businessman must think in terms of a range of reasonable rates, such as 6 to 25 percent. If the computed figure falls within this range, he accepts the number as computed by his colleagues; but if it falls outside the range, he must select an arbitrary rate, such as 10 percent, or he must reject the weighted average cost of capital approach. We are assuming, of course, that the person estimating the cost of capital of the common stock has used every practical and theoretical tool.

Under the weighted cost of capital system (the weights being determined by the relative market price of the components), retained earnings are included in the common stock component. That is, the market price of the common stock includes the expectation of stockholders that a firm will earn profits, distribute some of them, and retain the remainder to expand the future dividends paid by the firm. This means that the current market price reflects the stockholders' beliefs concerning future dividend patterns of the firm; the stockholders have anticipated that future retained profits will be handled in a certain manner. While other systems of taking retained profits into consideration are available, care should be used not to double count the role of retained profits in the cost of capital figure.

The Role of Dividend Policy

Nonetheless, management may change the pay-out ratio and otherwise engage in policies that vary from stockholders' expectations. Stockholders react in a manner that is reflected in the amount they will pay for the stock. A change in the pay-out ratio, for example, might lead to a change in both the numerator and the denominator of the ratio:

$$\text{Cost of common} = \frac{\text{Expected future earnings per share}}{\text{Proceeds per share}}$$

When this ratio changes, one of the major components of the weighted cost of capital changes and hence leads to a change in the combined weighted cost of capital. Furthermore, if there is a change in expectations concerning the amount of dividends to be paid, other components, such as the cost of long-term debt, might also change. Thus a sharp drop in the amount of dividends paid will increase the equity base of the company, a situation that might change the attitudes of bondholders toward the risk of owning bonds in this firm; the end result might be to lower the investor's yield to maturity. The point, once again, is that a change in any individual cost might lead to a change in the remaining ones.

The current market yield on preferred stock is usually considered to be an adequate approximation of the cost of this component. The formula is:

PREFERRED STOCK

$$\text{Cost of preferred} = \frac{\text{Anticipated future annual dividends per share}}{\text{Current market price}^2}$$

2. A more exact figure can be obtained by using proceeds per share in the denominator.

If the dividends per share are assumed to be $7 and the market price of the preferred stock $100, the cost is 7 percent. Since dividends on the preferred stock are usually fixed by contract, this figure is readily available; the market price of the preferred may be more difficult to obtain.

BONDS

The cost of bonds is the investor's yield to maturity (explained below), adjusted for the fact that the business obtains a tax deduction for interest paid on debt.

The Formula

The formula for determining this cost is:

$$\text{Cost of bonds} = (\text{Investor's yield to maturity}) \times (1 - \text{tax rate})$$

Assume that the bonds of a firm are yielding 6 percent to investors and that the corporate tax rate is 50 percent. The cost of the bond component would be:

$$\begin{aligned} \text{Cost of bonds} &= 6 \text{ percent} \times .5 \\ &= 3 \text{ percent} \end{aligned}$$

In this example, the cost of the long-term debt is 3 percent.

The Face Rate

When a corporation decides to float (issue) bonds, the matter of the rate of interest must be considered by the board of directors. Thus a corporation might promise to pay 4 percent on the outstanding bonds. The rate of interest a corporation agrees to pay is known as the *face rate of interest*, also called the *coupon rate of interest*. The face rate of interest determines how many dollars a firm must pay on each bond per year. If a 4 percent, $1,000 bond were under consideration, the firm would have to pay $40 per year on this instrument.

Percentage Paid
on the Proceeds
versus Investor's
Yield to Maturity

More important than the face rate of interest are the *percentage paid on the proceeds* and the *investor's yield to maturity*. Both of these take into consideration any premium or discount on the bonds.

If the bonds are sold at a premium, they are sold above face value. A $1,000 bond sold at $1,100 is sold at a premium of $100. On the other hand, if bonds are sold at a discount, they are sold below face value. If a corporation sells a $1,000 bond for $900, the amount of the discount is $100. Unlike shares of stock, there is no potential liability attached to the purchaser of a bond at a discount.

Assume that a firm sells a $1,000, 20-year, 4 percent bond to an investment banker for $1,020. Also assume that on this same day the banker in turn sells the bond to an investor for $1,025. First let us examine the transaction from the viewpoint of the issuing firm. There is a $20 premium on the bond. During the life of the issue the company will pay $40 in cash in interest each year. At maturity the issuer will be obliged to repay the principal of the loan, which is $1,000. Remember that the corporation originally received $1,020 and that at maturity it has to repay only the face value of the bond, $1,000. The corporation appears to have made a profit of $20 on this part of the transaction. If this amount is averaged over 20 years, the average gain amounts to $1 a year. Instead of considering this $1 as profit, it is customary to consider it as reducing the average interest cost to the corporation. The $1 is subtracted (only on the issuer's books) from the $40 cash outlay, making $39 the average yearly cost to the corporation. On the other hand, from the investor's viewpoint, he receives $40 in cash each year. But at maturity he receives only $1,000, despite the fact that he paid $1,025 for the bond. His "loss" of $25 is averaged over the 20 years, and his average annual interest becomes $38.75 ($40 − [$25 ÷ 20]).

The formula for determining the percentage paid on the proceeds received is:

$$\text{Percentage paid on proceeds received} = \frac{\text{Average yearly payments}}{\text{Average proceeds}}$$

$$= \frac{\$39}{\frac{1}{2}(\$1,000 + \$1,020)}$$

$$= \frac{\$39}{\$1,010}$$

$$= 3.86 \text{ percent}$$

The sale of bonds at a premium lowers the percentage paid on the proceeds below the face rate of interest of 4 percent.

The investor's yield to maturity views matters from that of the bond buyer. This rate is similar (but not identical) to the issuer's percentage paid on the proceeds, as can be seen in the following formula:

$$\text{Investor's yield to maturity} = \frac{\text{Average yearly return}}{\text{Average cost of bond}}$$

$$= \frac{\$38.75}{\frac{1}{2}(\$1,000 + \$1,025)}$$

$$= \frac{\$38.75}{\$1,012.50}$$

$$= 3.83 \text{ percent}$$

The slight difference in the two rates is caused by the different prices used in the formulas. The issuer stresses the price that it receives and the bond buyer stresses the price that he pays. Because of investment banking fees and other factors, the two prices may not be the same. Then there is the even more important factor that after the bonds are issued, the market price fluctuates, thus resulting in further variations between the percentage paid on the proceeds and the new holder's yield to maturity.

Next, assume that a corporation sells a $1,000, 20-year 4 percent bond to an investment banker for $980. Also assume that on this same day the banker sold the instrument to an investor for $985. From the issuer's viewpoint, the bond has been sold at a discount of $20. During the life of the bond the corporation will pay $40 in interest per year and in cash. In addition, at maturity, the corporation will be obliged to repay the principal of the loan, which is $1,000. Since the firm received only $980 when the bond was issued, and since it must repay $1,000, there is a loss of $20 on this aspect of the transaction. The $20, when averaged over the life of the instrument, amounts to $1 a year. The $1 is considered as increasing the average yearly interest cost. This $1 is added (only on the issuer's books) to the $40 cash outlay, resulting in an average yearly interest cost of $41 to the corporation. In contrast, from the investor's viewpoint, he receives $40 in cash each year. But at maturity he receives $1,000, despite the fact that he paid only $985 for the instrument. Hence, he has a gain of $15 on this phase of the transaction. His average gain per year is $0.75. Furthermore, his average annual income can be viewed as being $40.75.

Once again, the formula for determining the percentage paid on the proceeds received is:

$$\frac{\text{Investor's yield}}{\text{to maturity}} = \frac{\text{Average yearly return}}{\text{Average cost of bond}}$$

$$= \frac{\$40.75}{\frac{1}{2}(\$1,000 + \$985)}$$

$$= \frac{\$40.75}{\$992.50}$$

$$= 4.11 \text{ percent}$$

Therefore, the sale of bonds at a discount raises the percentage paid on the proceeds above the face rate of interest of 4 percent.

Once again, the investor's yield to maturity may be estimated by this formula:

$$\frac{\text{Percentage paid on}}{\text{proceeds received}} = \frac{\text{Average yearly payments}}{\text{average proceeds}}$$

$$= \frac{\$41}{\frac{1}{2}(\$1,000 + \$980)}$$

$$= \frac{\$41}{\$990}$$

$$= 4.14 \text{ percent}$$

Observe the closeness between the percentage paid on the proceeds and the investor's yield to maturity.

From the investor's viewpoint, the purchase of bonds at a premium lowers the yield to maturity below the face rate of interest; likewise, the purchase of a bond at a discount raises the yield to maturity above the rate of interest stated on the face of the bond. Thus, if at the time of issuance a purchaser acquired any of the 3¾ percent bonds of the Mission Corporation at $1015, the effective yield to the buyer would have been 3.71 percent. On the other hand, if at the time of issuance a buyer acquired at $990 any of the 3¼ percent, 10-year notes of Commercial Credit Company, the effective yield to the buyer would have been 3.37 percent. If bonds are sold at par value, the yield to maturity is the same as the face rate. One must use bond tables to compute yields accurately.

When a corporation borrows money through the issuance of bonds, it must pay the going rate of interest to sell them. *The sale of bonds at a premium or at a discount permits the corporation to make fine adjustments in the yield to maturity that the purchasers of the bonds will be able to receive, provided the bonds are held until maturity.* The rate of interest at which corporations are able to attract funds to themselves varies from company to company, depending mainly on the investors' appraisal of the risk involved in the loan. If a corporation is not too strong financially, it will have to offer a higher effective rate of interest on its bonds than another corporation that is stronger financially. In general, a relatively high yield to maturity is a reflection of a high degree of risk, while a low yield is a reflection of little risk.

Limits on Debt

One can see that at a point in time as debt continues to be issued, the interest rate on it will tend to increase and the price-earnings ratio on the common stock will tend to fall. The price-earnings ratio falls because the position of the common stockholder becomes weaker and riskier; interest on the debt and repayment of the principal precede any payments to the stockholders. Therefore, after a certain level debt is not as advantageous as it seems, despite the fact that interest rates may be quite low and despite the fact that interest is a tax deduction.

SHORT-TERM DEBT

The items included in short-term debt for the purpose of computing cost of capital are those on which the firm pays an interest fee or similar cost. Typically this would include notes payable to banks, notes to officers, and accounts payable if the firm is not taking its discounts. Generally, items such as accruals and accounts payable on which discounts are taken are excluded from the computations. In the case of a bank loan, the formula for estimating the cost of capital is:

Cost of bank loan = (Effective interest rate) $\times$ (1 − tax rate)

If the effective interest rate is 5 percent and the tax rate is 50 percent, the cost of the bank loan may be considered to be 2.5 percent. The same principles would apply to notes payable. An interesting point is that many firms exclude all current debt from cost of capital computations.

Combining the Component Costs into an Average for the Firm

As can be seen in Table 9-1, the weighted cost of capital is 13.55 percent, assuming the data given above. Many ingenious adaptations of the above description of the weighted cost of capital are in use. To recapitulate, the weighted cost of capital is the sum of the individual weighted costs of all the specific sources.

The concept of a weighted cost of capital is based on the realistic assumption that each project is financed in part with equity funds. This means that the financing of a project should be viewed as continuing through time. A firm that floats a bond issue today will have to plan on obtaining equity funds in the future if it is to maintain a balance between equity and debt and if the investing public is to use the same capitalization rate on the common stock.

OPTIMUM CAPITAL
STRUCTURE AND
THE WEIGHTED
AVERAGE COST
OF CAPITAL
The capital structure (proportion of debt to equity) is said to be at an optimum when the weighted average cost of capital is at a low point. Figure 9-1 shows the famous saucer-shaped curve, the essence of which is that the percentage cost of capital is at a minimum over a fairly wide range and that it is higher on either side of this range. The main conclusions to be inferred from Figure 9-1 are that the use of debt, in judicious amounts, lowers the weighted average cost of capital and that the best proportion of debt to equity is at the low point of the weighted average cost of capital line.

FIGURE 9-1
Debt to Equity
Ratio and Weighted
Average Cost
of Capital

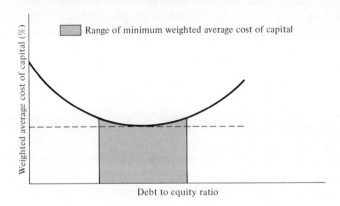

The reason for the weighted average cost of capital line sloping downward, reaching a low level, and then rising is that the curve reflects a mixture of high and low cost sources, debt being the low cost source—when used in moderation. To the firm, such debt is a cheap source because interest is a tax deduction and because investors will accept a low interest return on bonds. But after a point is reached in the proportion of debt to equity, the cost of using debt begins to increase because bondholders begin to demand higher interest rates to compensate for the extra risk. Furthermore, the cost of the common stock (to the issuer) begins to increase as large amounts of debt are issued. The reader will recall that as the proportion of debt to equity increases, investors are willing to pay less for each share of common stock in a firm. A sophisticated way to say this is that investors raise the capitalization rate on the common stock; they want a higher return to compensate them for the additional risk. Security analysts would condense all this by saying that ratio of price to future earnings per share would decline.

A comparatively low weighted average cost of capital is more desirable than a comparatively high one; the former is a signal that the investing public holds the firm in high esteem and will, therefore, advance funds to it at a moderate cost. If the firm seeks to raise additional funds through the sale of common stock, a fixed dollar amount can be raised by issuing fewer shares; if preferred stock is issued, investors will accept a moderate yield. Finally, if bonds are to be issued, the firm can raise the additional funds by paying a low interest rate. In summary, a low weighted average cost of capital is a signal that management is running the company efficiently, in the opinion of investors.

The weighted average cost of capital is future oriented because it attempts to measure what the cost would be if stocks and bonds were sold today. In other words, calculations are based on what the company would have to pay today— not what it cost the company at the time the securities were originally issued. Hence, the weighted average cost of capital comes close to being a marginal cost.

Estimate a firm's weighted average cost of capital, given the information in Table 9-2.

Problem

TABLE 9-2
Data Necessary to Estimate Weighted Average Cost of Capital

Securities	Aggregate Market Value	Cost Data (Percent)
Bonds	$100,000	5 (1)
Preferred	200,000	7 (2)
Common	200,000	8 (3)

(1) Investors' yield to maturity; corporation is in the 28 percent tax bracket.

(2) Future dividends per share divided by estimated proceeds per share, if new shares were sold.

(3) Future dividends per share divided by estimated proceeds per share, if new shares were sold.

Solution

TABLE 9-3
Determination of Weighted Average Cost of Capital

Securities	Weight (Percent)	After-tax Cost (Percent)	Weighted Average
Bonds	20	3.60	0.72
Preferred	40	7.00	2.80
Common	40	8.00	3.20
Weighted average cost of capital			6.72

The exact cost of capital (discount rate) that is used in evaluating a specific project depends mainly on how the firm prefers to deal with risk. The weighted

OTHER COST OF CAPITAL RATES

average cost of capital is assumed to be high enough to include a return for risk taking. Despite its historic importance, the weighted average cost of capital concept is beginning to diminish as a practical tool; more sophisticated cost of capital rates are being explored, particularly those that attempt to incorporate risk and utility analysis into the evaluation of each major project.

One substitute for the weighted average cost of capital is the *riskless rate of interest*, such as 6 percent. The riskless rate is usually considered to be the rate than can be earned on U.S. government bonds. When the riskless rate is used, extremely *conservative* estimates are made of future annual cash benefits. The capital budgeting procedures are then applied in the usual manner. Projects have their net present value computed by using the riskless rate in the discounting process. If the net present value is positive, the project is still in the running for acceptance. To repeat, in arriving at this judgment the riskless rate of interest is used rather than the weighted average cost of capital. In addition, the internal rate of return is estimated for a conservatively predicted flow of future cash benefits; but this rate is then compared with the riskless rate (rather than the weighted average cost of capital rate) to determine acceptance or rejection of the project. In practical situations, the riskless rate of discount is usually lower than the weighted average cost of capital rate.

A second substitute for the weighted average cost of capital is the concept of a managerially constructed table that classifies projects according to their degree of risk and suggests a proper discount rate for each risk category. Thus new products might require an 18 percent rate, new machines a 16 percent rate, and new laborsaving devices a 12 percent rate. High percentage rates are used on high-risk projects; low percentage rates are used on low-risk projects. The reader will recall that if all other factors remain constant, as the discount rate is raised, the firm is acting more conservatively; and as the discount rate is lowered, the firm is liberalizing its criteria for accepting projects.

For example, assume that a firm estimates its weighted average cost of capital to be 12 percent and that it will use this rate on projects of average risk. But also suppose that this same firm uses a 10 percent cost of capital (discount rate) on projects of very low risk and that it uses a 14 percent rate on high-risk projects. This particular firm is seeking to rank two projects, data for which are given in Table 9-4. If the risk adjusted rate of return is used in the discounting process, the net present values are:

					Risk Adjusted Rate of Return (Percent)	Weighted Average Cost of Capital (Percent)
TABLE 9-4 Ranking for Two Projects		*Net Annual*				
	Cash	*Cash*	*Life in*	*Risk*		
Project	*Cost*	*Benefits*	*Years*	*Class*		
A	$9,000	$2,000	7	Low	10	12
B	9,000	2,200	7	High	14	12

NPV = Present value of annual cash benefits − Present value of cost

NPV_A = ($2,000 × 4.8684) − $9,000
    = $9,736.80 − $9,000
    = 736.80

NPV_B = ($2,200 × 4.2883) − $9,000
    = $9,434.26 − $9,000
    = 434.26

Since project A has the higher net present value, it is given a higher ranking than B.

If the weighted average cost of capital is used, the ranking is reversed:

NPV_A = ($2,000 × 4.5638) − $9,000
    = $9,127.60 − $9,000
    = 127.60

NPV_B = ($2,200 × 4.5638) − $9,000
    = $10,040.36 − $9,000
    = 1,040.36

Since project B has the higher net present value and the same cost, it is given a higher ranking than project A.

Which discount rate should the businessman use, especially when each method gives contradictory answers? In this dilemma he should use the one that he feels will make the most money for his particular company.

A third substitute for the weighted average cost of capital is the borrowing rate, such as 8 percent, that would have to be paid on a bank loan. In a few kinds of transactions, such as whether to borrow and purchase an asset or whether to rent it from an owner for a specified period of time, the borrowing rate might be used. Again, the issue facing management is which discount rate to use in analyzing a particular problem in a specific company.

A college student working during the summer months for American Can Company is given the assignment of comparing two projects, A and B. Each has a cost of $10,000 and an economic life of four years. Data on annual cash benefits are in Table 9-5.

Problem

Year	Project A	Project B
1	$1,000	$8,000
2	1,000	1,000
3	8,000	1,000
4	1,000	1,000

TABLE 9-5
Annual Cash Benefits

(a) If the pay-back test is used as a preliminary screening device, should both projects be kept in the running for further consideration?

(b) If the net present value criterion is used, should the projects be accepted if the cost of capital is 10 percent? 5 percent?

Required: By using the interest tables in the previous chapter, show how these answers were obtained.

Solution

TABLE 9-6
Net Present Value
of Projects
A and B

Project A	Project B
10% Assumption	10% Assumption

Project A		Project B	
$1,000 × 0.90909 =	$ 909.09	$8,000 × 0.90909 =	$7,272.72
1,000 × 0.82645 =	826.45	1,000 × 0.82645 =	826.45
8,000 × 0.75131 =	6,010.48	1,000 × 0.75131 =	751.31
1,000 × 0.68301 =	683.01	1,000 × 0.68301 =	683.01
	$8,429.03		$9,533.49

NPV = $8,429.03 − $10,000   NPV = $9,533.49 − $10,000

   = −$1,570.97   = −$466.51

5% Assumption		5% Assumption	
$1,000 × 0.95238 =	$ 952.38	$8,000 × 0.95238 =	$7,619.04
1,000 × 0.90703 =	907.03	1,000 × 0.90703 =	907.03
8,000 × 0.86384 =	6,910.72	1,000 × 0.86384 =	863.84
1,000 × 0.82270 =	822.70	1,000 × 0.82270 =	822.70
	$9,592.83		$10,212.61

NPV = $9,592.83 − $10,000   NPV = $10,212.61 − $10,000

   = −$407.17   = $212.61

(a) Both A and B have a pay-back period of three years; since this is less than their economic life, both should be given further consideration.

(b) If the cost of capital is 10 percent, both should be rejected because the net present value is −$1,570.97 for A and −$466.51 for B. If the cost of capital is 5 percent, project A should be rejected because its net present value is −$407.17; but project B should be accepted because its net present value is +$212.61.

INCORPORATING COMMON SENSE IN THE CAPITAL BUDGETING PROCESS

Additional Constraints

Although the tools of *net present value*, the *index of profitability*, the *internal rate of return (yield)*, and the *pay-back test* have greatly improved the decision-making process, astute managers in a particular firm are reluctant to rely on these tools exclusively. This reluctance is based primarily on the belief that the above models do not include all the variables that the business community deems to be important. A solution to this predicament is to use capital budgeting as a major screening device and then to refine the process with further screening techniques, called constraints.

Assume that the management of a particular firm concedes that one of the primary goals of the company is to increase the market value per share. Furthermore, management imposes these constraints on itself: It will not accept projects with an index of profitability of less than 1.3; it will seek to increase annual earnings per share by at least $0.20 and annual dividends per share by at least $0.15; it will place a ceiling of 35 percent on its debt-to-equity ratio; and it will place a ceiling of $500,000 on major expenditures for the coming year. (When management places a ceiling on the amount of money it will spend each year, this self-imposed constraint is called *capital rationing*.) Obtaining a solution (the selection of a group of new programs) that includes the above constraints enables businessmen to live in the present as well as anticipate the future; the inclusion of a number of additional variables in the model enables them to make operationally meaningful decisions. The constraints may be thought of as additional standards of eligibility for acceptance of new programs.

Capital rationing, as previously noted, means that a firm decides at the beginning of the year that it will limit its major expenditures to a certain maximum, such as a total of $300,000 for the coming year. This limitation on total spending recognizes that the firm is able to expand by just so much without certain inefficiencies developing (new employees may not be trained as fast as expected, present employees may be assigned additional duties against their wishes, labor problems may develop, and competitors may take sudden and drastic counteractions). By placing a ceiling on the total amount to be spent, management is using good sense because the survival of the firm is more assured. In summary, although the firm foregoes the chance of enormous profits on new projects, it also lessens the chance of large catastrophic losses.

Capital Rationing

Decision makers for thousands of years have engaged in diversification, which, as is well known, means acquiring projects whose profits do not all decline at the same time. An example of diversification is the policy of investors placing their savings in banks, government bonds, defensive securities (securities whose price and dividends do not decline when the market as a whole is declining), convertible bonds, and land ventures. By diversifying, the investor obtains a mixture of investments; the incomes from the various components are unlikely to decline simultaneously. In a similar manner, business firms seek out projects whose profits do not all decline in the same year. Thus a firm might diversify into making machine tools, manufacturing chewing gum, owning apartment houses, and selling life insurance. This approach to business administration acts as a favorable force on the price of the firm's common stock—it causes the stock to rise with a minimum of fluctuation.

Diversification

Capital budgeting has certain limitations that should be kept in mind. One is the great difficulty encountered in predicting net cash inflow and net income for a

LIMITATIONS OF CAPITAL BUDGETING

span of years. Predictions become progressively unreliable as the period of time covered increases. Because of unknown future developments, such as wars, competition, and the business cycle, all predictions should be regarded as estimates rather than as precise expectations. A partial solution to this problem is to estimate the quantitative criteria as a range of rates. Thus management may estimate that a certain machine probably will yield a rate of return that is between 18 and 24 percent and that another project probably will yield between 10 and 14 percent. This type of planning places forecasting on a semiscientific basis while still giving management considerable flexibility.

Another limitation of capital budgeting is that if it is applied too literally, incorrect decisions may be made. Thus, suppose that E. I. du Pont de Nemours and Company is weighing the alternatives of spending cash to buy U.S. government securities yielding 6 percent or spending cash to acquire a machine that will earn 20 percent. If one takes the capital budgeting process too literally, the decision might be to acquire the machine that yields 20 percent. The fact that this firm at a recent date had $220 million of government securities that yielded approximately 6 percent is evidence that it acquired this low-yield investment for a reason. The explanation of this action lies in an examination of the goals of the firm; such goals include solvency as well as profitability. The investing public will pay more for the stock of a profitable company that is highly solvent than for the stock of a profitable company that is of only average solvency. In summary, then, a firm may elect to accept a lower-yielding alternative (such as the purchase of government bonds) if this course of action better advances its goals.

Yet another limitation, already mentioned, is that not all projects can be assigned specific quantitative rates or other objective criteria. The cement sidewalks, mentioned in Chapter 8, represent such an example. Another project like this is the construction of a recreation center for employees. In situations such as these the judgment of management must replace the quantitative labels that were developed in this chapter.

A further limitation of the capital budgeting process is that it may not predict the total consequences of the decision. Thus the addition of laborsaving machines may create resentment among the remaining employees to such an extent that they engage in an unobservable work slowdown or perhaps in other unobservable acts that are detrimental to the welfare of the firm. While theoretically capital budgeting should include such factors, anticipating all possible consequences of a decision is very difficult. Hence, sound managerial judgment is still necessary when a firm is weighing alternate projects.

Despite the limitations of capital budgeting, a firm that bases its decisions on this procedure is more likely to reach its goals than one that bases its decisions on hunches.

HIGHLIGHTS
OF THIS CHAPTER

The percentage cost of capital should be regarded as an estimate rather than an exact amount. This is because certain assumptions are necessary about future earnings per share and about how the public will capitalize the income if preferred stocks or bonds are issued. Yet even in crude form this concept is significant.

The percentage cost of capital may be defined as the minimum rate of return that a project should earn if the price of a share of common stock is not to fall. If a project earns more than the cost of capital, the price of the common stock will rise. But if a project earns less than the cost of capital, the price of the common stock will fall.

An important point to remember is that common stock and retained profits have a cost of capital, even though it is different from the cost concept in the accounting usage.

Management must decide on one of four major cost of capital rates: (1) weighted average cost, (2) the riskless rate, (3) rates according to the risk class of the asset being acquired, and (4) the borrowing rate. Actually, all of these can be made to work, provided corresponding adjustments are made in expected future annual cash flows.

In the final analysis, the decision maker should use a cost of capital that lies between 8 and 12 percent, unless he has good reasons for using a rate not in this range.

If management uses the capital budgeting process, selecting an unreasonable percentage cost of capital can have serious consequences. If the rate is unrealistically high, projects will be rejected that would have increased the profits and solvency of the firm. On the other hand, if the cost of capital percentage is unrealistically low, projects will be accepted that lower the firm's profitability and solvency.

In conclusion, the cost of capital concept has two main uses. First, it is used as the discount rate when determining the net present value and the index of profitability; second, it is used as a standard of comparison after the internal rate of return has been estimated. If the internal rate of return is greater than the cost of capital, the project is accepted; if the internal rate of return is less than the cost of capital, the project is rejected. It is not necessary to compute the cost of capital if the pay-back period test is used. The cost of capital concept is a vital one in the individual firm, if the capital budgeting process is being used.

9-1. Define the term *weighted average cost of capital*.
REVIEW QUESTIONS

9-2. Suggest several substitute discount rates for the weighted average cost of capital.

9-3. Explain the use of the cost of capital (discount rate) in the following: (a) net present value, (b) index of profitability, (c) internal rate of return (yield), (d) pay-back test.

9-4. If bonds are issued in relatively large amounts, does the price-earnings ratio on the common stock tend to increase or decrease? Why?

9-5. What is meant by *capital rationing*? Why do so many successful firms use this constraint?

REVIEW PROBLEMS   Answers to some of the problems appear at the end of this section. *For each problem, show how you obtained the answer.*

Handwritten margin note: $i(1-t) = i_{post\,tax}$
$6\%(1-.38) = 3.72\%$

9-1. Company M has a short-term bank loan outstanding on which it pays interest of 6 percent. If this firm is in the 38 percent federal income tax bracket, what is the approximate after-tax cost of this source of funds to the company?

9-2. The following data apply to Company J: face value per bond $1,000; face rate of interest 4 percent; maturity date of bond 20 years from now. Assume that the firm is in the 38 percent federal income tax bracket. (a) If the bonds are selling in the market at $1,020, what is the investor's yield to maturity and what is the approximate unweighted cost of capital of the bonds (on an after-tax basis)? (b) If the bonds are selling in the market at $980, what is the investor's yield to maturity and what is the approximate unweighted cost of capital of the bonds (on an after-tax basis)? The investor's yield to maturity is determined by the formula:

Handwritten margin note: Determine yield to maturity of bond. Premium. Disc.

$$Y = \frac{D + [(\$1,000 - M)/N]}{(M + 1,000)/2}$$

Handwritten calculations:
$Y = D + \dfrac{1000 - 1020}{20} = \dfrac{-20}{20}$

$\dfrac{1000 + 1020}{2} = \dfrac{2020}{2}$

$= \dfrac{40 + 20}{1010} = \dfrac{40-1}{1010}$

$= \dfrac{39}{1010} = 3.86\%$

where Y equals investor's yield to maturity, D equals dollar interest received per year by investor, M equals current market price of the bond, and N equals number of years until bond matures.

Handwritten margin note: Bonds 100 .00 .... 50% / CS 100 .50% / 200 T.Cap.

9-3. What is the weighted cost of capital of Firm X, given the following data: market yield on bonds 8 percent; total market value of the bonds $100; tax rate on the firm 50 percent; market value of each share of common stock $10; number of shares of common stock 10; and expected future dividends per share $1. Assume that only stocks and bonds enter into the computations.

Handwritten margin note: $8(1-.5) = .04 \quad .50 \times .04 = .02\% \quad 7\%$
$\dfrac{1}{10} = .10 = .05$

9-4. Assuming that the following data apply to Company N, determine the firm's weighted average cost of capital. (The company is in the 40 percent tax bracket.) Common stock: aggregate market value $4 million; market value per share $25; expected future dividends per share $2.40; investment banking fees per share on new issue $1. Notes payable: average amount due $500,000; average annual interest rate 4 percent. Bank loans: average amount outstanding $500,000; true rate of interest 6 percent. First mortgage bonds: $500,000 face value; coupon rate 5 percent; market value per $1,000 of face value, $980; maturity date 10 years from now.

Handwritten margin note: 5% coupon $\$1000$ bond face. $\$50$

9-5. Given the following information, determine the weighted average cost of capital of Company Z, which is in the 42 percent tax bracket. Bonds outstanding: $100,000 face value; 6 percent face rate of interest (coupon rate); due in 10 years; current market price per $1,000 bond, $960. Bank loan outstanding: $100,000 at 7 percent true rate of interest. Preferred stock: aggregate market value $100,000; market price per share $20; dividends per share $1. Common stock: aggregate market value $500,000; expected future dividends per share $2; current market price per share $12; investment banking fees per share on a new issue $2.

Answers: 9-1, 3.72 percent; 9-2a, 3.86 percent and 2.39 percent, respectively; 9-2b, 4.14 percent and 2.57 percent, respectively; 9-3, 7 percent.

Selling Discount selling yield high

$$9\text{-}2, \quad y_a = \frac{40 + \frac{1000 - 1020}{20 yr}}{\frac{1000 + 1020}{2}}$$

$$y_B = \frac{40 + \frac{1000 - 980}{20 yr}}{\frac{1000 + 980}{2}}$$

$$\frac{990}{}$$

$$y_a = \frac{39}{1010} = 3.86\%$$

$$y_b = \frac{41}{990} = 4.14\%$$

MANAGING THE ASSETS 3

10 Managing Fixed Assets: General Considerations

Fixed assets are especially important because of the magnitude of the expenditures involved and because of the length of time management may have to live with decisions that have resulted in these acquisitions. The importance of the fixed asset area is indicated by the fact that in most firms middle management can make expenditures up to only a certain amount, say $3,000; expenditures beyond this amount may have to be approved by the president. Furthermore, if the expenditure is very large, say $100,000, even the president may need additional approval from the board of directors. In other words, top management reserves for itself many of the really important decisions in the acquisition of fixed assets.

The following will be discussed in this chapter:

1. Owning versus renting assets
2. Selling fixed assets to obtain cash (the sale-lease-back arrangement)
3. Selling idle assets
4. Conserving fixed assets
5. Reminder on the role of capital budgeting
6. Financing specific assets

OWNING VERSUS RENTING ASSETS

Rents Paid

A firm need not own an asset in order to have the use of it, for items of wealth may be rented. When capital is rented, there is an agreement whereby an owner permits, for a rental, a second party to have possession and exclusive use of the property for an agreed period of time. The rent paid by the tenant may be fixed or variable. If fixed, there is an agreement to pay a flat sum each month or year, as, for example, when a firm agrees to pay $300 per month for a storeroom. If, on the other hand, the rent is variable, the amount is contingent on some activity, usually sales. When this plan is in effect, the rental is often a percentage of sales, with a minimum to be paid regardless of volume. When real estate is rented, the variable arrangement protects the landlord in periods of inflation, for the rent increases as the dollar amount of sales increases; also, the landlord is protected during a recession because of the minimum rental that he is entitled to receive regardless of the tenant's sales. The occupant may also find the variable arrangement a satisfactory plan because his rent becomes a semifixed charge instead of a fixed one. Provided that the minimum rental is not too high, a tenant will, in many cases, find the variable arrangement the more satisfactory one.

In recent years there has been a growing tendency to lease many kinds of assets, including rugs, drapes, office furniture, machine tools, trucks, and accounting machines. For example, the Chesapeake and Ohio Railroad rents elaborate computing machines, the rentals being $25,000 a month. In many cases the lessee is given an option to buy the rented property. Thus United States Steel Corporation, which rents elaborate electronic machines, has an option to purchase the equipment and to apply the rentals to the purchase price. Another interesting example of leasing is that the New York Yankees pays rent to the Knights of Columbus, which owns the ground on which Yankee Stadium is built. The practice of renting an asset instead of owning it is increasing in importance, although revisions in the tax law permitting a firm to take larger depreciation allowances may lessen the advantage of leasing (to a tenant).

Several important terms follow:

1. Parties to a lease

  a. *Lessor.* The owner of the property or equipment, he receives the rent.
  b. *Lessee.* The user of the property (or tenant), he pays rent to the owner.

2. Aspects of the lease

  a. *Operating lease.* The lease can be terminated on a stipulated notice; it is often a short-term lease. Examples are: a student who rents an apartment, a family that rents a telephone, and a drugstore that has a one-year lease.
  b. *Financial lease.* The lease is a long-term one that often runs for the life of the asset or covers a period of time sufficient for the lessor to recover his cost by way of rents; it cannot be terminated; it is similar to debt. When American Can Company agrees to rent an office building for thirty years, a financial lease is in effect.
    1. *Net financial lease.* The lessee agrees to pay taxes, insurance, and repairs.
    2. *Gross financial lease.* The lessor agrees to pay taxes, insurance, and repairs.

When the lease expires, in the absence of any agreement to the contrary, the landlord is entitled to all improvements made by the tenant. Assume that Jones has been a tenant of a storeroom for 10 years and that during the period he

Status of Improvements at the Time the Lease Expires

made many improvements, including the addition of new windows and the construction of an attractive entrance. When the lease expires, all these improvements become the property of the landlord unless the lease provides otherwise. In some leases there is a clause stating that the tenant shall be reimbursed for any improvements made. Thus, if an owner leases land for a period of 50 years with the contractual agreement that the tenant will erect a building on the site, there may be a provision in the lease requiring that the tenant be paid the appraised value of the building at the end of 50 years. Clauses requiring that the tenant be compensated for improvements are most likely to appear in long-term leases.

Reasons for Renting instead of Owning Assets

Following are reasons why a firm might rent instead of own capital:

KNOW

Real Estate

1. Many business firms need only a relatively small storeroom or loft, neither of these being purchasable as a unit. This would be particularly true in cities, where the buildings tend to be large. Since a firm might not be able to use the remainder of the building or want to assume responsibility for renting it, the management may decide to rent only a part of the structure.

2. The lease arrangement permits more flexibility in moving to another location. If the property is rented, the tenant is free to move at the expiration of the lease or even before if there is the possibility of subletting the property. On the other hand, if the building were owned and the firm decided to move, the management might be reluctant to make the change if the building had to be sold at a loss.

3. A firm may find that desirable locations *must* be rented, if they are obtainable at all. Thus it might be necessary to rent a storeroom for a proposed drugstore if ideal locations are for rent only—not for sale. Businessmen often find this to be the case when they are seeking a desirable location for a retail store.

Equipment

1. In many cases, a manufacturer will not sell certain kinds of equipment; instead, he will only rent it—IBM being an example. A manufacturer is likely to encourage or insist on the lease arrangement when the unit cost of the equipment is high and when the property is so complex that the manufacturer is expected to provide continuous maintenance service.

2. The lease offers the advantage of placing the risk of obsolescence on the shoulders of the owner. If more efficient equipment becomes available, the tenant need not renew the lease. Obsolescence is especially important in the machine tool field. Kearney & Trecker, a manufacturer of machine tools, advertises that an advantage of leasing equipment from their company is that the lessee assumes no risk of obsolescence.

3. When accompanied by an option to purchase, the lease, in effect, permits the tenant to determine the productivity of the equipment before he purchases it. Kearney and Trecker, for example, advertises that its plan of rental gives an option to buy and that the tenant may exercise this option at any time. The privilege of obtaining machines on a trial basis is especially important when they are complex in nature.

Both Real Estate and Equipment

4. A firm can get along with fewer assets if it rents its buildings, storerooms, or equipment. There are several reasons why this might be important: The owners will not need to place as much of their own funds in the business; the firm will have more funds on hand with which to finance circulating assets; and the firm will not need to plan on raising funds from outside sources, such as bondholders. The possibility of renting capital is especially important during the promotion stage because at this time there is likely to be much difficulty in raising funds.

5. A firm might find it cheaper to rent capital than to own it. In order to determine the lower cost alternative, a businessman would have to study the facts in specific situations. In the case of real estate, professional landlords are often better managers than those who are not expert in this field. Therefore, even after allowing for the profit of a landlord, a businessman may find it cheaper to rent than to own his premises. The same principles may hold true for equipment that is rented. Reo trucks for example, may be rented or purchased. The lessor points out that it can achieve many economies in trucking costs that a small firm cannot. Table 10-1 shows several items that this specialized lessor can obtain at a lower cost than any one lessee.

Truck Ownership	Reo Truck Leasing
Interest	Interest
Depreciation	Depreciation
License Tags	License Tags
Property Tax	Property Tax
F. & T. Insurance	F. & T. Insurance
P.L. & P.D. Insurance	(P.L. & P.D. Insurance)
Collision Insurance	(Collision Insurance)
Painting and Lettering	(Painting and Lettering)
Garaging	(Garaging)
Washing	(Washing)
Polishing	(Polishing)
Gasoline	(Gasoline)
Oil and Grease	(Oil and Grease)
Tires	(Tires)
Maintenance	(Maintenance)
Damage Repairs	(Damage Repairs)
Road Service	(Road Service)
Spare Trucks	(Spare Trucks)
Administration	(Administration)

OUR COSTS WILL BE LOWER THAN YOURS ON MOST, IF NOT ALL, OF THE ITEMS IN PARENTHESES

TABLE 10-1
Truck Operation Costs

Source:
Reo Truck Leasing, Inc., "A New Concept of Truck Leasing" (booklet), p. 11.

6. If the money must be borrowed to buy the real estate or equipment, the lease has the advantage of not placing numerous restrictions on management, as might be the case if a long-term loan were obtained.

7. The management of the firm may save time in discussing various deductions

with agents of the United States Treasury if the property is rented. If the real estate or equipment were owned, there would probably be arguments over certain expenses, such as depreciation and capital expenditures. However, if the capital is rented, the entire rental can be deducted without considerable discussion.

8. Renting real estate or equipment has the advantage of lessening bookkeeping costs. There is no need to keep detailed records on depreciation, repairs, and the many other items that accompany ownership of property.

Reasons for Owning instead of Renting Assets

Following are some of the more important reasons why a firm might elect to own its capital instead of renting it:

Real Estate

1. If the property is owned, the possible problem of having to seek a new location at a disadvantageous time is avoided. Many people are acquainted with retail stores having sales because they "lost their lease." That is, landlords refuse to renew the lease or they ask terms that tenants decide not to accept.

Equipment

1. A firm that owns it equipment is in a position to adapt it to particular needs. For example, a firm that owns its own trucks can make changes in their structure so that coal can be hauled. Such radical changes may be difficult if the equipment is leased.

Both Real Estate and Equipment

2. In some cases, outright ownership will be cheaper than renting the property. As noted previously, this is a problem that has to be decided by analysis of the particular circumstances at hand. However, by eliminating the profit of the landlord, a firm may find that the better alternative is to own rather than to rent real estate and equipment.

3. Assuming that the property is paid for without any borrowing, there is the advantage of owning over renting in that fixed outlays are decreased. If a businessman owns his property, a number of ownership costs become variable expenses—as is true of major repair items. On the other hand, if the property is rented, most leases will require the payment of a minimum fixed sum each year. Businessmen find a certain amount of financial security in having a relatively large proportion of their outlays variable rather than fixed.

Impact of the Lease on Financial Statements

If a comparison is to be made between the statements of different companies, a problem arises when one firm makes extensive use of rented property and the other makes extensive use of borrowed money to finance the purchase of assets. Unless one is careful, a quick inspection of the balance sheets might lead one to think that the company without the debt is the stronger of the two. Insofar as the balance sheet is concerned, a company with debt outstanding appears to be weaker than the company without any debt, other factors being the same. However, this is not necessarily so, for an inspection of the profit and loss statement of the firm that obtains its assets from lessors might indicate that the lessee has heavy rental charges. These might even exceed the interest and principal repayments on the bonds of the other company.

Of special importance in analyzing a capital structure is the method of handling rents paid for the use of facilities. Rents paid constitute a fixed charge just as interest is a fixed charge. Rents and interest charges are very closely related in finance. A firm can issue bonds and use the proceeds to acquire assets, or it can rent the desired facilities. In order to compare the capital structure of one firm with another, the rentals paid must be capitalized at a certain rate, such as 5 percent. Then the sum of the bonds and capitalized rentals of one firm can be compared with the sum of the bonds and capitalized rentals of another firm. Only by capitalizing rentals can a valid comparison be made between two firms—one having heavy interest charges but relatively small rents paid, the other with heavy rental charges but small interest charges.

The *sale–lease-back* arrangement means that a corporation sells some or all of its buildings to a life insurance company, college, or other investor, the agreement stating that the buyer will immediately rent the acquired property to the seller for a long period of time, such as 30 years. In other words, the seller of the property becomes a tenant instead of an owner of the premises. In leasing arrangements of this sort, the tenant (former owner) may agree to pay all the taxes and to keep the property repaired. The tenant usually has the right to renew the lease at the expiration date. Furthermore, the rental for the new period is virtually always at a reduced rate. Some corporations that have sold their buildings are listed in Table 10-2.

SELLING FIXED ASSETS TO OBTAIN CASH: THE SALE-LEASE-BACK ARRANGEMENT

Meaning of the Sale-Lease-back Arrangement

TABLE 10-2 Corporations That Sold Their Buildings

Seller	Type of Property Sold	Buyer
Fruehauf Trailer Company	Plant	Equitable Life
Lit Brothers	Store buildings	University of Pennsylvania
Allied Stores Corporation	Store buildings	Union College

One of the most famous was the sale of buildings by Allied Stores to Union College. Union College, seeking a desirable investment, decided to invest in real estate. The deal was handled by having Union's Real Property Corporation acquire title to the assets. Allied Stores sold the buildings at a loss of $340,000, this loss being deductible for tax purposes. Union College agreed to rent the buildings to Allied Stores for a period of 30 years. Allied Stores had an option to renew the lease at the end of the 30 years. The provisions of Allied Stores' lease are typical of other leases of this kind.

Originally, colleges with endowment funds were the main purchasers of buildings as investments. However, life insurance companies are now the chief type of investor in the sale-lease-back arrangement. At first, department store buildings were the only important kind sold under the plan. Recently other types of buildings have been sold, such as laboratories, manufacturing plants, and office buildings. There have been some cases in which the life insurance company has built to the tenant's specifications. As part of the agreement, the tenant signs a long-term lease.

Reasons Corporations Sell Their Buildings

There are two main reasons why corporations may decide to sell their buildings to life insurance companies, colleges, and other investors:

1. *To raise additional cash.* Selling fixed assets brings cash into the business on advantageous terms. The cash is raised without issuing stocks or bonds or borrowing from banks. Companies that have been in need of more cash because of the rise in the price level have found the sale-lease-back arrangement very satisfactory.

2. *To gain a tax advantage.* This advantage may be demonstrated by comparing the sale of assets with a loan obtained through a bond issue. If a building is sold, the corporation must pay a fixed rental to the new owner of the premises, this rental being deductible in full for tax purposes. On the other hand, if a loan were obtained through a bond issue, only the interest would be an allowable expense, the payments on the principal not being allowed as a deductible item. In summary, the sale-lease-back arrangement has the very decided advantage of indirectly permitting the amortization of principal to become a deduction for tax purposes.

When a building is owned outright, for tax purposes the corporation can deduct such items as depreciation, repairs, insurance, and other similar expenses. Likewise, when a building is used by a corporation under the sale-lease-back arrangement, the corporation may have to pay for repairs, insurance, and perhaps other expenses that are agreed on in the lease. These items are also deductible for income tax purposes. Therefore, the rental charges for a leased property provide a tax advantage only to the extent that they exceed the expenses that would be deductible if the property were owned.

In the majority of cases, the first reason is the more important; that is, many corporations sell their assets to raise cash on advantageous terms.

Possible Dangers of the Sale-Lease-back Arrangement

Perhaps the greatest danger in the sale-lease-back arrangement is that the corporation may find it difficult to meet the heavy fixed rentals in a period of declining revenue. A number of corporations have found it difficult to pay their high rental charges (drug companies and cigar stores being examples of companies that encountered this difficulty). Another minor difficulty is that the Internal Revenue Service may hold the sale-lease-back arrangement to be a loan in disguise. If this should be the case, the entire rental would not be deductible as an expense. Despite the possible disadvantages, a number of companies have found the sale-lease-back arrangement a desirable method of raising cash.

Problem[1]

Upon request, Company X will buy an asset and immediately lease it to the firm making the request. Company X, the lessor, assumes no responsibility for repairs, taxes, or insurance on such assets; the tenant assumes these obligations. Company X receives such a request from Company Y. The asset would cost Company X $39,927 and would be rented to Company Y for five years, at the end of which time the asset would be considered worthless. If Company X desires to earn 8 percent on its money, how much annual rent should it charge Company Y?

Solution

Step 1. Use Table 8-2. The factor at the intersection of the fifth-year row and the 8 percent column is 3.9927.
   Step 2.

$$3.9927X = \$39,927$$
$$X = \$10,000$$

Answer: An annual rent of $10,000 would give the desired return.

Problem

A lessee has rented a property that he knows has a cost of $4,917.30; the property has a life of six years and the tenant pays an annual rent of $1,000. What rate of interest is the owner earning on his investment?

Solution

This is a capital budgeting problem; short-cut methods should be used rather than trial and error methods.
   Step 1. $4,917.30 ÷ $1,000 = 4.9173.
   Step 2. Begin with the sixth-year row and move to the right until the factor of 4.9173 is found. Then look to the top of the column; the rate of interest is 6 percent.
   Answer: 6 percent is being earned on the investment (this is also the rate of interest being paid by the lessee on the transaction).

SELLING IDLE ASSETS

In addition to economizing in the amount of cash, accounts receivable, and inventory, a firm should economize in the use of items such as land, equipment, and buildings. In any business idle assets should be sold for cash and the cash should be channeled into more productive assets or the funds should be withdrawn from the firm. Idle and obsolete trucks, unused buildings, and unused typewriters in storage should be liquidated for their auction value unless there is some special reason for keeping them. In addition to receiving needed cash, certain expenses of the company might decrease—property taxes and fire insurance premiums, for example. Of course, in economizing in the use of assets,

1. In this and the next problem, assume first rent is payable at the end of the first year.

the profit position of the firm should not be jeopardized; that is, the management should be reasonably sure that there is no further need for the fixed asset.

CONSERVING THE FIXED ASSETS

Risk management for fixed assets means establishing policies and procedures that will protect the firm against the hazards that might dissipate the fund of value represented by these assets. The major courses of action used to preserve the assets are these:

1. Establish a sound depreciation policy
2. Use insurance and establish funds and reserves for losses
3. Provide an adequate repair policy
4. Formulate a replacement policy
5. Design a meaningful set of preventive actions

The method that a firm uses to depreciate its assets affects the conservation of capital and the period in which federal income taxes are paid.

If no depreciation were ever recorded, profits would be overstated and profit distributions might include a return of principal. In time such a practice would lead to a gradual liquidation of the firm. In order to prevent this from happening, depreciation is recorded so that sufficient funds (the funds not paid in dividends) could be available for replacing the depreciated item, even though the funds may not be used to purchase assets identical to the ones being depreciated.

The effect of recording depreciation is to make costs larger and net profits smaller. Or, to state the matter in another way, depreciation is a noncash expense. Recording depreciation has as its ultimate effect the lessening of the amount of dividends that stockholders can possibly receive. In this sense, some cash has been "saved." However, recording depreciation does not guarantee that there will be cash available to replace assets when they no longer serve the needs of the business. Management may instead spend the retained cash on other items—repairs, repayment of bank loans, or expansion of inventories.

A second method of conserving the fixed assets is to carry insurance on the property that will indemnify the company in the event of certain kinds of losses, such as fire, explosion, and damage caused by riots. Or, in lieu of insurance, the firm may establish reserves and funds to pay for physical destruction. United States Steel Corporation is an example of a firm that uses the fund-and-reserve method of coping with physical losses on its properties. The insurance program on fixed assets is integrated with the insurance program on circulating assets, as well as the overall risk management of the firm.

A third method of conserving capital is to have a carefully designed policy on repairs. Some firms take great pains to engage in a preventive repair policy; other firms prefer to complete repairs as needed; still others attempt to average repairs over a period of time and thus try to stabilize profits; and still other firms integrate repairs with the amount of depreciation. This latter point means that a firm might expect low repairs in the early years when depreciation charges are high and high repairs in later years when depreciation charges are low. This arrangement results in a rather steady amount of charges to each year's revenue. In any event, the amount of money spent on repairs each year is not always left entirely to chance; instead, it may be subject to some control on the part of management.

A fourth method is to establish a replacement policy that leads to increased profits for the company. For example, the Sharon Steel Corporation announced that its capital expenditures for a two-year period would be $25 million. The firm went on to state that the company was not seeking an increase in capacity through this expenditure. Instead, it was modernizing and updating equipment to obtain increased efficiency. Large companies have a staff of employees who are constantly studying the possibility of replacing one asset with another. New machines may be superior to the ones already owned because of savings in labor costs and repair costs. In making a decision on whether to replace an asset, only future events should be considered; the fact that an old machine is still largely undepreciated is of no importance. The only significant point is whether the substitution will increase the net profits in the future. Past mistakes in buying the wrong machine or in constructing a building in a poor location are over and done with, and the sunk costs arising from these decisions should not affect the decision to make a change.

A fifth method of meeting risk is for the management to design a meaningful set of preventive actions. This phase of management includes the installation of fire sprinklers, the hiring of night watchmen, and the use of fire-resistant materials. Not only are such actions desirable in themselves but they may result in lower insurance premiums. These internal controls will play an important role in conserving the assets of the firm.

REMINDER ON THE ROLE OF CAPITAL BUDGETING

In planning for the expansion of fixed assets, the reader is reminded of the importance of capital budgeting as a decision tool. The capital budgeting process is useful in comparing the desirability of assets as well as in giving guidance on the amount by which total assets should expand. Several important techniques within the capital budgeting process are the yield method, the net present value method, and the pay-back test. (The yield is also known as the internal rate of return.)

Problem

Company X is considering buying a fixed asset that will have a cash cost of $3,889.60; the asset will have a life of five years, and it will result in annual cash benefits of $1,000 per year. Company X has a cost of capital of 6 percent. Determine (a) the yield; (b) the net present value; and (c) the pay-back period.

Solution

(a) The yield is 9 percent, for this is the rate that discounts the annual cash flows of $1,000 back to a present value equal to the cost of the asset. (The reader should use the short-cut method in arriving at this answer rather than the trial and error method.) (b) The net present value is found as follows:

Present value of cash benefits (6 percent)	
4.2123 × $1,000	$4,212.30
Less present value of cost	3,889.60
Net present value	$ 322.70

(c) The pay-back period is 3.9 years ($3,889.60 ÷ $1,000).

Problem Company G is considering purchasing an asset that will result in annual cash benefits of $1,000 per year for four years; the asset has no scrap value. If the firm has a cost of capital of 8 percent, what is the most that the firm could afford to pay for the project, assuming the project must earn at least the firm's cost of capital?

Solution *Step 1.* Find the intersection of the row for the fourth year and the 8 percent column. The factor at the intersection is 3.3121.

  Step 2. Let X equal the maximum purchase price.

$$X = 3.3121 \times \$1,000$$
$$X = \$3,312.10$$

The most the firm could afford to pay is $3,312.10; if the firm paid more, the return on the asset would be less than 8 percent; if it paid less, the asset would yield more than 8 percent.

Problem Company M is considering buying an asset for $10,000. The asset has a life of four years and has no scrap value. The annual cash benefits are $3,000 per year. Based on the yield test, should the firm purchase the asset?

Solution This problem cannot be solved because the firm's cost of capital is not given.

Problem Company J is considering buying an asset that has a cash cost of $8,000. The asset has a life of three years and has no scrap value. The firm's cost of capital is 10 percent. The asset is expected to have annual cash benefits of $2,000 per year. Based on the yield test, the net present value test, and the pay-back test, should the asset be purchased?

Solution By inspection, it is apparent that the firm will not even recover its capital. The firm must spend $8,000 to earn $6,000. The project should be rejected immediately. Since the firm does not recover its capital, the proposed expenditure will fail the three tests mentioned. It is not necessary to proceed with all the computations to know that the project will fail on all three tests.

Problem Asset M will cost $8,000 and asset Z will cost $8,000. The annual cash benefits of each are as follows:

	1st Year	2nd Year
M	$ 5,000	$10,000
Z	$10,000	$ 5,000

On the basis of the information shown, which asset should be given priority?

Asset Z should be given priority because the firm has the use of cash sooner. *Solution*

Insofar as the financial manager is concerned, the rent versus purchase decision is a financial one. This means that the basic need for an asset has already been demonstrated and that the management must decide which of the following financial alternatives to use: (a) buy the asset and finance it through borrowing, or (b) rent the asset. *FINANCING SPECIFIC ASSETS*

If the money is borrowed to acquire the fixed asset, the proceeds of the loan are used to pay the seller. Under the borrowing arrangement, the new owner of the asset can deduct for tax purposes both interest on the loan and depreciation on the asset. After the loan is repaid, the owner firm has title to the asset.

On the other hand, if the asset is acquired on a lease basis, the tenant pays rent for an agreed period of time. The entire rental is usually deductible for income tax purposes. At the end of the rental period, the lessee has no title to the equipment.

An analytical tool that gives guidance on which financial alternative to use is that of the net present value test. Although the net present value model provides guidance in deciding whether to buy or rent, unfortunately it does not provide a precise answer, because the vital information plugged into the model is largely a matter of conjecture. Among the information that is a matter of conjecture is: (a) the discount rate used to discount future cash flows, (b) the terminal value of the equipment, (c) future changes in the federal income tax structure, and (d) the rate of obsolescence caused by advances in technology.

Because of the large expenditures usually associated with fixed assets, this area of decision making is especially important. To give guidance to management, capital budgeting procedures may be used. The yield method, the net present value method, and the pay-back test are all useful techniques for determining the direction of optimum expansion, replacement, and evaluative policies. **HIGHLIGHTS OF THIS CHAPTER**

The lease enables a firm to have the use of real estate and equipment without having to purchase them. The lessee commits himself to pay a rental for the exclusive use of the property. There are several reasons for renting instead of owning capital: the owners have less of their own funds tied up in the business; the renting arrangement may be cheaper; the property may be available only on a lease basis. On the other hand, there are good reasons for owning instead of renting property: in some cases it is cheaper to own than to rent; fixed charges are decreased; and in the case of storerooms, the businessman will not run the risk of having to vacate when his lease expires.

A lease has some of the characteristics of debt, the main one being that the tenant commits himself to pay a fixed minimum rental for an agreed period of time. However, a lease is different from debt in the legal sense and therefore has received separate treatment in this chapter.

A firm in need of cash will find that selling its buildings is an alternative to outside financing. If a building is sold, additional working capital is obtained without having to pay interest on the money.

REVIEW QUESTIONS

10-1. Distinguish between the lessor and the lessee.

10-2. What is the difference between a gross lease and a net lease?

10-3. A board of directors is considering engaging in a sale-lease-back arrangement. What advantages and disadvantages of this transaction should the directors consider before making a final decision?

10-4. Arrange for an interview with a real estate agent and seek answers to these questions: (a) What business properties or storerooms are for rent? (b) How much is the monthly rental? (c) Is the rental a fixed amount, one based on sales, or one based on a combination of the previous two? (d) How long will the lease run? (e) Who pays for such items as heat, taxes, and insurance? (f) Who pays for repairs during occupancy? (g) Are there any restrictions imposed (by either the landlord or by zoning laws) on the kind of business that may be conducted on the property?

10-5. Visit an auto rental agency or a car dealer and try to obtain the answer to these questions: (a) What are the advantages (to a business firm) of renting a fleet of automobiles rather than owning such a fleet? (b) How is the monthly rental determined? (c) Who pays for gasoline, oil, and repairs? (d) Who pays for the major kinds of insurance? (e) Who is responsible if the car is wrecked? (f) In your opinion, what are some of the disadvantages (to a business firm) of renting instead of owning the cars?

REVIEW PROBLEMS[2]

Answers to some of the problems appear at the end of this section. *For each problem, show how you obtained the answer.*

10-1. A lessee has rented a property that he knows has a cost of $36,048; the property has a life of five years and the tenant pays an annual rental of $10,000. What rate of interest is the owner earning on his investment?

10-2. Upon request, Company P will buy an asset immediately and lease it to

2. In problems 10-1 and 10-2, assume that the first year's rent is paid at the end of the first year, not the beginning of that year.

the firm making the request. Company P assumes no responsibility for repairs, taxes, or insurance on such assets; the tenant assumes these obligations. Company P receives such a request from Company G. The asset would cost Company P $31,699 and would be rented to Company G for four years, at the end of which time the asset would be worthless. If Company P desired to earn 10 percent on its money, how much in annual rentals should it charge Company G?

10-3. Company Q is considering purchasing an asset that will result in annual cash benefits of $1,000 a year for six years; the asset has no scrap value. If the firm has a cost of capital of 10 percent, what is the most the firm could afford to pay for the project, assuming the firm must earn at least the cost of capital rate?

10-4. Company R is considering buying an asset that has a cash cost of $5,000. The asset has a life of four years and it has no scrap value. The firm's cost of capital is 10 percent. The asset is expected to have annual cash benefits of $1,000 per year. Based on the yield test, the net present value test, and the pay-back test, should the asset be purchased? The answer to this problem can be determined by inspection. Why?

10-5. Asset X will cost $5,000 and asset Y will cost $5,000. The annual cash benefits of each arc as follows:

	1st Year	2nd Year
X	$5,000	$2,000
Y	$2,000	$5,000

Which asset should be given priority, on the basis of the information shown?

10-6. Company A whose cost of capital is 6 percent, is attempting to determine whether to give asset X or asset Y preference. The following data apply to each:

	X	Y
Cash cost	$911.19	$1,354.88
Life of project	4 years	4 years
Annual cash benefits (net cash inflow)	$300	$400

Required: Rank the projects, using (a) the yield method, (b) the net present value method, and (c) the pay-back test.

10-7. The X Company, whose balance sheets (before sale of assets) is given below, sells $50,000 of its fixed assets. The proceeds are used to increase inventory by $10,000, to increase cash by $10,000, and to decrease accounts payable by $30,000.

Cash	$ 25,000	Bank loans	$ 30,000
Accounts receivable	25,000	Accounts payable	40,000
Inventories	25,000	Net worth	105,000
Fixed assets	100,000		
Total	$175,000	Total	$175,000

Required: (a) Prepare a *pro forma* balance sheet, (b) Determine the current ratio before and after the transaction, (c) Determine the net working capital before and after the transaction, (d) Determine the ratio of debt to net worth before and after the transaction, (e) If selling fixed assets is so advantageous, why is it that more firms do not engage in this practice?

10-8. Five years ago Company B bought a machine for $1,000. The machine has a life of 10 years; it has no scrap value; and it is depreciated on a straight-line basis. Today the management decides to acquire a more efficient machine for $2,000 and sells the old one for $100. If the firm is in the 50 percent tax bracket, how much is the net cash outlay (for capital budgeting purposes)?

10-9. Company M, a large firm, has $10,000 which it is considering investing in alternative A or alternative B. Alternative A is to invest in a fixed asset. If there is prosperity, the fixed asset will earn 10 percent; if there is a recession, the fixed asset will earn 3 percent. There is a 70 percent chance of prosperity and a 30 percent chance of recession. On the other hand, the firm may invest the $10,000 in alternative B, which consists of placing the money in government bonds on which 4 percent can be earned with 100 percent certainty. All the above percentage returns are on an after-tax basis. If the management uses expected value as its decision criterion, where should it place the $10,000?

10-10. Company C, a small firm, owns an airplane; it is considering the advisability of insuring the plane against loss. If the plane crashes, it will be a total loss. If the insurance policy is purchased, the premium is $2,000; if the insurance is not purchased, the expected loss is $1,500. The $1,500 was obtained in the usual manner of multiplying probabilities by losses. Should the firm buy the insurance, even though the premium is higher than the expected loss? Give reasons for your answer.

10-11. Company Z, with a cost of capital of 10 percent (the discount rate) buys an asset for $1,500. The firm pays $500 immediately, $500 at the end of the first year, and $500 at the end of the second year. What is the present value of the cost of the asset?

10-12. Company L enters into a contract whereby the firm receives $1,000 immediately, $1,000 at the end of the first year, and $1,000 at the end of the second year. If the firm has a cost of capital of 12 percent (the assumed discount rate), what is the present value of the receipts?

10-13. A firm buys an asset for $2,000. The asset will yield net cash benefits of $2,000 during the fourth, fifth, and sixth years. If the firm's cost of capital is 12 percent, what is the net present value of the project?

10-14. Company T has just purchased a machine for $1,000 in cash. The net cash savings are expected to be $500 a year for three years. The machine has a life of three years; the estimated junk value of the machine at the end of its life is $200. If the firm's cost of capital is 10 percent, what is the net present value of the project?

Answers: 10-1, approximately 12 percent; 10-2, $10,000; 10-3, $4,355.30; 10-9, alternative A, since A's expected return is $790 while B's is only $400; 10-10, yes; 10-11, $1,367.75; 10-12, $2,690.10; 10-13, $1,419.20; 10-14, $393.66.

James Robinson is president of the Claster Company, a firm whose main activities are selling building supplies to contractors and retailers. The firm was started in 1971 and has been expanding rapidly. The president believes that his company could expand its sales if it could increase its current assets. During the past year the firm's profits came to 20 percent of its total current assets. Hence, current assets are a precious item.

CASE ON LEASING VERSUS OWNING EQUIPMENT

The president has decided that his firm is in need of an $8,000 machine that will cut and drill holes in a special product—steel supports for basements in homes where floors are sagging. This cutting and drilling machine is subject to rapid obsolescence because of improving technology. Furthermore, Robinson is not sure that his firm will continue to manufacture the special steel supports beyond the second year from now. His problem is to make a decision on whether to rent or buy the machine under consideration.

If the machine is leased, the annual rental would be $2,000 a year for a five-year period, except that the tenant could cancel the agreement at the beginning of any fiscal period. The lessee would be responsible for repairs. Robinson is aware of the fact that he will pay a total of $10,000 for the machine that he could purchase for $8,000 cash. The extra $2,000 is the penalty he must pay for being a tenant rather than an owner.

The other possibility is to borrow $8,000 from a bank and pay cash for the machine. Under this alternative, the firm would repay the bank at the rate of $1,600 a year, plus 6 percent interest on the unpaid balance. The scrap value of the machine at the end of five years is estimated to be zero. If the machine were purchased, straight-line depreciation would be used for tax purposes.

The Claster Company is in the 50 percent federal income tax bracket.

Required:

1. Estimate the annual net cash outflow (lease payments minus tax deduction for the rentals) under the leasing arrangement. Estimate the net annual cash outlay under the purchasing arrangement (payment to the bank less tax deductions given for the interest and depreciation). Estimate the total cumulative cash outlays at the end of the fifth year for each of the alternatives.

2. Discuss the general pros and cons of the two alternatives. Which alternative would you select? Give your reasons.

Managing Working Capital— Capital— Cash (I)

The proportion of current assets and fixed assets to total assets varies considerably from one industry to another. In manufacturing, current assets constitute 53 percent of total assets; in public utilities, current assets constitute only 12 percent of total assets; and in retailing, current assets constitute 68 percent of total assets. The nature of the service or product sold determines to a large extent the relative importance of current and fixed assets. The proportion of current and fixed assets to total assets has a twofold significance—it affects the amount of officer time devoted to each of the two classes and it affects the kind of financing used. The three main current assets are cash, accounts receivable, and inventories.

Cash performs a number of functions. It makes possible the payment of money by check; it acts as a storage depot for earmarked funds, such as those to be used to buy a building; it is a reservoir from which funds may be withdrawn to meet emergencies, such as when a flood damages a plant and there is an immediate need for repairs; and it provides a storehouse for purchasing power to take advantage of profitable opportunities, such as buying a large amount of inventory at a bargain price.

The following will be discussed in this chapter:

1. Basic considerations in managing cash
2. Lockbox banking
3. Seasonal current asset requirements
4. Borrowing from commercial banks

One philosophy is to keep a generous amount of cash in banks so that the firm will be prepared for emergencies and for opportunities to absorb other companies and to buy large quantities of goods at reduced prices. Montgomery Ward is an example of a firm that carried relatively large cash balances before the new management changed the policy. Generally speaking, only the larger firms are able to maintain relatively high cash balances; many smaller firms are so pressed for cash that idle money is spent for additional assets, advertising, and research. On the other hand, many companies believe that although a reasonable amount of cash adds to a firm's debt-paying ability, excess cash for any extended period of time is largely a wasted resource because it is not earning a return. A wise move is to remove this idle cash and invest it in suitable short-term outlets. Thus the Chesapeake and Ohio Railroad Company plans its cash needs very carefully, and when it has excess cash, the money is invested in government securities. This firm had $990,000 of surplus cash; this was invested in Treasury bills for one day and earned interest of $104.17. Many of the large corporations follow a similar policy. The trend is to withdraw a large part of the idle balances from banks and to place the money in the short-term money market. This arrangement earns a return for the firm and does not destroy liquidity, because the instruments can be sold if necessary.

Efficiency in the Use of Cash

In the final analysis, the amount of sales is probably the most important factor in influencing the level of cash over a period of time. As the level of sales increases, the firm most likely will need additional cash to conduct the higher scale of operations. As a measure of the efficiency with which a firm uses its cash, the cash velocity test may be used:

$$\text{Cash velocity} = \frac{\text{Annual sales}}{\text{Average cash balance}}$$

If sales are $1,000 and the average cash balance is $100, the cash velocity is 10. For example, Raytheon Company, through more effective cash planning, increased its cash velocity from 28.8 to 52.7. This situation was the result of cash balances not expanding as rapidly as sales. Although the cash velocity ratio has pitfalls, the guarded statement may be made that if a firm has sufficient funds to pay its debts, a relatively high cash velocity is desirable.

Problem

Company Z, with annual sales of $1 million, is a heavy user of bank loans to finance current assets. The firm, through a more efficient billing system and by waiting until the last minute to write payroll checks, is able to increase its cash turnover from 10 to 20. If the company uses the extra cash to repay bank loans on which they are charged 6 percent interest, by how much are expenses reduced?

Solution

The increased turnover means that the average cash balance needed is now $50,000 instead of $100,000. Hence, an extra $50,000 is freed for managerial use. If management uses the money to repay bank loans, interest expenses are reduced by $3,000 (6 percent of $50,000).

The Cash Budget— Minimum Balances

The cash budget is the indispensable tool for managing cash, since this forward-looking statement takes into account the interplay of transactions. If the plans call for an increase in sales, all of the current assets are likely to be affected. For example, if credit sales will increase in the near future, the first impact is that cash on hand will decline because the company must pay for the goods that are sold before it receives the receipts from the sale. Similarly, a change in the amount of inventory to be held will affect not only cash and accounts receivable but also the amount of fixed assets. It is difficult to keep track of these inter-relationships without placing the variables, in writing, in the form of a cash budget.

There is, in addition, the policy matter of the minimum cash balance to be maintained. In establishing the minimum, consideration is given to the amount needed for clearing checks as well as for an emergency fund. This emergency portion becomes frozen and is in some respects similar to a fixed asset; that is, it is committed permanently to the firm's operations. Earmarking part of the cash account is a sound precautionary measure because of the considerable number of events that may cause a slowdown in cash intake. For example, general business conditions may result in customers being unable to pay their debts on the agreed dates or may result in a decrease in customers' orders, thus slackening the rate of conversion of inventory into cash; even in prosperous times, the selling depart-ment may not be selling enough goods to maintain a reasonable rate of con-version of inventory into cash; and the credit department may have granted credit to customers who are slower in paying their debts than had been ex-pected. While businessmen are fully aware that a low cash balance endangers the solvency of the firm, they are also aware of the fact that a large cash balance means lost interest on the funds. The minimum level of cash that is finally selected affects the amount of borrowing that will be required as well as the amount of excess cash that is available for whatever purposes management deems appropriate.

One phase of directing the use of working capital is to protect the company against theft and loss of cash and securities. The solution to this problem has two aspects: the use of preventive measures and of insurance. The use of pre-ventive measures means the establishment of procedures that will quickly bring to light any theft on the part of employees and that will place responsibility for the missing asset. As for the second point, many companies carry insurance that will reimburse the firm if cash or securities are stolen by an employee or by burglars, or if cash or securities disappear under mysterious circumstances. The process of taking out insurance to protect against loss caused by dishonest employees is called "bonding the employees," and the employees whose activi-ties are covered by such a policy are called "bonded employees." The use of insurance to protect the firm against loss of cash and securities is a widespread business practice.

Conserving the Cash against Loss

In recent years some large firms have attempted to obtain faster use of checks already mailed by customers. This is done by adopting a relatively new service

LOCKBOX BANKING

Purpose

Lock Box
Banking

called *lockbox banking*, offered by commercial banks. Let us first illustrate the normal lag between the time a customer remits a check and the time when the recipient firm actually has the use of the money and then show how lockbox banking shortens this time interval. To demonstrate the normal arrangement, assume that a customer in Texas mails his check to a New York City manufacturer. A three-day period may elapse before the check arrives in this city. The New York manufacturer may need another full day to record the check on its books. Then, after depositing the check in a New York City bank, the manufacturing firm may have to wait two more days before it can use the deposited money. Thus there may be a lag of six or seven days before the New York manufacturer has the use of the money. This situation is likely to be true of many hundreds of checks originating in other parts of the country.

Lockbox banking is a method of shortening the lag between the mailing of checks and time when the intended receiver has the use of the money. First, the New York manufacturer enters into an agreement with a large bank in each major region of the country, which acts as a central point of collection for receivables from that region. Then the New York manufacturer instructs all its customers, by a notation on the invoice, to send their checks to a certain box number at the appropriate regional bank. The staff at the bank opens the mail addressed to the New York manufacturer's box number, deposits the checks to the account of the manufacturer, and then telegraphs to the manufacturer the amount of the total daily deposit. Also, the regional bank sends by airmail to the New York manufacturer the name of each specific customer and the amount that he has paid on his invoice. The manufacturer then posts to his records from the data received by airmail from the regional bank. The gist of all this is that the New York manufacturer has the use of the funds in about three days rather than six or seven.

Having the use of the funds several days sooner is important to the New York manufacturer. If the firm is receiving an average daily amount of $40,000 under the normal method of collecting accounts receivable, a speed-up of three days means that the firm has an extra $120,000 in its bank account. Not all of this is available for spending, however, as the regional bank might insist on a compensating balance of, say, $60,000 as reimbursement for its services for acting as a collection center. (A compensating balance is a bank balance in the form of a demand deposit that a business firm owns but leaves dormant. The bank can earn interest on the $60,000, which is either lent to its customers or invested in securities. Most commercial banks prefer to be reimbursed for their services in the form of a dormant checking account rather than in fees.) But even if part of the funds are frozen in the form of a compensating balance, the New York manufacturing firm has an extra $60,000 which may be used to expand inventory, to acquire U.S. government bonds, or for some other purpose. Lockbox banking, therefore, has as its main aim the acceleration of the movement of accounts receivable toward cash.

Lockbox banking procedure gives additional advantages to the business firm. It reduces the exposure to credit losses by expediting the time at which data are posted to ledgers; it reduces overhead costs because of the clerical work done by the bank in receiving, processing, endorsing, and depositing remittance checks; and it facilitates auditing control by divorcing remittances from the accounting department. These further advantages must be given consideration when weighing the cost of entering into lockbox banking agreements.

Problem

Company L, located in New York, has annual credit sales of $18 million in Texas. The firm is considering lockbox banking. Company L has average receipts of $50,000 per day ($18 million ÷ 360 days). After making a study, the firm has concluded that it has an average float of seven days and that this could be reduced to three days if lockbox banking were adopted. The Texas bank that would handle the process insists on a balance of $100,000 for its services. If Company L uses the freed funds to repay its New York bank loans, on which 6 percent is paid, how much would be saved in interest.

Solution

$50,000 per day X 4 days = $200,000 (four days saved)

$200,000 − $100,000 = $100,000 (the saving in float less the regional bank's requirement of a balance of $100,000 for its services)

$100,000 at 6 percent = $6,000

Answer: Company L would save $6,000 in interest.

Lock Box Banking

SEASONAL CURRENT ASSET REQUIREMENTS

The use of short-term credit to finance current assets is considered sound financial policy because these assets will be converted into cash in the near future, thus providing the funds with which to pay creditors. Conservative financial policy dictates that short-term credit should not be used to finance permanently a major amount of fixed assets. The reason is that fixed assets are not intended to be converted into cash, thereby creating the problem of finding sources of cash to meet maturing short-term debt. However, a number of companies, such as public utilities, have borrowed from banks for the temporary financing of fixed assets; later, bonds or shares were issued and the proceeds used to repay the banks. Using short-term credit on a temporary basis to finance the acquisition of fixed assets is a sound arrangement.

The amount of current assets that a firm needs at its low point of operations is called *permanent current assets*. At certain seasons of the year, a firm may expand its total circulating assets. The amount of expansion in total current assets caused by seasonal factors is called *temporary current assets*. Short-term credit is especially suitable for financing a temporary expansion of circulating assets (see Figure 11-1).

Permanent current assets

Temporary Current asset.

BORROWING FROM COMMERCIAL BANKS

Selecting the Bank

The selection of a bank should be given careful thought, since, once the decision is made, it is improbable that a switch to another institution will be made. If the business is large, it may want to deal with two or more commercial banks. However, the smaller firms tend to limit their affiliation to one institution. When

FIGURE 11-1
Financing
Permanent
and Temporary
Assets

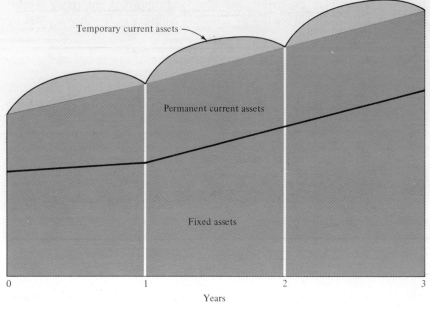

Temporary current assets

Permanent current assets

Fixed assets

0   1   2   3

Years

Code

Financed by short-term credit

Financed by ownership sources and by long- and intermediate-term credit

he is selecting a bank, a businessman will want satisfactory answers to such questions as these:

How much will the bank charge for checking account facilities?

Is the bank safe? Accounts are insured on only the first $20,000. Therefore, a company could lose much of its cash if the bank failed.

Can the bank supply special services that might be needed—for example, financing export shipments?

Do the officers appear favorably inclined toward making loans?

Is the bank large enough to make the size of loans that will be required?

Are the bank's officers reasonably well informed on the nature of the industry's financial and operating problems?

Is the bank's location convenient for making deposits?

Will the bank's officers cooperate in obtaining credit references for the depositor and in giving credit references on him?

Are the directors of any competitors on the board of directors of the bank?

In small towns, where there are usually only one or two banks, the selection is relatively simple, and the decision is based on friendship with the officers of one of the institutions. In larger cities, where there are more banks from which to choose, the selection is more likely to be based on impersonal factors.

After a bank has been selected, a businessman should cultivate a business friendship with some of the main officers of the financial institution and, if possible, with several members of the bank's board of directors. Among other advantages, friendly relationships may make it easier to obtain loans and favorable credit references. It is not difficult to become acquainted with bank officers, who are understandably anxious to know their customers better. *Cultivating Business Relations with Bankers*

A businessman should keep his banker posted on his major financial decisions, such as plans to expand or to take on new products. Also, he should give his banker his latest financial statements for the bank's credit files. The relationship should be maintained in an atmosphere of full disclosure; that is, unfavorable as well as favorable information should be given to the banker. Any attempt to withhold unfavorable information will make the banker distrustful of all data given to him.

Another concrete way of initiating and maintaining favorable relations with bankers is to keep a reasonably adequate balance in a checking account. The bank can invest this balance and earn a return on it. Although substantial balances please bankers, an excessive amount in the checking account means idle capital which is not contributing to the earnings of the depositor. Just how much should be kept on deposit is a matter for the management of each firm to decide.

A banker will usually study three aspects of the transaction before he grants the loan: the character of the applicant, the use for which the proceeds are intended, and the sources of funds with which to repay the loan. *The Banker's Investigation of the Applicant*

Before a banker will grant a loan, he must be assured that the debt will be repaid. In arriving at his conclusion, the first factor taken into consideration is the character of the borrower. Character encompasses honesty and a reputation for fair dealing. In some cases, a quick decision can be made if the applicant for credit is well known. On the other hand, there are many cases in which the banker cannot obtain much information on the borrower. In the absence of any glaring defect in a person's character, the banker will have to assume that the borrower is honest. *Character*

The banker will always want to know how the borrower intends to use the proceeds of the loan. The lender will be more inclined to make the loan if the money is to be used to expand inventory or to acquire more efficient equipment. On the other hand, if the proceeds are to be used to speculate in commodities, it is almost certain that the banker will frown on the loan. Whether the banker thinks the use of the proceeds is a worthy one depends not only on the firm's strength but also on economic and competitive conditions in the country. If the banker thinks business in general will decline, he might reject a loan that would be granted during a business upswing. *Use of the Proceeds*

The banker will make inquiries to determine where the borrower will obtain the cash to repay the loan. *Sources of Funds to Repay the Bank Loan*

Self-Liquidating Loans If the loan is self-liquidating, cash will be generated which can be used to repay it. In other words, the borrower uses the borrowed funds to acquire assets that will be converted into cash within a short period of time and in the normal course of business operations. For example, a ninety-day loan to acquire inventory during the Christmas season would be self-liquidating if the merchandise is sold and the proceeds are available to repay the bank loan. However, not all bank loans are self-liquidating. For example, a loan by a bank to a firm for the purpose of buying typewriters is not self-liquidating because the typewriters will not be converted into cash in the normal course of business operations. A loan whose proceeds are used to acquire fixed assets is often called a *capital loan*. When a loan of this sort is made, the bank expects the borrower's earning power to be sufficient to repay the loan. Banks prefer self-liquidating loans because their chances of being repaid are usually greater.

Banks are concerned with the shiftability of loans made to borrowers. *Shiftability* is a term used to describe the ability of the bank to sell the borrower's notes to another bank. When a loan is shifted, the lending bank obtains its money before the maturity data of the note. If the lending bank sells a borrower's note to another bank, the borrower must repay the loan to whatever party holds the note at maturity. Shiftability is related to the concept of a self-liquidating loan because such a loan is generally easier to shift (transfer) than a loan that is not self-liquidating. The sale of a borrower's note to a federal reserve bank enables a local bank to obtain cash quickly if the need for liquidity arises.

Earning Power of the Borrower Over a period of time the earning power of the borrower will provide cash with which to repay the loan. When the proceeds of a loan are used to acquire fixed assets, the bank normally expects to be repaid from earnings; but it must be willing to have the debt outstanding for a reasonable period of time, such as five years. It is then customary to require the borrower to amortize the loan by making regular monthly payments on it.

More Permanent Capital An external source of funds for the repayment of the loan is the injection of more permanent capital into the business. These funds may be obtained from the sale of stocks and bonds, additional investment by a single proprietor, or some other source. For example, in recent years, public utilities have been borrowing from banks and repaying them from the proceeds of security issues.

Accommodation Paper (Using Cosigners) Another external source of funds is from cosigners. To increase the safety of the loan, a bank may require that, in addition to the borrower's signing the note, a financially responsible person act as *cosigner*. The second signer becomes liable in the event that the borrower defaults. Officers and directors of small corporations may be asked to cosign notes when the corporation borrows from a bank. Then, if the corporation fails, the bank can look to the cosigners for payment of the debt. Such an arrangement reduces the possibility that the officers and directors will drain off corporate assets through high salaries and excessive dividend payments and leave the bank with a claim on a bankrupt corporation. Cosigners may also be required under two other circumstances. A wife may be required to place her name on her husband's note when she holds much of the family wealth in her name; and an officer or director of a parent company may be required to place his name on a note that arises when a bank lends to a subsidiary. When the lending bank obtains cosigners, it increases its chances of being repaid ultimately. When a borrower consents to obtaining cosigners, he increases his chances of securing the money from the bank. Borrowers with strong credit standings are not usually asked to furnish cosigners as a condition for obtaining a loan.

Collateral A supplementary source for repayment is collateral. If the business or its principals (owners) can supply collateral, the banker may decide his chances of being paid are good even if the company liquidates. Such assets as inventories, stocks and bonds, accounts receivable, real estate, equipment, and life insurance policies may be pledged as collateral. Except on life insurance policies, a bank will seldom advance a loan of more than 80 percent of the market value of the pledged items. When specific assets are pledged, the risk to the bank is decreased. If the borrower defaults, the bank can seize the collateral and sell it. If the proceeds from the sale of the collateral exceed the amount due the bank, the excess is returned to the borrower; should it be less, the bank, along with other creditors, can look for full satisfaction of the debt through claims on unpledged assets. A secured loan gives added protection to the bank because it now has priority over unsecured creditors to the extent of the pledged collateral. From the borrower's viewpoint, the offer to pledge collateral will increase his chances of obtaining the loan.

Information on these five sources of funds for repaying loans will usually be obtained from financial statements presented by the applicant for the loan. In addition to the balance sheet and the statement of profit and loss, a borrower may have to submit a budget that will show expected cash inflow and outflow. Even if the banker does not require a formal budget, he will expect the applicant for the loan to have a reasonably exact knowledge of the probable inflow and outflow of cash during the time the loan will be outstanding.

Inventories as Collateral

When inventories are used as backing for a loan, the transaction is usually accompanied by one of three documents—a warehouse receipt, a trust receipt, or a factor's lien.

Warehouse Receipts

The business of *warehousing* may be defined as the operation of a building or other facility in which the operator, for a profit, takes custody of property deposited therein by others.[1] A *valid warehouse receipt* is a document that

1. Committee on Banking Relations, *To the Bankers of America: Warehouse Receipts Can "Work" for You* (Chicago: American Warehousemen's Association, n.d.), p. 3.

acknowledges the receipt of goods deposited with a bona fide warehouseman. The Uniform Warehouse Receipts Act defines a *bona fide warehouseman* as a person or organization lawfully engaged in the business of storing goods for profit. The act further stipulates that a valid warehouse receipt can be issued only by a bona fide warehouseman as thus defined.

The warehouse receipt may be used as collateral for a loan from a bank or other lender. If so, insurance is taken out by the borrower on the stored goods, and the endorsed policy, along with the warehouse receipt, is delivered to the lender. The cost of the loan is measured by the interest rate charged by the lender plus the cost of the warehousing service, which is usually from 1 to 3 percent of the value of the goods stored. As the borrower needs the inventory, he pays the bank, which in turn authorizes the release of an equivalent amount of goods from the warehouse. The loan is beneficial to the borrower because the movement of inventory into cash is accelerated. The overall advantage of inventory loans is that the borrower can expand his operations with a given amount of permanent capital.

If the borrower defaults, the lender can claim the goods stored in the warehouse. The warehouse will release the goods to any holder of the warehouse receipt, provided all storage charges have been paid. The warehouse receipt enables a lender to accept collateral without having to be responsible for physical custody of it. Since the lender depends on the warehouse to take good care of the items stored, he will insist on the borrower's storing the goods with a warehouse that is financially strong.

From the lender's viewpoint, the safety of the loan depends on the value of the pledged collateral, the marketability of the inventory, the credit strength of the borrower, the integrity of the warehouseman, and the bond supplied by the warehouseman. Lenders have found the warehouse receipt to be a suitable type of collateral if the goods are standardized and have a ready market. However, inventory loans do present a problem because the goods are not yet sold; hence, there is more risk in lending on this type of collateral than on accounts receivable, which are only one step away from being converted into cash. As the risk in transactions increases, the lender advances a sum of money that is a smaller and smaller percentage of the market value of the inventories.

Negotiable and Nonnegotiable Warehouse Receipts   The warehouse receipt may be *negotiable* or *nonnegotiable*. It is the former if made out to bearer or to the order of a person or institution; it is the latter if made out to a specific person or institution.[2] The American Warehousemen's Association points out that there has been a decided trend toward the preference by banks for nonnegotiable warehouse receipts issued in the name of the lending bank.[3] The main reason for this preference is that merchandise may be released on written order of the party in whose name the receipt is issued, and for all or any part of the goods, without surrender or endorsement of the receipt.

2. Ibid., pp. 6-7.
3. Ibid., p. 5.

Field Warehousing Instead of sending goods to a public warehouse, a borrower may make arrangements to have warehouse facilities established on his own premises. If so, a so-called field warehouse operator rents a section of the borrower's facilities for a nominal rental and encloses the part in which the goods are stored. The cost to the borrower is approximately 2 percent of the value of the goods stored, although this percentage is less when the transaction is large. The warehouse company has control over the goods because it has the keys to the enclosure. The device of having the warehouse facilities on the premises of the borrower is known as *field warehousing*. Field warehousing is often described as "warehousing brought to the merchandise instead of merchandise brought to the warehouse." The main advantage of field warehousing is that it saves transportation costs to and from the public warehouse.

A bonded employee is placed in charge of the stored inventory so that the holder of the warehouse receipt is assured that the pledged collateral will be kept separate from the borrower's unpledged inventory. The bonded employee is often an officer of the borrowing corporation who has been placed on the payroll of the warehouse company. The warehouse company in turn bills the borrower for the cost of these services. In addition to the three arrangements described below, others are possible under which the bonded employee will release the pledged inventory.[4]

1. If the inventory has a quick turnover, the borrower and his bank may have an agreement with the warehouse company whereby the borrower can withdraw limited amounts of goods without first obtaining a release.
2. The borrower pays the bank, which in turn signs a release for all or part of the inventory, depending on the amount paid on the loan.
3. The borrower pays the warehouse, which then releases some or all of the inventory. The warehouse, by previous agreement with the lender, is obligated to send the remittance to the bank within twenty-four hours.

Trust Receipt

A *trust receipt* is a document that gives the lender title to the inventory but allows the borrower (as trustee) to have possession of the goods. The trust receipt is used when it is necessary for the borrower to have possession of the goods so that they may be sold or processed. An automobile dealer might obtain a loan on the basis of a trust receipt as collateral. If so, the car dealer makes arrangements with a lender to pay the manufacturer. The lender obtains a note from the dealer and at the same time obtains trust receipts for each vehicle. The result of the transaction is that the dealer obtains possession of the car but title is vested in the lender, often a bank or other lender. As each car is sold, the dealer, according to the agreement, turns the proceeds over to the lender. The trust receipt is especially adaptable for use when the inventory can be clearly indentified by serial number or some other means.

4. *Reconstruction Finance Corporation Loan Memorandum Bulletin*, distributed by Douglas-Guardian Warehouse Corporation, New Orleans, n.d.

Factor's Lien   The *factor's lien* is a document that gives the lender a lien (claim) on the inventory of the borrower. The factor's lien arrangement is often made the subject of special statutory rules and regulations. In the absence of these special state laws, it is difficult for a lender to obtain an effective lien on inventory. The lien must be recorded at the courthouse so that other creditors will be put on notice that some of the debtor's assets are already pledged for a loan. In many cases, there must be a sign over the pledged inventory stating that there is a factor's lien on it. When the borrower sells the pledged inventory, the factor's lien shifts to the accounts receivable or the cash received from the transaction. From the borrower's viewpoint, the saving in transportation costs and warehouse charges may make the factor's lien a more advantageous document than the warehouse receipt for goods stored in a public warehouse.

It will be recalled that the term *factor* also has a specialized meaning—a financial institution that buys accounts receivable.

Warehouse receipts, trust receipts, and factor's liens are similar in that all are used to secure short-term credit. Inventory is placed with a disinterested third party when the warehouse receipt is used; this does not occur when the trust receipt and the factor's lien are used, for under the latter two arrangements the inventory is in the possession of the borrower. Trust receipts are unlike factor's liens in that under the trust receipt arrangement, title is vested in the lender even though the inventory is in the hands of the borrower; under the factor's lien, both title and goods are in the hands of the borrower. These matters are of importance to lenders whose primary interest is in having first claim on the goods in the event of bankruptcy of the borrower or in the event of fraud.

Stocks and Bonds as Collateral   A borrower may pledge stocks and bonds as collateral for a loan. At the time the loan is negotiated, the borrower completes an assignment form which gives the lender the right to have the ownership of the securities transferred to itself. As long as the borrower's name is still on the corporation's books he is entitled to dividends, voting rights, and other incidents of ownership. When the loan is repaid, the securities are returned to the borrower and the assignment form is destroyed.

Stocks and bonds of large companies make excellent collateral because of the relative ease with which they may be converted into cash if the borrower defaults. On the other hand, if the securities are those of small companies or of companies whose stock is seldom traded, bankers and other lenders will be more hesitant about granting the loan. Even on loans secured by the stocks of large companies, the lender may insist that the collateral be greater than the amount of the loan, say, 125 percent of the debt. The lender will normally expect a larger margin of protection if the shares are those of small companies. If the stock used as collateral is quoted in daily newspapers, the lender will periodically review its value. Should the market price of the collateral fall below the agreed amount, the borrower will have to supply additional securities or pay off some of the loan—the course of action being determined by the contents of the loan agreement.

A borrower who pledges stocks or bonds had the alternatives of selling the securities or pledging them for a loan. Either action would have brought cash to the owner. There are at least two reasons why a firm may elect to borrow and use the securities as collateral instead of selling them: The stocks may be needed to maintain control over another company, and they may be giving a higher yield than the interest being paid on the loan. Using the securities as collateral enables the borrower to obtain cash and yet enjoy the advantages of owning the securities.

Accounts receivable may also be pledged as collateral for a bank loan. Lenders will not usually advance more than 75 or 80 percent of the face value of the pledged accounts. The customers whose accounts have been pledged may or may not be notified of the assignment. If the customers are notified, they must usually make payment direct to the lender. If the customers are not notified, the borrower collects the accounts and immediately turns over the proceeds to the lender. Many borrowers prefer that their customers not be notified of the assignment. Banks will usually charge a high rate of interest on an accounts receivable loan because of the amount of time and effort required to service it. *Other Types of Collateral*

Real estate may also be pledged for a bank loan. The mechanics of pledging real estate for a bank loan are similar to the pledge of property under a bond issue except that no trustee is needed. The bank and the borrower can deal directly with each other, thus eliminating the need for a trustee.

A financial institution or an individual may lend to a borrower and at the same time acquire a lien on the equipment that the borrower has acquired with the proceeds of the loan. In addition, the borrower may have to pledge other specified assets. Since equipment is usually specialized, the resale value is generally less than the cost, thereby making this type of collateral less desirable than collateral based on marketable stocks and bonds. The loan is often repaid on the installment basis. Banks and other lenders advance money to borrowers with equipment to pledge when this is the most convenient type of collateral the borrower has to offer. When the First National Bank of Kansas City lent money to Mid-Continent Airlines, Inc., the borrower gave a chattel mortgage on aircraft, spare engines, propellers, and radio equipment.

The cash surrender value of a life insurance policy is a form of collateral looked on with favor by many lenders. When such a loan is made, the borrower gives the policy and a completed assignment form to the creditor. In many cases, the lender must notify the life insurance company and receive approval before the assignment is valid. If the borrower dies, the proceeds of the policy are payable to the lender, who keeps only the amount necessary to cancel the loan. If the borrower defaults, the lender may cash the policy and reimburse itself for the unpaid balance on the loan. When the loan is repaid by the borrower, the insurance company is notified and the various documents are returned to the borrower.

Unsecured Loans   When a bank loan is obtained, the borrower promises to repay the bank according to the terms of the note. If the bank does not require the pledge of any specific collateral, the note is said to be unsecured. If the borrower fails to repay the loan, the bank shares in the available assets on a pro rata basis along with creditors of other unsecured loans. The available assets would be those not pledged as collateral for other loans. In general, borrowers with a high credit rating are able to obtain unsecured loans from banks. On the other hand, when a bank is in doubt about the ability of the borrower to repay the loan, the borrower may be required to pledge collateral as an added safeguard for the bank.

The Amount of the Loan   ***Limits on the Amount Lent by Any One Bank***   Conservative banking practice dictates that banks place a limit on the amount they will advance to any one borrower. This desirable practice is reinforced by banking legislation; national banks, for example, cannot make an unsecured loan of more than 10 percent of their capital and surplus to any one borrower. Limits on loans to any one borrower are not an end in themselves but instead are intended to force diversification. When loans are spread among many borrowers, the bank does not suffer a major calamity if one of its borrowers defaults.

Even though a particular bank cannot or will not make a loan because of the size of the sum sought, the bank's officers may still arrange a loan for the would-be borrower. In the case of a small bank, this is done by approaching a banker in a larger city. The small bank and the city bank both participate in the lending, and the borrower receives the amount he needs. In addition to cooperation between small banks and larger city banks, there is also some cooperation between large banks which participate in making loans to borrowers. Finally, in a few cities, banks have credit pools from which loans are made to the poorer risks, particularly small businesses. As a general statement, it may be said that if the credit strength of the borrower is sufficiently great, the chances of obtaining a loan are very good.

The Line of Credit   If a company is a frequent borrower, there arises the problem of negotiating each bank loan separately, thereby consuming both the bank officers' and the borrower's time. Furthermore, the borrower is not assured in advance that he will be able to borrow in order to finance his seasonal operations. To avoid frequent detailed negotiations, the bank may grant a line of credit. This means that the bank agrees to lend up to a certain amount (such as $100,000), the borrower having the privilege of using the funds at any time during the period when the money is at his disposal.

If the bank agrees to lend up to a certain amount and the borrower has the option of using the funds any time during a period of several years, a *commitment fee* is usually charged the borrower on the unused part of the available credit. A bank might agree to advance up to $100,000 any time during a two-year period, the borrower taking the funds as he needs them. If $80,000 of the loan were used the first year, it is possible that a commitment fee of about

Commitment fee

one-eighth of 1 percent would have to be paid on the remaining $20,000. Practice varies on whether a commitment fee will be charged and on its amount.

A balance sheet may not reveal the whole story about the ability of a firm to muster cash to pay its debts. Many businesses carry an abnormally low amount of cash in their asset structure. But the principals (proprietors, partners, or stockholders) may have substantial personal assets ready to be pumped into the business if the need arises.

A line of credit with a bank also enables a firm to avoid carrying large idle balances for emergency purposes. An annual report provides an example of the use of this device:

> Today's tight credit situation has increased the importance of an additional factor in the traditional three-way rivalry for treatment of dividends, capital improvements, and debt reduction. This is the requirement of keeping enough, but not too much, cash for working capital. Our payroll comes to some $45 million a month, and this must be met with cash. So must our equipment obligations as they fall due; so must the annual interest on our bonded debt. So must our tax bills. Obviously, this requires considerable working capital or "cash in the drawer"—and the bottom of the drawer can never be allowed to show. As "insurance" against this happening because of any sudden and unmanageable need for ready cash, we have an arrangement with banks for a so-called "stand-by loan" under which they have agreed to lend us $50 million upon demand. It was not intended that we should draw on this loan and we have not done so, but the fact that we have the arrangement to fall back on has allowed us to reduce our working capital to today's minimum.

Of course, the company must pay a small fee to the banks for the unused part of the line of credit. But this arrangement is cheaper than borrowing at 7 or 8 percent and then having the money lie idle in banks. Some firms, then, are in a stronger financial position than their balance sheets indicate.

Revolving Credit   Many banks permit and encourage the use of *revolving credit*. This means the borrower is allowed a maximum line of credit and that a business can borrow funds, repay them, borrow again, and continue the process, provided that not more than the agreed amount is outstanding in loans at any one time. Revolving credit is especially useful in financing accounts receivable and inventories. It is now common practice for large banks to enter into a joint agreement to advance funds on a revolving credit basis to business firms. The joint arrangement decreases the risk to all the banks.

Short-term Maturities   First, there are the 30-, 60-, and 90-day loans, which are still an important type of transaction entered into by banks. However, it should be noted that many of these loans are renewed indefinitely. Even though the banker and the borrower know that the note will be renewed, a short maturity has two advantages to the bank: the interest rate can be changed at any maturity

The Due Date on Bank Loans

date; and, if necessary, the bank can demand payment, although this second point is less important than the first. It can be seen that maturity dates are often only nominal in the sense that the borrower can use the funds for an unlimited period of time.

Some bankers insist that short-term loans be "cleaned up" once a year; that is, the borrower is expected to be fully out of debt to the bank at least once during each 12-month period. Borrowers are expected to have the cash available for repaying the debt even if the money has to be borrowed from another bank. Practice on cleaning up loans varies from one bank to another. The practice applies, of course, only to notes with a nominal duration of less than a year.

Indefinite Due Date A second plan is to have an indefinite due date. The borrower signs a demand note which provides that the loan will be repaid upon the occurrence of a certain event. Thus an automobile dealer might borrow from a bank to buy automobiles for his inventory. The agreement is that as each car is sold, the proceeds from the sale will be used to pay off the note.

Installment Loans (Term Loans) Banks, life insurance companies, and other institutions may lend to business firms under an arrangement known as "term lending," which has two distinguishing features: the loans run for longer than one year and they are repayable in installments. This is in contrast with the typical short-term loan, which is generally repaid in one sum on the maturity date. Term loans, which openly acknowledge the debt as being for a number of years, fill a need for intermediate credit. These loans have been used for such purposes as financing expansion of fixed assets, increasing circulating assets, redeeming preferred stock, and repaying short-term creditors.

The Kaiser Steel Corporation's term-loan arrangement will illustrate some of the highlights of term lending in practice.

1. The loan agreement was with three banks, which agreed to lend an aggregate of $24 million.
2. Kaiser Steel Corporation did not have to borrow all the money at once. But it agreed to pay a fee of three-quarters of 1 percent per annum on the unused part of the credit.
3. The borrower agreed to an annual interest rate of 7 percent on funds actually borrowed.
4. The loan was payable in equal installments over an eight-year period.
5. The bank agreement contained, among other protective provisions, the following: (a) the Kaiser Steel Corporation agreed not to incur any other bank indebtedness until the loans were repaid, (b) the corporation agreed to keep its net current assets above a certain amount, (c) the company was not allowed to buy any of its common stock, and (d) the company agreed not to pay dividends unless certain ratios were above the specified level.

The Cost of Bank Loans When a bank lends to a businessman, the interest on the loan may be paid when the loan is repaid or may be deducted from the proceeds at the time the loan is made. As an example of the first situation, assume that a company borrows $1,000 at 6 percent for 60 days. At maturity, the borrower would pay the bank $1,010. Of this sum, $1,000 would be on the principal, while $10 would be interest. In any note transaction, the amount repayable at maturity by the maker of the note is called the maturity value. In this illustration, $1,010 is the maturity value. It should also be observed that in computing interest, it is assumed that there are 360 days in a year.

Another way of handling the loan is for the bank to deduct the interest from the proceeds received at the time the loan is granted. When the loan transaction is handled in this manner, the bank is said to *discount* the borrower's note. Under this arrangement, the borrower does not receive in cash the full face value of the note. Assume that a company discounts its $1,000, 6 percent, 60-day note at its bank. How much will the company receive in cash? Since the interest is $10, the borrower will receive $990. How much will have to be paid the bank at the maturity date? In this illustration, the maturity value of the note is $1,000; therefore, this sum will have to be repaid the bank.

Discount note

Company X borrows $1,000 from a bank which charges 6 percent interest. Assuming that the loan is for one year, determine the effective rate of interest if (a) the interest is deducted at the time of the loan; (b) the interest is paid at maturity.

Problem

If the interest is deducted in advance, the proceeds are $940 and the dollar interest is $60. The effective rate of interest is:

Solution

$$\text{Effective rate} = \frac{\text{Annual dollar interest}}{\text{Proceeds}}$$
$$= \frac{\$60}{\$940}$$
$$= 6.38 \text{ percent}$$

If the interest is not deducted in advance, the effective rate of interest is determined as follows:

$$\text{Effective rate} = \frac{\text{Annual dollar interest}}{\text{Proceeds}}$$
$$= \frac{\$60}{\$1,000}$$
$$= 6.00 \text{ percent}$$

Roland Brown has been borrowing $10,000 from a bank that charges him an effective rate of interest of 8 percent. Brown has an insurance policy on which he could borrow this amount and pay an effective rate of interest of 5 percent; he also has $10,000 in a savings and loan association which pays him 4.5 percent. Explain why he prefers not to borrow on his life insurance policy and not to liquidate his savings and loan account, since both of these alternatives would save him interest.

Problem

Solution   Brown prefers not to borrow on his life insurance policy because he fears he does not have sufficient willpower to repay the loan; he has a similar fear about the savings and loan account, namely, he may never build the account to its present $10,000 level. It is common knowledge that there are other considerations in finance than minimizing interest costs.

The formula below may be used to determine the effective rate of interest (true rate of interest) on an installment loan. This formula is especially useful when the loan is to run for more than 12 months. Observe that the effective rate of interest attempts to relate the dollar amount of interest paid to the average amount of money or credit received. The formula is useful not only in computing the effective rate of interest on installment loans but also in determining the true rate of interest being paid on consumer credit:

$$R = \frac{2pc}{A(n+1)}$$

where R equals the true annual rate being paid by the debtor; p equals the number of equal installment payments in one year—exclusive of the first down payment (if payments are made monthly, p is 12; if payments are made weekly, p is 52); c equals the total interest or finance charges in dollars; A equals the amount of cash or credit actually received; n equals the total number of installment payments to be made by the debtor. (If someone buys an automobile on the installment plan and makes equal monthly payments over a 15-month period, then n is 15 and p is 12.)

Example: Arthur Jones buys a $2,300 automobile, making a down payment of $500. He is to pay off the debt by making 18 equal monthly payments of $109 each. If Jones buys on the installment plan, what equivalent annual interest is he paying for the use of the credit? $p = 12$, $c = \$162$, $A = \$1,800$, $n = 18$.

$$R = \frac{2 \times 12 \times 162}{1,800 \times 19}$$
$$= 0.1137 \text{ or } 11.37 \text{ percent}$$

Answer: Jones is paying 11.37 percent a year.

Finally, one other method of computing interest is of sufficient importance to mention here. In this plan, the borrower makes installment payments on the loan but he pays interest only on the unpaid monthly balance. This is the best type of installment loan for a borrower to obtain. Such a transaction is a likely arrangement on real estate loans from a bank. Assume that Howard Ricker buys a small plot of land for $10,000 for business purposes and that the bank charges 5 percent interest on the loan. Ricker's monthly payments, including interest, appear in Table 11-1.

	Loan Balance at End of Month	Payment on Principal	Interest Payment	Total Payment	
1st month	$10,000.00	$50.00	$41.67	$91.67	*TABLE 11-1*
2nd month	9,950.00	50.00	41.46	91.46	*Ricker's Monthly*
3rd month	9,900.00	50.00	41.25	91.25	*Loan Payments*

A loan of this sort results in the true rate of interest being equal to the quoted rate. Unfortunately for the borrower, the bank is apt to agree to these favorable terms only on real estate loans; it is unlikely to permit such an interest arrangement when the installment loan is on equipment.

Another aspect is that while a loan is in force, the bank may require the borrower to keep a certain percentage of it on deposit. As previously indicated, the portion of the loan that must be kept on deposit during the life of the loan is called the *compensating balance*. Generally, only the banks in the larger cities require compensating balances, and not all of these banks follow the practice. Thus a bank might require that the cash balance of the borrower be at all times at least 20 percent of the loan. Under these conditions, if a borrower wanted to borrow $50,000 from a bank that insisted on a compensating balance of 20 percent, it would be necessary to borrow $62,500 so the borrower could spend $50,000 of the loan and still keep $12,500 on deposit. A scheme of this sort makes the borrower pay a higher effective rate of interest, because interest is paid on $62,500 but only $50,000 is available in cash. If a bank quoted an interest rate of 5 percent on a one-year loan, the dollar interest would be $3,125 (5 percent of $62,500). However, since the borrower has the use of only $50,000, the effective rate of interest would be 6.25 percent ($3,125 ÷ $50,000). It can be seen that if the borrower has to keep a balance larger than he would normally maintain, a compensating balance has the effect of raising the cost of the loan. If, on the other hand, the borrower would normally keep on deposit the amount required by the compensating balance rule, there is no effect on the interest rate.

Compensating Balance and Rate of Interest

The C Company is planning to borrow $40,000 in cash for a one-year period from a bank that requires a compensating balance of 20 percent and that charges 6 percent interest. *Required*: (a) Determine how much will have to be borrowed in order to meet the compensating balance requirement and yet have the proceeds amount to $40,000. (b) What effective rate of interest is the borrower paying on the loan?

Problem

(a) X is the amount actually borrowed (a sum greater than $40,000); .20 is the compensating balance in percent; $40,000 is the specific amount of cash needed.

Solution

$$X - .20X = \$40,000$$
$$.80X = 40,000$$
$$X = 50,000$$

Answer: The firm will have to borrow $50,000.

(b) Effective rate of interest $= \dfrac{\text{Annual dollar interest on loan}}{\text{Actual proceeds of loan}}$

$$= \dfrac{(.06)\,(\$50,000)}{\$40,000}$$

$$= 7.50 \text{ percent}$$

Problem   Company A is in need of $190,000 for a one-year period. The first bank will lend the money at 5 percent, the note to be discounted (that is, the interest to be deducted in advance). The second bank offers to lend the money at 4 percent; the interest is not to be deducted in advance but instead is to be paid at maturity. However, the second bank will require a compensating balance of 20 percent. (a) Compare the respective amounts that would have to be borrowed from each bank so that the borrower would receive his $190,000. (b) Compare the annual rate of interest being charged by the respective banks.

Solution   (a) The amount to be borrowed from the first bank is determined as follows (let X equal the amount of the loan):

$$X - .05X = \$190,000$$
$$.95X = 190,000$$
$$X = 200,000$$

The amount to be borrowed from the second bank is determined as follows (let X equal the amount of the loan):

$$X - .20X = \$190,000$$
$$.80X = 190,000$$
$$X = 237,500$$

Answer: Company A would have to borrow $200,000 from the first bank and $237,500 from the second.

(b) The rate of interest charged by the first bank is approximately 5.26 percent, found by dividing the annual dollar cost of $10,000 by the proceeds of $190,000. The rate charged by the second bank is 5.00 percent, found by dividing the annual dollar cost of $9,500 by the proceeds of $190,000.

The Prime Rate
of Interest   The *prime rate of interest* is the rate charged by very large banks (on short-term unsecured loans) to their financially strongest business customers.

HIGHLIGHTS
OF THIS CHAPTER   *Much of financial policy is concerned with planning the sources of cash, the use made of cash, and the repayment of creditors. Although cash is not the only*

financial matter in a firm's economic life, it is the hub around which all other financial matters center. Not only must an appraisal of the cash position of the company take into consideration the cash available for spending but it must also consider the probable cash inflow in the near future. An analysis along these lines will take us into a study of the management of cash and the conversion of receivables and inventories into cash.

The modern practice is to seek a cash balance that enables a firm to meet its obligations and to meet emergency drains on the firm. A business that has too little in cash has trouble in meeting its payments on time and loses discounts. Furthermore, a chronic shortage of cash may interfere with obtaining credit and funds on advantageous terms. On the other hand, an excess of cash may be a costly luxury, for the excess is not earning any interest. Presumably excess cash should be placed in short-term marketable securities, inventories, or fixed assets or should be used to reduce debt. By carefully managing its cash, an enterprise can add to its profitability.

Commercial banks advance short-term credit when they make loans for stated periods, such as 60 days; they advance intermediate-term credit when they grant loans for periods such as five years. The borrower who wishes to obtain a bank loan should always remember that banks are in business to earn money for their stockholders. Therefore, the applicant must be able to present his proposal to obtain a loan in a manner that convinces the bank's officers that they can add to the institution's profits by advancing him the funds. This, of course, is true wherever credit is sought in a business transaction.

11-1. Identify these terms:
   compensating balance
   prime rate of interest
   lockbox banking
   field warehousing
   permanent current assets
   line of credit
   commitment fee
   term loan

11-2. What are the advantages and disadvantages of maintaining large balances in checking accounts?

11-3. A banker was discussing a loan with Mr. Carnahan, the proprietor of a small clothing store. The banker was willing to advance the loan, but he insisted that Mrs. Carnahan cosign the note. Suggest a reason why the banker insisted on the wife also signing the note.

11-4. Arrange for an interview with a commercial banker and seek answers to these questions: (a) Does the bank levy a charge on checking accounts of business firms? (b) What rate of interest does the bank charge on business loans? on consumer loans? (c) Under what conditions does the bank require a cosigner to a note? (d) What criteria must an applicant for a small business loan meet before the bank will grant the loan? (e) What are the advantages of having a safe-deposit box? What is the annual charge for one? (f) In your state, if husband and wife have both their names on a checking account or a savings account, what are the legal, the estate tax, and the inheritance tax implications if the following words or phrases appear on the account: *and, or, joint tenancy, joint tenancy by the entirety?*

REVIEW PROBLEMS The answers to the problems appear at the end of this section. *For each problem, show how you obtained the answer.*

11-1. A student bought an automobile on the installment plan. The car dealer sold him the car for $1,500 but allowed him a trade-in of $300 on an old car; hence, the net cost of the car was $1,200. The student agreed to make 15 monthly payments of $85 each. What rate of interest was he paying on the loan?

11-2. The K Company obtains from a loan firm a term loan of $3,600, payable in equal monthly installments over a three-year period. If the installments are $110 each, what rate of interest is being paid on the loan?

11-3. James Smith, a merchant, has his own one-year note for $5,000 discounted at his bank. The discount rate is 5 percent. Determine (a) the dollar interest cost of the loan; (b) the proceeds of the loan; (c) the amount that will have to be repaid at maturity; and (d) the effective rate of interest being paid on the loan.

11-4. Company Y borrows $1,000 from a bank that charges 5 percent interest. Assuming that the loan is for one year, determine the effective rate of interest if (a) the interest is deducted at the time of the loan (the note is discounted); (b) the interest is paid at maturity.

11-5. The B Company is about to borrow $85,000 in cash for one year from a bank that requires a compensating balance of 15 percent and that charges 5 percent interest. Determine (a) how much will have to be borrowed so as to meet the compensating balance requirement and yet have the proceeds amount to $85,000; (b) what effective rate of interest the borrower is paying on the loan.

11-6. Company Q, located in New York, has annual credit sales of $9 million in California. The firm is considering lockbox banking. Company Q has average receipts of $25,000 per day ($9 million ÷ 360 days). The firm concluded from a study that it has an average float of seven days and that this could be reduced to two days if lockbox banking were adopted. The California bank would insist on a balance of $100,000 for its services. If Company Q uses the freed funds to repay its New York bank loans, on which interest of 6 percent is paid, how much would be saved in interest?

11-7. A business firm has a checking account in a bank, and the firm has borrowed money from this bank. If the borrower fails to repay the loan, the bank has the right to seize the checking account and apply the balance to the loan. This right of the bank is called the *right of offset*.

The firm whose statement is given below has failed. On deposit in the bank from which the loan was obtained is $1,000 cash; "other assets" are liquidated for $3,500 in cash.

Cash	$ 1,000	Unsecured bank loan	$ 4,000
Other assets	9,000	Trade creditors	3,000
		Common stock	3,000
Total	$10,000	Total	$10,000

(a) What is the total amount of cash that the bank will receive from the liquidation, assuming that the bank has the *right of offset*? (b) How much will the trade creditors receive? (c) How much will the holders of common stock receive?

11-8. Many large banks are besieged with class action suits that claim a bank overcharges a borrower when the bank bases interest computations on a 360-day year instead of a 365-day year. The outcome of these suits is still in doubt. If a person borrows $10,000 for 60 days at 10 percent, how much more in dollars is he paying for the use of the money if the bank bases its computations on a 360-day year instead of a 365-day year?

11-9. Company K has annual sales of $1 million and a cash turnover of 10. What is the percentage of the average cash balance to annual sales?

11-10. Company L, with annual sales of $2 million, is a heavy user of bank loans to finance current assets. The firm, through a more efficient billing system and by waiting until the last minute to write payroll checks, is able to increase its cash turnover from 10 to 20. If the company uses the extra cash so generated to repay bank loans on which 6 percent interest is paid, by how much are expenses reduced?

Answers: 11-1, approximately 9.37 percent; 11-2, approximately 6.5 percent; 11-3a, $250; 11-3b, $4,750, ll-3c, $5,000; 11-3d, 5.26 percent; 11-4a, 5.26 percent; 11-4b, 5.00 percent; 11-5a, $100,000; 11-5b, 5.88 percent; 11-6, $1,500; 11-7a, $2,750; 11-7b, $1,750; 11-7c, nothing; 11-8, $2.29; 11-9, 10 percent; 11-10, $6,000.

12 Managing Working Capital— Cash (II)

The following additional aspects of cash management will be explained in this chapter:

1. Commercial paper houses
2. Commercial finance companies
3. Other sources of cash
4. Outlets for excess cash
5. An example of operations research in managing cash

COMMERCIAL PAPER HOUSES

General Nature of Commercial Paper Houses and Commercial Paper

The commercial paper house is a financial institution that has as one of its main functions the purchasing of short-term notes payable (called commercial paper) from well-known corporations; the commercial paper house in turn sells these notes at a profit, mainly to commercial banks that have idle funds to invest.[1] In some cases, the commercial paper house does not take title to the notes but instead acts as a selling agent in placing the paper. Medium- and large-sized corporations find the commercial paper house a convenient way of reaching the short-term money market. (Sales finance companies usually sell their notes without any assistance from commercial paper houses.) Whereas the facilities of commercial banks are available to all forms of organizations, both large and small, this is not true of commercial paper houses; these organizations tend to cater only to the large and well-known corporations.

Commercial paper supplements borrowing from the bank with which a firm normally does business. The borrowing business issues noninterest-bearing unsecured notes in denominations of $2,500, $5,000, and multiples of these

---

1. Commercial paper houses may engage in other activities, such as lending directly to companies.

amounts. The notes are then sold to a commercial paper house on a *discount basis*, the annual rate of discount being approximately 6 percent. Since, at the time of the issuance, the borrowing corporation cannot determine who will buy the commercial paper, the notes cannot be made out to the ultimate holder; therefore, the borrower makes the notes payable to the order of itself and then endorses them, thereby giving the commercial paper a bearer status.

The commercial paper house in turn sells the notes to buyers (usually commercial banks) on a discount basis. The notes often run for periods of three months, six months, or nine months. At maturity the issuing corporation must pay the maturity value of the notes to whatever parties hold the commercial paper. For its services, the commercial paper house charges a commission of approximately a quarter of 1 percent of the maturity value of the paper. This commission is paid by the borrowing corporation.

Cost of the Funds Acquired from the Sale of Commercial Paper

Assume that the Clark Company sells six-month notes with a maturity value of $1 million at a discount of 4 percent to a commercial paper house. How much will the Clark Company receive in cash, assuming that the commercial paper house charges a commission of a quarter of 1 percent for its services? The amount that would be received is computed as follows:

Maturity value of the commercial paper (notes)		$1,000,000
Less:		
Interest for six months at 4 percent	$20,000	
Fee of ¼ of 1 percent	2,500	
Total deductions		22,500
Proceeds to the company (borrower)		$ 977,500

It will be necessary for this firm to pay $1 million at maturity to the holders of the commercial paper.

From the viewpoint of the borrower, the effective rate of interest is 4½ percent, computed as follows:

Annual rate of discount at which notes were sold	4 percent
Annual rate paid commercial paper house (0.00¼ × 2 = ½ of 1 percent). Since the company has the use of the funds for only half a year, the fee of the commercial paper house must be converted to an annual basis— ½ of 1 percent in this illustration	½
Total	4½ percent

Commercial paper houses do not usually endorse the paper sold to financial institutions. However, it is common practice for them to sell this paper on a 10-day option to commercial banks. This means that the banks have 10 days to

The 10-Day Option

investigate the credit strength of the issuer and to decide on whether or not to keep the paper.

Reasons for Using Commercial Paper and Its Limitations

The main reason for using commercial paper to supplement bank loans is the low interest on this kind of loan. Not only is the annual rate of interest low; in addition, there is no compensating balance required. Second, a firm's bank may be unable to lend the amount required by the borrower. For example, the bank may have already lent all its available resources, or banking laws may prevent it from lending a sum greater than 10 percent of its capital and surplus on an unsecured loan. A third incidental advantage is the publicity received on the company's high credit rating.

On the other hand, there are three main reasons why a firm might hesitate or be unable to raise funds through the sale of commercial paper. First, this source of credit is not open to small firms that need to raise moderate amounts of cash. Commercial paper houses do not find small transactions profitable; or, stating the problem in different terms, the commercial paper house would have to raise its fee to a point that would make this source of credit too costly. A second complication is the highly impersonal approach to the transaction. The holders of commercial paper expect payment at maturity, and there is no possibility that the loan will be extended. If the loan is obtained directly from a bank, it is conceivable that an extension can be negotiated. Furthermore, if the loan is received from a bank with which the corporation regularly does business, it is possible that the lender will be more favorably inclined to assist the borrower in times of financial crisis. Third, and last, a minor reason for not using commercial paper is that the officers of the borrower may have to reply to questions by bankers who are considering buying the commercial paper from a commercial paper house.

COMMERCIAL FINANCE COMPANIES

General Nature of Commercial Finance Companies

Commercial finance companies have as their main function the lending of cash to borrowers who pledge accounts receivable as collateral for the loan. The borrowers are business firms, and the accounts pledged are those due from other business firms. Again, it should be noted that one cannot always determine from the name of an organization the activities conducted by it. Commercial finance companies may render additional services—outright purchase of accounts receivable, lending on the pledge of inventory, advancing funds on the pledge of fixed assets, and so on. Furthermore, commercial finance companies are not the only institutions that lend on the pledge of accounts receivable; commercial banks and sales finance companies may also extend credit on this basis. Although the commercial finance company will be used to illustrate the procedure of pledging accounts receivable for a loan, the same techniques apply regardless of where the accounts are pledged.

Pledge of Accounts Receivable

When a commercial finance company—or other lender—advances funds on the basis of a pledge of accounts receivable, the amount of the loan is approximately 70 to 80 percent of the value of the invoices pledged. The lender is thus protected by a margin of between 20 and 30 percent. The margin has a twofold effect: first, it increases the safety of the loan; and second, it prevents the borrower from realizing the full profit on the account before it is collected.

The customers whose accounts are pledged may be notified, although in most cases they are not. The disadvantage of notifying customers is that they may interpret the pledge as a sign of weakness on the part of the borrower. Even when they are not informed by the pledger, the lender reserves the right to notify the customers whose accounts have been pledged if the pledger becomes insolvent. If the accounts are pledged without notification, the borrower collects the accounts and remits the payment directly to the commercial finance company. The commercial finance company, by previous agreement with its own bank, endorses the checks in the name of a special person so that the customers whose accounts were pledged will be unaware of the assignment of their accounts. If, on the other hand, they were notified of the pledge, the customers whose accounts are involved will remit directly to the commercial finance company.

Permanent arrangements usually will be made by a borrower with a commercial finance company; that is, there is a standing agreement, the terms of which are that the commercial finance company will lend an agreed amount if the borrower can supply acceptable accounts receivable as collateral. An important aspect of this arrangement is that loans are automatically granted as the need arises (as sales are made). This results in a flexible arrangement insofar as the borrower is concerned.

The cost of obtaining a loan through the pledge of accounts receivable varies greatly, although it is often higher than the rate for an unsecured bank loan. It is customary to quote interest rates in one of two ways:

Cost of a Loan from Commercial Finance Companies

1. As a percentage of the average daily balance of the loan. The loan is increased as additional sums are borrowed; it is decreased as the pledged accounts are converted into cash and the proceeds used to reduce the loan. A commercial credit company may charge 1/30 of 1 percent per day, which is an annual rate of 12 percent (1/30 of 1 percent × 360—assuming a 360-day year).
2. As a percentage of the total of the accounts pledged. If $100,000 of accounts receivable were pledged for a loan of $80,000 and if the interest charge were 1/30 of 1 percent of the $100,000, the effective rate would be 15 percent per year (1/30 × 360 ÷ 0.80).

There are other plans in addition to these two methods, particularly when there is a minimum charge and when, in addition to the interest rate, a flat commission is charged on the accounts pledged or on the amount of the loan.

Although these interest rates may seem comparatively high, a businessman does not stop at this point in analyzing the merits of borrowing on the pledge of accounts receivable. More important than the interest rate is the dollar cost of the loan in relation to the amount of the increased net profit because of the transaction. If, over a period of a year, the interest cost is $4,000 and the amount added to net profits is $8,000 because of the expanded volume of business financed by the loan, the businessman would be satisfied even though the interest rate might have been 15 percent. As noted earlier, the percentage interest rate is of significance only in providing a measuring rod as to which source will supply credit at the lowest dollar cost.

The fact that the loan is decreased on certain days is important because this reduces the dollar cost of the funds. This is unlike bank loans, where a sum might be borrowed for 90 days and interest paid for the full period. Therefore, one cannot make a direct comparison between interest rates charged by a commercial finance company and a commercial bank because the base (the amount of the loan) to which the rate is applied constantly changes under the arrangement of the pledge of accounts receivable.

Another element that complicates the comparison of rates between commercial credit companies and commercial banks (which do not lend on accounts receivable) is that the effective rate at the bank becomes higher if a compensating balance is required. A bank that requires a compensating balance of 20 percent and that charges a nominal rate of interest of 6 percent is in reality charging 7.5 percent (6 percent ÷ 0.80).

In conclusion, a firm would prefer to borrow on an unsecured note from a bank because of the lower interest rate. However, banks may be "loaned up," the credit standing of the borrower may not be sufficiently high, or there may be other reasons why the commercial finance company's facilities are used.

Problem   Company Q has purchased $100,000 worth of goods, the terms being 10/10, N/70.[2] (a) Determine the dollar cost of the following alternatives. (b) Which alternative is the most expensive (in dollars)? (c) Which is the least expensive (in dollars)?

1. Pay the bill on the 60th day.
2. Borrow from a bank that charges 6 percent a year, on a discount basis.
3. Borrow, by pledging inventory, from a finance company. The finance company will lend 75 percent of the value of the goods pledged, and, in addition to its 6 percent interest charge on the $90,000, it also levies a fee of ¼ of 1 percent on the value of the goods pledged ($120,000).
4. Borrow, by pledging accounts receivable, from a finance company that charges 1/30 of 1 percent per day on the value of the accounts receivable pledged. The finance company will lend 90 percent of the face value of the receivables.

In order to shorten computations and focus attention on principles, assume that in 2, 3, and 4 the loan will be obtained for a full 60 days and the money received will be used to take advantage of the discount offered on the purchase.

2. The terms 10/10, N/70 mean that the buyer can reduce his bill by 10 percent if he pays it during the first 10 days. He obtains no discount if he pays between the 11th day and the 70th day. If he pays the bill after the 70th day, his account is overdue and his credit rating is impaired.

Solution

(a) The dollar cost of 1 is $10,000, because this is the amount of the discount that will be lost if the bill is not paid on time.

The dollar cost of 2 is $909.09. Observe that $90,000 in cash would be sought to take advantage of the discount; that this is a 60-day loan; and that the annual interest rate is 6 percent. Hence, the interest rate for 60 days is 1/6 of the annual rate, or .01. Since the loan is discounted, the firm will have to borrow more than $90,000 in order to obtain $90,000. The amount borrowed is determined as follows (let X equal the amount to be borrowed):

$$X - .01X = \$90{,}000$$
$$.99X = 90{,}000$$
$$X = 90{,}909.09$$

Therefore, the dollar interest cost is $90,909.09 – $90,000.00, which is $909.09.

The dollar cost of 3 is $1,200, determined as follows:

Interest cost	= (.06) ($90,000) 1/6	$ 900.00
Value of goods pledged:		
.75X	= $ 90,000	
X	= 120,000	
Fee on goods pledged	= ¼ of 1 percent × $120,000	300.00
Total cost		$1,200.00

The dollar cost of 4 is $2,000, determined as follows:

Amount of receivables pledged	= .90X = $ 90,000	
	X = 100,000	
Cost of transaction	= (1/30) (.01) ($100,000) (60 days)	= $2,000

(b) and *(c)* The most expensive alternative is 1; the least expensive is 2.

OTHER SOURCES OF CASH

Short-term loans may be obtained from other sources: parent companies, subsidiaries, the federal government, the firm's officers, and, on an emergency basis, consumer credit institutions.

Small business units are most likely to be hard pressed for cash, large companies finding it easier to borrow in the money market.

During a period of rising prices the problem of raising adequate working capital becomes acute for small and medium-sized companies. The costs of inventories, labor, and the replacement of assets all increase, but the increase in the selling price of goods is not adequate to bring the needed additional cash immediately into the business.

A borrower may enter into an agreement whereby both a bank and a life insurance company supply part of the loan. If a firm needs $300,000, a bank may supply $50,000, repayable in five years; and the life insurance company may provide the remaining $250,000, repayable between the fifth and fifteenth year. In a transaction of this kind, the commercial bank will prefer to hold the part of the debt that matures early, whereas the life insurance company will prefer to hold the long-term part of the loan.

The federal government has established a special unit to aid in financing small business firms that are unable to obtain loans from established institutions. The U.S. Small Business Administration (SBA) can lend money directly to small business firms or it can cooperate with financial institutions in supplying money on a loan basis. All loans must be of sound value or secured so as to reasonably assure repayment. Hence this federal agency is not a charitable institution. Generally, a small business seeks a loan at its local bank. If the bank is unwilling to lend, then the business firm is eligible to apply to the SBA for a loan. In addition to supplying small businesses with cash, the SBA has a staff of specialists to give advice on business problems.

OUTLETS FOR EXCESS CASH

Treasury Bills and Certificates

A widely used outlet for excess cash is United States *Treasury bills*. These instruments are sold weekly by the federal government on a discount basis; the investor's interest return is the difference between what he pays for the document and what he receives at maturity or what he receives if he sells it in the open market. Treasury bills have maturities ranging from 91 days to one year, and they earn an annual rate of from 3 to 5 percent. A purchaser, such as General Motors Corporation, can acquire Treasury bills that have a maturity date near the time when the money will be needed—such as a day before an income tax payment is due. Treasury bills that are nearing maturity are much in demand; hence, their price rises more than the normal increase generated by the interest factor. In addition to earning interest, an investor who sells these instruments before maturity may earn a second gain generated by the heavy demand for bills with short-term maturities. Reaping a profit on the latter is known as "riding the yield curve." In newspapers, Treasury bills are quoted on a yield basis rather than a price basis. This means that the reader can see at a glance the percentage return that he would obtain on these instruments if he purchased them; he does not need to refer to a bond table. Treasury bills meet all the criteria of a sound short-term investment. They are perfectly safe because they are issued by the federal government; they are marketable because they can be sold quickly at or near the current market price; they do not fluctuate much in price because they have relatively short maturities; and they offer a satisfactory yield.

While an investor in Treasury bills earns interest in the manner described, an investor in Treasury certificates usually receives his interest in the form of a check. Because there are not as many Treasury certificates outstanding as Treasury bills, the former are not as marketable as the latter. This means that a business firm holding Treasury certificates and then wishing to sell them before their maturity might have to dispose of them at a small loss. In most other respects, however, the two investment outlets are comparable. Both have a maturity of not more than one year; both earn about the same return; and both are quite safe. Both, therefore, provide an excellent place for the commitment of idle funds generated by seasonal operations. Typical yields on short-term investments are given in Table 12-1.

	Yield (Percent)	
Treasury bills:		TABLE 12-1 *Typical Yields on Short-term Investments*
3-month maturity	4.0	
Over 3 months	4.2	
Commercial paper	4.5	
Bankers' acceptances	4.1	
Certificates of deposit		
180 days and under	4.5	
Over 180 days	5.0	
U.S. government bonds	5.3	

Treasury Notes and Bonds

The federal government issues *Treasury notes* that have a maturity of from one to five years and *Treasury bonds* that have a maturity of more than five years. Both instruments earn a higher return than Treasury bills. Offsetting the advantage of higher yield, however, is that such documents may fluctuate considerably in market price. If an investor needs cash to meet an emergency and has to sell these notes or bonds, he may have to take a loss. Thus, in a two-month period, United States long-term bonds fluctuated between $1,005 and $925. The possibility of suffering a deterioration in principal does not make these outlets suitable for seasonally generated excess cash. Yet, if management is certain that it will not need the money in the near future, both Treasury notes and Treasury bonds may make a satisfactory investment. For example, if a firm is establishing a fund to purchase a building three years from now, both the notes and the bonds might make satisfactory investments.

Certificates of Deposit

Certificates of deposit (CDs), with maturities of from 30 days to one year, are debt instruments issued by commercial banks. Such documents, as their name indicates, are evidence that depositors have placed money in a time deposit in a bank and that the bank will pay whomever presents the certificates on the maturity date. A business firm may purchase CDs from a bank or in the open market. If the purchase is made from a bank, the business makes a time deposit and receives a negotiable certificate. Since the Federal Deposit Insurance Corporation insures only for the usual amount, a firm placing several million dollars in one of these outlets must consider the safety factor. As a result, many firms acquire only CDs issued by the very large commercial banks, on the presumption that these banks are safer than small ones. It can be seen, however, that CDs are not as safe as fully guaranteed United States government obligations. Because of this factor, the yield obtainable on CDs is higher than that on short-term government obligations of comparable maturity—The yield being approximately 4.5 percent. Although a commercial bank may issue either negotiable or nonnegotiable CDs, most business firms prefer the former because they may be sold in the open market if the owner needs the money before maturity. Because CDs meet the requirements for a sound investment for temporarily idle funds, it should be no surprise that these instruments are a popular form of investment for business firms (as well as for individuals).

Commercial Paper:
Bankers' Acceptances

Just as a corporation might issue bonds to obtain funds, so might it issue bearer notes to raise funds for a period of time from 30 days to a year. This means that a corporation sells notes at a discount and receives cash in return. Such instruments are commonly referred to as *commercial paper*. This form of debt is in turn purchased by other business firms as an investment, thereby allowing business firms to lend each other money. Thus a firm might raise funds by selling $1 million of its notes payable for $980,000 in cash. As explained earlier in this chapter, at maturity the issuer pays the note holders $1 million, the $20,000 representing interest. In the meantime, business firms and other investors are willing to purchase commercial paper because of the interest that can be earned on it. An investor may purchase commercial paper direct from its issuer or in the open market. Only the very large and prosperous firms issue commercial paper; hence, these documents are relatively safe but probably less safe than United States government securities and CDs (admittedly, a direct comparison of safety is quite difficult). Yet, commercial paper has an outstanding record for safety and is a relatively sound investment. Since there is an established market for commercial paper, an investor may sell it and receive his money before the due date; therefore, these investments have liquidity. The yield is approximately 4.5 percent, although commercial paper due in 30 days carries a lower rate than that which is due in 90 days. This differential is caused mainly by the economic law that there is more risk in owning an instrument due in 90 days than in owning one due in 30 days. (The same principle holds true for United States government securities.) In recent times, corporate treasurers have been seeking investment outlets that offer a higher yield than can be obtained on federal government securities; commercial paper meets this requirement.

Bankers' acceptances are drafts drawn on a bank and accepted by the bank. After a bank accepts a draft by placing its signature on the front of it, the original owner may sell it in the open market. Business firms with excess cash may purchase these instruments (at a discount), hold them until the due date, and then collect from the bank that accepted the draft. Interest is earned because the buyers receive at maturity more than was paid for the investment. Since banks generally have a high credit standing, bankers' acceptances are sound investments; since there is a market where they may be sold if the investor wants his money before maturity, these outlets have marketability; and since the investor earns approximately 4.1 percent on them, they provide an adequate return.

Other Investments

In addition to the investments already discussed, financial managers may find other outlets appropriate to their needs. This is especially true if the financial manager is willing to tolerate the hazard of a fluctuating market price in return for the extra yield. Such investments as municipal and high-grade corporate bonds may prove suitable. In the final analysis, the three elements of safety, market fluctuation, and return must be balanced so that profits will be optimized.

As an aid to the decision-making process, models may be used to give guidance on the number of times that a business should borrow during the year so as to minimize acquisition and holding costs, assuming the firm knows how much it will need to borrow during a one-year period. In applying the operations research process to solve this problem, cash is viewed as a form of inventory that is stored and gradually used. Just as there is an order cost for obtaining inventory, so is there a cost for applying for a loan; for example, the cost may consist of the value of officers' time and the expense of preparing special accounting statements. Also, as in the case of inventory, there is a kind of storage cost of having the money, called a holding cost. This latter cost is the difference between the rate paid to the bank for the use of the funds and the rate earned on the funds invested temporarily in the short-term money market. Let us illustrate the use of operations research, known as management science, with an example. Assume that a firm is in need of $50,000 in additional funds during the coming year, that it incurs an acquisition expense of $125 per loan (for officers' time and for preparing special accounting reports), that a bank charges 6 percent interest, and that the proceeds of the loan may be invested in government securities (until the money is needed for operating purposes) at 4 percent. Two questions must be answered by operations research: (1) What is the best amount to borrow at any one time? (2) What is the best number of loans to obtain? If an answer to the first question can be obtained, the answer to the second is easily derived.

The issue to be resolved is whether to borrow the $50,000 in one transaction, whether to obtain two loans of $25,000 each, or whether to use some other combination, assuming that the banker is willing to give the borrower a choice. If the borrower obtains few loans, one set of costs will decline, the other set will rise. The set of costs that will decline is the $125 expense incurred for each loan obtained. If the borrower obtains only 1 loan, this subset of costs will amount to only $125; if he obtains 2 loans, the subset will increase to $250; if he obtains 10 loans, the subset will rise to $1,250. Insofar as the acquisition costs are concerned, the fewer the number of loans, the lower the acquisition costs. But there is another subset of costs to consider, namely, the cost of not fully utilizing the borrowed funds immediately. The borrower is paying the bank 6 percent but earning only 4 percent on the money that is invested in government securities; hence, there is a holding cost of 2 cents on the average for each $1 invested in the short-term money market. Insofar as the second type of cost is concerned, it is better to obtain numerous small loans, each loan being acquired at the time the firm needs the money. If only the second kind of cost is considered, it is better to obtain 10 loans of $5,000 than to obtain 1 loan of $50,000; the holding costs of the former are $50 ($5,000 ÷ 2 × $0.02); the holding costs of

AN EXAMPLE OF OPERATIONS RESEARCH IN MANAGING CASH

the latter are $500 ($50,000 ÷ 2 X $0.02). In summary, if it takes into consideration only the first set of costs, the firm should obtain one or a few loans; if it takes into consideration only the second group of costs, the firm should obtain a number of small loans. The problem is to obtain a balance between these opposing costs so that the sum of the two kinds is at a minimum.

In this example, operations research will give an answer to only one part of the transaction, because simplifying assumptions are made; with this in mind, the next step is to apply the management science process to solving the problem. The goals of the firm should be considered; there should be a team approach to the problem or, in the absence of a team, all departments within the business should be informed as to the decision about to be made; the important variables should be quantified, placed in a formula, and the formula solved; and the answer obtained should be checked and double checked for reasonableness before a decision is made.

The following symbols will be used to represent the main variables in this problem:

U = Total amount of dollars to be borrowed ($50,000 in this example)
P = Cost in dollars for acquiring each loan ($125 in this example)
H = Cost of storing a dollar (in this example the cost is the difference between 6 percent and 4 percent; when the 2 percent is applied to $1.00, the answer is $0.02)
Q = Number of dollars to be borrowed with each loan so as to minimize the sum of the two kinds of costs

The optimum ordering quantity is found to be obtainable by the following formula:

$$Q = \sqrt{\frac{2UP}{H}}$$

Substituting the information in the formula, we have:

$$Q = \sqrt{\frac{2 \times 50,000 \times 125}{.02}}$$
$$= 25,000$$

The answer is that the best amount to borrow at one time is $25,000. If this is true, then the optimum number of loans to obtain is two ($50,000 ÷ $25,000).

HIGHLIGHTS OF THIS CHAPTER

Commercial paper houses have as their main activity the purchase of short-term notes issued by corporations. Commercial finance companies specialize in lending on the pledge of accounts receivable.

A firm that has excess cash may choose to invest it in short-term outlets, such as United States Treasury notes, CDs, and bankers' acceptances. When making such investments, the investor should give consideration to yield, risk, and maturity date. On the other hand, a number of corporations prefer to keep their idle balances in checking accounts, since, despite the lost interest, these depositors are likely to be given preferential loans by bankers.

A new development is the attempt to apply operations research to the management of cash.

REVIEW QUESTIONS

12-1. What is the main function of a commercial paper house? a commercial finance company?

12-2. What are the main advantages for a firm that obtains funds through a commercial paper house instead of borrowing from a bank?

12-3. Why do some firms acquire cash through the pledge of accounts receivable with a commercial finance company instead of borrowing from a bank?

12-4. What services does the SBA render to small business firms?

12-5. Company X, a large corporation, has $1 million in cash over and above its normal cash needs. Rather than use this money to pay cash dividends, the firm decides to hold the funds for emergency purposes and for purposes of adding new product lines, if such an opportunity should arise. Assuming that the firm must give consideration to both yield and safety: (a) Prepare a portfolio from the following list: United States Treasury bills, commercial paper, certificates of deposit, long-term United States government bonds, common stock of a new company formed to search for uranium, common stock of a public utility, common stock of Company X, and keeping the money in a safe-deposit box. (b) Suggest the annual return in dollars that your portfolio would earn. The answer to this problem will be a matter of judgment.

REVIEW PROBLEMS

The answers to the problems appear at the end of this section. *For each problem, show how you obtained the answer.*

12-1. The Chamberlain Company sells 90-day notes to a commercial paper house at a discount of 3 percent. The commercial paper company charges a commission of a quarter of 1 percent. What is the annual rate of interest being paid on this transaction?

12-2. The Galton firm, a partnership, is studying the interest rate that would be charged by a finance company that advances funds on the basis of the pledge of accounts receivable. The finance company charges a flat fee of $1/30$ of 1 percent a day on the daily loan balance. What annual rate of interest is being charged by the finance company?

12-3. Company L has purchased $200,000 worth of goods, the terms being 10/10, N/60. Determine the dollar cost of the following alternatives. Which is the most expensive (in dollars)? Which is the least expensive (in dollars)? (a) Pay the bill on the 70th day; (b) borrow from a bank that charges 6 percent a year, on a discount basis; (c) borrow, by pledging inventory, from a finance company (the finance company will lend 90 percent of the value of the goods pledged and in addition to its 6 percent interest charge on the $180,000, it levies a fee of ½ of 1 percent on the value of the goods pledged); (d) borrow, by pledging accounts receivable, from a finance company that charges 1/30 of 1 percent per day on the value of the accounts receivable pledged (the finance company will lend 90 percent of the face value of the receivables pledged).

In order to shorten the computations and focus attention on principles, assume that in (b), (c), and (d) the loan will be obtained for a full 60-day period and that the money received will be used to take advantage of the discount offered on the purchase.

12-4. Company R seeks to determine the optimum amount to borrow as each loan is negotiated at a bank. The management of the firm will need $250,000 in additional loans during the coming year. The expense of obtaining each loan is $100; furthermore, the bank charges 6 percent. Proceeds of the loan may be invested in government securities at 4 percent (until the money is needed for operating purposes). (a) What is the optimum amount to borrow at one time? (b) How many loans per year should the borrower seek?

Answers: 12-1, 4 percent; 12-2, 12 percent; 12-3 (answers may differ because of rounding)—12-3a, $20,000; 12-3b, $1,818.18; 12-3c, $2,800; 12-3d, $4,000; (a) is most expensive and (b) is least expensive; 12-4a, $50,000; 12-4b, 5.

CASE ON COMMERCIAL BANK LOAN TO A SMALL BUSINESS

A supplier makes an attractive offer to the vice president of the Zing Manufacturing Company (hereafter called Zing). If Zing will buy an extra $10,000 of raw materials and pay cash, a 30 percent discount will be given. This is in contrast with the usual discount of 15 percent given by this supplier. The vice president confers with the president, and they decide to purchase the materials, provided Zing's bank will lend them $7,000 to finance the deal. Zing has entered into transactions like this on previous occasions; hence, there is not a direct connection between an increase in inventory and an increase in accounts payable.

George Bender, Elmer Larsen, and the wives of these two parties are the only stockholders in Zing, a manufacturer of storm windows. Bender owns 90 shares, Larsen owns 50 shares, and each of the wives owns 5 shares. Zing has been a profitable company and has yielded a good income for the two men and their families. Bender is president; Larsen is vice president; Mrs. Bender is secretary. Mrs. Larsen is not active in the firm. Bender receives a salary of $18,000; Larsen a salary of $12,000; and Mrs. Bender a salary of $2,000. This corporation, like many others, is a family controlled enterprise.

Bender and Larsen are respected citizens in their community. Each has a reputation for paying his bills on time. Also, despite its chronic shortage of cash, Zing is respected by its suppliers. Both men participate in civic affairs, including charity drives. Bender has a heart ailment and he is especially interested in the heart drive. Larsen is active in fund raising for the local hospital. The excellent reputation of the two men and their company has helped them obtain credit in the past from the local bank.

Zing has several loans from its bank, all secured by the pledge of the firm's fixed assets and inventories. The terms of the loans are that the firm will pay no dividends, that it will limit salaries to the amount now in existence, and that it will not purchase any of its own common stock. Both Bender and Larsen sign the notes in their capacity as corporate officers. The notes due the bank are all of a six-month maturity. There is, however, an implied understanding that the bank will renew the notes at their maturity, although the interest rate might be changed. The local bank has been quite liberal in granting credit to Zing.

The bank would normally consider a request for a $7,000 loan as routine, and it would grant the money without delay. However, Zing is already heavily indebted to the bank. The loan committee of the bank has been called into special session to study this case. Even when the last loan was granted, some of the members of the committee thought the bank was lax in its dealings with Zing. The president of the bank pointed out to the loan committee that Zing is a valuable customer and that he hoped that whatever the outcome, Zing would not take his business to another bank.

Table 12-2 gives financial data for the business and for its owners.

	Five Years Ago	Four Years Ago	Three Years Ago	Two Years Ago	Last Year	TABLE 12-2 Balance Sheets and Other Business Data for Zing
Assets						
Current assets:						
Cash	$ 1,000	$ 2,500	$ 500	$ 500	500	
Accounts receivable	10,000	7,500	14,500	42,500	42,500	
Inventories	14,500	16,500	17,000	31,000	35,500	
Other current assets	500	500	1,000	1,000	1,000	
Total current assets	$26,000	$27,000	$33,000	$75,000	$79,000	
Fixed assets:						
Machinery	$ 7,000	$ 8,500	$10,000	$ 9,500	$12,500	
Cars and trucks	4,500	5,000	3,500	7,000	5,000	
Other fixed assets	500	500	500	500	500	
Total fixed assets	$12,000	$14,000	$14,000	$17,000	$18,000	
Total assets	$38,000	$41,000	$47,000	$92,000	$97,000	
Liabilities and Net Worth						
Current liabilities:						
Notes payable:						
First National Bank	$10,000	$ 7,000	$ 9,000	$46,000	$38,000	
Benner and Larsen	2,000	2,000	2,000	2,000	2,000	
Accounts payable	8,000	12,000	22,000	25,000	29,000	
Accrued taxes	1,000	2,000	1,000	2,000	5,000	
Total current liabilities	$21,000	$23,000	$34,000	$75,000	$74,000	

Capital:					
Stock, 150 shares,					
$100 par value	$15,000	$15,000	$15,000	$15,000	$15,000
Surplus	2,000	3,000	(2,000)	2,000	8,000
Total capital	$17,000	$18,000	$13,000	$17,000	$23,000
Total liabilities and net worth	$38,000	$41,000	$47,000	$92,000	$97,000

Other Business Data

Net sales	$154,000	$218,000	$170,000	$313,000	$331,000
Net profit after taxes	2,000	1,000	(5,000)	4,000	6,000

Zing estimates that its annual depreciation over the next few years will be at least $1,500. Furthermore, the management of Zing believes that its net profits after taxes will be at least $6,000 a year. The personal balance sheets of the owners of Zing are as follows:

	The Benders	The Larsens
Cash in bank	$ 1,000	$ 2,000
Savings and loan shares	2,000	3,000
United States government bonds	4,000	
Church bond		1,000
Residence	30,000	25,000
Stocks in business firms	10,000	1,000
Corporation bonds	1,000	2,000
Cash surrender value of life insurance	8,000	4,000
Shares in mutual funds	12,000	6,000
Total	$68,000	$44,000

Neither of the families have any debt, except for a few minor household ones. Furthermore, the face value of the life insurance on Bender is $100,000 while the face value of life insurance on Larsen is $60,000.

Required:
1. Should the bank grant the loan? Give reasons for your decision.
2. If the loan is granted, propose a repayment schedule for Zing (keep in mind that the bank does not want the entire loan repaid, as it earns interest on the debt).
3. What steps should be taken by the bank to strengthen its position?
4. What actions should the firm take to lessen its heavy reliance on debt?

Managing Working Capital — Receivables

The purpose of having receivables is to increase sales and hence increase profits; if a firm could have the same volume of sales without having receivables, there would be no point in selling on account. Since there is an interrelationship between sales policy and the extension of credit, the establishment of the level of receivables is a top-management decision. Because there are also many day-to-day activities that must be conducted, the operating team that handles this phase of the firm's activities is often grouped into a credit department. The finance person's interest in accounts receivable is severalfold. First, he determines whether accounts receivable add to the firm's earnings as much as would be the case if the funds were committed to some other asset. Second, he attempts to minimize the amount of accounts receivable without impairing sales. If accounts receivable can be reduced by $200,000, there is a savings of $12,000 to the firm, provided the firm uses the money to repay bank loans on which it is paying 6 percent. In the final analysis, the purpose in managing accounts receivable is to enable the firm to reach its goals.

The following aspects of accounts receivable will be studied in this chapter:

1. Considerations affecting the general level of receivables
2. Keeping the receivables moving toward cash
3. Conserving the receivables against loss
4. Credit bureaus
5. Operations research in managing receivables

The objective of managing accounts receivable is to maximize sales, speed cash inflow, and reduce credit risk.

The optimum amount of accounts receivable and notes receivable is determined by top management, often by the president and his advisers. Some firms, such as Sears Roebuck, follow a policy of extending generous terms; other companies,

CONSIDERATIONS AFFECTING THE GENERAL LEVEL OF RECEIVABLES

such as Greyhound Bus Corporation, sell almost entirely for cash. Several factors influence the amount of credit that a business extends:

1. The type of product or service sold has an influence on the amount of credit extended. If the item being sold has a high unit price, like jewelry, probably the seller will have to extend generous credit terms. On the other hand, if the unit price is low, such as that of a newspaper, there is little need for credit.

2. The customs of an industry influence the amount of credit that a particular firm extends to its purchasers. This is a factor that is to a large extent beyond the control of any one firm. If tradition permits the purchaser a relatively long period of time to pay his bill, the seller will have a relatively large amount of receivables on his books. Also, a firm's historical policy of extending credit has an impact on the amount of credit that it will extend in the future. Purchasers become accustomed to certain credit terms, an expectation that may be difficult to change.

3. The stage of the business cycle also has some bearing on the amount of credit extended. In prosperous times sellers are likely to find the amount of accounts receivable increasing because of new customers who are making purchases and old customers who are increasing their purchases. On the other hand, in a period of business decline, accounts receivable are likely to decrease because of the smaller amount of purchases by the firm's customers.

4. The amount of assets that an enterprise has will affect the amount of credit that it can extend to others. Thus a large firm is usually in a better position to extend credit than a small one. This arises from the probable situation that large firms find it easier to obtain funds in the capital markets than the small ones.

However, within the framework given above, there is some flexibility for each business in extending credit. Each firm must evaluate its policy on this matter and determine whether it should extend more liberal credit terms, make its credit terms more stringent, or keep its credit policy the same. In recent years the use of credit has grown tremendously. Consumers especially have come to expect more generous credit terms in the form of a lower down payment and a longer period of time in which to pay the debt. This new situation may mean the expansion of receivables for some selling firms. However, financial institutions have expanded their operations and have relieved retailers and other business firms of part of the burden of carrying large amounts of receivables. Many retail firms, for example, sell on generous credit terms and then immediately sell the receivables or notes so acquired to a financial institution. The seller in effect converts a credit sale into the equivalent of a cash sale. In seeking the optimum amount of receivables, the sales department and the credit department will be able to offer valuable advice. The sales department must be consulted because the extension of credit on favorable terms is often a competitive sales weapon (extending less favorable terms might adversely affect sales, and extending more generous terms might increase sales). The credit department also will have valuable advice to give because of its familiarity with the individual customers of the firm and with trade practices in the industry. In a particular situation, the course of action taken will be based on the alternative that will increase the net profits of the enterprise.

An important circulating asset that will be converted into cash in the ordinary operation of a business is accounts receivable. If all goes well, the customers will pay their debts, and the firm will have converted this claim into liquid resources. Management expects over a period of time that some of the accounts will be uncollectible. But this does not alter the fact that companies expect to convert their accounts receivable into cash in the near future. In manufacturing, wholesaling, and retailing, the accounts receivable must be collected promptly if the company is to have a steady inflow of funds.

KEEPING THE RECEIVABLES MOVING TOWARD CASH

Normal Movement of Accounts Receivable

Both management and creditors are interested in obtaining clues on the rate at which accounts receivable are being converted into cash. Such questions as these arise. How many days will it take to collect the accounts receivable on the books? Is the firm taking a longer or a shorter period to collect its accounts than in the previous year? How does the firm compare with other companies in the same industry insofar as number of days is required to collect accounts receivable? Answers to these questions provide useful information in directing the management of circulating assets, as well as in evaluating the performance of the credit and collection department.

Turnover of Accounts Receivable

Several methods can be used to answer the questions posed in the preceding paragraph. Assume that a firm has annual credit sales of $200,000 and that its accounts receivable average $25,000. A starting point in determining liquidity is to use the *accounts receivable turnover test*, computed as follows:

$$\text{Accounts receivable turnover} = \frac{\text{Sales on account per year}}{\text{Average accounts receivable}}$$
$$= \frac{\$200,000}{\$25,000}$$
$$= 8$$

The best figure to use in the numerator is sales on account. While this data is available to management, it may not be public information and hence might be unavailable to outsiders. Total sales (combined cash and credit) is a less desirable concept if a relatively large percentage of the sales are for cash, because it is possible that the formula will show a high accounts receivable turnover and yet have a credit and collection department that is very lax in its activities. Of course, a number of firms sell on account only, and in this situation the total sales figure may be used justifiably. The denominator of the formula (average accounts receivable) is obtained in a number of ways, none of which is entirely satisfactory. A simple plan is to add the accounts receivable at the beginning of the year to the accounts receivable at the end of the year and divide by two to obtain an arithmetic average. In the formula, opening accounts receivable is assumed to be $30,000 and closing accounts receivable is assumed to be $20,000. The difficulty with averages is that they may not be truly representative of accounts receivable for the year. According to the formula, the accounts receivable turnover is 8. This means that the average amount of $25,000 is collected each 1.5 months (12 months ÷ the turnover of 8). Furthermore, if the accounts receivable turnover is 8, then the average number of days necessary to collect the accounts is 45 (360 ÷ 8). (It is immaterial whether one uses a 360- or a 365-day year.) There is still another method of estimating the number of days necessary to collect the amount of accounts receivable on the books. It is shown below, in two parts:

$$\text{Average amount of credit sales per day} = \frac{\text{Sales on account per year}}{360}$$
$$= \frac{\$200,000}{360}$$
$$= \$555.55$$

$$\text{Average number of days necessary to collect accounts receivable} = \frac{\text{Accounts receivable on books}}{\text{Average daily sales on account}}$$
$$= \frac{\$25,000}{\$555.55}$$
$$= 45$$

After management computes the turnover of receivables, the next step is to compare the results with the same data in the firm for a previous period of time and with industry averages. One can compare the turnover of a jewelry store with its own data for an earlier period or with the turnover of other jewelry stores, but one cannot justifiably compare the turnover of a jewelry store with that of a grocery store. The turnover of a one-year period, as mentioned, may be compared with the turnover of several previous years. If the turnover figure is changing upward or downward sharply, this would be cause for investigation. Thus, if a firm's average collection period for the current year is 45 days and if the average for previous years never exceeded 35 days, management wants an explanation for this change. Also, the business may want to compare its own collection period with industry averages. Dun & Bradstreet, Inc., for example, releases an informative series on credit terms used in various industries and on the average collection period in these industries. One may make the guarded statement that for a particular industry a relatively high turnover of accounts receivable is usually a good sign while a relatively low turnover of accounts receivable is usually a bad sign.

The turnover of receivables analysis is a useful tool because it calls attention to the possibility of making changes in two policy areas: (1) changing the period of time for which credit is extended, and (2) changing collection policies.

Management ought to seek the optimum period of time it should allow its customers to pay their bills. The possibilities of shortening or lengthening the credit period should be investigated. If the collection period is shortened without disturbing the firm's volume of sales, the efficiency of the firm is increased. In general, a shortened credit period is desirable for two reasons. First, there is the probability that a larger percentage of the accounts receivable will be collected and the complementary possibility that there will be fewer losses from bad debts. The risk to the seller increases as he extends more and more generous credit terms (that is, when he gives the buyer a longer period of time in which to pay the bills). There is less certainty in collecting an account due in six months than in collecting one due in 30 days. Second, the shorter the collection period, the fewer accounts receivable are on the books. The freed funds can be used for other worthy purposes, such as acquiring more inventory or even distributing the funds to owners. On the other hand, there is the possibility that the firm should increase the number of days that it allows its customers to pay their debts. The extension of more generous credit terms can be a powerful inducement for new customers to buy from the firm. In other words, there is the possibility that sales are being lost because competitors are extending more generous credit terms. An increase in credit terms allowed will require additional capital to expand accounts receivable and will increase bad-debt losses. But the important point is whether gross income will be increased sufficiently to more than offset these factors. The key question is whether shortening or lengthening the credit period (or keeping the period the same) will increase net profits. Theoretically, a firm would prefer to sell for cash alone. But competitive conditions, tradition, and economic characteristics of the borrower have entrenched the sale on account, and hence many businessmen must plan on having a substantial amount invested in accounts receivable.

Management also ought to investigate the possibility of making changes in its future collection policies. The officers should compare the credit terms extended with the average number of days it actually takes to collect these accounts. If a firm extends terms of 3/10, N/30, and if the firm takes an average of 45 days to collect these accounts, the preliminary evidence is that this company is not enforcing its credit terms. Perhaps collection policies and procedures need to be revamped.

If the enterprise is undergoing rapid change in the rate at which it is making sales, caution must be used in interpreting the accounts receivable turnover test. Thus, if a firm's sales in December are increasing faster than usual, accounts receivable will increase sharply and will tend to lower the turnover ratio and perhaps give the impression that the firm is taking more than the normal number of days to collect its accounts. Likewise, rapidly falling sales in December would lower the amount of accounts receivable on the books and would raise the turnover ratio, perhaps giving the impression that the firm is more efficient in collecting its accounts. Both impressions could be incorrect. Since management is familiar with circumstances attending changes in sales and accounts receivable, it is in a better position than the general public to interpret data on turnover of accounts receivable.

The management of Company K is considering giving its customers 30 days *Problem* instead of 15 to pay bills. This policy is expected to increase sales and profits.

The immediate issue, however, is the impact of such a change on the total asset requirements of the firm and on the methods to be used to finance the expansion in total assets. (When sales increase, it is generally the situation that assets must increase to support the new level of sales.)

The following ratios apply to the company: cash is 10 percent of sales; accounts receivable are 10 percent of sales; inventories are 20 percent of sales; accounts payable are 100 percent of inventory. These ratios will also prevail after the change in credit policy except that accounts receivable will become 20 percent of sales.

The following is the firm's balance sheet before the change in credit policy:

Cash	$ 27,000	Bank loans	$ 27,000
Accounts receivable	27,000	Accounts payable	54,000
Inventories	54,000	Partners' equity	94,500
Fixed assets	67,500		
Total	$175,500	Total	$175,500

If credit terms are changed to 30 days, sales are expected to increase to $360,000; $22,500 of additional fixed assets will be needed.

Required: (a) Determine the new total asset requirements that will result if the change in credit policy is made. (b) How much in additional financing will be needed as a result of the change in credit policy?

Solution   First, prepare a revised asset section for a pro forma balance sheet:

Cash (10 percent of $360,000)	$ 36,000
Accounts receivable (20 percent of $360,000)	72,000
Inventories (20 percent of $360,000)	72,000
Fixed assets ($67,500 + $22,500)	90,000
	$270,000

At the end of step 1, the firm estimates that it will need a total of $270,000 in assets. This is an increase of $94,500 ($270,000 − $175,500). Hence, funds will have to be provided to the extent of $94,500. Accounts payable will increase by $18,000 ($72,000 − $54,000); this will lower the financing requirements by $18,000. (b) The firm still needs an additional $76,500 ($94,500 − $18,000). The additional $76,500 might be raised by obtaining additional bank loans, by increasing the partners' equity, and by any other reasonable means. The conclusion is that a change in credit policy had many repercussions. Total asset requirements increased, and planning had to be done on where to obtain the money to finance the expansion.

When a firm makes a sale on account, there may be a waiting period of 30 days (for example) before the money is collected. It is possible to receive this cash sooner by selling the account to another party. The buyer of the account then collects the receivable. Although a number of institutions will buy accounts receivable, *factors* are the main purchasers. The *factor* is an organization whose main activity is the outright purchase of a firm's accounts receivable. The word *factor* is also used as a verb and means to sell accounts receivable to this financial institution. These institutions will be used to illustrate the process of speeding up the circular flow of assets via the sale of accounts receivable.

The Role of Factoring

Although there are only about 20 large factors in the United States, they do several billion dollars worth of business each year. Most of the accounts receivable that they purchase are from textile companies, although in recent years the accounts purchased from the shoe, furniture, and equipment industries have greatly increased. Factors are not the only institutions that purchase accounts receivable; commercial banks and other institutions may also engage in this practice. However, the purchase of accounts receivable is most often associated with factors because this is their main function. In addition, however, factors may lend against the pledge of accounts receivable, advance funds against the pledge of inventory, and supply cash for the purchase of fixed assets.

Factoring is one of the methods available for speeding up the movement of accounts receivable into cash. The reason for the desirability of this speed-up is that circulating asset turnover is increased. This in turn means that a larger annual volume of business can be conducted on a given amount of permanent capital. Usually the added annual volume will raise net profits.

The factor that acquires the accounts receivable assumes responsibility for bad debts except those arising from a dispute over the quantity or the quality of the goods sold. Since the factor takes this risk, it is only natural that he would want to approve or disapprove each sale on credit. Factors can give their decision quickly because they maintain elaborate credit files on selected companies. The assumption of the credit risk by factors is another advantage of using their services.

Assumption of Bad-Debt Losses by Factors

After the factor has given its approval, the business firm ships the goods. Invoices are clearly marked with an inscription notifying the purchaser of the goods that the account has been sold and that payment should be made direct to the factor. The seller of the goods must supply the factor with proof of the transaction by submitting copies of the invoice and the proper shipping documents. On the day the factor receives the invoice, cash is available to the seller of the merchandise. From the merchant's viewpoint, each sale becomes a cash sale.

Mechanics of the Purchase of Accounts Receivable by Factors

Factors have two basic charges—a flat fee based on the total accounts receivable purchased and a discount rate that is imposed if the seller of the accounts

Charges by Factors

obtains funds before the factor collects the money. The flat fee levied on a particular seller of accounts receivable ranges from one-half of 1 percent to approximately 3 percent, depending on such matters as the credit strength of the seller, the volume of business transacted each year with him, and the average size of the accounts purchased from him. This fee is based on the "net amount," that is, the billed price less any discounts, as shown in the following example, which indicates (in general terms) how factors' charges are computed (in practice, many other methods are used):

Gross amount of invoice	$1,000.00
Less 3 percent discount, which it is assumed a merchant allows his customer if the bill is paid within 30 days	30.00
Net amount of the account	$ 970.00
Less factor's fee, which is assumed to be 2 percent	19.40
Difference	$ 950.60

In some cases, the factor remits the entire $970.00 and collects the $19.40 in the following month.

If the merchant is willing to wait 30 days for his money, he will receive $950.60. If he should leave the proceeds with the factor after the collection date (30 days in the above case), he will receive interest at the annual rate of 1 to 5 percent. But if he wants cash immediately, a 6 percent yearly interest charge is levied in the following manner:

Difference (as above)	$950.60[1]
Less 6 percent interest (for 30 days)	4.75
Total due	$945.85

From the $945.85, the factor may withhold a reserve of from 5 to 10 percent to guard against loss in the event of a dispute between the seller and the buyer over the quantity or quality of the goods.

In this illustration, the dollar cost of factoring is $24.15 ($970.00 − $945.85). In itself this is meaningless unless a comparison is made with the amount of profit added to the business because of the increased turnover of working capital. In this illustration, the annual rate of interest being paid is 30 percent, determined as follows:

2 percent for 30 days—converted to a yearly basis	24 percent
6 percent yearly for immediate receipt of cash	6 percent
Total	30 percent

1. A frequently used practice is to base the interest on the net amount of the account (in this case $970).

The rate is higher than that on unsecured bank loans. However, because of the many services rendered by factors, neither the annual interest rate nor the total interest cost in dollars can be used as the sole basis on which to compare these two sources of funds. The first important supplementary function performed by factors is that of credit investigation. This service lowers the overhead of the seller of accounts receivable because he does not need to maintain an elaborate credit department. A second significant service is that the factor collects the accounts, thus further lessening the personnel and overhead requirements of the seller of the accounts. Third, credit losses are eliminated. The value of all three functions must be subtracted from the factor's charges before a comparison can be made with the cost that would be incurred if funds were obtained from another source.

Factors also lend to business firms on the basis of the pledge of accounts receivable. When factors act in this capacity, the loan granted resembles a loan granted by a commercial finance company or by a bank that lends on the pledge of accounts receivable. Although "factoring" and "lending on the pledge of accounts receivable" are different, the two functions often are conducted by the same financial institution.

A merchant can sell his *notes receivable* and hence obtain cash before the maturity date of the documents. Sales finance companies, banks, and other institutions will buy notes from businessmen. In the discussion to follow, the sales finance company will be used to illustrate this procedure. *Role of the Sales Finance Company*

A *sales finance company* is an institution whose principal activity is the purchase of installment *notes* from dealers who sell at retail. The dealers have obtained the notes from their customers who have bought goods (automobiles, television sets, and so on) on the time-payment plan. For example, if Fred Jones acquires an automobile on the installment plan and gives the car dealer notes amounting to $1,200, the dealer will probably sell the notes to a sales finance company and Jones will then make his payments directly to the new owner of the paper. The buyer of the automobile usually knows from the beginning that he is to present his payments to the sales finance company. In the discussion to follow, the term *dealer* will include any car dealer, merchant, or retailer who sells on the installment plan and receives notes or their equivalent from the transaction. The document the customer gives the dealer is often a note, although it is sometimes referred to as paper and other times as a sales agreement. Sales finance companies seek business by approaching dealers; they do not attempt to reach car buyers (or other consumers who buy on the time-payment plan). These companies are anxious to buy installment notes because of the interest that can be earned on them. Dealers are willing to sell the notes acquired from their customers for a number of reasons, although at this point it might be observed that one advantage of this operation is that dealers convert a sale on credit into the equivalent of a cash sale. Three sales finance companies that operate on a national scale are Commercial Credit Company, CIT Financial Corporation, and General Motors Acceptance Corporation. In addition, there are other sales finance companies that limit their operations to a certain region, as well as a great many others that operate on a local basis only.

Sales finance companies are also called discount houses, commercial credit companies, and automobile finance companies. Only rarely can one determine from the name of a financial institution the kinds of activities conducted by it (commercial banks are an exception). Also, it should be noted that sales finance companies are not the only organizations that buy installment notes. A number of other institutions, such as commercial banks, may be anxious to acquire prime-risk notes resulting from the sale of goods to ultimate consumers on the time-payment plan.

Role of Credit **The basic reason** for using short-term credit is to increase the firm's profits. By *in Earning Profits* using this form of credit, a business can expand the scale of its operations and thereby earn more profits than if operations were conducted at a lower level. The following example demonstrates this point.

> A has a capital of $800 in cash. He must purchase $400 in materials, which he buys on credit on 30-day terms. In order to produce an article from those materials which he will sell for $1,000 he must spend $400 for labor. It takes 30 days to produce the article and labor must be paid in cash. Competitive conditions require A to sell his product on 30-day terms. Therefore, at the end of the first 30 days A will have expended $400 for labor, the bill for the materials amounting to $400 will be due and have to be paid, and therefore A will have expended his entire capital of $800. He will not receive payment of the sale price of his product until 30 more days have elapsed, and even though he could obtain additional materials he would not have the cash to pay for the labor necessary to process the same. Consequently, he would have to limit his production to one article every 60 days, or 6 articles a year, which would give him annual sales of $6,000 and a gross profit of $1,200. On the other hand, if this same manufacturer had arranged to finance his accounts receivable, he would at the end of the first 30 days have created an account receivable in the amount of $1,000, against which the finance company would advance $800. Therefore, A would have funds available with which to pay for the labor required to produce another article during the next 30 days, and the process would be constantly repeated so that the cycle of cash flow would be reduced from 60 days to 30 days. Consequently, A could produce 12 articles per year and have sales of $12,000 instead of $6,000, and a gross profit of $2,400 instead of $1,200.[2]

As a business gains momentum and begins to earn profits, the extra cash generated is generally used to replace receivables financing.

2. Walter S. Seidman, *Sales Finance Companies and Factors* (New York: National Conference of Commercial Receivables Companies, Inc., 1949), pp. 14-15.

A firm conserves its accounts receivable and notes receivable in a number of ways, some of which are:

1. Precautions before the sale is made
   a. Using the line of credit
   b. Obtaining reports on the financial strength and integrity of the buyer
2. Precautions after sale is made
   a. Using commercial credit insurance
   b. Having the customer pledge collateral
   c. Taking special steps to protect the accounts against physical loss

A *line of credit* is an informal advance commitment by a creditor to extend credit or to lend money up to a designated amount. Thus a seller might allow a buyer to purchase goods on account as long as the amount of indebtedness does not exceed $10,000; or a bank might permit one of its customers to borrow up to $8,000. The line of credit is good for a limited period of time, such as six months or one year. It is established after taking into consideration the financial strength of the buyer, his past paying record, and other factors. In trade credit, the line of credit is used when a debtor has relatively frequent occasion to buy goods on account. The seller is then freed of the detailed work of conducting a credit investigation for each transaction. The line of credit is a form of revolving credit; that is, the debtor can make a number of purchases of goods on account as long as the total amount owed does not exceed the limit imposed by the seller. Firms that earn profits on inventory turnover have occasion to extend lines of credit.

Using the Line of Credit

The maximum line of credit for every customer is determined and then placed on the proper accounting records. As each order is received, a clerk inspects the records to see if the line of credit is exceeded; if not, the order is approved. But if the order would raise the buyer's indebtedness above the line of credit, an officer must review the situation. It is possible that the order will be approved if circumstances warrant. It can be seen that the line of credit is more of a management tool than an absolute limit on the amount of goods that can be bought on account. The overall purpose of the line of credit is to systemize the sale of goods on account and to reduce the bad-debt losses of the seller.

A number of agencies investigate the probable debt-paying ability of *business units*. This service is sold to businessmen and bankers throughout the country. Dun & Bradstreet, Inc., is one of the well-known organizations that sells these credit ratings. These services are important to the businessman, because he may refer to the credit ratings when granting credit to his customers, and because his own credit rating in Dun & Bradstreet may influence the amount of credit he can obtain from his suppliers.

Obtaining Reports on the Financial Strength and Integrity of Buyers

Dun & Bradstreet, Inc., gathers data on the ability of business firms to pay their bills on time—especially bills that have been incurred as a result of purchasing merchandise on account. Dun and Bradstreet, therefore, is basically a data bank with information on millions of businesses stored on computer tapes; the information is available to those who subscribe to the service. The data are useful to credit managers who must give their approval to selling goods on account to another business firm.

The credit manager is especially interested in two of the services—the *Reference Book* and the *Business Information Report*. The Reference Book contains the names of nearly three million business firms located throughout the United States and Canada, although a subscriber may elect to receive a Reference Book on firms in a certain region. Individual firms are listed alphabetically by town within each state. Each of these firms receives a credit rating, and most ratings consist of letters and a number. (See Figure 13-1 for the *Key to Ratings*.) The letters stand for estimated financial strength (net worth). For example, in the rating FF1, the letters "FF" indicate that the financial strength of the business is between $10,000 and $20,000. The number stands for composite appraisal of the business. In this example, the "1" indicates a high composite credit appraisal. In other words, this firm, although small, has paid its bills in the past and will probably continue to do so in the future. Figure 13-2 shows the rating of an actual company as it appears on a line in the Reference Book. One application of Dun & Bradstreet ratings is that a seller might automatically give his approval for the sale of *small orders* if the prospective buyer has a certain minimum credit rating. Thus a policy might be to grant immediate trade credit to a prospective buyer in the $20,000 to $30,000 range of financial strength if his composite credit appraisal is 1 or 2.

In addition to being useful to credit managers, the Reference Book is useful to those in the marketing and purchasing areas, because the service also states the products each firm makes or sells.

Professions, such as accounting or law, or certain services, such as barbershops, are not listed, since their credit buying of merchandise is for their own use.

If the credit manager needs more information than is given in the Reference Book, he can obtain it from the second of the two mentioned services—the Business Information Report, an example of which is shown in Figure 13-3. This report gives a more detailed picture of a firm. Of special interest is the payments section, which gives information on whether the firm is paying its specific bills on time. HC is the highest credit a particular supplier has extended; OWE indicates the amount currently owed to that supplier; PPT means the customer is prompt in his payments; and DISC reveals that the business is paying in time to take the cash discount. The material in the Business Information Report is sufficient for most purposes; however, an even more detailed report—the Analytical Report—is available on larger and more complex businesses.

Other sources of information on firms seeking to purchase goods on account are:

Past experience with the debtor. When goods are sold on account, heavy emphasis is given to the past experience (if any) with the would-be purchaser.

FIGURE 13-1
Key to Ratings

Key to Ratings

ESTIMATED FINANCIAL STRENGTH			COMPOSITE CREDIT APPRAISAL			
			HIGH	GOOD	FAIR	LIMITED
5A	Over	$50,000,000	1	2	3	4
4A	$10,000,000 to	50,000,000	1	2	3	4
3A	1,000,000 to	10,000,000	1	2	3	4
2A	750,000 to	1,000,000	1	2	3	4
1A	500,000 to	750,000	1	2	3	4
BA	300,000 to	500,000	1	2	3	4
BB	200,000 to	300,000	1	2	3	4
CB	125,000 to	200,000	1	2	3	4
CC	75,000 to	125,000	1	2	3	4
DC	50,000 to	75,000	1	2	3	4
DD	35,000 to	50,000	1	2	3	4
EE	20,000 to	35,000	1	2	3	4
FF	10,000 to	20,000	1	2	3	4
GG	5,000 to	10,000	1	2	3	4
HH	Up to	5,000	1	2	3	4

**CLASSIFICATION FOR BOTH
ESTIMATED FINANCIAL STRENGTH AND CREDIT APPRAISAL**

FINANCIAL STRENGTH BRACKET

1 $125,000 and Over

2 20,000 to 125,000

EXPLANATION

When only the numeral (1 or 2) appears, it is an indication that the estimated financial strength, while not definitely classified, is presumed to be within the range of the ($) figures in the corresponding bracket and that a condition is believed to exist which warrants credit in keeping with that assumption.

ABSENCE OF RATING DESIGNATION FOLLOWING NAMES LISTED IN THE REFERENCE BOOK
The absence of a rating, expressed by two hyphens (--), is not to be construed as unfavorable but signifies circumstances difficult to classify within condensed rating symbols. It suggests the advisability of obtaining a report for additional information.

EMPLOYEE RANGE DESIGNATIONS IN REPORTS OR NAMES NOT LISTED IN THE REFERENCE BOOK

Certain businesses do not lend themselves to a Dun & Bradstreet rating and are not listed in the Reference Book. Information on these names, however, continues to be stored and updated in the D&B Business Data Bank. Reports are available on these businesses but instead of a rating they carry an Employee Range Designation (ER) which is indicative of size in terms of number of employees. No other significance should be attached.

**KEY TO EMPLOYEE
RANGE DESIGNATIONS**

ER 1	Over 1000 Employees
ER 2	500 - 900 Employees
ER 3	100 - 499 Employees
ER 4	50 - 99 Employees
ER 5	20 - 49 Employees
ER 6	10 - 19 Employees
ER 7	5 - 9 Employees
ER 8	1 - 4 Employees
ER N	Not Available

© **DUN & BRADSTREET, INC.** 1973

99 Church Street, New York, N.Y. 10007

18B-7(720801)

FIGURE 13-2
A Line in the
Reference Book

A line in the reference book tells you:

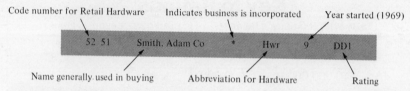

Code number for Retail Hardware   Indicates business is incorporated   Year started (1969)

52 51   Smith, Adam Co   *   Hwr   9   DD1

Name generally used in buying   Abbreviation for Hardware   Rating

Dun & Bradstreet rating:
Most Ratings consist of letters and a number. The LETTERS are known as the capital rating and denote the estimated financial strength of the business. For example, the letters "DD" mean the estimated financial strength of this concern is between $35,000 and $50,000. The **Number** stands for the composite credit appraisal of the business based upon information contained in the Business Information Report. In this example, the "1" indicates the composite credit appraisal is "High".

Analysis of financial statements. Many progressive credit managers study the financial statements of the prospective buyer of goods on account. These statements may be obtained directly from the applicant, from investment manuals, and from other sources.

Ledger experience. Ledger experience means the debt-paying record of the applicant with other creditors. If the applicant has paid others promptly, this is a sign of financial strength.

Direct interview. The prospective creditor may personally interview the applicant. In many cases, it is possible to appraise the overall situation better when there is personal contact with the management that is seeking to buy the goods on account.

Miscellaneous sources of information. These include information obtained from the applicant's bank, information at courthouses on bankruptcies, the general reputation of the applicant in the industry, and credit bureaus.

The appraising of a credit risk is primarily an art and cannot be determined or measured by mechanical formula. Successful appraising of the applicant's credit strength can be accomplished only by those with mature judgment, and even they often find their conclusions invalid when extraneous factors such as wars and depressions suddenly strike the economy.

*Using Commercial
Credit Insurance*

Phelps, in an authoritative work, has defined *commercial credit insurance* as "an arrangement between an insurance company and a business firm under which the firm as the insured (1) is guaranteed indemnification against abnormal credit losses arising from a failure of business debtors to pay, and because of this relationship, (2) receives other auxiliary services or benefits."[3] In addition to rendering the insurance function, then, credit insurance companies offer other services, such as the collection of overdue accounts. The insurance is available only to business firms; furthermore, only accounts receivable due from other

3. Clyde William Phelps, *Commercial Credit Insurance as a Management Tool* (Baltimore: Commercial Credit Company, 1961). p. 10.

business firms are insurable. If a manufacturer sells goods to wholesalers, the accounts receivable represented by the transaction would be insurable. On the other hand, if a grocer sells goods to housewives, these accounts would not be eligible for insurance. A large, well-known credit insurance company is American Credit Indemnity Company of New York, a subsidiary of Commercial Credit Company.

FIGURE 13-3
A Business
Information
Report

PLEASE NOTE WHETHER NAME, BUSINESS AND STREET ADDRESS CORRESPOND WITH YOUR INQUIRY

Dun & Bradstreet® BUSINESS INFORMATION REPORT

RATING UNCHANGED

SIC	D-U-N-S	© DUN & BRADSTREET, INC.	STARTED	RATING
34 61	04-426-3226	CD 13 APR 21 19--	1957	DD1
	ARNOLD METAL PRODUCTS CO	METAL STAMPINGS		

53 S MAIN ST
DAWSON MICH   66666
      TEL 215 999-0000

SAMUEL B. ARNOLD   )
GEORGE T. ARNOLD   ) PARTNERS

SUMMARY

PAYMENTS	DISC PPT
SALES	$177,250
WORTH	$42,961
EMPLOYS	10
RECORD	CLEAR
CONDITION	STRONG
TREND	UP

PAYMENTS	HC	OWE	P DUE	TERMS			APR 19--	SOLD
	3000	1500	1	10	30	Disc	Over 3 yrs
	2500	1000	1	10	30	Disc	Over 3 yrs
	2000	500	2	20	30	Disc	Old account
	1000				30	Ppt	Over 3 yrs
	500				30	Ppt	Over 3 yrs

FINANCE

On Apr 21 19-- S.B. Arnold, Partner, submitted statement Dec 31 19--

Cash	$	4,870	Accts Pay	$	6,121
Accts Rec		15,472	Notes Pay (Curr)		2,400
Mdse		14,619	Accruals		3,583
		------			------
Current		34,961	Current		12,104
Fixed Assets		22,840	Notes Pay (Def)		5,000
Other Assets		2,264	NET WORTH		42,961
		------			------
Total Assets		60,065	Total		60,065

19-- sales $177,250; gross profit $47,821; net profit $4,204. Fire Insurance mdse $15,000; fixed assets $20,000. Annual rent $3,000. Signed Apr 21 19-- ARNOLD METAL PRODUCTS CO by Samuel B. Arnold, Partner Johnson Singer, CPA. Dawson
                    -----0-----
Sales and profits increased last year due to increased sub-contract work and this trend is reported continuing. New equipment was purchased last Sept for $8,000 financed by a bank loan secured by a lien on the equipment payable $200 per month. With increased capacity, the business has been able to handle a larger volume. Arnold stated that for the first two months of this year volume was $32,075 and operations continue profitable.

BANKING

Medium to high four figure balances are maintained locally. An equipment loan is outstanding and being retired as agreed.

HISTORY

Style registered Feb 1 1965 by partners. SAMUEL, born 1918, married. 1939 graduate of Lehigh University with B.S. degree in Mechanical Engineering. 1949-50 employed by Industrial Machine Corporation, Detroit, and 1950-56 production manager with Aerial Motors Inc., Detroit. Started this business in 1957. GEORGE, born 1940, single, son of Samuel. Graduated in 1963 from Dawson Institute of Technology. Served U.S. Air Force 1963-64. Admitted to partnership interest Feb 1965.

OPERATION

Manufactures light metal stampings for industrial concerns and also does some work on a sub-contract basis for aircraft manufacturers. Terms net 30. 12 accounts. Five production, two office employees, and one salesman. LOCATION: Rents one-story cinder block building with 5,000 square feet located in industrial section in normal condition. Housekeeping is good.
4-21 (803 77) PRA

In an effort to obtain a moderate-sized premium, a business firm generally seeks insurance only on abnormal credit losses; that is, the firm may insure itself on 10 to 20 percent of its accounts receivable (called coinsurance) and may also assume its normal bad-debt losses of, say, 1 percent. Or, if it is willing to pay the increased premium, the business firm may obtain 100 percent protection. Most business firms, however, prefer to pay the reduced premium and to bear some of the risk themselves. The premium cost of credit insurance is generally less than 1 percent of the insured accounts, the exact cost depending on such factors as the mercantile rating of the debtors whose accounts are insured, the size of the accounts, and the percentage of the accounts insured.

Table 13-1 shows how a policyholder is reimbursed for four accounts receivable that were uncollectible. Customers A, B, C, and D have not paid their debts, and the policyholder has filed a claim with its credit insurance company. The amount each customer owes and the amount of the insurance on each account is shown in the table. Thus A owes $15,000, and his account is insured for $12,500. In this typical policy, the insured agreed to act as coinsurer for a certain percentage of each account and also to assume the normal bad-debt losses up to $5,050. (This firm's bad-debt losses are assumed to be $5,050.) Hence, the policyholder will not expect to collect the full $12,500 on the A account. Also, the insured assigns the four accounts in Table 13-1 to the insurance company, which in turn attempts to collect from the delinquent customers. The policyholder shares in the collections to the extent shown in the table. Thus, if the insurance company collects some of the overdue debt from A, the insured company receives 25 percent of the salvage value (the amount so collected). In summary, the policyholder receives a check from the insurance company for $25,400, with the possibility of receiving more, depending on the final salvage value of each account.

<table>
<tr><td rowspan="2">TABLE 13-1
Example of a Loss
Adjustment under
Commercial
Credit Insurance</td><td rowspan="2">Account</td><td rowspan="2">Amount
Owed</td><td rowspan="2">Coverage
Stipulated
in Policy</td><td>Percent of
Coverage
Allowed after
Coinsurance</td><td>Net
Allowed
Loss</td><td>Policyholder's
Salvage
Interest
(Percent)</td></tr>
<tr><td></td><td></td><td></td></tr>
<tr><td></td><td>A</td><td>$15,000</td><td>$12,500</td><td>90</td><td>$11,250</td><td>25</td></tr>
<tr><td></td><td>B</td><td>15,000</td><td>15,000</td><td>90</td><td>13,500</td><td>10</td></tr>
<tr><td></td><td>C</td><td>1,000</td><td>1,000</td><td>90</td><td>900</td><td>10</td></tr>
<tr><td></td><td>D</td><td>6,000</td><td>6,000</td><td>80</td><td>4,800</td><td>20</td></tr>
<tr><td rowspan="3">Source:
Clyde William Phelps,
Commercial Credit Insurance
as a Management Tool
(Baltimore: Commercial Credit
Company, 1961), p. 37</td><td>Total</td><td>$37,000</td><td>$34,500</td><td></td><td>$30,450</td><td></td></tr>
<tr><td colspan="3">Less primary loss</td><td>5,050</td><td></td></tr>
<tr><td colspan="3">Amount of loss paid policyholder</td><td>$25,400</td><td></td></tr>
</table>

The terms of a credit insurance policy are subject to wide flexibility. Hence the specific provisions may vary from case to case. In general, the insured has to balance the merits of increased protection and increased services against the increasingly larger premium for the added protection or services.

Business firms find credit insurance useful under a number of conditions, a few of which are when sales are concentrated in a few large accounts, in customers who are all in the same line of business, and in customers who are all in the same economic region. On the other hand, credit insurance may not be useful to a business firm whose customers are government units or public utilities. But on the whole, the use of credit insurance is growing, and firms in more than 150 lines of activity now use this service.

A seller may diminish the risk to himself by having the purchaser pledge as collateral the property so purchased, or the seller may retain title to these goods until the buyer has paid for them. First is the *chattel mortgage*. Under this plan, title to the property is pledged with the selling merchant or other creditor. If the debtor defaults, the property may be seized; if the buyer makes his payments promptly, the mortgage is void after the final payment. Second is the *conditional sale*. Under this arrangement, title remains with the creditor until all the installments have been paid. The sale is conditioned on the completion of all the payments. After the last payment, title is vested in the purchaser. The mechanical differences between a chattel mortgage and a conditional sale vary from state to state. Merchants tend to use the arrangement that makes repossession easier. Third is the *lease plan*. Under this arrangement, the purchaser rents the property for a certain period of time. Then, according to the agreement, after the last rental is paid, title moves to the tenant. All three of these arrangements are for the protection of the merchant or other party allowing the installment credit.

Having the Purchaser Pledge Collateral: Maintaining Title to the Goods

Although accounts receivable and notes receivable records are less subject to theft and loss than is cash, management usually takes special precautions to keep these records in a place that is fire resistant and beyond the reach of malicious mischief-makers. While burglars and others would find little use for receivable records, the absence of such records could cause serious financial loss to their owner. Hence, a great deal of care must be used in protecting records of accounts and notes receivable against theft or physical destruction. Also, a firm may elect to carry valuable document insurance on the records that contain receivable data. Many interesting problems arise in protecting accounts and notes receivable against loss, especially in an age threatened by atomic warfare.

Taking Special Steps to Protect Receivables against Loss

Before extending consumer credit that generates accounts or notes receivable, the businessman should determine if the potential purchaser of the goods is creditworthy. Among the ways he does this is by checking his own records, by telephoning other merchants with whom the consumer has done business, and by seeking relevant information from a data bank maintained on consumers by a local credit bureau. The local credit bureau is an especially helpful place from which to obtain information to evaluate the debt-paying ability of new customers.

CREDIT BUREAUS AND THE MANAGEMENT OF ACCOUNTS RECEIVABLE

Function of Credit Bureaus

A credit bureau's prime function is to assemble information that is relevant to predicting the ability and willingness of individuals to repay *consumer credit*. A typical file on an individual might contain this information:

His name, social security number, and birthdate

His record of employment for the past five years and approximate current income

Whether he pays his bills on time

Whether he has been sued for a debt and whether he has gone bankrupt

Adverse information must not be kept on file for more than 7 years, except that bankruptcy incidents may be kept on file for 14 years.

There are approximately 2,100 credit bureaus; most of these belong to the national trade association, Associated Credit Bureaus, Inc.

Included in the list of names of individual citizens maintained by a local credit bureau might be the name of the professor teaching this course, the names of young married couples in the class, and hundreds of other local citizens. Credit reports on consumers are more widely used than is generally realized.

The credit bureau does not evaluate a person's debt-paying ability; instead, it supplies information on an individual to those who subscribe and pay for the service. The user of the service of the credit bureau extends or refuses credit based on his own criteria. Those who use the service include retail merchants, banks, physicians, dentists, hospitals, and national credit card companies. In addition to the above, life insurance companies and potential employers may wish to see a credit report on a person before life insurance is sold to him or before he is hired for a responsible position. But despite the above two supplemental uses, credit reports issued by credit bureaus are used mainly as a source of information by which businessmen control the quality of accounts and notes receivable.

Government Regulation of Credit Bureaus[4]

The U.S. government regulates the role of credit bureaus by:

1. Limiting the use of information in the file of each individual
2. Obliging merchants who use credit reports obtained from a credit bureau to inform consumers when credit is denied
3. Granting rights to persons whose names are on file in the credit bureau

Thus the management of accounts receivable has numerous legal as well as financial aspects.

The U.S. Fair Credit Reporting Act limits the use of a credit report on a consumer to these purposes: to consider him for credit, to review his overdue account, to consider him for employment, and to consider him for life insurance. Federal law prohibits neighbors and relatives who are curious about a person's financial standing from obtaining a credit report. Similarly, neither a newspaper reporter nor a politician may obtain a credit report on his enemies. Even a subscribing member to a credit bureau's services must state in writing that he has a legitimate business use for the information.

4. See *What the Credit Granter Needs to Know about the Fair Credit Reporting Act* (circular) (Houston, Tex.: Associated Credit Bureaus, Inc., 1973).

The obligation of the merchant (credit granter) is that he must inform the consumer when credit is denied based on a report from a credit bureau. Under the law, it is mandatory for the credit granter to provide the consumer with the name and address of the credit bureau if the consumer is denied credit based wholly or partially on information from that credit bureau. The law does not require the consumer to request this information. However, the credit granter has the option of providing verbal or written information about the credit bureau.

The U.S. Fair Credit Reporting Act also gives the consumer the right to know what information is in his file and the right to have erroneous information corrected or removed. Furthermore, the individual consumer is entitled to know the name of employers who have received credit reports on him within the past two years and the names of all others who have received credit reports on him within the past six months. The spirit of the Fair Credit Reporting Act is to have a law that protects consumers without placing undue restrictions on credit granters and credit bureaus.

The question may arise whether a firm should sell to a group of poor-risk buyers. One criterion on which to base such a decision is to determine whether such a package of transactions will add to the net profits of the firm. If marginal revenues exceeds marginal costs, then the package will add to the net profits. The problem, however, is to estimate the data so that one can compare marginal costs with marginal revenues. Let us illustrate these statements with a problem. Assume that the credit department of Company K believes that by selling to a poor-risk group the firm will be able to collect $50,000 in cash from these accounts. Sales will actually total $60,000, but only $50,000 is estimated to be collectible. Assume also that variable selling costs are 10 percent of sales, variable administrative costs are 20 percent of sales, variable production costs are 30 percent of sales, federal taxes are 50 percent of profits, and fixed expenses for the firm are $98,649.99 (consisting of officers' salaries, rent, and so forth). Should the firm proceed with the opportunity to sell to this group of potential buyers? Marginal analysis, also known as incremental analysis, provides guidance on the matter:

OPERATIONS RESEARCH IN MANAGING RECEIVABLES

Marginal Analysis

Cash to be received from selling to poor-risk group		$50,000
Less:		
Selling costs	$ 6,000	
Administrative costs	12,000	
Production costs	18,000	36,000
Taxable income		$14,000
Tax		7,000
Net marginal income, also known as net gain		$ 7,000

(Observe that the fixed costs of $98,649.99 are not relevant to the analysis.)

Since marginal revenue is positive (amounting to $7,000), this is a signal to proceed with the proposition of selling to the new class of buyers.

Use of Expected Value (Minimizing Expected Losses) Assume in still another and different situation that Company P has decided to sell to a certain class of poor-risk customers because, despite the bad-debt losses, the firm will add to its profits. The firm plans to do this because marginal revenue is expected to exceed marginal costs. Company P expects these bad-debt losses from this particular group of accounts:

Probabilities	$\frac{1}{8}$	$\frac{1}{2}$	$\frac{1}{4}$	$\frac{1}{8}$
Outcomes—bad-debt losses	$960	$2,000	$3,000	$4,000

This means that the firm estimates there is a one-eighth chance of bad-debt losses of $960; a one-half chance of bad-debt losses of $2,000, and so on. Observe that the probabilities must add up to 1. Company P is considering installing an intensive billing system that would cost $100; this improvement should lessen bad-debt losses. Management believes that by installing this system, the new distribution of outcomes and their probabilities will be:

Probabilities	$\frac{1}{8}$	$\frac{1}{2}$	$\frac{1}{4}$	$\frac{1}{8}$
Outcomes—bad-debt losses	$720	$1,600	$2,400	$3,200

The question under consideration is whether management should proceed with the expenditure of $100. The concept of expected value provides guidance (but not conclusive proof) as to the more desirable course of action, that is, whether to spend or not to spend the $100. Let A represent the alternative of not spending the $100, and let B represent the alternative of spending it.

Preliminary expected Loss of (*A*)
$$= \frac{1}{8}(\$960) + \frac{1}{2}(\$2,000) + \frac{1}{4}(\$3,000) + \frac{1}{8}(\$4,000)$$
$$= \$120 + \$1,000 + \$750 + \$500$$
$$= \$2,370$$

Preliminary expected Loss of (*B*)
$$= \frac{1}{8}(\$720) + \frac{1}{2}(\$1,600) + \frac{1}{4}(\$2,400) + \frac{1}{8}(\$3,200)$$
$$= \$90 + \$800 + \$600 + \$400$$
$$= \$1,890$$

By making an expenditure of $100, the firm would lower expected bad-debt losses by $480 ($2,370–$1,890). Hence, it would be advantageous to make the expenditure because there would be a net saving of $380 ($480–$100). A reasonable decision would be to instigate the chain of events that would lower expected losses; this course of action would lower expenses and raise profits.

Capital Budgeting   Capital budgeting may make a contribution to the area of the management of receivables. Suppose that a firm is considering selling to a high-risk group of customers because, despite the additional bad-debt losses, additional cash profits will be generated. Assume in a new example that Company M's best estimate of the future is that if accounts receivable are increased by $100,000, this new class of customers will add $30,000 annually (after deducting all cash expenses and federal income taxes) in net cash benefits (net cash inflow) for a period of five years. If the firm estimates that it has a cost of capital of 8 percent, should it proceed with the granting of the credit? This question must be answered in two steps:

Step 1 Evaluate the project by using techniques such as the net present value test and the yield test.

Under the net present value test, the value of the undertaking is $19,781, found as follows:

$$NPV = \text{Present value of annual cash benefits} - \text{Present value of cost}$$
$$NPV = (\text{PV of } \$30,000, 8\%, 5 \text{ years}) - \$100,000$$
$$= \$119,781 - \$100,000$$
$$= \$19,781$$

Under the yield method, 15 percent is the rate that discounts the $30,000 receipts back to a present value equal to the outlay of $100,000 ($30,000 × 3.3522 = $100,566, and we will accept 15 percent as being sufficiently close in this example).

Since the net present value is positive, this is a signal not to reject the proposal; since the yield is 15 percent in comparison with a cost of capital of 8 percent, this is also a favorable preliminary sign. Despite the fact that both the net present value test and the yield test are favorable, at this point one cannot say for sure what the ultimate decision would be, because the investment of additional funds in accounts receivable must first be compared with alternative uses of the $100,000. Perhaps there are even better alternatives than using this money to expand accounts receivable.

Step 2 Compare the returns that would be earned on the accounts receivable with the returns that would be obtained from competing projects. If, for example, the firm could use the $100,000 to acquire fixed assets that would give a net present value of $25,000 and a yield of 20 percent, then the money might be better spent on the fixed assets. But if the net present value test and the yield test indicate that there are no better alternatives than expanding the accounts receivable, then this would be a sound investment from Company M's point of view. In the absence of any information to the contrary, it would be beneficial to the firm to commit the funds to accounts receivable. Of course, management might have to temper the decision with sound judgment, because it has to consider factors that might have been omitted from the model.

The application of capital budgeting to the management of accounts receivable is a new and coming field; at present not much has been done in this area on a practical basis. But as management becomes more familiar with operations research, the procedures mentioned above will be incorporated more and more into the decision-making process.

Accounts receivable and notes receivable must be collected at the planned rate if the firm is to remain solvent and if it is to attain a profitability status. The rate at which a firm plans to collect its accounts and notes receivable is determined largely by the credit terms it extends to its customers. Management directs the efforts of the firm to meet these plans through effective collection procedures. Unless the receivables are collected according to plan, the firm will be unable to pay its expenses and debts. Also, a serious slowdown in the collection of receivables may cause bad-debt losses, which means that the capital of the firm may be dissipated.

Factoring differs from the pledge of accounts receivable in that under factoring (1) no loan is involved as the accounts receivable are purchased, whereas when accounts receivable are pledged, a loan is in effect; (2) many managerial and clerical services are rendered, whereas no such services are usually rendered when accounts are pledged for a loan; (3) customers whose accounts are sold to the factor are usually instructed to make payment directly to the factor, whereas when accounts are pledged for a loan, the firms whose accounts are pledged are seldom notified and make their payments to the seller of the goods; and (4) the purchaser of the accounts usually assumes responsibility for bad-debt losses, whereas when accounts receivable are pledged, the pledger generally assumes this loss.

The pledge of accounts receivable and the outright sale of accounts receivable (factoring) are alternate ways of converting accounts receivable into cash. There are two main advantages of the pledge of accounts receivable over factoring:

1. Customers are not notified of the assignment of the accounts.
2. The costs are less (although it should be noted that fewer services are received.)

On the other hand, a factoring has two main advantages over the pledge of accounts receivable:

1. Factoring is a form of credit insurance; that is, there is a guaranty that there will be no bad debts.
2. The business firm is relieved of any credit investigation and collection expenses.

However, factoring and the pledge of accounts receivable do have an important similarity. Under both arrangements the seller of merchandise converts his accounts receivable into cash, thus accelerating the circulation of current assets. The phrase accounts receivable financing *includes borrowing on the pledge of accounts receivable and outright sale of the accounts to a factor.*

13-1. Identify the following terms:
accounts receivable turnover test
days necessary to collect the amount of accounts receivable on the books
factor
Dun & Bradstreet ratings
sales finance company
line of credit (trade credit)
ledger experience
commercial credit insurance

13-2. The Walton firm, a partnership, sells textile goods to wholesalers. The firm operates on a small amount of permanent capital and therefore has to keep the current assets circulating in order to have enough cash to pay current bills. The partners are weighing the alternatives of borrowing from a commercial finance company on the pledge of accounts receivable or of selling the accounts receivable to a factor. Discuss the advantages and the disadvantages of each.

13.3 Business men who sell to the ultimate consumer are concerned with the amount of accounts receivable that becomes worthless because individuals voluntarily go bankrupt. *Bankruptcy* means basically that a person turns over his assets to the court and is forgiven virtually all his debts. If possible, invite a lawyer to speak to your class and seek answers to these questions: (a) Will he give several short examples (without revealing names) of persons who have filed for *personal* bankruptcy? (b) If the bankrupt is married, must his wife also file for bankruptcy? (c) Can a person give his assets to his children, be declared bankrupt and have his debts forgiven, and then have the children return the assets to him? (d) If a person has his debts forgiven by way of bankruptcy and a few years later inherits $80,000, is he legally obligated to use this money to pay old debts? (e) How often can an individual go bankrupt?

Answers to some of the problems appear at the end of this section. *For each problem, show how you obtained the answer.*

13-1. Company A has already purchased credit insurance. The terms of the policy are that the insured will bear two parts of the losses: (1) it will assume an amount of the losses equal to $28,000 (its normal bad-debt losses), and (2) it will act as coinsurer for 10 percent of the losses. This particular policy does not provide for any salvage return to the firm. How much will the insured receive from the insurance company, assuming the information shown in Table 13-2?

Debtor's Name	Amount of Insurance on Each Account	Amount of Loss on Each Account
Smith	$20,000	$15,000
Hobson	18,000	3,000
King	10,000	12,000
Arthurs	8,000	8,000

TABLE 13-2
Insurance and Losses for Company A

13-2. The president of Company R notices that the company is borrowing more and more to support a given level of sales. He suspects that his credit and collection department is not collecting accounts on time. The firm grants its customers terms of 2/30, N/40. The company has annual sales of $2,160,000, and its accounts receivable average $360,000. Is the credit department enforcing the firm's credit policies?

13-3. The management of Company M is considering giving its customers 60 days instead of 30 to pay bills. Such a policy will increase sales and perhaps profits. The immediate issue, however, is the impact of such a change on the amount of financing that will be needed. The following ratios apply to the company: cash is 10 percent of sales; accounts receivable are 10 percent of sales; inventory is 10 percent of sales; accounts payable are 100 percent of inventory. These ratios will prevail after the change in credit policy except that total accounts receivable will average 20 percent of sales.

Following is the firm's balance sheet before the change:

Cash	$ 54,000	Bank loans	$ 54,000
Accounts receivable	54,000	Accounts payable	54,000
Inventories	54,000	Partners' equity	162,000
Fixed assets	108,000		
Total	$270,000	Total	$270,000

If credit terms are changed to 60 days, sales are expected to increase to $810,000; $54,000 of additional fixed assets will be needed. (a) Determine the new total asset requirements as a result of the change in credit terms. (b) How much in additional financing will be needed as a result of the change in credit policy?

13-4. Assume that the credit department of the Banton Company is considering selling on account to the extent of $100,000 to a poor-risk group. Bad-debt losses will be 15 percent in this category of accounts. Assume that variable selling expenses are 12 percent of sales, variable administrative costs are 20 percent of sales, variable production costs are 28 percent of sales, federal taxes are 50 percent of profits, and fixed expenses of the firm are $40,000. Should the firm proceed with the opportunity to sell to the poor-risk group?

13-5. George Robinson, a college student, is considering starting a small business in order to help defray his expenses. He has $400 in cash. He must purchase $200 in materials, which he can buy on credit on 30-day terms. In order to produce an article from these materials, which he will sell for $500, he must spend $200 for labor. It takes 30 days to complete the article, and labor must be paid in cash. Competitive conditions require Robinson to sell his product on 30-day terms. Therefore, at the end of the first 30 days, he will have expended $200 for labor; the bill for the materials amounting to $200 will be due and will have to be paid. The student will at this point have spent his entire capital of

$400. He will not receive payment for the sales price of his product until 30 more days have elapsed; even though he could obtain additional materials, he would not have the cash to pay for the labor necessary to process them. Consequently, he would have to limit his production to one article every 60 days, or six articles a year, which would give him an annual sales of $3,000 and a gross profit of $600. The student would like to expand his operations, and the only source of outside funds is to sell his accounts receivable to a finance company, which will give him $480 on each $500 of accounts receivable. The student could apply the $80 profit toward his living expenses. If Robinson used this procedure, he would have funds to pay for the labor required to produce another article during the next 30 days, and the process would be constantly repeated so that the cycle of cash flow would be reduced from 60 days to 30 days. If the student pledged the accounts receivable: (a) How many articles could he produce per year? (b) What would be his annual sales? (c) What would be his annual net profit?

13-6. Company P sells $1 million of accounts to a factor. The factor charges an annual interest rate of 7 percent and a flat fee of 1 percent. The accounts receivable of the company would be due in six months. If the company sells the accounts receivable to a factor on the day it makes the sale, the true annual interest rate being paid by the firm is 9 percent.

Required: Show how the answer 9 percent was obtained.

13-7. Company K is considering buying a credit insurance policy at a cost of $3,000, which will require that the insured bear 10 percent of the losses. The management estimates the bad debt losses and their probabilities to be:

Bad Debts	Probabilities
$1,000	.10
2,000	.30
4,800	.50
5,000	.10

Should the management buy the policy, if it is using expected value as its decision criterion?

13-8. Given the following information, find the number of days' sales uncollected: assets $720,000; net worth $360,000; current ratio 2 to 1; turnover of assets 2; and accounts receivable $72,000.

Answers: 13-1, $4,400; 13-3a, $486,000; 13-3b, $216,000, of which additional accounts payable will provide $27,000; 13-4, yes, because the firm will add $12,500 to its earnings after taxes; 13-5a, 12; 13-5b, $6,000; 13-5c, $960; 13-6, 9 percent; 13-7, Yes, because expected loss will be lower by $240; 13-8, 18 days.

A grocer evaluating his accounts receivable finds that one of his customers owes $918.02. The grocer decides to do the best he can to collect all or part of this account. He has three main options: (a) Turn the bill over to a collection agency (the agency will keep 50 percent of the proceeds, if it collects the money); (b) use the garnishment approach (start court proceedings to have a certain amount deducted from the debtor's paycheck); (c) urge the customer to borrow from a finance company to "consolidate his debts" and use some of the money to pay the grocer. The grocer is aware of the problem of bad public relations that might arise from too drastic an approach; he is also aware of the borrower's option to go to the courts and have himself declared bankrupt, a procedure that results in his being forgiven forever the $918.02, and certain other of his debts. Since the customer has virtually no assets except his old automobile, the bankruptcy route is a real possibility. Discuss the advantages and disadvantages of the options open to the grocer. Also, which option do you recommend?

Richard and Mary Bressler incorporated three businesses in 1974, succeeding a partnership organized in 1965. The husband and wife are the sole stockholders of (1) the Bressler Paint Company, (2) the Bressler Varnish Company, and (3) the Bressler Real Estate Company. Paint manufacturing, varnish manufacturing, and real estate holdings, respectively, are accounted for by the above three corporations, which were set up separately for tax purposes and to insulate the risk of each enterprise.

Although the enterprises have been profitable over the years, there is currently a shortage of cash, as can be seen by the balance sheet of each company (see Table 13-3). The enterprises have been unable to pay their accounts payable on time, thus losing the discount. What is even worse, some of these accounts are now overdue. Most of the accounts payable have terms of 3/10, N/45.

Bressler is considering the following alternatives: First, he could sell the real estate of the Bressler Real Estate Company. Although this structure is carried on his books at·$75,000, he recently had an offer to sell it for $100,000. The local real estate syndicate that offered to buy it indicated that it would be willing to lease the structure to the Bressler Real Estate Company for an annual rental of $8,000 a year for a 10-year period. If the present owner sold the building, the syndicate would be responsible for taxes, repairs, and insurance. Second, he could factor the accounts receivable of the Bressler Paint Company, whose annual credit sales average $840,000. Bressler recently investigated this possibility and found that a factor would charge a flat fee of 2 percent on all accounts purchased, plus interest at 6 percent a year. The paint firm sells on terms of 2/10, N/60. Therefore the yearly 6 percent interest would actually be levied for approximately 60 days on each account, since the factor would have to wait this long for payment on some of the accounts and since the paint company would expect payment on the day it makes the sale. Bressler estimated that if he factored the accounts receivable of the paint firm, he would save $8,000 in bad-debt losses and another $7,000 by abolishing his credit and collection department. The factor insisted, however, on buying all future accounts receivable and on approving in advance all future sales on account. Finally, the agreement would be that either party could terminate the arrangement upon notice of 30 days.

TABLE 13-3
Financial Data
on the Three
Enterprises

	Bressler Paint Company	Bressler Varnish Company	Bressler Real Estate Company
Assets			
Cash	$ 8,000	$ 1,000	$ 1,000
Accounts receivable	235,000	20,000	
Less allowance for bad debts	(10,000)		
Inventory	160,000	40,000	
Total current assets	$393,000	$ 61,000	$ 1,000
Fixed Assets			
Land and buildings (net)			$ 75,000
Machinery (Net)	$115,000	$180,000	30,000
Total fixed assets	$115,000	$180,000	$105,000
Total assets	$508,000	$241,000	$106,000
Current Liabilities			
Accounts payable	$190,000	$ 90,000	$ 2,000
Bank loan	30,000	20,000	
Accrued items	10,000	10,000	1,000
Total current liabilities	$230,000	$120,000	$ 3,000
Net Worth			
Capital stock	$120,000	$ 60,000	$ 50,000
Surplus	158,000	61,000	53,000
Total net worth	$278,000	$121,000	$103,000
Total liabilities and net worth	$508,000	$241,000	$106,000
Purchases	$500,000	$105,000	
Sales (all on credit) previous year	$840,000	$210,000	$ 16,000
Net profit previous year after taxes	$ 20,000	$ 15,000	$ 10,000

Third, he could increase the discounts that the Bressler Paint Company gives its own customers and at the same time shorten the period of time in which they have to pay their bills. The firm is considering changing the terms from 2/10, N/60 to 4/10, N/30. This plan might speed up collections and hence give additional funds to take advantage of the discounts the firm is now missing on its accounts payable.

Fourth, Bressler could look into the operations of his own credit and collection department. There is the possibility that this division is lax in its collection procedures.

If any one of the firms can generate cash, this money could be immediately lent to either or both of the other two, since the three firms are under the ownership of the Bresslers.

Required: Discuss the advantages and the disadvantages of each of the proposed alternatives. Should any other alternatives be considered? Which alternative or combination of alternatives would you recommend?

Managing Working Capital— Inventories

The finance person is interested in inventories to the same degree that he is concerned with accounts receivable. First, it is his duty to determine whether incremental amounts of inventory are earning as much as could be earned if the funds were diverted into some other use. Second, he attempts to minimize the amount of inventory on hand without impairing sales; if inventories can be lowered, funds are released to pay off bank loans or to use in some other way. All the major departments of the firm have an interest in inventories. The sales department likes a large inventory of finished goods because of the increased possibilities of making sales. The production department generally prefers a large inventory of raw materials so as to minimize the possibility of interruptions in production. The finance department leans in the direction of preferring a minimum amount of inventory (without interfering with the profitability of the firm) because of the high costs of storing large quantities of goods. At times the views of these three departments conflict; a method of eliminating the conflict is to work in terms of models that prevent suboptimization.

The following aspects of inventory management will be discussed in this chapter:

1. Considerations influencing the level of inventory
2. Managing the inventory
   a. Keeping the inventory moving toward cash
   b. Conserving the inventory
   c. Improving the inventory
   d. Diversifying the inventory
3. Financing the inventory
   a. Financing inventory expansion
   b. The nature of trade credit

c. Role of sales finance companies

d. Acquiring inventory on consignment

4. Operations research in managing inventories

CONSIDERATIONS INFLUENCING THE LEVEL OF INVENTORY

The production department in a manufacturing concern or the buying department in a merchandising concern will have to be aware of the sales budget so that arrangements can be made to have the goods available for delivery when the sales are made. The amount of inventory needed in relation to a given volume of sales varies from industry to industry and is affected by a number of factors. An important factor is the perishability of the inventory. If the inventory spoils easily (such as fruit), an effort will be made to keep it at a minimum. A grocery store, for example, might buy just enough fresh fruit to meet the requirements for a particular Saturday. On the other hand, canned tomatoes may be purchased and stored for several months. The hand-to-mouth buying of perishables decreases the chance of loss on goods that might spoil. A further factor is the extent of the assortment that the business firm wishes to have in its inventory. Particularly in the clothing line, a company might decide that volume would be increased if customers had a wide assortment from which to select. If this is the case, inventory requirements will increase. Still another factor is the distance of the business firm from its source of inventory. If the inventory, such as raw materials, comes from a distant source that cannot be depended upon, it may be necessary to stockpile the items. Manufacturing companies have attempted to stockpile such materials as rubber, tin, and copper. Yet another factor is the length of time needed to produce or grow a product. A firm tends to carry a relatively large inventory of items that require a considerable time to acquire or produce. The rubber processing companies carry relatively heavy inventories of crude rubber, partly because of the long period of time necessary to develop rubber plantations. On the other hand, it is not necessary for a grocery store to stockpile bread because the supply of this food is readily expanded. The businessman's experience as to the environmental conditions under which he operates and the industry averages give him guidance on his optimum inventory.

A firm attempts to avoid having excess inventory on hand because such a situation leads to unnecessary expenses, such as insurance premiums, bank interest to carry the inventory, and taxes in some states. In a somewhat classical example of inventory control, the management of the Glidden Company put on a drive to eliminate unneeded stocks of goods. The *Wall Street Journal* reported the Glidden plan as follows:

> For ages, most businessmen have rewarded employees with bonuses and contest prizes for sales-boosting efforts. Now the Glidden Co. has come up with a unique contest for executives only—to find those making the best use of money.
>
> Only a score of Glidden executives—regional and divisional managers are eligible for the exclusive-sounding contest. First prize is $4,000, followed by

awards of $2,500, $1,250, and $750. All prizes are after deduction of withholding taxes.

Dwight P. Joyce, chairman and president of the paint, food and chemical concern, says he is chiefly looking for the manager who reduces his inventories and accounts receivable but at the same time maintains or increases sales and profits. Merely reducing the amount of money used in a region's or division's business is not enough, he stresses.

Why a contest like this? Mainly, the high cost of borrowing money to carry inventories and accounts receivable, says Mr. Joyce. "It's a brainchild of mine that's been incubating for a long time," he adds. This past August, Mr. Joyce discussed the idea with other company officials and it was agreed a contest should be started.

Mr. Joyce explains the problem of high borrowing costs with a few statistics. For each $1 million of borrowed money, Glidden shells out about $56,000 in interest payments. Additionally, consider the fact, he says, that Glidden's inventories rose to $47,387,605 at the end of August, or nearly $9 million greater than a year earlier. To carry an extra $9 million of inventory with borrowed money costs Glidden about $500,000 in interest charges alone, he says.

If in the current fiscal year we could reduce our inventories by $3 million, through this contest, for example, that could mean an increase in pretax profits of $150,000, comments Mr. Joyce. That, he figures would be an excellent return on a $10,366 (before taxes) investment in contest prize money. . . .

On the other hand, firms are careful not to cut their inventory to a level that would interfere with sales to such an extent that net profits would be decreased. Each firm must experiment with the level of inventory that is best for it.

It is expected that inventories will be sold and cash will be received from the sale. To measure the rapidity with which inventories are sold within a year, the turnover test is sometimes used. *Inventory turnover* is found by dividing total cost of goods sold during a year by the average inventory. If cost of goods sold is $100,000 and average inventory $10,000, the turnover is 10.

Usually a high inventory turnover is a favorable indicator. The inventory turnover ratio enables a company to compare the operations of a given period with those of a previous period and with operations of other companies in a comparable economic position. Another important aspect of inventories is that they are a step further away from cash than are accounts receivable. Accounts receivable are definite in amount. However, there is no assurance that the inventories will be sold at the expected prices. Many a company has failed because its inventory became frozen or had to be liquidated at a loss, thus disrupting the flow of circulating capital.

The proprietor or officers expect that the circulation of assets will result in a profit being earned for the company. Thus for each $100 in cash invested in

KEEPING THE
INVENTORY MOVING
TOWARD CASH

Inventory Turnover

inventory, the business might expect a return of $175 to the cash account. This gross profit or markup would be possible because of the sale of inventories or services at a profit. After the cash is collected, the process will be repeated over and over; that is, there will be a constant movement of cash to inventories, to accounts receivable, and then back to cash. However, management may withdraw part of the cash from circulating assets, as would happen if profits were distributed to owners, debts were repaid, or some of the cash were used to buy fixed assets, such as a building (see Figure 14-1).

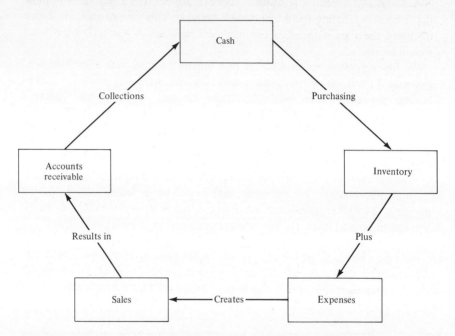

FIGURE 14-1
The Circular Flow
of Current Assets

A quick way to raise cash is to unload inventories at reduced selling prices. Cash is received and the financial position of the firm is more liquid. Management frowns on this type of distress selling because it makes a bad impression on customers, who tend to lose their respect for a supplier so financially weak that he must resort to major price reductions to make sales. Consequently, buyers may decide to do business elsewhere.

In addition to creating a bad impression, the dumping of inventories is an expensive method of raising cash. The goods may be sold below cost or at a price just above it. The lost gross profit should be compared with the cost of alternative methods of raising cash. In some situations the best plan will be to liquidate the inventory, in others to raise the cash through a less expensive method.

Problem A new and aggressive financial manager of Company C proposes to raise the inventory turnover to 10; he believes that current inventories could be lowered without injuring sales. Cost of goods sold is $180,000; average inventory is $20,000; total assets are $1 million. If inventory turnover can be increased to 10 while sales stay the same: (a) How much in funds would be released from inventory? (b) If the released funds were used to reduce a 6 percent bank loan, how much in interest would be saved each year?

Solution

(a) New average inventory $= \dfrac{\text{Cost of goods sold}}{\text{New turnover}}$

$= \dfrac{\$180,000}{10}$

$= \$18,000$

Decrease in inventory is $2,000 ($20,000 − $18,000). Therefore, funds released are $2,000.

(b) Interest saved is $120 ($2,000 × .06).

CONSERVING THE INVENTORY

Management usually takes two steps in protecting the firm against losses in inventory—establishing preventive measures and purchasing insurance. Thus one internal control intended to discourage employees from making unauthorized removals of inventory for personal use is to require that before inventory can be removed from a stock room, both a supervisor and an employee may have to sign a form that is presented to the stock clerk. The stock clerk in turn is not authorized to issue inventory unless he receives the form signed by the two previously mentioned parties. A practice such as this tends to prevent fraud; and in the event that there is fraud, the procedure enables management to trace the misdeed to those who are responsible for it. Many firms are finding theft of inventory a problem of increasing significance. One estimate is that over $1 billion in inventory is stolen by employees each year. An example is the stealing of inventory by seven employees of Ford Motor Company. At the end of each day these persons would wrap stolen inventory in cloth bags and bind the bags with tape so that the contents would not jiggle. They then strapped the bags to their bodies and walked unchallenged out of the plant. A ready market for the goods was provided by an automobile dealer in New York City, who paid the thieves 10 percent of the retail value. In another example, four stock clerks in a Chicago department store stole $40,000 worth of merchandise. The store has a rule that an employee cannot carry out a parcel unless it bears an official stamp. One member of the group had a duplicate of the stamp made. Thereafter, the four thieves blandly displayed the stamped parcels to the guard at the door. They were caught only when a store detective opened the wrong locker and found the duplicate stamp.[1] Even hiring a night watchman and enclosing plant property by a fence are part of the preventive internal controls that are frequently used to conserve inventory. Then, of course, there are the usual insurance policies from which protection may be obtained from losses caused by fire, water damage, theft, and many other kinds of risks. Insurance provides one

1. See Irwin Ross, "Thievery in the Plant," *Fortune*, October 1961, p. 140.

of the main pillars for protecting the firm against certain kinds of losses in inventory.

IMPROVING THE INVENTORY

If a manufacturing or processing firm is to maintain or expand its profit position, it must improve its products and perhaps even develop new ones. An annual report of National Dairy Products Corporation states, "Businesses operate in a constantly changing environment. Their degree of success is measured in the ability to anticipate change, prepare for it, and influence the direction it takes. Those that excel in this ability form the vanguard of industrial leadership, for they are the innovators." Manufactured or processed products are constantly changing; in a number of cases the products or services rendered have a life of only about five years, as is represented in Figure 14-2. In some companies, over 25 percent of annual profits are being derived from products not in existence five years ago. An annual report of North American Rockwell Corporation stated that the firm introduced 50 new products in a recent year and that during the next three years over 30 percent of the products now being made will be reengineered or completely new. Some firms formalize the quest for product improvement and for the development of entirely new products by establishing a research and development department; others have no such department but instead follow a policy of giving continuous attention to improving products.

FIGURE 14-2
The Basic Life
Cycle of
New Products

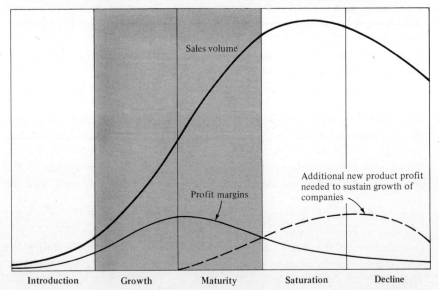

Source:
Management
Research
Department,
Booz, Allen and
Hamilton

Stockholders and management now view a research budget as indispensable for the survival of the firm. Efforts expended on product development are measured by several criteria: dollars spent per year, percentage of sales used on research, number of employees spending their time on research, and number of square feet of space devoted to research activities. Thus an annual report of Olin Mathieson Chemical Corporation stated that the company planned to spend $28 million per year on research; a Rexall Drug and Chemical Company annual report stated that in the field of drugs, it spends 12 percent of sales on research, in comparison with an average of 8 percent for the pharmaceutical industry; and an annual report of the Reliance Electric and Engineering Company stated that its research center provides 50,000 square feet for this activity. A firm that is looking ahead must assume that the future will continue to bring forth changes in product design as well as new products; an opposite point of view is likely to mean that the firm will fall behind competitors or even fail.

The trend today is for a firm to manufacture or sell a wide range of different types of products rather than one product or a line of related products. A company that handles a wide variety of different inventories is hedging against the possibility that a particular one might be unprofitable as well as making it possible for the firm to participate in products created as a result of the information explosion. A business firm that engages in diversified activities is known as a *conglomerate*. One well-known conglomerate is Textron, Inc., which makes, among other items, cologne, pencils, helicopters, eyeglass frames, and bathroom towel racks—and raises chickens. The president of this company states that a firm is in business to make money and that the best way to accomplish this objective is to use the conglomerate device because it provides a mechanism for directing resources quickly into a profitable area. Textron has a policy of buying other firms rather than developing products from within; one example is its purchase of the W. A. Sheaffer Pen Company. Textron acquires a firm only if it offers (over a period of time) a 25 percent return before taxes on the funds invested by Textron. Each purchased company is operated separately and is headed by a president whose annual bonus depends on whether or not his division earns the required 25 percent. In summary, one method of quickly diversifying inventories is to purchase other firms.

Corporations have virtually unlimited capacity to buy other firms, because unissued stock may be used as the medium of payment. For example, Litton Industries, Inc., uses common stock (in the main) to purchase other companies. Of course, acquirer firms attempt to be selective in the firms being acquired so as not to dilute earnings per share of the buyers; in fact, the expectation is that earnings per share of the purchaser will increase after the completion of the transaction. There is thus a direct connection between diversifying inventory, raising earnings per share, and eventually raising the market price of the common stock of the buyer firm.

DIVERSIFYING THE INVENTORY

As a general rule, when a firm expands its inventories for sale, provision must be made for additional financing. This means that total assets will increase because of the additional activity and, therefore, that total liabilities and net worth will have to increase so as to make the balance sheet balance. The amount by which the total liabilities and net worth must be expanded is the amount of additional financing required; management's problem is to determine which of the liability

FINANCING INVENTORY EXPANSION

and net worth accounts will increase. The items on the right-hand side of the balance sheet, such as accounts payable, bank loans, and common stock, do not necessarily increase automatically; negotiation may be necessary to obtain funds from these sources. Hence, planning for expansion in sales and inventory usually requires concomitant planning for sources of funds to finance the expansion.

Problem   A retailer is planning to increase his sales by $540,000. His problem is to determine the amount of additional financing needed to implement this change in policy. Below is information applicable to the new product line (not the old):

Assumed number of days in a year	360
Collection period	20 days
Relation of inventory to sales	10 percent
Relation of cash to sales	3 percent
Additional fixed assets needed	$15,000

The following is the firm's balance sheet data before the expansion:

Cash	$ 30,000	Accounts payable	$ 60,000
Receivables	45,000	Bank loans	20,000
Inventories	60,000	Other payables	5,000
Fixed assets	90,000	Retained earnings	40,000
		Common stock	100,000
Total	$225,000	Total	$225,000

Solution   *Step 1* Prepare a revised assets section for a pro forma balance sheet:

Cash—$30,000 + (.03 × $540,000)		$ 46,200
Receivables:		
Old	$45,000	
Additional:		
$540,000 ÷ 360 = $1,500 = average daily sales		
$1,500 × 20 = $30,000		
$45,000 + $30,000 = $75,000		75,000
Inventories—$60,000 + (.10 × $540,000)		114,000
Fixed assets—$90,000 + $15,000		105,000
		$340,200

Step 2 At the end of step 1, the firm estimates that it will need a total of $340,200 in assets; at this stage total liabilities and net worth are only $225,000. The amount of $115,200 ($340,200 − $225,000) is necessary to make the statement balance; hence, $115,200 is the amount of additional financing needed. This amount might be raised by increasing accounts payable by a reason-

able extent, by increasing bank loans, by selling stock, and by other means. In conclusion, when sales increase substantially, virtually all the assets increase; furthermore, management must make provision for financing this increase.

Trade credit is credit advanced by one business firm to another when goods are sold on account. A simple but important example of trade credit would be the purchase of goods on account by a retailer from a wholesaler. On the other hand, consumer credit is granted by a business firm to a consumer. Thus, when the housewife buys her groceries on account, we have an example of the use of consumer credit. Trade credit and consumer credit are fundamentally the same in that both types of credit result in (1) the lender's advancing goods to the debtor, and (2) the debtor's agreeing to repay the creditor in the future. Strictly speaking, credit means the power to acquire control over goods or money, thereby leading to the conclusion that credit is a power possessed by the debtor.

THE NATURE OF TRADE CREDIT

Trade Credit versus Consumer Credit

Companies with large inventories tend to use trade credit to a greater extent than those that sell only services. *The main reason for this is the convenience of using trade credit when inventories are purchased.* After the buyer makes arrangements with his suppliers to obtain the goods, the later transactions are relatively simple; that is, goods are ordered, then received, and then paid for—all steps being completed with a minimum of red tape. Particularly important to the buyer is that he has an opportunity to inspect the goods before he has to pay for them.

Companies Using Trade Credit

Another factor leading to the use of trade credit is that many firms find it easier to obtain than bank loans because banks, as a rule, are stricter than business firms in their lending policies. This is so for a number of reasons, three of which follow:

1. The markup on goods sold is sufficiently great to cover some bad-debt losses and still leave a profit for the seller. On the other hand, the interest rates charged by banks are usually so low that there is little margin of allowance for bad debts. Therefore, banks tend to lend to borrowers who are the better risks and to limit the amount of loans they will advance to any one borrower.
2. Those who grant trade credit are free from government regulation as to the amount of risk assumed. Commercial banks, in contrast, are influenced by banking laws in the amount of risk assumed. Also, bankers are sensitive to adverse reports by bank auditors when there are overdue notes in the portfolio.
3. Still another factor worth noting is that many small businesses must use trade credit extensively because they are unable or unwilling to obtain funds or credit from other sources. Since small firms are unstable and have a tendency to fail, the more cautious creditors, such as commercial banks, place a very conservative limit on the amount of funds they will advance.

Actually, the problem of a firm is not whether to use bank credit or trade credit to the exclusion of one or the other; instead, the managerial decision is to determine the most advantageous combination of bank loans and trade credit.

The Cost of Trade Credit   The terms of trade credit vary from industry to industry and from company to company. However, regardless of the industry, the following two factors must be considered when analyzing the terms of trade credit: the length of time the purchaser of the goods has before the bill must be paid and the discount, if any, that is offered for prompt payment. Thus the terms 3/10, N/30 on a $1,000 purchase mean that if the bill is paid within 10 days from the date of the invoice, the payment may be reduced by 3 percent; that is, the bill will be considered as paid in full if 97 percent of the original amount is sent to the seller. This means that $30 is deducted from the $1,000 and that the seller considers the account as settled in full upon the receipt of $970. The entire bill must be paid in full within 30 days—no discount being allowed for any payment made between the 11th and the 30th days. Likewise, the terms 2/10, N/45 mean that 2 percent may be deducted from the amount of the bill if payment is made within 10 days from the date of the invoice. The entire amount must be paid within 45 days. Numerous other trade credit terms may be used in a particular industry.

Trade credit may be costly in at least two ways. A saving is lost if the company fails to take advantage of the discount offered, and the purchase price of the goods may be higher if bought from a supplier that grants generous credit terms. Only by investigation of facts can one determine whether or not the purchase price of goods is higher because of generous credit terms. However, it is possible to compute the cost of credit when a firm fails to take advantage of discounts offered. Assume that a company buys $1,000 worth of goods and the terms are 3/10, N/30. If the company takes advantage of the discount, 3 percent of the purchase price is saved. However, if the bill is not paid during the 10-day period but instead is paid on the 30th day, it may be said that 3 percent was lost because the company waited an additional 20 days. Since there are 360 days in an interest year, and since there are eighteen 20-day periods in a year, it may also be said that the annual cost of the lost discount is at the rate of 54 percent (18 × 3). Likewise, if the terms were 4/15, N/60 and if payment were made on the 60th day, the annual rate of the lost discount would be 32 percent (8 × 4). It can be seen that from a financial viewpoint, the practice of failing to take advantage of discounts is very costly. It can also be seen that it would be sound economics for a company to borrow from a bank at perhaps 6 percent and use the proceeds to pay trade creditors within the discount period.

Problem   A supplier offers to sell goods at a bargain price of $100,000 to Company P; the offer has been accepted. Terms are 4/30, N/60. The firm does not have the cash to take advantage of the offer but can borrow from a bank that charges 6 percent per year and that will not make a loan for less than one month. If the bank loan is obtained, by how much in dollars will expenses be reduced?

Discount taken	$4,000
Less interest on bank loan for one month	480

.06 × $96,000 = $5,760
$^{1}/_{12}$ × $5,760 = $480

Expenses are reduced by	$3,520

ROLE OF SALES FINANCE COMPANIES

Dealers who sell automobiles and merchants who sell refrigerators, television sets, and other appliances are often in need of "wholesale financing" or "floor plan financing"; that is, they need to borrow money to pay the manufacturer. This is especially true of automobile dealers, whose high-cost inventories necessitate large amounts of capital or access to financial institutions that will lend money—generally the latter. Sales finance companies, banks, and other institutions may supply the needed cash by granting loans based on trust receipts, although we are concerned here with only the first of these institutions. The car dealer, for example, may place his order for the required number of cars or he may be given a quota to sell. After supplying about 10 to 20 percent of the required cash, he makes arrangements so that the manufacturer is paid by the sales finance company. In some cases, the sales finance company will supply all the credit needed to pay the manufacturer. In the meantime, the dealer signs a demand note and a trust receipt for each car and gives the documents to the sales finance company. The effect of the trust receipt arrangement is that the cars belong to the sales finance company even though the dealer has possession of the various vehicles. As the automobiles or trucks are sold, the dealer remits cash to the sales finance company; or if the cars are sold on the installment plan, the installment notes are used to repay the holder of the trust receipts. Auditors periodically check the dealer's storeroom to be sure that the same number and kind of cars are on hand as indicated by the trust receipts held by the sales finance company.

ACQUIRING INVENTORIES ON CONSIGNMENT

A company may acquire inventory on consignment; title remains with the owner and the consignee will use his best efforts to sell the goods. The consignee must keep the consigned goods separate from his inventory. If the consignee sells the goods, a commission is earned; if the goods are not sold, they are returned to the owner. Manufacturers may introduce new products by shipping them on consignment, for retailers hesitate to risk their money in a new and untried product. From the consignee's viewpoint, handling goods on consignment lessens the amount of money that will have to be tied up in current assets, but from the owner's viewpoint, shipping goods on consignment expands the amount of current assets needed.

The Inventory Model

One inventory model in use, already mentioned, gives information on the optimum amount to purchase with each order. Should the firm order 10 units, 20 units, or some other number when an order is placed? Remember that the basic problem is to minimize the sum of these two costs:

1. Acquisition cost (cost of preparing purchase order and similar expenses)
2. Holding cost (cost of storing, insuring, and other similar costs)

Since this subject has already been covered, only a review problem will be worked here.

Problem

A firm uses 100 units of inventory a year; the cost of preparing a purchase order is $10 and the storage cost per unit is $5 for a one-year period. What is the optimum number of units to order?

Solution

The formula for determining the optimum quantity to order is:

$$EOQ = \sqrt{\frac{2UP}{H}}$$

where U equals total units sold each year; P equals cost in dollars of preparing a purchase order; H equals cost in dollars of storing a unit of inventory; and Q equals number of units that should be purchased with each order so that costs will be minimized.

$$EOQ = \sqrt{\frac{2 \times 100 \times 10}{5}}$$
$$= 20$$

It might be well to observe that there are other, more sophisticated inventory models.

Heuristic Programming

In many situations, mathematical models are difficult to apply, whether in managing cash, receivables, inventories, or other assets. The reader may have already developed some reservations on the actual applicability of the mathematical model to determine the optimum amount to borrow from a bank or to buy with a particular purchase order. Mathematical models sometimes depend on assumptions that turn out to be far removed from reality, that rely on data not available (such as the cost of preparing a purchase order), or that turn out to be so complicated as to defy solution, even with computer assistance. In a situation such as this, a heuristic approach may be used. "A heuristic approach is any device or procedure used to reduce problem solving effort—in short, a rule of thumb used to solve a particular problem."[2] A heuristic approach may not give

2. Jerome D. Wiest, "Heuristic Programs for Decision Making," *Harvard Business Review*, September-October 1966, p. 130.

optimum solutions, but it will give reasonable solutions with considerably less expense and effort.

Some examples of heuristics are: Never permit the current ratio to decline below 2 to 1; when the Dow-Jones Average goes above 700, this is the time to begin taking profits; a student should be dropped from college when his cumulative average is less than D; purchase more inventory when the amount on hand falls below 10. All these statements are heuristics; they are rules of thumb that sidestep many of the complicated issues in determining expected value, in using calculus, and in using intensive linear programming analysis. Heuristics have been used for many years. Lately, however, they have been carefully studied, combined into a series of constraints, and fed into a computer, which then uses the heuristics as a set of instructions.

One application of the heuristic approach is to use a computer decision to replace the decision of a trust officer of a bank, who buys securities (inventories for the various trust accounts). Many of the cat and dog type of securities are ruled out; perhaps a list of 100 top-grade companies are fed into the computer and stored in its memory. Then various formulas for computing, say 10 key ratios, are recorded and stored in the computer. Also stored is information concerning the needs of investors, which we will assume are safety, income, and capital appreciation. As information about the various corporations is received by the bank, it is fed into the computer. The computer is able to find securities suitable to the needs of the various investors; furthermore, the computer will give advice on whether securities in an account should be changed. The entire process is called a heuristic approach because (1) not all the securities of the 1 million corporations in the United States need be evaluated—only the 100 originally agreed on; (2) only 10 key ratios are considered, not the several hundred or so that might be abstracted from the firm's financial statements; and (3) investors' needs are limited to the three possibilities rather than the numerous considerations that the trust officer might weigh when selecting securities for the accounts. In other words, a heuristic program eliminates many of the alternatives that would have to be considered in a thorough analysis. But the loss of thoroughness is offset by the speed in obtaining the information and in lowering the cost of obtaining it. "Heuristic programming is not so concerned with finding the one best answer after a lengthy search as with rapidly reaching a satisfactory one."[3] If the computer makes a decision that is as good as the trust officer would make, then the simplifications have not injured the quality of the decision-making process. There is considerable research going on in this very type of problem, that is, whether a computer by using a heuristic approach can make equally good or even better decisions than an individual in the executive hierarchy.

Similarly, a heuristic approach may be used in determining the optimum amount of inventory to purchase with one order. Perhaps experience indicates that some simple rule such as "purchase 100 units when the inventory level falls below 10 units on hand" will provide as good an answer as an elaborate inventory model.

3. Ibid., p. 131.

The above information on the heuristic approach should not be interpreted as grounds for discarding such sophisticated models as the inventory model and expected value models; rather, this approach should be viewed as being useful when for reasons of cost or insufficient information it is not possible to use analytical methods.

HIGHLIGHTS OF THIS CHAPTER

Because of the amount of funds invested in inventories, the management of this current asset assumes special importance. Among other features of managing inventories are these: determining the optimum inventory; keeping the inventory moving toward cash; conserving the inventory; and financing the inventory.

Special consideration must be given to improving and diversifying the inventory, mainly because of competitive pressures and because of a rapidly changing technology.

The finance person is interested in a balance in the level of inventory. The amount on hand should be adequate to meet all reasonable needs; yet excessive inventory should be avoided because of the expense of having inventory on hand (such as insurance, taxes, space requirements, interest on the funds borrowed to obtain the inventory, and so on).

REVIEW QUESTIONS

14-1. Explain the meaning of these terms:
inventory turnover
conglomerate
trade credit compared with consumer credit
floor plan financing
consignment
heuristic programming

14-2. Is it easier for a business firm to obtain trade credit or bank credit? Why?

14-3. Why is trade credit used so extensively by business firms?

14-4. Summarize the main features of the Glidden Company's inventory control project, mentioned in this chapter.

REVIEW PROBLEMS

Answers to some of the problems appear at the end of this section. *For each problem, show how you obtained the answer.*

14-1. Below is the statement of income and expenses for the Zenio Corporation:

Sales	$240,000
Less cost of goods sold	160,000
Gross profit	$ 80,000
Less expenses (light, heat, rent, supplies, and so on)	60,000
Net profit	$ 20,000

If the average inventory turnover for this type of company is 10, is Zenio above or below this average? Assume that the average inventory is $20,000.

14-2. A hardware store has purchased $2,000 of goods on account, the terms being 2/10, N/30. Assuming that the firm could borrow from its local bank at 5 percent, would you recommend that it do so in order to be able to pay its debt of $2,000 on or before the 10th day? If the bill is not paid on the 10th day, assume it will be paid on the 30th day.

14-3. A supplier offers to sell goods at a bargain price of $50,000 to Company P; the offer is accepted. Terms are 3/30, N/60. Company P does not have the cash to take advantage of the offer but can borrow from a bank that charges 7 percent per year and that will not make a loan for less than one month. If the bank loan is obtained, by how much (in dollars) will expenses be reduced?

14-4. A business is planning to increase its sales by $1,080,000 by expanding its inventory. Determine the amount of additional financing needed as a result of the expansion in sales. Below is information applicable to the new product lines (not the old ones):

Assumed number of days in a year	360
Collection period	18 days
Relation of inventory to sales	10 percent
Relation of cash to sales	2 percent
Additional fixed assets needed	$20,000

The following is the firm's balance sheet before expansion:

Cash	$ 40,000	Accounts payable	$ 70,000
Receivables	50,000	Bank loans	25,000
Inventories	70,000	Other payables	15,000
Fixed assets	90,000	Retained earnings	45,000
		Common stock	95,000
Total	$250,000	Total	$250,000

14-5. A retailer is planning to increase his sales by $810,000. His problem is to determine the amount of additional financing needed to implement this change in policy. Below is information applicable to the new product line (not the old one):

Assumed number of days in a year	360
Collection period	15 days
Relation of inventory to sales	10 percent
Relation of cash to sales	3 percent
Additional fixed assets needed	$15,000

The following is the firm's balance sheet before the expansion:

Cash	$ 30,000	Accounts payable	$ 60,000
Receivables	45,000	Bank loans	20,000
Inventories	60,000	Other payables	5,000
Fixed assets	90,000	Retained earnings	40,000
		Common Stock	100,000
Total	$225,000	Total	$225,000

14-6. The manager of the Z Company has proposed raising the inventory turn-over to 15; he believes that current inventories could be lowered without injuring sales. Cost of goods sold is $180,000, average inventory before the change is $20,000, and total assets are $1 million. If inventory turnover can be increased to 15 while sales stay the same: (a) How much in funds would be released from inventory? (b) If the released funds were used to reduce a 6 percent bank loan, how much in interest would be saved each year?

14-7. Company R, which has an average of 20 days' purchases on its books (in the form of accounts payable), has annual purchases of $180,000. What is the average amount of accounts payable?

14-8. Company X, which has an average of 20 days' purchases on its books (in the form of accounts payable), has annual purchases of $360,000. What is the average amount of accounts payable?

14-9. Company R is able to pay most of its bills within the discount period. But on approximately $500,000 of its purchases, the firm is unable to take advantage of the terms 4/10, N/40. The firm pays these bills on the 40th day. Company R is unable to obtain any additional bank credit and its owners are unwilling to increase the net worth or funded debt. The company is able to sell the $500,000 worth of goods for $1,500,000. On this increment of sales, the following data apply: selling expenses $100,000; general expenses $200,000; administrative expenses $200,000. Should the firm eliminate the $500,000 segment of purchases because it "loses" $20,000 in cash discounts and because it is paying an "effective rate of interest" of 48 percent?

14-10. Company F has annual purchases of $720,000; the suppliers of the company extend it terms of 4/30,N/50. This company has average accounts payable of $30,000. Is the firm following a wise policy in paying its bills?

14-11. Wallace Blackmer, an energetic president, plans to increase his inventory so that his sales will increase. Previous to the proposed expansion, the firm had annual purchases of $720,000; it also received the terms of 3/10, N/20 from its suppliers. The president estimates that under his program the firm's purchases will increase to $1,080,000. The firm has an average of $80,000 in accounts payable. Is Blackmer on safe ground in assuming that his suppliers will be delighted because of the additional orders they will receive?

14-12. Company Z, which has annual purchases of $1,080,000, has average accounts payable of $135,000; the company's suppliers grant terms of 2/30, N/45. Is the company paying all its bills in time to take the 2 percent discount?

14-13. Company A has annual purchases of $360,000; the suppliers of the company extend it terms of 5/20, N/40. The company has average accounts payable of $10,000. Is the firm following a wise policy in paying its bills?

14-14. Assuming that the data given below apply to Company Z, determine the optimum amount of inventory to order at one time.

Number of units used per year	32
Cost of preparing one purchase order	$8
Cost per unit charged by seller	$80
Storage costs as a percentage of purchase price of one unit	10 percent

14-15. Company X buys goods on account, the terms being 4/10, N/30. If the firm pays on the 30th day, the annual cost of the trade credit, expressed as a percentage, is 72 percent. *Required*: Show how the answer was obtained.

Answers: 14-1, inventory turnover is 8—below the average; 14-3, $1,217.08; 14-4, $203,600; 14-5, $154,050; 14-6a, $8,000; 14-6b, $480; 14-7, $10,000; 14-8, $20,000.

MANAGING
FOR
EXPANSION

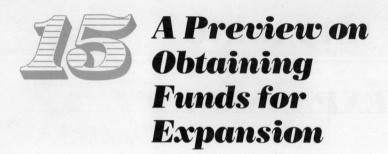

A Preview on Obtaining Funds for Expansion

Assume a conviction by management that it could increase the firm's earnings by a substantial amount if it had additional current or fixed assets. A situation of this kind would make management lean in the direction of going ahead with the expansion. This is the same as saying that a firm expands when the net present value of the project is positive. In less sophisticated terms, this means that the firm accepts projects if the end result will be to raise the price of the shares of common stock or to raise the market value of a single proprietorship or a partnership. A major and very interesting part of this analysis is the determination of the sources of funds to be used to finance this expansion. In other words, management can further advance the financial welfare of the residual owners by seeking the ideal percentage of each individual source of assets to the total assets used in the firm.

At this early point it might be well to give a periscopic view of where American industry actually does obtain funds for its growth. As can be seen in Table 15-1, the classification used is that of internal and external sources—a dichotomy that is frequently used in financial literature and government reports. Internal sources consist of retained profits and depreciation. A common expression is that depreciation is a source of funds, despite the irrationality of implying that an expense creates funds. External sources consist of debt and stock issues, that is, funds obtained from sources outside the business. For the period covered, internal sources came to 62 percent, while external sources came to only 38 percent. Perhaps the most important conclusion to be drawn from these data is that retained profits and depreciation allowances are a far more important source of funds than are stocks or bonds.

The following matters will be discussed in this chapter:

1. Planning the amount and timing of the funds
2. Using the firm's past as a planning tool

3. Surveying the sources of assets
4. Determining what the financial ratios should be
5. Using trading on the equity as a planning tool
6. Seeking the optimum capital structure

Source	Percentage	
Internal:		*TABLE 15-1*
Retained profits	24	*Percentage*
Depreciation	38	*Sources of Funds*
		for Corporations,
	62	*1963-1973*
		(Estimated)
External:		
Short-term debt	16	
Long-term debt	14	
Stock	8	
	38	*Source:*
Total	100	*U.S. Department*
		of Commerce

PLANNING THE AMOUNT AND TIMING OF THE FUNDS

One of the first steps in the planning process is to determine the amount of funds needed. This in turn depends on the size of the project being considered or the amount of expansion in circulating assets being contemplated. Data for estimating the amount of funds needed to finance the expansion are obtained from the capital budget and the cash budget. The capital budget gives clues as to which projects should be accepted, while the cash budget gives clues as to the time when the funds will be needed to pay for the assets. The cash budget must be prepared for a commensurate period of time to include the point of time at which the funds will be expended. The funds required to support a project are often thought of in terms of minimum and maximum amounts. Thus, if management is thinking in terms of constructing a new factory, the estimate might be that the edifice will cost $260,000, with a minimum of $250,000 and a maximum of $270,000. This is a sound type of analysis because it permits some variation from the target figure, yet keeps the firm financially prepared to pay for the project.

An example of planning based on minimum and maximum amounts of funds needed is the New York Stock Exchange's projection of its space needs for a five-year period. A special committee of the exchange predicted that the volume of this institution would increase by 50 percent in the next five years. Since the members earn commissions on volume, this report had the effect of stating that the amount of business in this institution would increase substantially in the period for which the projection was made. Such a large increase in volume would require additional space facilities. The committee of the exchange did not specify any specific new site. But it did estimate that such a new location would cost a minimum of $50 million and a maximum of $78 million. Furthermore, the exchange had assets of $29 million. The committee suggested that the balance of the amount needed be financed by immediately increasing initiation fees and annual dues and that any additional amounts needed be borrowed through the issuance of a mortgage on the building to be acquired. In summary, the New York Stock Exchange made a set of plans based on the minimum and maximum amount of funds needed rather than on a specific amount.

Also important is when the funds will be needed to pay for the expansion. If a firm is committed to a major capital expenditure, payment may be made immediately, deferred until the project is finished, or spread over a period of many months. As an example of the latter, a firm may pay 20 percent of the purchase price when approximately 20 percent of the project is completed, another 60 percent when the project is approximately 80 percent completed, and the final 20 percent after the project is 100 percent completed and approved. If a deferred payment schedule is to be used, the firm may attempt to synchronize its fund raising with its fund disbursements. One approach, used by Chrysler Corporation, is to obtain a special kind of bank loan in which the borrower takes down (uses) the funds as needed, thus saving an interest cost that would be incurred if all the money were borrowed at once. Another possibility is to borrow money from a bank as the need for payments arises and to float a stock or bond issue at a later date, using the proceeds to repay the bank. (For example, the Pauley Petroleum Company borrowed $7 million from banks to finance a drilling program in the Mexican Tidelands. At the end of the year in which this drilling occurred, the firm raised $9,540,000 from the sale of stock, the proceeds being used to repay the bank loan and add to the corporation's general funds.) Or the officers of a firm may believe that just prior to engaging in a major capital expenditure program is an opportune time to raise long-term funds because money market conditions are such that capital is cheap. Such a firm would obtain funds immediately and invest the proceeds in safe securities of proper maturities until the need to make cash payments arises. Still another firm may not be in a strong enough financial position to make a commitment to engage in a major capital expenditure program until the funds are actually on hand. Such a firm may enter the money market even at a disadvantageous time. In any event, planning the timing of the cash expenditure is an important step in the process of fund raising.

USING THE FIRM'S PAST AS A PLANNING TOOL

The firm's past must be used as a planning tool in the quest for an optimum source of capital mixture. The stability of a company's past net operating income has an important bearing on the future source of capital mixture. A firm whose earnings are highly variable will have to use caution in the selection of sources such as bonds that require fixed cash payments for interest and repayment of principal. With revenue uncertain, diligence must be exercised so as not to assume too heavy a burden in fixed charges.

The size of the firm's past net operating income also influences the range of choices of sources of capital. A large firm with a net operating income of $1 million is in a more flexible position to bargain for funds than a firm with a net operating income of $10,000. Big firms are generally quite diversified and able to hire specialized and talented management. Small firms, as a class, are unlikely to have either of these advantages. In many cases the public assumes that large firms are relatively more prosperous and stable than small ones. Such an outlook broadens the number of sources of capital available for large companies, and it may lead suppliers of capital to advancing funds or credit on more lenient terms to the larger enterprises.

The stage of the life cycle of the firm has some bearing on the source of capital mixture that will be used. For example, a newly promoted firm has a different problem in raising funds than does an old, established, profitable company. A lack of demonstrated earning power may mean heavy reliance on common stock and other forms of financing that do not require an agreement to pay definite sums of cash on specific dates. At a time when the well-established General Motors Corporation was selling bonds at a low rate of interest, the newly formed but ill-fated Tucker Corporation (a firm that proposed to manufacture automobiles) had to sell common stock to raise funds. Also, a newly established firm may be forced into a simple mixture of sources of capital, as investors may avoid complex financial patterns. In situations like this promoters are limited in the range of sources of capital. Furthermore, in a new firm the matter of control is of such great importance that care must be exercised not to lose it to rivals. If control is important in a specific case, common stock may be issued with limited voting rights but with full rights to share in dividends. When a young firm is raising capital, many compromises must be made, and the owners may have to be satisfied with less than their first choice of an optimum source of capital mixture.

The amount of prior financing in which a firm has engaged may also influence future financing. A firm that has floated a bond issue or a preferred stock issue may have agreed not to issue any securities with claims on income or assets prior to securities now outstanding. In other words, contractual provisions entered into in the past may limit the sources of funds and their terms.

The main advantage of acquiring assets from owners instead of creditors is that the firm is put in less danger of failing. If a large outlay is needed to meet the interest payments and the principal of debts, the company is in danger of failing if sales should suffer a drastic slump or if a substantial proportion of the accounts receivable should be uncollectible. Management is conscious of the possibility of failure because it represents the owners, whose equity will be wiped out first if there is insufficient cash to pay debts.

A second advantage of obtaining assets from owners instead of creditors is that the management of the debtor may be freer to make policies. Although creditors do not participate in the day-to-day decisions of managing a firm, when there is considerable debt the lenders may place some restrictions on the activities of the borrower. Thus a bank that is lending to a firm might require that the management of the borrower agree to a limit on the officers' salaries and on the amount

SURVEYING THE
SOURCES OF ASSETS

Reasons for Obtaining
Additional Assets
from Owners
Instead of Creditors

of profits withdrawn from the business. Even though these restrictions may not be unreasonable, the management of the firm needing the capital may believe that these outside influences on policy-making should be avoided.

A third advantage of ownership sources of assets is that the smaller the debt, the better the chances of borrowing in an emergency. That is, the firm saves one of its best sources of funds until an acute need arises. Other factors being equal, a firm with a small amount of debt is, in an emergency, in a better position to borrow than one that is heavily indebted.

Reasons for Obtaining
Additional Assets
from Creditors
Instead of Owners

One reason for acquiring assets from creditors instead of owners is that business firms may find that creditors will accept a rate of interest that is low in relation to the return expected by suppliers of ownership capital. For example, AT&T borrowed money at 7 percent while its common stock was yielding almost 8 percent. Similarly, a small partnership was able to obtain a 6 percent loan when proposed additional partners expected a return of at least 10 percent on any money that they might inject into the firm. When assets can be attracted to the business on cheap terms, the position of the owners is always strengthened. That is, assuming a given level of profitability, the profits to the owners will be increased or losses reduced if some of the capital can be acquired from low-cost sources.

A second reason for obtaining assets from creditors instead of owners is that those who lend nearly always will advance funds without expecting to participate in the control of the enterprise. For example, General Foods Corporation obtained a $35 million long-term loan without giving the lenders the right to vote for directors at annual meetings. Although banks may place a few restrictions on the borrower, these lenders do not normally insist on any voting rights. Generally speaking, creditors are viewed as outsiders and are not expected to participate in the management of the business. If instead of borrowing money a business acquired the funds by bringing in new partners or selling voting stock, those in control of it might find their position endangered.

The third reason for going into debt instead of raising funds from ownership sources is the tax advantage: interest is a deductible expense for income tax purposes. Interest paid to bondholders and bankers is an example of interest that is deductible. On the other hand, dividends paid on both preferred and common stock are not deductible, as these items are regarded as distributions of profit and not as expenses.

Fourth, some forms of credit are used because of convenience, as is the case when merchandise is purchased on account. Even if the buyer has sufficient cash, he may prefer to have 10 days or so to make the payment so that he will have time to check the quantity and quality of the goods. In the meantime, the purchaser is in debt to the seller of the commodities.

A Threefold
Classification of Credit

Credit may be classified on the basis of the length of time the debtor has use of it. The following threefold division of credit is based on the time factor:

1. Maturity of more than 10 years (long-term credit)
2. Maturity of more than 1 year but not more than 10 years (intermediate-term credit)
3. Maturity of 1 year or less (short-term credit)

As shown in Table 15-2, the same groups of creditors tend to supply both short- and intermediate-term credit.

Long-term	Short- and Intermediate-term	TABLE 15-2 Creditor Sources of Assets
Individuals	Trade creditors	
Life insurance companies	Commercial banks	
Commercial banks	U.S. Small Business Administration	
Mutual savings banks	Commercial paper houses	
Investment companies	Commercial finance companies	
Trustees	Others	
Pension funds		
Others		

Long-term Credit

Long-term credit is used most often to finance the purchase of assets with a long life, although this form of credit may be used to finance the acquisition of any class of assets—even current assets. A public utility raising funds to finance the purchase of a new office building might find long-term credit a suitable mode of financing. When a firm desires to have the use of the money longer than 10 years, long-term credit is sought.

The main reason for using long-term credit instead of borrowing from short- or intermediate-term sources is that the firm will not be threatened with insolvency because of the unwillingness of creditors to renew the loan. The case for long-term credit may be summarized by stating that it should be used when the management of the borrower expects that the firm will need a long period of time to generate sufficient earnings to repay the debt.

Long-term credit may be used by all forms of organization, although it is most often associated with a firmly established corporation. This is in contrast with short- and intermediate-term credit, which are used extensively by all forms of organization. The difficulty with single proprietorships and partnerships using long-term credit is that these forms of organization are relatively impermanent, thereby creating a problem for the lender. Even small corporations have difficulty in obtaining long-term credit if creditors believe that the firm is unstable because its success depends on one or two key men. Lenders may compensate for the risk of lending to impermanent organizations by requiring the borrowers to pledge collateral and repay the loan in installments.

Intermediate-term Credit

Intermediate-term credit is used to finance the acquisition of both current assets and fixed assets and to retire debt and preferred stock. When intermediate-term credit is used to finance the purchase of current assets, the management of the borrower believes that the circular flow of these assets will provide sufficient funds to repay the debt. When intermediate-term credit is used to finance the purchase of fixed assets, the assets acquired are usually those with a relatively short life, such as a delivery truck. These fixed assets are expected to add to the stream of income a sum that will be sufficient to pay the interest and the principal and to expand earnings available for the proprietor, the partners, or the stockholders. When intermediate-term credit is used to retire debt or preferred stock, the management of the borrower believes that the earning capacity of the firm will be sufficient to pay the creditors who advanced the intermediate-term credit.

The main reason for using intermediate- instead of short-term credit is that the firm has the use of the funds for a longer period of time; the main reason for using intermediate- instead of long-term credit is that the latter may not be available, that is, creditors may insist on a maturity of five years or less because they think the risk is not as great on an intermediate-term loan.

Short-term Credit   There are a number of reasons why a firm might use short-term credit instead of the other two forms. First, short-term credit may lower the interest cost to the business because the extra funds may be borrowed for the exact period of time they are needed. The National Dairy Products Corporation, for example, makes heavy use of short-term credit. This company's inventory requirements are at their peak during the summer months, at which time the firm borrows from commercial banks. Since this is the only period of the year that the enterprise needs the additional funds, the management borrows for the busy season only, thereby paying interest on the funds for only a fraction of a year. A further factor is that the interest rate on short-term bank loans may be lower than that which would have to be paid on intermediate- or long-term credit. Assuming that such is the case, the profits available for owners would be increased if short-term credit were used.

Second, short-term credit may be used because of necessity; that is, no other source of funds may be available on terms suitable to the management. A business, for example, may have to buy on account and take advantage of the maximum credit period because intermediate- and long-term credit are not available. When short-term credit is obtained under such strained circumstances, the indirect interest cost is generally high.

A third reason for using short-term credit is that this arrangement at times allows management to do business with other people's money without having to pay interest. If no discount terms are offered to the debtor, he might delay making the payment for, say, 30 days, and thereby have free use of the funds during the one-month period. In effect, the buyer of the goods has acquired a "costless" loan for a 30-day period.

Problem   Company B has $700,000 in current assets and $300,000 in current liabilities. How much in short-term debt can the company assume before violating a current ratio constraint of 2 to 1 (assuming the proceeds are used to increase current assets)?

$700,000 + x = 2(\$300,000 + x)$

$700,000 + x = \$600,000 \quad + 2x$

$700,000 \quad\quad = \$600,000 \quad + x$

$100,000 \quad\quad = x$

Solution

Answer: $100,000.

Company W has $100,000 in assets. It also has $25,000 in current liabilities, $15,000 in 4 percent bonds outstanding, and $60,000 of common stock outstanding. The company has average annual earnings of $30,000 before interest but after taxes. If it is assumed that a company of this kind should earn interest on its bonds six times, how much in *additional* 5 percent bonds could this company issue and still meet the suggested standard?   *Problem*

Answer: $88,000. The company can stand total interest charges of $5,000. However, $600 of this total is already used up, leaving a maximum additional amount of $4,400. This $4,400 can support $88,000 of bonds ($4,400 ÷ .05).   *Solution*

The determination of financial ratios depends on the type of industry under consideration as well as the specific circumstances surrounding each firm. Table 15-3 gives suggested guidelines for industrials and public utilities. The reader should understand that these ratios must be adapted to the particular operating characteristics of each firm within the above industries.   ***DETERMINING WHAT THE FINANCIAL RATIOS SHOULD BE***

	Industrials	Public Utilities	*TABLE 15-3 Suggested Standard Ratios*
Fixed obligations should not exceed this percentage of the capital structure	25 percent	60 percent	
Preferred stock should not exceed this percentage of the capital structure	25 percent	35 percent	
Fixed charges (mainly bond interest but in many cases also rent) should be earned at least this number of times	3	2	
Preferred stock dividends should be earned at least this number of times	2½	1½	
For each $1,000 of funded debt, there should be at least this amount of net current assets	$1,000	$1,000	
For each $1,000 of funded debt, there should be at least this much in fixed assets	$1,000	$1,000	
The current ratio should be at least this	2:1	1½:1	

Trading on the equity means using funds on which a limited return is paid. For example, a firm is said to be trading on the equity when it uses a bank loan, preferred stock, or bonds. This is because the suppliers of these sources are paid a limited amount for the use of their money. In a similar manner, a limited partnership trades on the equity when it pays a limited partner a given return on his contribution. On the other hand, when a firm raises funds through a common stock issue, this is not trading on the equity because there is no limit on the amount that can be received by this group of owners. The concept of trading on the equity is applicable to any firm that pays a limited return on funds that it uses, whether from short- or long-term sources. The concept is likewise applicable to all forms of organization, including the single proprietorship, the partnership, and the corporation. A firm that obtains a high percentage of its assets from creditors and preferred stockholders trades on the equity to a higher degree than a firm that obtains a smaller percentage of its assets from these sources. Public utilities have been heavy users of debt, thereby engaging in the process of trading on the equity. A company is said to trade on the equity because creditors and preferred stockholders are willing to advance funds to the firm on the strength of the equity supplied by the residual owners, equity embracing the residual proprietors' capital and the earning power of the business.

A convenient way to approach the complex problem of trading on the equity is to seek answers to these questions:

1. For a firm with a given capital structure, does trading increase the returns to residual owners?
2. For a firm with a given capital structure, how do specific changes in EBIT affect the percentage returns to residual owners?

Table 15-4 supplies answers to the above queries. Observe that there are several financial plans in this table. Plan A contains 60 percent debt, plan B 50 percent, and plan C no debt. If the firm has $500,000 in debt, it must pay 6 percent interest; if it has $600,000 in debt, it must pay 6½ percent. In all three plans, assets are assumed to be $1 million. A point of further importance is that under each plan, the level of EBIT is first assumed to be $40,000 and second assumed to be $80,000. Also, the tax rates used in the table are 30 percent on all net profits plus 22 percent on all net profits above $25,000.

*For a Firm with a
Given Capital Structure,
Does Trading on
the Equity Increase
Returns to Owners?*

Trading on the equity is advantageous if the market price of the common stock is higher than would be the case without trading on the equity.

Let us assume that we are analyzing plan A, where it can be seen that the profit to owners from trading on the equity depends on the level of EBIT. At the $40,000 level, earnings per share on the common stock are $0.17½ and the market price per share is $1.75. These data can be compared with the situation that prevails under plan C. Under this latter capital structure, earnings per share are $2.47 and the market price per share is $29.06. Hence, at the $40,000 level of EBIT, trading on the equity is not profitable to the extent engaged in under plan A. This is because the firm is not earning on its assets the rate (6½ percent) that is being paid to the bondholders.

		Assumed Sources of Funds			TABLE 15-4
		Plan A	Plan B	Plan C	Examples of Trading on the Equity
A.	Debt	$600,000	$500,000	$0	
B.	Interest rate on debt	6½%	6%	0%	
C.	Common stock ($100 par value)	400,000	500,000	1,000,000	
D.	Shares of common	4,000	5,000	10,000	
E.	Total assets	$1,000,000	$1,000,000	$1,000,000	
F.	EBIT	$40,000	$40,000	$40,000	
G.	Interest	39,000	30,000	0	
H.	Taxable income	1,000	10,000	40,000	
I.	Tax	300	3,000	15,300	
J.	Net for common	700	7,000	24,700	
K.	Earnings per share on common	0.17½	1.40	2.47	
L.	Price-earnings ratio	10.00	10.526	11.765	
M.	Market value of common (K × L)	$1.75	$14.74	$29.06	
N.	EBIT	$80,000	$80,000	$80,000	
O.	Interest	39,000	30,000	0	
P.	Taxable income	41,000	50,000	80,000	
Q.	Tax	15,820	20,500	36,100	
R.	Net for common	25,180	29,500	43,900	
S.	Earnings per share on common	6.29½	5.90	4.39	
T.	Price-earnings ratio	10.99	11.364	11.765	
U.	Market value of common (S × T)	$69.18	$67.05	$51.65	

A 100 percent increase in EBIT results in these percentage increases:

	Plan A	Plan B	Plan C
Earnings per share	3,497%	321%	78%
Market price of common	3,853%	354%	78%

But if the level of earnings is $80,000, still under plan A, we have a different story. Earnings per share on the common are $6.29½ and the market value is $69.18. Again these results should be compared with those of plan C, which indicate lower earnings per share and a lower market price—still assuming EBIT at the $80,000 level. Hence, at the $80,000 level of EBIT, trading on the equity is profitable to the residual owners. This is because the company is earning a higher rate on its assets than is being paid on the bonds.

Under plan A an increase of $40,000 in EBIT is followed by an increase in the market price of the common from $1.75 to $69.18, an increment of $67.43. This gain is actually caused by two basic factors: (1) increased earning power of the firm and (2) trading on the equity. We are especially interested in the second of the two points. The guarded statement may be made that at the

$80,000 level of EBIT, trading on the equity accounts for $17.53 ($69.18 − $51.65) of the increase of $67.43. This reasoning is based on a comparison of plans A and C. That is, if no trading on the equity is used, as in plan C, the market price of the common stock is $51.65. But if trading on the equity is used, the market price of the common is $69.18. The difference in results is caused by the use of debt. For this reason, financial management is especially concerned with the optimum source of capital mixture.

Of significance is the fact that the price-earnings ratio on the common stock probably increases as EBIT increase, for the reason that common stock becomes safer as the times interest is earned increases. Thus, in plan A, the price-earnings ratio on the common is 10.00 at the $40,000 level of EBIT and 10.99 at the $80,000 level. This change in the price-earnings ratio further magnifies the impact of trading on the equity. Also, notice that as a firm uses trading on the equity on an increasing scale, at a given level of EBIT the price-earnings ratio on the common tends to decrease. The price-earnings ratios used in Table 15-4 are purely arbitrary and are intended only to illustrate the phenomenon that the price-earnings ratio on the common is unlikely to stay the same regardless of the relative amount of debt used. Thus the price-earnings ratio on the common in plan A is less than the ratio on the common in plan B. For example, at the $80,000 level under these two plans, the price-earnings ratio in plan A is 10.99 and in plan B is 11.364. This is because plan A contains a larger proportion of borrowed funds, a factor that increases the risk to the common stockholders.

A word of caution should be injected at this point. Very little is known about how price-earnings ratios on common stock actually change with different proportions of debt to total assets. It is entirely possible that price-earnings ratios on the common stock change to a greater extent than is shown in Table 15-4. That is, there is the possibility that as a firm has a larger and larger percentage of debt to total assets, the public might decrease the price-earnings ratio on the common to such an extent that the benefits of trading on the equity are substantially neutralized.

For a Firm with a Given Capital Structure, How Do Specific Changes in EBIT Affect the Percentage Returns to Residual Owners?

To illustrate how specific changes in EBIT affect percentage returns to residual owners, let us examine plan A in Table 15-4. Since this situation does contain considerable debt, we have an example of trading on the equity, and we would expect leverage to appear in earnings per share and in the market price per share of common stock. As EBIT increase from $40,000 to $80,000 (a 100 percent increase), earnings per share on the common stock increase from $0.17½ to $6.29½ (an increase of 3,497 percent) and the market price of the common rises from $1.75 to $69.18 (an increase of 3,853 percent). Here we have an example of how a change in one amount, EBIT, causes a relatively large change in other amounts. In contrast, in plan C there is no trading on the equity because all the funds have been obtained from residual owners. A 100 percent increase in EBIT causes the earnings per share to increase by 78 percent and the market price of the common to increase by the same percentage. (This is not a relatively large differential in percentages.) In general, it may be said that in prosperous times trading on the equity is advantageous to the firm; in periods of recession and declining earnings trading on the equity is disadvantageous.

Of equal importance is that when a firm is trading on the equity, any percentage decline in EBIT will result in a larger percentage decline in earnings per share and in the market price per share.

Residual owners (common stockholders, single proprietors, and partners) stand to make large gains if trading on the equity is a success. As previously indicated, success comes in a number of forms, mainly in the increase in the market price of the shares of common stock.

Risks of Trading on the Equity

On the other hand, the use of trading on the equity entails certain risks and annoyances which need to be examined. If trading on the equity is unsuccessful, this means that over a span of years the firm is unable to earn as high a return on its assets as is being paid on the debt and preferred stock. In time, the firm's cash becomes so low that there is default on interest, on sinking funds for debt, on maturity values of debt, and on preferred stock dividends. When these contingencies happen, the following are some of the penalties, from the viewpoint of the common stockholders:

1. If the firm is unable to meet its commitments to creditors, this group may seize the assets of the firm and sell them at public auction. Furthermore, if the firm is unincorporated, the single proprietors and partners may lose personal belongings such as their home, furniture, stocks and bonds, and even automobile.
2. If commitments to preferred stockholders are not met, this group obtains voting rights.
3. In the event that commitments are not paid on either bonds or preferred stocks, dividends on the common cease and the market price of the common falls sharply.

Even if trading on the equity is profitable, the suppliers of funds on which a limited return is paid may impose certain annoying restrictions on management, including limitations on the amount of dividends that can be paid, on salaries of officers, on purchase of treasury stock, on sale of new senior securities, on sales of assets, and on merging with another firm.

The optimum capital structure may be defined as that combination of debt to equity which results in the lowest weighted cost of capital. The traditional view states that there is some combination of debt to equity at which bondholders will be satisfied to such an extent that they will accept a moderate yield and that the common stockholders will be satisfied to such an extent that the price-earnings ratio of the stock will be reasonably high. This view holds that it is possible for a firm to issue moderate amounts of debt without jeopardizing the solvency of the company, that debt is a cheap source of funds, and that by

SEEKING THE OPTIMUM CAPITAL STRUCTURE

trading on the equity a firm is able to generate more profits and dividends for the owners. Thus, if a company can borrow $100 at 6 percent and use this money to buy assets that yield 10 percent, the bondholders are paid their 6 percent while the profit of 4 percent accrues to the benefit of the stockholders. Public utilities are frequently cited as an example of an industry that has successfully used trading on the equity. The traditional view continues by stating that moderate amounts of debt do not change stockholders' views of the risk of owning stock in the firm, or if it does lead to the opinion that there is more risk, the increased earnings per share will more than offset the decline in the price-earnings ratio. In summary, the traditional view states that a reasonable amount of debt is an advantage to the issuing firm. American businessmen are convinced of the soundness of using debt. This conviction is based on the belief that bonds are a cheap source of funds because (1) investors take a low return on them (2) because the interest on them is tax deductible to the issuing corporation, and (3) because they tend to make the firm's weighted cost of capital lower than would be the case if the firm had only common stock outstanding.

HIGHLIGHTS OF THIS CHAPTER

A common classification of sources of funds is internal versus external. Internal sources consist of retained profits and depreciation; external sources consist of funds raised from outside the business and include stocks, bonds, short-term debt, and so on. Many small and intermediate-sized firms prefer to expand through internal sources exclusively. But if the firm has numerous profitable projects, it may seek outside sources of funds, thereby raising the market price of the common stock of the present stockholders.

Although there may be advantages to obtaining funds from owners over creditors, and vice versa, each firm must seek a balance in the proportion of debt to equity.

If the firm uses debt, the repayment date should synchronize with the cash flows of the firm. That is, the addition of certain kinds of assets to the firm will only gradually increase cash flow; hence, the repayment schedule should be established with this point in mind.

Trading on the equity means obtaining funds on which a limited return is paid. This process results in leverage; that is, certain percentage changes in operating income result in larger percentage changes in earnings per share and in market price of the common stock. The use of a moderate amount of debt, therefore, is an advantageous procedure from the viewpoint of the common stockholders.

REVIEW QUESTIONS

15-1. What are the advantages of trading on the equity? the disadvantages?

15-2. What are the advantages of obtaining funds from owners? from creditors?

15-3. Which supplies the more funds for business firms: retained profits or common stock?

15-4. Do external sources supply more funds for business firms than internal sources?

REVIEW PROBLEMS Answers to some of the problems appear at the end of this section. *For each problem, show how you obtained the answer.*

15-1. Company K has $300,000 in current assets and $100,000 in current liabilities. How much in short-term debt can the company assume before violating a current ratio constraint of 2 to 1 (assuming the proceeds are used to increase current assets)?

15-2. Company M has EBIT of $200,000 a year. The firm has $100,000 of 4 percent bonds outstanding. Assuming that EBIT in this type of company should be five times greater than total bond interest, what is the maximum amount of additional bonds at 5 percent that this company could issue and still meet the suggested coverage test?

15-3. Below are data for Company P, whose earnings before interest and taxes are $30,000:

Current assets	$ 80,000	Current liabilities	$ 30,000
Fixed assets	220,000	5 percent first mortgage bonds	100,000
		6 percent preferred stock	30,000
		Common stock and retained profits	140,000
Total	$300,000	Total	$300,000

An investor maintains the following standards for bonds: (a) earnings before interest and taxes should be at least five times greater than the bond interest; (b) the mortgage bonds should not be more than one-half the fixed assets; (c) the net current assets (net working capital) should be at least as great as the bonds outstanding; and (d) there should be at least $2 of stock and surplus for each $1 of bonds outstanding. For preferred stock, the investor maintains these standards: (a) earnings before interest and taxes should be seven times greater than the sum of the interest requirements and the preferred stock dividend requirements; (b) the fixed assets, after deducting bonds, should be at least as great as the amount of preferred stock outstanding; and (c) there should be $3 of common stockholder equity for each $1 of preferred stock outstanding.
Required: Determine whether or not the above company meets these standards.

15-4. Given the following information for Company X, determine the total net worth: sales $800,000; turnover of assets 2; current liabilities $100,000; long-term bonds $100,000; no other liabilities.

15-5. Given the following data, determine the amount by which the common stock has risen as a result of trading on the equity.

	Actual Sources	Alternate Sources
Debt	$100,000	0
Interest rate on debt	6%	0
Common shares	4,000	10,000
Income tax rate	50%	50%
EBIT	$100,000	$100,000
Price-earnings ratio	10	12½

Answers: 15-1, $100,000; 15-2, $720,000; 15-4, $200,000; 15-5, $55 ($117.50 − $62.50).

CASE ON PLANNING FOR SEASONAL FINANCIAL NEEDS

Seymour Thompkins is president and Albert Bressler is vice president of the Thompkins Department Store. For the first five years of its life, the department store was operated as a partnership. In the sixth year, the firm was converted into a corporation. The change was advantageous because the owners obtained limited liability and yet could elect to be taxed as an unincorporated enterprise. Thompkins owns 500 shares out of a total of 1,000 shares outstanding. Bressler, his former partner, owns 400 shares. The remaining 100 shares are owned by key employees. The two main stockholders each receive a salary of $1,000 a month.

This firm does not plan to expand permanently, although because of its seasonal operations, there is a rapid expansion of assets during certain months of the year. In December of each year the two officers reevaluate their policy of making heavy use of bank credit. They consider these general alternatives:

1. Selling voting stock to employees who are not now stockholders. These new stockholders would expect 10 percent on their money.
2. Obtaining funds from long-term creditors through the sale of 5 percent bonds.
3. Borrowing money from intermediate-term creditors who would expect 7 percent.
4. Continuing to borrow from the local bank, which charges 6 percent.
5. Liquidating some of their personal assets (see Table 15-5) and pumping these additional funds into the business.

TABLE 15-5 Personal Balance Sheets of the Two Officers

	Thompkins	Bressler
Cash surrender value of insurance	$10,000	$15,000
Market value of home	25,000	20,000
Market value of stocks, other than in department store	7,000	5,000
United States government bonds	4,000	1,000
Shares in local bank	8,000	2,000
Total assets	$54,000	$43,000

Required: Discuss the advantages and disadvantages of the five proposals under consideration. Which alternative would you select? Give reasons.

16 Securities Markets

This chapter will be devoted to the securities markets. These markets are analyzed because of their importance in providing a machinery for the determination of prices of securities, a most important element in measuring the cost of capital. The following will be discussed in this chapter:

1. Who has the money to buy stocks and bonds
2. The transfer of securities among investors
3. The nature of stock exchanges
4. The operation of the over-the-counter market
5. Practices in buying and selling securities

WHO HAS THE MONEY TO BUY STOCKS AND BONDS?

The main purchasers of corporate securities are individuals, life insurance companies, commercial banks, mutual savings banks, investment companies (mutual funds), trustees, and pension funds.

Individuals

Individuals are an important segment of the capital market because they hold large blocks of common and preferred stocks. Individuals have always been an important source of equity capital for the small corporation. In recent years, large firms have succeeded in broadening the ownership base, that is, increasing the number of shareholders in the economy.

If the national income continues to increase over the next several years, the middle-income group will have more money to invest and therefore will be a potent force in the capital market. Another factor encouraging further stock purchases by the middle-income group is the employee stock ownership plans of many large companies, which encourage the rank and file of their workers to buy limited amounts of corporate shares. Against these two factors must be weighed the tendency of individuals to place their money in institutions such as life insurance companies and commercial banks.

Employee stock ownership plans A corporation may decide to embark on a special program to sell securities to employees—either key officers or the rank and file of the employees. The securities sold virtually always consist of common stock.

When a corporation offers to sell securities to employees, there must be some special feature about the plan which excites the employees' interest so that they will take advantage of it. Otherwise, any employee could buy the shares in the market and there would be no special reason for buying direct from the company. Some special features that the corporation might use to stir the employees to action are the sale of stock below its current market price, the sale of stock on the installment plan, and the sale of special stock which is slightly safer than ordinary common stock. The first and second plans are much more important than the third. An illustration of the first and second plans is the stock offering plan of the General Telephone Corporation. The employees of this organization could buy the stock of this company on the installment plan at $3 below market price, provided, however, that the company would not charge more than $35 nor less than $25 per share. No employee could buy more than 250 shares.

A corporation may get the stock it sells from two sources. It may sell unissued stock, or it may have to buy the stock in the market.

Corporations with relatively stable profits seem best suited to encourage the rank and file of their employees to buy their stock. A company with stable profits can go through a depression period and still continue to pay dividends. AT&T is an example of a stable organization which has encouraged employee stock ownership. Stability is an important factor because employees are likely to expect dividends and a relatively stable market price through both prosperous and depressed periods.

Not all employees are eligible for participation in a given employee stock purchase program. The employee may have to be with the company for a stated period of time (such as six months), he may have to be an officer of the corporation, he may have to be in a stated wage bracket, or the like.

If the employee is eligible for the program, there are always upper limits on the amount of stock that can be purchased. Usually the employee can buy so many shares for each $1,000 of annual wages, and usually there is an upper limit on the unpaid balance. When the Dow Chemical Company sold stock to employees, each worker could buy one share for each $200 of his annual wages.

Since insurers contract to pay fixed amounts in the future, they must be careful to place their cash in investments that are safe. Also, life insurance companies must seek investments that pay a steady income. In contracting to pay the beneficiaries certain sums, the insurers have assumed that their investments will yield a certain rate of return each year. Although life insurance companies must seek conservative investments that pay a regular income, there is no pressure on

Life Insurance Companies

them to seek highly liquid investments, since their agreements to pay the policy-holders fall due over a great many years. The actual investments that a particular life insurance company will make are determined by the judgment of its own investment department and by the state insurance laws. In general, the state laws that apply to life insurance companies require that the insurers follow a conservative investment policy.

For many years life insurance companies were not allowed to acquire common stocks. Recently this rule has been relaxed in some states; in New York, for example, life insurance companies may buy a limited amount of common stock. Life insurance companies have increased the demand for *blue chip stocks* (supposedly the safest ones). In addition to supplying business firms with funds through the purchase of their securities, life insurance companies supply funds through mortgage loans on business properties. They also hold some of their assets in the form of cash, a great deal of their assets in government securities, a large part in mortgages on residences, and a small part in direct ownership of housing projects.

Commercial Banks Commercial banks are another important holder of corporate securities—mainly bonds. Four important considerations affect bank investments—safety, liquidity, rate of return, and government regulation. First, commercial banks must make sound investments, for the community looks on these institutions as pillars of strength. Banks have a social responsibility to invest wisely so that depositors can be assured that their savings are safe. The second consideration, that of liquidity, is still an important factor in the selection of investments. Since those with checking accounts may withdraw their money on demand and since those with savings accounts can withdraw their money either on demand or within 30 days, the bank management must be ready to meet these demands. Commercial banks meet the liquidity problem by keeping large sums of cash on hand and in other banks, by investing in such liquid assets as United States government bonds, and by borrowing from other banks if the need arises. The third consideration, that of keeping the assets earning a return, is a problem that confronts all banks. Banks are in business to earn a return for their stockholders, and the income earned on total assets must be great enough to meet all expenses, including taxes, and still leave a profit for the stockholders. Finally, and quite important, are the government rules and regulations on what kinds of investments a bank can make. These include the rule that banks can buy bonds only from the top four ratings and the general rule that, with a few unimportant exceptions, a bank cannot buy common stock. As is true of life insurance laws at the state level, laws regulating bank investments stress conservatism.

Mutual Savings Banks *Mutual savings banks* are cooperative savings institutions in which savers pool their funds, the funds being used to acquire conservative investments. A mutual savings bank has no stockholders; any "profits" are paid out to depositors or kept as reserves. There are at least three structural differences between commercial banks and mutual banks. Mutual savings banks are nonprofit institutions, whereas commercial banks are operated for profit; the deposits in a mutual savings bank are mostly time deposits, whereas deposits in commercial banks are mainly in the form of checking accounts; and mutual savings banks tend to pay a higher return on savings accounts than do commercial banks. Most state laws provide that mutual savings banks can invest only in the "legal list," that is, specific investments released by state officials. The legal list consists mainly of debt instruments, although in recent years mutual savings banks have been allowed to purchase limited amounts of corporate stock. Since mutual savings banks are not under as much pressure as commercial banks to maintain liquidity, they can invest in nonliquid assets that have a relatively high average yield.

Instead of buying stocks and bonds of corporations engaged in production, marketing, or financial activities, an investor may buy securities in an investment company, which in turn owns securities of companies engaged in these activities. Investment companies hold large blocks of corporate stocks and bonds and are therefore an important part of the securities markets. The income of an investment company comes from dividends, interest, and profits on the sale of securities. From this gross return are subtracted the expenses of the investment company. The net profit is available for distribution to the stockholders of the investment company. The present tax laws are such that investment companies are encouraged to pay 90 percent or more of their net income to stockholders. It can be seen that when an investor buys shares in an investment company he is indirectly purchasing stocks and bonds. What are the advantages of this plan of investment?

Investment Companies

1. Supposedly there is expert management in the selection of securities because investment companies are in a position to hire experts to give advice on what stocks and bonds should be acquired. Since the cost of hiring expert advisers can be spread over a large dollar volume, the cost per unit of purchase is relatively low.
2. Investors are able to obtain diversification even with small sums. Once an investor purchases securities from an investment company, he has an indirect fractional claim on a great many different issues. It is almost impossible for an investor of moderate means to obtain satisfactory diversification by directly purchasing stocks and bonds.
3. Constant supervision is another advantage of owning shares in an investment company. Expert advisers are retained to review the investment merits of the securities in the portfolio. Such supervision is difficult for investors who directly own either shares or corporate bonds.

These three advantages are so impressive that many investors are convinced that investment companies provide the best outlet for those who have only small sums to invest in stocks.

Trustees   "Trust" is the name given to an arrangement under which title to property is held by one person or institution for the benefit of another person. The one holding title (called the *trustee*) usually invests or manages the property and makes payments to the beneficiary as provided in the trust agreement or instrument. Trusts can be divided into two main kinds—*testamentary* or *death trusts* and *inter vivos* or *living trusts*. The testamentary trust is established in a will and takes effect upon the death of the creator.

Example   George Smith's will provides that $200,000 of his estate should be turned over to the First National Bank, that his wife should receive the income from the fund as long as she lives, and that upon her death the $200,000 is to be divided equally between his two sons. This is a testamentary trust. In this illustration, Smith is the creator or settlor; the First National Bank is the trustee; and the two sons are subsequent beneficiaries or remaindermen. An *inter vivos* or living trust is created during the lifetime of the creator or settlor.

Example   Earl and Ruth North were people of considerable wealth. They desired to give financial assistance to the construction of a home for old people. Many of the expenditures for the project were of a nonrecurring type, although these outlays would be quite large during the first five years. After the home was constructed and placed in operation, the Norths were confident that a number of others would contribute to its support. To give financial aid for a limited period of time, the couple established a trust and contributed 2,000 shares of General Motors Corporation common stock. In this case the trust had a life of 10 years and at the end of this time the principal of the estate reverted to the couple or their heirs. During the life of the trust the income produced by the securities was used to establish and improve the facilities of the home.

The living trust may be *revocable* or *nonrevocable*. If a person creates a trust by transferring $50,000 to a trustee for a stated purpose but reserves the right to revoke this agreement, the trust is revocable. If the creator reserves no right to revoke, an irrevocable trust exists. The reasons for the establishment of trusts, both testamentary and living, are many. A common one is to obtain expert management of a fund of capital. Trustees hold large blocks of corporate securities, particularly bonds; therefore, like life insurance companies, they play an important role in their capacity as holders of securities.

Pension Funds   *Pension funds* consist of money and investments earmarked for payment of retirement benefits to retired employees. The employees, employers, or both may make contributions to a fund that is distributed eventually to eligible employees. The methods of making financial arrangements so that the money will be available vary, although a few arrangements are very popular.

First, the funds may be turned over to a trustee, who will invest the money in the legal list, according to the "prudent man rule" or according to instructions of the employer. After considering such factors as the age of the workers and the probable return on investments, an actuary figures the annual contribution that will have to be made to the trustee. The trustee must use prudence in investing the fund, but he cannot guarantee that there will be a certain amount of money in the fund when employees begin to retire. If there is not enough money available, the employer may have to add to the fund. As a practical matter, the trustee, as noted earlier, makes such safe investments that there is little likelihood that the principal of the fund will be dissipated. This type of trustee arrangement generates a demand for corporate securities; that is, pension funds hold billions of dollars of securities and probably will continue to increase in significance over the coming years.

In another financial plan, the employer makes yearly payments to a life insurance company, the payments being used to buy annuities for the employees. Like payments to trustees, the payments made to life insurance companies are determined by an actuary. When the plan is handled by the life insurance company, the insurer is responsible for having enough cash on hand to make payments to the retirees. The insurance company places the payments it receives along with other funds and makes the usual investments. Indirectly, then, pension funds find their way into the capital markets, because life insurance companies place some of their assets in corporate securities.

Other Investors

Estates, colleges with endowments, hospitals with endowments, educational foundations (such as the Ford Foundation), business corporations, partnerships, religious organizations, and fraternal societies may also hold corporate securities for investment purposes.

TRANSFER OF SECURITIES AMONG INVESTORS

Holders of stocks and bonds may decide to obtain cash for their investments by selling their securities to other investors. Similarly, others in the economy have cash to invest and are desirous of buying stocks and bonds. The problem is to bring together the order of prospective sellers and buyers so that an exchange of securities for cash may take place. An efficient system whereby investors can convert their securities into cash quickly and at or near the current market price makes investors more ready to put their savings into stocks and bonds. Indirectly, then, an efficient system of transferring securities aids corporations in selling stocks and bonds to investors.

One way of transferring the ownership of securities is for the prospective buyer and the prospective seller to deal directly with each other. Thus someone who has stocks and bonds to sell may get in touch with a buyer who will buy the securities for the agreed price. Or someone who wants to buy stocks or bonds may purchase them directly from the seller at the agreed price. Stocks and bonds of smaller corporations are often traded in this manner; that is, the prospective seller and the prospective buyer agree on the sale or purchase without the intercession of any middlemen.

The second and by far the more usual method of buying or selling securities is to deal with middlemen known as brokers and dealers. Transactions in the securities of large and well-known companies are generally conducted through these middlemen. If, for example, someone wants to buy stock in General Motors Corporation, he can obtain these securities through a broker or a dealer. Or if someone has stock in General Motors Corporation for sale, the securities can be quickly sold through a broker or a dealer.

A *broker* acts as a middleman who matches buying and selling orders, thereby serving both buyers and sellers. He does not take title to the securities involved in the transaction, but he charges a commission for his assistance in consummating the transaction. On the other hand, a *dealer* does take title to the securities. He buys securities at one price and expects to sell them at a higher price. The same person may act as a broker in one transaction and a dealer in another. The business of facilitating the transfer of securities among investors is known as the brokerage business.

THE NATURE OF STOCK EXCHANGES

The Function of Stock Exchanges

Brokers and dealers in large cities may band together and form stock exchanges, which provide a central meeting place where they may deal efficiently with each other in the buying and selling of securities. Each member of the exchange has numerous clients—some wanting to sell securities, others wanting to purchase them. By having direct contact with each other the members of the exchange are able to match, in an orderly manner, the thousands of buy-and-sell orders that come from all over the country. Even though these institutions are called stock exchanges, bonds, rights, and voting trust certificates may also be traded on the floor of the exchange. A stock exchange, then, facilitates the transfer of ownership of securities among investors.

Stock exchanges do not set or determine the price of securities traded under their jurisdiction. Supply and demand determine stock prices. Buyers and sellers set the prices at which they are willing to trade, and the members of the exchange execute these orders. Security holders' expectations as to the future determine the prices at which they will buy or sell stocks and bonds and other securities.

Corporations do not, however, sell their new issues of stocks and bonds on stock exchanges. Generally, a security must be "seasoned" before it is eligible for trading on an exchange; that is, the security must have been outstanding for some time and there must be considerable trading in the issue. Because of these requirements, new issues are not eligible for direct sale through a stock exchange.

Exchanges encourage the purchase or sale of securities in quantities that are known as "round lots." A round lot usually means 100 shares, although each exchange is free to determine the unit of trading on it. For example, the unit of trading on the New York Stock Exchange is 100 shares, except for a few inactive stocks in which 10 shares is considered a round lot. Odd lots consist of transactions in a number of shares less than round lots. An example of a round lot would be the purchase or sale of 100 shares of General Motors common stock; an example of an odd lot would be the purchase or sale of 3 shares of General Motors common stock. The exchange encourages trading in round lots by making it more expensive to purchase shares in odd lots and by lessening slightly the amount received from the sale of securities in odd lots.

If the board of directors decides that it will be to the advantage of the corporation and investors to have the corporation's stocks or bonds listed, formal steps *The Listing* must be taken to have the securities admitted to the trading privileges of the *Procedure* exchange on a listed basis. After an invitation is received from officers of the exchange, an application is sent to them giving a detailed analysis of the corporation's affairs. Some of the important information that is part of the application for listing on the New York Stock Exchange consists of the following: name of the applicant, history and description of the business, description of the property, description of the amount and kinds of securities outstanding, and balance sheets and profit and loss statements. The American Stock Exchange and other exchanges require similar information in the application for listing.

If the application is approved by the stock exchange authorities and the SEC, the securities are admitted to trading privileges on the stock exchange. The corporation then must pay a fee prescribed by the exchange. The listing fees, although substantial, are not a major factor influencing management's decision on whether or not to list its securities.

As part of the agreement, the corporation makes certain promises to the exchange, the most important of which are to notify the exchange of any variation in the character or nature of the business or of any alteration or proposed alteration in the capital structure and to publish informative financial reports at frequent intervals. The exchange extracts these and other promises from the corporation so that the public interest will be served.

Just why might a board of directors consider listing the corporation's securities? *Advantages and* The answer is that both the holders of the company's securities and the corpora- *Disadvantages of Listing* tion may benefit from the listing.

Advantages to the Holders of the Securities First, the marketability of the securities may be increased or maintained when listing results in increased trading in the issue. However, it should be observed that listing a security does not assure or guarantee that it will always be marketable, as it is possible for a listed security to decline gradually in marketability because of such factors as bankruptcy of the issuing company, decline in popular interest in the security, and changes in the capital structure of the issuing corporation.

Second, stockholders are better able to keep informed on the market value of their securities when these securities are listed. For example, the prices at which transactions take place on the New York Stock Exchange are given wide publicity in newspapers throughout the United States. It is an advantage to stockholders to have this information so readily available.

Third, bankers and others are more likely to lend if listed securities can be presented as collateral. Bankers can follow the market value of the collateral in the daily newspapers, thus adding to the safety of the loan. Bankers may hesitate to accept as collateral securities of unknown companies whose market value cannot be readily ascertained.

Fourth, corporations that have their securities listed are required to release financial statements to stockholders. In the past, corporations were reluctant to make public their financial reports because of a fear that competitors might obtain useful data. The stock exchanges and the SEC insist that corporations whose securities are listed on a registered stock exchange publish their financial statements.

Advantages and Disadvantages to the Corporation The most important advantage to a corporation in having its securities listed is that the corporation may be able to sell future issues on more favorable terms. If stockholders benefit from the listing of an issue, the investing public will be inclined to pay a little more for new issues that are also intended to be listed. This favorable attitude may make it possible for the issuing company to sell its issues on more advantageous terms. In other words, the cost of raising capital may be lowered.

A second advantage of listing a security is that investment bankers may charge a smaller commission for marketing the securities of a firm whose shares are listed on, for example, the New York Stock Exchange.

A third advantage that a corporation may obtain from listing its securities is publicity, which will gain customers for the corporation. When there is frequent mention of the name of a corporation in the financial section of newspapers, it is entirely possible that new customers will be added to the corporation's list of purchasers or clients.

Listing also has at least three major disadvantages to the corporation: it must agree to submit detailed financial reports to the stock exchanges and to the United States government (SEC); it must agree to submit to certain regulations, such as the requirement to meet SEC standards in the solicitation of proxies; and it must bear the cost of listing. Minor disadvantages of listing are that it might encourage speculation in the issue by officers and it might make it possible for outside groups to gain control of the corporation when the shares are selling at depressed prices.

The securities of only a small fraction of the approximately 500,000 corporations are traded on stock exchanges; the securities of most corporations are traded on the over-the-counter market—that is, off the stock exchanges.

THE
OVER-THE-COUNTER
MARKET (I)

The over-the-counter market consists of transactions in securities off the stock exchanges. Brokers and dealers who engage in over-the-counter market operations are located in major cities throughout the United States and are closely linked with each other by telephone. The over-the-counter market, then, is not limited to one place but embraces the entire United States; it is also broader in scope than stock exchanges. It will be recalled that stock exchanges limit their activities to trading in securities already issued. In contrast, the over-the-counter market handles both securities already issued and new securities being sold to the public. Whereas the stock exchanges are auction markets, the over-the-counter market is primarily a negotiated market; that is, buyer and seller may haggle over prices before the transaction is completed. Dealers in the over-the-counter market buy securities with the hope of being able to resell them at a higher price. This process resembles any merchandising activity in which the trader buys goods in the hope of reselling them at a higher price.

Generally, when a client wants to buy a security not traded on an exchange, a dealer will handle the transaction in one of two ways. He will sell the securities from his own inventory, or, if he does not own the desired securities, he will immediately get in touch by telephone with other dealers who are likely to have them for sale. Both methods make it possible for the client to purchase the securities quickly if he finds the price satisfactory. Similarly, when a client has securities for sale, the transaction will in all probability be handled in one of two ways. The dealer will buy the securities for his own account (inventory), or if he does not want the securities for his own account, he will get in touch by telephone with other dealers who are likely to be interested in buying them. Again, this arrangement makes possible the speedy sale of securities, provided the price is satisfactory to all parties concerned.

THE OVER-THE-COUNTER MARKET (II)

The *third market* refers to over-the-counter trading in listed securities, usually in large blocks. There is no rule or regulation that forbids the trading of listed securities in the over-the-counter market. Large institutional investors (such as mutual funds, life insurance companies, and pension funds) frequently buy or sell securities in this manner, rather than through a stock exchange. The main benefits to this group of buyers and sellers are: the commission paid to brokers is lower; there is less chance that such large transactions will depress the market price of the securities; and there is more privacy, in the sense that there is no immediate publicity release concerning the transaction.

There is also a *fourth market*, which refers to large institutional investors buying and selling directly with each other, rather than through the over-the-counter market or the stock exchanges. When large institutional investors bypass all the brokerage machinery, the entire brokerage fee is saved, although there is still a small fee payable to the parties that establish the information system necessary for the operation of the fourth market.

The National Association of Securities Dealers Automated Quotations (NASDAQ) is a computerized electronic system that links together thousands of brokers and dealers who trade in over-the-counter stocks and bonds. The system assembles price information on numerous over-the-counter issues and selected issues traded on the stock exchanges. Subscribing brokers and dealers in their respective local branch offices are able to use a desk-top computer terminal that gives instant price information on any of thousands of specific securities. The NASDAQ central information file relays to the desk-top computer the various bid and asked prices of securities that are submitted by brokers and dealers throughout the country. This information is beneficial to the investor. If he is selling his securities, he can sell to the purchaser who offers the highest price; if he is buying securities, he can acquire them from the source that sells at the lowest price. Because of the NASDAQ, the local dealer in the over-the-counter market is able to serve his clients more effectively.

A *central market*, also called a *national market*, is an ideal that will be reached when there exists a central reporting system that will give instant information on the market price of all the securities traded on all the stock exchanges and of a very large number of securities traded on the over-the-counter market. Physically, this means that a dealer, sitting at a computer terminal in his local office, will be able to immediately tell an investor where he can obtain the best deal, whether he is buying or selling. The *central market*, when fully operational, will give even more information than the NASDAQ, which is already a giant step forward in disseminating security prices.

Finally, it should be noted that numerous issues of corporate securities are traded on both the stock exchanges and on the over-the-counter market.

PRACTICES IN BUYING AND SELLING SECURITIES

Margin Buying

Stock may be paid for in full at the time of purchase or it may be purchased on margin. Buying stock on margin means that one does not pay the full purchase price at the time the securities are bought. Instead, a down payment is made, the balance being payable at a later date. Thus a stockholder might purchase $5,000 worth of stock and pay the broker $2,500, the balance being payable later. Margin is also expressed as a percentage, when used in this sense, it means the proportion of the cost price that must be made as a down payment. A 50 percent margin means that half of the cost price must be made as a down payment; a 75 percent margin means that three-quarters of the cost must be paid in cash. The margin requirements for securities listed on a registered stock exchange vary between 50 and 100 percent. When securities are purchased on margin, a broker lends the client the money and keeps the purchased securities as collateral. The investor must pay the broker interest on the unpaid balance. The main reason that securities are purchased on margin is that title can be acquired to a larger amount of securities with a given cash outlay. One purchases securities on margin when he expects the price of the purchased securities to rise. If the acquired securities rise in price, the gain is magnified; on the other hand, if the price of the purchased securities declines, the loss is magnified.

Short Selling

In a short sale the seller does not deliver the stock certificate when he has the broker sell the shares for him. An arrangement is made whereby the broker lends the stock certificate so that delivery can be made to the buyer. A short sale may take place when a seller does not even own the stock, when the stock is located at a distant point, or when the stock is in transit or not obtainable for some other reason. After the short sale, the short seller owes the broker a certain number of shares of stock. If a person sells short shares he does not even own, he expects that he can later acquire the stock at a price less than that for which the shares were sold at the time of the short sale. The usual time when a person sells short is when he expects the price of the shares to fall.

Assume that the stock of Company A can be sold today for $32 per share. Also assume that someone who does not own any stock in this company believes that the shares are about to decline in value. Under these conditions he might order his broker to sell short 100 shares of this stock at $32 per share. Since the buyer wants his certificate, it will be necessary for the broker to supply this document. Ordinarily, the broker will obtain the shares by borrowing them from another broker, one of the "loan crowd" that lends shares. Brokers in the loan crowd who lend stock will demand cash collateral equal to 100 percent of the market value of the shares lent. The broker who is borrowing the shares has received cash from the sale of the shares and can use this cash as collateral.

Eventually, the short seller must purchase shares in the market to replace the shares borrowed from the broker. If the market price of the shares goes down to $28, the short seller has made a gross profit of $4 per share because he has sold stock at $32 per share which cost him $28 a share. On the other hand, if the price goes up to $35 per share, the short seller will have a gross loss of $3 per share because he sold at $32 a stock that cost him $35. As in the case of margin purchases, a broker will permit a trader to engage in short selling only if the short seller is a reputable person and only after the short seller has made a deposit with the broker.

When the investor orders his broker to buy or sell *at the market* he is ordering the broker to buy or sell at whatever the price of the particular securities might be when the order reaches the floor of the exchange. An order of this type will be completed in a short period of time, although one cannot be sure of the price at which the transaction will take place. That price is the price at the exact second the order is consummated.

Types of Orders

A trader may give the broker specific instructions as to the price to buy or sell securities. This type of order is known as a *limit order*. Thus he may order his broker to buy shares of a specific stock at a price not exceeding $38. This means that the broker must not pay more than $38 per share for the stock but that he will be obliged to acquire the shares at a lower price if possible. Likewise, the trader may place a lower limit on the price of securities for sale. He may instruct the broker to sell specific shares of stock but at a price not lower than $40. This would mean that the broker could not sell the shares below $40 but that he would be obliged to sell at a higher price if possible. When a limit order is placed with a broker, it is necessary to state the period of time the order is to be in effect. Limit orders may be good for a day, a week, some other period of time, or until canceled (GTC).

In dollar averaging a person *periodically* invests a fixed sum of money in corporate stock, in order to be sure that he is buying securities at representative prices.

Dollar Averaging

The theory is that if prices fluctuate over a period of time, it will be possible to buy some of the shares at low prices and thus lower the average price of the shares held. Therefore, under dollar averaging an investor hopes that the market price of the shares will fall (and later rise). Dollar averaging is supposed to be an automatic solution to the difficult problem of deciding when to buy securities and at what price.

HIGHLIGHTS OF THIS CHAPTER

Stocks and bonds have marketability when they meet a twofold test: they can be sold quickly because there are always a number of purchasers ready to buy, and they can be sold at or near the prevailing market price. Marketability is a desirable characteristic from both the investor's and the corporation's viewpoints. It is important to security holders because it permits them to convert their securities into cash with a minimum amount of delay and loss. From the corporation's viewpoint, marketability of its securities is important because if its outstanding securities have this desirable characteristic, the corporation can sell additional issues on more advantageous terms.

The stock exchanges facilitate the transfer of securities among investors. The New York Stock Exchange is the largest stock exchange in the United States.

REVIEW QUESTIONS

16-1. Explain the meaning of the following terms:
stock exchange
over-the-counter market
third market
fourth market
national market
central market
dollar averaging
blue chip stock
trust

16-2. Who has the money to invest in stocks and bonds?

16-3. (a) What is the difference between margin buying and short selling? (b) What is the difference between a market order and a limit order?

16-4. Why does General Motors Corporation pay to have its common stock listed on the New York Stock Exchange?

16-5. Visit a stock brokerage firm and obtain answers to these questions: (a) Does the firm give advice in taking advantage of the "gift to minors" act—an act whereby parents transfer ownership of shares to a child, thereby making the dividends nontaxable to the parents? (b) Does the brokerage firm belong to a stock exchange as well as participate in the over-the-counter market? (c) Will the broker take small orders, such as two shares of General Motors common stock?

(d) How are brokerage fees determined? (e) Does the brokerage firm have a rack of pamphlets and circulars containing information on specific stocks that are likely to rise in price?

The board of directors of William McCormick Company, a restaurant chain, is considering whether or not to have its 1,073,000 shares of common stock listed on the New York Stock Exchange. A vice president of the exchange recently had lunch with the company's president, at which time the stock exchange official explained the advantages of listing. The president then reported the contents of this discussion to his board of directors.

CASE ON LISTING COMMON STOCK

William McCormick Company began operations about 40 years ago. At that time McCormick, who owned a small store, began to manufacture and market a quality ice cream that gained steady acceptance, first locally and then nationally. Over the years the complexion of this company changed as the firm began to establish restaurants and hotels. The company now makes extensive use of the license arrangement. Fundamentally, this means that the company permits its name to be used by an operator of a restaurant or hotel. As part of the agreement the licensee makes these promises: to pay a fee to the company for the use of its name; to buy certain products from it; and to maintain certain standards of quality and uniformity. Presently the company's restaurants are established primarily on the basis of serving motorists with food and shelter of an assured quality. Of the 626 restaurants, 284 are company owned and operated, and 342 are operated under a licensing arrangement (that is, the company permits other parties to use its name for the considerations mentioned above). Also, all of the company's 124 motor courts are operated under licensing arrangements. The firm continues to expand its operations.

The initial cost of listing the shares on the New York Stock Exchange would be $7,900; the annual fee thereafter would be approximately $1,075. These would be nominal expenses for the firm, which has annual sales of over $105,000,000.

Required: 1. Discuss the advantages and the disadvantages of William McCormick Company's listing its stock on the New York Stock Exchange. Which course of action should the board of directors take—list or not list the shares? 2. What is the effect of the board's decision on these groups: (a) common stockholders of the company, (b) officers of the company, (c) brokers who are members of the New York Stock Exchange, (d) rank and file employees of the company, (e) labor union officials, (f) licensees of the company, (g) other restaurant chains, and (h) the public at large?

 # Managing Asset Expansion via Retained Earnings

After the firm's profits have been measured by the accountants, there is the further problem of how these gains should be administered. A common practice is to reinvest a percentage of the profits in the firm. The amount of funds retained in a specific firm is determined by management when it establishes the pay-out ratio for each year. The balance of profits not paid out to stockholders is "retained" in the enterprise. In a corporation, the expectation is that the money reinvested in the business will generate earnings that in turn will add to the value of the common stock. In a similar manner, retained earnings in a single proprietorship or partnership are expected to add to the value of the owner's equity. Whether these expectations ever materialize depends on the rate of return earned on the funds kept in the business. If the firm is in a growth industry, chances are good that the incremental earnings will materialize and that the price of the common stock will increase. A rather spectacular illustration of how retained profits may be used to good advantage by growth companies is shown in Table 17-1. The data show how several insurance companies with a low pay-out ratio fared during a 10-year period. The optimum or ideal dividend policy is one of unusual complexity, and in the final analysis it is determined largely by the judgment of management.

TABLE 17-1
Increase in Market
Value of Selected
Life Insurance Company
Stocks, 10-Year Period

$5,000 Invested in Shares of	Worth
Philadelphia Life	$320,391
Bankers National	132,987
U.S. Life	179,136
Commonwealth Life	134,493
Franklin Life	193,987
Liberty National Life	109,534

In order to expand, small business must ordinarily rely heavily on retained earnings. Small business is at a special disadvantage in that the funds can be raised only from local sources and the investment banking machinery is not geared to financing small business. Therefore, retained earnings may be the only source of funds available.

Because they are limited in the return they can earn on their assets, public utilities cannot depend on retained earnings as a major source of funds. The utilities, in general, have relied on stock and bond financing to expand their fixed and current assets. (See Figure 17-1 for a comparison of the use of retained profits by public utilities and other industries.)

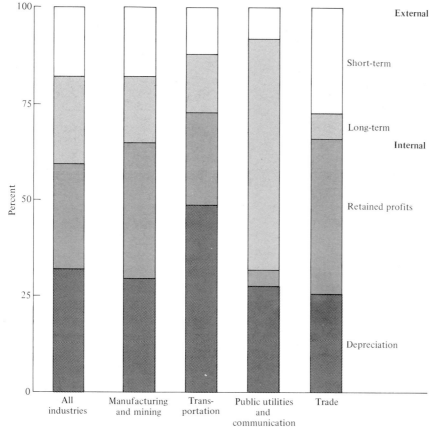

FIGURE 17-1
The Importance of Retained Profits as a Source of Funds, 1967-1972 (Estimated)

Source:
U.S. Department of Commerce and SEC

The following will be discussed in this chapter:

1. Kinds of dividends
2. Mainstreams of profit allocations
   a. Segment distributed to the government
   b. Segment distributed to stockholders
   c. Segment retained in the business

3. Integrating dividend policy with the goals of the firm
4. Factors influencing dividend policy
5. Mechanics of a dividend payment
6. Nature of stock dividends
7. Standards for appraising retained profits as a source of funds
8. Automatic dividend reinvestment plans
9. Repurchasing of common stock by original issuers

KINDS OF DIVIDENDS

Dividends may be classified as cash dividends, stock dividends, property dividends, scrip dividends, and dividends payable in bonds. A *cash dividend* means that the stockholders receive checks for the amounts due them. A *stock dividend* has these features: (1) the stockholders receive additional shares of the company paying the dividend; (2) the distribution of shares is accompanied by a reduction in earned surplus; and (3) the stockholders do not have to pay for the shares received. A *property dividend* means that the corporation pays the stockholders in assets other than cash. Examples of assets that have been paid as property dividends are a company's own products and the securities of subsidiaries. *Scrip dividends* mean that the corporation issues notes promising to pay dividends at a later date. The scrip may be interest-bearing or not. Scrip dividends are rarely used. A dividend in which the stockholders receive bonds is a rare event in finance. Cash dividends are by far the most important kind of dividend, with stock dividends ranking second in importance.

MAINSTREAMS OF PROFIT ALLOCATIONS

Segment Distributed to the Government

The corporation tax rate ranges from 22 to 48 percent, depending on the size of the taxable income. Many businessmen are of the opinion that high taxes skim away much of the profit that might have been used to expand assets. This, of course, is a problem for individual firms. Recently, however, the dollar amount of profits has increased so substantially in prosperous years that, although the government is taking a larger percentage of profits, the dollar amount remaining after taxes has remained adequate to finance a great deal of business expansion.

After a particular tax rate has been in effect for a period of time, it is probable that management can adapt its policies to the tax so that there is no particular hardship encountered by the firm. It is the large, unexpected increases in tax rates or changes in collection procedures that lead to a strain on the cash position of individual firms.

Management is interested in postponing the payment of taxes as long as possible, thereby having the use of the funds on an interest-free basis. Assume that a corporation is in the 50 percent income tax bracket and that it elects to measure depreciation by the declining balance method instead of by the straight-line method. If in a certain year $20 instead of $10 is charged as depreciation, profits will be $10 less. This will save the firm $5 in taxes for that year. (But notice that taxes will increase in later years as the amount of depreciation decreases.) This $5 may be used for any purpose deemed expedient by the management. If fast write-off plans are used instead of straight-line methods, the following results occur during the first half of the life of the assets: current expenses (depreciation) increase, current taxable profits decrease, current federal income taxes decrease, circulating assets increase (because of lower taxes), and current earnings per share decrease. During the last half of the life of the asset, the following results occur: current expenses (depreciation) decrease, current taxable profits increase, federal income taxes increase, circulating assets decrease, and earnings per share increase. It might seem as if the advantages gained during the first half of the life of the asset are offset by the disadvantages appearing during the second half. But fast write-off plans are more advantageous than straight-line methods for two reasons: the firm recovers its capital at a faster rate, and it can earn interest on the extra cash retained due to temporarily lowered tax payments. Because of these two advantages, many boards of directors elect to compute depreciation under the newer plans.

Stockholder Preferences Management must decide what part of the profits (after income taxes) to pay out to stockholders as dividends. Table 17-2 indicates the percentage of net profits paid by three companies to their stockholders.

Segment Distributed to Stockholders

Over a period of time the success of a company is measured by the amount of cash that it pays out as dividends, even though in the short run earnings per share are the more significant figure.

Company	Recent Price	Latest 12-Month Earnings	Indicated Dividend	Payout Ratio (Percent)	Yield (Percent)
Budd Company	$13.00	$1.66	$0.80	48	6.2
Champion Spark Plug	36.75	3.33	2.20	66	6.0
Chrysler Corporation	33.50	4.64	2.00	43	6.0

TABLE 17-2 Payout Ratios of Three Firms

On the one extreme is a group of owners who prefer to receive the largest possible amount of profit distributions in the shortest possible time. These persons have a certain sum of capital which they wish to preserve, but they also hope to receive high current investment income. Such groups prefer a 100 percent payout ratio. One example of such a group might be elderly people who are living off social security checks and dividend checks. These people are interested in short-run benefits because they might not live long enough to enjoy long-run gains.

At the other extreme is a group of owners who have no need at all for current income in the form of profit distributions. An example of this group might be wealthy corporate executives who have high current salaries. Such persons prefer a zero payout ratio. Members of this group are willing to forego current profit distributions so that the firm can reinvest profits, thus causing future dividends to increase and, even more important, causing the market price of the stock to rise sharply. This group often finds it advantageous to be taxed at capital gain rates rather than at regular income tax rates.

Between the above two extremes are most owners, who prefer a balance between profit distributions and the reinvestment of profits in the firm. These investors expect to receive some current income in the form of profit distributions but at the same time assume that the firm will retain some of the annual profits. Furthermore, it is the expectation of this group of owners that the firm will reinvest the earnings in a manner that will lead to moderate increases in future dividends and in the market value of the stock. Investors in this middle-of-the-road classification are pleased if the firm distributes about half of its annual profits (a payout ratio of 50 percent). Most firms have a policy of paying some cash dividends to stockholders each year when the money is available.

There may be a conflict of interest if stockholders with varying needs all own stock in the same company. No one firm can please all three groups at the same time. The solution for the individual investor, therefore, is to seek out companies whose dividend policies are most likely to suit his needs.

Stockholders' Criticism of Corporate Dividend Policy   Some stockholders are critical of the practice of retaining earnings in corporations to finance expansion. While these stockholders do not object to the retention of profits in the business to act as a buffer against the vicissitudes of the business world, they do feel that the retention of profits to finance expansion results in forcing the stockholders to reinvest in the business. They argue that they should be allowed to decide on whether they care to reinvest more money in the same company. Stockholders who are critical of the practice of retaining earnings for purposes of expansion have offered a twofold solution to the problem.

The first proposed solution is to have the corporation distribute as dividends all profits, after setting aside a reasonable amount for future contingencies. If the corporation needs additional funds for expansion, it should issue additional securities which the stockholders who want to increase their investment in the company could buy. On the other hand, those who do not care to increase their commitment in the company would be free to invest elsewhere. Under this scheme, the corporation would have to compete in the market against other corporations for the use of the investors' money.

A second proposed solution is for the corporation to pay a stock dividend. In this approach the stockholder receives a dividend not in cash but in shares of stock. After the receipt of the stock dividend the shareholder has his original shares plus the additional shares received as a stock dividend. If the stockholder does not care to have his share of the profits reinvested, he can sell the shares. On the other hand, if a person keeps the shares received as a stock dividend, he is in effect consenting to the permanent reinvestment of some of the profits in the business.

Segment Retained in the Business   *Uses of Retained Profits*   Assuming that the firm retains profits in the enterprise, management can put them to a number of uses that are expected to advance the goals of the business. One use is to expand the assets of the firm, thus adding to the earning power of the enterprise. Another similar use is to engage in a major program of repairing and remodeling, with the purpose of making the equipment more efficient, this in turn resulting in lower costs and higher profits. A firm that retains a considerable percentage of its profits is expected to expand the earning power of the enterprise.

A second area that is less important than the first (but often more interesting) is to use profits for profit-sharing plans. General Motors Corporation, for example, has a profit-sharing plan which it calls a bonus plan. Under this plan, selected key employees are allowed to share in profits to a limited extent. First, a sum equal to 5 percent of the firm's capital is earmarked for stockholders and then subtracted from net profits. Then, 12 percent of the remaining available profits are distributed to key employees, partly in cash and partly in stock, over a period of several years.

A third general use of profits is to lower debts. Railroads, for example, use a large percentage of their profits for this purpose. But since debt is such a cheap source of capital (because of the low yield that investors accept and because of the tax deduction allowed the issuer), this use of retained profits has decreased in importance in the larger firms. In small firms, however, there appears to be some tendency to use profits to repay bank loans, especially term loans. Many small businesses still view debt as a temporary expedient; these firms pay off their loans as soon as possible.

A fourth use of profits is for research. The welfare of the firm is advanced if the research results in new products or the improvement of old products (and if more efficient methods are found to produce old products). Although research may not appear in near-term balance sheets or near-term profit and loss statements, such outlays are definitely advantageous to the firm. In many situations success begets more success. Successful firms, such as du Pont and IBM, have high profits, part of which are used for research, which in turn leads to even higher profits.

The Economics of Retained Earnings If a portion of the profits is retained in the business, management should be able to prove that the stockholders will, over a period of time, benefit from this action. There is deductive evidence that a firm which builds up its surplus account by withholding dividends from the common stockholders may be better able to weather adverse business conditions than a firm which pays out all available earnings to the common stockholders. Such a presumption is based on the condition that the retained earnings are used to improve the efficiency of the plant and equipment. If the retained earnings are put to this use, then the cost structure may be lowered, the competitive position of the firm strengthened, and the ability of the business to survive depressions increased. Retained earnings do not always result in these favorable conditions because they may be put to other uses, such as raising salaries and increasing plant capacity beyond its most profitable point.

The board of directors must decide in each individual case what proportion of the profits should be retained in the business. On theoretical grounds, it can be argued that directors are justified in retaining earnings only if the rate of return earned on the withheld profits would be as high as or higher than that which could be earned on the funds if invested elsewhere by the stockholder. In practice, directors give virtually no weight to this theoretical principle.

Retained Earnings and the Compound Interest Factor Management should put the retained earnings to a use that will expand earning power. At least 5 percent should be earned on the segment of the profits retained in the business, because this much could be earned if the idle cash were invested only in government securities. Obviously, management is expected to have enough business acumen to earn more than an annual average of 5 percent. In any event, stockholders should expect concrete benefits from the portion of the profits retained in the business. The following quotation from an annual report of a large steel company indicates how the management of this firm views its responsibility to earn an additional return on profits returned to the business.

> The Board of Directors voted to increase the dividend paid in the fourth quarter from the 75 cents per share previously paid to $1.00 per share, thus placing National Steel Corporation's stock on a $4.00 annual basis. This was done in the belief that the return to the stockholder should reflect the increased investment of the stockholder resulting from the retention of earnings in the business and their expenditure for plants and facilities necessary to the growth and improvement of the company. The rapid progress of steelmaking methods and facilities makes mandatory a continuous program of replacement and additions for maintenance of a steel company's competitive position. In view of the extremely high cost of building today, compared with former times, retained earnings are and must continue to be one of the important sources of the very large sums required. In our opinion, the use of the stockholder's money in this manner should not only preserve the value of his investment but also bring him a higher return.

Ambition of Officers In connection with dividend payments, a factor of some importance is the personal ambition of the officers. Probably the politics of being successfully elected to office depends on some of each year's profits being retained in the business. These profits in turn can be used for future dividends or to increase the earning power of the firm, which also leads to increases in future dividends. If this is so, management might avoid paying large but erratic dividends, even if this were the best policy for stockholders. In other words, company officers might believe that the best dividend policy for them is the one that keeps them in power. This is a difficult type of variable to measure, even though its presence is a factor in the large publicly held corporation.

Problem Company K is planning its financial requirements three years in advance. Among other matters, this means preparing a *pro forma* balance sheet. Management is especially interested in the liability and net worth section of the balance sheet because of the information gained on the amount of financing that will be needed. The firm has the following sales projection: next year $500,000; two years from now $600,000; three years from now $700,000. Below is the firms balance sheet as of the present:

Current assets	$200,000	Bank loans	$ 40,000
Fixed assets	200,000	Accounts payable	40,000
		Mortgage	50,000
		Common stock	100,000
		Retained profits	170,000
Total	$400,000	Total	$400,000

The following ratios apply to the firm: current assets are 50 percent of sales; fixed assets are 50 percent of sales; bank loans are 10 percent of sales; accounts payable are 10 percent of sales; net profit after taxes is 10 percent of sales; and the firm has a 50 percent payout ratio.

Required: (a) Determine the following information as of the end of the third year: the total amount of assets that will be needed to support the expected level of sales; the amount of the retained profits; the amount of bank loans outstanding; and the amount of accounts payable on the books. (b) The expansion in the accounts just mentioned will result in supplying some of the funds for expansion. How much in additional financing will be needed over and above the automatic expansion in short-term credit and retained earnings? (c) Suggest a few places where the funds might be obtained.(See Table 17-3).

Solution

TABLE 17-3 Funds Needed by Company K

	Present Year	1 Year from Now	2 Years from Now	3 Years from Now
Expected sales		$500,000	$600,000	$700,000
Current assets (50%)	$200,000	$250,000	$300,000	$350,000
Fixed assets (50%)	200,000	250,000	300,000	350,000
Total	$400,000	$500,000	$600,000	$700,000
Bank loans (10%)	$ 40,000	$ 50,000	$ 60,000	$ 70,000
Accounts payable (10%)	40,000	50,000	60,000	70,000
Mortgage	50,000	50,000	50,000	50,000
Common stock	100,000	100,000	100,000	100,000
Retained profits	170,000	195,000*	225,000	260,000
Funds needed to make the statement balance	0	55,000	105,000	150,000
Total	$400,000	$500,000	$600,000	$700,000

*Amount of profits earned in this period is $50,000 (10 percent of $500,000). Half of the profits are retained in the business. Hence, $25,000 is added to the present year's retained profits ($170,000 + $25,000 = $195,000). The same procedure is used for subsequent years.

Answers: (a) Assets needed at the end of the third year $700,000; retained profits $260,000; bank loan $70,000; accounts payable $70,000. (b) The firm will still need $150,000 to support the proposed expansion in sales. (c) These funds might be obtained by selling more stock, increasing the mortgage, retaining even more profits in the business and so on.

INTEGRATING DIVIDEND POLICY WITH THE GOALS OF THE FIRM

The optimum dividend policy for a business firm is that which advances the goals of the firm. The primary goals of the firm are expressed as follows:

$$\frac{\text{Primary goals}}{\text{of firm}} = \frac{\text{Increase financial}}{\text{welfare of owners}} + \frac{\text{Assume social}}{\text{responsibility}}$$

Increased Financial Welfare of Owners

The financial welfare of the owners is increased when they receive a high composite rate of return on their investment. The formula for this rate is:

$$\frac{\text{Composite rate of return on cost of owners' equity}} = \frac{\text{Profits received} + \text{Capital gains} + \begin{matrix}\text{Higher than}\\ \text{normal salaries}\\ \text{and fringe benefits}\end{matrix}}{\text{Cost of investment}}$$

In other words, the financial welfare of the owners is increased when they receive any of the three items mentioned in the numerator of the above formula. Management seeks to increase the sum of the items in the numerator; management can do nothing about what investors paid for their commitment. A point of great importance is that management has some control over the composition of the total of the items in the numerator. Thus some firms intentionally pay small current dividends (profit distribution), others pay large current dividends, and others follow a middle-of-the-road policy. When a firm over a period of several years distributes a small percentage of available profits, the expectation is that future profit distributions and future market price of the stock will increase. In summary, a high composite rate of return is one goal of the owners *after* they have purchased stock in a particular company.

Assumption of Social Responsibility

The assumption of social responsibility is given some weight in determining the pay-out ratio. At certain times, such as when the economy is in a slump, firms are urged to distribute profits as dividends so as to create additional purchasing power in the economy. Actually, the impact of dividends on the economy is still largely undetermined. Much depends on what the firm would have done with the profits if they had been retained in the business versus what the owners would have done with the profits if they had received them in cash.

A certain amount of social responsibility is probably a good idea; too much of it might be open to question in a large firm in which there are a number of stockholders. This may be illustrated by reference to the now-famous Ford Motor Company case. Henry Ford, the founder of the company, followed a policy of paying a very small amount of dividends out of very large profits. A stockholder sued the firm in an attempt to force larger dividend payments. Ford argued that he was reinvesting the profits so that society could have the benefit of low-priced cars that would result from large-scale production. He also argued that he was seeking to advance the welfare of his workers by providing them with steady work at good rates of pay. The court held these motives to be contrary to the goals of the firm, that is, to earn money for the stockholders. Ford lost the case; the Ford Motor Company was forced to pay a large dividend. This, however, is one of the relatively few cases wherein a court interfered with management's policy on dividends.

Dividend policy refers to the attitude of the directors concerning how much of the profits should be distributed as dividends. Similarly situated companies with the same amount of profits pay varying proportions of their earnings as dividends in a given year. Some companies are known to pay a large proportion of the profits as dividends while other companies have the reputation of paying a relatively small proportion; still others have the reputation of paying a steady dollar amount of dividends each year. Ideally, a corporation should be financially able to pay steady dividends to stockholders. A steady dividend policy, such as that followed by AT&T, makes it possible for the company to raise additional capital on advantageous terms and also raises the credit standing of the company. Factors that influence directors in establishing a dividend policy are: the legality of the proposed dividend payment, the cash needs of the corporation, covenants in indentures, the welfare of the investor, Section 531 of the Internal Revenue Code, and the previous year's dividends.

FACTORS INFLUENCING DIVIDEND POLICY

Necessity of Having a Surplus One main factor influencing the amount of dividend payments to owners is the legality of the proposed payment. Directors must determine whether or not the dividend will be in accordance with the law of the state from which the charter was obtained. When the law is violated on this point, creditors and stockholders may take legal action against the directors. The general rule is that dividends should be paid only out of surplus. Or, in negative terms, if there is no surplus or profits, cash dividends cannot legally be paid.

Another legal problem in the payment of dividends is whether or not dividends can be "distributed" from paid-in surplus. In general, paid-in surplus arises from the sale of par-value stock at a premium, and from the sale of no-par-value stock above its stated value. Some states permit the payment of dividends from paid-in surplus; other states forbid this practice; still other states permit it but with definite restrictions. The payment of cash dividends from paid-in surplus is risky, and directors should be sure of the legality of the practice in the domicile of the corporation.

Legality of the Proposed Dividend

Cash Needs of the Corporation   Directors must consider the cash needs of the corporation when deliberating on what portion of the profits to retain and what portion to pay as dividends. Directors rarely pay the maximum possible amount of dividends; instead, it is the practice to retain a substantial part of the profits in the business. The present and future cash needs of the corporation must be considered.

Is a Dividend Payment Warranted?   The cash position of the corporation may not warrant a cash dividend despite the existence of a substantial surplus. Cash may have been used for other purposes, such as expanding inventories, acquiring additional fixed assets, or paying off debt. A corporation with large profits does not necessarily have large cash balances at the end of the year for the reason that the cash may be already spent. This idea has been expressed in an annual report of the Clevite Company, as follows:

> It will be noted that the Reinvestment of Profit account now stands at $16,767,231, representing money earned, but withheld from our stockholders, over the entire 31 years of our company's existence. It should not be thought, however, that this large sum represents cash, or assets easily convertible into cash. Actually, this is the money which has primarily financed the expansion of the company, and on which we do our business. By far the greater part of it is represented by our real estate, buildings, machinery, equipment, and raw materials, by quantities of bearings and bushings in different stages of completion, and by the money required to carry our accounts receivable. In these various forms, this multi-million-dollar investment finances our business and is, therefore, of direct and daily benefit to stockholders and employees alike.

Amount of Cash Flow   Perhaps of equal importance with profits as a determinant of dividend policy is cash flow (net profits after taxes plus depreciation). With liberalized depreciation schedules, many firms are writing off their assets at a faster rate. This is resulting in a larger cash flow because of increased depreciation charges and lower federal income taxes. Such a situation creates the paradox of firms having lower earnings per share on the common but higher cash flow per share on the common. Thus Universal Cyclops Steel Company found that as a result of taking advantage of the new depreciation schedule, during the first half of a recent year its earnings per share fell by 5 cents but its cash flow per share increased by 10 cents. This is not an unusual example; many firms are having lower profits but more cash for distribution to owners or for retention in the business. As for the economy as a whole, there is some evidence that dividends show a remarkably stable relationship to cash flow—between 30 and 40 percent in recent years.

Cash May Be Needed to Tide the Business over Contingencies   Uncertainty about the future may lead to the retention of all or part of the profits in the corporation. Just as an individual saves for a rainy day, so do corporations accumulate cash to meet future contingencies. For example, corporations expect that their earnings will fall during depressions. If part of the retained earnings are kept in the form of cash, the corporation has increased its chances for survival. In many cases, it is the company with the largest cash balance that survives—not necessarily the most efficient company. One reason given by the American Radiator and Standard Sanitary Corporation for withholding a considerable part of the profits in the business was the uncertainty on the amount of foreign losses that would eventually be incurred because of unsettled international conditions.

The Board of Directors May Want to Expand the Corporation's Capacity to Produce Goods and Services During a four-year period, the Gillette Safety Razor Company used $4,500,000 of retained earnings to expand fixed assets. The Ford Motor Company is one of a number of companies that have grown to be large and powerful corporations by retaining earnings.

During a Period of Rising Prices, the Cost of Replacing Assets Increases, thereby Making It Necessary to Retain Large Amounts of Profits in the Business During a period of rising prices, many corporations must use profits to replace worn-out assets. Accountants base their depreciation allowances on the cost of the assets, with the result that accumulated depreciation allowances are less than the cost of replacing the assets. Therefore, management needs more cash to replace assets than was expected. One source of this cash is dividends withheld from stockholders. In one year, United States Steel Corporation, for example, set aside 60 percent of its net income for use in replacing worn-out assets, the usual depreciation allowances being inadequate. The directors may retain the profits in the form of surplus, or a reserve may be established. In either case, cash is retained in the business that might have been paid in the form of dividends.

Covenants in Indentures and Provisions in Charters There may be an agreement with the bondholders placing restrictions on the amount of dividends paid stockholders. An agreement of this type would be found in the indenture. The purpose of such restrictions is to place limits on the amount of cash that leaves the corporation via the dividend route. By placing a limit on the amount of dividends that can be paid, stockholders are prevented from draining cash away from the business to such an extent that the liquidity position of the company would be impaired. For example, the indenture for the Wheeling Steel Corporation 3½ percent bonds provides that as long as any of the debt is outstanding, the corporation shall not pay any cash or property dividends on the common stock unless after the payment the net current assets are at least equal to the amount of bonds outstanding.

Similar provisions may be found in the charter when there is preferred stock outstanding. Preferred stockholders are thereby given the added protection of preventing directors from dissipating cash through excessive dividend payments to common stockholders. The charter of James Lees and Sons Company provides, among other dividend restrictions, that as long as the preferred stock is outstanding, the total dividends paid on the common in any one year shall not exceed $90,000.

Section 531 of the Internal Revenue Code

For some corporations, Section 531 of the Internal Revenue Code is a factor to be considered in determining how much of the profits should be retained in the business and how much should be paid as dividends. This section of the code penalizes the accumulation of profits in the business *if* the retention is for the purpose of lowering income taxes for stockholders. Each corporation must check up on itself to see if it is subject to the provisions of this law. When profits are retained for legitimate business needs, no penalty is imposed on the corporation. When the corporation is penalized, the rates vary from 27.5 to 38.5 percent and are applied to a base defined in the law.

The government's campaign against the unreasonable accumulation of surplus has been relaxed in two important respects: there is no penalty until accumulated earnings exceed $100,000, and the burden is now on the government to prove that the amount of accumulated earnings in excess of $100,000 is unreasonable. Corporate directors must be careful not to incur the penalties of Section 531. If the corporation is forced to pay this tax, minority stockholders may sue the directors and attempt to force them to reimburse the corporation.

Previous Year's Dividends

A study by John Lintner indicates that directors seek to avoid a policy that results in sharp changes in dividends per share each year.[1] This means that if a firm's earnings per share are gradually rising, the dividends per share will not be increased proportionately until management is sure that the changes in earnings per share are reasonably permanent. Likewise, if earnings per share begin to fall, dividends per share will not be cut proportionately until management is reasonably certain that the decline in profitability will continue for some time. Therefore, an important starting point in determining the current year's dividends per share is the amount paid in the previous year.

MECHANICS OF A DIVIDEND PAYMENT

The Directors' Meeting

At one of its meetings the board of directors discusses the possibility of paying a dividend to the stockholders. If the directors decide that a dividend should be paid, a resolution is adopted declaring that the stockholders shall be paid a certain amount. Stockholders then become creditors of the corporation to the extent of the dividend.

Preferred stockholders must be paid before common stockholders can receive any return. Furthermore, neither preferred stockholders nor common stockholders can receive dividends unless all interest on debt has been paid. It is also customary to forbid dividend payments on common and preferred stock when sinking fund installments on bonds and preferred stock are in arrears.

Date of Record and Ex-Dividend

The directors meet on a certain date, such as April 15, and declare a dividend for the first quarter. An announcement is made that dividend checks will be mailed to those who have their names on the books as of a certain date, such as April

1. John Lintner, "Distribution of Income among Dividends, Retained Earnings and Taxes," *American Economic Review Proceedings*, May 1956, pp. 97-113.

30. This latter date is known as the date of record. If a person buys stock in time to get his name on the books by April 30 (the date of record), he will receive the dividend. Anyone who buys the stock too late to get his name on the books buys the stock ex-dividend.

When a stock goes ex-dividend, the market price tends to fall by the amount of the dividend (theoretically); this factor, along with the consideration that an investor must pay a brokerage fee both when he buys and when he sells securities, makes it unprofitable for him to buy stock about to pay a dividend, hold the stock until the dividend is paid, sell the stock, and then buy and sell in other companies about to pay a dividend.

A corporation may declare a regular dividend and an extra dividend. The regular dividend is the amount that the corporation usually pays on its shares. When profits are unusually good, the corporation may declare an additional dividend, called an extra dividend. The following excerpt from an annual report of Swift & Company indicates the nature of extra dividends:

Regular Versus Extra Dividends

> During the fiscal year, shareholders received regular quarterly dividends of 40 cents a share, totaling $1.60 plus an extra dividend of 75 cents a share. Our dividend policy is to pay as liberal dividends as earnings and financial needs of the company permit. Swift & Company's objective is to maintain a steady rate of quarterly dividends; to pay an extra dividend in March when and to the extent that the previous year's earnings warrant it. Swift & Company has paid dividends every year since 1886, with the single exception of 1933.

A corporation distributes its profits in the form of an extra dividend when it does not want to create the impression that dividends are to be increased permanently. If profits continue at high levels, management will eventually increase the regular dividends and discontinue the extra dividend.

Melons   In the financial world, an unusually large dividend is known as a *melon*. There is no exact meaning of this term; it is used to describe any unusually large dividend payment. Melons are paid on common stock, not on preferred stock.

A *stock dividend* is an official notice to the stockholders that part of the corporation's surplus has been permanently committed to the business. The stock may be either common or preferred. Strictly speaking, stock dividends are not dividends at all, but instead are a technique for changing the capital structure of the corporation.

NATURE OF STOCK DIVIDENDS

Stock Dividends and Surplus

The most important reason for paying a stock dividend is to give the stockholders something on a dividend date and yet conserve the cash of the corporation. A stock dividend accomplishes this objective because the corporation mails only pieces of paper (stock certificates) to the stockholders. For example, when

Reasons for Paying a Stock Dividend

the Petroleum Heat and Power Company paid a 5 percent stock dividend, the president of the company said payment of a dividend in stock instead of in cash was deemed advisable to permit the company to conserve available cash in order to finance its expanding development program in Texas.

Another objective in paying a stock dividend may be to lower the market price per share. Shares that are selling at very high prices do not appeal to the average investor. By paying a large stock dividend a corporation can lower the market price per share, thereby possibly stimulating interest in the issue. Although a large stock dividend substantially lowers the price of outstanding shares, shareholders are not harmed by it because the fact that each stockholder holds proportionately more shares will offset the decline in the market value per share.

A third reason for paying a large stock dividend is to lower the dividends and earnings per share so that the public will not think the corporation is earning excessive profits. By increasing the number of shares outstanding, the earnings and dividends per share may be decreased proportionately. Supposedly the general public will be less critical of a corporation that does not have unusually large earnings and dividends per share.

Some corporations also pay stock dividends to cut the earned surplus to a relatively modest figure, again avoiding the possible criticism that the corporation has been earning exorbitant profits.

Impact of a Stock Dividend on the Corporation

When a corporation sends stock dividends to stockholders, accountants make important changes on the books. More specifically, the amount of the stock dividend being paid is subtracted from the surplus account and added to the capital stock account. The result of this change is to permanently commit a portion of the surplus (an amount equal to the stock dividend) to the business, stockholders being given shares to represent the undistributed profits permanently committed to the business. The impact of a stock dividend may be seen in Table 17-4, assuming a 100 percent stock dividend.

TABLE 17-4
Financial Position Before and After Stock Dividend

Before

Assets			Liabilities and Net Worth		
Current assets:			Current liabilities		$ 50,000
Cash	$50,000		Bonds payable		100,000
Accounts receivable	25,000		Net worth:		
Inventories	25,000	$100,000	Common stock	$100,000	
Fixed assets		300,000	1,000 shares, $100 par value		
			Earned surplus	150,000	
					250,000
Total assets		$400,000	Total liabilities and net worth		$400,000

Assets			Liabilities and Net Worth		
Current assets:			Current liabilities		$ 50,000
Cash	$50,000		Bonds payable		100,000
Accounts receivable	25,000		Net worth:		
Inventories	25,000	$100,000	Common stock	$200,000	
Fixed assets		300,000	(2,000 shares, $100 par value)		
			Earned surplus	50,000	
					250,000
Total assets		$400,000	Total liabilities and net worth		$400,000

It should be stressed that the payment of the stock dividend as shown in this table did not result in the stockholders' receiving any cash; instead, the corporation sent an additional 1,000 shares of $100 par-value stock to those who were already stockholders. Before the stock dividend there were 1,000 shares outstanding; after the 100 percent stock dividend there were 2,000 shares of stock outstanding. Before the stock dividend the amount in the capital stock account was $100,000; after the change the amount in the capital stock account was $200,000. Before the stock dividend the amount in the surplus account was $150,000; after the stock dividend the amount in the surplus account was $50,000.

Tax Aspects of a Stock Dividend Stock dividends are not taxable income to the recipient at the time the shares are received unless the dividends are received as a payment on preferred stock dividend arrearages or as an alternative to dividends in cash. Formerly, the rule was that stock dividends would be tax-free only if the stockholder's relative position was not changed.

The investor is also confronted with the problem of computing profit or loss on the sale of shares after a stock dividend is received. Assume that James Abbott bought 100 shares of stock at $150 per share, making a total cost of $15,000. Assume further that a 100 percent stock dividend is declared. Several years later, Abbot sells 10 shares at $110 per share. How much did he gain or lose on the sale? The first thing to observe is that for purposes of determining gain or loss, the average cost per share changes from $150 to $75. The new average cost of $75 per share is found by dividing $15,000 by the new number of shares held (200). Therefore, the gain on the transaction is computed as follows:

Selling price per share	$110
Cost per share	75
Profit per share	$ 35
Total profit (10 shares at $35)	$350

For tax purposes, this is the way Abbott would compute his gain on the sale of 10 shares.

What Is the Cost of the Additional Capital?   Retained profits should be thought of as having a percentage cost of capital. This cost, however, should be viewed as a crude estimate rather than as a precise percentage. Despite its inexactness, the use of this concept leads to better decisions than the assumption that retained profits have no cost at all.

Assume the following for Company Z:

Previous dividends per share	$ 4
Earnings per share for the current year	8
Current market price of the common stock	20
Tax bracket of stockholders	30 percent

According to previous policies, management has paid out about $4 per share and retained about $3 per share. This year, management is considering declaring an extra dividend of $1, thus increasing the dividend per share to $5. Accordingly, management has already decided to retain the usual $3 per share, and this specific issue is not under consideration. If a stockholder received the extra dividend of $1, he would actually have 70 cents, after taxes, to invest in another company; or to look at it another way, he would now have $20.70 worth of stock ($20 to begin with, plus 70 cents of additional stock). Therefore, if the company has the stockholder's interests at heart, it will retain the extra $1 only if the money can be invested in projects that will lift the stock of the company above $20.70; otherwise the stockholder would have been better off to have received the dividend. Notice that it is not sufficient for Company Z to reinvest the $1 and make the price of its stock rise to, say, $20.50; the company must do better than this to surpass the results of the stockholder having $20.70 in value if he had received the dividend. In other words, management should look at the matter (in theory) from the veiwpoint of the common stockholder. If the stockholder would be able to increase his wealth more by receiving the dividend, the company should pay it; if the stockholder's wealth would be increased more by maintaining the money in the business, the firm should withhold the money.

Generally, retained profits are a cheaper source of funds than common stock, preferred stock, or bonds. The main reason for this is that there are no flotation costs incurred when profits are retained; another reason is that it does not raise personal income taxes.

Must the Firm Make Fixed Periodic Cash Payments for the Use of the Funds?   The answer to this question is no. In this respect, retained earnings are similar to common stock and preferred stock. Retained earnings are unlike debt, on which a fixed return must be paid under most circumstances. The fact that a firm does not have to make fixed periodic payments for the use of retained earnings is an advantage of this source of funds.

How Long Does the Firm Have the Use of the Money?   Another major advantage of retained earnings is that the firm has the use of the money indefinitely. In this respect retained earnings are like common and preferred stock but unlike most forms of debt. Although all retained earnings might eventually be paid out as dividends, this seldom occurs, because most firms consider a major part of earned surplus to be committed to the business permanently.

How Much Control Must Be Sacrificed?   Still another advantage of retained earnings is that no change takes place in the control of the firm. Those who already own the stock maintain their relative voting positions. This is one reason why small corporations rely heavily on retained earnings as a source of funds. If additional common stock were sold, outsiders would be given voting rights. If preferred stock were sold, the owners of these shares would be given a very small amount of voting privileges. If money were borrowed, the creditors would have no voting rights but in the event of a default on either the interest or the principal, the creditors might be entitled to take over the business. If the owners of a business want to be completely free from outside control, they will rely heavily on retained profits as a source of funds.

Are Restrictions Imposed on Managerial Freedom?   Another outstanding advantage of retained profits is that no restrictions are placed on management's freedom to make decisions. This situation makes retained profits similar to common stock but unlike preferred stock and debt.

Must Collateral Be Pledged?   Still another advantage of retained profits is that this source of funds requires no pledge of collateral.

Many large companies are now giving stockholders—both common and preferred—an opportunity to reinvest their dividends in the company's common stock; these arrangements are known as *automatic dividend reinvestment plans.* Stockholders who join these plans use their dividends to buy additional common stock in the firm. The shares are purchased in the open market for the participating stockholders; hence the corporation does not receive the proceeds. Over 4 million stockholders in over 400 large corporations now participate in these plans. For example, the *Wall Street Journal* reported that 100,000 stockholders in General Telephone and Electronics reinvested approximately $2 million in a recent quarter. While mutual funds and monthly investment plans have had automatic dividend reinvestment plans for years, the concept is relatively new as applied directly to corporations.

The dividend-paying corporation usually turns over the administration of the plan to a bank, called the trustee. By doing this the corporation saves time, paperwork, and money; instead of writing thousands of small checks (or paying the transfer agent to write them), it writes one large check, which is sent to the trustee bank. In speaking about the automatic dividend reinvestment plan, the manager of shareholder relations of Gulf Oil Company said, "It's 22,000 fewer dividend checks that I have to handle." But even more important than the

AUTOMATIC DIVIDEND REINVESTMENT PLANS

savings in paperwork is the goodwill generated with stockholders who take advantage of these plans.

Stockholders who participate in automatic dividend reinvestment plans receive several specific benefits. First, they pay a very low brokerage fee. American Can Company, in explaining its plan, said, "Your funds are consolidated with the funds of others for the purchase of stock in bulk and the commission savings on large purchases are passed on to you." An example of such a savings would be the purchase of five shares of stock selling at $31 a share. If an investor bought these shares through a regular broker, he would pay a commission of $8.14; but if he bought them through an automatic dividend reinvestment plan, he would pay a commission of only $4.13. In addition, the stock buyer does not have to pay the odd lot penalty cost. Because the trustee bank buys stock in quantity for all participants, an individual's savings in commission fees can amount to anywhere from 50 to 60 percent as compared with usual brokerage house rates on small orders.

A second advantage to stockholders is that they earn dividends on fractional shares held in their account. Ford Motor Company gave this information to its stockholders: "Your invested funds are fully utilized, since the bank credits your account with fractional interests in shares (computed to three decimal places) on which, in turn additional dividends are prorated and invested for you."

Other advantages to participating stockholders are that investors with small holdings can dollar average, and they obtain free custodial services from the trustee bank, thereby giving protection against the certificates being lost, misplaced, or stolen.

Even though stockholders reinvest their dividends, these dividends are subject to the usual federal income taxes.

Automatic dividend reinvestment plans appeal mainly to small investors; large institutional investors believe they themselves can do a better job of reinvesting the dividends.

REPURCHASING OF COMMON STOCK BY ORIGINAL ISSUERS

Reasons for a Corporation to Buy Its Own Shares First, a corporation may want to have on hand treasury stock (see Chapter 4) for executive stock option plans. The Mead Corporation recently purchased 250,000 shares of its own stock "solely to cover stock options that have been granted but not yet exercised." This firm (like General Motors Corporation and Exxon Corporation) prefers not to increase the total number of authorized and issued shares outstanding in order to implement stock option plans.

Second, a corporation may want to build a stockpile of shares that will be used for future acquisitions. When one company buys another, the buying corporation often pays with its own shares, rather than with cash. For example, the board of directors of Sonesta International Hotels Corporation authorized the purchase of up to 150,000 shares of its common stock and up to 20,000 of its preferred. The chairman of the board of directors of this firm said, "We are talking to the owner of an existing hotel which we might like to acquire for stock."

Third, a *Wall Street Journal* survey has confirmed that much of the buying of stock for treasury purposes "results from the belief of executives and directors that current stock prices do not reflect the improved earnings prospects of their companies." Another way to say this is that executives believe the stock of their company is undervalued because the current price-earnings ratio is not reflecting the potential earnings of the firm. An officer of White Consolidated Industries, Inc., whose stock was selling at eight times the estimated current year's earnings said, "What kind of a multiple is that for a company likely to more than double earnings over a couple of years?" He stated that the board of directors would buy $5 million of its own stock. When a corporation buys its own stock and does not resell the shares in the current year, earnings per share increase, because total profits are divided among fewer shares. Since security analysts and investors are impressed with an increasing level of earnings per share, the price-earnings ratio is likely to increase. This chain of events, corporate management believes, will raise the market price per share of the common stock.

Somewhat similar to the above is the practice of a company buying its own shares to head off a dilution in earnings per share. If a particular firm has recently used its own unissued stock to pay for a growth company, the buying company runs the risk of having its current earnings per share decline, because (by definition) a growth company is not expected to begin paying dividends to its parent company until several years in the future. For example, when Textron Corporation acquired the shares of American Research and Development Corporation, a venture capital company, it was well known that the acquired company would not immediately contribute to the quarterly earnings of Textron Corporation. If Textron had taken no action, its own earnings per share would have declined because its total profits would have been spread over a larger number of shares (the ones used to buy American Research and Development Corporation). To prevent this from happening, Textron purchased 1.8 million of its own shares, hence spreading its own total profits over fewer shares.

Fourth, a firm may buy its own stock because this outlet is a better investment of the company's money than other alternatives, such as buying another company or developing a new product. The president of Fuqua Industries, Inc., said, "Our earnings are good and rather than invest in something that we did not know anything about, we decided to buy some stock in our own company, which we do know something about." The board of directors of this company authorized the firm to buy up to 500,000 shares of common; the *Wall Street Journal* reported that about 1,500 shares a day were being purchased.

Numerous other reasons exist for a corporation to purchase its own stock. Raytheon, for example, purchased 750,000 of its shares to help offset dilution resulting from the conversion of preferred stock.

Purchasing Shares Versus Paying a Large Cash Dividend   A firm with permanent excess cash has an option of distributing this cash to its stockholders through a large cash dividend or through a program of buying its own stock. From the corporation's viewpoint, a disadvantage of distributing the surplus cash through a large extra dividend is that investors might think a precedent is being established and might expect the large dividend to continue in the future. But if the surplus money is used to purchase common stock, there is no implication that a precedent is being established, for investors look on major repurchase programs as being of an episodic nature. The stockholder may prefer to sell his shares to the company, rather than receive a large cash dividend, because of tax considerations. The capital gains tax that he pays on the sale of his securities to the company is less than the tax he would pay on the receipt of dividends (although the first $100 of dividends is tax-free). Because of the above considerations, managerial decisions on disposing of large sums of idle cash must be considered concurrently with the dividend policy of the firm.

Methods of Acquiring the Stock   A corporation that is purchasing its own stock may use one of three methods. First, it may make a *tender offer* to all stockholders. Under this arrangement, the firm gives notice that it is willing to buy a certain number of its shares at a fixed price, which is usually several dollars above the current market value. For instance, A-T-O Inc. announced to its stockholders that it was offering to purchase at $10.60 (market price $8) any and all shares up to a maximum of 1,000,000 shares. The tender offer is widely used, despite the fact that the company must pay several dollars above the market price per share. With this method, stockholders are apprised of why the firm is acquiring its own stock, and all stockholders are given an equal opportunity to sell their shares back to the firm.

Second, a firm may buy the shares in the open market. And third, it may buy the shares from institutional investors.

Corporate financial policy on repurchasing its own common stock was formerly an incidental problem in financial management; it is now a significant area of decision making, because a large number of firms are now acquiring their own common stock.

HIGHLIGHTS OF THIS CHAPTER   *From a financial viewpoint, profits are channeled in three main directions: paid to the federal government as income taxes, retained in the business, and paid as dividends to stockholders. This threefold classification applies to the single proprietorship, the partnership, and the corporation.*

Dividends may be classified into five types: dividends payable in cash, dividends payable in stock, dividends payable in property (assets) other than cash, dividends payable in bonds, and dividends payable in scrip. Cash dividends are by far the most important kind of dividends.

Stock dividends result in a permanent commitment of part of the accumulated profits in the business. Stockholders will benefit from a stock dividend if the corporation increases its total dividend payments or if the market price per share is reduced to such an extent that there is an increase in the demand for the shares, thereby increasing the aggregate market value of the shareholders' commitment.

The advantages of retained profits as a source of funds are: (1) they are a low-cost source; (2) no voting rights are given; (3) no restrictive provisions are imposed on management; (4) the firm has the use of the funds indefinitely; (5) the issuer pays no fixed return, as would be the case if bonds were issued; and (6) no collateral need be pledged.

REVIEW QUESTIONS

17-1. What are the advantages of financing expansion through retained earnings?

17-2. What are the main reasons for a corporation paying a dividend in stock, instead of in cash?

17-3. Into what three mainstreams do corporate profits flow?

17-4. If you were on the board of directors of Ford Motor Company, what are some of the factors you would consider before voting for a $5-a-year dividend rate?

17-5. How much in annual dividends is AT&T common stock now paying? What is the current market price of these shares? (Look these up in a newspaper.)

17-6. A balance sheet contained this item:

Profits retained in the business $1,000,000

Explain how the firm might have retained a sum much greater than this. That is, what kind of a transaction lowers retained profits below the true amount actually "retained" in the business?

REVIEW PROBLEMS

Answers to some of the problems appear at the end of this section. *For each problem, show how you obtained the answer.*

17-1. Assume that a company is subject to these federal income tax rates: 30 percent on all profits *plus* 22 percent on all profits over $25,000. The profit and loss data for this company are as follows:

Sales		$200,000
Less expenses:		
Labor	$40,000	
Material	10,000	
Depreciation	40,000	
Interest	1,000	
Other	9,000	
		$100,000
Taxable profit		$100,000

Compute this firm's income taxes under the conditions given in the statement. (a) If this firm changed its depreciation policy in a manner to increase its depreciation to $50,000 for the year given, how much in taxes would be saved for this one year? (b) Why is this saving so important if in later years the company will have to pay larger annual taxes?

17-2. Following is a summary of the financial position of the Holman Company:

Cash	$ 50,000	Liabilities	$100,000
Other assets	350,000	2,000 shares of common,	
		par value $100	200,000
		Retained earnings	100,000
Total	$400,000	Total	$400,000

Assuming that this company pays a cash dividend of $10 a share: (a) What total amount in cash dividends will be paid by this company? (b) How much are retained earnings after the dividend payment? (c) What is to prevent an investor from making a profit by buying this stock a few days before the company mails the cash dividend, holding the stock until he receives the check, and then selling the stock and placing the proceeds in another company's stock that is about to pay a dividend, and repeating the process over and over (that is, switching his money in and out of stocks and holding the stocks just long enough to receive the dividends)?

17-3. General Motors Corporation has a bonus plan (executive compensation plan) which permits key employees to share in profits. The bonus is in addition to regular salaries. The main features of the plan are as follows.

The aggregate amount of the bonus is 12 percent of the yearly earnings after subtracting 5 percent on capital from the net earnings. However, the total bonus cannot exceed dividends paid to the common stockholders. The bonus committee, which is composed of five directors, has discretion with respect to giving bonuses to individual employees. Only employees with a salary of over $500 per month are eligible for the bonus. Any individual who receives a bonus of $1,000 or less is paid in cash at the time the bonus is distributed.

Assuming capital of $2,387,379,115 and net earnings in one year of $558,949,188, determine the total bonus award of General Motors. (Dividends on the common stock amounted to $350,249,851 for that year.)

17-4. The Gilbert Manufacturing Company has earned a profit of $50,000 (after taxes) in a certain year. Management is undecided on how much of this profit to retain in the business, although undoubtedly it will keep a large part of the money in the company. The final decision hinges mainly on the rate of return the firm can earn on this money if it is retained in the business. Management breaks down the $50,000 into units of $10,000 and estimates the amount of additional profit that will be added to the firm's earnings from each unit. The estimated data appear in Table 17-5.

Unit of Money Retained in the Business	Total Profits Retained in the Business	Amount of Profit Added as a Result of the Addition of a $10,000 Unit	Cumulative Earnings Added as a Result of Earnings Retained in the Business
First $10,000	$10,000	$1,000	$1,000
Second $10,000	20,000	900	1,900
Third $10,000	30,000	800	2,700
Fourth $10,000	40,000	500	3,200
Fifth $10,000	50,000	200	3,400

TABLE 17-5
Gilbert Manufacturing Company Profits

Other companies in the industry are able to earn 7 percent on investment. Assuming that management is interested in maximizing the returns of stockholders, how much of the $50,000 should be retained in the business?

17-5. Company M is planning its financial requirements three years in advance. Among other matters, this means preparing a *pro forma* balance sheet. Management is especially interested in the liability and net worth section of the balance sheet because of the information gained on the amount of financing that will be needed.

The firm has the following sales projection: next year $1 million; two years from now $1,200,000; three years from now $1,600,000. The basic question to be answered is the amount and type of financing that will be needed to finance the expansion in sales. Below is the firm's balance sheet as of the present:

Current assets	$480,000	Bank loans	$ 80,000
Fixed assets	320,000	Accounts payable	80,000
		Mortgage	100,000
		Common stock	200,000
		Retained profits	340,000
Total	$800,000	Total	$800,000

The following ratios apply to the firm: current assets are 60 percent of total sales; fixed assets are 40 percent of sales; bank loans are 10 percent of sales; accounts payable are 10 percent of sales; net profit after taxes is 10 percent of sales; and the firm has a 50 percent pay-out ratio.

(a) Determine the following information as of the end of the third year: the total amount of assets that will be needed to support the expected level of sales; the amount in the retained profits account; the amount of bank loans outstanding; the amount of accounts payable on the books. (b) The expansion in the accounts just mentioned will result in supplying some of the funds for expansion. How much in additional financing will be needed over and above the automatic expansion in short-term credit and retained earnings? (c) Suggest a few places where the extra funds might be obtained.

17-6. The following is a summary of the financial position of the Godfrey Company:

Assets	$1,000,000	Liabilities	$ 200,000
		Common stock, $100	
		par value	600,000
		Retained profits	200,000
Total	$1,000,000	Total	$1,000,000

The company pays a 10 percent stock dividend. After the stock dividend is paid, determine (a) the number of shares of common stock outstanding; (b) the amount of retained profits; (c) the amount of assets; (d) the amount of liabilities; (e) the book value per share of common.

17-7. The New York Bank paid a stock dividend of 4 ⅙ percent. Before the payment of the stock dividend, the company had 7,200,000 shares of $20 par-value stock outstanding. The directors announced that they would continue the annual payment of $2 per share on the new number of shares to be outstanding after the stock dividend.

Compute (a) the number of additional shares that would be issued as a result of the stock dividend; (b) the total par value of all shares to be outstanding after the completion of the transaction involving the payment of the stock dividend; (c) the total annual dividend requirements on the new number of shares outstanding; (d) how much an individual shareholder would gain in dividends received, assuming he held 24 shares prior to the stock dividend.

17-8. A recent newspaper report stated that the directors of the American Tobacco Company had declared a quarterly dividend of 85 cents per share. In addition, the directors declared an extra dividend of $1 per share. Although the paper did not say so, the stockholders were to receive separate checks for the regular dividend and the extra dividend.

Suggest a reason why the company paid the extra dividend by a separate check rather than combining the dividends into one check.

17-9. Below is the financial position of an oil company:

Cash	$ 8,789,204.12	
Other current assets	16,878,107.00	
Total current assets		$25,667,311.12
Investments in other companies		2,040,487.65
Fixed assets		62,342,806.51
Other assets		965,545.87
Total assets		$91,016,151.15
Current liabilities		$11,640,587.45
Long-term debt		25,000,000.00
Capital stock		12,469,223.29
Earned surplus		41,906,340.41
Total liabilities and equities		$91,016,151.15

The company had debenture bonds outstanding. Among other provisions, these bonds limited the amount of dividends that could be paid to holders of common stock. The following are the restrictions on paying dividends. Dividends cannot be paid unless after the payment (1) the net working capital is at least $7,500,000, (2) the remaining current assets are at least 200 percent of the current liabilities, and (3) the earned surplus is at least $20,229,963.

What is the maximum dividend that could be paid by this firm?

17-10. Company P is in the 40 percent income tax bracket. Determine the amount of tax due, assuming the following:

Income before interest and taxes	$140,000
Preferred stock dividend requirements	5,000
Amount of interest due on bonds	10,000
Dividends paid on common stock	15,000
Sinking fund requirements on bonds	20,000

17-11. Company X has assets of $1,000,000 and earnings per share of $5.67; it pays a dividend of $2.88 a year; it obtains 25 percent of its assets from 6 percent bonds and 75 percent from common stock. Company X can support this level of earnings per share and dividends per share with an EBIT of $100,000. Company B, a similar company, imitates X by seeking the same earnings per share and the same dividends per share. But Company B obtains 35 percent of its assets from 6 percent bonds and 65 percent from common stockholders. Both firms are of the same size, both are in the 50 percent tax bracket.

Data for both firms are:

	Company X	Company B
Assets	$1,000,000	$1,000,000
6% bonds	$ 250,000	$ 350,000
Common stock—$100 par	$ 750,000	$ 650,000
Shares of common	7,500	6,500
EBIT	$ 100,000	
Interest	$ 15,000	
Taxable income	$ 85,000	
Tax	$ 42,500	
Net profits	$ 42,500	
Earnings per share	$ 5.67	$ 5.67
Dividends per share	$ 2.88	$ 2.88

If X can support its earnings per share and dividends per share with an EBIT of $100,000, what level of EBIT is needed by B to earn $5.67 a share and to pay a dividend of $2.88 a share?

Answers: 17-1a, $5,200; 17-2a, $20,000; 17-2b, $80,000; 17-3, $52,749,628; 17-4, $30,000; 17-6a, 6,600; 17-6b, $140,000; 17-6c, $1 million; 17-6d, $200,000; 17-6e, $121.21; 17-7a, 300,000; 17-7b, $150 million; 17-7c, $15 million; 17-7d, $2; 17-9, $2,386,136.22; 17-10, $52,000; 17-11, $94,710.

Managing Expansion via Common Stock

Although the subject of stock is given broad treatment here and in the next chapter, it should be remembered that stock issues are basically a method of raising funds to be used in acquiring current assets and fixed assets.

The issuance of stock by a corporation is generally a very special event. In many instances a corporation may issue shares only two or three times during its life. Since this is the case, it is important to note that investors usually acquire stock that has already been issued; that is, the stock is purchased from some other stockholder. These transactions do not affect the corporation, because it has already received its money for the shares. If, for example, Tom Andrews buys 100 shares of United States Steel Corporation stock from Jack Bell, the corporation does not enter into the deal; only Andrews and Bell are involved.

When a corporation is selling units of ownership, the needs of investors must be considered. The corporation can cater to different classes of investors by issuing stocks with varying rights and degrees of risk. One kind of stock contract may be designed to appeal to investors who are willing to take much risk because of the hope of an unlimited return, while another type may be drafted to appeal to relatively conservative investors. The time-honored classification is common stock and preferred stock.

Common stock, preferred stock, and retained profits are important forms of equity capital (nondebt sources of funds). These three kinds of capital are a foundation on which a debt structure can be erected. That is, a firm must have a reasonable amount of equity capital before it can expect lenders to supply funds. For example, when a single proprietor or a partner seeks a bank loan, among the first questions asked by the banker will be, "How much of your own money have you invested in the firm?" Or in the case of the corporation, the question will be, "How much is your net worth?" For these reasons the discussion of equity capital will precede that of debt capital.

Should a particular firm sell common stock to obtain funds? The answer depends on what the needs of management are and on the ability of common stock to meet them. In many situations, common stock is the best alternative for fund raising; in other situations it falls short of being satisfactory.

The following standards will be used for evaluating common stock as a source of funds (from the management viewpoint):
1. What is the cost of the additional funds?
2. How much control must be sacrificed?
3. Must the firm make periodic payments for the use of the funds?
4. How long does the firm have the use of the money?
5. Are restrictions imposed on managerial freedom?
6. Must collateral be pledged?

Relative to preferred stock and debt, common stock may be a costly source of capital. The expensiveness of common stock under some money market conditions is a disadvantage of this source of funds.

WHAT IS THE COST OF THE ADDITIONAL FUNDS?

A firm bargains over the cost of capital when it fixes the price at which it will sell the common shares. The issuer prefers to receive a high selling price for its new common stock; the purchaser prefers a low price. A relatively high selling price for the shares lowers the cost of capital to the issuer; a relatively low selling price for the shares raises the cost of capital to the issuer. But from the investor's viewpoint, a relatively low purchase price increases the probability that he will earn a high composite rate of return; a relatively high price decreases the probability of his earning a high composite rate of return.

Management has a duty to obtain funds on terms that are advantageous to the existing owners. Obtaining funds at a low cost is one application of this principle. If, for example, a firm plans to raise $100,000, the existing owners (single proprietor, partners, or stockholders, as in this case) are benefited if the company has to pay $4,000 instead of $6,000 for the use of the money. The $2,000 savings gained in this illustration increases the amount of earnings on the owners' equity. While those who advance money to a firm are anxious to obtain the largest number of dollars for the use of their funds, the management is anxious to pay the least number—assuming that the suppliers of capital are a different group from the present owners.

An indirect clue as to the cost of capital to a firm is to study national averages, which give some information on this problem for groups of firms. One approach is to study how many times greater the market price of the stock is than the earnings per share. This concept is called the price-earnings ratio, also known as the multiple. In the discussion to follow we will use the latter term. If average market prices are $50 and average earnings per share are $5, the multiple is 10. From management's viewpoint, a good time to sell additional stock is when the multiple is high.

Another way to express the multiple is: earnings per share as a percentage of the market price. If earnings per share are $8 and the current market price of the stock is $80, the earnings-price relationship is 10 percent.

HOW MUCH CONTROL MUST BE SACRIFICED?

One disadvantage of common stock as a fund-raising device is that voting rights must be given to those who buy it. If a small firm or a family-owned firm is selling the shares to persons other than the present stockholders, control of the corporation may eventually be lost. But if a large firm sells shares with voting rights, control is seldom disturbed, because the new stock is usually distributed among a considerable number of purchasers. Hence, the matter of control must be analyzed in the light of each firm's circumstances. But certainly the managements of hundreds of thousands of corporations are concerned with the possibility that control of the firm may be lost if common stock is issued.

Stockholders' Meetings

Stockholders' meetings may be divided into two classes—regular meetings and special meetings. Regular meetings are held once a year under conditions prescribed in the bylaws of the corporation. At the regular meeting of the stockholders of large corporations, there is often a bitter battle of words between some of the stockholders and the management. Thus at an annual stockholders' meeting of the New York, New Haven, and Hartford Railroad, an aroused stockholder denounced the management for not paying a dividend and for the way certain information was presented in the annual report. Another friction that may develop at the regular annual meeting involves the size of pensions and the profit-sharing schemes enjoyed by officers. A considerable minority of the stockholders believe that officers are enjoying unreasonably excessive incentive plans. Stockholders holding this viewpoint do not hesitate to express their dissatisfaction at the annual stockholders' meeting. In many respects, the regular stockholders' meeting is the most important one for the owners of the business. Directors have the right to call a special stockholders' meeting when matters come up that must be attended to by the stockholders. The bylaws also contain rules and regulations for calling and conducting the special stockholders' meeting.

Methods of Voting: Noncumulative versus Cumulative

Stockholders may cast their votes in either of two ways: on a noncumulative basis or a cumulative basis.

Noncumulative Voting

It is customary for each common stockholder to have 1 vote for each share held. If there are 15 candidates for 9 directorships, a stockholder with 1 share may cast 1 vote for each of 9 candidates. Although a stockholder under these circumstances may be said to cast 9 votes, these votes cannot be cumulated on any one candidate. In other words, under the assumption that a stockholder has 1 share, no candidate could get more than 1 vote from this stockholder. If this stockholder owned 100 shares, he would be entitled to cast 100 votes for each of 9 candidates. No candidate for the position of director could receive more than 100 votes from this stockholder. Under noncumulative voting, stockholders cannot cumulate their votes and concentrate them on one or a few candidates. However, a stockholder who owns more than half the shares of the firm can always elect all the directors. We may illustrate this by assuming the following:

There are 9 directors to be elected; there are 100,000 shares of stock outstanding; Louis Jones owns 50,001 of these shares. Jones could elect all 9 directors because the candidates he backs will always receive 2 more votes than the opposition candidates could possibly receive. The 9 candidates backed by stockholder Jones will each receive 50,001 votes. The maximum number of votes any opposition candidate could receive is 49,999. The problem of domination by a single stockholder is alleviated by the fact that only rarely do we find more than half the stock of a large corporation owned by a single individual. Yet the problem of granting minority representation remains.

A method of voting known as cumulative voting has been designed to grant *Cumulative Voting* minority representation on the board of directors to minority stockholders who own substantial numbers of shares. Cumulative voting means that each shareholder has a number of votes equal to the number of shares owned multiplied by the number of directors to be elected *and* that, furthermore, the number of votes possessed by a stockholder may be divided in any desired manner among the candidates. Under cumulative voting, if 9 directors are to be elected and if a stockholder has 1 share of stock, the stockholder has 9 votes which may be distributed among the candidates in any desired manner. The stockholder might even cast all 9 of his votes for 1 candidate. If the stockholder owns 100 shares and if there are 9 directors to be elected, the voter would have 900 votes which could be cast for 1 candidate or spread out among the candidates in any manner suitable to the stockholder. The term *cumulative* is applied to this kind of voting because a stockholder may cumulate his votes on selected candidates.

A formula has been devised to indicate the number of shares necessary to elect a desired number of directors under cumulative voting. A group of stockholders, for example, might want to know how many shares it would need to muster in order to elect 3 directors on a board of 9 in a corporation that has 100,000 shares outstanding. The formula that will give this information is as follows:

$$\frac{\text{Desired number of candidates to be elected to the board of directors}}{1} \times \frac{\text{Number of shares of stock outstanding}}{\text{Total number of directors to be elected at the stockholders' meeting}} + 1 = \text{Number of shares needed to elect desired number of directors.}$$

Substituting, we have:

$$\frac{3}{1} \times \frac{100,000}{9} + 1 = 30,001$$

The minority group would need to muster 30,001 shares to be assured of selecting 3 directors.

Under cumulative voting, the holders of a majority of the shares can select a majority of the directors, but not necessarily all of them, as under noncumulative voting. Some uncertainty is injected into the formula when the number of votes that will be cast is not definite and when either the majority or the minority spreads its votes over too many candidates, thus enabling the other side to win more than its theoretical share of directorships. Yet the mathematics of cumulative voting is such that stockholders with a substantial number of shares are able to place some representatives on the board of directors.

The Case against Cumulative Voting The management of a company is generally against cumulative voting. Insiders say that minority directors tend to create friction on the board. When a stockholder of Standard Oil Company of New Jersey proposed that cumulative voting be allowed, the management opposed the idea and gave the following reasons for its view:

> The Company's management continues to believe that a change in the voting rights of stockholders as now proposed is neither appropriate nor in the best interest of the stockholders. Directors elected through cumulative voting tend to be representatives of separate groups of stockholders, each looking after special interests, and not working together as the most effective team for the maximum benefit of all stockholders. The management believes it to be quite important to the stockholders that the Board continue to be a cohesive group of directors who can work together cooperatively and effectively, and that every director represent all stockholders of every type rather than any special group. The management is convinced that the election of directors under the present voting procedure ensures a Board which wholeheartedly can give careful attention to the collective interest of all the stockholders.

In a number of states, some legislators have gone so far as to propose legislation that would abolish laws which make cumulative voting mandatory.

Defense of Insiders against Cumulative Voting Those in control of the corporation try to prevent individuals on an opposing slate from gaining membership on the board of directors. They put up their own slate of candidates and expect the entire ticket to be elected. In some elections, minority groups campaign for an opposition ticket in the hope of placing one or more of their candidates on the board of directors.

In the ensuing contest the insiders do all they can to defeat each and every member of the opposition. One scheme is to reduce the number of persons on the board of directors from, say, nine to seven. If minority stockholders have 6,500 out of 60,000 shares in a company that has nine directors, they could elect one director and still have a few shares to spare. But suppose that the directors have the power to amend the bylaws and that they vote to reduce their membership to seven. As a result of this change, the minority group, with its 6,500 shares, could elect no directors; it now needs 7,501 votes to place one man on the board. This form of strategy is legal, although it does seem to violate the spirit of cumulative voting.

Another subterfuge is to classify the board so that the terms of office are staggered. Suppose that minority stockholders have 6,500 shares out of 60,000 in a company that has nine directors. Again the minority could elect one director and have a few votes to spare. But if the insiders want to neutralize cumulative voting, they might amend the bylaws so that the board is classified into three groups, each containing three members: one group to be elected for a one-year term, another group for a two-year term, and the third group for a three-year term. Furthermore, the bylaws can state that stockholders must vote separately for each of the three groups. Again the minority would lose its chance to win a directorship because 6,500 shares would not be enough to place one director on a board of three. Minority owners would now need 15,001 to be assured of electing one director to each group. Classifying board membership was declared to be illegal in an Illinois case (Montgomery Ward & Company) but in some other states it is not so considered.

A corporation that has a large number of stockholders readily willing to sell their stock is known as an *open* corporation; a potential buyer can always acquire shares in an open corporation (General Motors Corporation meets this specification). On the other hand, a *close* corporation is one in which there are only a few stockholders, these stockholders being unwilling to sell their shares to the general public. When stockholders sell their shares in a close corporation, they usually sell their entire interest, as, for example, did Branch Rickey when he sold his equity in the Dodgers baseball club.

Publicly Owned Corporations

In some companies, there are more women then men stockholders, as in the case of United States Steel Corporation (see Table 18-1).

Registered in Name of	Holders	Shares
Individuals:		
Women	123,679	12,851,935
Men	95,882	12,375,758
Joint accounts	91,308	7,834,389
Total Individuals	310,869	33,062,082
Nominees	1,546	12,152,804
Brokers	330	5,172,430
Others	31,105	3,782,146
Total	343,850	54,169,462

TABLE 18-1 Stockholders in United States Steel Corporation

The Proxy System   The proxy system permits stockholders to cast their votes at stockholders' meetings without attending in person. A proxy is a form signed by a stockholder and given to another person so that he can vote the shares of the absentee voter. The person who votes the shares is also known as a proxy.

The Nature of Proxies

When a stockholders' meeting is to be held, a stockholder is likely to receive, through the mail, a proxy form along with a request that it be signed and returned to the sender, who is asking permission to represent the stockholder at the meeting. Usually the sender is a stockholder who owns stock, although any person may solicit the votes of stockholders. Corporate management, upon the receipt of the signed proxies from the stockholders, in turn will cast the votes at the meeting. The management will vote the shares for the present board of directors or for their nominees. Also, the management will vote the shares favorably on any actions recommended by the board of directors unless the absentee stockholders instruct otherwise. As long as the stockholders are satisfied with the amount of dividends they are receiving, they are likely to sign the proxies and return them to the existing management. From these comments it can be seen that the proxy system permits management to maintain control over the corporation with relatively small holdings in its own name.

If a stockholder signs a proxy and mails it to the sender and then later changes his mind, can the stockholder revoke the proxy? The answer is yes under most circumstances. A stockholder, by giving notice in writing, can revoke the proxy. Also, if a stockholder signs a proxy and then later changes his mind and appears at the stockholders' meeting, his personal appearance usually supersedes any proxies previously signed.

The importance of proxies in modern times cannot be overemphasized. Not only does this device make absentee voting possible, but it also allows the management of the corporation to become almost self-perpetuating. Proxies continue to grow in importance with the development of large corporations.

Proxy Contests The field of corporation finance contains many instances of different groups competing with each other for proxies. Proxy contests develop when an outside group is attempting to wrest control of the corporation from the existing board of directors. A famous proxy fight was won by John D. Rockefeller, Jr., when he campaigned at his own expense for proxies so that he could oust the management of the Standard Oil Company of Indiana. Proxy fights often develop when the company is not making sufficient profits or paying adequate dividends, and an outside group thinks it can do a better job than the present board of directors in managing the affairs of the corporation.

Proxy contests are conducted in an atmosphere charged with bitterness. The opposition slate drafts its charges and circulates them among stockholders. The charges often include these telling points: earnings and dividends are too low; the management is of only average competence and hence unable to keep up with competitors; the insiders are bleeding the company through high salaries, lavish expense accounts, and overgenerous retirement plans; and the management is not reporting honestly the financial position of the company. As a counterattack, those in control will charge the opposition with being reckless speculators seeking control for their own selfish ends. Also, insiders will point out that they have experience in managing the company, whereas the opposition has none. These charges and countercharges are generally hurled regardless of the specific issues under consideration. In a number of battles, each side sues the other for slander or libel. The debate between contestants fighting for control of a large company arouses national interest, as in a Montgomery Ward & Company proxy fight.

Each group puts on a vigorous campaign to win the votes of the stockholders, who are bombarded with literature from each camp urging them to sign and return the proxy and not to sign a proxy at a later date for the other side. In some clashes, each side sends five or six communications to stockholders. If there are a large number of owners of stock, both sides hire firms of proxy solicitors to get in touch with each owner. These organizations are well versed in the techniques of persuading stockholders to vote for one side or the other. When there is a battle for control over a large company, advertisements are inserted in newspapers and magazines. Employees who own stock are pressed by both sides. Every effort is made by each group to win a decisive victory. Insiders have a special advantage because they can charge most of their proxy expenses to the company; only if the outsiders win can they also require the company to pay these expenses.

The SEC in Action on Proxies The commission has found that contestants in a proxy fight are likely to be guilty of giving out false or misleading information. To control this problem, the SEC requires that the contestants submit to it material intended for distribution as campaign literature. If the literature contains false or misleading information, the SEC will not approve it.

Among the offenses uncovered in a number of proxy fights is the misuse of statistics by one side or the other or both. In one contest, the SEC found that an opposition group planned to challenge the ability of the company to earn profits under the present management. The insurgents sought to illustrate the existing management's lack of ability by means of an income statement that included a sinking fund payment as a charge against income, an accounting procedure contrary to sound accounting practice. The distorted statement indicated a loss in the firm's operations for six years when, in fact, if the income account had been stated in accordance with accepting accounting practices, it would have shown that losses occurred in only two of the years. The commission objected to this procedure and the opposition group amended its charges before actually mailing them to the stockholders.

The SEC does not require that the contestants maintain a front of outward piety. Instead, as the SEC puts it, the struggle for control should be conducted in an atmosphere of "contentious advocacy." The commission's only function is to do as much as possible to get the facts before the stockholders so that they can reach a reasonably sound conclusion on the issues under consideration. It should be remembered, however, that the SEC has jurisdiction over the proxy contests in only a limited number of companies.

Class A and Class B Stock

Class A and Class B stock present ways of giving one group of shareholders special privileges, such as priority in the receipt of dividends and special voting privileges. The terms *Class A stock* and *Class B stock* have no fixed meaning, and one must consult the charter or a summary of it to get an exact description of these securities. In some cases, Class A stock has priority over Class B stock in the receipt of dividends. Class A or Class B may be voting or nonvoting, depending on the terms of the charter. Bon Ami Company has the following classes of securities outstanding:

Class A stock outstanding—94,583 shares.

Class B stock outstanding—200,000 shares.

Class A has preference over Class B in the receipt of dividends. Class B can receive no dividends until Class A has received $4.00 per share. Then Class B is entitled to $2.50 per share. After Class B stock receives $2.50 per share, both classes participate equally in any further distributions.

Holders of Class A stock and Class B stock have one vote for each share held.

These two kinds of common stock may also be used to classify control. For example, the Sinclair Finance Company was formed by Thomas Sinclair, with an initial capital of $50,000. During the first year of operations, three offices were established to lend money to the general public. The Sinclair Finance Company has two classes of common stock outstanding, Class A stock and Class B stock. The Class A stock has all the voting rights while Class B stock has no voting rights. Thomas Sinclair and Elizabeth Sinclair (his wife) control 56.8 percent of the Class A stock. The Class B stock is widely held by a number of investors, including the two Sinclairs. As for dividends, each share of Class A stock receives the same dividends as each share of Class B stock. In this situation, the Class A stock is used to keep control of the firm in the Sinclair family.

The use of classified common stock has been increasing in recent years, particularly among the medium-sized firms.

ADDITIONAL STANDARDS FOR APPRAISING COMMON STOCK

Must the Firm Make Periodic Payments for the Use of the Funds? A corporation does not have to make periodic payments for the use of stockholders' funds. If the corporation earns profits, the stockholders can, over a period of time, expect returns in either the form of dividends or capital appreciation. But if the corporation suffers losses or if the directors decide not to distribute the profits, the stockholders have no recourse. The fact that the firm does not have to pay any fixed return on the common stock is one of the outstanding advantages of using this method of raising funds. This advantage becomes even more striking when common stock is contrasted with debt—a source of capital that usually requires specified interest payments.

Guaranteed stock means shares whose dividends are guaranteed by a second corporation, the second corporation contracting to pay a specified rate of return on the shares of the first corporation. The stockholder, in effect, becomes a creditor of the guaranteeing corporation. A corporation cannot guarantee dividends on its own shares; the guarantee must be made by a corporation other than the issuing company. Guaranteed stock is prevalent in the railroad field.

Why does a corporation assume liability for paying dividends on another corporation's shares? We find that the guarantee takes place primarily when one company rents the entire assets of another company. Suppose Railroad A wants to use Railroad B's facilities. Railroad A might rent the entire B system, paying rentals to B for the use of the property. As part of the terms of the lease, Railroad A would probably guarantee the stock of railroad B. Table 18-2 lists a few guaranteed stocks.

	Price	Yield in Percentages	
Philadelphia, Germantown & Norristown RR	$93.50	6.41	
Little Miami RR	70.00	6.14	
Delaware & Bound Brook RR	33.00	6.06	

TABLE 18-2 Selected Guaranteed Stocks

How Long Does the Firm Have the Use of the Money? The corporation does not make any promise to return the common stockholders' money at a specified time, the funds being committed to the company permanently. Hence, the firm has the use of stockholders' money for an unlimited period of time. The stockholder has no power to require that the firm return his funds. If he wants to obtain money for his shares, he must find another investor who will purchase them from him. From the management point of view, a major advantage of common stock as a fund-raising device is that the firm is never confronted with a maturity date on this form of financing.

Are Restrictions Imposed on Managerial Freedom? An outstanding advantage of common stock is that it places no restrictions on managerial freedom other than those arising from corporation law and stockholders' voting rights. If the money were borrowed from bondholders or banks, there is the possibility that the management would have the following restrictions imposed on it: a limitation on the amount of dividends that can be paid, restrictions on mergers or consolidations, a limit on the salaries of the officers (especially those in small firms), and so on. No such limitations are placed on managerial freedom when common stock is sold.

Must Collateral be Pledged? When common stock is sold, no collateral is pledged by the management. Under the present legal structure, common stockholders cannot have property pledged for their benefit because this group of investors owns the firm—not specific assets in it. A major advantage (to management) of issuing common stock is that no collateral need be pledged. The company's assets are therefore available to pledge to other investors who might advance funds to the business on advantageous terms if collateral can be pledged for their benefit.

The main advantages of common stock as a source of funds are: (1) since common stock has no maturity date, the issuer has the use of the funds forever;

HIGHLIGHTS OF THIS CHAPTER

(2) the issuer is not committed to pay a fixed return on the securities, as would be the case if a bond issue were floated; (3) common stock is not accompanied by restrictive provisions, as is usually the case with a preferred stock issue or a bond issue; (4) an issuer never pledges collateral for a common stock issue.

The main disadvantages of common stock as a source of funds are these: (1) common stock may be an expensive source of funds, particularly if the point is taken into consideration that new common stockholders will share in future profits; and (2) common stock generally carries full voting rights, a potential disadvantage to the current management.

Common stock is a widely used device for raising funds. Actually, there must be a solid base of common stock or retained earnings before a firm can sell preferred stock, issue bonds, or borrow from commercial banks.

REVIEW QUESTIONS   18-1. What are the advantages of raising funds through the sale of common stock? the disadvantages?

18-2. Can common stock have collateral pledged for it?

18-3. Answer these questions: (a) What is the difference between cumulative and noncumulative voting? (b) If noncumulative voting now exists, is management usually in favor of changing to cumulative voting? (c) What is a proxy?

18-4. United States Steel Corporation, like many other firms, has more women stockholders than men stockholders. How do you suppose women obtained so much stock?

18-5. Arrange for an interview with a major executive in a firm that has recently floated a common stock issue. Seek answers to these questions: (a) How does the company plan to use the proceeds? (b) What factors were considered in establishing the selling price? (c) What practical problems had to be overcome in completing the transaction? (d) Why did the firm use common stock instead of preferred stock or bonds?

REVIEW PROBLEMS   Answers to some of the problems appear at the end of this section. *For each problem, show how you obtained the answer.*

18-1. The net profits after taxes of the Statler Company are $100,000. This company has 20,000 shares of common stock outstanding and pays an annual dividend of $2.50 on each share of stock. The current market price of these shares is $50. Determine (a) the earnings per share; (b) the price-earnings ratio; and (c) the yield on the stock.

18-2. Company F has 1 million shares of common stock outstanding; the firm has 11 directors. Assume that all the shares are voted at the annual election.

(a) Under noncumulative voting, how many shares would be needed to be certain of electing all 11 directors? (b) Under noncumulative voting, how many shares would be needed to be certain of electing 3 directors? (c) Under cumulative voting, how many shares would be needed to be certain of electing 3 directors?

18-3. Company F needed $40,000 for permanent expansion. The firm believed it could earn 25 percent (before taxes) on the additional assets to be purchased with the money. Below is the firm's balance sheet before financing:

Current assets	$100,000	Current liabilities	$ 50,000
Fixed assets	100,000	$5 par-value common	50,000
		Retained profits	100,000
Total	$200,000	Total	$200,000

Before financing, the firm's EBIT were $80,000; the company is in the 50 percent tax bracket. The company sold to the general public additional stock at $40 a share; if the firm had waited another nine months, it could have sold the common stock for $50 a share. (Ignore investment banking fees in the questions to follow.) (a) How many fewer shares of stock would have been issued had the stock been sold for $50 a share? (b) How much lower were earnings per share as a result of selling the stock at $40 a share instead of at $50 a share? (c) What was the opportunity cost (in terms of earnings per share) of selling the stock at $40 instead of $50? Use the following format in solving this problem:

	Pro Forma Data	
	Common Sold at $40	Common Sold at $50
EBIT	$90,000	$90,000
Tax	————	————
Net profit after taxes	————	————
Shares of common outstanding	————	————
Earnings per share on common	————	————

18-4. Company G is in need of $40,000 for permanent expansion. The firm believes that it can earn 25 percent (before taxes) on the additional assets to be purchased with the money. Below is the firm's balance sheet before financing:

Current assets	$100,000	Current liabilities	$50,000
Fixed assets	100,000	5 percent bonds	50,000
		$5 par-value common	50,000
		Retained profits	50,000
Total	$200,000	Total	$200,000

Before financing, the firm's EBIT were $50,000; the company is in the 50 percent tax bracket; the common stock is currently selling at $50 a share.

The firm is considering whether to issue 6 percent preferred stock or to issue common stock (ignore investment banking fees). Assuming that the management will select the course of action that will result in the largest earnings per share on the common stock, which of the two sources should it use to finance the expansion? Use the following format in solving this problem:

	Prefinancing Data	Pro Forma Data Preferred Stock Issued	Common Stock Issued
EBIT	$50,000	$60,000	$60,000
Interest on bonds	___	___	___
Taxable income	___	___	___
Tax (50 percent)	___	___	___
Net profit after taxes	___	___	___
Less preferred stock dividends	___	___	___
Available for common stock	___	___	___
Shares of common outstanding	___	___	___
Earnings per share on common	___	___	___

18-5. Determine the dividends per share on the common stock of Company L, given the following data: market price per share $100; par value $150; earnings per share $20; yield per share 10 percent.

18-6. Determine the yield on the stock of Company P, given the following information: market value $100; earnings per share $20; book value per share $200; pay-out ratio 50 percent.

18-7. Company Y, in the 50 percent tax bracket, is planning to expand its assets by $100,000. As a result of the expansion, total sales will increase to $1 million; earnings before interest and taxes are expected to be 10 percent of sales. The financial position of the firm before the additional financing is given below:

Total assets	$1,000,000	Common ($10 par value)	$100,000
		Retained earnings	900,000

The decision to be made is whether to sell common stock or bonds to raise the funds. Bonds can be sold at par and with a coupon rate of 7 percent; additional stock can be sold at $100 a share. If bonds are sold, the price-earnings ratio is expected to be 26; if additional common stock is sold, the price-earnings ratio is expected to be 30. If market value per share is used as the criterion, which kind of security should be issued? The answer is that stock should be sold because it will result in a market price per share of $136.50; if bonds are sold, the market price per share will be $120.90. *Required*: Show how the answer was obtained. Use the following format:

	Pro Forma Data	
	Bonds Issued	Stock Issued
Earnings before interest and taxes	$100,000	$100,000
Interest	$ 7,000	0
Taxable income	$ 93,000	$100,000
Tax	$———	$———
Net profit after taxes	$———	$———
Shares of common outstanding	———	———
Earnings per share	$———	$———
Price-earnings ratio	26	30
Market price of common	$ 120.90	$ 136.50

18-8. Mr. Y would like to become a director in a small company that is required to grant cumulative voting to its stockholders. This firm has 11 directors and 60,000 shares of common stock outstanding. How many shares does Mr. Y need to accomplish his objective?

18-9. The recent percentage return on high-quality corporate bonds has been 6 percent; at the same time the yield on many blue chip stocks issued by the same companies has been approximately 4 percent. If bonds are safer than stocks (within the same company), why is the yield higher on the lower risk instruments?

18-10. The common stock of Company R is selling at $15 a share; the common stock of Company M is selling at $55 a share. Suggest several reasons why there is such a wide disparity in the price of the respective shares.

18-11. Company A is incorporated in a state that requires cumulative voting. The firm has 3,600 shares of common stock outstanding, and it has a board of directors of 11 members. The bylaws give the directors the power to reduce their number. A dissident group of stockholders have 601 votes on their side; the outsiders plan to elect several directors. If the incumbent management wishes to limit the dissidents to electing one director, what should be the size of the board of directors?

Answers: 18-1a, $5; 18-1b, 10; 18-1c, 5 percent; 18-2a, 500,001; 18-2b, 500,001; 18-2c, 250,001; 18-3a, 200; 18-3b, 8 cents; 18-3c, 8 cents; 18-5, $10; 18-6, 10 percent; 18-8, 5,001; 18-11, 5.

The Amacorp Industrial Leasing Company, Inc., is planning on expanding its activities. After negotiations are completed with a client, the company will buy an asset and then immediately rent it to the customer for the agreed rental. *CASE ON PLANNING TYPES OF FUNDS NEEDED*

Typical items purchased by this leasing company are electronic office equipment, cash registers, air conditioning equipment, portable steel buildings, and oil-field equipment. In fact, the leasing company will make arrangements to buy almost any kind of fixed asset and then rent it to the business firm that agrees to the terms of the lease. Most of the leases are written primarily on the credit standing of the lessee, with only secondary consideration being given to the repossession value of the equipment. Typical customers of the leasing company are factories, supermarkets, banks, department stores, and bowling alleys. The firm is in need of approximately $1 million for permanent expansion. The basic issue confronting the management is whether to raise the funds from short-term, creditor sources, intermediate-term creditor sources, long-term creditor sources, or equity sources. Data on the firm are given below in Tables 18-3 and 18-4:

TABLE 18-3 *Earnings Summary*		
Total current assets		$2,500,000
Total fixed assets		1,000,000
Total rentals receivable in future years		6,000,000
Total assets		$9,500,000
Total current liabilities		2,300,000
Total intermediate-term credit		6,800,000
Net worth		400,000
Total liabilities and net worth		$9,500,000

TABLE 18-4
Latest Summary
of Financial
Position

	One Year Ago	*Two Years Ago*	*Three Years Ago*
Income	$687,000	$371,000	$156,000
Net income per share	0.26	0.11	0.03

Required: (a) Discuss the pros and cons of the sources of funds being considered by management. Which alternative would you select? Give your reasons. (b) If common stock were issued, suggest the probable selling price to the public. If bonds were sold, suggest the probable rate of interest on the issue.

Managing Expansion via Preferred Stock

In the preceding chapter we studied the nature of common stock from both the corporation's and the investor's viewpoint. In this chapter we will analyze preferred stock. Preferred stock closely resembles common stock on a number of points, although there are sufficient differences to warrant a separate treatment.

Preferred stock resembles common stock in that (1) both common stockholders and preferred stockholders are part owners of the business; (2) the corporation is not obligated to pay a fixed return on either of these securities, the returns depending on the availability of profits and the willingness of the directors to pay dividends; and (3) both are entitled to a return only after all costs have been provided for or paid.

Three main differences between preferred stock and common stock are: (1) preferred stockholders have priority over common stockholders in the receipt of dividends; (2) there is usually an upper limit on the amount of dividends that can be received by preferred stockholders; and (3) preferred stockholders do not usually have the permanent right to vote for directors. Other differences will be pointed out in the ensuing discussion.

If preferred stock is issued to finance expansion, the expectation is that this course of action will in time increase the price of the common stock. This expectation may be summarized by describing the impact of the issuance of preferred stock on two variables: earnings per share on the common stock and the price-earnings ratio on the common stock. Since preferred stock is a low-cost source of financing, its use usually will result in higher earnings per share on the common stock than if additional common stock were issued to provide funds for the expansion. This is a favorable situation, because an increase in earnings per share tends to raise the market price of the common stock. The issuance of preferred stock may, however, have an adverse effect on the price-earnings ratio on the common stock. A decrease in the price-earnings ratio tends to lower the price of the common shares. The expectation is that the increased earnings per share on the common stock will more than offset the decrease, if any, in the price-earnings ratio. Finally, there is the factor, previously mentioned, that the investment market may not make fine gradations in risk and that a firm may issue a reasonable amount of preferred stock without any decrease in the price-earnings ratio on the common stock. If this is the case, preferred stock is an advantageous source of funds.

The following questions will be discussed in this chapter:

1. What is the cost of the additional funds?
2. How much control must be sacrificed?
3. Must the firm make periodic cash payments for the use of the funds?
4. How long does the firm have the use of the money?
5. Are restrictions imposed on managerial freedom?
6. Must collateral be pledged?

WHAT IS THE COST OF THE ADDITIONAL FUNDS?

Extent of Participation in Corporation Profits

Nonparticipating preferred stock means that the preferred shareholders' participation in dividends is limited to an amount stated in the charter. This is the usual type of provision found in preferred stocks. The $3.75 preferred stock of General Motors Corporation means that the holders of preferred shares can never receive more than $3.75 for any one year, assuming that dividends are paid regularly. The common stockholders of General Motors, on the other hand, hope to receive large dividends in highly profitable years. When preferred stock is participating, the holders of these securities may share in corporate dividends to an extent greater than the minimum amount stated in the charter. The extent to which preferred stock participates in corporate dividend distributions depends on limits imposed by the charter.

Why Will Preferred Stockholders Accept a Lower Return Than Common Stockholders?

There are several reasons to account for the popularity of preferred stock with some investors: preferred stock has certain priorities over common stock in the receipt of dividends, its dividends are usually cumulative, and it is usually slightly safer than common stock (within the same company). (See Table 19-1 for the yield on selected preferred stock issues.)

TABLE 19-1

Issue	Price	Yield (Percent)
Alabama Power 4.60%	$78.00	5.90
Consolidated Edison 5.75%	98.00	5.87
Consumers Power 4.50%	80.00	5.63
Crown Zellerbach 4.20%	79.50	5.29
Louisiana Power & Light 6.44%	99.50	6.48
Pacific Lighting 4.36%	74.00	5.89

The Preference Feature

One outstanding and indispensable feature of preferred stock is that it has priority over common stock in the receipt of dividends. This means that before common stockholders can receive any cash dividends, the preferred stockholders must be paid a certain amount. To illustrate this point, let us examine the $3.75 series of General Motors preferred stock. According to the terms of this issue, the preferred stockholders must receive $3.75 for each share before the common stockholders can receive any dividends in any year. But the fact that a preferred stock issue has priority in the receipt of dividends does not mean that the corporation must pay steady dividends. On the contrary, the corporation is never under any obligation to pay dividends on any ownership security unless there is some unusual provision in the charter. All the preference feature does is to state that if any group of stockholders receives dividends, then the preferred stockholders will receive their dividends first.

The preference feature is usually accompanied by what is known as the cumulative feature. This means that if the corporation does not pay dividends in a designated period, it must pay these arrearages before common stockholders can receive any dividends. The cumulative feature, then, means that in the absence of any charter provisions to the contrary, dividends on the preferred stock accumulate with the passage of time regardless of whether or not profits are being earned. On the other hand noncumulative preferred stock loses its claim to dividends when not paid by the directors regardless of whether or not profits are being earned. *The Cumulative Feature*

The preference feature is greatly strengthened when accompanied by the cumulative feature. Because investors look for this feature in their preferred stock, corporations, whenever possible, will include this provision in the contract with the preferred stockholders.

Corporations that are financially strong do not issue noncumulative preferred stock. The lack of the cumulative feature would raise substantially the cost of this source of capital. If we looked into the origin of noncumulative preferred stock, we would find that most of these securities originated in railroad reorganizations.

Some preferred stock issues contain a deferred cumulative provision. This means that the issue is noncumulative for a few years after its sale; then the preferred stock dividends are automatically put on a cumulative basis. For example, the Maxson Food Systems, Inc., 50 cent convertible preferred stock was noncumulative the first four years after it was issued; after this waiting period the dividends were cumulative. From the corporation's viewpoint, provisions of this nature prevent burdensome accumulations of dividends in the period immediately after the stock has been issued.

Although the cumulative feature is supposed to prevent the payment of dividends on common stock until all accumulated dividends on the preferred have been paid, we find that after large sums of dividends are accumulated on its preferred stock, a corporation may seek to make an arrangement with the preferred stockholders under which all or part of the dividend arrearages will be voluntarily canceled. Preferred stockholders are frequently offered additional securities and cash in lieu of the accrued dividends on their preferred stock.

Along with this offer might be the promise to resume dividend payments on the preferred stock. A proposal of this sort is tempting to the preferred stockholders because it means the resumption of dividend payments on their investment. In addition, the holders of preferred shares would now have securities in place of their accumulated dividends. These securities could be sold in the market if the new owners cared to sell them.

Although the cumulative feature is an advantage to the preferred stockholders, its presence may be an obstacle to the successful flotation of future issues of common stock. If, after issuing preferred stock, the company suffers a financial setback and defaults on the preferred shares, it is difficult to sell common stock as long as these arrearages exist. Also, if there is a relatively large amount of preferred stock outstanding, the company may have difficulty in selling common stock even if there are no arrearages on the preferred. A large amount of cumulative preferred stock outstanding is always a threat to the holders of common shares.

The Safety Factor
The safety factor in preferred stock stems from the position of this stock in a liquidation. It is customary to grant preferred stockholders preference in the receipt of assets in case the corporation is liquidated (the company dissolved and the assets sold for cash). This means that in the event of liquidation the common stockholders cannot receive any assets until the preferred stockholders receive their stated preference.

Cost of Preferred Stock Issuable in Series
Some charters authorize the issuance of more preferred stock than will be needed in the immediate future. Thus a corporation might be authorized to issue $600,000 in preferred stock and yet issue only $100,000 of 5 percent series A preferred stock at a particular time, the remaining $500,000 being issuable when the need arises in the future. The $100,000 in preferred stock that has been issued is known as Series A stock to distinguish it from other amounts of preferred shares that may be issued in the future. At a later date the corporation might issue $150,000 of 4½ percent series B preferred stock. The outstanding preferred stock would be $250,000 and the authorized but unissued preferred stock would be $350,000. Shares issued in series are usually the same except for the dividend rate. In the above case, the series A preferred stock carries a 5 percent dividend rate while the series B carries a 4½ percent dividend rate. But in all other respects the two series would be similar. Series A would not have any priority over series B in the receipt of dividends or in any other respect. When the charter permits the issuance of preferred stock in series, the directors are permitted to sell these shares under conditions prescribed in the charter. As for the cost of the preferred stock issued in series, although the company will pay the least return possible at the time the additional shares are issued, it must set the return high enough to induce investors to buy the stock.

If the issuer can make the preferred stock more attractive to investors, the firm can lower the return on the securities. One way of increasing the attractiveness of preferred stock is to make it convertible. If preferred stock is convertible, the issuing corporation will exchange other securities for it at the option of the preferred stockholders under conditions stated in the charter. If convertible, preferred stock is almost always convertible into a junior security—particularly common stock. The Bush Manufacturing Company 4½ percent cumulative convertible prior preferred stock is convertible at the option of the holder into two shares of common stock of the company. From the point of view of the issuing corporation, the conversion feature is expected to act as an added inducement for the purchase of preferred stock and thus make it more salable. From the point of view of the preferred stockholders, the conversion feature permits them to share in any future growth of the corporation. Since both the security purchaser and the corporation appear to benefit from the inclusion of the conversion feature, it is understandable why many preferred issues contain this provision.

Convertible Preferred Stock—the Matter of Cost[1]

A major advantage of obtaining funds from preferred stockholders is that it is generally possible to do business with other people's money without giving them an opportunity to control the corporation. There is, however, the fact that preferred stockholders do have some voting rights, even though these voting privileges are not sufficient to give this group control of the firm. The voting rights of preferred stockholders fall into three classes: permanent voting rights, temporary voting rights, and consent voting rights. A preferred stock may have one or more of these classes of voting rights.

HOW MUCH CONTROL MUST BE SACRIFICED?

Permanent voting rights give the preferred stockholders the perpetual right to participate, through the voting process, in corporate activities as designated in the charter. For all practical purposes this means the right of preferred stockholders to participate in the election of directors. The right is perpetual in that it cannot be taken away from the preferred stockholders as long as the articles of incorporation remain unchanged. A preferred stockholder whose stock carries the permanent voting right may cast his votes either in person or by proxy. An illustration of a preferred stock issue carrying the permanent voting right is the Greyhound Corporation preferred stock, which entitles each shareholder to one vote per share. The preferred stockholders in this company may vote on all matters on which the common stockholders are entitled to vote. On the other hand, the H. J. Heinz Company preferred stock specifically provides that the holders of preferred shares shall not have permanent voting rights. The general rule is that preferred stockholders of industrials lack the permanent right to participate in the selection of directors.

Permanent Voting Rights

1. Convertible securities are explained in Chapter 21.

Temporary Voting Rights

When certain events occur, (or fail to occur) temporary voting rights give the preferred stockholders the right to participate in the selection of directors, such voting rights continuing until the condition that brought them into existence has been remedied. An example of an issue that vests temporary voting rights in the preferred stockholders when a certain event occurs is the Robert H. Graupner, Inc., 6 percent cumulative preferred stock. This issue provides that the preferred stockholders can select a majority of the directors if the company's business of brewing ceases as a result of a revocation of licenses not applicable to all brewers within the jurisdiction of the licensing authority taking the action.

Usually it is the failure of certain events to occur that causes the temporary voting rights to become effective. Often the failure of the corporation to pay dividends for a stated number of quarters, to keep up the sinking fund agreement, or to maintain certain financial ratios will result in the preferred stockholders being granted temporary voting rights. An example of an issue that vests temporary voting rights in the holders of preferred stock upon the failure of an event to occur is the H. J. Heinz Company preferred stock, which grants the holders the right to select two additional directors if at any time the unpaid dividends on the preferred are in arrears for six quarters or more, such voting rights to continue until all back dividends on the preferred have been paid. The failure of a corporation to pay dividends on its preferred stock is the usual contingency that results in the preferred stockholders exercising their temporary voting rights.

Consent Voting Rights

Consent voting rights exist when certain actions proposed by the board of directors must be approved by the preferred stockholders before the actions may be completed. These voting rights suggest that corporate policies may not always be to the advantage of preferred stockholders. Since directors are usually representatives of common stockholders, the preferred stockholders must resort to contractual limitations on management; that is, certain proposed actions must first be approved by the preferred stockholders.

One group of consent voting rights is concerned with limitations on the issuance of additional securities by the corporation. The corporate charter may require that under certain conditions the consent of the preferred shareholders must be given before additional bonds or additional preferred stock may be issued. For example, the Wesvaco Chlorine Products Corporation $3.75 preferred stock provides that, with certain exceptions, the holders of a majority of the outstanding preferred shares must give their consent to the issuance of securities that result in placing liens on the assets. It is also customary to require the consent of the preferred shareholders before the corporation can issue additional preferred stock that would have preference over the shares already issued.

Another group of consent voting rights provides that the approval of the preferred stockholders must be obtained before certain types of transactions take place that will result in removing assets from the business. For example, the Midwest Rubber Reclaiming Company 4½ percent cumulative preferred stock provides that the holders of at least 90 percent of the outstanding preferred shares must approve a dividend on the common stock if certain financial ratios are not satisfactory. Other restrictions on the removal of assets may also exist.

A third set of consent voting rights is concerned with the right of the preferred stockholders to approve amendments to the charter. The usual provision is to require that the holders of a stated percentage of the preferred shares must approve charter changes that affect the rights of preferred stockholders. Common requirements are that three-fifths, two-thirds of three-fourths of the preferred shares outstanding must be voted affirmatively before changes which are deemed to affect the preferred stockholders can be made in the charter. General Motors Corporation $3.75 preferred stock provides that no amendments can be made to the charter if the rights of the preferred are involved unless three-fourths of the outstanding preferred shares are voted affirmatively for the change.

An advantage of preferred stock is that the firm does not have to make fixed payments to the preferred stockholders. This situation is in contrast with the many forms of debt that require fixed payments to those who have supplied the money.

MUST THE FIRM MAKE FIXED, PERIODIC PAYMENTS FOR THE USE OF THE FUNDS?

If dividends on the preferred stocks are not paid, can the preferred stockholders take any legal action against the corporation? The answer is no. Courts hesitate to substitute their judgment for that of the board of directors. Only on very special occasions will courts force a board of directors to declare a dividend. Generally speaking, when a corporation misses a payment on the preferred stock, there is nothing for the holders to do but sell their stock or keep it in the hope of better days ahead.

Although boards of directors are not compelled to pay dividends on preferred stock, they usually make every effort to do so. There are three pressures that cause directors to make dividend payments on the preferred stock when such payments can be made without harming the welfare of the corporation. First, there is the moral obligation, for when a corporation sells preferred stock to the public the implication is that the preferred stockholders will receive dividends if the corporation is prosperous. Second, penalties are imposed on the corporation after dividends are in default on the preferred stock for a certain number of quarters. One penalty is that the common stockholders cannot receive returns if dividends are not being paid on the preferred stock. Also, it is customary to grant preferred stockholders representation on the board of directors after dividends have been in default on the preferred stock for a certain number of quarters. Third, passing (not paying) a preferred dividend will depress the price of both the common and the preferred stock. In addition to making for disgruntled stockholders, this state of affairs might hurt the sale of stocks or bonds in the future. Although there are pressures on the directors to pay dividends on the preferred when earnings are available, the directors may still deem it to be in the best interest of the corporation to delay dividend payments to preferred stockholders.

Like common stock, preferred stock does not have a maturity date. The absence of a fixed maturity date is an advantage of using preferred stock as a fund-raising device. In many cases preferred stock is callable; that is, the company at its option can return the funds to the preferred stockholders. Also, there is the fact that many issues of preferred stock have a sinking fund, meaning that the issuer promises to repurchase some of its shares each year. If the firm is unable to keep the promise to purchase the agreed number of shares, certain penalties are imposed on it.

A disadvantage of preferred stock is that it restricts management's freedom to make decisions. Typical restrictions are these:

1. Limitations on paying dividends to common stockholders when certain financial ratios are unsatisfactory.
2. Provisions forbidding the payment of dividends to common stockholders when sinking fund installments on the preferred stocks are in default.
3. Limitations on the purchase or redemption of junior securities as long as there is preferred stock outstanding.
4. Features of the charter that require the approval of the preferred stockholders before assets can be sold or leased to another firm.
5. Provisions forbidding the issuance of additional securities, particularly bonds, prior preferred stock, and *pari passu* preferred stock. *Pari passu* preferred means preferred stock ranking equally with the preferred issue already outstanding.

All of these restrictions are found in the corporation's charter rather than in the bylaws. Of course, the exact restrictions vary from one firm to another, except in public utilities, where there is a considerable amount of standardization.

Preferred stock is similar to common stock in that no collateral is pledged under either type of security. In fact, when preferred stock is sold, the assets available for pledging to creditors actually increase. Preferred stockholders, like common stockholders, own the company, which in turn owns the assets. The fact that no collateral has to be pledged for preferred stock is an advantage of this source of funds.

In recent years preferred stock has been declining in importance, for when the alternative of bond financing is available, management generally floats bonds rather than preferred stock. The reason for this course of action is that bond interest is deductible for federal income taxes whereas preferred stock dividends are not.

Yet, preferred stock does have its uses. First, public utilities still issue this instrument of financing on an extensive scale. Second, preferred stock (convertible) is widely used when one firm acquires another. The common stockholders of the firm that is being acquired may prefer to be paid in convertible preferred stock of the surviving firm because the preferred is safer than the common shares of the surviving firm and still has potential market appreciation. Third, finance companies make frequent use of preferred stock because of their great need for a variety of funds. Other specific circumstances may lead to the issuance of preferred stock.

How does preferred stock measure up to the preferences of management? In many respects, it satisfies management's needs; in other respects, it does not. Preferred stock meets the preferences of management on these scores: it is a cheap source of funds; it does not have a specific maturity date, so that for practical purposes the firm has the use of the money for an unlimited period of time; it does not require the fixed periodic payments to the suppliers of capital; it does not require that the new owners have permanent voting rights; and it does not require that collateral be pledged. All these factors are advantages of financing through a preferred stock issue.

On the other hand, there are several points on which preferred stock falls short of meeting the wishes of management.

First, the management of a corporation may fear the intrusion of preferred stockholders in the management if this class of security holders has temporary voting rights and if the corporation passes preferred stock dividends. Although preferred stockholders may obtain only minority control of the board of directors, even this is resented by the majority members. Consequently, far-sighted management may be reluctant to use preferred stock to raise funds.

Second, when typical preferred stock is issued, annoying restrictions are imposed on the officers: the corporation cannot pay dividends on common stock unless selected financial ratios are satisfactory; the corporation cannot issue long-term debt instruments; and the corporation cannot buy its own stock unless designated financial ratios are satisfactory. Because of these and other such restrictions, many firms avoid the use of preferred stock as a fund-raising device.

HIGHLIGHTS OF THIS CHAPTER

19-1. What are the main differences and the main similarities between common stock and preferred stock?

19-2. Are dividends paid on preferred stock tax deductible to the issuer?

19-3. Outline the main kinds of voting rights that preferred stockholders may have.

19-4. What are the main restrictive provisions imposed on a firm that issues preferred stock?

REVIEW QUESTIONS

Answers to some of the problems appear at the end of this section. *For each problem, show how you obtained the answer.*

REVIEW PROBLEMS

19-1 The following is a summary of the financial position of the Menker Company:

Assets	$1,000,000
Liabilities	$ 200,000
4 percent preferred stock, 2,000 shares, $100 par value	200,000
Common stock, 6,000 shares	600,000
Total	$1,000,000
Income after income taxes is $100,000.	

(a) How many times have the preferred stock dividends per share been earned?
(b) Compute the earnings per share on the common stock.

19-2. Assume that the Menton Company, whose financial position is given below, is liquidated. After liquidation of the assets, $42,000 is available for distribution. This company is forced to liquidate because of inability to pay its debts.

Assets		$210,000
Creditors	$ 85,000	
Preferred stock, 250 shares of $100 par value (the involuntary liquidation value is $100 per share, while the voluntary liquidation value is $102 per share)	25,000	
Common stock, 1,000 shares of $100 par value	100,000	
Total		$210,000

(a) In the above liquidation, how much would the creditors receive? How much would the preferred stockholders receive? How much would the common stockholders receive? (b) Assuming that there was $120,000 in cash available for distribution and that the liquidation was voluntary, how much would the creditors receive? How much would the preferred stockholders receive? How much would the common stockholders receive?

19-3. The Samson Company has 1,000 shares of $100 par-value preferred stock outstanding and 2,000 shares of $100 par-value common stock outstanding. The preferred stock carries a dividend of 5 percent and is cumulative but nonparticipating. At the end of each year, the company distributes all available profits as dividends. Below are the profits of this company for five years. Compute the total annual amount of dividends paid to the preferred stockholders as a class and the total annual amount of dividends paid to the common stockholders.

Year	Total Profits	Paid to Preferred	Paid to Common
1974	$20,000	—	—
1975	15,000	—	—
1976	0	—	—
1977	4,000	—	—
1978	25,000	—	—

Answers: 19-1a, 12½; 19-1b, $15.33.

20 Managing Expansion via Bonds

When a business seeks a low-cost source of funds, long-term credit may be the answer. The following are examples of long-term credit that one might see on a balance sheet: money received from the general public for bonds maturing in 10 to 15 years; money received from a life insurance company in return for promissory notes, the notes maturing in 10 to 20 years; and money received from a bank in the form of a term loan, the repayment schedule calling for the gradual extinguishment of the debt over a specified period of years. The documents to support the loan may consist of bonds, notes, indentures, loan agreements, or other contracts.

Since the same financial principles that apply to bonds also apply to other forms of long-term debt, corporation bonds will be used to illustrate the impact of long-term debt on the firm. Below are two examples of the use made of the proceeds from bond issues.

1. The Wheeling Steel Corporation 3½ percent bonds. The company raised approximately $14 million from the issue. The proceeds were used mainly "to increase capacity and to lower costs."
2. The Wisconsin Power and Light Company 3⅜ percent bonds. The proceeds to the company were $4,025,600. The company used the money to repay bank loans incurred for construction purposes and to pay for additional construction.

Managements differ in their outlook on the amount of bonds that should be issued. Some managements fear the possibility of default so much that they avoid long-term debt almost entirely. On the other hand, many corporate officers favor the use of long-term debt in moderation. This philosophy is based on the belief that a reasonable amount of bonds outstanding is a sign of sound financial management.

These aspects of bonds will be discussed in this chapter:

1. General nature of bonds
2. Parties to a corporation bond issue
3. The terms of the indenture
4. Criteria for evaluating a bond issue
5. Tax-exempt pollution-abatement revenue bonds

Perhaps the most important aspect of a bondholder is that he is a creditor of the corporation; that is, the corporation has borrowed money and has issued the bonds as evidence of the debt. This is in contrast with holders of stock—both preferred and common—who are owners of the corporation, not its creditors. A number of important differences between bonds and shares arise from this fundamental distinction.

*GENERAL NATURE
OF BONDS*

*Bondholders
Are Creditors*

The bondholder expects to receive a return for the use of his money, the return being interest, not dividends. Holders of stock, both preferred and common, receive dividends on their shares, not interest. The terms *interest* and *dividends* have a fixed meaning in finance in the United States and should not be confused with each other.

*Bondholders
Receive Interest*

The amount of interest to be paid on each bond outstanding is a fixed charge[1] and must be paid whether or not profits are available, if the corporation is to avoid failure. (An exception to this rule is "income bonds," where the interest is payable only if earned.) Thus, if a corporation has $100,000 of 5 percent bonds outstanding, the company would have an annual interest outlay of $5,000 (paid to the parties who own the bonds) even though the business is not making any profit. If the corporation failed to make the required interest payments, bondholders could take legal action against it. Stocks, unlike bonds, do not have a fixed rate of return that must be paid each year; the amount of dividends depends on surplus and the willingness of directors to pay dividends out of it.

Not only is the bondholder entitled to a fixed rate of return, he is also entitled to his interest before holders of stock (both preferred and common) can receive any dividends. This priority is one of the factors that makes bonds safer than stocks within the same company.

Individual bondholders receive a sum of money for their interest, the amount depending on the par of the bond and the rate of interest stated on the bond. If a person owns a $1,000 3 percent bond of National Steel Corporation, he would expect to receive $30 for each full year the bond is held. The fact that the bondholder paid more or less than $1,000 for the bond does not affect the amount of interest received. Corporations compute their interest obligations on face value, not market value.

1. The bonds of the Christiansen Corporation, offered to its employees, contain unusual provisions in that the amount of interest payments and the amount of principal repayment are tied to the consumer price index. Each bond is given an original value of $100. The value is recalculated twice a year, with a ceiling of $150 and a floor of $100. Interest is at the rate of 4½ percent of the adjusted value. This means the interest cannot be less than $4.50 but might be as high as $6.75 per year.

There is an upper limit to the amount of interest that a bondholder can receive, the limit being the rate stated on the bond certificate. In this respect, bonds resemble preferred stocks, which usually have a ceiling on the amount that can be received by the owner. Bonds are unlike common stock in that there is no upper limit on the amount that can be received by the common stockholders. Bondholders are willing to accept a limited return because of the belief that bonds are a safer investment than stocks within the same company.

An unimportant exception to the general rule that bondholders can receive only a limited return is the participating bond, which promises to pay a fixed return and in addition permits the bondholders to share in corporate profits up to a certain amount.

Priority in Liquidation

In liquidation caused by failure, creditors always have priority over owners in the distribution of the cash proceeds. Therefore, bondholders, being one class of creditors, will always have priority over both the preferred stockholders and the common stockholders in a liquidation.

Bonds Usually Have a Maturity

Virtually all corporation bonds have a maturity date; that is, the corporation agrees to pay off the outstanding bonds in cash at a certain date in the future. Although bonds have a maturity, the corporation usually reserves the right to repay the bonds ahead of the due date. Many corporation bonds mature between 15 and 30 years after the date of issuance. There are, however, a few exceptional cases in which bonds have been issued without a maturity. (Stocks can never have a maturity date.) Since bonds are evidence of loans, we would expect that provision would be made for the repayment of the loan.

Voting Rights of Bondholders

Bondholders do not usually have the right to vote for directors at all annual meetings. But bondholders may have two types of voting rights: (1) the right to vote for directors when interest payments are in default for a certain number of periods, and (2) consent voting rights, where they can approve or disapprove certain proposed actions of the directors. The bondholders, for example, might have to approve a proposal to issue bonds with a claim ranking ahead of the bonds already issued. However, for practical purposes, bondholders are viewed as outsiders and are not expected to have any influence on policy-making decisions.

Bonds May Be Secured by Collateral

Some corporation bonds are secured by collateral, while others are not. The 7 percent bonds of the Consolidated Edison Company of New York are secured by buildings, franchises, and other property; the 4½ percent Debenture Bonds of Mid-Continent Airlines do not have any collateral pledged for them. The fact that a document happens to be a bond does not necessarily mean that there is collateral pledged for the loan. In contrast with bonds, stocks cannot be secured by collateral because stockholders are the owners of the corporation, which in turn owns the assets.

Bondholders, being creditors and not owners, are not entitled to detailed information about the annual operations of the corporation in which they hold bonds. In small corporations, bondholders do not receive any annual report. However, the financial statements of nearly all large corporations are published in the financial press and manual services, and many such corporations mail copies of their annual report to those bondholders whose addresses they have.

Bondholders Are Limited in the Amount of Information They Receive

There are three parties to a corporation bond issue—the debtor corporation, the trustee, and the bondholder.

PARTIES TO A CORPORATION BOND ISSUE

The corporation is the borrower, giving bonds in exchange for cash.

The Corporation

To solve the problem of dealing with large numbers of bondholders, corporations deal with a *trustee*, who represents all the bondholders. The trustee is usually a large bank, although an individual is often appointed as a co-trustee. An agreement, called the *indenture*, is drawn up between the issuing corporation and the trustee for the benefit of the bondholders. The indenture states in detail the rights and obligations of the issuing corporation the duties of the trustee, and the rights of the bondholders. The issuing corporation is not obliged to send indentures to the bondholders. Instead, the bondholders look to the trustee for specific information about the terms of the indenture. The trustee is appointed by the corporation or the investment banker and is paid a fee by the corporation.

The Trustee

As long as the corporation is meeting its interest and principal payments, the duties of the trustee are highly mechanical in nature: (1) to sign each and every bond issued, (2) to make sure that no more bonds are issued than authorized, (3) to collect cash from the corporation and then pay this cash to the bondholders as interest and principal repayments, (4) to check on the corporation to see if the terms of the indenture are being carried out, and (5) in the case of large bond issues, to submit an annual report to the bondholders stating that the corporation appears to be conforming to the terms of the indenture.

The third party to a bond issue is the bondholder, the creditor of the corporation.

The Bondholder

When a bondholder buys a bond, he expects two main economic benefits: interest to be paid by the corporation on specified dates and payment of the face value of the bond at a definite date in the future. This expected flow of payments is the main determinant of bond values.

As already noted, in the opinion of investors bonds are safer investments than stocks within the same company. This view is held because of certain priorities that bondholders are given, particularly priority in the receipt of cash when the suppliers of money are paid for the use of their funds and priority in the return of money when the company is liquidated. The bondholder accepts a limited return and gives up an opportunity to share in the management of the company because of the compensating factor of expected safety.

When newspapers and periodicals quote bond prices, the quotations are not in dollars but in percentages of face value. Thus a quotation of 98 for a bond with a face value of $500 means the bond has a value of $490. To take another example, a closing quotation for National Steel bonds was 101 7/8. This quotation indicated a market value of $1,018.75 per $1,000 of face value. A point in the corporation bond market is 1 percent of face value; in contrast, a point in the stock market is $1.

A number of services rate bonds according to their relative investment merit. These services are sold by professional organizations whose main function is the rating of securities. Moody's rates bonds into nine classes:

Aaa	Baa	Caa
Aa	Ba	Ca
A	B	C

These symbols designate risk, the first indicating the least risk, the last indicating considerable risk. Thus a rating of Aaa indicates that a bond is very strong, whereas a C rating indicates that a bond is very weak. There is no such thing as a bond that is riskless; safety is a matter of degree. Therefore, investment rating services rate bonds in relation to each other, some bonds being relatively safer than others.

The bond itself contains the name of the issuing corporation, the title of the bond, the denomination of the bond, the rate of interest to be paid on it, the bank where the interest is payable, the serial number of the bond, and signatures. Bond denominations may be for any amount, although $1,000 is a very common face value. The advantage of issuing bonds in small denominations is that the savings of the small investor can be tapped; the disadvantage of issuing such bonds is the heavy clerical costs incurred in servicing a large number of bonds.

The name of the person who owns a *registered bond* is on the records of the corporation; furthermore, the corporation or its paying agent will mail the interest checks to the bond owners whose names appear on its records. Hence, it is extremely important to have one's name on the trustee's or the corporation's records, if a registered bond is owned. Registered bonds must be properly endorsed before title can pass to a different bondholder.

The main feature of a *bearer bond* is that it has a set of interest coupons attached to it. The bondholder, prior to each interest date, cuts off a coupon and deposits it in his local bank. The bank in turn collects from the trustee. The holder of a bearer bond, in contrast with the holder of a registered bond, must take the initiative in collecting the interest. If a person does not send in his coupons on time, the interest can be collected later because the corporation sets aside a sum of cash with the trustee for the payment of all coupons. Usually neither the corporation nor the trustee keeps an official list of the holders of bearer bonds. All the corporation knows is the total amount of bonds outstanding. In this respect, bearer bonds resemble paper money, the federal government not knowing who owns the five dollar bills and the ten dollar bills, and so on, but knowing only the total amount of money outstanding. Title to bearer bonds passes upon delivery, thereby creating a problem of safekeeping. Because bearer bonds are so transferable, they may sell at a slight premium over registered bonds. Usually the bondholder can select either a registered bond or a bearer bond. Furthermore, the bondholder can change his bond from one to the other of these forms for a small fee.

THE TERMS OF THE INDENTURE

As already indicated, the indenture is a lengthy document that describes in detail the terms of the loan. An alternate document, the *deed of trust*, serves the same purpose as the indenture. The terms of a bond issue are given in one or the other of these. Some of the provisions that may appear in the indenture are the rate of interest to be paid on the bonds; the nature of the collateral pledged, if any; covenants on the part of the issuer to pay taxes on and keep repaired the firm's properties; provisions permitting the redemption of the bonds before maturity; provisions establishing a sinking fund; convertibility aspects, if any, of the bonds; and the maturity date of the bonds.

The *acceleration clause* is a provision in the indenture stating that the trustee or a certain percentage of the bondholders may declare the entire debt due and payable if the corporation defaults on the terms of the indenture. Thus the indenture for the Harrisburg Gas Company bonds provides that if the corporation defaults on its agreements, the trustee or the holders of 25 percent of the amount of bonds may accelerate the maturity date. The indenture lists a number of events that will be construed as default, some of which are: (1) failure to pay interest or principal on the bonds, (2) failure to make payments into a sinking fund, (3) breach of a covenant for 90 days after being warned in writing by the trustee, (4) filing of a bankruptcy petition or a petition to be reorganized, and (5) assignment of assets for the benefit of certain creditors. The indenture defines what is meant by an act of default, thereby clarifying the rights of the bondholders and the responsibilities of the trustee.

CRITERIA FOR EVALUATING A BOND ISSUE

1. What is the cost of the funds?
2. Must the firm make fixed periodic cash payments to bondholders?
3. How long does the firm have the use of the bondholders' money?
4. Do bondholders have collateral pledged for their benefit?
5. Do bondholders place restrictions on managerial freedom?
6. Do bondholders have voting rights?

An outstanding advantage of bonds issued in reasonable amounts is that under most money-market conditions they are a cheaper source of funds than either common stock or preferred stock.

In most cases corporations must offer investors a yield to maturity that is between 5 and 10 percent in order to make the bonds attractive. The lowest yield that a corporation can offer on its bonds is influenced by the rate of interest that investors can obtain on long-term government bonds. If government securities are yielding 5 percent, the rate offered by corporations on new issues will normally have to exceed this; otherwise bond buyers would place all their funds in government securities because government bonds carry no risk of loss of principal if they are held until maturity. As the risk of owning corporate bonds increases, investors expect a larger and larger spread between the prospective yield on the two classes of securities.

On the other hand, yields offered on new bond issues seldom go above 10 percent, for two reasons. If the offered rate of interest has to be this high, bonds become too expensive a method of raising funds, and there is the probability that the company is so weak that investors will not buy the bonds under any conditions (since they do not believe that the issuer will have sufficient earnings to pay the promised interest and return the principal). Table 20-1 shows the yield to maturity on several bond issues.

*TABLE 20-1
Yield to Maturity
on Several Bonds*

Security	Approximate Price	Yield to Maturity (percent)
Central of Georgia 4s	$ 750	5.67
General Acceptance 6¼s	1000	6.25
Hilton Hotels Corp. 6s	890	6.97

Included in the list of factors that make one security more risky than another are the size of the corporate income in relation to the interest requirements, the stability of the gross revenue, the nature of the industry, and the length of time the bonds are expected to be outstanding. This latter point deserves brief comment. The distant future has more uncertainties than the near future. Therefore, the longer the bonds have to run, the greater the risk to the investor. In order to be compensated for the risk, investors generally expect a higher return on bonds that will be outstanding longer.

In some periods bondholders demand a relatively high return for the use of their money. From the corporation's viewpoint, the best time to sell bonds is when bond yields are low. During periods of low interest rates, for each $100 borrowed a firm will have to offer relatively few dollars (such as $3 instead of $5) to make the new bonds attractive to investors. If a corporation decides to sell bonds when interest rates are higher than usual (but lower than stock yields), usually the firm can call the bonds when interest rates are lower and replace the high-cost money with low-cost money. If a firm borrows at 6 percent and three years later can borrow at 4 percent, the management may decide to prepay the 6 percent loan from the proceeds of a 4 percent loan. This is a common practice among large corporations, especially public utilities.

Most bonds can be called, but if money is extremely scarce, purchasers of new corporation bonds may insist that the debt be noncallable; that is, the company cannot pay off the bond issue before the scheduled maturity date. If this is the case, then the company becomes "locked in" with the contract in about the same manner as it would if common stock or noncallable preferred stock had been issued.

The general rule is that a corporation must make regular payments on its bond issue or face bankruptcy. Since the corporation agrees to make such fixed payments, it is taking some risk in that it may not be able to keep up the payments. This provision of bonds, however, is an advantage to the bondholders, who believe that it adds to the safety of their investment. For example, National Dairy Products Corporation makes an unqualified promise to pay interest annually on its bonds. On the other hand, this same firm makes no promise to pay any fixed return on its 14,112,213 shares of common stock outstanding. Because of the safety factor in bond issues, bondholders will accept a lower return than stockholders. This means that the corporation agrees to these fixed payments because such a promise lowers the cost of capital on a bond issue below that of a common or preferred stock issue.

Must the Firm Make Fixed Periodic Cash Payments to Bondholders?

General Rule

An *income bond* is a bond on which the interest is payable only if earned. This type of bond is an exception to the general rule that bond interest must be paid whether or not it is earned. Some income bonds outstanding are the Atchison, Topeka and Santa Fe Railway Company 4 percent adjustment bonds due 1995 and the Western Pacific Railway Company 4½ percent bonds due 2014. The interest on income bonds is usually cumulative for three or four years, whether or not profits are being earned. Income bonds, also known as adjustment bonds, often are issued during a corporate reorganization, a procedure to be studied later.

The Exception— Income Bonds

From the investor's viewpoint, income bonds resemble preferred stock in that the return on both of these securities depends on earnings. From the corporation's viewpoint, the most important difference between income bonds and preferred stock is that interest paid on income bonds is a deductible expense for federal income tax purposes, while dividends on preferred stock are not.

Until recently, as a general rule income bonds were issued only when a corporation failed and a court forced these bonds on bondholders. In the past, management seldom voluntarily issued these securities because investors held income bonds in such low esteem. That is, investors expected such a high rate of interest on these bonds that management avoided using them. Recently, however, several large companies have been calling in preferred stock and issuing income bonds in their place so as to take advantage of the possible tax savings. The Chicago, Milwaukee, St. Paul and Pacific Railroad, for example, called in its 5 percent preferred stock and replaced it with 5 percent income debentures.

How Long Does the Firm Have the Use of the Bondholders' Money?

Management prefers to have the use of bondholders' money indefinitely but with the right to repay the debt at its option. A firm's promise to establish a sinking fund and to repay the balance of the debt as of a certain date increases the risk of failure; officers agree to include these provisions in the indenture because such an action will lower the cost of capital of the bond issue.

Sinking Funds

A bond issue with a sinking fund requires that each year or each half year the corporation set aside a certain sum of money for the retirement of a portion of the debt. Instead of having all the debt come due at one time, the corporation makes provision for paying off some of the bondholders each year. The sinking fund may be designed to retire all the bonds or a large portion of them by maturity. Sinking funds, therefore, result in the gradual retirement of all or a part of the debt during the life of the bond issue.

Some bonds contain the sinking fund feature, but others lack it. Industrial bonds are likely to contain a provision for the establishment of a sinking fund. However, many outstanding bonds of public utilities and railroads do not. There is a trend toward the inclusion of the sinking fund feature in all bond issues, including industrials, public utilities, and railroads.

A sinking fund differs from voluntary redemption in that under the sinking fund arrangement the corporation is obligated to retire a portion of the bonds each period, whereas in a voluntary redemption the corporation reduces the amount of outstanding bonds at its option. The final result is the same under both procedures: the outstanding bonds of a given indenture are decreased. The voluntary redemption feature is included in the indenture for the benefit of the corporation, whereas the sinking fund provision is included in the indenture for the benefit of the bondholders.

Serial Bonds

A corporation, through the issuance of serial bonds, may have definite bonds come due each year or each half year. For example, the Montana-Dakota Utilities Company has an issue of serial bonds outstanding, $100,000 of these bonds maturing annually on April 1 until 1982. The effective rate of interest offered on the serial bonds that mature in the near future is lower than that offered on the longer-term serial bonds, because from the investor's viewpoint the risk increases as the time factor increases. This may lead to a relatively low interest rate for the entire issue.

From the corporation's viewpoint, the main reason for issuing serial bonds is that the funds may be attracted to the business at a lower average rate of interest than would be the case if all the bonds matured at one time. From the investor's viewpoint, the main reason for favoring serial bonds is that the bonds have a definite maturity—banks and life insurance companies, for example, favoring investments that will result in a return of cash on a specific date.

The pledge of collateral gives one group of creditors limited priority over another group. Hence, the group whose claims are so secured have a slightly safer investment than those whose claims are unsecured. In return for safety, this special group of creditors may be satisfied with a lower return. A firm, therefore, pledges collateral because of benefits to itself; that is, the cost of capital of the bond issue is reduced.

Do Bondholders Have Collateral Pledged For Their Benefit?

In addition to having priority over owners, some creditors may have priority over other creditors in claims against assets when a firm is liquidated. This priority may arise from:

1. Statutes
2. Agreements
   a. Subordination of some claims
   b. Pledge of collateral

Priority by statute means that the law gives certain groups, known as *preferred* creditors, automatic priority over all other creditors. An example of a preferred creditor is the United States government for unpaid taxes. Preferred creditors have an exceptionally strong position because they must be paid before other claimants.

Priority by agreement means that certain creditors have priority over others by virtue of provisions in the note, the loan agreement, or the indenture. First, one group of claimants may agree to *subordinate* its claims to those of other creditors. This means that the subordinated group will not be paid until those with superior claims have been paid in full.

Second, a firm may pledge collateral for the additional protection of certain creditors. Those creditors whose claims are supported by the pledge of collateral have priority over creditors of unsecured claims to the extent of the pledged collateral (except that preferred creditors have priority over all creditors). The kinds of property offered as collateral for debt are real property and personal property. *Real property* consists of immovable items of value such as land and buildings; the document that contains the agreement to pledge real property is the *mortgage*. Thus the long-term debt of the Texas Electric Service Company is accompanied by a mortgage that pledges land and buildings as collateral. Real property is more often pledged for long- and intermediate-term credit than for short-term credit. *Personal property* consists of movable items of wealth, such as stocks, bonds, delivery equipment, passenger cars, and freight cars; the document that contains the pledge of personal property is often called the *chattel mortgage*. Personal property is more often pledged for short- and intermediate-term credit than for long-term credit. In some cases, the lender will insist that the borrower pledge collateral; in other cases, the borrower will volunteer to pledge collateral, thereby hoping to obtain a lower rate of interest or other advantageous terms.

A mortgage bond is a debt instrument that is accompanied by the pledge of property by the issuing corporation. The collateral pledged is usually land and

Mortgage Bonds

buildings, although other assets may also be pledged. The mortgage, which gives the pledge, is filed in the county courthouse so that the public will be put on notice that selected assets of a particular corporation have been pledged for the payment of certain debts. If only one specific asset is pledged as collateral for the loan, the mortgage is sometimes said to be a *specific mortgage*; if the mortgage covers a number of assets it is called a *blanket or general mortgage*. The exact legal nature of the pledge varies from state to state.

As a practical matter, holders of corporation bonds rarely take the drastic step of seizing and selling pledged property at public auction even when the corporation defaults on its interest or principal payments. Bondholders hesitate to exercise their legal right to sell the pledged property because the proceeds from the public sale may be very small, particularly if the property is of a specialized nature or if it is sold in a period of depressed prices. When bondholders find themselves in the predicament of owning bonds in a corporation that is not meeting its obligations, they may, and often do, decide that they will eventually get more money if they reorganize the company. In other words, bondholders may decide that the value of their pledged assets in a going concern would be greater than their value at an auction sale. Bondholders, acting in self-interest, will elect to take the alternative that will minimize their losses, and this alternative is often an attempt to rehabilitate the corporation rather than liquidate it. Besides, courts will not permit the assets of railroads and public utilities to be seized by creditors; they will insist on reorganization of these public service corporations. Yet, we must not underrate the significance of the pledge of real estate as collateral for bond issues even though bondholders may not always be able or willing to exercise their legal right to seize pledged collateral.

Priority of Holders of Mortgage Bonds over Each Other

A *lien* is a claim that one party has on the assets of another party. In corporation finance, holders of secured bonds have a lien against certain assets when the corporation specifically pledges these assets as collateral for the loan. Furthermore, there are different degrees of claims on pledged property. Thus first-mortgage bondholders have a first lien on pledged property, second-mortgage bondholders have a secondary claim on the same property, and a third-mortgage bond issue has a third-ranking lien on this same property. For example, a $100,000 building might be used as collateral for three different bond issues, each having a different lien on the pledged property:

$40,000 first-mortgage bonds
 25,000 second-mortgage bonds
 10,000 third-mortgage bonds

If this corporation defaults on the interest or principal of all issues, any of the three groups theoretically could seize the building and sell it at public auction in the lien theory states. If the building sold for $65,000, the first-mortgage bondholders would be paid in full; then the second-mortgage bondholders would be paid in full; but nothing would be left for the third-mortgage bondholders. However, they would still have a general claim against the corporation for the amount due them. Assume that the pledged building sold for only $30,000. Under these circumstances, the first-mortgage bondholders would get the entire $30,000, the second- and third-mortgage bondholders receiving nothing from this transaction. At this point the first-, second-, and third-mortgage bondholders would have a combined unpaid claim of $45,000 against the corporation, although this claim does not have any precedence over any other group of creditors of unsecured claims. The rule is that holders of mortgage bonds become creditors of unsecured claims for the balance of their claim.

Under the open mortgage, the corporation can issue additional bonds as the need arises, there being no upper limit to the amount of bonds of a given lien that can be issued; bonds are issued in "series" from time to time. For example, the Public Service Company of Oklahoma has the following series bonds outstanding: *Series Bonds*

> First-mortgage bonds:
> Series B due February 1, 1978 $10,000,000
> Series C due April 1, 1981   10,000,000

Each of these bonds is a first-mortgage bond, because it is necessary to have all bonds issued under the same indenture equal in rank. None of the bonds would have precedence over the others in liquidation or reorganization even though they were not issued at the same time. Each set of series bonds may carry a different interest rate. *Series bonds*, then, are bonds issued under the same indenture but at different times, each series having the same lien as all the other series, but perhaps differing in other provisions such as the interest rate, the sinking fund, and the call features. About the only limitation imposed on the directors when drafting the terms of series bonds is that a new issue of series bonds cannot mature ahead of an issue already outstanding. Series bonds are widely used by public utilities where it is necessary to have available a means for financing the acquisition of additional facilities to meet the secular increase in demand for service.

The indenture may place certain checks on the issuance of bonds in series, the checks being intended to prevent the overissuance of bonds to the detriment of existing bondholders. Their position would be jeopardized if the corporation issued bonds to such an extent that interest charges or principal payments would be difficult to meet. Before a firm can sell additional series bonds, the indenture may force the firm to meet these financial requirements: EBIT must be two or three times greater than interest requirements; the current ratio must be at least 2; and the additional bonds may not be issued for more than 50 percent of the value of the property being acquired.

Leasehold bonds are credit instruments secured by pledging a building on leased ground. Since the pledged real estate has been erected on leased land, the land is not part of the pledge. Because the lessor (owner of the land) has first claim on *Leasehold Bonds* the building if the ground rent is not paid, the position of holders of leasehold bonds is not as strong as that of holders of first-mortgage bonds.

Collateral
Trust Bonds
Collateral trust bonds, also called *collateral trust notes*, are bonds for which other securities have been pledged as collateral. The issuing corporation pledges stocks and bonds instead of real estate. The securities pledged are usually those of a company other than the issuer of the collateral trust bonds, although a corporation may pledge its own securities for a bond issue. In addition to the pledge of stocks and bonds, collateral trust bonds occasionally have other intangibles pledged as collateral for them, such as a patent. Even though physical custody of the securities is transferred to a trustee, the pledger, as long as it conforms with all the terms of the indenture, is entitled to all voting rights of the pledged collateral and also to all income on the securities so pledged. Holding companies have been the chief users of collateral trust bonds.

Debenture Bonds
A *debenture*, sometimes called a plain bond, has no specific pledge of property as collateral for the loan. A debenture bond issue represents an unsecured loan. In this type of bond, as in a mortgage bond and a collateral trust bond, the corporation promises to pay interest on specified dates and to repay the principal at a specified time.

Recently the very strong corporations have been issuing debenture bonds to raise cash. Companies that have high earning power can issue these bonds at a low rate of interest because there is no doubt in the purchaser's mind concerning the ability of the corporation to meet its obligations. Some well-known companies that have issued debenture bonds at low rates of interest are AT&T and Firestone Tire and Rubber Company. From a corporation's viewpoint, there is no reason to pledge collateral for a bond issue if investors are willing to purchase the securities without such a pledge.

In recent years, a number of corporations have been issuing *subordinated debentures*, that is, bonds which will not be paid until those with superior claims have been paid. The indenture states the specific groups that rank ahead of the holders of subordinated debt. Bondholders purchase these instruments because the interest that can be earned on them is usually higher than that on a first-mortgage bond issued by a company of comparable strength. If a strong corporation found that it could issue preferred stock and subordinated debentures by offering the same return, it might choose to issue the subordinated bonds because of the federal income tax advantage.

Corporations also favor subordinated debentures because their issuance does not hinder future financing. When money is borrowed later, those who advance the funds can be given a superior rank. When a firm is in a position to offer creditors a superior rank, funds can be attracted at relatively low rates of interest.

Do Bondholders
Place Restrictions
On Managerial Freedom?
Theoretically, a firm prefers not to have to agree to restrictive provisions (agreements whereby the management limits its freedom of action). Such restrictions,

however, are an advantage to bondholders because this group believes that the safety of their investment is thereby increased. Because restrictions on management increase the safety of the bond issue, bondholders may accept a lower rate of return than they would accept without such provisions.

Bonds are similar to preferred stock, which also limits managerial freedom. Typical major restrictions are as follows: dividends cannot be paid on the common stock or the preferred stock unless designated financial ratios are above minimums stated in the indenture; the company cannot purchase its own stock unless certain financial ratios are above a specified minimum; the company cannot issue additional bonds unless a certain percentage of the bondholders approve; and the company cannot merge or otherwise combine unless a certain percentage of the bondholders approve. If the bonds are callable, the company can, of course, extinguish the debt if its terms prove to be too onerous.

As already indicated, bondholders are viewed as outsiders, and they do not have any inherent right to participate in the voting process. Therefore, when a corporation sells bonds, there is no direct danger of the common stockholders losing their control of the firm. On this score, bonds have an advantage over additional common stock.

Do Bondholders Have Voting Rights?

A recent development in financial management is the use of *tax-exempt pollution abatement revenue bonds.* These bonds provide a roundabout but low-cost method for corporations to finance the acquisition of equipment that alleviates pollution.

TAX-EXEMPT POLLUTION ABATEMENT REVENUE BONDS

The bonds are not issued by a corporation; instead they are issued by a specially created regional or local political entity, under the rules and regulations promulgated by a specific state. The special political units have the power to engage in activities that lure new industries into the area and induce industries to stay in the area. To accomplish these ends, the political units have the power to assist local companies in obtaining low-cost financing, by issuing revenue bonds; the savings in interest is passed on to companies that obtain the use of this money.

Viewpoint of the Political Unit

A revenue bond is one on which the interest and principal is payable only from a specified source—as will be illustrated. The taxing power of the sponsoring local unit (county or municipality) is not pledged for the bond issue. For example, the County Court of Tyler, West Virginia, issued $7,500,000 of 5.2 percent industrial development revenue bonds, due in 1998. The proceeds were used to buy antipollution equipment, which it immediately rented to Union Carbide Corporation. The issuer expected the cash from the rentals to be sufficient to pay interest and principal on the bonds and to cover a small amount of miscellaneous operating expenses. The prospectus for the bond issue stated that the bonds "were not a charge against the general credit or taxing power of the issuing county."

In addition to promising to pay rent for the use of the equipment, owned by the local or regional political unit, the local company (lessee) may guarantee the interest and principal on the bonds. This supplemental feature adds to the strength of the bond issue, and it eliminates any temptation on the part of the benefiting corporation to stop paying the rent and abandon the equipment.

Generally, *tax-exempt pollution abatement revenue bonds* have these characteristics: they are serial bonds; they have a minimum denomination of $5,000; they are always tax-free (that is, the holder need not pay any federal income tax on the interest collected); and they are purchased mainly by commercial banks and life insurance companies.

The main benefits to the citizens of an area that issues these bonds are: the quality of the regional environment may be improved; industry may be persuaded not to close down a plant that is polluting the area; and the whole process is completed without any cost to the taxpayers in the immediate area.

Viewpoint of the Benefiting Corporation

In most cases the benefiting local company pays low rent for the use of the equipment owned by the local or regional political entity. For example, International Paper Company had to acquire special equipment for its plant in Mobile, Alabama, in order to keep operating; the equipment consisted of new boilers that would throw off less fumes and odors. To discourage International Paper Company from closing the plant to avoid the cost of the new equipment, businessmen in the area offered the paper company a plan for low-cost financing of it. The businessmen formed the Industrial Development Board of the City of Mobile. This nonprofit corporation sold $8,500,000 of 5.81 percent serial bonds. The proceeds were used to buy the boilers needed by the paper company. Simultaneously, International Paper Company agreed to pay rent for the use of the equipment. The rentals were high enough to service the debt obligation and to meet a small amount of overhead. To further strengthen the agreement, International Paper Company also unconditionally guaranteed the interest and principal on the debt issued by the Industrial Development Board of the City of Mobile.

International Paper Company, however, had another alternative; it could have floated its own bond issue, purchased the equipment, and repaid the interest and principal. If it had floated its own bond issue, the net interest cost would have been 7.52 percent. But by having the bonds floated by the Industrial Development Board of the City of Mobile, the net interest cost (upon converting the annual rentals to a percentage interest cost) was 5.81 percent. Thus International Paper Company saved $1.8 million over the life of the bond issue. This is a significant savings and comes about because of the ability of local governmental agencies to issue bonds at a lower rate of interest than profit-seeking corporations; this can be done because the interest on the bonds is tax-free. Because of this tax-free status, investors will accept a low rate of interest; and the savings in interest is passed on to the management of the local plant in the form of lower rents charged for the use of the facilities.

In addition to the lease arrangement, other plans are possible. For example, Gulf Oil Corporation needed $25 million to obtain equipment that would decrease the pollution in the Philadelphia area. The Philadelphia Authority for Industrial Development, an agency of the city of Philadelphia, sold $25 million of tax-free bonds and used the proceeds to buy the equipment. The unique feature of this transaction is that Gulf Oil Corporation then purchased the antipollution facilities from the Philadelphia Authority and could claim depreciation on the equipment (for tax purposes). In this transaction, the oil company did not pay annual rentals. The bonds floated by the Philadelphia Authority for Industrial Development were issued at a cost of 5.24 percent; if the oil company itself had floated the bond issue, the interest cost could have been 7.36 percent. Over the life of the issue, the savings to Gulf Oil Corporation is 9.8 million.

In summary, a company with a plant in a particular area can reduce the net interest cost of financing a project if it has the regional or local government unit issue the bonds.

Viewpoint of the Investor

The buyers of tax-exempt pollution abatement revenue bonds obtain a reasonable yield that is entirely tax-free. Furthermore, these investors believe the bonds to be safe for the following reasons: first, the rents are expected to be adequate to cover interest and principal payments on the bond issue; second, the benefiting local company may guarantee the interest and principal on the debt; third, in some cases the revenue bonds may be accompanied by a first mortgage on the facilities. An example of an issue with a high rating is the one issued by the City of Salem, Illinois; this issue, used to finance facilities for Beatrice Foods Company, received a Moody rating of "A."

HIGHLIGHTS OF THIS CHAPTER

Advantages of bond financing, from the management point of view, are these: bonds are often a cheap source of funds, and they do not carry voting rights. Disadvantages are these: bonds carry a fixed interest charge, they often have a sinking fund, and they often contain restrictions on management.

When the corporation repays the debt at maturity, no special problems arise. The bondholders receive the sums due them, and the terms of the loan are no longer binding on either the corporation or the bondholders. Generally, the corporation deposits the required cash with a trustee, who takes care of the mechanics of paying the bondholders.

If there is a sinking fund for the bonds, the corporation is required to set aside a sum of money each year and use this money to acquire bonds. The acquired bonds are usually canceled, although some indentures provide that these bonds shall be kept alive. Sinking funds are especially prevalent in industrials, but there is a growing tendency to have the bonds of public utilities and rails accompanied by a sinking fund.

Serial bonds are bonds which have spaced maturities; that is, a certain portion of the debt comes due each year or half year.

20-1. Explain the meaning of the following terms:
point in the corporation bond market
bond rating
trustee
preferred creditor
real property
personal property
lien
leasehold bond
registered bond
indenture
yield to maturity
serial bond
series bond
mortgage bond
collateral trust bond

20-2. From the management viewpoint, what are the main advantages and disadvantages of long-term debt (bonds) as a source of funds?

20-3. What are the two main promises made by an issuer of corporate bonds?

20-4. Why do some corporations secure their bonds with a pledge of collateral?

20-5. Answer these questions: (a) What are two examples of *covenants* found in the indenture? (b) What is the acceleration clause? (c) Is it legal for the indenture to place limitations on the amount of cash dividends that can be paid?

20-6. Metropolitan Edison Company issued 8 1/8 percent debentures, series due in 1997 at 101.342 percent. Answer these questions: (a) How much in dollars would an investor pay for one of these $1,000 par-value bonds? (b) Is the investors' yield to maturity greater or less than 8 1/8 percent? (c) What is the nature of a debenture bond? (d) Suggest several reasons why this firm elected to pay 8 1/8 percent, rather than float an issue of common stock.

Answers to some of the problems appear at the end of this section. *For each problem, show how you obtained the answer.*

20-1. The 5 percent bonds of Company D are selling in the market at $960. If the bonds have 10 years to run until maturity, what is the yield on them after taking into account premium or discount?

20-2. The 6 percent bonds of Company K are selling in the market at $1,020. If the bonds have 20 years to run until maturity, what is the yield on them after taking into consideration premium or discount?

20-3. Company L, a growth company, is in need of $40,000 for permanent expansion; the firm believes that it can earn 25 percent (before interest and taxes) on the additional assets to be purchased with the money. Below is the firm's balance sheet before financing:

Current assets	$100,000	Current liabilities	$ 50,000
Fixed assets	100,000	$5 par-value common	100,000
		Retained profits	50,000
Total	$200,000	Total	$200,000

Before financing, the firm's EBIT were $50,000; the company is in the 50 percent tax bracket; the common stock is currently selling at $25 (a price-earnings ratio of 20). The firm is wondering whether to sell additional common stock or a 5 percent bond issue (ignore investment banking fees in this problem.) (a) Compare the merits of bond financing with stock financing for this firm. (b) What would be the *pro forma* earnings per share under each alternative? (c) Is the price-earnings ratio likely to fall as a result of the issuance of bonds (in this problem)? (d) Since the firm believes it has numerous profitable outlets for the funds, it would like to release as little cash as possible to the new stockholders or the bondholders; assuming that the bonds would not have a sinking fund and the current dividend rate of 50 cents a share would continue indefinitely, which alternative would result in the least cash outflow over the next five years? Use the following format in assembling data for this problem:

Pro Forma Data

	Prefinancing Data	Common Issued	5 Percent Bonds Issued
EBIT	$50,000	$60,000	$60,000
Interest on bonds	0	–	–
Taxable income	$50,000	–	–
Tax (50%)	$25,000	–	–
Net profit after taxes	$25,000	–	–
Shares of common outstanding	20,000	–	–
Earnings per share	$1.25	–	–
Dividends per share	$0.50	–	–

20-4. A certain company issued serial bonds, due between 1970 and 1980. The portion due in 1975 yielded the investor 6 percent. What is the most likely yield on the part of the debt maturing in 1978: (a) 2 percent, (b) 3 percent, (c) 4 percent, (d) 6.19 percent, (e) 2.25 percent, or (f) 5 percent.

20-5. The 5½ percent first mortgage bonds of Company K are selling at $665; the 4½ percent first mortgage bonds of Company B are selling at $975. Indicate a number of factors that might explain the wide divergence in the price of these two bonds.

Answers: 20-1, 5.51 percent; 20-2, 5.84 percent; 20-4, d.

21 The Role of Convertibles and Warrants

In order to make stocks and bonds more attractive to investors, two supplementary inducements may be offered. First, the issuer may provide that the bonds and preferred shares be exchangeable (convertible) into common stock, at the option of the investor. Second, the firm may issue warrants which accompany bonds, preferred stock, or common stock.

The above two supplementary features have one basic similarity. Both are devices for permitting the investor to benefit from an increase in the market price of the common stock. More specifically, convertible securities and warrants are similar in that they represent an option to buy a given amount of stock at a specified price; this option will be of value if there are good prospects that the market price of the common has exceeded or will exceed the specified price.

The following will be discussed in this chapter:

1. Convertible bonds
2. Convertible preferred stock
3. Warrants

Since convertible securities and warrants are being issued at an increasing rate, these instruments will be analyzed from both the issuer's viewpoint and the investor's viewpoint.

THE ROLE OF
CONVERTIBLE BONDS

A *convertible bond* is one that is exchangeable into other securities at the option of the bondholder. Convertible bonds are virtually always exchangeable into common stock, although on rare occasions a convertible bond is exchangeable into preferred stock. The bondholder will usually convert when he sees a chance to increase his economic worth by making the switch. Some bonds contain the conversion privilege while others lack this feature.

When a corporation includes the conversion privilege in the indenture, something extra has been added to the bond issue. Not only is the bondholder given a bond with all its promises; in addition, he can exchange his instrument for shares of stock if he cares to do so. This extra feature makes bonds more attractive to investors and thus makes it possible to issue the securities on more advantageous terms. Therefore, the corporation also benefits by including the conversion feature in the bond, even though it appears as if this feature were added only for the benefit of investors.

From the bondholder's viewpoint, the conversion privilege gives him an opportunity to benefit from any future increase in the earning power of the corporation. Under this arrangement, not only does the bondholder have the right to receive fixed interest payments but, in addition, he is given an opportunity to become a stockholder instead of a bondholder if he thinks this course of action is desirable. Convertible bonds are especially popular when inflation is expected. If disastrous inflation should strike the economy, bondholders could exchange their fixed interest-bearing investments for stocks, which, being ownership documents, tend to rise with the price level. Bonds are also likely to contain the conversion privilege if issued during a period of rising stock market prices. The conversion feature, then, gives the bondholder an opportunity to stay a creditor and receive a fixed return or to change his mind and become a stockholder.

When the corporation includes the conversion feature in its indenture, it must have available sufficient unissued shares to accommodate all bondholders who elect to convert.

If the common stockholders have the preemptive right, the corporation will have to give them first choice on the purchase of newly issued convertible bonds; even if the preemptive right does not exist, the management of the firm may voluntarily give them first choice.

Convertible bonds are seldom backed by the pledge of collateral; they are usually in debenture form, and they are often subordinated to other forms of debt.

After a bondholder converts, he cannot reverse the process and reobtain the bonds he surrendered when he converted.

Convertible bond financing is used by both large and small corporations and by both strong and weak ones.

The *conversion ratio* is the number of shares for which a $1,000 par-value bond may be exchanged; the *conversion price* is the amount of face value of a bond that must be surrendered for one share of common stock. An alternate way to state this is that the conversion price is the price at which a convertible bondholder may buy shares from the company and that he pays this price not with his cash but with the bond he holds. Furthermore, the corporation will not accept less than $1,000 face value of bonds in any single transaction. The 4½ percent Ford Motor Credit Company bonds, due in 1996, are convertible into shares of the parent firm (the Ford Motor Company). The conversion ratio is 12.80; the conversion price is $78.125. This means that a bondholder who converts will receive 12.80 shares of common stock of the parent company;

Basic Concepts

Conversion Ratio and Conversion Price

alternately stated, he may buy shares from the parent company at $78.125 and pay for them by surrendering his bond. Two formulas are:

$$\text{Conversion price} = \frac{\$1,000}{\text{Conversion ratio}}$$

$$\text{Conversion ratio} = \frac{\$1,000}{\text{Conversion price}}$$

The original conversion ratio and conversion price are stated in the indenture and on the bond certificate; they are alternate methods of expressing the basic provisions of a convertible bond issue.

Like most convertible bond issues, the Ford Motor Credit Company indenture provides that upon conversion no fractional shares of common stock shall be issued; instead, Ford Motor Company (the parent organization) will pay the bondholder cash in lieu of fractional shares.

The conversion ratio and the conversion price may change under conditions specified in the indenture and on the bond certificate. On the one hand, the conversion ratio may decrease with the passage of time. For example, a $1,000 face value bond might have a conversion ratio of 50 for the first five years, 48 for the second five years, and 47 thereafter. As the conversion ratio declines, the conversion price increases. On the other hand, the indenture may provide for an increase in the conversion ratio, such as when there is a stock split, a stock dividend, or the sale by the company of additional common stock below the conversion price. Thus, if there is a two for one stock split, the conversion ratio would be doubled and the conversion price cut in half. Similar adjustments are made for stock dividends. When adjustments must be made in the conversion ratio and the conversion price for stock splits, stock dividends, and other designated changes in the capital structure, the indenture is said to contain an *anti-dilution* clause.

At the time the bonds are issued, the *conversion price* is 5 to 20 percent above the market price per share of the common stock. In the case of the Ford Motor Credit Company, at the time the securities were issued the conversion price was $78.125, while the market price of the underlying common was $68. Hence, the new bondholder would not convert immediately (since he would have to pay the company $78.125 for shares that could have been purchased in the open market for $68). But this investor, looking ahead, might believe that over the next several years the market price of the common might rise to a high level, such as $85 or $90. If these are his beliefs, then the conversion feature would have a definite value to him, because he or his assignees could buy from the parent company shares that have a market value of $85 or $90 for only $78.125. To conclude, the conversion price is the option price at which the bondholder may buy shares from the company. Since at the time the convertible bonds are issued the option price is above the market price per share of common stock, the bondholder must wait for a substantial increase in the market price of the common to obtain a substantial financial gain.

Another way to express the above interrelationships is to view the matter from the side of a bondholder who owns a $1,000 face value bond, currently selling at $1,005. Assume that the conversion price is $25, the conversion ratio is 40, and the current market price of the common stock is $20. The bondholder will not convert at this time, because he would be giving up a bond worth $1,005 for shares with an aggregate market value of $800 (40 X $20). But if the market price per share of the common goes higher than $25, such as to $30, the value of the bond will rise to at least $1,200. Thus, at this point, the holder of the convertible bond may find it desirable to convert, because he will receive shares with an aggregate market value of $1,200 (40 X $30) upon surrendering his bond. The shares can be held for expected dividend payments or sold at a gross profit of $200. If the bondholder decides to realize on the $200 profit, he will sell his bond directly in the market at $1,200.

The *conversion value* of a bond is the aggregate current market value of the total *Conversion Value* shares into which a $1,000 face value bond can be converted; it is determined by *and Conversion* multiplying the conversion ratio by the current market price per share of the *Premium* common stock. To phrase it another way, the conversion value is the aggregate market value of all the common stock that the bondholder will receive if he converts his bond. If a $1,000 face value bond is covertible into 40 shares of common stock, which is selling at $24 per share, the conversion value is $960 (40 X $24). Observe that the *conversion value* is different from the *conversion price*. In the above example, the conversion price is $25 ($1,000 ÷ 40), but the conversion value is $960. Conversion value changes daily and is affected by changes in the current market price of the common; conversion price changes only under conditions stated in the indenture.

The market value of a $1,000 face value bond frequently exceeds its conversion value; this excess is called the *conversion premium*. Assume that an outstanding $1,000 face value bond is convertible into 40 shares of common stock, that the market price of the common is $27, and that the current market value of the bond is $1,125. The conversion value of the bond is $1,080 (40 X $27); the conversion premium is $45 ($1,125 − $1,080). The formula is:

Conversion premium = Current market value of bond − Conversion value of bond

The conversion premium, therefore, is the amount by which the market value of a bond exceeds its conversion value.

Even at the time of issuance, the selling price of the bond (market price) is above the conversion value.

An investor is willing to pay a premium over conversion value because he believes that the underlying common will increase even further in price; he becomes leery of the worth of the premium as the market price of the bond goes far above its face value and far above its call price.

The *investment value* of a convertible bond is the estimated price at which the *Investment Value* bond would sell if it were not convertible. Hence, the investment value of a *and Premium over* $1,000 face value bond is the price at which a nonconvertible bond (of the same *Investment Value* company) would sell in the open market. There is no way for an individual investor to determine investment value; he must rely on the financial advisory services to estimate this figure. Financial advisory services periodically release their opinion on the investment value of a specific convertible bond; this value varies somewhat from week to week because national interest rates change and because future prospects of the issuer change. The investment advisory services arrive at investment value by estimating the price at which the bond would have to sell to provide a yield to maturity equal to that on a straight bond of equivalent quality and maturity. The market price of a convertible bond is unlikely to fall below the price of nonconvertible bonds of the same quality and maturity. *The significance of investment value, therefore, is that it gives an estimate, as of a particular time, of the lowest value to which a particular convertible bond could fall.*

The market value of a convertible bond frequently exceeds its investment value; this excess is called the *premium over investment value*. The formula is:

Premium over investment value = Market price of bond
— Investment value of bond

A financial service reported that the bonds of the Georgia Pacific Corporation had a market value of $942.50, an investment value of $770.00, and a premium over investment value of $172.50. The significance of the premium over investment value is that it gives the investor an estimate of the maximum amount that his bond could decline; that is, it places a tentative upper limit on his losses. In the Georgia Pacific Corporation situation the investor's risk is limited because his bond would not be expected to decline below $770. Stating the matter differently, the maximum loss he could incur is $172.50, the amount of the premium over investment value. If this investor had purchased $942.50 of common stock in the Georgia Pacific Corporation, there would be no assurance that if the firm suffered a financial setback, his loss would be limited to $172.50. The premium over investment value, therefore, measures the degree of price risk— that is, the amount by which a bond might decline in price under adverse conditions. It is measured by the difference between the current market price of the bond and its investment value. To recapitulate, the premium over investment value is an alternate method of expressing the component of the market price of the bond that is subject to the risk of decline in the price of the associated common stock; it is the amount by which the market price of the bond could drop before reaching its intrinsic value; it gives the investor an estimate of the maximum loss he might incur if he purchased a specific convertible bond.

Although the convertible bond is not expected to fall below its investment value at any point, investment value is not a fixed amount; therefore the bondholder cannot be assured that his bond will not decline below the investment value as of the time he purchased it.

Table 21-1 reviews several terms discussed in the preceding sections.

A.	Market price of bond	$803.80	
B.	Market price per share of common	$ 27.00	
C.	Conversion ratio (shares)	20.00	
D.	Conversion price	$ 50.00	
E.	Conversion value (C × B)	$540.00	
F.	Premium over conversion value (percent) (A − E) ÷ E	49.00	
G.	Investment value ($)	$640.00	
H.	Price risk (percent) (A − G) ÷ A*	20.00	

TABLE 21-1
Witco Chemical
4½ percent
Convertible Bonds,
Due in 1993

*Price risk is the percentage by which a bond could decline in market value before it reaches its investment value.

Because of the attractiveness of the conversion feature to investors, the interest rate that an issuer has to pay on a convertible issue is lower than it would have to pay on a nonconvertible bond. The Ford Motor Credit Company simultaneously sold two bond issues at the face value of $1,000 per bond. One was a nonconvertible issue on which the company had to pay 7½ percent interest; the other was a convertible subordinated issue on which the firm had to pay only 4½ percent interest. An investor is willing to accept a relatively low yield to maturity on a covertible bond because he believes that this kind of bond offers a medium for reasonable price appreciation. From the issuer's viewpoint, the lower the offering yield, the less cash the firm will have to use to service the debt. This benefits the holders of common shares because there is more cash available for dividends, either presently or eventually.

Four Reasons for Issuing Convertible Bonds

The company might be able to float a new issue with fewer indenture-imposed restrictions on management.

This may be the only form of financing that will bring funds to the company.

Most important, convertible bonds are a method of selling common stock between 5 and 20 percent above its current market price (provided matters work out as the company would like them to). This point will be discussed further.

In one sense, the issuance of convertible bonds is a deferred method of issuing stock. Assume that a company needs to raise $900,000 in cash and that the following data pertain to the securities of the corporation:

1. The common stock of the company is selling at $90.
2. It is expected that the price of the common will increase to $110 in the next few years.
3. The company can issue bonds at a reasonable rate of interest and at par. These bonds, if issued, would be convertible; the conversion rate would be 10 shares of common stock for each $1,000 of bonds.
4. These bonds are callable at 105 percent.

Would it be better to raise the $900,000 from the sale of stocks or from the sale of convertible bonds?

Although the answer might depend on factors not given above, we will conclude that it would be advantageous (to the common stockholders) to have the corporation issue bonds. The reason for this decision will be demonstrated by comparing the alternatives of a stock issue versus a bond issue. If the money were raised from a stock issue, it would be necessary to issue 10,000 shares of common stock to raise $900,000, assuming that the current market price of the common was $90. As an alternative, the company could raise the money by selling bonds. After the bonds are issued, assume that the market price of the common increases to $110. With the market price of the common at $110, the value of the bonds is $1,100 per $1,000 face value. At this stage, the corporation could call the bonds at 105 percent. However, prior to the redemption, the bondholders would be given an opportunity to convert. It would be in the self-interest of the bondholders to convert, because by converting they could receive common stock with a market value of $1,100, whereas if they allowed their bonds to be called, they would receive only $1,050 per $1,000 of bonds. Assuming that all the bondholders convert, the company would issue 9,000 shares. However, if the company had issued stock in the first place, it would have been necessary to issue 10,000 shares to raise the money. Therefore, the common stockholders have benefited, because the dividends and earnings per share are spread over 1,000 fewer shares.

After a bondholder converts his bond into common stock, the corporation's total amount of securities outstanding does not change. But the composition of the capital structure is altered as the amount of bonds outstanding decreases while the amount of common stock outstanding increases. In effect, the corporation has paid off part of the debt in shares of stock. This change in the composition of the capital structure is important, because interest payments are thereby decreased.

Policy Decisions

Assuming that high-ranking officers of the firm decide to proceed with selling a convertible bond issue, the next step is to make two interrelated and simultaneous decisions. First, the conversion price and conversion ratio must be determined; second, the offering yield must be established.

Specifying the Conversion Price and the Conversion Ratio

The conversion price (as already noted) is set at approximately 5 to 20 percent above the current market price of the common stock. Thus, if the market price of the common is $32, the conversion price might be $40. Since this is the case, the bondholder would not convert immediately. If the conversion price is not too far above the market price of the common, this is an advantage to the bondholder but a disadvantage to the issuer. The advantage to the bondholder is that he need not wait as long for the market value of the common to rise above the conversion price and, furthermore, when he does convert, he will receive relatively more shares of common stock. The disadvantage to the issuer is that when the bonds are converted, the corporation must issue a relatively larger number of shares, thus causing more dilution in earnings and dividends per share. The converse holds true if the conversion price is comparatively high at the time the bonds are issued. Nonetheless, the terms of the conversion are only one aspect of the ultimate cost to the issuer; the other and equally important aspect of the transaction is the rate of return the firm offers on these securities.

Simultaneously with the task of fixing the conversion ratio and the conversion price is the matter of establishing the yield on the bonds—at the time of their issuance. Because a bondholder is often a highly sophisticated investor, he will insist on a high yield to maturity if the conversion price is comparatively high in relation to the market price per share of the common stock. If the conversion price is high, the bondholder wants a good current income while he is waiting for the market price of the common to exceed the conversion price.

The issuer would like to sell convertible bonds with a low yield to maturity and a high conversion price, while the investor would like to buy a newly issued bond with a high yield to maturity and a comparatively low conversion price.

As the corporation and the investor bargain with each other over the terms of the new bond issue, each side must compromise; if the issuer insists on a relatively high conversion price, it will have to offer a high yield to maturity, such as 8 percent; but if the issuer is satisfied with a moderately high conversion price, the investor will accept a moderate return, such as 5 percent.

A corporation may eliminate a bond issue by redeeming it. When convertible bonds are redeemed, the investor is given a choice between receiving the redemption price in cash or converting his bond into common shares; he is given about 60 days in which to make up his mind. If the conversion value of the $1,000 face value is sufficiently above the redemption price, the firm need not plan on paying off the bonds in cash; instead, it can plan on paying off the bondholders with shares of common stock. In this situation, the corporation is said to "force" conversion, because the bondholder will find it to his advantage to convert rather than to receive the call price in cash.

The 4½ percent convertible subordinated debenture bonds of McDonald's Corporation (the hamburger specialist) due in 1996, had a conversion price of $70.50 and thus a conversion ratio of 14.1844 shares per $1,000 face value of bonds. Several years after the issuance of the bonds, the market price per share of the common stock was $94. Based on this information, the conversion value per bond was $1,333.33. McDonald's Corporation called the bonds at the redemption price of $1,045. It was to the bondholder's advantage to convert and receive common shares, rather than to receive cash. If he converted, he would receive $1,333.33 in value: if he mailed in his bond for redemption, he would receive only $1,045 in cash. McDonald's Corporation advertised in the major newspapers, urging all holders of these bonds to convert rather than redeem. In this and similar situations, the firm redeeming the bonds hopes that it will not be called on to pay out a large sum of cash; the issuer hopes that nearly all the bonds will be converted rather than redeemed. Only a few careless bondholders of McDonald's Corporation overlooked the announcement of redemption; they received only $1,045 for their bonds.

If, during the life of the issue, the common stock has no prospects of rising above the conversion price, the bond issue is said to be *overhanging*, a term designating the situation where the firm cannot force conversion through redemption. Of course, the issuer could call the bonds and pay the bondholders in cash, obtaining the funds through the flotation of another stock or bond issue. But in many cases corporations prefer not to follow this course of action because of the expense in floating a new issue of securities. Nevertheless, if the outstanding issue has onerous terms in the indenture, the corporation may decide to go ahead with redeeming the bonds and paying off the bondholders in cash.

Holding Strategies The owner of a convertible bond may select from several holding period strategies; the length of time he actually keeps the bond is influenced strongly by whether the market price of the underlying common stock rises or falls.

Common Stock Rises A first strategy is to plan to hold the bond indefinitely and to collect the two interest payments each year; in the meantime, the bond is increasing in value. A segment of the investor's wealth remains in the bond because he prefers this medium over other investment opportunities. If at a later date he needs the money or finds a better investment opportunity, he can sell the bond. Thus an investor need not sell or convert his bond in the near future to have a successful commitment in this type of security.

A second strategy is to plan to hold the bond for a short period of time—several years at the most, but always more than six months. While the investor is pleased to receive the interest check every six months, he is interested primarily in quick capital gains. He really buys the bond for the purpose of selling it at a quick profit. In other words, he seeks turnover, selling one convertible bond, perhaps buying another, thereby moving from one issue to another. The second strategy, therefore, is to plan to sell the bond (after a minimum holding period) as soon as it rises substantially in market price.

A third strategy is to plan to keep the bond for several years and then convert it into common stock. This action is expected to take place when the firm has raised the dividends per share on the common stock to a level such that aggregate annual dividend income on the shares acquired through conversion is higher than the annual interest income that would be received if the bond were retained. For example, if an investor has a bond that pays $50 a year in interest, he might be tempted to convert if he could obtain a total annual dividend income of $96. Of course, he takes more risk when he does this, because owning common stock is riskier than owning bonds in the same company (though not necessarily much more if the convertibles are also subordinated).

Common Stock Falls If instead of rising sharply, the common stock falls sharply, in price, the bondholder will still receive his two interest checks a year. If the decline in common stock price is permanent, the investor has little hope of making a profit from the convertibility aspect of the bond. In fact, the bond itself might decline to its investment value. Table 21-2 shows how varying changes in the underlying common stock prices affect the market value of the bond, including the impact of a catastrophic drop in the market price of the common. A critical problem facing the bondholder is that a collapse in the

TABLE 21-2
Summary on Convertible Bonds Courtesy of New York Stock Exchange (Figures Rounded)

		Firm Sells Bonds at Par	Common Rises to		Common Falls to
			$40	$60	$16
A.	Market price of 5% bonds	$1,000	$1,200	$1,500	$750
B.	Market price per share	32	40	60	16
C.	Conversion ratio (shares)	25	25	25	25
D.	Conversion price	40	40	40	40
E.	Conversion value (B × C)	800	1,000	1,500	400
F.	Conversion premium (A − E)	200	200	0	350
G.	Conversion premium (A − E) ÷ E[a]	25%	20%	0%	87½%
H.	Investment value	750	750	750	750
I.	Premium over investment value (A − H)	250	450	750	0
J.	Premium over investment value (A - H) ÷ H	33%	60%	100%	0%
K.	Market yield ($50 ÷ A)[b]	5%	4.17%	3.33%	6.67%
L.	Redemption price	$1,050	$1,050	$1,050	$1,050

a. The conversion premium gradually disappears as the market price of the bond becomes very high, because (1) the risk of owning the bond increases and (2) the market yield declines.

b. Market yield is found by dividing the annual dollar interest on the bond by the current market price of the bond. Hence, market yield is different from yield to maturity.

market price of the common stock is likely to be accompanied by a decrease in the investment value of the convertible bond.

Summary on Price Behavior The market price of a convertible bond may behave in a manner different from that of a bond without the conversion feature. A convertible bond will not fall below its investment value. Furthermore, such a bond has potential price appreciation, for as the market price of the common exceeds (or has prospects of exceeding) the conversion price of the common, the bond will begin to rise sharply in price. The current market price of most convertible bonds is tied closely to the appreciation potential of the underlying common stock. Also of interest, as already mentioned, is that a convertible bond typically sells at a premium over its conversion value, but this premium gradually disappears as the bond price soars to high levels. Finally, the fact that a bond is redeemable at the option of the issuer does not place a ceiling on the market price; instead, its impact is to cause the market price of the bond and its conversion value to converge; that is, the premium over conversion value disappears. In summary, convertible bonds offer the prospect of capital appreciation but with limited risk in a drop in the market price.

Three Conditions under Which a Bondholder Will Convert Like the holders of convertible preferred stock, those who own convertible bonds will switch their investments into common stock under three main conditions: when the yield that can be obtained on the common is sufficient inducement to make it worthwhile to take on the added risk that accompanies common stock; when the bonds are being redeemed and the redemption price is less than the value of the common stock into which the bonds could be converted; and when the conversion privilege is about to expire and the value of the shares into which the bonds could be converted is greater than the sale value of the bonds after the expiration of the conversion privilege.

Problem An investor owns a convertible bond in Company R, data for which are given below:

Market price of convertible bond	$1,050
Number of shares into which bond is convertible	25
Market price per share of common	$41
Redemption price (call price) of bond	$1,000

Required: (a) If the bondholder converted immediately, how much money would he make or lose? (b) By how much must the common stock rise in price before the bondholder would just break even by converting (assuming the market price of the bond remains at $1,050)?

Solution (a) If the investor converted immediately, he would lose $25, because he would be giving up a bond worth $1,050 to receive stock worth $1,025 (25 shares × the market price of $41). (b) The common stock must rise to $42 per share ($1,050 ÷ 25) for the bondholder to be able to receive $1,050 stock value for his $1,050 bond. At $42 per share, the bondholder would receive $1,050 in value if he converted. The answer is that the market price of the common must rise by $1 ($42 − $41).

Potential Profits Surprisingly, if an investor is 100 percent certain that the market price of the common stock will increase substantially, he will make more money by purchasing the common stock at the time of the financing, rather than the convertible bond itself. The reason is that at the time the bond is issued, the market price of the common is below the conversion price; in essence, the conversion price gives the bondholder an option to purchase common stock at 5 to 20 percent above its current market price. If, at the time of financing, the market price of the common is $40 and the conversion price is $50, an investor who has total faith in the future of the company should buy the stock immediately in the open market for $40, rather than buy it later from the firm at the conversion price of $50.

But the investor may not be 100 percent certain that the market price of the common will increase. If this is his belief, he might want to compromise and acquire a convertible bond in that specific company, so that he will have a fixed annual interest income; furthermore, he hopes his bond will not decline in price below its investment value, as estimated by an investment advisory service. As pointed out by the New York Stock Exchange in one of its circulars, when a person buys a convertible bond he believes that the market price of the common will rise in the future, but his belief is not strong enough to buy the common stock in the first place.

Problem

Company X, a very strong firm, has $5 million of 5½ percent convertible debentures outstanding; each $1,000 bond is callable at $1,100; each $1,000 bond has a conversion price of $40. The bonds are now selling at 120 percent; during the past 12 months they ranged between 107 percent and 125 percent. The common stock of Company X is now selling at $48; during the past year it ranged between $35 and $50. (a) What does the term *conversion price* mean? What is its practical significance? (b) What is the *conversion rate* in the above example? What is its interrelationship with the *conversion price*? (c) If the market price of the common goes above the conversion price, can Company X assume that there will be a rush to convert? (d) How could Company X "force" the bondholders to convert? (e) While Company X could eliminate interest charges by forcing conversion, it did not do so. Suggest a reason why the management did not force conversion. (f) Would it have been sound financial management for Company X to have issued these convertibles without the call (redemption) feature? (g) Why would a bondholder pay the current market price of $1,200 when he knows the firm can redeem the bonds at $1,100? (h) The convertibles of Company X contain an anti-dilution clause, if this firm has a two for one stock split, what would be the new conversion ratio? (i) What is the main reason for the wide fluctuations in the price of the bonds during the past 12 months? (j) Why are convertible bonds (as a group) said to be a reasonably good hedge against inflation?

Solution

(a) The *conversion price* is the dollar amount of bonds that must be surrendered for each share of common stock; its practical significance is that it is an indirect method of stating how many shares a bondholder will receive for each $1,000 bond surrendered; also, when the market price of the common exceeds the conversion price, the market price of the bond begins to rise. (b) The *conversion rate* is the number of shares of common that will be received for surrendering a $1,000 bond. Its relation to conversion price is that the conversion ratio can be determined by dividing the par value of the bond by the conversion price. (c) If the market price of the common goes above the conversion price, the management of Company X cannot assume that there will be a rush to convert; instead, bondholders may keep their bonds, which in the meantime have increased substantially in price. (d) Company X could force conversion by calling the bonds; it would then be more profitable for the bondholder to convert rather than receive $1,100 in cash. (e) Company X did not call the bonds and force conversion because such a course of action (in this example) would dilute the earnings per share on the common. (f) It would not have been sound financial management to issue convertibles without a call feature because the lack of a call feature would limit the flexibility of management to get rid of the bond issue if such a course of action should prove desirable in the future. (g) Bondholders were willing to pay $1,200 for the bond which is callable at $1,100 because of the guarantee that the bonds could be converted within 60 days (usually) prior to the exact redemption date. (h) A two for one split would mean the conversion ratio would be changed to 50. (i) The bonds fluctuated in price because of the fluctuation in the price of the common stock. (j) Convertibles are a hedge against inflation because the stock market tends to rise in inflationary periods; as stock prices rise, convertibles tend to rise.

THE ROLE OF CONVERTIBLE PREFERRED STOCK

Convertible preferred stock is exchangeable into common stock at the option of the investor.

Many of the terms that apply to convertible bonds also apply to convertible preferred stock; hence these instruments will be discussed only briefly. Table 21-3 provides an illustration .

TABLE 21-3
Northern Illinois Gas $1.80 Preferred Stock

A. Market price of preferred	$30.63
B. Market price of common	$28.50
C. Conversion ratio (shares)	1.00
D. Conversion value (B × C)	$28.50
E. Conversion premium (percent) (A − D) ÷ D	7.00
F. Investment value	$26.00
G. Price risk (percent) (A − F) ÷ A	15.00

As noted earlier, price risk is the percentage by which the market price of a convertible preferred stock could fall before reaching its investment value.

The chief use of convertible preferred stock occurs during a merger, when the buying coporation gives convertible preferred shares to the common stockholders of the selling firm.

From the investor's side of the fence, convertible preferred stock has potential price appreciation. But the dividends are not as assured as is bond interest; furthermore, there is less downside protection, for as one investment advisory service stated "the floor can be a long way down."

THE ROLE OF WARRANTS

A *warrant* gives its owner the right to purchase a designated number of shares of stock from the corporation (or shares of beneficial interest of a business trust, which also issues warrants) at prices and within the time limit prescribed in the document. This instrument generally has a limited life, such as five or ten years; in a few rare cases it has no expiration date. Although there are a few nontransferable warrants, most of them are negotiable, and they are traded in the open market, just like common stock.

A warrant does not carry voting rights; it does not entitle its holder to any dividends; and it has no claim on assets.

These instruments are exercised at the option of the holder, not the corporation; the corporation must reserve a sufficient number of shares so that it can keep its agreement to sell shares to warrant holders.

When the warrant is exercised, the investor surrenders it to the company, along with the designated purchase price. The price is usually payable in cash, although in some cases other forms of consideration are accepted, such as the company's bonds.

One example of the use of warrants is provided by the Zayre Corporation. This firm sold a large 8 percent debenture issue at $976.25 per bond. The bonds were due in 1996. The buyer of each $1,000 face value of bonds received 12 warrants; each warrant entitled its holder to purchase one share of common stock at $40. The warrants were good for five years. Zayre Corporation believed that this package offer was in the best interest of the firm; since all the bonds were sold, investors believed that this package was a promising opportunity for them.

Just as the basic provisions of a preferred stock issue and a common stock issue are found in the corporate charter and the basic provisions of the bond issue are found in the indenture, the basic provisions of a warrant are found in the warrant agreement, a document that is kept with the warrant agent (usually a bank).

Warrants from the Corporation's Viewpoint

Uses of Warrants

First, if the warrants accompany a new bond issue, the offering yield may be lower and there may be fewer indenture-imposed restrictions on the management. Some bonds are issued with warrants included as a supplementary feature, while other bonds lack this feature. The warrant may be a document which is detachable from the bond, or it may be nondetachable. If the warrant is detachable, it may be bought and sold separately in the open market. If it is nondetachable, it usually appears as a clause in the bond, and the debt instrument must be surrendered when the warrant is exercised; then, a new bond without the warrant feature is issued to replace the surrendered document. If the warrant is nondetachable, the market value of the bond includes any value the warrant might have. In short, when a firm gives warrants with a bond issue, the company is making the bonds more attractive to investors.

Second, warrants may be issued along with preferred stock, especially when a merger takes place and the common stockholder of the selling firm receives preferred shares for his common shares. The receivers of the new preferred shares are likely to insist that these securities be either convertible or accompanied by warrants. When Allegheny Airlines acquired Mohawk Airlines, the following were the terms: for each 4.25 shares of Mohawk surrendered, the stockholders of Mohawk received 1 share of common stock of Allegheny and 2/3 of a warrant in Allegheny. Each warrant entitled the holder to buy 1 share of Allegheny at $18 for the first five years and at $25 for the subsequent five years. The use of warrants during a merger is a growing practice.

Third, in order to obtain funds under any conditions, it may be necessary to give warrants with a new security issue. Both individual and institutional investors are becoming more sophisticated in demanding a share in the future profits of the firm, even when these investors purchase fixed-income securities.

Fourth, warrants may be given to investment bankers who buy an issue of either stocks or bonds from the company and who, in turn, intend to sell these securities to the ultimate investor. The investment banker may buy stock from an issuer for $10 a share and hope to resell it to the general public for $13. In addition to his gross profit of $3 a share, he may be given 10,000 warrants to buy stock from the firm at $10 a share, the warrants being good for, say, 10 years. Presumably the investment banker would have insisted on even more profit than $3 a share if the warrants had not been given to him.

In addition to the above, two other possible uses of warrants are: (1) after a corporate failure they may be given or sold to common stockholders, and (2) they may be used in certain special transactions as an immediate method of raising cash.

There is no limit to the creative use of warrants by business firms; thus the *Wall Street Journal* reported that Cerro Corporation eliminated its common stock cash dividend to save cash for its domestic diversification program. The metals company said it would try to hold the loyalty of shareholders who are dividend conscious by giving them a chance to trade their common stock for preferred stock and warrants. Under the exchange offer, Cerro said a new class of cumulative preferred stock would be swapped for common stock. An unusual feature of this plan was that the warrants could not be exercised until the value per share has doubled on the New York Stock Exchange; at the time of the offering, the common stock was selling at $17 a share on this exchange. Hence, the holder of the warrant could not exercise it until the stock had reached $34 a share, which was the price at which the company would sell the shares. The company went on to say that the dollar dividends promised on the new preferred stock would exceed the average dollar dividends being paid on the common stock during the previous several years. Cerro Corporation released a statement pointing out that those common stockholders who retained their shares would be in a better position to participate in Cerro's recovery, if there was one. But the economic price to be paid by the common stockholders was the sacrifice of current dividend income.

Basic Decision The basic decision of management is to establish the *option price*, also called the *exercise price*. This is the price at which the warrant holder may buy shares from the corporation or the business trust. At the time the warrants are issued, the option price is usually above the market price of the common. If the market price per share of common stock is $10, the option price might be $14. Under these conditions, the option to buy the stock would not be exercised, because no investor would pay the firm $14 a share when identical shares could be purchased in the open market at $10. Nevertheless, the warrants are not empty rights issued by the firm, for they have a value even at this time if their holders anticipate an eventual rise in the price of the common stock.

Basically, when a firm issues warrants, it opens the possibility of selling shares in the future at a price higher than the current market quotation.

Although the option price is stated in the contract, this price is subject to certain kinds of prearranged changes. One such change is the stepped-up option price, which means that the option price may change with the passage of time; for example, it might be $35 for the first five years and $40 thereafter. Also, a few warrants contain the "flush out" clause which permits the management to lower the option price, thus encouraging early action on the part of the warrant holders and thereby getting rid of the outstanding warrants. As in the case of convertible bonds and convertible preferred shares, the exercise price of a warrant may also be protected against dilution by stock splits, stock dividends, and other designated changes in the capital structure.

When the holder of a warrant exercises his right to buy stock from the corporation, the corporation usually receives cash and in turn issues more common stock. The newly acquired cash can be put to whatever use is deemed best by the management, although the indenture may require that the proceeds be used to call bonds. The capital structure is expanded to the extent of the additional stock which is issued. If, however, the corporation uses the proceeds from the sale of the stock to redeem some of the outstanding bonds, the effect on the corporation is the same as if a conversion had taken place; that is, the amount of outstanding bonds is decreased while the amount of common stock is increased.

The corporation is not sure of how many shares it will be called on to sell to the holders of the warrants. Nor is the corporation sure of when, if ever, the cash will be received. It can be seen that there is much uncertainty about the ultimate effect of warrants on the capital structure.

Warrants from the Investor's Viewpoint

The *initial* recipient of the warrant usually receives them as part of a package of economic benefits. If he is a security holder, he has already received bonds, preferred stock, common stock, or shares of beneficial interest; if he is an investment banker, he has already received a commission for his efforts in selling the securities.

An investor who owns warrants or who is considering buying them, is concerned with two practical problems—the factors that influence the market price of the warrants and the opportunities for making money in them.

Factors Influencing the Market Price of Warrants

Warrants have a *theoretical value* (also called a formula value) and a *market value*. The theoretical value is found by the following formula:

$$\text{Theoretical value} = \begin{pmatrix} \text{Market price of common stock} \\ - \text{ Exercise price} \end{pmatrix} \times \begin{array}{l} \text{Number of} \\ \text{shares each} \\ \text{warrant} \\ \text{entitles owner} \\ \text{to purchase} \end{array}$$

The theoretical value of a warrant is always defined as zero when the stock is selling for less than the exercise price.

Several years after Greyhound Corporation issued warrants, the common stock of this firm was selling at $25; each warrant entitled the holder to buy one share of common stock at the option price of $23.50. The theoretical value of a warrant at this time was $1.50. Most warrants have a market price greater than their theoretical value; the Greyhound warrants mentioned above had a theoretical value of $1.50 but a market value of $8. Investors were willing to pay this premium over theoretical value because they believed that the market price of the common would continue to rise; furthermore, as will be explained in the next section, the purchaser of warrants has the possibility of earning high percentage gains on his warrants with a limited amount of his funds committed to them.

In summary, the main (but not only) determinants of the market value of a warrant are the current level and the anticipated future level of the market price of the common.

Opportunities
for Making Money
in Warrants (I)

If the investor is lucky, he makes money in one of two ways; selling the warrants at a profit or exercising them and obtaining common stock. If he makes a profit on selling the warrants, one of the factors affecting the level of his gain is the phenomenon of leverage. The reader will recall that *leverage* means that a percentage change in one value leads to a larger percentage change in another value; in the current discussion, leverage means the possibility that a certain percentage gain in the market price of the common will be followed by a larger percentage gain in the market value of the warrant.

To illustrate the leverage factor, assume that the market price of the common is $15, the exercise price is $20, and one additional share may be purchased by submitting one warrant. Although the theoretical value of this warrant is zero, in practice it will probably sell at a premium of approximately $5; hence, let us assume that the current market price of the warrant is $5. Assume an investment of either $15 in a share of this stock or $5 in a warrant of this same firm. If the market price of the common rises from $15 to $45, the gain is 200 percent. But the warrant will rise to $30 (its theoretical value of $25, plus an assumed $5 premium), which is an increase of 500 percent over the original investment of $5. Hence, a 200 percent increase in the price of the common stock results in a 500 percent increase in the price of the warrant. The possibility of obtaining high percentage gains on warrants is one of the reasons they frequently sell at a premium over their theoretical value.

A highly astonishing (though not typical) example of how leverage can benefit the investor is this: If a person had bought $500 of Tri-Continental Warrants and had held them for 20 years, this investment would have grown to $1,212,000 at the end of this time period.

The degree of leverage is most dramatic when the market price of the common is not too far from the option price. As the market price of the common far surpasses the option price, the degree of leverage declines; at this point the market value of the warrant and its theoretical value converge and become almost equal. When the market price of the common is at comparatively high levels, a certain percentage change in the price of the common, such as 14 percent, will result in about a 14 percent change in the market value of the warrant. Leverage has disappeared.

Along with the advantage of leverage, and related to it, is the low amount of cash needed to acquire warrants. Assume, as previously, that a warrant entitles its owner to purchase one share of common stock at the option price of $20, that the current market price of the common is $15, and that the current market value of a warrant is $5 (this warrant is selling at a premium of $5). If the market price of the common is $15 and then rises to $45, the gain is $30. If a person acquired the warrant for $5 and it rose to $30 (its theoretical value, plus a premium of $5), the profit is $25. On a small initial investment of $5, he made almost as much dollar profit as if he had made a $15 investment in the common stock. The fact that investors can make large dollar gains by investing limited amounts of cash is a further advantage of buying warrants.

On the negative side, a sharp drop in the market price of the common stock can be followed by an even sharper decline in the market price of the warrant. The investor can suffer substantial losses if the future prospects of the firm take a turn for the worse. An investment advisory service gave this warning to its readers: "The purchase of a warrant is a venture to be undertaken only by those willing to accept unusually heavy risk." This advice was given because of the possibility of suffering huge losses from the purchase of warrants.

In summary, an investor in warrants can obtain economic gains without having to exercise them, for he can sell them in the open market to new investors.

The second way to profit from ownership of warrants is to exercise them and receive the shares from the company. One situation that leads to exercising them is when the warrants are about to expire, because after the expiration date they are worthless. Another situation is when the dollar dividends on the common stock are increasing. A person who needs current income rather than sporadic capital gains will exercise the warrants and obtain the common stock. Yet another situation is when the exercise price is about to be increased because of a "stepped-up" clause. An investor might find it to his advantage to acquire the shares of common stock just prior to the increase in the option price.

In summary, the warrant holder can make money in one of two main ways—by selling the warrant in the open market or by exercising it and obtaining the underlying common stock. If he follows this latter course of action, he may hold the newly acquired common stock for its dividends, or he may eventually sell it.

Opportunities for Making Money in Warrants (II)

A convertible bond is exchangeable into common stock, at the option of the investor. The issuer includes the conversion feature because of benefits to itself; These are: a lower rate of interest, fewer restrictions in the indenture, and the possibility of later selling common stock at a figure above its current market value.

The investor is attracted to the conversion feature because of benefits to himself. These are: the possibility of reasonable price appreciation and a floor beyond which he hopes his bond will not fall. In other words, he has the

HIGHLIGHTS OF THIS CHAPTER

possibility of capital appreciation but he is protected against catastrophic loss in this quest; in the meantime, he expects to receive a steady income in the form of interest.

As pointed out by the New York Stock Exchange, a bondholder need not convert his bond to enjoy its advantages. These bonds are frequently sold many times before they are finally converted into stock, and many investors have actively participated in the convertible bond market without ever exercising the conversion privilege.

Convertible preferred stock is exchangeable into common stock at the option of the investor. A deluge of convertible preferreds has arrived on the open market, most of them arising from the exchange of securities in a merger. Many of the expectations that apply to convertible bonds also apply to convertible preferred stock.

Warrants give the holder the right to buy shares of common from the company at a specified price and usually within a limited period of time—such as five or ten years. Warrants may be issued along with bonds, along with preferred stock, along with common stock, as compensation to investment bankers, after a reorganization, and even by themselves as a method of raising cash.

Because of leverage, if an investor is lucky, he can make fabulous dollar and percentage profits on warrants; but if he is unlucky, he can suffer severe losses.

From both the issuer's and the investor's viewpoint, the ultimate success of convertible securities and warrants depends on the extent to which the common stock rises in price.

One of the trends in finance is the accelerated use of convertible securities and warrants.

REVIEW QUESTIONS 21-1. Explain the meaning of the following terms:
convertible bond
conversion ratio (rate)
conversion price
conversion value
conversion premium
investment value
premium over investment value
overhanging issue
warrant

21-2. From the management viewpoint, what are the potential advantages of adding the conversion feature to a bond issue?

21-3. Under what conditions will an investor convert his bonds into common stock?

21-4. What two policy decisions must management make after it has decided to float a convertible bond issue?

21-5. Suggest several holding strategies that an investor in convertible bonds might use.

The answers to the problems appear at the end of this section. *For each prob-*
lem, show how you obtained the answer.

21-1. Company C has 6 percent convertible bonds outstanding. The conversion price is $20; market price of each bond is $1,250; par value is $1,000; market price of each share of common stock is $25. If a bondholder converts, how many shares of common stock will he receive?

21-2. Company D has 5 percent convertible bonds outstanding. The par value of each bond is $1,000; market value of each bond is $1,005; conversion price is $40; conversion ratio (rate) is 25; market price per share of common is $39. If this firm declares a 10 percent stock dividend, what is the adjusted conversion ratio (rate)?

21-3. Company N has 6 percent convertible bonds outstanding. The par value is $1,000; call price is $1,050; market price of each bond is $1,200; conversion price is $25; conversion ratio (rate) is 40; market price of each share of common is $29. The issuer plans to call the bonds and thereby force conversion. What is the lowest price at which the common stock can sell and still not make it advantageous for the bondholder to send in his bonds for redemption, in the event of a call?

21-4. Company R has 5 percent convertible bonds outstanding; each bond has a face value of $1,000. The terms are that each bond is convertible into 10 shares of common stock; the market value of the common is now $80. If bonds (without the conversion feature) issued by companies of comparable risk are selling at $996, what is the market value of the bonds of Company R?

21-5. Company Z has 6 percent convertible bonds outstanding; each bond has a face value of $1,000. The terms are that each bond is convertible into 20 shares of common stock; the market price of the common stock is now $60. Suggest an approximate market value of the bond on the basis of the information given.

21-6. An investor owns convertible bonds in Company Z, data for which are given below:

Market price of convertible bond	$1,160
Number of shares into which bond is convertible	20
Market price per share of common	$54
Redemption price (call price) of bond	$1,050

Required: (a) If the bondholder converted immediately, how much money would he make or lose? (b) By how much must the common stock rise in price before the bondholder would just break even by converting, assuming the market price of the bond remains at $1,160?

21-7. Company R's warrants permit the warrant holders to buy three shares of common stock at $6 each from the company. The market price per share of the common is $8. What is the theoretical market value of a warrant?

21-8. Company B's warrants permit the holders of a warrant to buy two shares of common stock at $10 each from the company. The market price of the common stock is $14; the market price of the warrants is $2 above their theoretical market value. What is the market value of a warrant?

21-9. A warrant offered with a bond issue permits its holder to purchase 2.5 shares of common stock; the current market price of the common is $10; the theoretical value of each warrant is $15. What is the subscription price of the common stock?

21-10. Merrill Lynch, Pierce, Fenner and Smith, in pointing out the implications of converting preferred stock into common stock, suggests that upon conversion there may be a decline or an increase in the earnings per share on the common stock, depending on the circumstances.

The following data apply to Companies A and B, each of whose convertible preferred stock is exchangeable into one share of common stock (before any conversion has taken place):

	A	B
Earnings after taxes	$10,000,000	$10,000,000
Shares of common outstanding	1,000,000	1,000,000
Shares of convertible preferred outstanding	500,000	500,000
Annual dividend requirements on preferred	$ 2,000,000	$ 3,750,000
Earnings available for common	$ 8,000,000	$ 6,250,000
Earnings per share on common	$8	$6.25

If all the preferred stock of Company A is converted, the new earnings per share on the common stock will be $6.67, a drop of $1.33. If all the preferred stock of Company B is converted, the new earnings per share will be $6.67, an increase of $0.42.

Required: Show how the new earnings per share on the common stock were obtained for each firm.

Answers: 21-1, 50; 21-2, 27.5; 21-3, $26.25; 21-4, $996; 21-5, $1,200; 21-6a, lose $80; 21-6b, $4; 21-7, $6; 21-8, $10; 21-9, $4.

CASE ON A FAMILY-CONTROLLED BUSINESS: CONVERTIBLE BONDS OR BONDS WITH WARRANTS?
The Kay Company is a family enterprise, controlled by Arthur Kay, who owns 3,000 shares of the common stock. The firm, in need of approximately $20,000 for expansion, is considering three possibilities: (1) Selling common stock for $20 a share, a figure that is $2.50 below the current market price of $22.50. If common stock is sold, 1,000 additional shares will be issued. (2) Selling, at par,

$20,000 of 5 percent convertibles with a conversion feature. Each $1,000 bond would be convertible into 30 shares of common stock. If the convertibles are issued and then converted, a total of 600 shares of common stock will be issued. Since there are 20 bonds with a denomination of $1,000 each, the number of shares to be issued is 20 X 30. (3) Selling, at par, $20,000 of 5 percent debentures with 10 warrants attached to each $1,000 bond. One warrant gives its holder the right to buy one share of stock at $32 a share. After the sale of the debentures there would be a total of 200 warrants outstanding. If all the warrants are exercised, the warrant holders will buy 200 shares and will pay a total of $6,400 for the shares (200 X $32).

The above securities would be sold to buyers other than Kay and his associates. Before the financing, the firm's EBIT are 15 percent of total assets; after the financing the firm expects its total EBIT to become 20 percent of total assets. Kay will consider many factors in making his final decision, although the data in the following table will be of special interest.

Required: (a) Complete the data in Table 21-4. (b) What is your opinion as to the best form of financing for the firm? (c) Give the reasons for your answer to (b).

TABLE 21-4
Data on the Kay Company

	Prefinancing Data	Common Issued	Postfinancing Data — Debentures Issued — Immediately after Issue	Debentures Converted	Warrants Exercised
Total assets	$80,000	$100,000	$100,000	$100,000	$106,400
Current liabilities, non-interest-bearing	$10,000	$ 10,000	$ 10,000	$ 10,000	$ 10,000
5 percent debentures	0	0	20,000	0	20,000
Common stock, $5 par	20,000	25,000	20,000	23,000	21,000
Retained earnings	50,000	50,000	50,000	50,000	50,000
Paid-in surplus	$0	$ 15,000		$ 17,000	$ 5,400
EBIT	$12,000	$ 20,000	$ 20,000	$ 20,000	$ 21,280
Less interest	0	0	1,000	0	1,000
Taxable income	12,000	20,000	19,000	20,000	20,280
Tax (50 percent)	6,000	10,000	9,500	10,000	10,140
Net after taxes	6,000	10,000	9,500	10,000	10,140
Shares of common outstanding	4,000	5,000	4,000	4,600	4,200
Earnings per share	$———	$———	$———	$———	$2.41
Shares owned by Kay	3,000	3,000	3,000	3,000	3,000
Percent of total shares held by Kay	75	———	———	———	———
Times interest earned after taxes	———	———	———	———	———
Percent of debt to total assets	———	———	———	———	———
Price-earnings ratio	15	15	15	15	———
Market price of common	$22.50	$30.00	$35.62	$———	36.15

# Managing Expansion: Implicit Costs of Long-Term Funds

In this chapter we will examine the issues involved in computing the cost of capital of several *individual* sources of funds for expansion. The assumption will be made that the company is planning on acquiring one very large asset and that it is comparing different sources of funds to finance this project. While this approach is perilous because of the difficulty of actually incorporating all the implicit and explicit costs in the answer, such an approach is useful in calling attention to the following highly important elements in finance:

1. The importance of keeping market value of the stock in mind when making decisions
2. The importance of timing when selling stocks and bonds
3. The impact of changing capitalization rates (as well as price-earnings ratios) when additional funds are raised
4. The relationship between the incremental cost of capital and the rates earned on the projects acquired with the new funds

Table 22-1 shows data that will be used throughout this chapter to explain how the cost of a number of different sources, including common stock, may be estimated.

Since the market price of the stock is $12 and the expected *future* earnings per share are $1, the modified price-earnings ratio is 12. The phrase *modified price-earnings ratio* is used here to indicate that the ratio is based on anticipated annual future earnings per share rather than current earnings per share, which are used generally to determine the price-earnings ratio.

Capitalization rates on common stock are often a source of difficulty for the reader. A useful formula for providing a pattern of analysis on this problem is:

$$I = PRT$$

Where I equals income, interest, earnings, or other returns (in this chapter I is assumed to equal expected earnings per share on the common stock); P equals principal or market value (in this chapter P will equal the current market price of the common stock); R equals rate earned on the principal (in this chapter R will mean the capitalization rate on the common stock); T equals time period (in the discussion in this chapter T is equal to one year; hence, T is equal to 1 and may be dropped from the formula). Therefore, the shortened formula is:

$$I = PR$$

Given any two elements in the formula, the third can be found. For example, what is the capitalization rate on common stock if its market value per share is $12 and its expected future earnings are $1?

$$I = PR$$
$$R = \frac{I}{P}$$
$$R = \frac{\$1}{\$12}$$
$$R = 8.33 \text{ percent}$$

What is the value of I (expected future earnings per share) if the market price of a share is $12 and its capitalization rate is 8.33 percent?

$$I = PR$$
$$I = \$12 \times 8.33 \text{ percent}$$
$$I = \$1$$

The reader should keep in mind that as the risk of owning common stock increases, investors are willing to pay less for each share—a force tending to raise capitalization rates. If, in the above example, the price per share fell to $10, the capitalization rate would rise to 10 percent. Thus increased risk generally leads to increased capitalization rates.

An alternate way to express this is to state that investors expect to earn 8.33 percent, through a future span of time, on the current market value of their investment. In establishing market value, investors capitalize future rather than historic earnings per share. Also observe that the expected future earnings per share of the Clark Corporation, shown in Table 22-1, are those that investors anticipate without any additional expansion. If there is any expansion, changes might occur in both anticipated future earnings per share and the rate at which these expectations are capitalized.

Assume that the Clark Corporation is studying a project that will cost $1 million and that the firm is considering selling stock to the general public to raise the money for this project. Although the market price of the common stock is $12, we will assume that the firm would receive only $10 from the sale of each share, because the bankers who handle the issue will charge $2 a unit for their assistance in marketing the issue. The firm, therefore, will have to sell 100,000 shares to obtain the proceeds of $1 million; and there will be 1,100,000 shares of common stock outstanding after the financing. Finally, assume that after the financing the investors will still expect earnings of at least 8.33 percent on the current market price of their investment, which they do not want to fall below $12 a share.

Balance Sheet Data—Before Financing

Assets:

Current assets	$ 8,000,000
Plant and equipment, net	8,000,000
Total	$16,000,000

Liabilities and net worth:

Current liabilities	$ 3,000,000
Common stock, 1 million shares, $5 par value	5,000,000
Earned surplus	8,000,000
Total	$16,000,000

Estimated Average Annual Future Data If Expansion Is Not Undertaken

Sales	$ 5,000,000
Cost of goods sold	3,000,000
Net operating income	$ 2,000,000
Federal income tax, 50 percent rate assumed	$ 1,000,000
Net income	$ 1,000,000

Other Data

Estimated future earnings per share on common stock	$ 1
Current market price of common stock	$ 12
Modified price-earnings ratio (the multiple)	12
Rate at which estimated future earnings per share on common stock are capitalized (percent)	8.33

The computations for estimating the percentage cost of capital of common stock are shown in the first column of Table 22-2. The formula for obtaining this estimate is:

$$\text{Cost of capital} = \frac{\text{Sacrifice}}{\text{Proceeds}}$$
$$= \frac{\$100,000}{\$1,000,000}$$
$$= .10$$
$$= 10 \text{ percent}$$

The $100,000 of additional earnings required to prevent the price of the common stock from falling can be viewed as a future payment per year that must be made to stockholders if the price of the shares is not to decline below $12 each. In determining the cost of capital, an assumption is made that earnings are eventually paid out to the owners. It is true, of course, that in the short run only a part of the earnings is distributed as dividends, the balance being retained in the business. But when earnings are withheld from owners, a reasonable belief is that future distributions will increase as a result of these withholdings. Over a span of time earnings of successful companies probably are distributed to owners, even though the future recipients may not be the same owners who held the stock at the time the earnings were withheld. If the $100,000 of additional annual earnings are ultimately distributed to owners, then such distributions can be regarded as a sacrifice by the company for the use of the money supplied by the stockholders.

TABLE 22-2
Estimating the Percentage Cost of Capital of an Incremental Common Stock Issue

		Current Market Price of Common $12; Bankers' Fees $2 a Share	Current Market Price of Common $16; Bankers' Fees $2 a Share	Current Market Price of Common $12; Bankers' Fees $1 a Share
A.	Proceeds of issue	$1,000,000	$1,000,000	$1,000,000
B.	Required value per share of common	$12	$16	$12
C.	Capitalization rate (percent) on common stock	8.33	6.25	8.33
D.	Required earnings per share on common stock to maintain price (B× C)	$1	$1	$1
E.	Additional shares of common needed to raise $1,000,000	100,000	71,429	90,909
F.	Shares of common outstanding prior to financing	1,000,000	1,000,000	1,000,000
G.	Total number of shares of common outstanding after financing (E + F)	1,100,000	1,071,429	1,090,909
H.	Required earnings on common stock to prevent a decline in price (G × D)	$1,100,000	$1,071,429	$1,090,909
I.	Earnings before expansion	$1,000,000	$1,000,000	$1,000,000
J.	Additional earnings required to prevent price of common stock from falling. Such additional earnings may also be viewed as a sacrifice (H − I)	$100,000	$71,429	$90,909
K.	Cost of Capital = $\dfrac{\text{Sacrifice}}{\text{Proceeds}}$ =	$\dfrac{\$100,000}{\$1,000,000}$	$\dfrac{\$71,429}{\$1,000,000}$	$\dfrac{\$90,909}{\$1,000,000}$
	=	.10	.071	.0909
	=	10 percent	7.14 percent	9.09 percent

As indicated in the first column of Table 22-2, the amount of money actually received by the firm was $1 million. Since the cost of capital of common stock is 10 percent, any project financed from this source must earn at least this rate to prevent a decline in the market price of the common stock. Any lower percentage earned on a project would cause the market price of the stock to fall; any higher percentage would cause the market price of the stock to rise. As can be seen in Table 22-3, if the project under consideration promises a rate of return of only 9 percent, the price of the common stock will fall to $11.89; if the project promises a rate of return of 12 percent, the market price of the common stock will increase to $12.22; if the project promises a rate of 10 percent, the firm will neither gain nor lose. Therefore, under these cost of capital conditions, a project that promises more than 10 percent should be accepted;

TABLE 22-3 Minimum Rate That Must be Earned on Project to Maintain Market Value of a Share of Common Stock (Financing through a Common Stock Issue That Has a Percentage Cost of Capital of 10 Percent)		Rate Earned on Project		
		9 Percent	12 Percent	10 Percent
A.	Existing earnings before expansion	$1,000,000	$1,000,000	$1,000,000
B.	New earnings on $1,000,000 project	$90,000	$120,000	$100,000
C.	Earnings after financing (A + B)	$1,090,000	$1,120,000	$1,100,000
D.	Total number of shares of stock outstanding after financing	1,100,000	1,100,000	1,100,000
E.	Earnings per share of common stock after financing (C ÷ D)	$0.991	$1.018	$1.00
F.	Capitalization rate (percent) on common stock	8.33	8.33	8.33
G.	Market value per share of common stock after financing (E ÷ F)	$11.89	$12.22	$12.00

one that promises less than 10 percent should be rejected. The capital budgeting process should be used to determine whether the project actually promises a return of at least 10 percent. In this chapter we will limit our computations to estimating the cost of capital; the reader should be able to use the material developed earlier on estimating the rate of return on a project.

A Short-cut Method of Computation

If the capitalization rate on the common stock is not expected to change as a result of the expansion, a simpler method of determining the percentage cost of common stock may be used. This formula is:

$$\text{Cost of capital} = \frac{\text{Sacrifice}}{\text{Proceeds}}$$
$$= \frac{E}{P_s}$$
$$= \frac{1}{10}$$
$$= .10$$
$$= 10 \text{ percent}$$

where E represents management's best estimate of what future earnings per share would be without the additional financing, and P_s represents proceeds per share to the issuer. In our example, we will assume that $1 per share represents expected future earnings. As is well known, the future level of earnings is not apt to be the same as its present or past level. Hence, when determining the cost of capital, only future earnings should be considered. The use of future figures explains why the cost of capital can be computed for a firm that has no earnings in the year in which the stock is issued and for a firm whose current earnings are temporarily depressed. Also, the use of future data gives a more realistic picture of the cost of capital for growth companies, that is, those whose current earnings per share are much less than future earnings per share are expected to be.

The short-cut formula usually gives the same results as the longer method previously explained. Since the capitalization rate on the common stock is unlikely to change much as a result of expansion through the issuance of these instruments, many people prefer this shorter method. But if the capitalization rate on these shares is expected to change as a result of the financing, the short-cut method cannot be used. Because the longer procedure of calculating the cost of capital has wider applicability, we will stress it in this chapter.

After a project is accepted and financed in some manner, the price of the common stock probably will change; therefore, after this happens, the new price is used in making new decisions.

Proper timing means selling the securities when their market price is relatively high. Assume that the Clark Corporation is considering financing the $1 million project at a time when the market price of the common stock is $16 rather than $12 and that the investment bankers still charge $2 a share for their services in assisting with the sale of the issue. As can be seen in the first column of Table 22-2, if the stock is floated when its market price is $12, the cost of capital is 10 percent. But, as can be seen in the second column of the table, if the stock is floated when its market price is $16, the cost of capital drops to 7.14 percent. Since management attempts to minimize the cost of capital, the financial interests of the common stockholders are advanced by obtaining the funds at 7.14 percent. The best time to sell common stock, from the issuer's viewpoint, is when its price is relatively high. When the price is high, a company needs to sell fewer shares to obtain the money. This is beneficial to the firm because earnings on the new project will be spread over a smaller number of shares; it is an advantage to existing stockholders because there are more earnings per share available for them.

Although national averages for stock prices give clues as to the best time to sell the securities, each firm must study its own situation when the cost of common stock is being considered. One approach is to observe the trend in the market value of a company's shares. But because of stock splits and stock dividends, dealing with only the market price of the stock is inadequate. A solution to this difficulty is to deal with capitalization rates on the common shares or with the modified price-earnings ratios. Low capitalization rates mean that the price of the firm's stock is relatively high; high capitalization rates mean that the price of

Proper Timing of the Issue and the Cost of Capital

the firm's stock is relatively low. Or, alternately, a high modified price-earnings ratio means that the price of the stock is high; a low modified price-earnings ratio means that the price of the stock is low.

Low capitalization rates and high price-earnings ratios go together; high capitalization rates and low price-earnings ratios go together. The best time for a company to sell common stock is when the capitalization rate is low (the price-earnings ratio is high); the worst time to sell common stock is when the capitalization rate is high (the price-earnings ratio is low). One should not forget, however, that we are assuming that a project is able to earn a specific rate of return, such as 20 percent.

Flotation Expenses and the Cost of Capital

In many situations the management of a firm must hire financial specialists, called investment bankers, to sell the securities. These middlemen have salesmen who make every effort to convince potential purchasers of the wisdom of buying the shares of stock being offered. In some cases the services of investment bankers are not used. Although management saves the fee charged by the investment bankers, the officers must themselves take some of their time to complete this task. In addition to the fee just mentioned, other costs such as printing, legal fees, and transfer taxes are incurred in selling securities.

A saving in the amount paid for floating the issue will lower the cost of capital. Assume that the Clark Corporation is selling shares for $12 and that investment bankers charge $1 a share. If the bankers charge $2 a share for their services (see column 1 in Table 22-2), the percentage cost of capital is 10 percent. But if the bankers charge $1 for their services (see column 3 in Table 22-2), the percentage cost of capital is 9.09 percent. Basically, then, a low investment banking fee results in a lower cost of capital. This situation benefits common stockholders, because the cheaper the source of capital, the more likely is the price of the common stock to increase (assuming that the rate of return earned on the project is higher than the percentage cost of capital).

Selling costs vary considerably, depending on the type of security being marketed. The SEC estimates that for issues under $250,000, the flotation costs are $8.80 for each $100 of bonds sold, $16.40 for each $100 of preferred stock sold, and $22.80 for each $100 of common stock sold. From these data, it can be seen that flotation costs consume a relatively large portion of the proceeds of a common stock issue, thereby raising the cost of capital to the issuing firm.

ESTIMATING THE PERCENTAGE COST OF CAPITAL OF INCREMENTAL RETAINED PROFITS (A DANGEROUS PROCEDURE)

Retained profits also have a cost, although it is an elusive one to measure. Even though management need not pay any specific return to stockholders, there is a lost opportunity for them to have received the money and invested it elsewhere. In analyzing the cost of retained profits, we will use the same general approach as in measuring the cost of common stock. That is, we will look at the matter as an attempt to preserve the market value of what the owner's financial position would have been if he had received the dividend in cash and immediately reinvested in another company of comparable risk. Suppose that the Clark Corporation (data for which are shown in Table 22-1), does not issue the $1 million of common stock but instead is considering financing a project through $1 million of retained profits. The firm, then, is weighing the alternative of retaining the $1 million of profits against the alternative of paying a dividend of $1 on each of the outstanding shares. What is the cost of retained earnings? An answer to this question will also indicate the minimum rate of return that must be earned on the project in order to advance the goals of the firm.

Data for estimating the percentage cost of capital of retained earnings are shown in Table 22-4. Assume that the stockholders of the Clark Corporation are all in the 48 percent income tax bracket. As shown in the first column of this table, if they received a dividend of $1, they would pay 48 cents in federal income taxes and have 52 cents which could be invested elsewhere. Also, assume that if they did make such an investment, a brokerage fee of 2 cents would be paid, leaving a net investment of 50 cents. Hence, the financial position of the stockholders would be worth $12.50 if the dividend were reinvested in another company ($12 of stock of the Clark Corporation plus 50 cents of new stock). Therefore, stockholders would benefit from retaining the earnings only if the price of their Clark Corporation stock increased to at least $12.50. Otherwise these owners would have been better off to have received the dividend. The question arises as to what is the cost of capital of retained earnings.

As can be seen in the first column of Table 22-4, the cost of capital of retained profits is 4.10 percent, determined as follows:

$$\text{Cost of capital} = \frac{\text{Sacrifice}}{\text{Proceeds}}$$
$$= \frac{\$41,000}{\$1,000,000}$$
$$= 0.41$$
$$= 4.10 \text{ percent}$$

Furthermore, as demonstrated in Table 22-5, if the cost of capital is 4.10 percent, then any project financed from the proceeds of this source must earn at least this rate if the financial position of the stockholders is to be preserved or increased. Table 22-5 shows that if the firm earns 4.10 percent, the market value of the shares will move to $12.50. But investors are not gaining because, as indicated, they would have this much in invested value if they received the $1 in dividends. Hence, in any comparison, $12.50 is the investment value that must be maintained or increased. Table 22-5 also shows that if the project earns 2 percent, the investor's position will have deteriorated because the market value of his commitment will have declined to $12.24; if it earns 8 percent, the investor's position will have improved because the market price of the stock will have risen to $12.96. In summary, assuming that the percentage cost of capital is 4.10 percent, projects that offer a prospective return of more than this should be accepted; projects that offer less should be rejected.

TABLE 22-4 Estimating the Percentage Cost of Capital of Retained Profits		If All Stockholders Are in One of These Tax Brackets		
		48 Percent	30 Percent	60 Percent
A.	Proceeds (amount reinvested)	$1,000,000	$1,000,000	$1,000,000
B.	Original value of a share of common	$12	$12	$12
C.	Dividends per share on common	$1	$1	$1
D.	Tax on dividend, paid by stockholder	$0.48	$0.30	$0.60
E.	Amount of dividends available for reinvestment (by stockholder)	$0.52	$0.70	$0.40
F.	Brokerage fee paid by stockholder	$0.02	$0.02	$0.02
G.	Net invested in another company	$0.50	$0.68	$0.38
H.	Value of stockholder's investment (old stock of $12 plus new stock) (B + G)	$12.50	$12.68	$12.38
I.	Capitalization rate (percent)	8.33	8.33	8.33
J.	Required earnings per share to maintain market value of stockholder's investment (H × I)	$1.041	$1.056	$1.032
K.	Total number of shares of common stock outstanding after financing	1,000,000	1,000,000	1,000,000
L.	Required total earnings to prevent decline in market value of stockholder's investments (K × J)	$1,041,000	$1,056,000	$1,032,000
M.	Earnings before expansion	$1,000,000	$1,000,000	$1,000,000
N.	Additional earnings required to prevent a decline in market value of owner's financial position. (Such additional earnings may also be viewed as a sacrifice.) (L − M)	$41,000	$56,000	$32,000
O.	Cost of capital = $\dfrac{\text{Sacrifice}}{\text{Proceeds}}$ =	$\dfrac{\$41,000}{\$1,000,000}$	$\dfrac{\$56,000}{\$1,000,000}$	$\dfrac{\$32,000}{\$1,000,000}$
	=	.041	.056	.032
	=	4.10 percent	5.60 percent	3.20 percent

TABLE 22-5 Minimum Rate That Must be Earned on Project to Maintain Owner's Financial Position (Financed through Retained Profits That Have a Percentage Cost of Capital of 4.10 Percent)		Rate Earned on Project		
		4.10 Percent	2 Percent	8 Percent
A.	Earnings before expansion	$1,000,000	$1,000,000	$1,000,000
B.	New earnings on project	$41,000	$20,000	$80,000
C.	Earnings after financing (A + B)	$1,041,000	$1,020,000	$1,080,000
D.	Total number of shares of common stock outstanding after financing	1,000,000	1,000,000	1,000,000
E.	Earnings per share (C ÷ D)	$1.041	$1.02	$1.08
F.	Capitalization rate (percent) on common stock	8.33	8.33	8.33
G.	New market price of a share of common stock (E ÷ F)	$12.50	$12.24	$12.96

The cost of retained earnings is difficult to measure because stockholders of the firm are not in the same income tax bracket and they might not pay the same brokerage fees. This raises the interesting point that the cost of capital of retained profits depends on the tax bracket of the stockholders, as well as the amount of brokerage fees they would pay to invest their dividends in additional stock. Table 22-4 indicates how the percentage cost of capital varies with the income tax bracket of the recipient stockholders. The simplifying assumption again is made that the brokerage fees are still 2 cents a share. As can be seen in the table, if stockholders are assumed to be in the 48 percent tax bracket, the cost of capital is 4.10 percent; if they are in the 30 percent tax bracket, the cost of capital is 5.60 percent; if they are in the 60 percent tax bracket, the cost of capital is 3.20 percent. Since a firm with many stockholders may not know the federal income tax bracket of its residual owners, it cannot measure accurately its cost of capital. But a family-owned corporation might have sufficient information to make such a calculation. In other words, the cost of retained earnings is a realistic concept, even though it cannot be measured to a high degree of accuracy, mainly because of the varying tax brackets of the stockholders. In any event, retained earnings should be viewed as having a cost, even though this cost may not be identical to the accountant's usage of this term. The decision-making process is facilitated if the estimated percentage return on a proposed project can be compared with the estimated percentage cost of capital of retained earnings.

Although retained earnings are a cheap source of funds, a firm that retains much of its profits may displease potential owners who prefer current income in the form of dividends. There is the possibility that this segment of the investment market may reflect its displeasure by raising the capitalization rate on the common stock, an event that would lower the market price of these shares.[1] Whether the investing public will actually raise the capitalization rate depends mainly on the probable profitability of the particular company. If the public really believes that it will eventually receive the retained earnings, the capitalization rate may not increase (as in the case of IBM). But if the public does not really believe that it will receive the retained earnings in the future, the capitalization rate probably will rise (as in the case of the Pennsylvania Railroad Company).

Generally, retained profits are a cheaper source of funds than common stock, preferred stock, or bonds. The main reason for this is that there are no flotation costs incurred when profits are retained. Other reasons, such as the stockholders' income taxes and brokerage fees, may also account for the relatively low percentage cost of capital of retained earnings.

The framework used for estimating the percentage cost of capital of common stock and retained profits may be applied to bonds and other forms of long-term debt. Once again our attention will be focused on the market price of a share of common stock, and again the cost of capital will be presented in a form that

Impact of Personal Income Taxes and Brokerage Fees on Cost of Capital

ESTIMATING THE PERCENTAGE COST OF CAPITAL OF AN INCREMENTAL BOND ISSUE

1. Recall that a rising capitalization rate means a declining price-earnings ratio.

sheds light on the rate that must be earned on a project in order to prevent a decline in the price of the common stock. This minimum rate is the percentage cost of capital of the bonds. Assume that the Clark Corporation (see Table 22-1) does not use common stock, use retained earnings, or preferred stock to finance expansion, but instead is considering financing the project with the proceeds of a 4 percent, $1 million bond issue. Assume (temporarily) that the capitalization rate of 8.33 percent on the common stock will continue in effect after the bonds are issued. Finally, assume that the $1 million, 4 percent bonds are sold to the public for $1,050,000 but that the investment bankers charge $50,000 for marketing the issue. Hence, the firm receives $1 million in cash from the transaction. What is the percentage cost of capital of the bond issue under these circumstances?

The first column in Table 22-6 shows how the cost of capital is estimated. The formula is:

$$\text{Cost of capital} = \frac{\text{Sacrifice}}{\text{Proceeds}}$$
$$= \frac{\$20,000}{\$1,000,000}$$
$$= .02$$
$$= 2 \text{ percent}$$

Observe that in the first column of Table 22-6 the federal income tax rate is assumed to be 50 percent. Hence, although the firm pays $40,000 in interest, it receives a deduction of $20,000 on its tax return for this payment. The net interest dollar cost then becomes $20,000. A 50 percent tax rate is also assumed in the second and third columns of this table.

We must now relax an assumption that was made in computing the percentage cost of capital of the bond issue. We assumed that the capitalization rate of 8.33 percent on the common stock would not change as a result of issuing bonds. Actually, with such a large bond issue, the position of the common stock becomes weaker and riskier because interest on the bonds and repayment of principal on them precedes any payments to stockholders. The investment market may raise the capitalization rate on the common stock to compensate for the added risk. Assume that management believes that the capitalization rate on the common stock will rise to 8.90 percent as a result of the bond issue. If this is the case, the firm must plan to raise the earnings per share on the common stock to a level that will compensate for the increase in this capitalization rate. As can be seen in the second column of Table 22-6, if the capitalization rate on the common rises to 8.90 percent, the percentage cost of capital of the bonds becomes 8.80 percent. In contrast, if the capitalization rate on the common had stayed at 8.33 percent, the percentage cost of capital of the bond issue would have been only 2 percent.

How does management know what the new capitalization rate on the common will be? The officers must study data of similar companies to determine the relation between capitalization rates on common stock and the capital structure of these companies. If no direct comparison can be made, management must again use its judgment in estimating what the new capitalization rate on the common will be under the new conditions.

TABLE 22-6
Estimating the Percentage Cost of Capital of a Bond Issue

	Bonds Sold at a 4 Percent Rate, No Change in Capitalization Rate on Common	Bonds Sold at a 4 Percent Rate, Capitalization Rate on Common Changes	Bonds Sold at a 6 Percent Rate, Capitalization Rate on Common Changes
A. Proceeds of issue	$1,000,000	$1,000,000	$1,000,000
B. Required value per share of common	$12	$12	$12
C. Capitalization rate (percent) on common stock	8.33	8.90	8.90
D. Required earnings per share on common stock to maintain price of $12 (B × C)	$1	$1.068	$1.068
E. Total number of shares of common stock outstanding after financing	1,000,000	1,000,000	1,000,000
F. Required earnings on common stock to prevent a decline in price of $12 (D × E)	$1,000,000	$1,068,000	$1,068,000
G. Required earnings to cover bond interest (50 percent tax rate)	$20,000	$20,000	$30,000
H. Required total earnings to prevent a decline in the price of the stock (F + G)	$1,020,000	$1,088,000	$1,098,000
I. Earnings before expansion	$1,000,000	$1,000,000	$1,000,000
J. Additional earnings required to prevent price of common from falling below $12. (Such additional earnings may also be viewed as a sacrifice.) (H − I)	$20,000	$88,000	$98,000
K. Cost of capital = $\frac{\text{Sacrifice}}{\text{Proceeds}}$	$\frac{\$20,000}{\$1,000,000}$	$\frac{\$88,000}{\$1,000,000}$	$\frac{\$98,000}{\$1,000,000}$
=	.02	.088	.098
=	2 percent	8.8 percent	9.8 percent

If the capitalization rate on the common does increase to 8.90 percent, then the sacrifice of $88,000 (see column 2 of Table 22-6) includes two items:

1. $20,000 to cover the bond interest ($40,000 total interest but $20,000 net because interest is a tax deduction)
2. $68,000 to increase the earnings per share on the common stock to a level that will compensate for the increase in the capitalization rate (so that the price per share of common will not fall below $12).

The concept of cost of capital is broader than the dollar amount paid the bondholders for the use of their money.

A firm might be able to issue a moderate amount of debt without this action resulting in a change in the capitalization rate on the common stock. This is probably the case in many situations because the investing public does not always make fine gradations in risk and then increase the capitalization rate, assuming that after the issuance of bonds the total amount of debt is still nominal. In situations like this, debt clearly is an advantageous method of financing. When not overdone, the financing of sound projects through the use of debt tends to increase the price of the common stock. This happens because the differential between the rate earned on the project, say 20 percent, and the cost of capital, say 8.90 percent, accrues to the owners. The greater the differential, the greater the benefit to the common stockholders. The differential becomes greater as the cost of capital decreases. A moderate amount of debt keeps the cost of capital low, a situation that in turn tends to raise the market price of each share of common stock.

But one can readily see that as debt continues to be issued, both the interest rate on the debt and the capitalization rate on the common stock will increase. These two factors cause the cost of debt capital to rise. After a certain point debt is not as advantageous as it seems, despite the fact that the interest rates are quite low and that interest is a tax deduction. The main reason why debt begins to lose its attractiveness is that the future earnings on the common stock are capitalized at a higher rate. In view of this, management must, then, consider the impact of debt financing on the capitalization rate of the earnings on the common stock.

The concept of the cost of capital as used in this chapter explains why a firm like General Motors Corporation does not raise huge sums of money through the issuance of bonds at a nominal rate of 4 percent but instead uses an after-tax rate of 2 percent (assuming a 50 percent tax). If one focused his attention entirely on the 2 percent cost, an erroneous impression might be gained that the firm would be ahead if it accepted all projects that yield 2 percent or more. This policy would soon react against the best interests of the common stockholders because it would give too low a cutoff point in the selection of capital expenditures. Such incorrect decisions would soon lower the price of the common stock because the rate earned on the project would not be covering the cost of the bonds.

IMPORTANCE OF
MARKET PRICE
PER SHARE

A firm is continuously seeking the optimum or ideal source of capital mixture, that is, the combination of individual sources that advances the primary goals of the firm. If, for example, a person paid $50 for a share of common stock of a certain corporation, his financial welfare is increased if the market price of the issue rises to, say, $80. The investor seeks to maximize the positive spread between the current market price of his stock and the amount that he paid for it. This is the same as saying that he seeks to increase the net present value of his commitment. The optimum source of capital mixture is the combination that results in the highest market price of a share of common stock, assuming a given number of shares are outstanding. Eli Schwartz has stated this succinctly: "An optimum capital structure for any widely held company is one which maximizes the long-run value per share of the common stock on the market."[2]

Since we are focusing attention on the price of a share of common stock, an important point is the formula for determining the price of a unit of ownership. One formula is:

$$\text{Market price of a share of stock} = \frac{\text{Expected earnings} \times \text{Price-earnings ratio}}{\text{per share}}$$

In planning the strategy for raising funds, the impact of each source must be traced to each of these variables:

1. Anticipated earnings per share on the common stock
2. The price-earnings ratio

Some sources of capital, such as bonds, affect both variables. Thus, if a certain company sells $1 million of 4 percent bonds instead of 6 percent preferred stock, the earnings per share on the common will be higher under the bond issue than under the preferred stock issue. But such a transaction might lead to more risk in owning the common stock because of the prior claims of creditors. If this is so, the investing public might lower the price-earnings ratio on the common stock. Hence, the price of the common stock might not rise to the full extent warranted by the increase in earnings per share. The view taken in this discussion may be summarized as: What is the impact of the sources of funds on the price of a share of common stock?

In financing expansion, several variables must be analyzed concurrently: the cost of capital of the incremental amount of funds; the use to which the funds will be put and the rate of return earned on the assets acquired with the funds; and the final impact on the market price of each share.

If bonds are issued, management must keep in mind the impact on the price-earnings ratio of the common stock (or, what is the same thing, the capitalization rate on expected future earnings per share). If an excessive amount of bonds is issued, the common stockholders will hold riskier securities; hence, they will lower the price-earnings ratio, that is, raise the capitalization rate. But if a moderate amount of debt is issued, there may be no additional risk in owning the common stock.

The timing of a security issue is important, since the number of shares issued to raise a given sum of money can vary considerably; similarly, the rate of interest paid on bonds and the dividend rate paid on preferred stock may vary

HIGHLIGHTS OF THIS CHAPTER

2. Eli Schwartz, "Theory of the Capital Structure of the Firm," *Journal of Finance,* March 1959, p. 20.

considerably. The timing of a security issue has important implications, because the securities so issued remain outstanding for many years.

22-1. Which is more important in evaluating a share of stock, past earnings per share or future earnings per share?

22-2. As the risk of owning common stock increases, does the price-earnings ratio tend to rise or fall?

22-3. A firm recently raised an additional $1 million through the sale of 100,000 shares of common stock. Even with the extra 100,000 shares outstanding, the market price per share did not fall. Explain why the shares did not decline in price.

22-4. Why are retained earnings considered to be a cheap source of funds?

REVIEW PROBLEM

No answers are given for this problem.

22-1. Company R is in need of $60,000 for permanent expansion; the firm believes that it can earn 25 percent (before taxes) on the additional assets to be purchased with the money. Below is the firm's balance sheet before financing:

Current assets	$100,000	Current liabilities	$ 50,000
Fixed Assets	100,000	$4 par-value common	40,000
		Retained profits	110,000
Total	$200,000	Total	$200,000

Before financing, the firm's EBIT were $60,000; the company is in the 50 percent tax bracket; the common stock is currently selling for $30 a share (a price-earnings ratio of 10).

The firm is considering whether to issue additional common stock, preferred stock, or bonds to raise the $60,000. If common stock is sold, the firm will receive $30 per share; if preferred stock is sold, the company will receive $100 per share and the dividend rate will be 6 percent; if bonds are sold, the issuer will receive $1,000 for each bond, and the interest rate will be 5 percent.

If additional common is sold, the price-earnings ratio will remain at 10; if preferred stock is issued, the price-earnings ratio will fall to 9.75; if bonds are issued, the price-earnings ratio will fall to 9.50.

(a) Compare the impact of each form of financing on earnings per share on the common and on the market price of the common. (b) Which of the three alternatives do you recommend? Use the following format in assembling the data:

388 Managing for Expansion

	Prefinancing Data	Pro Forma Data		
		Additional Common Issued	6 Percent Preferred Stock Is Issued	5 Percent Bonds Are Issued
EBIT	$60,000	$75,000	$75,000	$75,000
Interest on bonds	0	—	—	—
Taxable income	$60,000	—	—	—
Tax (50%)	30,000	—	—	—
Net after taxes	$30,000	—	—	—
Less preferred dividends	0		—	—
Available for common	$30,000	—	—	—
Shares of common outstanding	10,000	—	—	—
Earnings per share of common	$3	—	—	—
Price-earnings ratio	10	10	9.75	9.50
Market price of common	$30	—	—	—

 # Distributing Stocks and Bonds to the Public at Large

In our discussion of stocks and bonds little was said about how corporations sell their securities. In many respects, the movement of securities from the corporation to the investor resembles the flow of manufactured goods from producer to consumer, a large number of middlemen often aiding in the distribution of both commodities and securities. The following aspects of the movement of securities from issuer to investor will be explained in this chapter:

1. Services rendered by investment bankers
2. The distribution of stocks and bonds to the public at large
   a. Outright sale to investment bankers, who in turn sell the securities to the general public
   b. The use of investment bankers as selling agents—another way of moving the securities to the general public
   c. The sale of securities to the general public without any assistance from investment bankers
3. The Securities Act of 1933

The sale of securities to special select groups will be studied in the next chapter.

SERVICES RENDERED BY INVESTMENT BANKERS

Since investment banks may aid in the distribution of corporate securities, it will be useful to discuss briefly their nature and functions. An *investment bank* is a financial institution whose main purpose is to help corporations and government units sell securities. These institutions are called banks because they aid business in acquiring funds for relatively long periods of time, unlike commercial banks, which stress the supplying of funds for relatively short periods of time. Furthermore, investment bankers do not accept deposits as do commercial banks. In addition to their main function, which is to deal in new securities, investment bankers engage in a number of other related activities for corporations, investors, and society.

The most important service rendered by investment bankers is their purchase of issues of stocks or bonds from a corporation. Investment bankers then sell the securities to the public, making a gross profit on the difference between the price paid to the corporation for the securities and the price at which they are sold to investors. The financing of Kaiser Steel Corporation may be cited as an example. The company sold 1,600,000 shares of preferred stock and 800,000 shares of common stock to a group of 234 investment bankers. The investment bankers paid the Kaiser Steel Corporation a total of $37,320,000 for all the shares. The investment bankers in turn sold the stock to the public for a total of $40 million.

Services Rendered for the Corporation

When acting in this capacity, investment bankers are basically merchants whose inventory consists of stocks and bonds. In one sense, investment bankers are like any other merchants who buy inventory at one price and hope to sell it at a higher price. In addition to earning profits from the sale of their inventory, they may also have additional income from fees earned by advising corporations on matters pertaining to long-term fund raising and by acting as selling agents for a corporation. (The bankers do not take title to the securities; instead, they receive a fee for each unit they are able to persuade the public to buy.) Directly or indirectly, investment bankers play a role in most large stock and bond issues being sold in today's market.

Investment bankers are expected to make a study of corporations whose securities they are selling to the public. This checkup on the corporation is made so that the investment bankers will not be in the position of marketing securities of corporations that have no prospects of economic success. This service of weeding out the weakest companies saves the investing public many a dollar. It should be noted, however, that investment bankers do not guarantee the securities they are peddling. In fact, purchasers may be put on guard by a notation in the advertising material that the issue is a speculation.

Services Rendered to Investors

Investment banking firms may be members of the various stock exchanges. If so, they are in a position to facilitate the transfer of securities already issued by corporations. When a security holder desires to sell securities, or when a potential security holder wants to acquire them, he can complete the transaction by contacting an investment bank that maintains brokerage offices.

Investment banking houses may participate in the over-the-counter market; this type of activity also facilitates the transfer of ownership of securities already issued by corporations.

Investment banks may have research departments which render advice to clients, both corporations and investors. Many research departments turn out numerous analyses of industries, corporations, and current political and economic developments. Much of this information is free and is intended to keep investor-clients satisfied as well as to attract new clients.

Investment banks may assist holders of large blocks of securities to sell their stocks or bonds, usually the former. Thus, 27 investment bankers bought 200,000 shares of common stock of the Opelika Manufacturing Corporation from 8 stockholders. They paid the stockholders $11.70 per share and resold the stock to the public at $13.00 per share. No portion of the proceeds accrued to the corporation. Shareholders with large holdings may want to sell part of their holdings for a number of reasons: to raise money to pay inheritance taxes, to increase the marketability of the shares not sold, or to convert from a close corporation to an open corporation, with the object of later raising funds from the general public. In another case, investment bankers purchased $12 million of Cone Mills stock from 3 heirs of the founder and from an endowed hospital; the reason given by the heirs for selling was to increase the marketability of the shares they retained, which represented two-thirds of their original holdings.

Investment bankers may initiate mergers among various companies by bringing together the parties involved and proposing terms that appear advantageous to the owners of the several companies.

Investors look to investment banking houses for the rendering of many of these services. Like all other private profit-seeking enterprises, investment banks strive to build up a large clientele, and in striving for this goal they compete with each other in the quantity and quality of the services they offer.

When investment bankers assist in the flotation of security issues, they are engaging in the *investment banking function*. When they help investors transfer their securities to other investors, they are engaging in the *brokerage function*. The investment banking function and the brokerage function are completely different even though a particular firm may carry on both, as does the firm of Merrill Lynch, Pierce, Fenner & Smith.

OUTRIGHT SALE TO INVESTMENT BANKERS, WHO IN TURN SELL THE SECURITIES TO THE GENERAL PUBLIC

The Investment Banker as a Middleman

A corporation may decide to sell the entire new issue to an investment banker or to a group of investment bankers. When investment bankers are acting in this capacity they are merchants who buy the securities at one price and sell them at a higher price. For example, when E. I. du Pont de Nemours and Company decided to sell preferred stock to the public, investment banks handled the entire transaction. The company disposed of 700,000 shares of preferred stock by selling these securities to investment bankers. The terms of the transaction are summarized in Table 23-1.

TABLE 23-1
Sale of du Pont
Preferred Stock

	Price to the Public	Underwriting Commissions	Proceeds to the Company
Total	$71,400,000	$1,400,000	$70,000,000
Per unit	$102	$2	$100

As indicated, the investment bankers paid the corporation $100 for each share. They expected to (and did) sell these securities to the public at $102 per share, making a gross profit of $2 on each security sold. The difference between the price paid the corporation and the selling price to the public is known as the *spread*; in the du Pont transaction it was $2. Looking at the transaction in the aggregate, we find that the investment bankers purchased 700,000 shares of preferred stock from du Pont, paying a total of $70 million to the company. They expected to sell these securities to the public for $71,400,000, making a gross profit $1,400,000. This is a typical transaction entered into by large corporations.

A second example of this nature may be found in an issue of bonds by the Consolidated Edison Company of New York, Inc., the terms of which are given in Table 23-2.

	Price to the Public	Underwriting Commissions	Proceeds to Consolidated Edison	
Total	$101,050,000	$320,100	$100,729,900	*TABLE 23-2 Sale of Consolidated Edison Bonds*
Percent per unit	101.05	0.3201	100.7299	

The underwriters paid the corporation 100.7299 percent of par for each bond purchased. This means that the corporation received an average of $1,007.299 for each $1,000 of bonds sold to investment bankers ($1.007299 \times \$1,000$). The investment bankers in turn expected to resell these bonds at 101.05 percent of par, which amounted to $1,010.50 per $1,000 of bonds ($1.0105 \times \$1,000$). The spread per $1,000 of bonds averaged $3.201. When compared with a par of $1,000 the spread amounts to 0.3201 percent. Again looking at the aggregate figures, we find that the investment bankers paid the corporation $100,729,900 for bonds that were resold to the public for $101,050,000. The bankers' gross profit on the transaction was $320,100.

The outright sale of securities to investment bankers has three main advantages to the corporation. First, the investment bankers, being specialists in the distribution of securities, can do a highly satisfactory job of distributing them at a reasonable cost. With their specialized experience they are in an excellent position to give advice to the corporation on the best type of security to offer, the most satisfactory terms to be included in the security, the timing of the issue, and the class of investors to be sought as purchasers. However high the cost of investment bankers' services might seem, a large corporation would probably pay even more to distribute its securities, for such a project would entail the hiring of specialist salesmen and specialist lawyers and other expenses.

Advantages of Selling Securities to Investment Bankers

Second, by selling an issue of securities direct to investment bankers the corporation is assured of a fixed sum of cash; the investment bankers take the risk of finding investors who will purchase the securities. This is an important service for the corporation, because it might need a definite sum of money at a definite date. Any delay in the receipt of cash could delay spending plans. The investment bankers spare the corporation this risk by guaranteeing that it will receive a stated sum of cash regardless of the speed with which the securities are sold to investors.

A third group of miscellaneous benefits also accrues to industrial corporations that sell their new securities outright to investment bankers—free advice to the corporation on operating policies, on future financial programs, and perhaps on other matters. All these advantages make it worthwhile for the corporation to give serious consideration to using investment bankers' services when planning to issue securities.

Negotiation versus Competitive Bidding
There are two main ways in which a corporation may sell its securities to investment bankers. The first method is negotiation; the investment banker and the representatives of the corporation agree over the conference table that the corporation will sell securities to the investment banker. The second method is competitive bidding; a corporation with securities to sell requests bids for the stocks or bonds, and the group of investment bankers that offers the most attractive bid is awarded the issue. The most attractive bid is the one that offers the best combination of the most money and the lowest interest or dividend rate. The process is highly impersonal under competitive bidding. The direct negotiation method predominates in the industrial field, but competitive bidding is typical of railroad, public utility, and municipal financing.

Negotiation
When stocks or bonds are to be sold to investment bankers under the negotiation method, the process of getting the securities from the corporation into the hands of investors has three main stages—origination, underwriting, and distribution.

Origination Origination is concerned with the preliminary steps leading to the purchase of the securities from the corporation by the investment bankers. A company needing funds may seek out an investment banker; or, perhaps, investment bankers, who are constantly on the lookout for new business, will seek out the company. The investment banker is interested in selling securities for the corporation, but before he makes a final decision he must investigate the company and the securities it proposes to sell. This investigation is necessary because the investment banker must be reasonably sure that the securities he purchases from the corporation will have sufficient appeal to be resold at a profit to investors. The investment banker who conducts this investigation is known as the *originator*. He makes a thorough study of the corporation, reviewing all factors that to his knowledge will have a bearing on the financial success of the company.

During the early stages of the negotiations, the originator and the corporation must agree on the approximate selling price of the security to the public, the spread (gross profit) that the investment banker will receive, and the approximate amount that the corporation will receive for each security. At a later date more exact information is available on the selling price to the public. Setting the price at which a security will be sold to the public is an art which comes only after long years of experience in the investment banking field. Consideration must be given to such factors as the market price of the company's already outstanding securities, the market price of similar securities in comparable companies, and anything else that will shed light on the most appropriate price for the new issue. The originator and the corporation finally agree on a price to the public which will be satisfactory to the corporation but which will not be so high as to drive potential purchasers out of the market.

The spread is deducted from the price at which the security is expected to sell to investors in order to determine how much the corporation will receive for each security. The spread, as noted earlier, is the investment banker's gross profit and is determined by such factors as (1) the financial strength of the issuing corporation, (2) the kind of security being offered, (3) the risk to the investment banker, (4) the selling effort anticipated, and (5) the bargaining power of the originator and the issuer. Financially strong companies like AT&T can get investment bankers to market their securities with a small spread because the bankers know that investors will take advantage of an opportunity to purchase new securities in a well-known and financially strong corporation. In general, the spread is less for bond issues than for stock issues; that is, the spread is less in terms of percentage of the selling price. The spread is large when the investment banker feels that there is considerable risk in the transaction. Thus, new issues that have an unknown market usually have a relatively large spread. The spread is relatively large if the investment banker thinks he will have to exercise a great deal of selling effort to dispose of the securities. This would be especially true for a company in a declining industry. Finally, the bargaining power of the corporation and the investment banker affect the spread. The corporation attempts to minimize the spread while the originator bargains for what he considers an adequate amount. All five factors have significance to the corporation, because the amount of spread is one of the determinants of the amount of cash that it will receive for its securities (the other determinant being the selling price of the securities to the public).

The Underwriting Phase When it becomes apparent that the issue will be purchased from the corporation, the originator gets in touch with other investment bankers who are invited to join the originator in the formation of a syndicate. The *syndicate* is a group of investment banking firms that band together for the purpose of purchasing securities from the corporation with the expectation of reselling these securities to the public at a higher price. Why does the originator invite other investment bankers to join him in purchasing the securities from the corporation? The main reason is that the originator decreases his risk of being caught with sticky (slow-moving) merchandise; if a number of investment bankers participate in the process of marketing the securities, they all share the risk. Also, the more investment bankers who participate, the greater the distributive power of the syndicate. Thus, when the American Tobacco Company sold bonds, there were 148 investment banking houses in the syndicate. Investment bankers who join the syndicate are expected to have either selling power or sufficient capital to carry the securities purchased for a reasonable period of time in the event that the issue turns out to be sticky. Although the corporation deals with the originator, the stocks or bonds are actually sold to the members of the syndicate—each member agreeing to buy a certain portion of the securities. As would be expected, the originator generally buys at least as much of the securities from the corporation as any other member of the syndicate.

The Distribution Stage The final and most important step in the distribution of securities is their sale to investors. Although the corporation has turned this step over to investment bankers and is assured a fixed sum of cash regardless of the success with which the securities are sold to the public, corporate management usually follows this final stage with keen interest. The members of the underwriting syndicate may have salesmen who get in touch with potential purchasers of the securities. Investment banking houses that deal directly with the ultimate purchasers are sometimes called retail houses. Other members of the syndicate are wholesale houses; that is, they do not sell directly to the public but instead sell to other investment houses and dealers.

"Out" Clauses in Contracts with Investment Bankers Even when investment bankers contract to buy securities from a corporation, the contract often contains a number of "out" clauses. If market conditions change adversely any time up to the public offering of the securities, the investment bankers are relieved of their obligation to go through with the deal. In the final analysis, investment bankers cannot be expected to buy securities that cannot be resold to the public at a profit. The weaker the issue, the more out clauses there are in the contract. A large number of out clauses lessens the certainty of receiving the money from the transaction.

Competitive Bidding   Under competitive bidding, when a corporation has securities to sell, it makes all the preliminary preparations and then offers to sell the securities to the highest bidder. Generally, investment bankers bid against one another for the securities. The corporation then sells the issue to the syndicate that offers the best terms. The main advantage alleged for this method is that the corporation receives better terms on its securities than it would under the negotiated sale.

THE USE OF INVESTMENT BANKERS AS SELLING AGENTS   When the selling agent plan of distributing securities is used, the amount of cash to be received by the corporation is not definite but depends on the number of securities sold by the investment bankers. The use of investment bankers as selling agents is of some importance in raising capital for small businesses and is also highly important in raising venture capital. The Lexa Oil Corporation sold common stock under an arrangement whereby an investment banker used his best efforts to sell the shares. The selling price of the stock was 20 cents. For each share sold, the investment banker received a commission of 5 cents. The investment banker did not take title to the securities, so the corporation was not assured of a fixed sum of cash.

Corporations may attempt to sell their securities to the general public without assistance from investment bankers. This procedure is often used by new companies floating their first issue and by established ones that are offering additional stocks or bonds to the public. Corporations that are so small as to be of local interest only must usually get along without investment bankers, as the services of these specialists may be very costly or not available at all. Therefore, the directors and officers must themselves plan a program for the sale of the securities.

After determining the kind of securities to be issued and their price, the next step is to register the stocks or bonds with a state securities commission. In most states it is illegal to sell new securities without first registering them with a state regulatory body whose duty it is to supervise the flotation of stocks and bonds. The management generally hires a lawyer to draft the documents necessary to complete the registration.

When the officers sell the securities on company time, they do not usually receive any fee for their services, although if the selling is done after office hours, a small fee may be received. The officers will, in any event, canvass prospects who might be interested in buying the stocks or bonds. The prospects will be reached by personal interview, telephone, newspaper advertising, and mail. This method of selling securities may take several months to complete.

Figure 23-1 shows how a small corporation reached the public in an attempt to sell bonds. Investment bankers did not participate. Potential investors approached the management of the issuer.

The main purpose of the Securities Act of 1933 is to force nonexempt issuers of securities to supply investors with complete and accurate information. The act also provides for the punishment of those who engage in fraudulent practices when marketing securities that are regulated by it. The act is based on the assumption that forcing an issuer to supply adequate and truthful information is as far as the federal government should go in protecting the purchasers of newly issued securities.

THE SECURITIES ACT OF 1933

Generally speaking, the following issues are exempt from the Securities Act of 1933: small issues, issues already subject to government regulation, issues being traded on stock exchanges, and issues sold to 25 or fewer persons.

A corporation is said to file a *registration statement* when it submits certain information with the SEC. After the registration statement is filed there is a waiting period of 20 days before the securities may be sold to the public, although the commission has the power to shorten this period in certain cases. As a practical matter, very few people ever see a registration statement. Instead, the general public usually gets its information from the *prospectus*, which is a summary of the registration statement. However, the public does benefit from the registration statement in that a great quantity of financial data is available for the financial services, which in turn pass this information on to the investing public.

The annual reports of the SEC reveal some of the specific types of protection that are given to investors by this government agency. Two incidents are listed below to give an idea of the practical operations of the SEC when enforcing the Securities Act of 1933:

The commission discovered that a company showed properties on its balance sheet at $700,000. The cost of the properties was $200,000. The commission required the company to amend its balance sheet and to carry the property at $200,000.

FIGURE 23-1

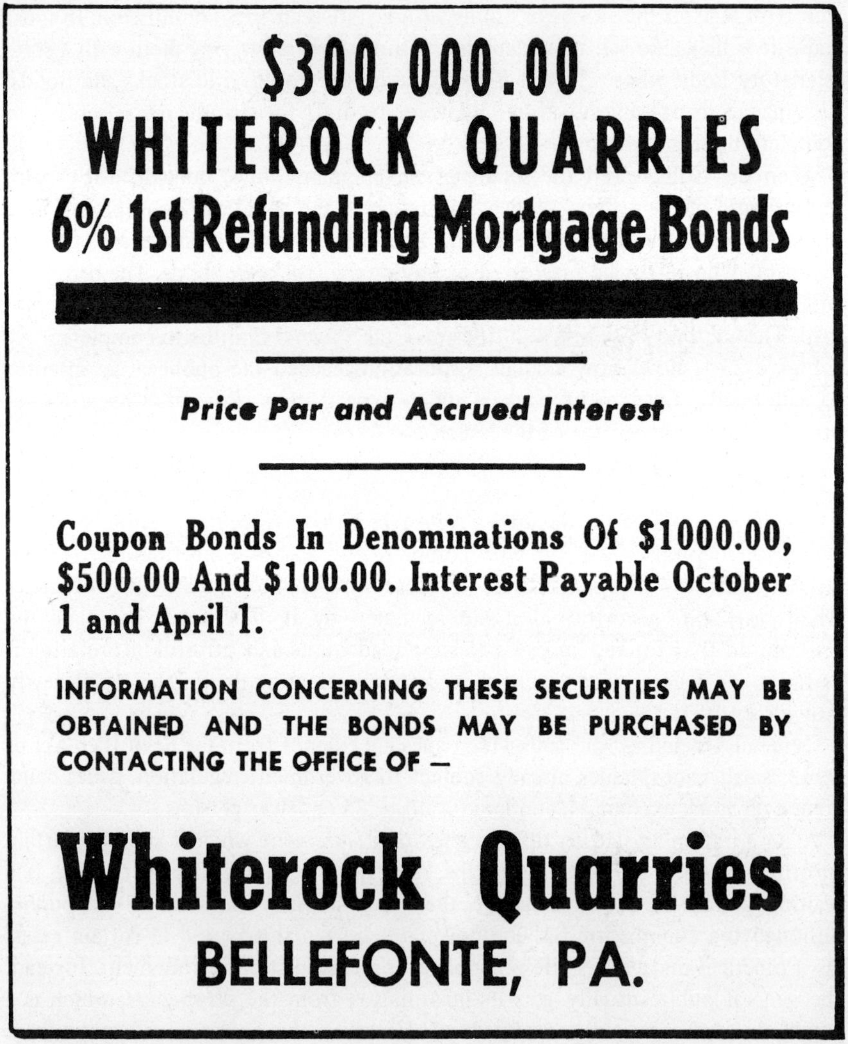

$300,000.00
WHITEROCK QUARRIES
6% 1st Refunding Mortgage Bonds

Price Par and Accrued Interest

Coupon Bonds In Denominations Of $1000.00, $500.00 And $100.00. Interest Payable October 1 and April 1.

INFORMATION CONCERNING THESE SECURITIES MAY BE OBTAINED AND THE BONDS MAY BE PURCHASED BY CONTACTING THE OFFICE OF —

Whiterock Quarries
BELLEFONTE, PA.

A mining company filed a registration statement and a prospectus with the SEC. The commission forced the company to add to the registration statement and the prospectus a section stating that the company had been selling stock to the public for over 20 years and that only a small percentage of the receipts had been used for actual development of the properties, most of the money having been used for salesmen's commissions, office expenses, and salaries.

Investment bankers render a number of services to corporations, investors, and the general public. From the viewpoint of society, the most important service rendered by investment bankers is that of facilitating the process of capital formation. Acting in this capacity, they are contributing toward a higher standard of living for the country.

When securities are offered to the general public, the distribution may take place in one of three ways: by outright sale to investment bankers, by the use of investment bankers as selling agents, and by sale to the public without any assistance from investment bankers.

A corporation may sell its securities to investment bankers through either negotiation or competitive bidding. Negotiation is prevalent in industrial finance, but competitive bidding predominates in public utilities.

HIGHLIGHTS OF THIS CHAPTER

REVIEW QUESTIONS

23-1. Explain the meaning of the following terms:
investment banking function
brokerage function
spread
origination
syndicate
registration statement
out clause
selling agent
prospectus

23-2. Does the U.S. government forbid the sale of speculative common stocks?

23-3. Discuss the nature of the services rendered by investment bankers to corporations and investors.

23-4. Suggest the main factors that will influence the amount of spread charged by investment bankers.

23-5. Distinguish between a negotiated sale and a competitive bidding sale.

23-6. Why does an originator often form a syndicate, rather than keep all the securities and sell them himself?

23-7. What are the main advantages to the issuer of selling an entire issue outright to investment bankers rather than selling direct to the general public?

23-8. Company Z is planning to issue_____ percent bonds. All the bidders (investment bankers) stated a rate of 5 percent and offered the bids given below. The best bid from the issuer's viewpoint is (a) 99.35 percent; (b) 90.75 percent; (c) 97.62 percent; (d) 102.733 percent; (e) 101.35 percent; (f) 100.73 percent; (g) 100.948 percent.

REVIEW PROBLEMS   See end of next chapter.

CASE ON SELECTING   The Esquire Company is in need of approximately $229,000 for permanent
A METHOD OF   expansion; the firm has decided on the sale of common stock as the method of
ISSUING SECURITIES   financing. Some data on the firm are given in Table 23-3.

TABLE 23-3
Data on
Esquire Company

	One Year Ago	Two Years Ago	Three Years Ago
Sales	$510,000	$267,000	$235,000
Net income after taxes	26,000	7,000	2,600
Earnings per share	0.208	0.09	0.03
Dividends	0	0	0

Two basic decisions had to be made. (1) Since there was no market in the common stock, the offering price to the public had to be determined. (2) A decision had to be made on which one of the following three methods of distributing the securities would be used: (a) selling the issue outright to an investment banker, (b) using the selling-agent services of an investment banker, (c) advertising the securities in the *New York Times* and instructing interested readers to write to the home office of the firm for a prospectus. Regardless of the method selected for issuing the securities, the company would have $18,000 in expenses for printing, legal fees, and other expenses.

An investment banking firm made this proposal to the issuer. It would either buy the entire issue outright at the agreed selling price to the public, less a commission of 80 cents a share; or it would act as a selling agent, charging the sum of the following:

1. It would charge a fee of 37½ cents for each share it could persuade the public to purchase.
2. For a payment of $250 to the issuer, it could, over a period of five years, purchase an aggregate of 25,000 shares of common stock at prices ranging from $2.75 to $3.50 per share, depending on the year the warrant was exercised.

Required: (a) Suggest the price at which these shares were to be sold to the public. (b) Give the advantages and disadvantages of each of the three alternative methods of selling the shares, and select the one you think most appropriate, giving reasons. (c) Based on your estimate of the price the public would be willing to pay, determine the approximate number of shares to be issued.

Distributing Stocks and Bonds to Special Buyers

The main theme of the previous chapter was the distribution of securities to the public at large, often with the aid of investment bankers but in some cases without the assistance of these middlemen. We will continue this general discussion by indicating how a corporation distributes its securities to select groups. The following will be discussed in this chapter:

1. Selling securities to those who are already stockholders in the firm
   a. The meaning of privileged subscriptions
   b. Comment on some important terms
   c. Privileged subscriptions from the corporation's viewpoint
   d. Privileged subscriptions from the investor's viewpoint
   e. Additional aspects of privileged subscriptions
2. Selling securities to a select group through direct placement
3 Factors in decision making

An established corporation may sell additional securities through privileged subscriptions. For example, the Pennsylvania Power and Light Company offered its stockholders the right to buy one additional share of common stock for each seven shares held. The selling price to the stockholders or their assignees was $24 per share and the offer could be taken advantage of within a two-week period.

THE MEANING OF PRIVILEGED SUBSCRIPTIONS

To stimulate the purchase of the securities being offered, the common stockholders are often given an opportunity of buying the stocks or bonds at what appears to be bargain rates; that is, the stockholders can often buy the securities from the issuing corporation at a price lower than identical securities are selling for in the market. When the Granite City Steel Company sold shares through privileged subscriptions, the additional stock was offered to stockholders at $35 per share; the closing price of the stock on the day prior to the offering to the stockholders was $40.37½. The new securities are not always sold below market price; a number of recent issues have been sold through privileged subscriptions at a price that was the market price the day before the offering.

The corporation mails to the stockholders a document known as a *subscription warrant*, which notifies the stockholders that they or their assignees will be entitled to purchase a certain amount of new securities from the corporation at a given price within a stated period of time. The subscription warrants often have a life of two weeks (see Figure 24-1).

FIGURE 24-1

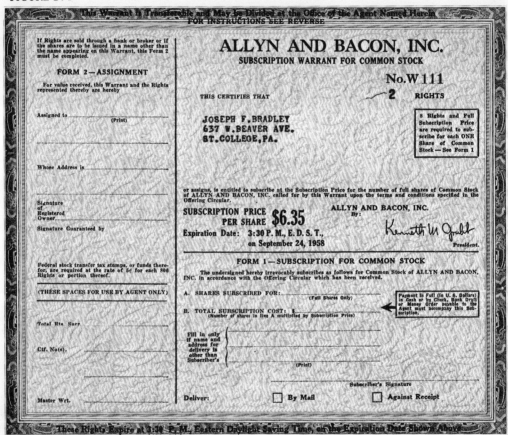

Usually the holders of the subscription warrants must send cash with their order for the securities, although occasionally the corporation gives them a year or so in which to pay for the securities. The subscription warrants of the Wheeling Steel Corporation may be cited as an example of the full cash payment method of handling privileged subscriptions. The holders of common stock could subscribe for convertible debentures, but the order for the securities had to be accompanied by cash. On the other hand, when Montgomery Ward & Company sold stock through privileged subscriptions, those who owned shares had the right to buy additional stock at $50 per share on the basis of one share for each four shares held. Half the purchase price had to be paid when the warrants were exercised; the balance had to be paid in two equal installments within a seven-month period.

The security holders who receive transferable subscription warrants should use them to purchase the securities being offered by the corporation or should sell them in the market. The subscription warrants have value in the market when they make it possible for the holder to purchase securities from the corporation at a price below market value. The warrants are usually transferable, and the corporation will honor them by selling new securities (common stock, convertible preferred stock, or convertible bonds) at the prearranged price to anyone who presents these warrants, whether or not he is the person to whom they were originally sent.

If additional common stock is being offered below market price, the shares originally held by the stockholders may decline in price. If there is a decline in the market value of the shares, it is caused by a dilution that takes place when a corporation sells shares and does not receive equivalent values. It stands to reason that the average market price per share will fall if the company offers a considerable number of additional shares below market value. However, in a number of cases the sale of additional shares slightly below market price has no appreciable effect on the market value of the shares. If investors believe that the corporation can earn a high profit on the additional funds being raised, the market value of all the shares may even increase slightly. In a given period so many factors influence the price of shares that other forces may offset or magnify the theoretical effect of privileged subscriptions on market price.

Under the privileged subscription arrangement, stockholders are not obliged to purchase the securities being offered by their corporation. For a variety of reasons a shareholder may not care to invest more money in the same corporation. If this is the case, he should sell his subscription warrants to another party.

COMMENTS ON SOME IMPORTANT TERMS

It will be worth our while to study some of the terms frequently used in any discussion of privileged subscriptions: subscription price, rights, subscription warrants, rights on, and ex rights.

Subscription Price

The price at which the corporation has agreed to sell the securities to existing security holders or their assignees is known as the subscription price. A corporation, for example, might offer to sell a certain number of shares to a given stockholder at $80 per share. If the market price of this stock is $92, the corporation might offer to sell a limited number of shares through privileged subscriptions at $80 per share.

Rights

When a corporation issues additional shares and sells them through privileged subscriptions, each shareholder receives 1 "right" for each share held. Thus, if a stockholder owned 100 shares of common stock, he would receive 100 rights.

Likewise, a stockholder who owned 500 shares of stock would receive 500 rights.

It is necessary to submit a certain number of rights along with the cash order for the shares to be purchased from the corporation at the special subscription price. The arrangement might be that the warrant holders can subscribe for 1 share of stock for each 4 shares held. This would mean that a warrant evidencing 4 rights would have to accompany the order for the shares. Under these assumptions, if our stockholder held 100 shares, he would receive a subscription warrant evidencing 100 rights, and with these rights he would be entitled to buy 25 additional shares of stock from the issuing corporation at the issuing price. For example, during a two-week period, warrant holders of the Granite City Steel Company could send 4 rights along with the subscription price for each share purchased from the company.

The number of rights that one must have in order to subscribe for 1 share depends on the relationship between the number of new shares to be issued and the number of shares already issued. Assume that a corporation already has 100,000 shares of common stock outstanding and that 25,000 more shares of common stock are to be issued.

The formula is:

$$\begin{aligned}\text{Number of rights needed to buy 1 share} &= \frac{\text{Number of shares outstanding prior to rights offering}}{\text{Additional shares to be issued}} \\ &= \frac{100{,}000}{25{,}000} \\ &= 4\end{aligned}$$

This would mean that each shareholder would be entitled to purchase 1 additional share for each 4 shares held. Another way of stating this is to say that the stockholders may purchase 1 additional share for each 4 rights held. The stock subscription warrant will state the number of rights one must have in order to buy 1 additional share.

Subscription Warrants

The document mailed to the common stockholders which evidences the right to participate in the privileged subscriptions is known as the *subscription warrant*, sometimes called the *warrant*. This document permits the holder to buy additional common stock, convertible preferred stock, or convertible bonds—depending on its terms.

Rights On

The term *rights on* means that the buyer of shares of common stock in the market is entitled to the rights about to be issued by the corporation. The buyer is said to buy the shares with rights. The terms *with rights* and *rights on* are synonymous. Assume that on March 15 the board of directors announces that on March 31 a list of stockholders' names will be prepared and rights mailed to the parties who have their names on the corporation's records at that time. If a person buys the stock after March 15 and in time to get his name on the records, he is said to buy the stock with rights. On the other hand, the seller of the stock gives up an opportunity to receive rights because his name will be removed from the list of stockholders before the warrants are mailed.

The term *ex rights* means that the buyer of the stock is not entitled to any rights. Assume, as in the above case, that the directors announce on March 15 that rights will be mailed to those whose names are on the books as of March 31. Also assume that the rights are to have a life of one month; that is, the warrants will be good until the end of April. Under these conditions, the corporation will mail the rights to those who have their names on the corporation's records at the close of business on March 31. Anyone buying the stock too late to get on the mailing list buys the stock ex rights. The stock will be said to sell ex rights until the end of April. Ex rights means that the buyer of the stock does not obtain the privilege of receiving the rights, because the corporation has already taken from its records (or the transfer agent's records) a list of those who are entitled to the rights.

Ex Rights

From the corporation's viewpoint, the privileged subscription is a success if all the securities are sold. Anything the corporation can do to stimulate the sale of the securities contributes to the success of the transaction. Four main factors determine whether or not all the securities offered will be sold: the spread between the market price and the subscription price, the future profit prospects of the issuing corporation, the number of additional shares being offered in relation to the number of shares already outstanding, and arrangements made for selling any of the securities not subscribed to by the existing security holders.

PRIVILEGED SUBSCRIPTIONS FROM THE CORPORATION'S VIEWPOINT

The first and most important requirement for success of privileged subscriptions is that the market price of the securities being offered stay above the subscription price. A large spread between the subscription price and the market price at the time the rights are issued will permit the market price to decline without falling below the subscription price. If the market price falls below the subscription price, no more shares can be sold by the corporation. A large spread, therefore, contributes to the success of the privileged subscription plan.

Spread between the Market Price and the Subscription Price

The pricing of shares to be issued under privileged subscriptions is a difficult art. As indicated, the subscription price should not be too high in relation to the market price; on the other hand, it should not be too low. A corporation could assure the success of the privileged subscriptions by setting the subscription price so low that the market price could not possibly fall below the price at which the shares could be purchased from the issuing corporation. Yet corporations do not follow this line of action. Corporate officers and directors try to raise the maximum amount of cash through the issuance of a limited number of shares. If all the stockholders bought their allowed quota of shares from the issuing corporation, it would not matter how low the subscription price was, because each shareholder's relative position would remain the same. But if some stockholders (for one reason or another) let their rights lapse, we would find that this group would be harmed by the use of a very low subscription price.

One more feature of the subscription price deserves brief comment. The subscription price should be at or above the par value of the shares being sold. If the shares being offered lack par value, then the directors have more freedom in fixing the subscription price.

Profit Prospects of the Corporation

A second requirement for the successful flotation of securities through privileged subscriptions is that the corporation must appear to have profitable years ahead. If the corporation does not, those who receive rights will be likely to sell them in the market. Investors are more apt to exercise their warrants if the issuer is a profitable corporation.

Number of Shares Being Offered

A third important factor that influences the success of privileged subscriptions is the number of shares being offered in relation to the number of shares already outstanding. Security holders are likely, for example, to take advantage of an offer to buy 5 shares for each 100 shares held. But if stockholders were offered an opportunity to buy an additional 100 shares for each 100 shares already owned, they might hesitate to make such a big commitment, even if the shares were offered below market price; in fact, stockholders would tend to sell their rights under these conditions. Therefore, we can say that a factor contributing to the success of privileged subscriptions is that the corporation issue relatively small amounts of new securities in relation to the number of securities outstanding.

Arrangements for Selling Unsubscribed Shares

A fourth factor that influences the success of the privileged subscriptions is what arrangements, if any, are made to sell the shares not purchased by holders of warrants. Some of the arrangements used by corporations are: (1) permitting oversubscription; (2) permitting employees to subscribe for any shares not purchased through the exercise of warrants; (3) entering into a standby agreement with investment bankers; (4) entering into an agreement with investment bankers whereby they will get in touch with stockholders and urge them to exercise their warrants; and (5) using privileged subscriptions without help from investment bankers.

Oversubscription Privilege

Stockholders may be given the right to oversubscribe for the new securities being offered. Under this plan, a stockholder buys his quota of securities and at the same time applies for additional securities at the subscription price. For example, the Barr Rubber Products Company sold shares through privileged subscriptions under a plan whereby the stockholders were given the right to oversubscribe to the shares. In addition to subscribing for the shares covered by the warrant, the holders of warrants could subscribe for additional shares that would be available if others did not exercise their warrants. Of the 24,200 shares offered to common stockholders, 19,014 shares were subscribed for through the primary subscription. However, the oversubscriptions amounted to 5,809 shares. Since there were only 5,186 shares not subscribed for through exercising the warrants, the stock had to be allotted to those who oversubscribed. From the corporation's viewpoint, the oversubscription was a success because it made possible the selling of the entire, 24,200 shares.

Another plan that may be used by the corporation to promote the sale of securities is to allow employees to purchase any shares not subscribed through the exercise of warrants. For example, the Long Island Lighting Company issued common stock through privileged subscriptions, with the additional provision that employees could subscribe for any shares not purchased by the stockholders. The company had 524,949 shares for sale, each stockholder being entitled to buy 1 additional share for every 6 shares held. Warrant holders purchased 511,583 shares, leaving a balance of 13,366 shares unsold. Then employees were invited to subscribe for these shares, the total subscriptions amounting to 30,781 shares. Since there was not enough stock to accommodate the employees fully, the shares were allotted to them.

Purchase by Employees of Any Stock Not Sold to Holders of Stock Subscription Warrants

To assure itself a minimum sum of cash, the corporation may enter into a standby agreement with investment bankers. Any shares not sold to holders of warrants are purchased by the investment bankers, thus guaranteeing the corporation a minimum sum of money. When the New Hampshire Fire Insurance Company offered to sell 75,000 shares of capital stock through privileged subscriptions, investment bankers entered into a standby agreement with the company. The outcome of this case was that stockholders subscribed for 93 percent of the shares. The 5,250 unsubscribed shares were purchased by a syndicate headed by the First Boston Corporation.

Standby Underwriting Agreements with Investment Bankers

Investment bankers charge a fee for underwriting a security issue offered through privileged subscriptions. There may be a flat fee on the entire amount of the securities being sold; in addition, there will probably be another fee based on the amount of securities actually purchased from the corporation. The Montana-Dakota Utilities Company case is an example of one way of compensating underwriters. This company offered 236,755 shares of common stock at $14.50 per share through privileged subscriptions, with investment bankers agreeing to purchase at the subscription price of $14.50 any shares not sold to holders of subscription warrants. The investment bankers received a fee of 40 cents per share on the entire 236,755 units, or a total of $94,702. Warrant holders purchased 226,853 shares; the investment bankers bought the remaining 9,902 shares. The bankers agreed with the corporation that if the shares were sold to the public at a price above $15.50 per share, the corporation would be entitled to 75 percent of the excess over $15.50. When the investment bankers decided to sell each of the 9,902 shares at $16.75, the company was entitled to an additional $9,283.13. In this case the bankers received the twofold gross profit of the 40 cents on all the shares underwritten and the markup on the 9,902 shares sold to the general public. Under a plan of this kind, which is typical, the issuing corporation is not assured of a fixed sum of cash, although it is guaranteed a minimum amount and possibly an extra sum if the new issue is well received.

Under another plan, the corporation is guaranteed a fixed amount regardless of how well the new issue is received. When the Stromberg-Carlson Company offered 72,025 shares of convertible preferred stock through privileged subscriptions at $50 a share, the corporation was guaranteed a fixed sum of cash. The contract with the investment bankers provided that they would buy any unsold shares from the corporation at $50 each. The investment bankers charged a fee of $1.40 a share on each of the 72,025 units being offered, or $100,835. The corporation was assured of $3,500,415 (72,025 × $48.60).

Efforts of Dealers in Contact with Stockholders

By getting in contact with stockholders, urging them to take advantage of the rights and to purchase securities from the corporation, investment bankers and brokers may assist corporations to sell securities through privileged subscriptions. They receive a commission on every share that is purchased because of their efforts. Investment bankers and brokers do not have a complete list of the stockholders; hence, not all the stockholders may be reached. Each broker or dealer can reach only his own customers who own shares in that particular company. The sale of Central Telephone Company common stock through privileged subscriptions was not underwritten, but dealers throughout the country received a fee of 55 cents for each share subscribed to through their efforts. Of this amount, approximately 5 cents went to the managing dealer (Paine, Weber, Jackson and Curtis) and the remaining 50 cents went to the participating dealers throughout the country. The company was not sure of a fixed sum of money under this arrangement.

Lack of Assistance from Investment Bankers

On the other hand, the corporation may attempt to dispose of securities through privileged subscriptions without any assistance from investment bankers. For example, when Montgomery Ward & Company offered 1,304,286 shares of common stock, it did so without the aid of investment bankers. Existing security holders and their assignees purchased 98.5 percent of the shares, the remainder being unsold. Likewise, AT&T has been offering convertible debentures through privileged subscriptions unassisted by investment bankers. Small corporations also tend to sell their additional securities without the aid of investment bankers. The reason is that the services of investment bankers are geared to the larger corporation's needs and are too costly for small companies. If a corporation offers the additional shares at an attractive price, management may believe that it can get along without the services of investment bankers and thus save the fees that would have to be paid to these middlemen.

PRIVILEGED SUBSCRIPTIONS FROM THE INVESTOR'S VIEWPOINT

As long as rights permit the holders to buy shares from the corporation below the market price, they will have a value in the market. Let us demonstrate how rights have value in a hypothetical situation. Assume the following:

1. Herbert Arnold already owns 100 shares of common stock in Company X.
2. Arnold is permitted to purchase 1 additional share for each 5 shares held; that is, he can purchase 20 shares direct from the company at the subscription price.
3. The price at which the shares can be purchased from the corporation is $80 per share.
4. The market value of the shares is $92 before the rights are issued.

If Arnold takes advantage of his privilege to buy shares of stock from the company, his position will change in the following manner:

Market value of original 100 shares at $92	$ 9,200
Cost of additional 20 shares at $80	1,600
Total investment	$10,800
Average value per share ($10,800 ÷ 120)	$ 90

It will be noted that the new market value after the issuance of rights will be $90 per share, the price having fallen by $2.

Since the rights permit the holder to buy stock at $80, it is possible to purchase the shares from the corporation at a saving of $10 per share ($90 − $80). However, in this illustration it takes 5 rights to be able to take advantage of the offer. Therefore, each right will have a value of $2 under the conditions mentioned above.

As soon as an announcement is made that rights are to be issued, it is possible to place a value on them, provided that one knows the subscription price and how many rights are needed to purchase 1 additional share.

As soon as it is officially announced that rights will be issued, trading may begin in them. To determine the value of a right during this period, the following formula has been developed:

$$\frac{M - S}{n + 1} = \text{theoretical value of a right}$$

where M represents the market price of the securities before the rights are issued, S represents the subscription price, and n represents the number of rights necessary to buy 1 share from the corporation. Substituting the information given in our hypothetical example, we have:

$$\frac{\$92 - \$80}{5 + 1} = \$2 \text{ per right}$$

After the rights have been issued, the value of each right may be determined by the following formula:

$$\frac{M - S}{n} = \text{theoretical value of the right}$$

Substituting, we have:

$$\frac{\$90 - \$80}{5} = \$2 \text{ per right}$$

The value of a right depends on two main factors: (1) the difference between the market price of the securities being offered and the subscription price of the securities being offered; and (2) the number of rights necessary to buy 1 share of stock from the issuing corporation.

As a concrete example, let us examine the value of the rights of the Long Island Lighting Company. When this company issued subscription warrants to its stockholders, the holders of warrants could subscribe, at $13 per share, for 1 additional share for each 7 rights held. The closing market price of the stock on the first day of the offering was $13.75. On this same day, the rights were selling at 12½ cents, their approximate theoretical value.

The theoretical value of a right will approximate its market value, although the two may never be exactly the same. Brokers' commissions and market forces may cause the market price of the right to vary slightly from its theoretical value. Yet the market price of a right will not vary greatly from the theoretical value because of arbitrage operations by those in the financial world.

In practice, not many stockholders sit down and attempt to place a value on their rights. Instead, the stockholder will merely look in the financial section of a newspaper and find the quotation that applies to him. If the quotation cannot be found in the newspaper, the stockholder can seek the advice of his broker on the matter.

An Appraisal of the Theoretical Impact of Rights on the Stockholder's Position

Suppose, as above, that Herbert Arnold owns 100 shares, that under a privileged subscription plan shares are to be offered at a subscription price of $80 each, and that the market value of identical shares is $92 each. Also assume that it takes 5 rights to buy a share of stock at the subscription price. Our object is to point out that Arnold does not really get something for nothing in this transaction.

Before the stock goes ex rights he will have 100 shares of stock with a market value of $92 per share.

After Arnold gets his 100 rights he will find that the market value of each of his shares will decline by the value of 1 right. Since the value of a right under the assumptions given above will be $2, the market value of the shares will fall from $92 to $90. But to offset this decline of $200 in the total amount of shares owned, Arnold now owns 100 rights worth $2 each, or a total of $200. At this stage he has not gained anything, because the $200 in rights he received is offset by a decline of $200 in the market value of the stock already owned.

If Arnold sells his rights in the market he will receive about $200 in cash. But this cash is not profit, because his shares have declined in value by about $200. He is in effect selling part of his principal when he sells his rights.

Suppose that Arnold uses his rights to buy 20 shares of stock from the corporation at the subscription price. He can acquire these shares at a saving of $10 each after the rights have been actually received ($90 − $80). Since he buys 20 shares, he has a saving of $200 on the shares purchased. But we have already seen that the value of the original 100 shares will decline by $2 each, for a total decline of $200. Arnold's saving of $200 on the transaction is offset by a decline of $200 in the market price of the original 100 shares.

Because the receipt of rights does not give the stockholders income in the usual sense of the word, rights are not taxable income; however, the sale of these rights at a profit may result in the seller receiving some taxable gain.

When a large corporation sells securities through privileged subscriptions, it is customary to appoint an agent to handle the details. When the Armco Steel Corporation sold its shares through privileged subscriptions, the Guaranty Trust Company of New York was appointed as agent. Warrant holders had to send their money along with the warrant to the agent, which was paid a fee by the Armco Steel Corporation for rendering this service.

ADDITIONAL ASPECTS OF PRIVILEGED SUBSCRIPTIONS

Role of the Agent

Most corporations do not issue fractional shares of stock when offering to sell shares through privileged subscriptions. Therefore, the stockholders are usually confronted with the problem of disposing of rights or acquiring additional ones. Assume that a person owned 9 shares of Armco Steel Corporation stock. This company offered to sell 1 additional share for each 5 rights but would not issue fractional shares. Thus our stockholder would have 4 rights left over and would have to buy 1 additional right or sell the 4 rights. The Armco Steel Corporation, to accommodate its stockholders, entered into an agreement with its agent stating that a warrant holder might place an order with the agent either to buy for his account sufficient rights (not exceeding 4) which, with the rights presented by the warrant, would permit him to subscribe for 1 or more full shares or to sell for his account those rights (not exceeding 4) that are insufficient in number to permit him to subscribe for a full share. The execution of such orders was subject to the agent's being able to find a seller or purchaser for the rights, as the case might be. Brokerage commissions and other service charges paid or incurred by the agent in this connection were paid by the Armco Steel Corporation. If the warrant holder wanted to sell all 9 rights, he would have to sell them through a broker, because the agent was interested in assisting only those who exercised their warrants.

Acquiring and Selling Rights

A *direct placement*, also known as a *private placement*, has two distinctive features: (1) the securities are sold to one or a few buyers who intend to hold them for investment purposes; and (2) the issuer and the purchaser negotiate with each other over the terms of the issue. Just how many buyers there must be before a transaction becomes a public offering instead of a private placement is a

SELLING SECURITIES TO A SELECT GROUP THROUGH DIRECT PLACEMENT

Nature of Direct Placement

little uncertain. The SEC studies the facts in each transaction and then decides on the classification of the issue. However, investment bankers generally feel that any issue purchased by more than 25 buyers is rightly classified as a *public offering* and therefore possibly subject to the provisions of the Securities Act of 1933.

An example of a private placement was the sale of $1 million of debentures by the Cuneo Press directly to the Equitable Life Assurance Society. In this case, the issue was sold to one buyer, who intended to hold the bonds for investment purposes; also, the Cuneo Press and the life insurance company negotiated directly with each other over the terms of the issue.

In many instances, investment bankers put the corporation in touch with life insurance companies that have funds to invest. When bankers intercede and render services in the transaction, they are paid a fee of approximately 1/8 of 1 percent by the issuing corporation. Basically, this fee is for giving advice rather than for taking risk.

Advantages of Private Placement to the Corporation

Selling securities by private placement eliminates much of the bankers' profits, thereby inspiring the hope that the corporation will receive a higher price for the securities thus sold. This will be the case unless the purchasers of the securities are such good bargainers that they can buy the securities at prices low enough to offset the savings made by eliminating the investment bankers' profits.

It has been suggested that if the entire bond issue is held by one or a few institutional investors, in the event that the corporation is unable to abide by all the terms of the indenture, the holders of the bonds will agree to its amendment. The representatives of the life insurance companies can meet with the representatives of the corporation, and perhaps the two parties in accordance with the self-interest of each will agree to modify some of the provisions of the indenture. From the corporation's viewpoint, it is simpler to deal with several life insurance companies than with numerous individual and institutional bondholders. This, however, is a minor advantage of private placement.

Another advantage of private placement is the bypassing of the Securities Act of 1933. This act requires corporations to both register their securities and wait 20 days before selling them. The waiting period creates uncertainty, because market conditions may change to such an extent that the securities cannot be sold at the desired price. Since private placements are exempt from the act, the corporation can assure itself of a fixed sum of cash through the private sale.

Disadvantages of Private Placement from the Corporation's Viewpoint

Private placement is not without its disadvantages to the issuing corporation. First, it may be a disadvantage to have all the bonds owned by one or a few life insurance companies. There is a financial advantage if the securities of a corporation are widely diffused among investors. Supposedly, if a corporation's securities are held by many investors, it can later sell additional securities more easily, because it is better known.

A second disadvantage of private placement is that there is no possibility of buying some of the bonds in the market at a discount, thus making a profit for the corporation. Such a scheme may have importance when the indenture contains a provision for a sinking fund. For example, Capital Airlines announced in an annual report that it made a profit of $847,493 through the purchase of debentures from the public for sinking fund requirements at a price less than par. This amount, along with profits from operations, was transferred to earned surplus. When life insurance companies hold the bonds, the corporation is unable to buy the bonds at bargain prices, that is, at a price less than par.

How does a firm decide on which of the alternatives to use?

FACTORS IN DECISION MAKING

First, there are the legal factors, which include state and federal laws. If a state law requires that the preemptive right be granted to stockholders, the issuing firm will have to sell additional common stock and convertible securities through privileged subscriptions. If the issuing firm is a public utility or a railroad, the additional securities may have to be sold through competitive bidding. In other words, the freedom of management to make decisions may be severely limited by legal factors.

Second, there is the cost of the alternative methods of marketing the issue. Cost is difficult to measure because of the varying amounts of services that investment bankers render for their fees. While competitive bidding may be a cheap method of selling securities, the issuing firm receives fewer advisory services for its money. Likewise, the use of investment bankers on a selling-agent basis might appear to be a cheap method of distribution, until one realizes that offsetting this possible low-cost alternative is the disadvantage that the issuing firm is not assured of a given sum of money on a specific date. Furthermore, while investment bankers might charge a moderate fee for their services under an outright purchase, if they distribute the securities in an orderly manner, this proper distribution might lower the cost of capital of future security distributions. Other complex relationships may arise in weighing the cost of alternative methods of distributing an issue.

Third, once an investment banker assists a firm in selling securities, there is a tendency for the issuing firm to use the services of the same banker in subsequent flotations. This is a rather common practice in finance. In some cases the investment banker may have a contract with the firm to distribute its future issues, such as for the next five years. In the main, however, any such agreements are implied rather than contractual.

Fourth, there is the desire of some firms to avoid the red tape of the Securities Act of 1933, as well as the uncertainty of the amount of money that will be received by waiting until the effective date of the registration statement. A firm that thinks in this manner would lean toward a private placement.

Finally, if the firm needs the money as of a certain date, it would avoid such arrangements as the use of investment bankers as selling agents. Instead, a method of distribution would be sought which would enable the issuer to receive the money at a time that conforms with the issuer's planned needs.

HIGHLIGHTS OF THIS CHAPTER

A corporation generally issues its securities through one of the following five methods: (1) outright sale to investment bankers, (2) sale through privileged subscriptions, (3) sale through private placement, (4) sale through the use of investment bankers as selling agents, and (5) direct sale to individual investors without the aid of investment bankers.

A corporation may sell securities on a privileged subscription basis; that is, those who already own securities are invited to purchase additional securities being offered by the corporation. Common stock and securities convertible into common stock are the usual kinds of securities offered through privileged subscriptions. The additional securities are generally offered to common stockholders.

The only way a corporation can guarantee itself a fixed sum of cash when selling securities through privileged subscriptions is to enter into a standby agreement with investment bankers or some other party.

Theoretically, the issuance of rights has a tendency to decrease the price of the shares. However, in practice there may not be any significant change in the price of the shares after the issuance of the rights. If the company is very profitable and appears to be able to earn a high rate of return on the additional money, the theoretical impact of the issuance of rights may be nullified.

REVIEW QUESTIONS

24-1. Explain the meaning of the following terms:
subscription warrant
subscription price
right
rights on
with rights
oversubscription privilege
standby agreement
ex rights
privileged subscription

24-2. Suggest the facts that make a privileged subscription a success.

24-3. Explain the advantages and disadvantages of a private placement (direct placement) to the issuer of the securities.

24-4. The board of directors is considering several alternative methods of issuing common stock. (a) Outline these alternatives, as explained in this and in the previous chapter. (b) What factors should management consider in selecting one of the alternatives?

The answers to the problems appear at the end of this section. *For each prob-* *REVIEW PROBLEMS*
lem, show how you obtained the answer.

24-1. Company A is going to raise funds by the sale of common stocks. Prior to
the offering, the company has 350,000 shares of stock outstanding. The company plans to issue 10,000 shares. How many rights would a stockholder need to
buy 1 new share?

24-2. The Putner Company announced on January 1 that it would sell 60 additional shares of common stock at $90 per share. The rights to the shares would
be mailed on January 15 and would be good for two weeks. The market price of
the shares just prior to the mailing of the rights was $100 per share. The com-
pany already has 300 shares outstanding, 100 of which are owned by Lawrence
Warner. (a) How many rights will Warner receive? (b) What is the theoretical
value per share after he subscribes? (c) What is the theoretical value of a right on
January 17? (d) What is the value of a right on March 15?

24-3. Company Z is in the process of selling additional shares of common stock
through privileged subscriptions. Prior to the privileged subscription offering, the
firm had 100,000 shares of common stock outstanding and planned to sell an
additional 10,000 shares at a subscription price of $6. After the stock had gone
ex rights, the market price dropped to $8. What was the price of the common
just prior to its going ex rights?

24-4. Company P has 1,000 shares of common stock outstanding; it needs to
raise an additional $10,000. The firm will raise the money by selling the new
common shares through a privileged subscription offering; the subscription price
will be $50. Before the rights were issued and before the stock went ex rights,
the market price of the common was $56 a share. After the stock goes ex rights,
what will be the new theoretical market price of the common stock?

24-5. Company R, in which the stockholders have the preemptive right, has 1
million shares of common stock outstanding; it plans to sell an additional
100,000 shares. The management announced on April 1 that the rights would be
mailed to holders of record as of April 24 and would be good for several weeks,
expiring on May 12. The firm stated that the subscription price would be $10;
the market price of the stock prior to the ex rights date was $12.20. James
Cooper owned 15 shares of stock as of April 10. (a) How many rights would
Cooper receive? (b) What is the total number of rights issued by Company R?
(c) How many rights are needed to buy 1 share? (d) What was the value of a
right before the shares sold ex rights? (e) What was the theoretical market price
of the common, after it went ex rights, but before the rights expired? (f) What
was the value of a right after the shares sold ex rights, but before the rights
expired? (g) What was the subscription price, after the shares sold ex rights, but
before the rights expired? (h) How many full shares could Cooper buy with his

15 rights? (i) If Cooper decided to buy only 1 share, how much would he receive from the sale of his extra 5 rights?

Answers: 24-1, 35; 24-2a, 100; 24-2b, $98.33; 24-2c, $1.67; 24-2d, no value; 24-3, $8.20; 24-4, $55; 24-5a, 15; 24-5b, 1 million; 24-5c, 10; 24-5d, 20 cents; 24-5e, $12; 24-5f, 20 cents; 24-5g, $10; 24-5h, 1; 24-5i, $1.

Asset Expansion via Business Combinations

In recent years business fusion has assumed a role of central importance in financial management. One reason for this is the need for American businesses to diversify and the urgency of accomplishing this objective. A quick method of diversifying is to combine with a firm that manufactures or sells the kinds of products the initiator of the combination would like to add to its own line of activities. A new analyst described the business fusion movement in these terms:

> A massive hunt is going on in the field of business.
>
> Corporations are tracking down other companies with the intent of buying or merging.
>
> And, paradoxically, in many cases the quarry has taken to stalking the hunter, hoping to be bagged.
>
> This is diversification, a highly popular means of changing the face of a corporation by adding new products through acquisition of other firms. Currently, it is one of the most significant influences in business.[1]

Generally speaking, a business combination is good news for the common stockholders of the surviving firm, because of the hope that the transaction will increase the market value of the common stock.

In order to raise the price of a share of stock (or keep it from falling) a firm must be on constant guard to meet competition. This is true in preserving the firm's share of the market, in selling new products, and in improving the quality of the products already being sold. The business combination provides a tool for survival of the firm. In general, medium- and large-sized firms must expand and grow or perish. Instead of growing entirely from within, a firm that combines with another engages in the very interesting practice of taking over another

---

1. Courtesy of *The Philadelphia Inquirer.*

whole enterprise. Such a course of action enables the purchasing firm to make a speedy entrance into another activity; the purchaser then does not need to engage in the slow process of building from within. Many banks are combining, because the acquiring bank has decided that this is the quickest way to expand. A firm that combines with another instead of growing from within is actually buying time.

The following will be explained in this chapter:

1. Planning the combination
   a. Integrating business fusion with the goals of the firm
   b. Estimating future earnings
   c. Determing the area in which the firm would like to expand
   d. Timing the combination
   e. Keeping the proposed fusion within the antitrust laws
   f. Keeping the combination tax-free
2. Directing the combination
   a. Managerial uses of the holding company
   b. Managerial uses of mergers and consolidations
   c. Management's defenses against takeovers
3. Evaluating the success of the combination: taking remedial action

PLANNING THE COMBINATION

In planning for a promotion, the main factor to be considered is the primary goals of the firm, which we have expressed by the following equation:

Integrating Business Fusion with the Goals of the Firm

$$\text{Primary goals of firm} = \text{Increase financial welfare of owners} + \text{Assume social responsibility} + \text{Engage in nonfinancial activities}$$

As explained earlier, this formula may also be expressed as

$$\text{Primary goals of firm} = \text{Increase net present value of owners' equity} + \text{Assume social responsibility} + \text{Engage in nonfinancial activities}$$

The reader will further recall that net present value of owners' equity tends to increase when the market price of their shares increases. Hence, insofar as the financial welfare of the owners is concerned, a firm works for the best interests of its owners when it engages in policies that increase the market price of the stock.

When a firm proposes to acquire another firm, the above formulas are useful as planning tools. If the proposed acquisition increases the net present value of the acquiring firm, this is evidence that the fusion will be advantageous to the acquirer. When Ford Motor Company acquired Philco Corporation, Ford stockholders expected to gain from the transaction by having the market value of their stock increase through time (or at least not decrease). The Ford stockholders would not have gone through with the fusion if the price of their firm's stock would have been diluted as a result of the transaction. In summary, the expected increase in the net present value of the owners' equity is the most important inducement for firms to combine with each other.

As for assuming social responsibility, the federal antitrust laws provide protection for the public on this point.

The element of the formula expressing nonfinancial activities of the firm takes on importance in business combinations. Apparently it is human nature for many businessmen to desire the prestige that accompanies the management of a "big" business. In our culture, one of the ways of gaining the respect of one's associates is to hold a responsible position in a large company. The prestige factor is difficult to measure, for management tends to divert the spotlight of publicity from itself by advancing other reasons for the expansion program.

Although future market price of the surviving company's stock is of prime concern, management keeps in mind this price is determined (mainly) by the formula: *Estimating Future Earnings*

$$\frac{\text{Future market}}{\text{price}} = \frac{\text{Expected average future earnings per share on the common}}{\text{Capitalization rate on the common}}$$

The formula focuses attention on the factors that influence market price. Probably the expected future earnings per share on the common is the more important of the two variables that generate market price. This is because the numerator in the formula can be subjected to a reasonable amount of control and measurement. Thus, when International Silver Company planned to acquire W. H. Hutchinson, Inc., the president of the silver firm said that the jointure would add $0.50 to earnings per share of common stock in the company that he represented. Since the price-earnings ratio of the silver firm was 15 to 1 (a capitalization rate of 6.66 percent), the market price of the shares of the silver company should increase by $7.50 ($0.50 divided by 6.66 percent).

Of course, the capitalization rate is also important, but management has less influence over this factor; hence, there may be less emphasis on this variable in an actual business transaction. Management hopes that the capitalization rate on the common stock will not increase; it may even hope that it will actually decrease because of the increased stability of profits as a result of the jointure. (The reader will recall that a low capitalization rate leads to a high value and that a high capitalization rate leads to a low value.) The purpose of a business fusion, then, is also to: (1) increase earnings per share, (2) stabilize earnings per share, and (3) minimize a potential decrease in earnings per share.

Generally, the profits of the combined companies are expected to be greater than the sum of what the future net profits of the constituent firms would have been without the combination. Suppose that Firm A has expected future profits of $1 million and that Firm B has expected future profits of $1 million. If these two companies combine, it is possible that the combined profits will be

$2,300,000. From where does the extra $300,000 come? One source is a cost-cutting program. Instead of having two vice presidents in charge of finance, one person could do the job; likewise, if each firm had 20 salesmen, perhaps a total of 30 such persons would be sufficient after the fusion. In addition to the possibility of lowering costs, there may also be the expectation of increasing sales at a faster rate than costs. This can happen when the products or managerial talents of different companies complement each other. (Thus, when Ford Motor Company acquired Philco Corporation, the main purpose of the fusion from the viewpoint of Ford was to acquire the excellent electronics research staff of Philco.) Very often a firm that is strong in marketing will acquire a smaller firm that lacks distributive power but has an excellent product. Expected future decreases in costs and increases in sales are translated into rough estimates of changes in earnings per share. In any event, the usual hope is that the post-fusion earnings per share on the common stock will exceed the pre-fusion combined earnings per share of the constituent companies. If this happens, the value of the stock of the surviving company will be greater than it would have been without the fusion.

Of course, when management is focusing attention on future earnings per share on the common, the emphasis is on average future performance over a span of years. Thus there might even be a temporary decline in the combined earnings per share for, say, the first year after the jointure. But after temporary dislocations are ironed out and after there is sufficient time to make other adjustments, the level of earnings per share should increase.

A purchasing firm may explicitly take into consideration the exact amount of the future earnings of the company being acquired. Here is an example of how this is done:

GENESCO PLANS TO BUY KNITTED FABRIC MAKER IN EXCHANGE OF STOCK

Genesco, Inc., Nashville, Tenn., would acquire Flagg-Utica Corp., a New York maker of knitted fabrics, yarns, underwear and outerwear, in an exchange of stock, according to an agreement reached by officials of both concerns.

If Flagg-Utica shareholders approve the plan, Genesco, a shoe and apparel maker, initially would issue 190,000 shares of common stock on the basis of 35 shares for each 100 Flagg-Utica shares. Genesco closed Friday on the New York Stock Exchange at $35. Based on that price the transaction would involve about $6.5 million.

Genesco also would issue between 3 shares and 27 shares per 100 Flagg-Utica shares, depending on the average net income of Flagg-Utica during the three years ended Jan. 2, 1965.

Of the 190,000 Genesco shares involved initially, 150,000 are Treasury shares. The company filed a registration statement with the Securities and Exchange Commission covering the issuance of the remaining 40,000 shares.

In other words, the basic terms of this combination were worked out in mid

1962. But if the firm being acquired should show good results between 1962 and 1965, a bonus would be given in 1965 to those who were stockholders of Flagg-Utica Corporation as of 1962.

Business combinations may be classified as vertical, horizontal, circular, and conglomerate. If *vertical*, the combination is for the purpose of acquiring control over additional stages in the production or distribution of a particular article. Thus a steel company might acquire control over coal mines, ore deposits, and even the railroads that haul the coal and ore. Specific companies that have expanded vertically are United States Steel Corporation, General Motors Corporation, and Bethlehem Steel Company.

Determining the Area in Which the Firm Would Like to Expand

If the combination is *horizontal*, one organization acquires another engaged in the same stage of production or distribution of an article. Thus, when Prentice-Hall, Inc. (book publishers), acquired Allyn and Bacon, Inc. (also book publishers), a horizontal combination took place.

Circular combination means that one company takes over other companies because of the belief that the products of all companies can be marketed more successfully if the advertising procedure is put under centralized control. Thus General Foods Company has grown through circular combination, taking over companies engaged in the distribution of such products as coffee, canned vegetables, and breakfast cereals. The main motive behind circular combination is to take advantage of the economies that result from large-scale marketing, particularly in the food lines.

Conglomerate combinations consist of a fusion of companies in unrelated lines. The main reason for the conglomerate combination is to obtain diversification for the surviving firm. Corporations seek to stabilize their profits by taking over a variety of companies engaged in diversified activities. This policy of expansion keeps the company's eggs from all being placed in one basket. An example of a conglomerate fusion was Revlon, Inc. (a company engaged primarily in selling cosmetics) taking over the manufacture of Esquire Shoe Polish.

Four general factors create an environment that is conducive or not conducive to business combination:

Timing the Combination

1. A period of high business stock prices stimulates business combinations, since high stock prices generate prospects for even higher prices from proposed combinations.
2. Idle cash is a factor encouraging the absorption of other companies.
3. The attitude of the U.S. Justice Department and the Supreme Court is a factor to be considered. At times the federal government appears especially strict in campaigns against combinations that might possibly result in the restraint of interstate commerce. This situation would, of course, discourage combinations.
4. Certain tax factors encourage combinations. Corporations can carry forward operating losses for five years and apply these losses against profits for the five

years; they can also carry the losses back for three years. A firm may have to file an amended return for the previous years if it incurs a heavy loss in the current year. Corporate management does not mind this detailed work, for the tax refund may be substantial. The tax privilege of carrying losses backward and forward has led profitable firms to combine with firms operating at a loss, for by so doing the profitable company lowers its federal income taxes. Assume that Company L has a deficit of $1 million on its books and that the federal income tax rate is 50 percent. If Company P, a very profitable enterprise, acquires Company L, the former would lower its federal income tax by $500,000 as a result of the acquisition. Although the federal government allows two companies to combine and to offset their profits and deficits, it will not allow the tax reduction if the purpose of the fusion was solely to lower taxes.

Keeping the Proposed Fusion within the Antitrust Laws

There are strict federal laws on activities of *competitors* that would restrain *interstate* commerce. One activity that is forbidden is a combination of such competitors. Hence, it would probably be illegal for United States Steel Corporation to combine with Bethlehem Steel Company. Most combinations today, however, are between firms that are not competitors. Many interesting problems arise in attempting to determine whether or not firms compete with or supplement each other.

Although some states, such as New York, also have laws forbidding the combination of certain competitors, the general rule is that intrastate commerce is exempt from laws that limit business combinations. Thus, if one small independent grocery store combined with another small independent grocery store, the combination probably would be legal—even though one of them would drop out of existence and the other would raise its prices as a result of lessening competition. It therefore makes a great deal of difference whether interstate or intrastate commerce is involved.

Keeping the Combination Tax-Free

An important factor in the holding company type of combination is the federal income tax. There is a tendency to make the combination a tax-free reorganization, that is, one in which the stockholders are not subject to an immediate federal income tax when they give up their securities in one company and receive securities in another company. Assume that Company B wants to gain control over Company A. One likely plan is for B to offer to exchange a generous amount of its stock for the stock of A. This offer is made directly to the stockholders of A, who will be interested if they do not have to pay a federal income tax at the time they switch their securities. If the business combination is a tax-free reorganization, no such tax is paid at the time the securities of B are received for those of A. But when the stockholders eventually sell their shares of B, they will have to pay federal income tax. Here is an example of how it works for the individual stockholder. Suppose that Andrew Smith paid $100 for his stock of Company A, that a tax-free reorganization takes place, and that he receives $200 (market value) of the stock of Company B. Smith pays no tax on this transaction at the time he receives stock of B. Instead, he pays a tax only when he sells the stock of B. If, several years later, he sells the B stock for $300, he has a capital gain of $200; according to tax regulations he may report only half the gain ($100) in his regular taxable income or he may pay a flat tax of $50 and not report any of the gain in his regular taxable income.

The federal government has several requirements that must be met before a combination is considered to be a tax-free reorganization; the most important one is that 80 percent or more of the shares held by the selling stockholders must be switched into the stock of the company seeking to acquire the shares.

A *holding company* is an organization that controls one or more corporations through stock ownership. The organization that owns the shares is usually a corporation, although joint-stock companies, Massachusetts trusts, and other forms of organization may be holding companies. The controlled company is known as a *subsidiary*; the company doing the controlling is the holding company. The number of shares that must be owned by the holding company to control the subsidiary company varies. Theoretically, the holding company should own one more than half the shares so as to be sure of control. However, in practice, holding companies can control subsidiaries by owning considerably less than one more than half the shares, as low as 15 percent ownership often being sufficient for control purposes. Holding companies can control subsidiaries with ownership of relatively small portions of the total stock mainly because of the proxy system. An organization is in a position to control a subsidiary when it can elect enough of the board of directors of the subsidiary to influence policy-making activities. Organizations that own substantial blocks of stock in corporations but do not attempt to control these corporations are not generally considered to be holding companies.

GENERAL NATURE OF HOLDING COMPANIES

The parent company may pay for the shares of the subsidiary in at least two ways: it may offer to pay cash for the shares or it may offer its own securities in exchange for the shares of the subsidiary. In an exchange offer, the proposed parent company makes the offer directly to the stockholders of the company over which control is desired. If the shareholders of the subsidiary accept the exchange offer, the parent company is spared the necessity of raising cash.

Method of Payment for Shares Acquired by a Holding Company

The holding company arrangement does not depend on the approval of the minority stockholders and creditors of the subsidiary about to be acquired. As long as the parent company can buy sufficient shares to control the subsidiary, the stockholders in the subsidiary who object to the combination have no recourse. However, the parent company must respect the rights of the minority stockholders and creditors of the subsidiary. If, instead of a holding company, the parent company has decided on a merger or a consolidation, it would be confronted with the problem of satisfying minority groups of the company over

ADVANTAGES OF THE HOLDING COMPANY

Minority Groups Cannot Block the Combination

which control is desired. Minority groups of a company about to be fused with another company (through an arrangement other than the holding company) tend to argue that their shares are being undervalued. Arguments of this sort delay the completion of the fusion. The holding company arrangement eliminates this particular problem when control is sought over the fixed and circulating assets of another company.

The Holding Company Provides a Plan for Insulating the Risk of Certain Activities of the Holding Company

Since each subsidiary is a legal entity, its failure does not result in the bankruptcy of the entire system. After failure of a subsidiary, the parent company will, of course, find that the stocks and other securities of the subsidiary have become worthless or nearly worthless. Although this is a severe loss, the predicament would be even worse if the affairs of the parent company and the subsidiary were carried on by the same corporate entity. By engaging in designated operations through a subsidiary, a parent company can partially insulate itself against risk of failure. Thus the Henry J. Kaiser empire consists mainly of two holding companies and a number of subsidiaries. The subsidiaries engage in such activities as making ships and steel. If one of the subsidiaries should fail, the loss to the parent company would be great but would probably not result in the collapse of the entire holding company system.

The Holding Company Offers a Plan for the Operation of Certain Types of Business by Nonresident Corporations

Some states require railroads, public utilities, and other forms of industry to be conducted by corporations that have received their charter in these states. A way of circumventing this kind of requirement is to form a subsidiary in the state in which operations are to be conducted. Since the holding company is simply a stockholder in the subsidiary, no rule or law is being violated, for operations are being carried on by the subsidiary, which has received its charter from the state in which its operations are conducted.

The Holding Company Provides a Method of Preserving Goodwill

Individual corporations may build up valuable goodwill over a period of time. This means that the company has acquired a reputation for selling high-quality goods or rendering excellent services. When a company with goodwill is purchased, the absorbing company may decide to acquire the desired company as a subsidiary so as not to disturb its goodwill. The National Dairy Products Corporation owns a number of subsidiaries, many of them having well-known products:

Kraft Foods Company	Cheese, Parkay Margarine, and Miracle Whip
Sheffield Farms Company, Inc.	Milk
Breyer Ice Cream Company	Ice cream

The National Dairy Products Corporation has numerous other subsidiaries. Both parent company and subsidiaries use the trademark Sealtest in their advertising.

If a state has unfavorable laws, their effect can be minimized by having a subsidiary conduct part of the operations of the holding company system. Thus, if a state should have a high income tax on profits, the rate would apply only to the taxable portion of the profits earned by the subsidiary rather than to the taxable portion of the profits of the entire system.

There are four main disadvantages of the holding company as a method of expansion. First, the holding company may be an expensive organization to maintain, for each must pay income, franchise, and other taxes; it must also pay the salaries of officers of the corporations in the holding company system. The expense of maintaining separate subsidiaries has led many holding companies to disband them as legal entities and to have the parent company or another subsidiary assume the operations of the disbanded company or companies. In 1916, to reduce administrative costs, the original General Motors Company and its subsidiaries were combined into General Motors Corporation.

A second disadvantage of the holding company is the federal income tax on intercorporate dividends; 15 percent of the income received in the form of dividends is taxable income to the recipient corporation. As federal taxes increase, the tax disadvantage becomes more important. When four Greyhound subsidiaries were fused into the parent company, one reason given for the action was to save taxes on intercompany dividends.

Third, the holding company is not always a complete fusion, for there may be minority interests whose rights must be respected. Minority groups may prevent the holding company from using the subsidiary to the best advantage of the parent in such matters as intercompany sales and purchases. Minority groups are perfectly justified in preventing the parent from exploiting the subsidiary. Therefore, the parent company may find it difficult to coordinate its activities fully with those of the subsidiary, despite a controlling interest.

A fourth disadvantage of the holding company is the public antipathy to size and monopolistic tendencies which this type of organization suggests.

However, the holding company continues to be used by American industry as a device for combination, the advantages apparently outweighing the disadvantages. As long as the holding company is not used to restrain commerce, it may be safely used as a method of expansion.

The board of directors of the subsidiary has the right to declare dividends. However, because the subsidiary is controlled by the parent company, the dividend policy of the subsidiary is determined by the holding company. Provided that profits are available in the subsidiary, the parent can feed dividends to itself at whatever rate is desired. If a parent owns a number of subsidiaries, minority holdings in each other may be held by the subsidiaries. The parent can also channel the flow of dividends from one subsidiary to another. Since the holding company's main source of income is usually dividends, one would expect to find dividend payments of the subsidiary quite liberal.

Services Rendered by the Holding Company for Subsidiaries	Parent companies may enter into agreements with subsidiaries whereby the parent company will, for a fee, render services to the subsidiaries. Under another arrangement subsidiaries may render services for each other. For example, AT&T and Western Electric Company own the Bell Telephone Laboratories, Inc., which does research work for both.
Common Officers	Since the parent company owns a controlling interest in the subsidiaries, all officers of the subsidiaries must have the approval of the top control body. Often the same persons serve as officers in the parent company and in the subsidiaries. Not only is this arrangement economical, but it also serves to solidify relations between the parent company and the subsidiaries.
Financing Subsidiaries	Parent companies may assist subsidiaries to raise cash through a number of plans: (1) The parent company may issue its own securities, either stocks or bonds, and then use the proceeds to buy securities from the subsidiary. This arrangement is used when the parent company is better known and has greater earning capacity than the subsidiary. Under these conditions, the parent company can issue the securities on more advantageous terms than could the subsidiary. This plan also keeps control of the subsidiary in the hands of the parent company. (2) The subsidiary may issue its own securities, with the parent company guaranteeing the stocks or bonds (primarily the latter). The guarantee by the parent company strengthens the issue and makes it possible to offer the securities on more advantageous terms than would be possible without the guarantee. (3) The parent company may lend directly to a subsidiary. Sometimes the process is reversed and the subsidiary lends to the parent (upstream loans). Parents and subsidiaries are likely to lend to each other when the rate of interest charged on the loan is lower than could be obtained if the loan were secured from an outside source; when it is desired to have a loan without numerous restrictive provisions, as might be the case if the loan were obtained from an outside source; or when the loan cannot be obtained from an outside source on any terms. AT&T is an example of a holding company that has the current policy of advancing funds to subsidiaries through loans or purchases of stock.
Intercompany Sales	The parent company may buy all or a major part of the output of its subsidiaries. Or the subsidiary may buy all or a major part of the output of the parent. The main advantages of intercompany sales are that the buying company is assured of a reasonably steady source of supply and that goods may be acquired cheaper (if the parent company orders parts of the organization to sell to each other at cost). Western Electric Company, a subsidiary of AT&T supplies the AT&T system with equipment, telephones, cable, switchboards, and the like.
GENERAL NATURE OF MERGERS AND CONSOLIDATIONS	Mergers and consolidations are a form of combination of corporations in which one or more of the fusing corporations drop out of existence, the remaining

corporation or corporations taking over the assets and customers of the constituent company or companies giving up their charter. If the fusion is a *merger*, one of the constituent companies remains while the others are legally dissolved. Thus, if Company A and Company B are to merge, Company A might take over Company B. If this happens, Company A would survive and Company B would give up its charter and become nonexistent. An example of a merger is the fusion of the Yellow Truck and Coach Manufacturing Company into General Motors Corporation. If the fusion is a *consolidation*, a new corporation is formed to take over all the constituent companies, and all the constituent companies are dissolved. If Company D is formed to take over Companies A, B, and C, consolidation occurs, and Company D is the only remaining corporation. Companies A, B, and C have given up their charters, thereby terminating their legal existence. An example of a consolidation is the present General Motors Corporation, which in 1916 was formed to take over the former General Motors Company and its subsidiaries. The term *amalgamation* is used by some people as being synonymous with *consolidation*. In newspapers, the terms *consolidation, merger,* and *amalgamation* are often used interchangeably. Despite the legal differences between merger and consolidation, the final outcome is substantially the same, for the operations of the constituent companies are combined under centralized control.

In a number of cases the holding company is an intermediate step toward a merger or a consolidation. After a firm acquires the stock of another organization, the next step is often to merge or consolidate the subsidiary into either a new corporation or the parent firm.

The various states have set up procedures for fusing one company into another and for fusing a number of companies into one new corporation. The general procedure for completing a statutory merger or consolidation is as follows: (1) The directors of the constituent companies agree on the terms of the proposed fusion. The stockholders of the selling corporation may be paid in cash, securities of the surviving corporation, or other assets. In many cases, stockholders receive a combination of cash and securities. Also there might be an informal agreement to give jobs to the officers of the displaced company. Only if officers and directors give full support to the fusion is it likely that the plan will be accepted by the stockholders. (2) If agreement is reached on the terms of the merger or consolidation, the boards of directors of all companies pass resolutions recommending that the plan be adopted by the stockholders of the constituent companies. (3) After approval by the boards of directors, the plan is submitted to the stockholders for their approval. The stockholders of all the constituent companies must give their approval to the plan for fusion—approval often meaning that the holders of at least two-thirds of the shares must vote affirmatively for the plan. Those who vote for the plan are urged to send their certificates to a trustee, who will hold the securities pending the outcome of the voting. If the plan fails to receive the required number of votes, the trustee returns the certificates to the owners. (4) If the plan is approved by the required majorities, the final major step is to notify the proper state authority, usually the secretary of state. If the entire procedure has been in accordance with state law, a statutory merger or a statutory consolidation will have taken place. The constituent companies are now united in both the legal and the economic sense.

THE VALUATION PROBLEM IN MERGERS AND CONSOLIDATIONS

The valuation problem arises when the decision is about to be made on how much one company is willing to pay for another company. Thus, if a new company is being formed to consolidate a number of other companies, the problem arises as to the proportion of the securities of the new company to be received by the stockholders of the constituent companies. Similarly, if Company A is proposing to take over Company B in a merger, the problem is to decide how much should be received by stockholders of Company B from the sale of their business.

The value of the new corporation may be determined by capitalizing the income, by adding the combined value of the assets, or by some other method. Capitalizing income is the most logical method of determining the value of a consolidated company. The capital structure of the consolidated company may consist of bonds, preferred stock, and common stock. The valuation problem is the proportion of the securities to be given to the stockholders of the constituent companies. These stockholders are more interested in their relative position in the new company than in the absolute number of shares received. The value placed on the constituent companies determines the proportion of the common stock of the consolidated company that will be received by the stockholders.

Amount of Net Assets Contributed to the Consolidated Company

One would expect that the corporation or corporations contributing heavily in net assets would be rewarded accordingly. Net assets are measured by subtracting all debt from total assets. Another important problem is the method of valuing the assets. An appraiser may be hired to evaluate them so that there will be fewer questions about the worth of the assets being contributed. This procedure eliminates the possibility that book values will vary widely because of differences in bookkeeping procedures.

Suppose that Company A and Company B are to consolidate into Company C and that Company A has net assets of $2 million and Company B has net assets of $1 million. Also assume that the consolidated company is to issue 30,000 shares of common stock. If assets contributed were the only factor to be considered, the stockholders of Company A would expect to receive two-thirds of the shares of Company C while the stockholders of Company B would expect to receive one-third of the shares of Company C. This would mean that the stockholders of Company A would receive 20,000 shares in the new company, while the stockholders of Company B would receive 10,000 shares in the new company.

Net Earnings of the Contributing Companies

The relative earning power of the constituent companies is the most important factor influencing what proportion of the securities of the consolidated company will be received by the stockholders of the constituent companies. After adjustments are made for differences in accounting procedures, it is possible to compare the earnings of one company with those of another. Even more important than past earnings are prospective earnings. Therefore, some estimates must be made as to what future earnings will be. The past earnings are significant only in that they shed light on probable future earnings.

Suppose that Company A and Company B are about to consolidate into Company C and that the earnings of Company A are $200,000 per year while those of Company B are $100,000 per year. Also assume that Company C is to issue 30,000 shares of common stock. On the basis of earning power, the stockholders of Company A would expect to receive two-thirds of the shares, while the stockholders of Company B would expect to receive one-third of the shares. This would amount to 20,000 shares for the stockholders of Company A and 10,000 shares for the stockholders of Company B.

One or more of the constituent companies may make special contributions to the consolidation that may not be reflected in the earning power of the constituent companies. An unusual talent on the part of management, an excellent location of a plant, or the possession of an unusual franchise are possible special contributions to the earnings of the consolidation. Even though these special contributions are difficult to measure, they cannot be ignored.

Special Contributions by the Constituent Companies

The market value of the shares of the constituent companies strongly influences the proportion of the shares to be received by their stockholders. Assume that Company A and Company B are to consolidate into Company C and that the shares of Company A are selling for $200, while those of Company B are selling at $100. Also assume that Company A and Company B have the same number of shares outstanding. Under these circumstances, the stockholders of Company A would expect to receive twice as many shares in the new company as would be received by the stockholders of Company B. The market value is to a large extent included in the earning power test. However, as a practical matter, stockholders of the constituent companies are likely to give independent weight to market value because this value is easy to comprehend, thereby enabling stockholders to make direct comparisons of their own position with that of stockholders of other constituent companies.

Market Value of the Shares of the Constituent Companies

In mergers, as in consolidations, market value per share is given heavy consideration in preparing the terms of the proposed fusions. The Philadelphia National Insurance Company was merged into the Fire Association of Philadelphia. About a month prior to the announcement of the proposed merger, the stock of the Fire Association of Philadelphia was selling at approximately $60 while the stock of Philadelphia National Insurance Company was selling at 25 percent of this value, or approximately $15. The terms of the merger were that the holders of Philadelphia National Insurance Company would receive 0.353 of a share of stock in the surviving company; this was obviously an advantageous switch. Furthermore, the management of the surviving company promised to increase dividends on its stock so that the former holders of Philadelphia National Insurance Company stock would receive 26.9 percent more in dividends than they had formerly received.

The price-earnings ratio combines the market price factor and the earnings per share factor. For this reason, considerable attention is given to the price-earnings ratio when the price is established for the shares of the company being purchased. Table 25-1 indicates the role of this concept in selected mergers. The

Industry	Number of Mergers	Price–Earnings Paid
Food	112	19.8
Electronics	62	22.9
Building products and materials	61	11.7
Finance-banking-insurance	60	22.8
Service	58	22.1
Machinery and equipment	57	12.6
Chemicals, paints, and coatings	43	14.5
Petroleum	41	13.5
Wholesale and retail	40	17.8
Automotive products	39	16.0

Source:
W. T. Grimm and Company,
Chicago, Illinois

purchasing company prefers a low price-earnings ratio; the stockholders of the company being acquired prefer a high price-earnings ratio.

Bargaining Power of the Stockholders of the Constituent Companies

Bargaining is always present in a proposed merger or consolidation. The shareholders of the constituent companies hope to improve their economic position regardless of the consequences of this action on the stockholders of other constituent companies. Each company stresses its strong points, some companies stressing the assets contributed, some their earning power, some their management, others the market value of the shares. There may be so much disagreement about the valuation of the constituent companies that the proposed merger or consolidation has to be abandoned. However, most mergers and consolidations are completed after lengthy discussions and many compromises.

USE OF CAPITAL BUDGETING IN COMBINATIONS

The cost of capital concept gives information on whether a firm should expand its total assets. If expansion opportunities arise in which the anticipated yield on the proposed acquisition exceeds the firm's cost of capital, then the expansion should be undertaken. For example, if Company X is considering purchasing another company, a model may be established whereby the variables are quantified and a decision made on the basis of objective information. Suppose that Company X has an opportunity to purchase another firm for $100,000 and that this other firm has promise of returning $15,000 in net annual cash benefits to its purchaser, for an indefinite period. If these are the anticipations, then the firm about to be acquired is offering a yield on investment of 15 percent. (In the event that the $15,000 net annual cash inflow is not expected to continue indefinitely, then the yield would be determined by finding the rate that discounts the net cash benefits of $15,000 back to a present value equal to the outlay of $100,000.) Assuming that Company X has a cost of capital of 12 percent, the purchase of the firm would be desirable. The expected yield of 15 percent is above the cost of capital of 12 percent. Such an acquisition would create profits for Company X and would increase the market value of the stock of the acquiring firm.

Of increasing interest is the strategy used by an incumbent management to maintain its power by protecting itself against "raids" by other companies that would like to purchase the firm. As long as antitrust laws are not being violated, it is possible for one firm to contact the stockholders of another and buy their stock. It is not necessary to obtain approval of the management of the firm being sought, although approval by incumbent management will increase the buyer's chance of success. In many cases, the management of the sought-after firm gives its approval and blessing to the transaction; but in about as many cases, the incumbent management objects because it is likely to lose its job or face demotion after the transaction is completed. In this section, we will be concerned with situations in which the incumbent management fights the proposed take-over.

MANAGEMENT'S DEFENSES AGAINST TAKE-OVERS

   A few of the defensive devices used to fend off the flirtations of the would-be purchaser are these:

1. Launch a counterpublicity program
2. Raise the dividends on the common stock
3. Repurchase some of the outstanding shares
4. Undertake a defensive merger
5. Delay in making available the list of stockholders

Typically, the incumbent management launches a publicity campaign stating that the would-be buyer is not offering enough for the shares of stock of the sought-after firm. If a company offers $15 a share for the stock of Company Y, the management of Company Y buys space in newspapers and writes to its stockholders, stating that the stock is worth at least, say, $25 a share. The incumbent management proceeds to advise the stockholders of Company Y against tendering their stock. If the stockholders are convinced of the argument, they will not tender their stock in sufficient amounts to lead to the consummation of the transaction; the proposed take-over will collapse, and the incumbent management will maintain control of the firm.

The second strategy, raising the dividends on the stock, has a twofold effect. It encourages stockholder loyalty and may raise the market price of the stock. For example, if the stock of Company Y is selling at $12 a share, the would-be acquirer may offer $15. But if the incumbent management raises the dividend on the stock of Y, the market price may rise to, say, $14. If this happens, then the stockholders of Company Y have less incentive to give up their shares, possibly feeling that a profit of $1 is not sufficient inducement. When a group attempted to gain control of Sharon Steel Corporation, the management of the steel enterprise raised the annual dividends from 60 to 80 cents a share.

The third defensive maneuver, repurchasing some of the shares of the company, lessens the amount of stock in "nervous hands" and sometimes pushes up the market price of the remaining shares. If the market price of the remaining shares does increase, then the attractiveness of the offer by the would-be acquirer is diminished. For example, National Vulcanized Fibers spent $6 million to acquire 34 percent of its own shares in order to fend off a raid by Victor Posner's Security Management Corporation.[2] In this transaction, National Vulcanized Fibers borrowed $6 million from a bank to finance the transaction.

Still another device is to split the stock, an action that stockholders interpret as good news, because the split may result in the price of the new shares being somewhat above their theoretical level. Thus, if the current market value of Company Y stock is $12 a share and the take-over bid is $15, the incumbent management might split the stock four for one. The new price should be $3 per share, but in practice it might be, say, $3.75 per share. Since the stockholders of Company Y now have stock with a market value of $15, they lose their incentive to exchange the stock for $15 per share from the would-be purchaser. When American Electric Power Company bid $100 a share for the outstanding stock of the Michigan Gas and Electric Company, the latter promptly split its stock seven for one.[3]

The fourth maneuver, undertaking a defensive merger, means getting into a line of business that would make it illegal for the would-be acquirer to take over the firm. If a large steel firm attempted to take over a candy manufacturer, the latter could conduct a raid of its own and buy a steel company. Since it would be illegal for the would-be acquirer to take over a firm that competes in the same industry, the take-over would be thwarted and the incumbent management would maintain control over the firm.

The fifth defensive tactic is delaying the distribution of the list of stockholders to the would-be purchaser. A usual situation is for the would-be purchaser to buy shares of stock and then demand the list of stockholders, a hypothetical

2. Samuel L. Hayes, III, and Russell A. Taussig, "Tactics of Cash Takeover Bids," *Harvard Business Review*, March-April 1967, p. 143.

3. Ibid.

right granted to all common stockholders. The officers of the sought-after firm could procrastinate and delay relaying this information until ordered to do so by a court. If the delay is for a sufficiently long period of time, the campaign efforts of the would-be acquirer are stymied.

While the modern firm is supposed to be operated primarily for the benefit of the stockholders (not to retain the officers in power), it would be naive to assume that the battle for executive survival is not an important part of the financial operations of the firm, whether in the corporation, the partnership, or the single proprietorship.

A business combination is successful if there is a net gain in the value of the common stockholders' position. In simple terms, the jointure is a success if the market price of the common stock of the surviving company increases; if the dividends per share on the common stock of the surviving company increase; or if salaries and fringe benefits of the surviving company increase (this third factor is important only in small firms). Stated in different terms, the fusion is a success if the composite rate of return on the cost of the common stockholders' investment increases. Admittedly, the measurement of the success of a fusion is difficult, mainly because there are so many other factors affecting the composite rate of return earned by stockholders. A few of these are international conditions, stock market psychology, strikes, changes in technology, and fierce competition.

EVALUATING THE SUCCESS OF THE COMBINATION: TAKING REMEDIAL ACTION

If the combination is not a success, then there arises the question of what type of remedial action should be taken. The actions taken are similar to the ones used in managing capital. Examples are:

1. Using package programs to increase sales and lower costs
2. Changing the product mix
3. Replacing the management
4. Using the business combination device again
5. Disposing of unprofitable divisions or unprofitable subsidiaries

The best brains in American industry are often unable to make the combination a success, even after different forms of remedial action have been tried. In cases like this, the firm staggers along, earning only moderate profits or even incurring losses.

The steps of planning, directing, evaluating, and taking remedial action may be applied to the process of combining business firms. Of all the steps, perhaps planning is the most important, for it is at this stage that the basic decision is made on whether or not to go ahead with the fusion. Perhaps the most difficult of the four aspects of the administrative process is that of taking remedial

HIGHLIGHTS OF THIS CHAPTER

action. Many of the functions of the two enterprises are irrevocably melted together so that after a jointure is completed, there is no separating them.

25-1. Why are the profits of the combined companies expected to be greater than the sum of what the future net profits of the constituent firms would be without the combination?

25-2. What is to prevent Sears Roebuck & Company from combining with Montgomery Ward & Company—both companies competing in many communities?

25-3. What is a conglomerate?

25-4. What defensive actions can a management take to avoid having its company taken over by another company?

REVIEW PROBLEMS Answers to some of the problems appear at the end of this section. *For each problem, show how you obtained the answer.*

25-1. Company Z, whose weighted average cost of capital is 10 percent, is considering purchasing Company Y for $100,000. If Company Y appears to promise annual net cash benefits of $20,000 to Company Z for the foreseeable future, should Company Z proceed with acquisition?

25-2. Company A is about to purchase the common stock of Company B for $13 a share. The common stock of Company B has averaged $10 during the past several years. Explain how Company A can afford to pay this much and yet not dilute the market value of its own stock.

25-3. Company P offers to buy out Company M and to pay the common stockholders of Company M $58 a share. Data for Company M are as follows:

Earnings after taxes	$100,000
Shares of common outstanding	20,000
Earnings per share	$5
Price-earnings ratio	10
Current market price	$50

The stockholders of Company M rejected the offer. Suggest several factors that might have influenced the stockholders of Company M.

25-4. Below are data for Companies X and Y, before they combined operations:

	X	Y
Sales	$1,000	$2,000
Less expenses:		
Officers' salaries	100	200
Salesmen's salaries	200	400
Other labor expenses	100	400
Other expenses	300	500
Total expenses	$ 700	$1,500
Net profit before taxes	$ 300	$ 500
Taxes (50 percent)	150	250
Net after taxes	$ 150	$ 250

After the firms merge, the expectations are that sales will increase by 10 percent, officers' salaries will decrease by 5 percent, and salesmen's salaries will decrease by 3 percent. Assume that there will be no other savings in expenses. (a) After the fusion, determine the net profits after taxes for the combined enterprises. (b) If net profits after taxes are capitalized at 10 percent both before and after the fusion, how much in additional value has been generated by the combination?

25-5. The *New York Times* reported the following information concerning a proposed business combination. (The names of the companies have been deleted.)

Company A has just offered to buy the shares of Company X on this basis: 0.20 shares of common stock of Company A, plus 0.40 shares of $2.80 convertible preferred stock of Company A (convertible into 1 share of common of Company A) for each share of Company X surrendered. The common stock of Company A is selling at $76.25.

B, a rival of A, also is seeking control of X. The common stock of B is selling at $78.75. The officers of B have decided that the common stock of X is worth $51.19.

On the basis of this information: (a) How much do the officers of A think the stock of X is worth? (b) How many shares or fractional shares of common stock of B should be offered for each share of X?

25-6. Companies X and Y were consolidated into Company Z. Stockholders of the two original firms were given one share in the new firm for each share in the old. The following applied to Companies X and Y before the combination (expand the format below in assembling data to answer the required parts of this problem):

	X	Y	Pro Forma Data — Price-Earnings Ratio of 10	Pro Forma Data — Price-Earnings Ratio of 12
Earnings after taxes	$10,000	$25,000	$35,000	$35,000
Shares of common stock	5,000	10,000	———	———
Earnings per share	$2	$2.50	———	———
Price-earnings ratio	10	8	———	———
Market price per share	$20	$20	———	———

(a) If earnings after taxes (after the fusion) are $35,000 and the price-earnings ratio is 10, did the stockholders of Company X or Company Y get the better bargain? (b) If earnings after taxes are $35,000 and the price-earnings ratio rises to 12 (after the fusion), did the stockholders of Company X or Company Y obtain the better bargain? The solution to this problem depends on judgment.

25-7. After much study, the board of directors of the Ford Motor Company approved in principle the intent to purchase Philco Corporation. Ford, in a public release, said that its aim in acquiring Philco was to make possible a fuller participation in the national defense and space efforts. Philco had considerable experience in this area, as well as a team of highly skilled scientists. While Ford could develop this area from within its own company, such a course of action would take several years. By acquiring Philco, Ford could plunge into this area almost immediately. Hence, Ford was prepared to offer generous terms to the stockholders of Philco. Concurrently with the Ford announcement, the management of Philco sent a letter to its stockholders recommending the fusion because "Philco lacked the financial resources needed to operate its business to advantage." All indications were that a fusion of the two companies would be to the mutual advantage of stockholders of both firms. (See Table 25-2.)

TABLE 25-2
Comparison of Ford Motor Company and Philco Corporation

	Ford Motor Company — Most Recent Year	Ford Motor Company — One Year Ago	Ford Motor Company — Two Years Ago	Philco Corporation — Most Recent Year	Philco Corporation — One Year Ago	Philco Corporation — Two Years Ago
Earnings per share	$7.79	$8.23	$2.12	$0.47	$1.67	$0.61
Dividends per share	$3.00	$2.80	$2.00	0	$0.25	0
Price of common (in dollars):						
High	92⅞	93½	50¾	38¼	36¾	26⅜
Low	60⅝	50¾	37⅜	15⅞	21	12⅜
Price-earnings ratios:						
High	11.9	11.4	29.0	*	22.0	43.2
Low	7.8	6.2	21.4	*	12.6	20.3
Payout ratio (percent)	38.5	34.0	94.3	0	15	0
Operating income as a percentage of sales	15.6	17.4	7.6	2.8	5.7	3.6

*Over 50 and hence not computed in financial service.

Suggest the number of shares of Ford that owners of Philco should be offered for each share of their Philco common stock.

25-8. Company K is in the 40 percent tax bracket; it has ordinary taxable income of $148,500; in addition, it receives $10,000 in dividends from stock that is held as an asset. (a) How much of the dividends must be reported as taxable income? (b) How much in income taxes will the firm have to pay?

25-9. Company R, with a cost of capital of 7 percent, is considering buying one of three companies; the finance department of Company R has estimated the range of internal rates of return that might be earned by each:

	High	Low
Company A	20%	10%
Company B	24	8
Company C	18	14

Which one should Company R acquire if it uses (a) the maximin criterion? (b) the maximax criterion?

25-10. The *Wall Street Journal*, in explaining the nature of a pooling of interest, gave this example:

	Company A	Company B
Shares of common	1,000,000	1,000,000
Net after taxes	$1,000,000	$1,000,000
Earnings per share	$1	$1
Price-earnings ratio	30	10

Company A offered to buy the stock of Company B and to pay for it with the stock of Company A; one-half share of Company A was offered for each share of Company B; all of B's stockholders accepted. Company A now has 1.5 million shares outstanding and $2 million of net profits. The day before the fusion, the stock of Company A was selling at $30 a share. What was the market price of the stock of Company A one day after the fusion, assuming that the price-earnings ratio remained at 30?

Answers: 25-4a, $566.50; 25-4b, $1,665; 25-5a, $45.75; 25-5b, 0.65; 25-8a, $1,500; 25-8b, $60,000; 25-10, $40.

Company A, located in Wisconsin, is engaged mainly in manufacturing auto-matic-control equipment for air transport companies and for the United States Air Force. It is very active in research and consequently has assembled a staff of

CASE ON TERMS OF A BUSINESS COMBINATION

top-notch scientists. The president of A receives a telephone call from the president of Company B, suggesting that it might be to the advantage of the two firms to combine. Company B, a California corporation, is engaged in substantially the same activities as A, electronics. Because the president of B did not want to send a written communication about this matter, he used the telephone.

Company A is seven years old; Company B is only two years old. Each firm is making profits, but neither has paid any cash dividends. Although B is younger, its profits are larger; however, it has considerably more shares of stock outstanding than does A.

Company A, the seller, has several reasons for being interested seriously in the proposal. First, if B makes an attractive offer, the stockholders of A will improve their financial position. Second, the officers of A are promised substantial pay increases if the combination goes through. Since the executives of A are also large stockholders of their company, there may be a double economic advantage for them.

From their viewpoint, however, there are two possible disadvantages. First, the president of Company A will become vice president of Company B. His position in the new company will not carry as much prestige as the presidency in the old firm. Moreover, there is no guarantee of tenure for the major officers of Company A in the combination. The management of A weighs the pros and cons of the proposal and decides to support it.

Company B, the buyer, is very anxious to gain control over Company A because of the latter's excellent research facilities and because the combination offers B an opportunity to diversify its activities further.

Company B plans to offer its own common stock directly to the stockholders of A. Hence, no cash is needed to finance the acquisition. Company B plans to operate A as a subsidiary for the time being; later, it might abolish A as a corporate entity.

The offer by B is set up so that if the combination is completed, the transaction will qualify as a tax-free reorganization. That is, the stockholders of A who receive stock of B will not incur a taxable gain in the year in which the exchange of securities is made. The main factor necessary to qualify the exchange of securities as a tax-free reorganization is that 80 percent of all classes of the stock of A be given up for the common stock of B.

In addition to its common stock, A also has 507 shares of $50, 6 percent preferred stock outstanding. Hence, in addition to obtaining the approval of the required percentage of common stockholders of A, it is also necessary for Company B to obtain the approval of the same percentage of the preferred stockholders. This problem is simplified because the officers of A own about 40 percent of its common stock and about 30 percent of its preferred stock.

The market price of B's common stock ranged between $5 and $10 in a period of several months before the proposed combination. The common stock of A was so inactive that there was no accurate measuring rod of its worth in the market. However, a small block of common stock of A did change hands at $50 a share. There was no trading in the preferred stock of A.

Table 25-3 shows data of both companies for the year before the proposal to combine, or for the latest year-end, as the case may be:

	Company B	Company A
Current assets	$1,586,000	$ 557,400
Current liabilities	$1,143,000	$ 249,400
Total liabilities	$1,198,000	$ 249,400
Fixed assets after depreciation	$ 441,000	$ 124,800
Net worth	$ 848,000	$ 460,800
Number of shares of preferred stock, 6%, $50 par value		507
Number of shares of common stock	259,255	16,675
Inventories	$1,007,000	$ 89,700
Annual sales	$2,658,000	$1,757,700
Profit before taxes	$ 263,000	$ 65,400
Current ratio	1.39	2.23
Book value per share	$ 3.27	$ 27.63

TABLE 25-3
Data for Company A and Company B

Required: (a) Assume that you are a preferred stockholder in Company A. How many shares of Company B would you demand for each share of preferred you own? (b) Assume that you are a common stockholder of Company A. How many shares of Company B would you demand for each share you relinquish? Bear in mind that the management of B must make the exchange offer so attractive that 80 percent or more of the stock of all classes in A will be exchanged for that of B. On the other hand, the management of B is not willing to go to extremes in winning the favor of A's stockholders. There are other electronics firms that B can absorb if the stockholders of A are unwilling to accept a reasonable offer.

EVALUATION AND REMEDIAL ACTION 5

Evaluating the Capital Structure: Bond Refunding and Stock Splits

Periodically, management should evaluate the source of capital mixture it is using. As indicated in previous chapters, the optimum source of capital mixture includes the terms of the agreements, as well as the specific owners and creditors. Although great care may have been exercised in obtaining funds in the past, a source of capital mixture quickly becomes obsolete in a dynamic business world. Changes in either the external or the internal situation may call for a new mixture. Examples of external changes are a declining or rising bank interest rate, rising or falling stock market prices, and a changing federal income tax structure. Examples of internal changes are an increase in the size of the firm and a desire to convert a close corporation into an open one. In other words, what was an optimum source of capital mixture last year may not be an optimum one now. The evaluation of the source of capital mixture is always made with the intent of taking remedial action, if necessary.

Changes are made in the composition of the source of capital mixture and the terms with each supplier of assets when management believes that such a course of action will increase the value of the stock. Any increase in the market price or decrease in the cost of the stock will be a step toward advancing the goals of the firm.[1]

The following will be explained in this chapter:

1. Guideposts for evaluating the source of capital mixture
2. Voluntarily retiring bond issues
3. Capital budgeting as a tool in debt management
4. Splitting the stock
5. Replacing stocks with bonds: other changes in the capital accounts

1. The "cost" of a share of stock is considered to be lower after a stock split.

The evaluation of the source of capital mixture must be made while evaluating the firm in other matters. That is, it is difficult to separate the appraisal of the effectiveness with which assets are used from the effectiveness of the source of asset mixture. Thus the level of operating income is a result of managing the assets efficiently. But the level and stability of operating income determines to some extent the design of an optimum source of capital mixture.

The following guideposts, presented in the form of questions, assist in scrutinizing a particular firm's source of capital mixture:

1. Is trading on the equity profitable?
2. Can the firm obtain funds from other sources at a lower cost than is now being paid?
3. Are the maturity and interest patterns within the firm's probable ability to pay?
4. Does the bank loan, preferred stock issue, or bond issue have an undue number of restrictions?
5. Can the firm obtain funds from another source by pledging less collateral?
6. Does the firm have an optimum number of shares outstanding?

These tests may be applied most fruitfully by management, which has a knowledge of the history, the current problems, and the prospects of the firm.

Is Trading on the Equity Profitable?   A firm trades on the equity when it uses sources of funds on which a limited return is paid. The basic issue is whether trading on the equity is actually advancing the welfare of the residual owners. This practice is advantageous if the percentage rate of return earned on the residual owners' equity is higher by trading on the equity than would be the case if the firm did not trade on the equity.

Yardsticks for Evaluating the Source of Capital Mixture

Can the Firm Obtain Funds from Other Sources at a Lower Cost Than is Now Being Paid?   There is the possibility that money market rates have declined since the firm obtained funds from creditors or preferred stockholders. If this is the case, these sources of funds may be paid off with the proceeds of lower interest-bearing loans or lower dividend-paying preferred stock. Thus a firm that floated a 6 percent bond issue might find that if bonds were sold today, a rate of 4 percent would be sufficient to induce investors to buy the securities. Under these circumstances, the firm could issue 4 percent bonds and use the proceeds to pay off the issue now outstanding. Likewise, if stock market prices are now abnormally high, this would mean that the cost of capital of this source is low. Hence, a firm might consider selling common stock to pay off preferred stockholders. Similarly, business firms are constantly on the alert for the possibility of replacing one short-term source of credit with another but lower-cost short-term source. Actually, most managements are quite quick to detect opportunities for lowering the amount paid by the firm for the use of funds.

Problem   Company S renegotiated a $100,000 bank loan; previously the bank charged 6 percent, now it charges 4 percent. The following data applied to the company before renegotiation: total sales $400,000; EBIT $26,000; corporation tax rate 50 percent. (See Table 26-1.) *Required*: (a) By how much did profits after taxes increase as a result of the change in the interest rate? (b) If the firm had not renegotiated the interest rate, by how much would sales have had to rise to increase profits by the amount of your answer to (a)?

Solution (a)

TABLE 26-1

	Prenegotiation	Postnegotiation
Sales	$400,000	$400,000
EBIT	26,000	26,000
Interest	6,000	4,000
Taxable income	20,000	22,000
Tax (50 percent)	10,000	11,000
Net after taxes	10,000	11,000

Profits increased by $1,000 as a result of saving $2,000 in interest charges.

(b)

Step 1. Net profits after taxes (before renegotiation) are 2½ percent of sales ($10,000 ÷ $400,000).

Step 2. If net profits are to be $11,000, sales must be $440,000, determined as follows:

Let X = new level of sales desired

$.02\frac{1}{2}X$ = $11,000

X = $440,000

Hence, lowering interest charges by $2,000 has the same impact (in this problem) as raising sales by $40,000 ($440,000 − $400,000).

Are the Maturity and Interest Patterns Within the Firm's Probable Ability to Pay?

This problem is concerned with relating future cash inflows to future cash outflows, using the past and the present as a guide. Several of the following tests shed light on the solvency position of the firm: (1) number of times preferred stock dividends are earned, (2) number of times interest requirements are earned, (3) number of times cash needed to service the debt is earned, and (4) number of times cash needed to service the preferred stock is earned. If the margin of protection declines below the safety point established by the officers, the solvency position of the firm is endangered. A firm must earn sufficient profits and generate sufficient cash to support its source of capital mixture.

It is customary to look to the earning power of the firm to pay bond interest and preferred stock dividends; it is also customary to look to current assets to pay current liabilities and the interest on them, if any. A common rule of thumb is that the firm's current liabilities should not exceed half its current assets. This is the same as saying that the current ratio should be at least 2 to 1. As most persons in finance know, however, there are a number of firms with a higher current ratio that are in financial difficulty and a number of firms with a lower current ratio that are highly solvent.

In the event that the evaluation of the solvency position of the firm shows a need for improvement, several types of remedial action may be taken, including these: call the bonds and replace them with common stock, retain a larger proportion of the earnings in the business, and refund a bond issue that is coming due in the near future.

Does the Bank Loan, Preferred Stock Issue, or Bond Issue Have an Undue Number of Restrictions? When the management agreed to the restrictive provisions for the protection of the suppliers of capital, it did so because such agreements tended to lower the cost of the funds. But as time goes on, these restrictions may begin to block progress in a manner not anticipated at the time of the original financing. For example, one of the protective provisions of a preferred stock issue may be that the company will not merge without the consent of two-thirds of these shareholders. When management encounters restrictive provisions that turn out to be handicaps, an effort may be made to negotiate new terms; or failing in this approach, the business firm might pay off the suppliers of these funds.

Can the Firm Obtain Funds from Another Source by Pledging Less Collateral? When a firm raised funds in the past, it may have pledged a relatively large amount of capital as a condition for obtaining the loan or as a condition for obtaining a low-cost loan. But as the firm grows, it might need credit from other sources that are reluctant to lend if the firm has already pledged its best collateral. This kind of a predicament is difficult to solve; it may require recasting the entire source of capital mixture.

Does the Firm Have an Optimum Number of Shares Outstanding? For each firm there is an optimum number of shares of common stock outstanding, assuming the firm is of a given size and a given level of profitability. For example, the profits or expected profits of a firm might drive the price of the common stock up to $400. While this is good news to common stockholders, such a high price tends to lessen the marketability of the issue. A solution, discussed later in this chapter, is to increase the number of shares by a stock split, a technique that lowers the unit price of each share by increasing the number of shares outstanding. Similarly, a firm that begins on a small scale might prosper over the years and now be ready to sell part of their holdings. The firm might have a stock split to lower the price of each share to a level that will encourage public participation in purchasing the shares about to be sold. A number of other interesting problems arise in seeking the best number of units of ownership to be outstanding. Management has an obligation to design a source of capital mixture that contains an optimum number of shares of common stock.

There are several important reasons for redeeming bonds.

1. The corporation may find that it can sell new bonds at a lower rate of interest than that being paid on the outstanding bonds. Assume that a corporation issues bonds on which it pays 5 percent interest. At a later date, the corporation may find that it can borrow at 3½ percent interest. If the bonds outstanding are redeemable, the corporation can redeem the 5 percent bonds and pay off this issue with the proceeds of the new issue (on which the corporation will have to pay only 3½ percent interest); this refunding operation results in a substantial saving to the corporation. Interest charges are often reduced when bonds are refunded. Any reduction in the rate of interest paid on a given sum of money is always beneficial to the stockholders, because the profits of the corporation are thereby increased (or losses reduced).

2. It may want to eliminate the bond interest entirely.

3. It may want to have the indenture voided. If there is some particular provision in the indenture that turns out to be unsatisfactory, the next move will be to have the indenture canceled. Some of the provisions of an indenture that might be considered burdensome are restrictions on paying dividends on common stock, the after-acquired clause, and limitations on disposing of the voting stock of a subsidiary. These restrictive provisions will no longer be in effect when the bonds are redeemed.

4. It may want to simplify the capital structure.

5. It may want to pave the way for refinancing. If there is a small closed mortgage issue outstanding, the corporation might redeem the entire issue with the objective of selling a larger open-end issue of bonds. In practice, we find many instances of redemption in anticipation of a major refinancing program.

In conclusion it should be noted that although many provisions in the indenture are for the benefit of investors, this is not true of the voluntary redemption feature, which is included for the benefit of the issuer, for the various reasons mentioned above.

Forced Conversion through Redemption

A corporation may force conversion by redeeming the bonds at a time when it is more profitable for the bondholders to convert rather than surrender the bonds and receive cash. Under these conditions, when a firm redeems its bonds, it does not need to plan on paying cash to all bondholders; instead, in effect, the company pays the bondholders with shares of common stock.

Problem

Company B is considering redeeming a bond issue. Data for the firm are given below:

Call price of convertible bond	$1,000
Market price of convertible bond	$1,090
Number of shares into which bond is convertible	10
Market price per share of common stock	$108
Price-earnings ratio before redemption	18
Anticipated price-earnings ratio after redemption	22
Shares of common stock outstanding prior to redemption	10,000
6 percent convertible bonds outstanding	$500,000
Earnings before interest and taxes (operating income)	$150,000
Tax rate	50 percent

Should this company redeem its bonds, assuming that the firm uses the impact of the transaction on the market value of the stock as the decision criterion?

Solution

	Preredemption	Postredemption
EBIT	$150,000	$150,000
Interest	$ 30,000	0
Taxable income	$120,000	$150,000
Tax	$ 60,000	$ 75,000
Net after tax	$ 60,000	$ 75,000
Shares of common stock outstanding	10,000	15,000
Earnings per share on common	$6	$5
Market price per share (price-earnings ratio X earnings per share)	$108	$110

In a situation like this, the bondholders would be forced to convert because they would receive $1,080 in stock (10 shares X the market price of $108); if the bondholders elected to receive cash, they would receive only $1,000. If all the bondholders converted, the new number of shares of common stock outstanding would be 15,000 (10,000 old + 5,000 new). The 5,000 new shares were obtained by first determining that there are 500 outstanding $1,000 bonds. For each bond the company would issue 10 shares of stock during the conversion process. This means that the firm would issue an additional 5,000 shares (500 X 10).

In this example, it would be advantageous for the firm to call the bonds, because the market price of the common stock would then be $110, an increase of $2 a share.

CAPITAL BUDGETING AS A TOOL IN DEBT MANAGEMENT

Problem

The following data apply to Company X: market price of a 6 percent bond $990; issue price of these bonds at a par value of $1,000; cost of capital of the firm 8 percent; the firm is in the 32 percent tax bracket; the bonds have five years to run before maturity. If Company X purchases one of these bonds in the market, it will have a profit of $10 per bond, which will be subject to the income tax. The management of the company is considering buying one of these bonds in the open market and retiring it. *Required*: Based on the net-present-value test, should the bonds be retired in this manner?

Solution

Outlay to buy the bond	$ 990.00
Plus tax on profit (32 percent of $10)	3.20
Total outlay	$ 993.20
Cash savings:	
Annual interest cost on an after-tax basis (68 percent of $60)	$ 40.80
Cash savings by not having to pay the principal at maturity	$1,000.00
Present value of cash savings (cash benefits):	
Interest (3.9927 × $40.80)	$ 162.90
Principal (.68058 × $1,000)	$ 680.58
Present value of cash benefits	$ 843.48

Since the present value of the cash benefits is $843.48 and the cash outlay required to obtain this benefit is $993.20, the net present value is −$149.72. Because the net present value is negative, the firm would not proceed with the possible transaction (it should proceed only if the net present value is positive).

Problem The following data apply to Company Y: market price of each 8 percent bond $980; issue price of these bonds $1,000; cost of capital of the firm 6 percent; the firm is in the 50 percent tax bracket; the bonds have a life of eight more years. If the firm buys these bonds in the market, it will have a profit of $20 a bond, which will be subject to the income tax. The management of the company is considering buying the bonds in the market and retiring them. *Required*: Based on the net-present-value test, should the bonds be retired in this manner?

Solution

Outlay to buy bond	$ 980
Plus tax on profit (50 percent of $20)	10
Total outlay	$ 990
Cash savings:	
Annual interest cost	$80
Tax (50 percent)	40
After-tax cost (cash benefits—that is, cash savings per year)	$ 40
Cash saving by not having to pay principal at maturity	$1,000
Present value of cash benefits (cash savings):	
Interest (6.2098 × $40)	$248.39
Principal (.62741 × $1,000)	$627.41
	$875.80

Since the present value of the cash benefits is only $875.80 and the cost is $990, the net present value is negative. Hence, the company should not retire the bonds in the manner being considered.

A *stock split*, also called a *split-up*, takes place when the corporation sends unissued shares to the stockholders without the stockholders having to pay for the stock and when the corporation reduces the par or stated value of all the shares. For example, a corporation with 1,000 shares of common stock with a par value of $100 might decide to split the stock two for one. A two for one split means that there will be twice as many shares outstanding after the split. In this hypothetical illustration the results after the split-up would be 2,000 shares outstanding with a par value of $50 each. It should be noted that the increased number of shares outstanding is accompanied by a reduction of the par or stated value of each share so that the balance in the capital account does not change. Before the stock split, the balance in the common stock account is $100,000 (1,000 shares × $100 par value). After the stock split, the balance in the common stock account is still $100,000 (2,000 shares × $50 par value). Furthermore, no cash has entered or left the business as a result of the split-up. A stock split resembles a stock dividend in that under both arrangements the corporation issues additional shares of its own stock without receiving any money or property for them. The chief difference between a stock split and a stock dividend is that the surplus is reduced in a stock dividend, whereas in a stock split the par or stated value of each share is decreased.

Before the Eaton Manufacturing Company split its stock two for one, the stock had a par value of $4; after the split-up the stock had a par value of $2. Before the split-up there were 896,260 shares outstanding and 4,439 shares in the treasury; after the split-up there were 1,792,520 shares outstanding and 8,878 shares in the treasury. Some additional split-ups are du Pont two for one split, General Motors Corporation two for one split, and Bethlehem Steel Corporation three for one split.

The main reason for a stock split is to decrease the market price of the shares to a level that will stimulate trading in the issue. Stocks that are very high (such as $150 per share) discourage most investors from trading in them. Investors prefer a large number of medium-priced shares to a few high-priced securities even though the aggregate investment is the same. Because of these preferences we find corporations making stock splits to bring down the market value of their shares. When the Atchison, Topeka and Santa Fe stock was split two for one, the reason given for this action was to "lower the price of the shares and thus make them more attractive to the average investor and to provide a wider distribution."

How does a stock split reduce the market value of the corporation's shares? If a corporation has a stock split of two for one or any other ratio, the earnings and dividends must be spread over a larger number of shares; the value of each share is diluted and the market value falls accordingly. Assume the following facts about a particular corporation: There are 2,000 shares outstanding, with a par value of $100. The market value of each share is $150. Assume further that this stock is split four for one. How will this stock split-up affect the value of the shares? First, the number of shares outstanding will be increased to 8,000 and the par value of each share will be reduced to $25. The balance in the capital account will not change—it is $200,000 both before and after the stock split. Since the corporation's earning capacity is not increased by the stock split, earnings will have to be spread over four times as many shares. We would therefore expect the market value of each share to fall to approximately one-fourth its previous level. This would result in a new market value of about $37.50 per share. It is the investor who benefits from a stock split, although taking action to decrease the market value of the shares may help the corporation in any future financing by getting the shares into a trading range that appeals to more investors. After du Pont split its stock two for one, stockholders increased by 15,000 within a year.

Two other circumstances may lead to a stock split-up—when a merger or consolidation is about to take place and it is desired to exchange shares on a share-for-share basis and when a close corporation is about to be changed into a publicly owned corporation. The stock of the Book of the Month Club, Inc., was split 2,000 for 1 just before the company became publicly owned. Soon after the split-up, key stockholders sold 200,000 of their shares to the general public.

Stock Splits from the Investor's Viewpoint

The immediate effect on a stockholder is that he owns more shares than previously. In a four for one split, an investor will have four times as many shares as before the split. Assume that a stockholder owned 100 shares of stock which had a market value of $150 each. The total market value of the commitment immediately before the split would be $15,000. After the stock split, the stockholder would have 400 shares, but the market value of each share would fall to approximately $37.50 per share. As far as aggregate market value is concerned, the investor has neither gained nor lost on this part of the deal. Just what benefits do stockholders expect to derive from a stock split?

Three main benefits are expected to accrue to stockholders after a stock split. First, with the market price of the shares decreased to a smaller amount, more investors are expected to become interested in the stock. This interest is often translated into a decision to purchase. Increased purchases may increase the demand for the shares and drive up the price. Thus the investor mentioned in the previous paragraph might find the market value of his shares increasing to $39.75. If so, the market value of his commitment would now be $15,900. If it could be definitely determined that the increase in market value was a result of the split, then the split would have been profitable to the stockholder, because the aggregate market value of his investment would have increased by $900. Even though shares may advance in price after a stock split, it is hard to prove that the increased market value is an outcome of the stock split. It is difficult to isolate certain factors and say that they are responsible for an increase in the market value of the shares.

A second advantage that stockholders hope for is that the corporation will not cut its dividends proportionately after the split. Thus, if a company is paying $9 per share in dividends prior to the split, one would expect the dividends to be cut to $2.25 after a four for one split. However, the corporation might pay $2.50 per share after the split. If this is the case, the stockholders will be ahead financially, because the aggregate dividends paid by the corporation will increase. For example, the Texas Company, which split its stock two for one, formerly paid a dividend of $1 per quarter. After the split, the quarterly dividend was 65 cents. In other words, the dividends per share increased $1.20 per year.

A third advantage that stockholders may expect from a stock split is that increased trading in the shares will add to their marketability. When the price of the shares is very high, there may be only a limited amount of trading in the issue. If one shareholder decides to sell a large block of securities, the market might not be able to absorb the issue except at a depressed price. After a stock split, when a shareholder decides to sell, it may be possible to dispose of the shares without depressing their price unduly because supposedly a larger number of individuals will be trading in the issue.

The market anticipates the three benefits mentioned above, and as a result we may encounter cases where the market value of the shares will increase substantially upon the announcement or even the rumor that there will be a stock split. Thus, if the shares are selling at $145 each, the market value might increase to $150 upon the announcement of a stock split. However, after the split, the stock will fall to approximately its theoretical market value.

Stock splits require the approval of the shareholders. Often the holders of two-thirds of the shares must approve these changes, which require amendments to the charter. Boards of directors recommend that there be a stock split; stockholders are usually agreeable to the stock split and are generally willing to cast their votes for the proposal.

At times, a corporation may go through a reverse stock split, meaning that the number of shares outstanding is decreased. Under this arrangement, stockholders turn in their shares and receive fewer shares with a higher par or stated value. The purpose of a *reverse stock split* is to increase the market value of each share. Reverse stock splits are not as common as stock split-ups.

Since interest on debt is a deductible item for federal income taxes, a number of companies have been altering the composition of their capital structure by decreasing the amount of stock and increasing the amount of bonds. Fairbanks, Morse and Company, for example, issued $15 million debentures and used the proceeds to buy its own common stock. The shares so purchased became treasury stock. The effect of this transaction was to substitute low-cost capital for high-cost capital. The end result was that earnings per share increased, even though the total earning power of the firm did not change.

REPLACING STOCKS WITH BONDS

Corporations may voluntarily acquire and then cancel their own common stock. This line of action is taken when the corporation has idle cash on which it is

OTHER CHANGES IN THE CAPITAL ACCOUNTS

earning no return or possibly a very low return. For example, Warner Bros. Pictures, Inc., had a net working capital of slightly over $43 million. The corporation offered to buy about 15 percent of its common stock from stockholders. Stockholders were invited to submit tenders to the corporation not exceeding $15 per share. The corporation bought from the stockholders who offered to sell at the lowest prices. The final outcome was that the corporation bought over a million shares at a price of $15 or less. The shares were then canceled.

At times, the provisions of a preferred stock issue outstanding may prove burdensome to the issuer. It is then necessary to attempt to get the preferred stockholders to agree to amend the terms of their contract. This assumes that the preferred stock is noncallable or that it is not expedient to call the issue. For example, the Atlantic Richfield Company had two issues of preferred stock outstanding—Series A preferred and Series B preferred. However, any additional preferred stock to be issued would have a secondary claim on dividends, thus raising the prospective dividend that would have to be offered to attract capital. The company persuaded the holders of the outstanding preferred to exchange their shares for a new issue, the terms of which permitted the company to issue additional *pari passu* preferred. As compensation to the preferred stockholders, the company waived its right to redeem the shares. Also, those who exchanged old stock for new received slightly more in dividends.

A survey of daily newspapers will reveal some of the following changes taking place: increasing the authorized common stock, increasing the authorized preferred stock, and accepting tenders for the sale of preferred stock.

HIGHLIGHTS OF THIS CHAPTER

Just as management must evaluate its use of assets, so must it evaluate its source of capital mixture and take remedial action, if necessary. With the passage of time, there may be a need for changing the composition of the sources of capital or for changing some of the terms with those who supply the capital. Several examples of remedial action are: (1) voluntarily retiring preferred stock, (2) voluntarily retiring a bond issue, (3) splitting stock, (4) eliminating a deficit, (5) replacing stocks with bonds, and (6) making other changes.

When a stock split takes place, the number of shares outstanding increases while at the same time the par or stated value per share decreases. Looking at the matter from the stockholder's viewpoint, we may say that he receives more shares without having to pay for them. Since the corporation issues shares without receiving any cash or other consideration for them, it follows that a stock split will lead to a dilution in the market value per share, which falls because earnings must be spread over a larger number of shares.

REVIEW QUESTIONS

26-1. Give several reasons why corporations split their common stock.

26-2. What is the difference between a stock split and a stock dividend?

26-3. Why does the market price of the common tend to rise when a stock split is about to take place?

26-4. Why might a company substitute a moderate amount of bonds for its outstanding common stock?

26-5. Robert Starbuck noted in a newspaper five years old that the stock of IBM was selling for $510. He became curious and found that the current market price of this firm's stock is $360. Is this reasonable proof that the earning power of the firm has declined?

Answers to some of the problems appear at the end of this section. *For each problem, show how you obtained the answer.* **REVIEW PROBLEMS**

26-1. Below are financial data for the Singer Company:

Assets	$1,000,000	Liabilities	$200,000
		Common stock, $100 par	500,000
		Earned surplus	300,000
Total	$1,000,000	Total	$1,000,000

This company has a two for one stock split. After the split, determine the following: (a) the total amount (in dollars) of common stock; (b) the total surplus; (c) the total liabilities; (d) the total net worth; (e) the total number of shares of common stock outstanding; (f) the par value of each share; (g) the book value per share.

26-2. The stock of Company X was selling at $100 a share just prior to a stock split of four for one; the stock has been paying an annual dividend of $10 per share. At the time of the split, the firm announced that the new postsplit annual dividend rate would be $3 a share. Assume that Fred Jones had one share prior to the split. (a) How many additional shares would he receive? (b) After the split, how much in dividends would he receive per year? (c) Is the price of the stock after the split likely to be more or less than $25 a share?

26-3. Company R renegotiated a $100,000 bank loan; previously the bank charged 6 percent, now it charges 5 percent. The following data applied to the company before renegotiation: total sales $200,000; EBIT $46,000; a corporate tax rate of 50 percent. (a) By how much did profits after taxes increase as a result of the change in the interest rate? (b) If the firm did not renegotiate the interest rate, by how much would sales have had to rise to increase profits by the amount of your answer in (a)? The answer to (b) will be an approximation.

26-4. Company M is considering refunding a bond issue, that is, paying off an outstanding issue with a new issue that carries a lower rate of interest. After taking into consideration all the major factors and most of the minor ones, the following information applies to the firm: the new bonds will have a maturity of

10 years; the firm's cost of capital is 6 percent; the transaction will result in an immediate net cash outlay of $100,000; and the firm will save, on an after-tax basis, $14,000 a year in interest (for 10 years). On the basis of the net-present-value test, should the firm proceed with the refunding?

26-5. The following data apply to Company A: market price of each 6 percent bond $980; issue price of these bonds $1,000; cost of capital of the firm 10 percent; the firm is in the 50 percent tax bracket; and the bonds have five years to run before they mature. If the firm buys these bonds in the market, it will have a profit of $20 per bond, which will be subjected to the income tax. Management is considering buying the bonds in the market and retiring them. Based on the net-present-value test, should the bonds be retired in this manner?

26-6. A husband and a wife have a considerable part of their wealth tied up in a wholly owned and wholly controlled family lumber business. The couple would like to diversify its holding by selling some of the stock to the general public. The following data apply to the firm:

Net profits after taxes	$3,000,000
Shares of common of the firm	100,000
Price-earnings ratio for this type of firm as indicated by an investment banking firm retained as an adviser	10

The banker also indicated that the general public would be receptive to buying the shares at $10 each. How large a stock split would be needed in preparation for the firm's going public?

26-7. In a certain year, Company Y had 12,000 shares of common stock outstanding for 2 months and 18,000 shares outstanding for 10 months. Net profits after taxes are $34,000. If a weighted average is used in determining the number of shares outstanding, what are the earnings per share?

26-8. Company R has convertible bonds outstanding; the conversion ratio is 50 (the owner of a $1,000 bond can convert it into 50 shares of common stock when he surrenders it). If the firm has a two for one stock split, what is the new adjusted conversion price (the conversion price is the dollar amount of bonds that must be surrendered to obtain 1 share of stock)?

26-9. Company Z has convertible bonds outstanding; the conversion price is $25. If the firm has a two for one stock split, what is the new conversion ratio?

26-10. Company Q has $75,000 of net profits; 10,000 shares of common stock; a payout ratio of 50 percent; and earnings per share of $7.50. The firm declares a 50 percent stock dividend and at the same time announces the new dividend rate per share to be $2.80. (a) What is the new payout ratio? (b) How much cash will be needed to meet the new total dividend requirements?

26-11. Directors of the White Consolidated Industries voted a two for one stock split and stated their intention of increasing the quarterly dividend to 10 cents a share after the split was approved. The company had been paying 15 cents a share prior to the stock split. If a stockholder had 100 shares before the split: (a) By how much will his annual dollar income increase? (b) By what percentage will his annual income increase?

26-12. Mr. P owns 100 shares of common stock in a firm that is paying $6 a share in dividends and that will continue to pay this rate indefinitely. The firm will pay a 10 percent stock dividend for the next few years. Beginning immediately, stock dividends will be paid on the first of the year; cash dividends will be paid at the end of the year. The stock of the firm is yielding 5 percent and is assumed to continue at this rate indefinitely. Presently, Mr. P is receiving $600 a year in dividends; the market value of his holdings is $12,000. Two full years from now: (a) How much in dividends will Mr. P be receiving? (b) What will be the market value of his holdings?

26-13. Company C, located in New York City, is in the 50 percent tax bracket. The firm had been paying a dividend of 20 cents a share per quarter. The management said "stockholders have been beseiging us with requests for additional dividends." To pacify them, management approved a plan whereby each stockholder would be given $25 of 7 percent debentures for each share of stock surrendered to the company (with an overall limit of 200,000 shares). Approximately 200,000 shares were surrendered to Company C. (a) If a stockholder originally held 100 shares and surrendered all of them, how much additional annual income did he receive? (b) On the entire transaction, what was the net additional cash outlay (to the company) per year as a result of pleasing all these stockholders?

26-14. Company D is considering redeeming a bond issue. Data for the firm are:

Call price of convertible bond	$1,000
Market price of convertible bond	$1,195
Number of shares into which bond is convertible	10
Market price per share of common stock	$115
Price-earnings ratio before redemption	20
Anticipated price-earnings ratio after redemption	24
Shares of common outstanding prior to redemption	10,000
7 percent convertible bonds outstanding	$500,000
Earnings before interest and taxes (operating income)	$150,000
Tax rate	50 percent

Should this company redeem its bonds, assuming that the firm uses the impact of the transaction on the market value of the common stock as the decision criterion?

26-15. Company P is considering redeeming a bond issue. Data for the firm are:

Call price	$1,000
Market price of convertible bond	$1,160
Number of shares into which bond is convertible	20
Market price per share of common stock	$54
Price-earnings ratio before redemption	10
Anticipated price-earnings ratio after redemption	12
Shares of common stock outstanding prior to redemption	10,000
4 percent convertible bonds outstanding	$500,000
Operating income	$128,000
Tax rate	50 percent

Assuming that management will base its decision on the impact of the redemption on the market price of the common should the company proceed with the transaction?

Answers: 26-1a, $500,000; 26-1b, $300,000; 26-1c, $200,000; 26-1d, $800,000; 26-1e, 10,000; 26-1f, $50; 26-1g, $80; 26-2a, 3; 26-2b, $12; 26-2c, more; 26-6, 30 for 1 (i.e., 29 additional shares for each 1 held); 26-7, $2; 26-8, $10; 26-9, 80; 26-10a, 56 percent; 26-10b, $42,000; 26-11a, $20; 26-11b, 33 1/3 percent; 26-12a, $726; 26-12b, $14,520; 26-13a, $95; 26-13b, $15,000.

Measures of Managerial Performance: Remedial Action

In the administrative process management makes plans to direct the use of assets toward the goals of the firm, both primary and contributory. Then, actions are taken to direct the use of assets with the hope of attaining these goals. We are now ready to evaluate the success of the officers in making satisfactory progress toward the goals or in actually reaching them. Periodically, the persons in charge of directing the use of cash, accounts receivable, inventory, and fixed assets must render an accounting of their stewardship. The evaluation process is interspersed all through the business firm and the economic system. The lowest paid employee is evaluated by his supervisor, department heads are evaluated by vice presidents, vice presidents are evaluated by the president and by the board of directors, the board of directors is evaluated by the stockholders, and the firm is in turn evaluated by the general public. Our concern will be with one phase of evaluation—that of management's success or failure in making wise use of the firm's assets. The evaluation process looks back with one eye while the other eye is focused on the future. Evaluation is made with the intention of taking remedial action, a step that anticipates making changes so that future goals can be reached.

Two main themes will run through this chapter. First, we will limit ourselves to a broad type of evaluation and remedial action and hence be concerned with classes of data and remedial action rather than with details. We will paint with a broad brush, because this approach gives a better insight into administrative financial management than does focusing attention on the smaller subdivisions of the problems of directing the use of capital. Second, since we will be stressing the management approach, we will focus attention on the evaluation of people who are in charge of certain areas of activities. Thus, a vice president in charge of sales will be evaluated on the basis of the plans established for him at the beginning of the period. This approach is in step with the times, as more and more attention is being given to holding individuals responsible for certain areas of business activities.

In evaluating management's direction of the use of assets, certain standards of reference must be used. Evaluation is basically a process of making comparisons. Yardsticks must be used as a frame of reference for determining in an objective manner the progress that a firm is making in reaching its goals.

These tools are useful in evaluating managerial performance:

1. Evaluating progress toward primary goals
   a. Increasing the financial welfare of the owners
   b. Assuming social responsibility
2. Using other criteria
   a. The firm's budgeted goals as a yardstick
   b. Industry averages as a yardstick
   c. The previous year's performance as a yardstick
      1. Tests to compare profitability
      2. Tests to compare solvency
3. Taking remedial action

Since Chapter 4 contains an extensive discussion of financial ratios on profitability and solvency, items under c above will not be repeated in this chapter.

EVALUATING PROGRESS TOWARD PRIMARY GOALS

The primary goals of the firm may again be stated as:

$$\text{Primary goals} = \frac{\text{Increase financial}}{\text{welfare of owners}} + \frac{\text{Assume social}}{\text{responsibility}}$$

Furthermore, the financial welfare of owners is increased when they receive distributions in the form of profits, when they receive larger than normal salaries and fringe benefits, and when they receive or earn capital gains. An alternate but equivalent method of expressing the primary goals is:

$$\text{Primary goals} = \frac{\text{Increase net present value of owner's equity}}{} + \frac{\text{Assume social}}{\text{responsibility}}$$

The question to be answered is whether or not the firm has been making progress toward these goals.

Increasing Financial Welfare of Owners

Table 27-1 shows an evaluation of United States Steel Corporation insofar as one phase of its primary goals is concerned, that is, increasing the financial welfare of its owners. Observe that the table gives information on two vital aspects of the operations of this firm—profit distributions to the owners and the market price of the common stock. Since United States Steel Corporation is a large, publicly owned firm, the matters of high salaries and fringe benefits paid to owners are not included. Of course, the managers of this firm receive these two forms of benefits, but primarily in their capacity as employees rather than in their capacity as owners. If a family owned firm were involved, the above two matters would be shown.

	United States Steel Corporation			Bethlehem Steel Corporation		TABLE 27-1 Progress of Two Steel Companies toward Reaching One of Their Primary Goals
Year	Cash Dividends	Range of Price of Stock		Cash Dividends	Range of Price of Stock	
1959	$3.00	$108–88		$2.40	$59–49	
1958	3.00	97–51		2.40	54–36	
1957	3.00	73–48		2.40	50–33	
1956	2.60	73–51		2.13	49–35	
1955	2.15	62–33		1.18	42–25	

A comparison is made with this firm's own recent past and with another competing steel company. In this line of endeavor, a customary practice is to compare a company's operations with that of competitors rather than with industry averages. In certain other fields where conditions between companies are more uniform, industry averages would be a useful yardstick for comparative purposes. There is no widely accepted view as to what should be a satisfactory composite rate of return to owners. In general, one phase of the primary goals is to earn as high a rate of return as is possible under the conditions in which the firm operates.

One tool that may be used to measure a firm's progress toward one of its primary goals (increasing the financial welfare of the owners) is the actual composite rate of return. A formula for giving a quantitative estimate of this progress is:

$$\text{Actual composite rate of return} = \frac{\begin{array}{c}\text{Average annual} \\ \text{amount of cash} \\ \text{dividends} \\ \text{received}\end{array} + \begin{array}{c}\text{Average annual} \\ \text{capital gains} \\ \text{realized or} \\ \text{earned}\end{array} + \begin{array}{c}\text{Average annual} \\ \text{fringe and} \\ \text{salary benefits} \\ \text{in excess of} \\ \text{normal}\end{array}}{\text{Cost of investment}}$$

The average dividends per year for United States Steel Corporation for the five-year period were $2.75; the average dividends for Bethlehem Steel Corporation for the same period were $2.10.

In each of the cases in Table 27-1, we may assume that an owner purchased stock in 1955 at a price that was the average of the high and the low. Furthermore, we may assume that the stock was sold in 1959 at the average of the high and the low for that year. Next, we obtain the average capital gain on the stock for each of the firms. This was $10.10 for United States Steel Corporation:

$$\frac{\$98.00 - \$47.50}{5} = \$10.10$$

Likewise, the average capital gain on the stock of Bethlehem Steel Corporation was $4.10:

$$\frac{\$54.00 - \$33.50}{5} = \$4.10$$

The formula for computing the actual composite rate of return for United States Steel Corporation is:

$$\text{Actual composite} \atop \text{rate of return} = \frac{\$2.75 + \$10.10 + 0}{\$47.50}$$
$$= 27 \text{ percent}$$

For Bethlehem Steel Corporation, this rate is:

$$\text{Actual composite} \atop \text{rate of return} = \frac{\$2.10 + \$4.10 + 0}{\$33.50}$$
$$= 19 \text{ percent}$$

For the period of time under consideration, the actual composite rate of return earned on United States Steel Corporation stock was 27 percent; the rate earned on Bethlehem Steel Corporation common stock was 19 percent. Hence the former firm had the superior performance. The main difficulty with the above form of measuring rod is that a firm may not yet have been a success but is on the verge of being one. Thus, if one held the common stock of Bethlehem Steel Corporation for another five years, his composite rate of return might be much more than 19 percent. Or the converse might be true; that is, a firm might have been a success in the past but be on the verge of a decline. In summary, the actual composite rate of return is an excellent measure of a firm's past performance, but it is not always a good predictor of the future.

Sound judgment must be used in evaluating the progress of a firm toward its primary goals. Thus a relatively new firm in its second year of operation might be incurring a loss and paying no dividends and yet be making normal progress, because many new firms operate at a loss during the first few years of their life—firms in the publishing business, for example. Yet the expectations are that these companies will pass their break-even point in the near future and then begin to operate at a profit. Another point to observe is that a firm such as United States Steel Corporation cannot be judged by its performance in any one year. The span of time should be long enough to average the good and the bad years, that is, years of prosperity and depression. Generally speaking, there will be some adverse years in the life of every firm. Unless sound judgment is used, the evaluation process may lead to instigation of the wrong kinds of remedial action.

A segment of the primary goals is for the firm to assume social responsibility as well as to advance the financial welfare of the owners. A firm is also judged by its contribution to the community. This contribution is over and above the company's making a superior product and paying high wages to workers. An example of the assumption of social responsibility is that of United States Steel Corporation (and other steel firms) in the Pittsburgh area. For many years, the smoke from steel mills posed a serious dirt problem in this city. The steel firms adjusted their equipment to eliminate nearly all the smoke nuisance. Another example of social responsibility is the financial support given by automobile manufacturers to several nonprofit organizations that engage in research for safety on the highway. In recent years, the public has been expecting more and more social responsibility from business firms.

Assuming Social Responsibility

In planning the use of capital a firm may establish certain goals for itself. As time passes actual performance may be compared with the aspirations of the firm that have been previously placed in writing. Table 27-2 shows the performance of the Scott Company, a hypothetical firm, compared with the budgeted goals.

THE FIRM'S BUDGET AS A YARDSTICK

	Budget	Actual	Variance
Sales	$6,000,000	$7,000,000	$1,000,000
Cost of goods sold	3,110,000	3,500,000	390,000
Gross margin	2,890,000	3,500,000	610,000
Selling expenses	750,000	1,740,000	990,000
General and administrative expenses	500,000	585,000	85,000
Operating income	1,640,000	1,175,000	465,000
Federal income tax	853,000	611,000	242,000
Net income	787,000	564,000	223,000

TABLE 27-2
The Scott Company Comparison of a Firm's Performance with Its Budget

The data in the table show information at the end of the fiscal period. Actually, this type of control can be prepared monthly and cumulative amounts carried as time progresses. Most firms that use an elaborate budgeting system do make monthly comparisons of actual performance with planned performance. If this is done, remedial action can be instigated in time to try to remedy difficulties. In many large firms an executive committee studies monthly reports that evaluate the firm's progress toward its objectives as set forth in the written plans of the firm.

INDUSTRY AVERAGES AS A YARDSTICK Another method of evaluation is to compare actual performance with industry averages. Although not conclusive in themselves, these averages are of great interest in industries where there is sufficient uniformity to make a meaningful comparison of a specific firm with data for the group. The same sources that supplied industry averages for the planning process can be used to give information for the evaluation.

TAKING REMEDIAL ACTION A firm that is unable to reach its goals will engage in a program of remedial action. The general strategy of remedial action consists of these steps: defining the problem, seeking the basic cause(s) of the problem, considering all possible solutions to the problem, and selecting the most promising of the proposed solutions and putting them into action.

Defining the Problem This phase of the strategy is not difficult. Usually the problem takes on one of these forms: declining market price of the shares of common stock, declining dividends, declining earnings per share, or default on interest and principal. All of these difficulties (if they persist for a long period of time) are bits of evidence that the firm is not reaching its goals.

Finding the Basic Causes of the Problem The problems are usually so complex as to defy a clear-cut listing, due to the fact that they are generally caused by a number of events all taking place concurrently. Thus a machine-tool manufacturer may believe that his declining profits are caused by foreign competition, domestic competition, a domestic recession, or labor difficulties. But some effort must be made to isolate basic causes of a firm's predicament. Very often, informed and sincere persons on the management team will disagree on why the firm is unable to earn profits. A modern practice is to hire a firm of management consultants to give its disinterested opinion on the causes of a company's difficulties.

Seeking Out All Possible Solutions to the Problem, Even Though Some of These Solutions Will Later Be Rejected Creative thinking is required to assemble a pool of ideas out of which will come the remedial actions later placed in effect. When the New York, New Haven, and Hartford Railroad ran out of cash and had to seek rehabilitation under federal law, the railroad hired a firm of consultants to give an opinion on all possible lines of rehabilitation. These possible courses of action were presented:

1. Successful reorganization
2. A form of state and community subsidy of passenger traffic
3. Voluntary merger
4. An Interstate Commerce Commission decree that the New Haven be included in a merger.
5. Federal government control and ownership
6. Liquidation

The consulting firm gave all the major possibilities, even though it knew some of them would be highly repulsive to the railroad (government ownership, for example).

Selecting One or More Kinds of Remedial Actions from the Pool of Ideas Those ideas that seem best suited to increasing the market value of the common stock are accepted. Just as a physician's remedy depends on his diagnosis, so do remedies for business firms depend on the diagnosis of the firm's problems. In practice there are thousands of types of remedial actions; only a few of the major ones will be discussed here. Furthermore, discussion will be limited to kinds of actions that are likely to require the attention of top management.

Because of the close interrelationship among all functional and administrative areas of the enterprise, remedial action taken by the board of directors often assumes the form of broad classes of actions rather than detailed actions. Thus, if a firm is losing money because it is unable to sell its products on a sufficient scale, the board of directors is more likely to dismiss the president than to begin changing the composition of the sales force. By selecting a new operating official, the board of directors assumes that changes will be made in selling procedures.

The remainder of this chapter will be devoted to the following general types of remedial action:

1. Using package programs to increase sales and lower costs
2. Changing the product mix
3. Replacing the management
4. Using the business combination device
5. Revamping the information system

The Sinclair Oil Corporation encountered a period when the market value of the stock fell and profits were decreasing. The firm, however, had a large cash balance and hence had reached one of its goals—staying solvent. In an annual report, the president said that the eyes of the management were focused on the oil business, not the stock market. He went on to observe that despite the decline in the market price of the common stock, "there has been no fundamental change in the value of Sinclair's properties or plants." He further observed that he and his associates were greatly concerned with the drop in profits. The first step in alleviating the difficulty was to determine the cause of the decrease in net earnings. The president explained that the oil company's difficulty was caused by a number of factors, including price-cutting in the industry, overcapacity, and increased cost of many items—especially labor items. He went on to say that his firm had a program of remedial action to improve the profit position of the company, that actions were being taken to increase income from every available source and to reduce costs of producing this income.

To attain these objectives, the company engaged in a program of remedial action, by:

USING PACKAGE PROGRAMS TO INCREASE SALES AND LOWER EXPENSES

1. Increasing efforts to economize and reduce costs in every operation
2. Making maximum use of every piece of equipment, each facility and plant
3. Reviewing every operation, looking to greater efficiency and economy in manpower and otherwise
4. Seeking new methods, new products, and reduced cost of raw materials and supplies
5. Accelerating replacement of any obsolete equipment
6. Increasing profitable sales from every source
7. Reducing inventories of materials, supplies, and equipment to minimum workable levels

The very essence of this drive was to review all operations and functions of every department and to develop an overall program that would emphasize the items most likely to increase income or further reduce expenses. Considerable care was exercised to insure that the long-range growth of the company would not be hampered to achieve short-run gains.

CHANGING THE
PRODUCT MIX

A firm that is not making satisfactory profits might decide to change its product mix, that is, change the kinds of goods or services being sold. Armour and Company had been earning meager net profits for a number of successive years averaging only three-tenths of one cent on each dollar of sales and earning only 3 percent on its net worth. For many years this enterprise committed nearly all of its assets to meat packing. Under new management the firm began to diversify and to take on additional activities, so that while formerly about 100 percent of the assets were devoted to meat packing, as of a recent date only 70 percent of the assets were so used. The other 30 percent is now used to produce chemicals and household items. Armour and Company also introduced a new cost accounting system and decentralized its activities. Furthermore, it hired the management consulting firm of Robert Heller and Associates to make a six-month study on how the overall profitability of the company could be improved. In summary, a change in the product mix (diversification), is a rather common solution for a firm that is not earning adequate profits.

Another similar type of remedial action is that of discontinuing the production or sale of certain kinds of inventory. In 1962 the American Optical Company discontinued the production of 2,000 items for the reason that in some years the firm sold only 50 of them. Despite this decrease, the American Optical Company still carried 30,000 different items in its stock. The impact of the decrease was quite favorable, as sales actually continued to increase despite a decline in the amount of average inventory and in the number of products handled. Of course, firms are careful not to discontinue slow-moving items if such an action would interfere with the sale of high-turnover inventory or interfere in any other manner with the market price of the certificates of beneficial interest or with the market price of the shares of common stock.

A change in top management is often used as a remedial action device. Certain firms may have special problems that people with certain talents are best able to solve. A firm that has a problem in obtaining war orders might hire a retired general as president; a firm that has a problem in production might hire an engineer as president; a firm that has an especially nasty problem in labor relations might hire a personnel man as president, and so on. The case of Endicott Johnson Corporation may be cited as an example of how changes in management can be used as a type of remedial action. This shoe manufacturing company has been in existence for many years. But in the 1960s its profits began to decline sharply, mainly because of faltering distribution of the firm's excellent products. The officers hired the management consultant firm of Booz, Allen, & Hamilton to make recommendations on how the firm could improve its profitability. As a result of this study and of the conviction of the major stockholders, a number of changes were made in the top management. A person skilled in marketing was brought in and made president of the company. Furthermore, five out of the ten highest paid positions were filled by new personnel. Also, whereas before the changes only one of the board of directors was an outside director, after the changes five members were outside directors. An interesting sidelight is that Endicott Johnson Corporation also hired nearly all the Booz, Allen, & Hamilton staff that made the study. Similar changes in management are commonly made by other firms that are having financial difficulties.

In many cases the transition from old to new officers is accomplished without much unfavorable publicity to the firm. This is especially likely to be true when the president retires or is moved up to chairman of the board of directors. A number of other devices are also used to enable the incumbent officers to make a graceful exit.

REPLACING THE MANAGEMENT

A firm that is unable to reach its goals of profitability and solvency may decide that the best alternative is to combine with another company. Underwood Corporation is an example of a firm that chose this course of action. For many years this company was a leader in the field of manufacturing typewriters and other office equipment. Then, through a combination of circumstances, this enterprise lost its leadership in the industry. The firm had been incurring serious losses, and it was in default on its bank loans. Several factors were probably responsible for the decline of the company from its eminent position. One of the main ones was the fierce competition from IBM. Another factor was management's early policy of paying out about 85 percent of each year's profits as dividends, leaving very little retained earnings for research and development. Yet another was the fact that Underwood missed an excellent opportunity to make an early entry into the electric typewriter field. After being turned down by Underwood, one of the inventors of the electric typewriter licensed his version of the machine to IBM. By the time Underwood did break into the electric typewriter field, IBM had already preempted a large share of the market. Other difficulties also beset Underwood.

USING THE BUSINESS COMBINATION

The faltering company decided to sell out to Olivetti, a large Italian corporation that produced the same general line of machines. As a first step Olivetti acquired a 34 percent interest in Underwood by purchasing 405,000 shares of unissued common stock at a price of $21.50 a share. This transaction gave Underwood sufficient funds to pay its overdue bank loans. Soon after, Olivetti acquired sufficient stock to raise its holdings to the 67 percent level. Underwood still produces adding machines and typewriters, but its main function is distribution of Olivetti products. The stockholders of Underwood were glad to be bailed out of their predicament; Olivetti was satisfied with the arrangement because Underwood's fine technical knowledge, integrity, and distributive power aided Olivetti in tapping the American market. As a result of the combination, Underwood Corporation is once again a leading name in the field of office machines.

REVAMPING THE INFORMATION SYSTEM

Yet another form of remedial action is to revamp the information system on which management bases its major decisions. The system may be too skimpy, too detailed, or not in operation at all. Data systems have been undergoing spectacular changes in recent years, largely because of the introduction of electronic computers:

1. Management is receiving information faster; for example, inventory information can be obtained daily.
2. Information systems are being designed to evaluate persons responsible for certain areas of the firm's operations; for example, a vice president in charge of a division can be evaluated monthly.
3. Information is broader than just accounting data; for example, data on the cost-of-living index can be fed into a computer and the results integrated with the firm's sales forecast.
4. Information previously thought important is now pushed into the background, for example, information which overemphasizes the point that debits equal credits.

The essence of all this is that to keep up with competitors, modern management needs more and more information on which to base decisions.

An example of a firm in which an adequate data system was lacking is the REA Express. According to an article in *Business Week*, this firm had been suffering losses for many years in succession. Its owners, mainly railroads, decided to instigate a comprehensive plan of remedial action. First, a new president was hired and given broad authority to make the changes he thought necessary. "The first thing the company did was to get its own expert railroad cost accountant to find out for the first time what its costs were." A new and complete information system was developed; the firm was able to make changes that contributed to earning profits.

Of parenthetical interest is that rehabilitation plans generally are a combination of different types of remedial actions. In addition to hiring a new president and revamping the information system, REA Express also fired 5,000 employees (312 of whom were supervisory). Many of the supervisory employees "had worked so long under the old ways that they couldn't change with the new discipline." The point is that a package of solutions may be necessary to enable a firm to manage its assets in a profitable manner.

Periodically, management must be evaluated to determine if it is making satisfactory progress toward its goals. In the broad sense, the firm is reaching its goals if it is increasing the financial welfare of its owners and is assuming social responsibility. Of these, probably the most important to the owners is whether their financial welfare is being increased, as reflected by a composite rate of return.

HIGHLIGHTS OF THIS CHAPTER

Evaluation is based on comparisons; the comparison may be with the composite return being earned by owners of similar companies, it may be on the basis of a firm's actual performance with its budgeted goals; it may be on the basis of a firm's actual performance with industry averages; and it may be on the basis of comparing present with past performance.

Several types of remedial action for the solvent firm are these: using package programs to increase sales and lower costs, changing the product mix, changing the method of compensating the officers, replacing the management, using the business combination device, and revamping the information system.

One of the most important ways of avoiding business failure is efficient management. Management must be such that there is constant emphasis on catering to the needs of consumers. Management must be efficient at all levels—at the policy-making level, in production, in sales, in labor relations, and in finance. Furthermore, the efficiency of management is relative, for the most efficient management sets a pace that others must meet in order to survive.

27-1. What is meant by *composite rate of return*?

REVIEW QUESTIONS

27-2. Explain how industry averages and the firm's budget may be used to evaluate management.

27-3. Explain the general types of remedial action that may be taken to make a company more profitable.

27-4. *Business Week* and *Forbes* frequently contain articles on how companies with low profits are making a comeback. Obtain one of these magazines, select such an article, and answer these questions: (a) What caused the difficulties? (b) What forms of remedial action are being taken to improve the firm's profitability?

27-1. Evaluate the performance of the K Company, using its budget as the standard for comparison:

REVIEW PROBLEM

	Budgeted Amounts	Actual Amounts
Sales	$100,000	$120,000
Less expenses and costs:		
Cost of goods sold	40,000	60,000
Rent	2,400	2,400
Heat	1,000	1,500
Light	300	300
Wages	30,000	40,000
Advertising	4,000	3,000
Local taxes	500	800
Insurance	500	300
Total expenses	$78,700	$108,300
Profit	21,300	11,700

CASE ON TAKING REMEDIAL ACTION FOR A FALTERING COMPANY

Quality Company, Inc. manufactured typewriters and other office equipment (mainly manually operated). As can be seen , this firm's profits began to decline in a recent period, despite the fact that sales continued to increase. During the period of financial difficulty, earnings per share and market price of the stock declined (see Table 27-3).

TABLE 27-3 Decline in Profits of Quality Company, Inc.

	One Year Ago	Two Years Ago	Three Years Ago
Sales	$93 million	$90 million	$87 million
Earned per share on common	$0.24 (deficit)	$0.30	$1.51
Dividends per share	none	$0.85	$1.20
Price range of common	18⅞-11½	22¾-12½	23½-15⅜
Current ratio	2.95	4.41	2.63
Percent net income to total assets	none	0.69	3.21
Percent net income to net worth	none	1.46	7.12
Net income per dollar of sales (percent)	0.49 (deficit)	0.61	2.83

One of the difficulties of the firm was its relatively high production costs. A main plant, located in upstate New York, was highly inefficient. Several other plants, however, located in this country and abroad, were quite efficient. The management considered moving the upstate New York operations to another city. But many civic groups in this community urged the management to keep the plant operating, for considerable unemployment would result if these operations were discontinued.

Another difficulty was the lack of a diversified line of products to sell. The management considered establishing a research and development department and devoting 4 percent of annual sales to the activities of the department. This course of action seemed to offer great promise.

Also contributing to the company's plight was inability to compete effectively in the European market.

Required: (a) Suggest a general program of remedial action for Quality Company, Inc. (b) Should the management keep the upstate New York plant operating? Give reasons.

 # Reorganization or Liquidation

When a business fails, the officers and directors of the corporation are unable to manage the fixed and circulating assets in such a manner as to provide cash to pay creditors. In small corporations, trade creditors and bank creditors usually go unpaid. In large corporations, the default may take place on bond interest, bond principal, maturing bank loans, or trade accounts. The inability to pay debts is not usually a state of affairs that strikes a company overnight. Careful analysis will reveal that the shortage of cash has been developing over a period of time. Shortage of cash and inability to borrow it are not in themselves causes of failure. Instead, shortage of cash is a symptom of a more fundamental cause of the corporation's predicament.

In an economy such as ours, business failure is by no means unusual. Fundamentally, this state of affairs arises from the fact that we must have freedom of entry into all fields of activity except the public-service fields. This freedom of entry and the ensuing competition make it almost inevitable that more business units will enter a field than can survive, some of the firms being destined to fail. Although the failure of many firms causes individual hardship and loss, society gains from the competitive process, in that the standard of living of the country is raised because of the emphasis on efficiency under a capitalist economy.

When a business is unable to pay its debts, major changes are made in the composition of the sources of capital and in the contractual terms with these suppliers. The kind of remedial action taken will depend on the seriousness of the problem at hand. In this chapter, we will analyze remedial action by discussing these points:

1. Causes of financial difficulties
2. Remedial action outside the courts
3. Remedial action under court supervision

4. The nature of liquidation
5. Which alternative will creditors select—reorganization or liquidation?

One of the most important ways of avoiding business failure is efficient management, at all levels—in policy-making, production, sales, labor relations, and finance. Furthermore, the efficiency of management is relative, for the most efficient management sets a pace that others must meet in order to survive. Management must be such that there is constant emphasis on catering to the needs of consumers.

Despite efficient management, there are forces beyond its control that may lead to business failure. Four of these are broad economic forces, political forces, physical forces, and luck. Broad economic forces such as depressions may wreck even the best-managed firms. During the early 1970s many companies failed when the demand for their products declined to such an extent that failure was unavoidable. Unexpected political developments may also lead to business failure. Wars lead to shortages of materials, shortages of skilled workers, and even physical destruction of the fixed or circulating assets. Sudden changes in tariffs may lead to loss of markets and eventually business failure. Physical forces may take such forms as floods, storms, and other natural catastrophes. Some of these factors may be insured against, but others may not. Luck always plays an important role in business failure or success. Unexpected good fortune has enabled many a business firm to show huge profits; on the other hand, bad luck has contributed to many business failures.

Table 28-1 shows the results of a study on business failure by Dun & Bradstreet, Inc. Of interest and significance is the role that inadequate management

*CAUSES OF
FINANCIAL
DIFFICULTIES*

TABLE 28-1
Why Businesses Fail
(Percent Figures)

Apparent Causes	Manufacturing	Wholesaling	Retailing	Construction	Commercial Services	Total
Neglect	2.4	4.2	3.1	3.2	3.5	3.1
Fraud	1.0	2.9	1.3	1.4	1.0	1.4
Inexperience, incompetence	93.9	90.4	90.5	89.7	89.4	90.9
Inadequate sales	54.1	47.1	52.6	30.7	47.7	48.2
Heavy operating expenses	10.1	5.2	2.9	21.6	8.1	7.8
Receivables difficulties	13.1	21.8	5.4	17.2	6.1	10.3
Inventory difficulties	4.7	10.9	10.6	1.9	1.7	7.5
Excessive fixed assets	11.0	3.1	6.9	4.2	11.2	7.1
Poor location	0.5	0.6	4.5	0.5	2.6	2.6
Competitive weakness	16.0	18.9	22.0	21.4	21.3	20.6
Other	2.9	3.3	2.3	4.6	2.9	2.9
Disaster	1.1	1.2	1.1	0.3	0.9	1.0
Reason unknown	1.6	1.3	4.0	5.4	5.2	3.6
Total number of failures	2,695	1,703	8,109	2,745	1,424	16,676

plays in the process. Many of these financial disasters could have been averted if the proprietors were better trained in the various phases of management.

A number of symptoms may precede business failure; the most important of these include:

1. Declining current ratio
2. Decline in the amount of cash in relation to total current **assets** and total current liabilities
3. Decrease in the rate of inventory turnover
4. Decrease in the rate of collection of accounts receivable
5. Slowness in paying creditors
6. Resort to unfair trade practices
7. Long-run declines in the market value of the shares and bonds of the corporation

It should be observed that symptoms of failure will vary somewhat from one company to another. Only careful analysis will reveal the importance of these clues in individual cases.

REMEDIAL ACTION OUTSIDE THE COURTS
In a *composition*, creditors voluntarily scale down their claims against the company, part of the debt being forgiven. Thus creditors of Company X might settle for 40 cents on the dollar, the remainder of the debt being forgiven. The 40 percent of the debt that creditors accept may be in cash or in promissory notes.

Another remedy, the *extension*, means that the debtor is given a longer period of time in which to pay the debt, the maturity date being extended beyond the original date. In the extension, the debt is not forgiven; only the payment date is postponed. The extension keeps in business a customer whose future patronage might be very valuable.

A third but seldom used plan is that of the *creditors' committee*. Under this arrangement, the owners voluntarily turn over the management of the defaulting business to a committee consisting of creditors. The creditors' committee will make policy for the business, although operating personnel of the enterprise are usually retained.

The composition, extension, and creditors' committee have two main points in common: these remedies are formulated outside the courts, and they are especially applicable to small business firms.

REMEDIAL ACTION UNDER COURT SUPERVISION
In a *reorganization*, adjustments are made in the affairs of the corporation so that it can continue in business. It is hoped that the reorganized corporation will be able to make the grade as a going concern. The reorganization may take place on a voluntary basis outside the courts or it may be completed under the jurisdiction of a court. Most reorganizations at present are conducted under the supervision of a federal court. The remainder of this section will explain important financial aspects of corporate reorganization.

During a reorganization, one or more of the following changes may take place. In many cases, the amount of ownership claims and creditors' claims is scaled down (that is, some of the claims against the corporation become worthless); the interest charges of the corporation are often decreased considerably; in many cases the maturity date of part of the debt is extended; the corporation is customarily permitted to raise additional cash so that a fresh start may be made with adequate working capital; certain economies may be initiated, such as the introduction of cost-saving machines; and the competence of the management is scrutinized. The changes listed above are the most important features of a reorganization. These financial objectives are common to all types of reorganization, although some of the changes are given more emphasis than others in particular instances.

As part of the reorganization process, there is often a scaling down of the claims against the corporation. The word *claims* is used in a broad sense here and includes bonds, short-term credit, and even stock. Assume that the reorganized value of the corporation (based on capitalized earnings) is $2,000,000 and that the corporation has current liabilities, bonds, and stocks—all of which add up to $3,700,000. Under new reorganization procedures, the claims and securities must be scaled down so that their combined total does not exceed $2,000,000. Altogether, the suppliers of capital will lose $1,700,000. It can be seen that this is a drastic process, for it nearly always results in suppliers taking losses. It should be noted that the value assigned to the reorganized corporation is highly important, as this is one of the factors that determines the amount of scaling down that will take place. Modern procedure stresses capitalizing the income as the most logical method of determining the value of a business.

Scaling Down of Outstanding Claims Against the Corporation

Not all reorganizations stress a reduction in the combined amount of debt and stock. In some reorganizations the combined amount of debt and stock actually increases after the consummation of the plan. In the Waltham Watch Company reorganization the emphasis was on converting (funding) current liabilities into longer-term obligations. This is an objective quite often sought in the reorganization of industrials. The situation described in Table 28-2 existed in the Waltham Watch Company before and after the first reorganization.

A rule known as the *absolute priority rule* is used by the courts in determining the general principles of how losses shall be borne in a reorganization. The gist of the absolute priority rule is that senior security holders take precedence over junior security holders. The rule may be stated as a threefold proposition:

1. Creditors must receive full compensation, either in cash or in securities, for the value of their claims before stockholders can receive any securities in the reorganized company (except that old stockholders may be permitted to buy stock in the reorganized corporation).
2. Certain creditors have priority over other creditors; creditors of secured loans have priority over creditors of unsecured loans to the extent of the value of the property pledged as collateral for the secured loan.

TABLE 28-2
Waltham Watch
Company

Liabilities and Capital Before Reorganization

Current liabilities:

Secured bank loans	$4,310,000.00	
Accounts payable	286,911.66	
Accrued liabilities	425,048.98	
Accumulated debenture interest	226,482.61	
Total current liabilities		$5,248,443.25
Convertible debentures		3,881,040.00
Deficit after applying deficit to net worth		(944,087.19)
Total		$8,185,396.06

Liabilities and Capital After Reorganization

Current liabilities	$ 442,702.97
Funded debt	4,000,000.00
Capital stock and surplus	4,579,138.36
Total	$9,021,841.33

3. Generally, preferred stockholders must receive full compensation for the value of their claims before the common stockholders can receive any securities in the reorganized corporation.

Reduction in Interest Charges An important aspect of many reorganizations is a decrease in the interest charges that the corporation will have to pay after it has been reorganized. Perhaps there will also be a reduction in other fixed charges, such as rentals. When railroads are being reorganized, the matter of a reduction in interest charges is especially important. Likewise, when public utilities are being reorganized, the reduction in interest charges will be emphasized. However, for industrials the reduction of interest charges is not always an important matter, there is more emphasis on funding current debt.

Extending the Maturity Date of Some of the Debt In many corporate reorganizations, the maturity date of some of the debt is extended. Thus, a first mortgage bond issue maturing in 1976 might be extended until 1995. Delaying the maturity date takes pressure off the corporation's cash account during the period of rehabilitation. The debt is not canceled; the maturity date is merely postponed. Eventually the corporation will have to satisfy the holders of these bonds. It will be recalled that a bond issue whose maturity date has been postponed is known as an *extended bond*.

Initiating Internal Economies In many reorganizations there is a genuine attempt to improve the efficiency of the plant. Time-and-motion studies may be made; more efficient methods may be installed; and the plant arrangement may be adapted so as to be more efficient.

The announcement that a corporation is about to be reorganized generally drives down market values even farther than they have already fallen. In most cases, the market has discounted the failure of the business, so that when failure is officially announced, the securities have already drastically declined in value. At this stage, some investors will sell their securities, but others will hold them, hoping that some of the lost values will be retrieved.

The severity of the loss to security holders depends on a number of factors, the main one being the severity of the corporation's financial plight. If the plight appears to be temporary, the losses to investors will be small. But if the corporation has suffered a permanent decline in earning power, the losses suffered by security holders will be drastic. Some investors will come out of the reorganization with little or no losses, but others may be wiped out completely. Between these two extremes are those who suffer drastic but not total losses.

Holders of first mortgage bonds usually come through a reorganization with a minimum of loss. If the interest has been earned on these bonds prior to reorganization, and if the bonds are secured by valuable real estate, the bondholders may not suffer any loss in the reorganization. However, in many cases the interest is only partially earned on the first mortgage bonds and the worth of the pledged property is not equal to the face value of the bonds. Under these conditions, holders of first mortgage bonds will suffer losses. Ordinarily, they will be called on to exchange their securities for new securities of the reorganized corporation. For example, the holder of a $1,000 first mortgage bond might have to accept the following: $500 in new first mortgage bonds carrying a lower rate of interest than was carried by the bond originally held, $400 in income bonds, and $100 in preferred stock. These figures merely suggest what a bondholder may expect in a reorganization.

Holders of second mortgage bonds generally receive drastic treatment in a reorganization. Their claim on income and assets is secondary to that of the holders of first mortgage bonds. In a drastic reorganization the former may be given preferred stock in satisfaction of their claims. Thus the holder of a $1,000 second mortgage bond might receive 10 shares of $100 par-value preferred stock. Even though the holders of second mortgage bonds usually receive such severe treatment, they are still better off than either the preferred stockholders or the common stockholders.

Holders of debenture bonds and other general creditors of unsecured loans are also likely to receive drastic treatment in a reorganization. The corporation has not pledged any property for holders of debenture bonds or other unsecured creditors. In most reorganizations, all creditors of unsecured loans will have their claims reduced. In some reorganizations, they must accept stock in lieu of their claims.

In a large number of reorganizations, the preferred stockholders and the common stockholders suffer severe losses. Often these stockholders come out of a reorganization with considerably fewer shares. Although every effort is made to permit the stockholders to maintain some equity in the reorganized corporation, this may not be possible under the absolute priority rule. In some cases the preferred stockholders and the common stockholders are wiped out completely; that is, their stock certificates become worthless.

The plight of the stockholders is slightly less severe when they are permitted to participate in a reorganized company through the payment of an assessment, or permitted to participate in the reorganized corporation through the receipt of stock purchase warrants. Actually, the stockholders are purchasing an interest in the reorganized corporation when they take advantage of either of these two offers. Both plans give stockholders an opportunity to recapture lost values in the event that the corporation becomes profitable in the future.

Security holders will argue for the issuance of bonds by the reorganized corporation for two reasons: the interest on bonds is a deductible expense to the corporation, and the use of bonds maximizes the amount of securities that can be issued by a reorganized corporation. When bonds and stocks are issued, different segments of the income stream are capitalized at different rates.

The Importance of Future Earning Power

The core of the problem of corporate reorganization is estimating future earnings. This perplexing problem cannot be solved in any exact manner, for certain assumptions must be made as to the future. Some of the unknowns are these: Will there be war or peace? Will there be severe or moderate inflation? What will competition be in the future? Will the labor supply be adequate? Fortunately, the past provides some guidance on these matters. In estimating future earnings, it is necessary to take recent earnings and then make adjustments for expected future developments. Holders of junior securities will argue for a high estimate of future earnings, because under this assumption some of them will suffer less severe losses. The courts, on the other hand, urge conservatism in estimating future annual income.

A low estimate of future annual income will result in assigning a low value to the business, and a high estimate will result in assigning a high valuation to the business. These comments may be illustrated by observing the outcome of two hypothetical cases:

Case 1   *Facts:* A corporation is expected to have $100,000 per year available for security holders. The company will issue only common stock. The capitalization rate to be used is 10 percent.
Required: Find the value of the business.
Conclusion: The value of the business will be $1 million on the basis of capitalized earnings ($100,000 ÷ 0.10).

Case 2   *Facts:* A group of experts estimates that this same company can earn $200,000 per year. The company will issue only common stock. The capitalization rate to be used is 10 percent.

Required: Find the value of the business.
Conclusion: The value of the business will be $2 million on the basis of capitalized earnings ($200,000 ÷ 0.10).

In Case 1 a group of experts estimated the future annual income to be $100,000. This resulted in a value of $1 million based on capitalized earnings. In Case 2 a different group of experts estimated the future annual income of this company to be $200,000. This higher estimate of future annual income raised the value of the business to $2 million.

Comments

In the rehabilitation process, the courts, the SEC, and the Interstate Commerce Commission all stress the importance of the reorganization plan being *fair* and *feasible.* The Tenth Annual Report of the SEC makes the following comments on these two terms.

The Goals of Fairness and Feasibility

> **Fairness** In appraising the fairness of reorganization plans, the Commission has at all times taken the position that full recognition must be accorded claims in order of their legal and contractual priority, either in cash or new securities or both, and that junior claimants may participate only to the extent that the debtor's properties have value after the satisfaction of prior claims or to the extent that they make a fresh contribution necessary to the reorganization of the debtor. Hence, a valuation of the debtor is necessary to provide the basis for judging the fairness as well as the feasibility of proposed plans of reorganization. In its advisory reports, in hearings before the courts, and in conferences with parties to proceedings, the Commission has consistently stated that the proper method of valuation for reorganization purposes is primarily an appropriate capitalization of reasonably prospective earnings.

> **Feasibility** Although the representatives of security holders frequently regard the fairness of the plan as their principal concern, the provisions of the statute and the protection of investors' interests require also that the plan be feasible. To be feasible, a reorganization must be economically sound and workable. It must not hamper future operations or lead to another reorganization. . . . In this connection, the Commission is particularly concerned with the adequacy of working capital, the relationship of funded debt and capital structure to property values, the adequacy of corporate earning power in relation to interest and dividend requirements, and the effect of the new capitalization upon the company's prospective credit.

Industrials, public utilities, and small railroads are now reorganized under Chapter X of the National Bankruptcy Act. Chapter XI of the act provides a procedure for the reorganization of corporations with unsecured debt. This section of the law is intended to permit reorganization without the time-consuming procedure under Chapter X. The debtor takes the initiative and proposes the

Laws under Which Reorganization Takes Place

reorganization plan. The use of Chapter XI is generally limited to smaller corporations, which are most likely to have unsecured loans.

Large railroads are reorganized under Section 77 of the National Bankruptcy Act. However, if the railroad does not need a complete financial overhauling, it may be reorganized under the more simple Mahaffie Act.

THE NATURE OF LIQUIDATION

In *liquidation* the assets of the business are sold for cash, which is distributed among the claimants according to the strength of their claims against the debtor corporation. The land, buildings, fixtures, and other noncash assets are sold at auction for the best price obtainable. Creditors are paid first, and if any cash remains, it is distributed to preferred stockholders up to the liquidating value per share. Any balance remaining after the payment of creditors and preferred stockholders goes to the common stockholders. In a liquidation caused by failure, there is rarely enough cash to pay the creditors; therefore, the preferred stockholders and the common stockholders seldom receive a return after a forced liquidation has been completed. Liquidation is a harsh process. It is resorted to only if the debtor has no chance of earning profits in the future.

Bankruptcy in the Sense of Liquidation

The purpose of bankruptcy is to discharge the debtor from debts (except for a few items stated in the law) and to provide an orderly procedure for liquidation, thus protecting creditors.

The court may appoint a *receiver* to conserve the estate until a trustee is elected by the creditors. The *trustee* takes title to all the assets of the debtor and proceeds to convert them into cash. In addition to the trustee, there is another important party to bankruptcy proceedings—the *referee*. He is the representative of the court, and his duties are stated in the law. His main duty is to declare liquidating dividends.

In general, the proceeds are distributed as follows: (1) costs of carrying out the liquidation, (2) wages of workers earned three months prior to the bankruptcy, but not exceeding $600 per person, (3) certain expenses of creditors in opposing the discharge plan, (4) certain taxes, (5) a few other types of preferred creditors, (6) creditors of secured loans, to the extent of the value of the pledged collateral, (7) creditors of unsecured loans, and (8) stockholders.

Assignments

Debtors who cannot meet their obligations may assign their assets to a trustee, who will liquidate the assets in an orderly manner for the benefit of the creditors. An assignment does not lead to forgiveness of the unpaid debts unless there is a special agreement to this effect. In most cases, the trustee is appointed by the debtor, although the party appointed is usually a creditor. From the creditors' viewpoint, the assignment has two main advantages: the assets are liquidated in an orderly manner, thus bringing in the maximum amount of cash; and the administrative costs of liquidating the assets are relatively low. Assignments are more often used by small business firms than by large corporations.

In most instances, when large corporations default on their debts, creditors select reorganization in preference to liquidation. Why do they select this method of solving their problem? The answer is that creditors may minimize their losses by selecting reorganization, and courts usually will not permit railroads and public utilities to liquidate because of the hardship that would be imposed on the customers of these public-service corporations.

The valuation of the corporation as a going concern is often higher than the liquidation value of the company. In other words, the cash obtained from the sale of the assets is often less than the value of the business in operation. Thus a corporation might have a going concern value of $2,000,000 but a liquidation value of only $500,000. It is, then, to the advantage of the creditors to reorganize the corporation rather than liquidate it. Assume that a corporation in default has estimated earnings of $200,000 per year after the reorganization. Also assume that the assets are carried on the books at $3,700,000. In addition, assume that companies in a similar economic position are earning 10 percent on their common stock. Finally, assume that the assets, if liquidated, could be sold for $500,000. Under these assumptions, the corporation, if reorganized, would have a value of $2,000,000 based on earning power, the estimated income of $200,000 being capitalized at 10 percent. This value is based on the assumption that the corporation will have a capital structure of common stock only. If bonds were issued in addition to common stock, the value of the business would be even greater because part of the income would be capitalized at a lower rate.

Upon comparison, it can be seen that in this instance the reorganization value is greater than the liquidation value, and therefore the better alternative is to reorganize the corporation rather than liquidate it. Under either reorganization or liquidation, the creditors will suffer losses, but the losses will often be greater if the company is liquidated. Creditors will select the more desirable of the two undesirable alternatives.

Although the large corporations are usually reorganized instead of liquidated, this is not always true. It may be that the creditors will have no alternative but to liquidate the corporation.

If the corporation's inability to pay its debts appears to be temporary, creditors will apply mild remedies to protect their interests. The three main remedies that may be used are the composition, extension, and, at times, creditors' committee.

If the corporation is liquidated, the assets are seized and sold at public auction. The cash is divided among the claimants according to their legal priorities. The National Bankruptcy Act provides a systematic method of liquidating corporations that have failed and cannot be feasibly reorganized.

Modern reorganization stresses the importance of placing a value on the business to be reorganized. The valuation is important because it determines how much scaling down is necessary. The valuation of a reorganized corporation is subject to widespread and justified criticism.

When a firm is being rehabilitated, these goals are often sought: decrease in debt, lowering of interest charges, additional cash, internal economies, change in

WHICH ALTERNATIVE WILL CREDITORS SELECT–REORGANIZATION OR LIQUIDATION?

HIGHLIGHTS OF THIS CHAPTER

management, and extension of maturity dates. In this process of rehabilitation, creditors suffer fewer losses than do stockholders. This is in accordance with the absolute priority rule, which states that creditors must be compensated before stockholders.

REVIEW QUESTIONS
28-1. What are several causes of business failure?

28-2. What financial changes may take place when a firm is reorganized?

28-3. Explain why creditors may elect to reorganize a firm rather than liquidate it.

28-4. Explain the meaning of the following terms:
business failure
composition
extension
capitalization of income

REVIEW PROBLEM
28-1. The Paterson Company is in the following condition just prior to re-organization:

Current assets	$100,000
Fixed assets	600,000
Total	$700,000
Current liabilities	$250,000
4 percent first mortgage bonds	100,000
5 percent preferred stock	100,000
Common stock	250,000
Total	$700,000

The courts hold the business to be worth $350,000; this value is based on a combination of stocks and bonds to be issued. (a) What groups of security holders will be allowed to participate in the reorganized company? (b) What groups will be wiped out completely?

Glossary

Accelerated depreciation Depreciation method that writes off the cost of an asset at a faster rate than the write-off under the straight-line method.

Acceleration clause A clause in the indenture whereby all the remaining debt becomes immediately due if the borrower defaults on any of the payments.

Acid-test ratio Current assets minus inventory, divided by current liabilities.

Add on clause An oppressive clause found in consumer credit whereby the creditor may repossess items already purchased from him and paid for, if the borrower defaults on payments for additional items.

Aging schedule A report showing how long accounts receivable have been outstanding.

Amortize To pay off a debt, usually through a periodic payments of equal amounts. Each payment consists of some principal and some interest.

Annuity A series of equal payments to be received periodically for a specified number of periods.

Appraiser An expert in establishing current market value for property (such as a house), jewelry, or antiques—depending on his specialty.

Appreciation Increase in the dollar value of an asset over time.

Arbitrage Simultaneously buying and selling the same or equivalent securities in different markets to profit from a divergence in their prices.

Assignment   A relatively inexpensive way of liquidating a failing firm that does not involve going through the courts.

Authorized stock   The total number of shares of stock that a company's charter allows it to issue; any additional authorization requires approval of stockholders representing a majority of the shares outstanding.

Average collection period   Accounts receivable divided by sales per day.

Balance Sheet   A condensed statement showing the nature and amount of a company's assets, liabilities, and net worth on a given date.

Balloon payment   A loan in which the final payment is substantially larger than any previous payments.

Banker's Acceptance   A businessman's short-term promise to pay which has been guaranteed for payment (accepted) by his bank. Used largely in foreign trade to substitute a bank's known credit for the unknown credit of an individual firm.

Bankruptcy   A legal procedure for the formal liquidation or reorganization of a firm that is unable to pay its debts.

Bear   Someone who believes the market will decline.

Bearer bond   A bond which does not have the owner's name registered on the books of the issuing company.

Bear market   A securities market characterized by generally declining prices over a period of several months.

Blue chip   Common stock in a company known nationally for the quality and wide acceptance of its products or services and for its ability to make money and pay dividends.

Blue sky laws   A popular name for laws various states have enacted to protect the public against securities frauds.

Bond   A long-term debt instrument.

Book value   Value of a share of common stock as determined by the company's accounting records.

Broker   An agent, often a member of a stock exchange firm, who handles the public's orders to buy and sell securities and commodities. For this service, a commission is charged.

Bull   One who believes the market will rise.

Bull market   A securities market characterized by generally rising prices over a period of several months.

Buy on margin   To buy securities with a partial payment and borrow the rest of the required cash from one's brokerage house.

Call   (1) An option to buy from the seller a certain numer of shares of a stock at a certain price and within a certain period of time. (2) The process of redeeming a bond or a preferred stock before its normal maturity.

Callable   A bond issue, all or part of which may be redeemed by the issuing corporation under definite conditions before maturity. The term also applies to preferred shares which may be redeemed by the issuing corporation.

Call premium   The amount in excess of par which a corporation must pay to exercise the privilege of redeeming its outstanding debt or preferred stock.

Capital budgeting   The process of planning expenditures on assets whose returns are expected to continue beyond one year.

Capital gain or capital loss   A profit or loss on the sale of a capital asset. A capital gain, under current federal income tax laws, may be either short-term (six months or less) or long-term (more than six months).

Capitalization rate   A discount rate used to find the present value of a series of future cash receipts. Also known as the discount rate.

Capital rationing   A situation where a constraint is placed on the total size of the capital investment during a particular period.

Cash flow   Earnings after taxes plus noncash expenses.

Central market   An ideal that will be accomplished when there exists a central reporting system that will give instant information on the market prices of all the securities traded on all the stock exchanges and information on the market price of a very large number of securities traded in the over-the-counter market.

Certificate of deposit   In normal usage, a time deposit requiring a larger investment and yielding a higher return than a normal savings account.

Chattel mortgage   A mortgage on personal property.

Class A stock   Common stock with income rights but not voting rights.

Closed-end fund   An investment company with a fixed number of shares to be bought and sold, like common stocks, over-the-counter or through the stock exchanges.

Commercial finance company   A nonbank lender to business firms, which chiefly makes short-term loans secured by inventory or receivables.

Commercial paper   Unsecured promissory notes, usually maturing within 270 days, used by major corporations to raise short-term funds.

Commitment fee   The fee paid to a lender for a formal line of credit.

Compensating balance   A required minimum checking account balance that a firm must maintain with a commercial bank. The required balance is generally equal to 15 to 20 percent of the amount of loans outstanding.

Composition   An informal method of reorganization that voluntarily reduces creditors' claims on the debtor firm.

Conglomerate   A corporation seeking to diversify its operations by acquiring enterprises in widely varied industries.

Conversion price   The effective price paid for common stock when the stock is obtained by converting either convertible preferred stocks or convertible bonds.

Conversion ratio   The number of shares of common stock that may be obtained by converting a convertible bond or share of convertible preferred stock. Also known as the conversion rate.

Coupon bond   Bond with interest coupons attached. The coupons are clipped as they come due and are presented by the holder for payment of interest.

Covenant   Detailed promises contained in the indenture.

Credit report   A report on the credit worthiness of a present or potential customer.

Current assets   Those assets of a company which are reasonably expected to be realized in cash within a one-year period.

Current liability   An obligation due within a year.

Current ratio   Current assets divided by current liabilities.

Debenture   An unsecured bond.

Derivative suit   In corporation law, a suit by a stockholder on behalf of the corporation. The stockholder alleges that the officers of the corporation have failed to act to protect the interests of the corporation and that therefore he is suing on behalf of the corporation.

Dividend yield   The ratio of a stock's current annual dividend to its current market price.

Dollar averaging   The investment of fixed sums of money at regular intervals. Also known as dollar cost averaging.

EBIT   An abbreviation for "earnings before interest and taxes."

EPS   An abbreviation for "earnings per share."

Equity   Ownership interest in a corporation, consisting of the sum of all stock-holders' claims.

Eurodollars   Dollars deposited in a bank abroad.

Ex-dividend   A synonym for "without dividend." The buyer of a stock selling ex-dividend does not receive the recently declared dividend.

Factors   Financial concerns that supply funds by purchasing accounts receivable and in other ways.

Field warehousing   A method of financing inventories in which a "warehouse" is established at the place of business of the borrowing firm.

Funded debt   Long-term debt.

Funding   Converting short-term debt to long-term debt, usually by selling new long-term securities to replace the maturing short-term ones.

Growth stock   Common stock of a company whose future earnings are expected to increase at a relatively rapid rate.

Hypothecation   The pledging of securities as collateral for a loan.

Income bond   A bond that pays interest only if the current interest is earned.

Indenture   The contractual agreement between the corporation, the trustee, and the bondholders.

Insolvent   The inability to meet maturing debt obligations.

Internal rate of return The expected rate of return on an asset that is under consideration for purchase, it is calculated by finding the discount rate that equates the present value of future cash flows to the cost of the asset. Also known as yield.

Investment bank A financial institution that helps corporations sell new securities.

Investment company A company which uses its money solely to invest in other companies, consisting of two principal types—the closed-end and the open-end (mutual fund).

Legal list A list of investments selected by various states in which certain institutions and fiduciaries, such as insurance companies and banks, may invest. Legal lists are often restricted to high quality securities meeting certain specifications.

Lessee The user of the property, he pays rent to the owner.

Lessor The owner of the property, he receives the rent.

Leverage A percentage change in one variable which causes a greater percentage change in another variable.

Limit order An order to buy or sell a security at a specified price or at a better price.

Line of credit An arrangement whereby a financial institution (bank or insurance company) commits itself to lend up to a specified maximum amount of funds during a specified period.

Lockbox plan A procedure used to speed up collections of accounts receivable.

Margin The amount paid by the customer when he uses his broker's credit to buy a security.

Market order An order to buy or sell a security at the most advantageous price obtainable after an order is presented to the broker or dealer.

Money market Financial markets in which funds are borrowed or loaned for short periods.

Mortgage bond A bond secured by the pledge of real estate.

Multinational corporation   A corporation characterized by a global strategy of investment, production, and distribution.

Net change   The change in the price of a security from the closing price one day to the closing price on the following day (on which the stock is traded).

Net present value   The present value of the cash benefits minus the present value of the cost of the asset.

Net working capital   Total current assets minus total current liabilities.

Net worth   The sum of common stock, preferred stock, retained earnings, and all net worth reserves.

Open-end fund   An investment company that continually sells and redeems its shares according to investor demand and has no limits on the total number of shares bought or sold. Also known as a mutual fund.

Par   In the case of a common share, a dollar amount assigned to the share by the company's charter.

Pay-back period   The period of time, measured in years, an investment will take to return its cost.

Payout ratio   The percentage of earnings paid out in dividends.

Point   In the case of shares of stock, a point is $1. In the case of bonds, a point is $10.

Preemptive right   A provision in the charter that gives holders of common stock the right to purchase on a pro rata basis new issues of common stock and securities convertible into common stock.

Price-earnings ratio   The current price of a share of stock divided either by current earnings per share or by expected earnings per share.

Prime rate   The rate of interest which large commercial banks charge their strongest customers for loans.

Private placement   Selling new securities to a few large buyers rather than to the general public. Also known as direct placement.

Profitability index   The present value of future returns divided by the present value of the investment outlay.

Pro forma statement   A projected statement—usually a projected balance sheet or a projected income statement.

Prospectus   A publication issued by a company to describe the securities to be offered for public sale and under what conditions they will be offered, as well as a general description of the firm's recent operations.

Proxy   A written authorization given by a shareholder to someone else to represent him and vote his shares at a shareholders' meeting.

Put   An option to sell to a designated party a certain number of shares of stock at a certain price and within a specified period of time.

Refunding   Redeeming one bond issue with the proceeds of another.

Registered bond   A bond registered in the name of the owner on the books of the corporation or the trustee.

Registrar   Usually a trust company or bank charged with the responsibility of preventing the issuance of more stock than authorized by a company.

Registration statement   The information filed with a state or federal government agency before the securities can be publicly offered.

REIT   Real estate investment trust. A form of business trust used in real estate finance.

Return on net worth   Earnings after taxes divided by net worth.

Round lot   A unit of trading. On the New York Stock Exchange the unit of trading is generally 100 shares in stocks and $1,000 par value in bonds. For some inactive stocks, the unit of trading is 10 shares.

Sales finance company   A company whose principal business is purchasing the notes receivable of other businesses at a discount.

SEC   The Securities and Exchange Commission, established by Congress to help protect investors.

Serial bond   A serial bond issue consists of a number of bonds issued at the same time but with different maturity dates (serially due), usually with interest rates varying for the different maturity dates. Not the same as series bonds.

Series bonds   Groups of bonds usually issued at different times and with different maturities and interest rates but all issued under the authority of the same indenture.

Standby underwriting The purchase, pursuant to agreement by investment banking firms, of the unsold portion of an issue offered by the issuing company directly to its own security holders.

Street name Securities held in the name of a broker instead of his customer's name are said to be carried in a "street name."

Stock dividend A dividend paid in stock instead of cash.

Stockholder of record A stockholder whose name is registered on the books of the issuing corporation or the transfer agent of the corporation.

Stock split Issuance of new shares for each share outstanding. Par or stated value of original shares is decreased.

Subordinated debt Debt of lower rank in liquidation than senior debt.

Tender offer A proposal made directly by one firm to the stockholders of another firm to buy their stock at a specified price.

Term loan Loan made by banks and insurance companies for intermediate terms, usually from three to five years.

Trade credit Short-term credit extended by a supplier to a business customer in conjunction with the purchase of goods for ultimate resale.

Trading on the equity Raising funds from sources on which a limited return is paid (usually bonds or preferred stock).

Transfer agent Person who keeps a record of the name of each registered shareholder, his or her address, and the number of shares owned; he also sees that the certificates presented to his office for transfer are properly cancelled and new certificates issued in the name of the new transferee.

Treasury bill A short-term, noninterest-bearing promissory note sold to investors at a discount by the U.S. government.

Treasury stock Stock issued by a company but later reacquired. It may be held in the company's treasury indefinitely, reissued to the public, or retired.

Ultra vires An act by a corporation beyond its powers as stated or implied in the charter.

Underwriting Purchase of an entire issue of new securities by investment bankers for reoffer to investors at a markup in price.

Underwriting syndicate   A group of investment banking firms formed to spread the risk associated with the purchase and distribution of a new issue of securities.

Warrant   An option, often good for five to ten years, that gives its holder the right to buy a specified number of shares of common stock in a particular company at a specified price.

Weighted average cost of capital   A percentage that represents the average cost of raising funds from common stockholders, preferred stockholders, bondholders, and other long-term sources.

References

Ainsworth, Kenneth G., "Federal Grants-in-Aid and State Taxes: A Study of Their Impact upon Maine Industry." *Journal of Finance*, March 1959, pp. 78-80.

Anderson, Theodore A., "Trends in Profit Sensitivity." *Journal of Finance*, December 1963, pp. 637-646.

Ang, Henry S. "A Study of Financial Expansion in the Basic Chemical Industry." *Journal of Finance* March 1962, pp. 135-136.

Arellano, Richard. "The Edge Act Corporations: A Study of Their Equity Investment Activities." *Appalachian Financial Review*, Spring 1969, pp. 270-271.

Atamian, Elliott L. "Using Investment Bankers in Negotiating Private Placements." *Business Topics*, Spring 1966, pp. 67-79.

Austin, Ellis T. *Consideration of the Treatment of the Government in National Income Accounts*. Thesis, Michigan State University, 1955.

Bacon, Peter W. "The Subscription Price in Rights Offerings." *Financial Management*, Summer 1972, pp. 59-64.

Bailey, E. Norman. "Real Estate Investment Trusts: An Appraisal." *Financial Analysts Journal*, May-June 1966, pp. 107-114.

Ball, Richard E., and Melnyk, Z. Lew. *Theory of Managerial Finance: Selected Readings*. Boston: Allyn and Bacon, Inc., 1967.

Bartels, Robert. *Credit Management*. New York: The Ronald Press Company, 1967.

Bauman, W. Scott. "Investment Experience with Less Popular Common Stock." *Journal of Finance*, September 1962, pp. 520-521.

Bay, John. "Time Lapse and Cyclical Changes in Commercial Bank Investment Portfolios." *Journal of Finance*, March 1967, pp. 93-94.

Beidleman, Carl R. "Limitations of Price-Earnings Ratios." *Financial Analysts Journal*, September-October 1971, pp. 76-91.

Bennett, Robert L. "Financial Innovation and Structural Changes in the Early

Stages of Industrialization in Mexico, 1945-1959." *Journal of Finance*, December 1963, pp. 666-683.

Beranek, William. *Analysis for Financial Decisions.* Homewood, Ill.: Richard D. Irwin, 1962.

Bernhardt, Raymond S. "A Critical Evaluation of Stock Repurchase Programs of Unlisted Industrial Corporations." *Appalchian Financial Review*, Spring 1970, pp. 367-368.

Bicksler, James L. "The State of the Finance Field: A Further Comment." *Journal of Finance*, September 1972, p. 917.

Blank, Seymour. "Small Business and Tight Money." *Journal of Finance*, March 1961, pp. 73-79.

Block, Stanley B. "The Effect of Mergers and Acquisitions on the Market Value of Common Stock." *Journal of Finance*, December 1968, pp. 889-890.

Blum, James D. "An Analysis of the Price Behavior of Initial Common Stock Offerings." *Journal of Finance*, March 1973, p. 215.

Bolster, Richard L. "The Relationship of Monetary Policy to the Stock Market: The Experience with Margin Requirements." *Journal of Finance*, September 1967, pp. 477-478.

Bonner, Gordon R. "Some Notes on the Rehabilitation of Preferred Stock." *Appalachian Financial Review*, Spring 1966, pp. 32-37.

Bornhofen, John O. "Business Risk and the Corporate Demand for Liquid Assets." *Journal of Finance*, September 1970, pp. 934-935.

Bowlin, Oswald D. "The Refunding Decision: Another Special Case in Capital Budgeting." *Journal of Finance*, March 1966, pp. 55-68.

Bowyer, John W. *Investment Analysis and Management.* 4th ed. Homewood, Ill.: Richard D. Irwin, 1972.

Boyer, Patricia A. "Cost of Equity Capital to the Small Business: An Empirical Study of Behavorial Aspects." Paper delivered at Financial Management Association, October, 1972.

Bradley, Joseph F. "Voting Rights of Preferred Stockholders in Industrials." *Journal of Finance*, October 1948, pp. 78-88.

Broman, Keith L. *Some Effects of Noncontributory Pension Plans on Corporate Financial Policy.* Thesis, University of Nebraska, 1955.

Calkins, Francis J. *Role of the S.E.C. in Corporate Reorganizations under Chapter X.* Thesis, Northwestern University, 1947.

Campanella, Frank B. "The Measurement and Use of Portfolio Systematic Risk." *Appalachian Financial Review*, Spring 1971, pp. 67-68.

Carey, Kenneth J. *A Mathematical Model for Short-term Price Movements of Common Stocks.* Thesis, University of Kansas, 1972.

Cheney, Harlan L. "How Good Are Subscription Investment Advisory Services?" *Financial Executive*, November 1969, pp. 31-35.

Corrigan, Francis J., and Ward, Howard A. *Business Financial Management.* Boston: Houghton Mifflin Company, 1963.

Cossaboom, Roger A. "Let's Reassess the Profitability-Liquidity Tradeoff." *Financial Executive*, May 1971, pp. 46-51.

Cox, Edwin B. "Trends in the Distribution of Stock Ownership." *Journal of Finance*, December 1960, pp. 557-558.

Crum, Lawrence L. "Federal Regulation of Bank Holding Companies." *Journal of Finance*, September 1962, pp. 527-528.

Curley, Anthony J. "A Stochastic Simulation of the Personal Investment Decision." *Journal of Finance*, September 1969, pp. 723-724.

Dellenbarger, Lynn E. *A Study of Relative Common Equity Values in Fifty Mergers of Listed Industrial Corporations, 1950-1957*. Thesis, University of Florida, 1960.

Dier, Raymond J. *The Sale of Securities through Privileged Subscriptions.* Thesis, New York University, 1954.

Dilbeck, Harold. "A Proposal for Precise Definitions of Trading on the Equity and Leverage." *Journal of Finance*, March 1962, pp. 127-130.

Doenges, R. Conrad. "The Reinvestment Problem in a Practical Perspective." *Financial Management*, Spring 1972, pp. 85-91.

Dran, John J., Jr. "A Cost Study of Ohio Credit Unions." *Journal of Finance*, March 1971, pp. 178-179.

Drzycimski, Eugene F. "The Stock Repurchase Decision." *Marquette Business Review*, Winter 1969, pp. 159-167.

Ellis, Charles D., and Young, Allen E. *The Repurchase of Common Stock.* New York: The Ronald Press Company, 1971.

Ellis, Herman A. *Financial Management of Southeastern Greyhound Lines* Thesis, Indiana University, 1954.

Eubank, Arthur A., Jr. *A Model of Interdependent Capital Budgeting and Financing Decisions under Uncertainty*. Thesis, Pennsylvania State University, 1972.

Ewert, David C. "Trade-Credit Management: Selection of Accounts Receivable Using a Statistical Model." *Journal of Finance*, December 1968, pp. 891-892.

Ezzell, John R. *The Effect of Dividend Instability on the Market Price of Common Stock*. Thesis, Pennsylvania State University, 1970.

Facer, Elden J. *Trends in Financial Soundness of Utah Banks, 1929-1947.* Thesis, Stanford University, 1949.

Faerber, LeRoy G. "The Cost of External Common Stock Equity Capital for Small Business: An Empirical Study of New Common Stock Offerings." *Journal of Finance*, December 1964, pp. 691-692.

Fenlon, Paul E. *Cases in Financial Management*. Columbus, Ohio: Grid, Inc., 1974.

Fenstermaker, J. Van, and Roberts, Lloyd E. "An Analysis of Factors Influencing Student Performance in Business Finance." *Collegiate News and Views*, Winter 1972-1973, pp. 20-23.

Ferreira, Charles G. "Quantification and Measurement of Risk: An Empirical Study of Selected Common Stocks." *Journal of Finance*, September 1967, pp. 482-483.

Fichthorn, William H. *Management Problems of Bank Charge Account Plans.* Thesis, Harvard University, 1955.

Fischer, Donald E. and Wilt, Glenn A., Jr. "Non-Convertible Preferred Stock as a Financing Instrument, 1950-1965." *Journal of Finance*, September 1968, pp. 611-624.

Fisher, Horace H. "Would You Believe Fifteen Percent?" *Business Inquiry of San Diego State College*, 1967, No. 2, pp. 5-12.

Fogler, H. Russell. "Overkill in Capital Budgeting Technique?" *Financial Management*, Spring 1972, pp. 92-96.

Foster, Earl M. "Analysis of Common Stock Prices." *Journal of Finance*, September 1970, pp. 940-941.

Franklin, Charles B., Jr. "The Treatment of Security Holders under the Absolute Priority Rule in Chapter X Reorganizations." *Journal of Finance*, December 1966, pp. 745-746.

Fraser, Kenneth W. "Corporate Financing Methods: Principles and Practices." *Commercial and Financial Chronicle*, March 15, 1956, pp. 9 ff.

Frazer, W. J., Jr. "Large Manufacturing Corporations as Suppliers of Funds to the United States Government's Securities Market." *Journal of Finance*, December 1958, pp. 499-509.

Furst, Richard W. "An Investigation into the Effects of Listing on the Market Price of Common Stocks." *Journal of Finance,* May 1970, p. 69.

Gallups, William C. "Installment Lending by Commercial Banks: A Cost and Yield Analysis." *Journal of Finance*, March 1971, pp. 180-181.

Glubok, Allan. "A Second Look at Marginal Accounts." *Credit and Financial Management*, May 1970, pp. 18 ff.

Goodell, George S. *The Role of Trade Credit in the Financing of American Industry, with Special Emphasis on the Steel Industry.* Thesis, Northwestern University, 1959.

Goodman, Sam R. "The Marketing-Controller Concept: An Inquiry into Financial/Marketing Relationships in Selected Consumer-Goods Companies." *Appalachian Financial Review*, Spring 1969, pp. 267-268.

Gover, Timothy D. "The Use of the Stock Tender." *Marquette Business Review*, Summer 1967, pp. 70-83.

Gray, Rusk F., Jr. "A Study of the Sinking-Fund Covenant with Special Reference to Corporate Financial Planning." *Appalachian Financial Review,* Spring 1970, pp. 373-374.

Greenberg, Edward. "Business Investment in Plant and Equipment: An Empirical Study." *Journal of Finance*, March 1963, pp. 71-72.

Greenlaw, Paul S., and Frey, M. William. *Finansim,* Scranton, Pa.: International Textbook Company, 1968.

Greer, Carl C. "A Benefit-Cost Model for Credit Decisions." *Journal of Finance*, March 1967, pp. 100-101.

Hardin, William F., Jr. *Cash Management in a Small Manufacturing Firm.* Thesis, University of North Carolina, 1968.

Harris, George T. "The Capital Structure in American Banking." *Journal of Finance*, December 1954, pp. 425-426.

Harvey, R. K. "A Portfolio Model of Capital Budgeting under Risk." *Journal of Finance*, December 1968, pp. 893-894.

Hastings, Paul G., and Mietus, Norbert J. *Personal Finance*. New York: McGraw-Hill Book Company, 1971.

Haydon, Randall B. *An Analysis of the Cost of Capital*. Thesis, University of Illinois, 1962.

Herzog, John P. "Investor Experience in Corporate Securities." *Journal of Finance*, March 1944, pp. 46-61.

Hess, Joseph A. "Noncapital Programming: A Theory of Financial Interdependencies." *Journal of Finance*, September 1971, pp. 986-987.

Hill, Robert E. *The Growth and Development of Foreign Banking in Three Commercial Banks in Mobile, Alabama*. Thesis, University of Alabama, 1957.

Hines, Mary Alice. "Comparative Institutional Analysis: Short-term Mortgage versus Hybird R.E.I.T.S." Paper delivered at Eastern Finance Association, April 1973.

Horowitz, Ronald M. "Arrearages on Cumulative Preferred Stocks Listed on the New York Stock Exchange: An Analysis of Experience." *Journal of Finance*, March 1955, pp. 105-106.

Howe, Charles H. "Corporate Saving Behavior: A Study of Internal Financing." *Journal of Finance*, December 1960, pp. 565-566.

Hubbard, Charles L., and Hawkins, Clark A. *Theory of Valuation*. Scranton, Pa.: International Textbook Company, 1969.

Hund, James M. *Managerial Decentralization: A Case Study*. Thesis, Princeton University, 1954.

Hutchins, Robert C. "Measurement of Multicompany Diversification." *Journal of Finance,* March 1972, p. 141.

Jackendoff, Nathaniel. *The Use of Financial Ratios and Other Financial Techniques and Services by Small Business*. Philadelphia: Temple University Bureau of Economic and Business Research, 1961.

Jennings, James P. "The Role of the Controller in Sales Forecasting." *Appalachian Financial Review*, Spring 1971, pp. 60-61.

Johnson, Keith B. "Stock Splits and Price Change." *Journal of Finance*, December 1966, pp. 615-633.

Johnson, Ramon E. "Relationships of Financial Risk to the Term Structure of Corporate Bond Yields." *Journal of Finance*, September 1966, pp. 554-555.

Johnson, Rodney D. "The Extinguishment of Convertible Bonds: A Theoretical and Empirical Analysis." *Journal of Finance*, March 1971, pp. 186-187.

Jolivet, Vincent M. *Public Financing of Small Corporations*. Thesis, Harvard University, 1957.

Junk, Paul E. "Monetary Policy and Fluctuations in the Extension of Trade Credit." *Journal of Finance*, December 1962, pp. 677-678.

Jurgensen, Louis C. *An Analysis of Employee Stock Ownership*. Thesis, University of Iowa, 1951.

Karna, Adi S. "The Cost of Private versus Public Debt Issues." *Financial Management*, Summer 1972, pp. 65-67.

Keller, Frank R. "The Behavior of Individuals in Security Investment Decisions." *Journal of Finance*, September 1970, pp. 942-943.

Kennedy, Robert F., Jr. "The Concept of Growth in the Evaluation of Common Stocks as Illustrated by the Chemical Products Industry." *Journal of Finance*, September 1958, pp. 425-426.

Kerr, John R. "The Pre-Twilight Years." *Consumer Finance News*, August 1967, pp. 17 ff.

Kester, Henry I. *A Comparative Study of the Risk of Loss on Loans of Consumer Finance Companies and the Loans of Commercial Banks.* Thesis, Northwestern University, 1955.

Klein, Richard H. "A Perspective on the MESBIC Program." *Business Topics*, Autumn 1972, pp. 45-51.

Kolb, Burton A. "Problems and Pitfalls in Capital Budgeting." *Financial Analysts Journal*, November-December, 1968.

Krainer, Robert E. "A Neglected Issue in Capital Rationing—the Asset Demand for Money." *Journal of Finance*, December 1966, pp. 731-736.

Kreidle, John R. *Finance Problems: Basic Business Finance.* Belmont, Cal.: Dickerson Publishing Company, 1970.

Kreidle, John R., and Perlick, Walter W. "The Current Status of Participating Stocks." *Mississippi Valley Journal*, Winter 1968, pp. 1-7.

Krum, James R. "Who Controls Finance in the Industrial Giants." *Financial Executive*, March 1970, pp. 20 ff.

Kumar, Prem. "Market Power, Growth, Leverage and the Valuation of the Firm." *Journal of Finance*, March 1971, pp. 188-189.

Lambert, Eugene, Jr. "Financial Considerations in Choosing a Marketing Channel." *Business Topics*, Winter 1966, pp. 17-26.

Laudadio, Leonard. "Size of Bank Borrower, and the Rate of Interest." *Journal of Finance*, March 1963, pp. 20-28.

Lavely, Joseph A. "Comparative Usage of Bond-Warrant and Convertible Bond Issues." *Journal of Finance*, June 1971, pp. 796-797.

Lerro, Anthony J., and Swayne, Charles B., Jr. *Selection of Securities.* Morristown, N.J.: General Learning Corporation, 1970.

Leveson, Sidney M. "The Dividend-Payout Paradox." *Appalachian Financial Review*, Spring 1969, pp. 253-254.

Lishan, John M., and Crary, David T. *The Investment Process*, Scranton, Pa.: International Textbook Company, 1970.

Logue, Dennis E. "An Empirical Appraisal of the Efficiency of the Market for First Public Offerings of Common Stock." *Journal of Finance*, March 1972, p. 142.

Ma, James C., and Henry, H. D. "What It Takes to Come Out of Chapter XI." *Credit and Financial Management*, February 1972, pp. 10 ff.

Maledon, Elick N., Jr. "Toward a Theory of Investment Decision Making." *Appalachian Financial Review*, Spring 1971, pp. 58-59.

Marberry, Charles E. *A Study of Income Administration Practices of American Manufacturing Corporations, 1932-1948.* Thesis, University of Illinois, 1952.

Marrah, George L. "Managing Receivables." *Financial Executive*, July 1970, pp. 41-44.

May, Marvin. "An Investment Opportunities Stock Valuation Model Based on Growth Patterns of Equity." *Journal of Finance*, September 1971, pp. 993-994.

Mayo, Herbert B. "On the Use of Debt to Exercise Warrants." Paper delivered at Eastern Finance Association, April 1973.

McCullers, Levis D. "Convertible Securities—Debt or Equity." *Appalachian Financial Review*, Spring 1971, pp. 73-74.

McFerrin, John B. *Caldwell and Company: A Study in Southern Investment Banking.* Thesis, University of North Carolina, 1937.

McGuigan, James R. "Timing Strategies in the Call Option Market." *Journal of Finance*, March 1972, p. 143.

Melicher, Ronald W. "New Test for Diagnosing Marginal Accounts." *Credit and Financial Management*, September 1970, pp. 12 ff.

Minick, John B. "Consumer Credit Insurance in Nebraska." *Journal of Finance*, March 1960, pp. 84-85.

Mock, Edward J. *Readings in Financial Management.* Scranton Pa.: International Textbook Company, 1964.

Morgan, Bruce W. "Corporate Debt and the Evaluation of Corporate Earnings." *Journal of Finance*, March 1967, pp. 106-107.

Mosconi, David L. *The Financing of Industrial Development in Colorado.* Thesis, New York University, 1952.

Nast, Donald A. "An Econometric Study of Warrant Valuation." Paper given at Eastern Finance Association, April 1972.

Nelson, Roger H. *Personal Money Management.* Reading, Mass.: Addison-Wesley Publishing Company, 1973.

Newcomer, Hale L. *Trading on the Equity from the Point of View of the Investor.* Thesis, University of Illinois, 1939.

Nielsen, Carl C. "The Organization and Capital Financing of Chemical Company Foreign Affiliates." *Journal of Finance*, December 1966, pp. 753-754.

Niendorf, Robert M. "Changes in the Price Relationship between Investment Grade Bonds and Preferred Stocks." *Journal of Finance*, March 1970, pp. 117-178.

Olson, Alden C. "An Analysis of the Impact of Valuation Requirements on the Preferred Stock Investment Policies of Life Insurance Companies" *Journal of Finance*, September 1963, pp. 560-561.

Oppitz, Robert J. *Selected Cases in Finance.* Englewood Cliffs, N.J.: Prentice-Hall, Inc., 1956.

Owen, C. F. "Business Financing and Taxation Policies." *Journal of Finance*, September 1960, pp. 417-419.

Patterson, Harlan R. "New Life in the Management of Corporate Receivables." *Credit and Financial Management*, February 1970, pp. 15-18.

Perlick, Walter W., and Lesikar, Raymond V. *Introduction to Business.* Dallas, Tex.: Business Publications, Inc., 1972.

Peterson, Harold. "Risk and Capital Structure of the Firm." *Journal of Finance*, March 1964, pp. 120-121.

Peterson, Melville. *A Comparative Study in Debenture and Mortgage Bond Finance.* Thesis, University of Illinois, 1959.

Petrello, George J. "Suggested Enrichment Projects of the Introductory Business Finance Course." *Collegiate News and Views*, October 1970, pp. 11-13.

Philippatos, George C. *Financial Management: Theory and Techniques*, San Francisco: Holden-Day, Inc. 1973.

Pinches, George E., and Kinney, William R., Jr. "The Measurement of the Volatility of Common Stock Prices." *Journal of Finance*, March 1971, pp. 119-125.

Pitts, James E. "The Impact of Tax Policy on Investment Behavior in the Chemicals and Allied Products Industry." *Appalachian Financial Review*, Spring 1969, pp. 271-272.

Pogue, Thomas F. "The Corporate Dividend Decision: A Cross-Section Study of the Relationship between Dividends and Investment." *Journal of Finance*, September 1969, pp. 734-735.

Porter, R. Burr. "Application of Stochastic Dominance Principles to the Problem of Asset Selection under Risk." *Journal of Finance*, December 1972, pp. 1177-1178.

Potter, Roger E. "Motivating Factors Guiding the Common-Stock Investor." *Journal of Finance*, December 1970, pp. 1184-1185.

Prock, Jerry D. "An Evaluation of a Selection Technique for Common Stocks." *Appalachian Financial Review*, Spring 1971, pp. 1184-1185.

Raihall, Denis T. *A Stochastic Simulation Model for Capital Investment Analysis under Uncertainty*. Thesis, Pennsylvania State University, 1967.

Rankin, David F. "Security-Based Conglomerate Acquisitions: The Effect on Residual Ownership." *Journal of Finance*, March 1971, pp. 190-191.

Rapp, Wilbur A. "Treasury-Stock Purchases: Their Effects upon the Price-Earnings Ratio." *Appalachian Financial Review*, Spring 1969, pp. 255-263.

Raymond, Robert Hugh. "Financial Statements of Life Insurance Companies." *Journal of Finance*, December 1965, pp. 724-725.

Reiff, Wallace W. "Capital Allocation in Credit Decision Making." *Credit and Financial Management*, September 1967, pp. 20-23.

Reilly, Frank K. "An Analysis and Reconciliation of Bond Refunding Decision Models." *Marquette Business Review*, Summer 1969, pp. 76-88.

Reilly, Raymond R. *An Econometric Study of the Cost Function for the Security Commission Business of Stock Brokerage Firms*. Thesis, Pennsylvania State University, 1970.

Reints, William W. "Investment Criteria of Open-End Investment Companies: An Empirical Investigation." *Journal of Finance*, September 1967, pp. 490-491.

Rhodda, William H. and Nelson, Edward. *Managing Personal Finances*. Englewood Cliffs, N.J.: Prentice-Hall, Inc., 1965.

Rogoff, Donald L. "The Forecasting Properties of Insiders' Transactions." *Journal of Finance*, December 1964, pp. 697-698.

Schultz, Raymond G. *Readings in Financial Management*. 2d ed. Scranton, Pa.: International Textbook Company, 1970.

Scott, David F., Jr. "Evidence on the Importance of Financial Structure." *Financial Management*, Summer 1972, pp. 45-50.

Seligman, Barnard. "Some Tax Implications of State Pension Investment Policy." *Financial Analysts Journal*, March-April 1967, pp. 113-115.

Serraino, William J; Singhvi, Surendra S.; and Soldofsky, Robert M. *Frontiers of Financial Management*. Cincinnati: South-Western Publishing Co., 1971.

Shade, Philip A. *Common Stocks: A Plan for Intelligent Investing*, Homewood, Ill.: Richard D. Irwin, Inc., 1971.

Shattuck, LeRoy A. "The Recapture of Insiders' Profits." *Journal of Finance*, September 1953, pp. 319-332.

Sibley, A. M. "Call Risk and the Prediction of Pre-Maturity Bond Redemptions." Paper delivered at Eastern Finance Association, April 1973.

Sloane, William B. "Earnings, Dividends and Stock Prices: Review and General Model." *Marquette Business Review*, Fall 1967, pp. 93-105.

Smith, Huron. *Capital Budgeting: A Programmed Approach.* Braintree, Mass.: D. H. Mark Publishing Company, 1968.

Snell, David A. *Financial Problems and the Availability and Adequacy of External Financing Sources for Small Business.* Thesis, University of Texas, 1960.

Soldofsky, Robert M. "The Size and Maturity of Direct Placement Loans." *Journal of Finance*, March 1960, pp. 32-44.

Sosnick, Stephen H. "Stock Dividends Are Lemons, Not Melons." *California Management Review*, Winter 1971, pp. 61-70.

Sprecher, C. Ronald. "A Note on Financing Mergers with Convertible Preferred Stock." *Journal of Finance*, June 1971, pp. 683-685.

Stevenson, Harold W. *Common Stock Financing.* Ann Arbor, Mich.: University of Michigan, 1957.

Stevenson, Richard A., and Bear, Robert M. "Commodity Futures: Trends or Random Walks." *Journal of Finance*, March 1970, pp. 65-81.

Stillman, Richard J. *Guide to Personal Finance.* Englewood Cliffs, N.J.: Prentice-Hall, 1972.

Stubbs, Francis L. *Financing of Small- and Medium-Sized Wisconsin Manufacturing Corporations, 1946-1950.* Thesis, University of Wisconsin, 1958.

Sussman, M. Richard. *The Stock Dividend.* Ann Arbor, Mich.: University of Michigan. 1962.

Sweetser, Albert G. *Financing Goods.* New York: Simmons Boardman Books, 1957.

Tanner, Dennis A. *Skewness as a Measure of Opportunity in Warrants.* Thesis, Pennsylvania State University, 1973.

Tate, Curtis E., Jr. *Investment Banking in Tennessee.* Thesis, University of Tennessee, 1952.

Taylor, Walton R. L. *The Symmetric and Asymmetric Cash Balance Model of Miller and Orr with Fixed and Variable Transfer Costs Dependent on the Direction of Transfer.* Thesis, Pennsylvania State University, 1972.

Thornton, Jack E. "Financial Characteristics of Firms Following a Policy of Paying Small, Periodic Stock Dividends." *Appalachian Financial Review*, Spring 1970, pp. 370-371.

Townsend, Charles E. *Small Business Investment Companies of Missouri.* Thesis, University of Missouri, 1962.

Tracy, Truman. *Valuation of Illinois Oil Producing Properties for Tax Assessment.* Thesis, University of Illinois, 1947.

Trivoli, G. W. "A Survey of Investment Policy for Pollution Control." Paper delivered at Eastern Finance Association, April 1973.

Trumph, Guy W. *Impact of Securities and Exchange Commission on Corporate Reorganizations under Chapter X of the National Bankruptcy Act.* Thesis, State University of Iowa, 1951.

Tsai, Mau-Sung. "Models for Bond Optimum Investment Decisions under Uncertainty." *Journal of Finance,* March 1967, pp. 109-110.

Twark, Allan J.; Dukes, William P.; and Bowlin, Oswald D. *Security Analysis and Portfolio Management.* San Francisco: Holden-Day, Inc. 1973.

Tyree, Donald A. "The Small Loan Industry in Texas." *Journal of Finance,* March 1961, pp. 113-114.

Vinson, Charles E. "Pricing Practices in the Primary Convertible Bond Market." *The Quarterly Review of Economics and Business,* Summer 1970, pp. 47-60.

Voorheis, Frank L. "Investment Policy and Performance of Bank-Administered Pooled Equity Funds for Employee Benefit Plans." *Journal of Finance,* September 1967, pp. 492-493.

Walker, Clyde. *An Analysis of Common Trust Funds, 1941-1948.* Thesis, University of Pittsburgh, 1950.

Weller, Kenneth J. "An Analysis and Appraisal of Rights Offerings as a Method of Raising Equity Capital." *Journal of Finance,* September 1962, pp. 529-530.

Wentz, Arthur G. "Intrinsic Value and its Use as a Determinant of Cost of Capital: A Test." *Appalachian Financial Review,* Spring 1970, pp. 375-376.

West, David A. and Wood, Glenn L. *Personal Financial Management.* Boston: Houghton Mifflin Company, 1972.

Whalen, Edward L. "A Cross Section Study of Business Demand for Cash." *Journal of Finance,* September 1965, pp. 423-439.

Whetten, Leland C. *The Rise of Proxy Solicitors.* Atlanta, Ga.: Georgia State College, 1961.

Widicus, Wilbur W., Jr., and Stitzel, Thomas E. *Personal Investing.* Homewood, Ill.: Richard D. Irwin, Inc., 1971.

Wiley, Robert J. "An Analysis of Financing by a Multinational Group of Companies Manufacturing in Brazil." *Appalachian Financial Review,* Spring 1970, pp. 368-369.

Willcox, Tilton L. "Requisites for Survival and Growth for Small (New) Securities Broker-Dealers." Paper delivered at Eastern Finance Association, April 1973.

Williams, John D. "An Analysis of Premiums Paid in Industrial Mergers in the Period 1959-1968." *Appalachian Financial Review,* Spring 1971, pp. 63-63.

Wing, George A. "Capital Budgeting, Circa 1915." *Journal of Finance,* September 1965, pp. 472-479.

Wolf, Harold A., and Richardson, Lee. *Readings in Finance.* New York: Appleton-Century-Crofts, 1966.

Wubbels, Rolf. *Regulation of Stockholders' Proxies.* Thesis, New York University, 1949.

Wyatt, Arthur A., and Kieso, Donald E. *Business Combinations: Planning and Action.* Scranton, Pa.: International Textbook Company, 1969.

Yehle, Eugene C. "An Appraisal of Corporate Working Fund Requirements." *Journal of Finance*, December 1953, pp. 439-440.

Young, Allen E. "Managerial, Market, and Investor Problems Associated with Cash Tender Offers by Corporations for Their Own Common Stock." *Appalachian Financial Review*, Spring 1969, pp. 264-265.

Index